STUART STYLE

STUART STYLE

MONARCHY, DRESS AND THE SCOTTISH MALE ELITE

Maria Hayward

YALE UNIVERSITY PRESS
New Haven and London

First published by Yale University Press 2020

302 Temple Street, P.O. Box 209040, New Haven CT 06520-9040

47 Bedford Square, London WC1B 3DP

yalebooks.com | yalebooks.co.uk

ISBN 978-0-300-24036-8 HB

Library of Congress Control Number: 2019949035

10 9 8 7 6 5 4 3 2 1

2024 2023 2022 2021 2020

Designed by Isobel Gillan

Printed in China

Front cover: Daniel Mytens the elder, *James Hamilton, 3rd Marquis and 1st Duke of Hamilton*, 1623. Oil on canvas, 200.7 × 125.1 cm. Tate Britain, London.

Back cover: Detail from the wedding suit of James, duke of York, 1673. Victoria and Albert Museum, London.

Frontispiece: David Scougall, *Lord David Hay*, *c.*1665–70. Oil on canvas, 91.5 × 76.1 cm. Private collection, sold by Sotheby's.

Published with assistance from the foundation established in memory of Oliver Baty Cunningham of the Class for 1917, Yale College.

Contents

Stuart Family Tree

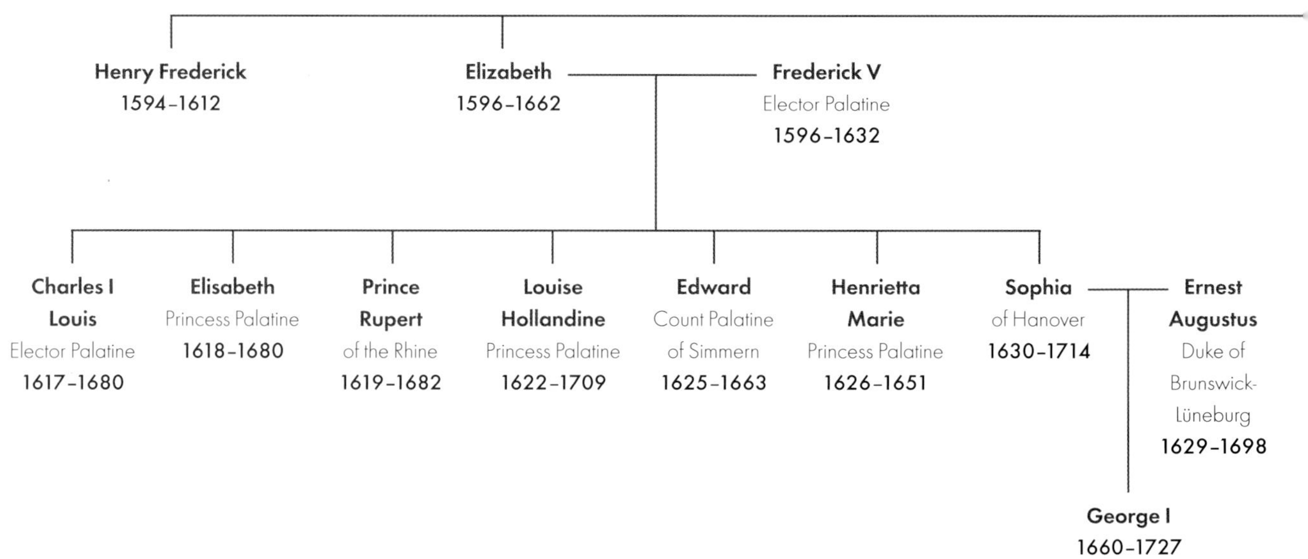

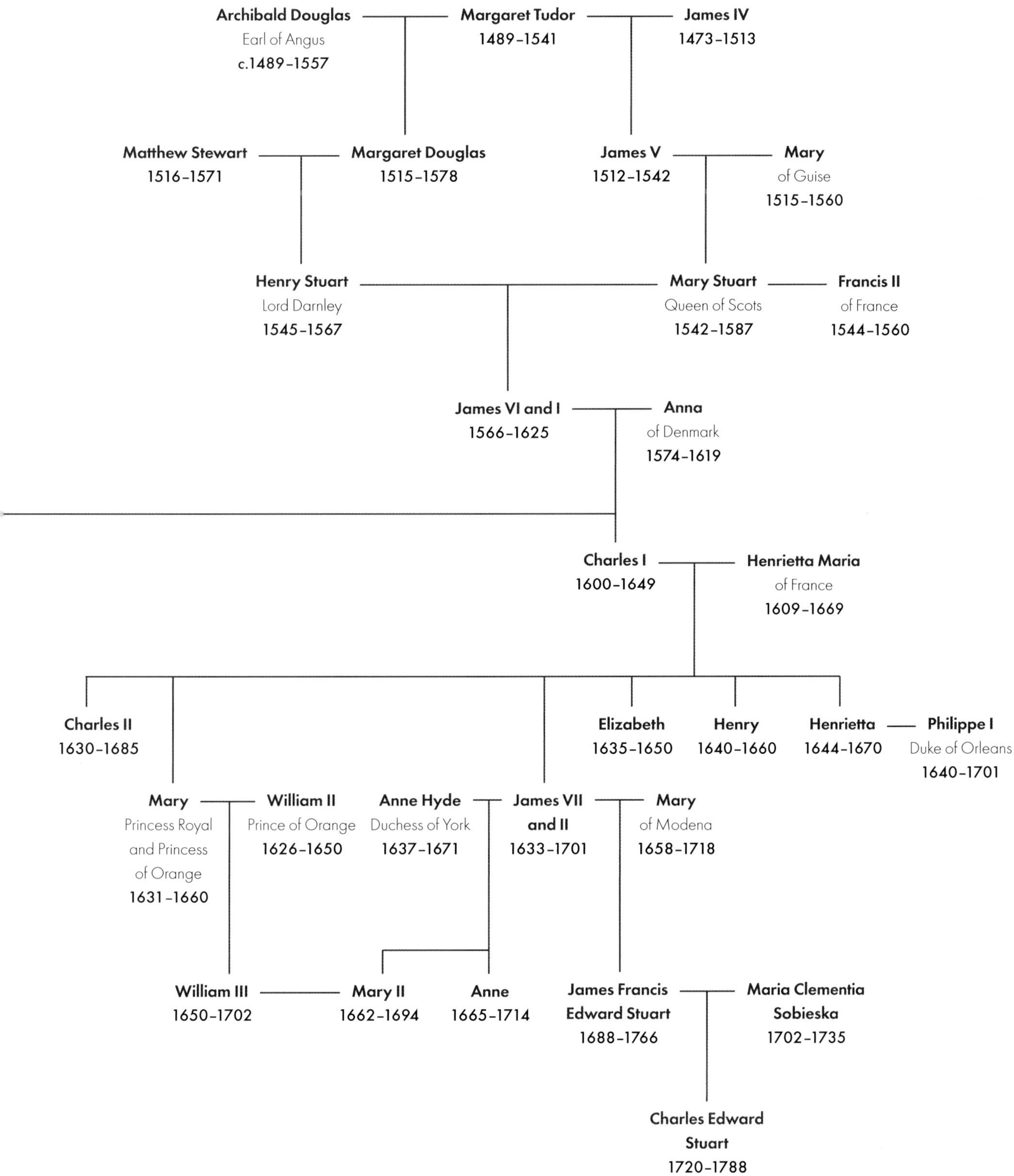
Archibald Douglas
Earl of Angus
c.1489–1557
Margaret Tudor
1489–1541
James IV
1473–1513
Matthew Stewart
1516–1571
Margaret Douglas
1515–1578
James V
1512–1542
Mary
of Guise
1515–1560
Henry Stuart
Lord Darnley
1545–1567
Mary Stuart
Queen of Scots
1542–1587
Francis II
of France
1544–1560
James VI and I
1566–1625
Anna
of Denmark
1574–1619
Charles I
1600–1649
Henrietta Maria
of France
1609–1669
Charles II
1630–1685
Elizabeth
1635–1650
Henry
1640–1660
Henrietta
1644–1670
Philippe I
Duke of Orleans
1640–1701
Mary
Princess Royal
and Princess
of Orange
1631–1660
William II
Prince of Orange
1626–1650
Anne Hyde
Duchess of York
1637–1671
James VII
and II
1633–1701
Mary
of Modena
1658–1718
William III
1650–1702
Mary II
1662–1694
Anne
1665–1714
James Francis
Edward Stuart
1688–1766
Maria Clementia
Sobieska
1702–1735
Charles Edward
Stuart
1720–1788

INTRODUCTION

Clothes Make the Man

The Stuarts, Scotland and the Scottish Male Elite

Stuart Style is not a conventional dress history book presenting the reader with a strongly London-focused, chronological overview of changing male fashions from James VI's accession to Elizabeth's throne in 1603 to the death of Anne in 1714. Consequently, it does not challenge the traditional narrative of how men's clothing styles evolved during the seventeenth century, a story that a number of scholars have told very well, most notably Aileen Ribeiro and Anna Reynolds.[1] However, *Stuart Style* does offer a new reading of who shaped these fashions by placing the later Stuarts, or more correctly Stewarts, centre stage from 1566 to 1701 (fig. 0.1). These dates, running from the birth of James VI and I to the death of James VII and II, emphasise the Scottish rather than an exclusively English contribution to the evolution and reception of male fashion in the British Isles. The Stuarts had a long, illustrious Scottish lineage stretching back to 1371 but they, and the clothing style they gave their name to during the seventeenth century, are usually studied within a British or English context (see Stuart Family Tree and Timeline of the Stuarts and Their People).[2] This book takes a different viewpoint, hence the use of 'Scottish' and 'English' rather than 'British', thereby reinserting the Scottish dimension, both of the Stuarts and their subjects from north of the border, into the familiar Stuart fashion narrative. As such, it is located within the 'cultural turn' of Scottish and dress history, and addresses the simple fact that to date there have been no detailed studies of later Stuart male royal clothing or of fashionable seventeenth-century male Scottish dress. It also follows in the footsteps of Sharon Adams and Julian Goodare's *Scotland in the Age of Two Revolutions* by focusing on a long seventeenth century and by exploring 'the history that the Scots themselves made'.[3]

Clothes are at the heart of *Stuart Style*, so there are many technical details relating to cut and construction (see Glossary), but the primary

0.1 Studio of Nicholas Hilliard and Isaac Oliver, *James VI and I and His Family*, 1612–14. Watercolour on vellum, with frame of ebony on oak, 27.5 × 19.4 cm. Victoria and Albert Museum, London. James VI and I, his sons and his son-in-law, Frederick, elector palatine, are dressed in fashionable doublets worn with ruffs or lace-edged collars.

purpose of investigating these garments is to assess what they reveal about social, religious and political attitudes rather than, for example, to pinpoint the specific style of the doublet at a particular moment in time. Many of the clothes in question belonged to five members of the Stuart royal line. James VI (1566–1625), Prince Henry (1594–1612) and Charles I (1600–49) were born on Scottish soil, James VI, Charles I and Charles II (1630–85) were crowned as king of Scots and Charles II and James VII and II (1633–1701) lived north of the border when staying in England was either not possible or unwise. Looking beyond these five royal wardrobes, the focus extends to the Scottish male elite as a means of assessing the dissemination and reception of royal style. Whether in Edinburgh, Westminster, Oxford or Saint-Germain-en-Laye, the royal court attracted both Scottish courtiers and Scottish artisans, and the two groups contributed to the distinctive style of Stuart fashion.

Scotland was the Stuarts' homeland, and its geography played a significant part in defining the distinct differences between the highlands and islands, in the north and west, and the lowlands, in the south and east. Indeed, Scotland's geography was central to the country's history. The 'highland divide' (fig. 0.2) was very significant, marking as it did more than a change in topography. This 'line' signified differences in land use, wealth, dress and language, with the Highlands favouring Scottish Gaelic and the Lowlands using Middle Scots. The physician, Archibald Pitcairn (1652–1713) mocked the various strands within Scottish society in his book *The Assembly, or The Scotch Reformation* (1691), with characters including Lord Whigridden, earl of Crawford; Laird Littlewit, a north countryman; Mr Novel, a Jacobite news-monger and Mr Wordie, a Presbyterian chaplain.[4] While the Scots were the first to acknowledge that location, religion and politics were significant in determining an individual's distinctive outlook, the Scottish monarchy and their people also had a strong sense of their nation and their self-worth.

Scottish identity was influenced by European ties forged through trade and royal marriages. James VI's parents had Scottish, English and French blood, Prince Henry and Charles I drew on their parents' Scottish and Danish heritage, while Charles II and James VII and II gained French and Italian influences from their mother. The lineages of the five men at the heart of this book reflect the Stuarts' selection of European brides, which strengthened cultural exchanges. The Stuarts were Francophiles, so it is not surprising that their style was heavily influenced by Paris – except when it temporarily suited them for it not to be. Prince Henry briefly pushed against French style in 1611, as did Charles II in 1666. However, their general preference for French fashion gradually caused the Stuarts to be out of kilter with strands of English society, in particular, who had a growing mistrust of the French, to match their long-standing dislike of the black-clad Spaniards. The playwright William Wycherley satirised such views in his *Gentleman Dancing-Master* (1673) by embodying the stereotypes of Spanishness, in the person of Don Diego, and Frenchness, in Monsieur de Paris.[5]

Scottish identity was also shaped by Scotland's larger and more populous southern neighbour: England. Scotland's approximately 30,000 square miles compared with approximately 50,300 square miles of English soil, while by the death of James VII and II, in 1701, Scotland's population was in the region of 1 million, a fifth of that to be found south of the Tweed. The nature of the relationship between the two countries changed in 1603 when James VI inherited the crowns of England and Ireland. Ruling over three kingdoms brought the Stuarts prestige, opportunities and challenges.[6] The latter included moving the court from Edinburgh to Westminster, thereby significantly changing how accessible the Stuart monarchs were to their Scottish elite. Edinburgh was approximately 420 miles by road from London. With good weather this journey took about a week, as William Douglas, 3rd duke of Hamilton (1634–94) noted in 1686. On 20 April he assured his wife that he had bought the satin and lace that

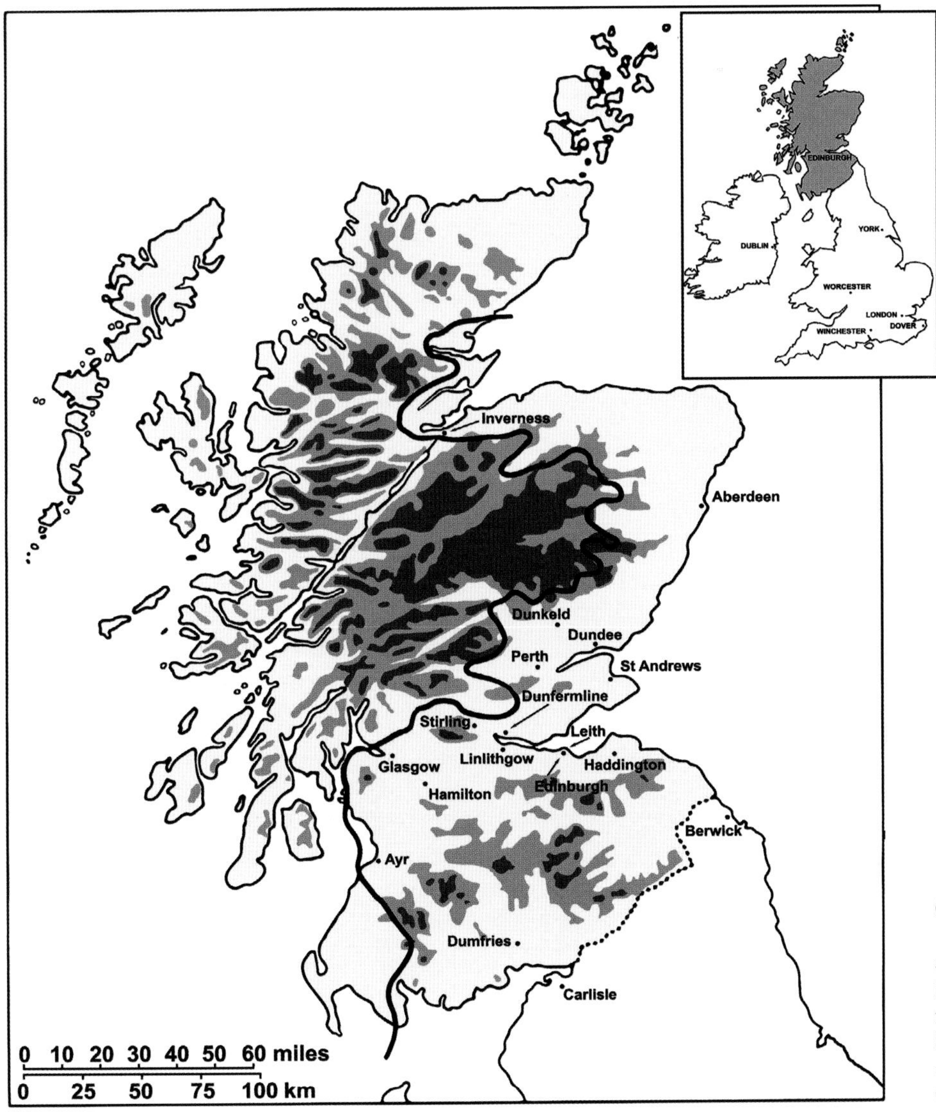

0.2 Main map: 16th- and 17th-century Scotland, showing the topography, Highland divide, the main towns or 'burghs' and the border with England; inset map: the location of other key towns and cities in England.

0.3 Unknown artist, *Archibald Campbell, 9th Earl of Argyll and Lady Anne (née Mackenzie, countess of Argyll)*, 1664–5. Oil on canvas, 110.1 × 163.2 cm. National Portrait Gallery, London. In addition to his elegant suit and lace collar, Argyll holds the staff of the Master of the Household in Scotland to stress his importance.

she wanted, adding that he would leave for home within the hour, and hoped to be in Edinburgh in eight days' time.[7]

In the late seventeenth century William, 3rd duke of Hamilton was a leading member of the Scottish male elite, a group that consisted of nobles, lairds and burgesses. Traditionally, Scotland had a strong nobility and a weak gentry, resulting in a tension between the long-established families, or *noblesse d'épee*, and the new men, or *noblesse de robe*.[8] Regardless of which group they came from, the elite's political influence was linked to their personal wealth, access to the king and connections with their kin. Interactions between the families or clans were dictated by geography, family and religion, which on occasion resulted in blood feud. As a social group, the Scottish elite did well during the long seventeenth century, increasing their influence from the Restoration onwards. The Scottish social structure was bound together by agnatic kinship, or descent through male ancestors. Beyond the immediate royal line, the earls and dukes of Lennox, and the house of Hamilton, had close ties to the Scottish crown, and were often found at court.

As Keith Brown and Julian Goodare demonstrate, the elite played an important role in Scottish government before and after 1603, namely in the Scottish parliament, the privy council and as the officers of state. Of the latter, the officials of the Scottish Treasury were especially influential because of their access to, and control of, royal funds.[9] Holding royal office or attending court made living close to the court desirable, as two substantial aristocratic town houses in Stirling reveal. The opulent frontage of Mar's Wark, built by John Erskine, 1st earl of Mar (*c.*1510–72), asserted Erskine's place in society, a position that was enhanced when he was appointed hereditary keeper of Stirling Castle. In contrast, the building known as Argyll's lodging passed through the hands of John Traill and Sir William Alexander before Archibald Campbell, 9th earl of Argyll (1629–85) bought it. He added to the lodging in the hope that Charles II would spend more time in Scotland after the Restoration. While these hopes were dashed, seventeenth-century Scottish courtiers like Argyll and the aristocracy are central to this study because their portraiture, household accounts, inventories, bills and a few pieces of extant clothing provide evidence of the creation, transmission and reception of the Stuarts' way of dressing.[10]

While Archibald Campbell hoped for preferment from Charles II, his strong Presbyterian beliefs placed him increasingly at odds with the king and his brother (fig. 0.3). Religion played a central role both in Argyll's life and in shaping early modern Scottish society, and so it features strongly in *Stuart Style*.[11] James VI was born six years after the Scottish Reformation of 1560, an event that brought about a complex and divided religious landscape dominated by the Scottish kirk. The differences between the Scottish and English churches were significant, but in 1603 they were irrevocably bound together. With Elizabeth's death, James's religious position changed overnight and he combined being an ordinary member of the kirk with being the supreme governor of the Church of England.[12] As Alan MacDonald has noted, James tried to bring the two churches closer together, but from the Scottish perspective, he was trying to impose unwanted English religious ways on his unenthused countrymen.[13] Least appealing of all was the Book of Common Prayer, often regarded as the most contentious book in the English language (fig. 0.4). The chapel at Stirling Castle was painted in 1628–9 by Valentine Jenkin in preparation for Charles I's planned visit after his coronation, so making it ready for Anglican worship following the Book of Common Prayer.

Moving from religion to the economy, while Scotland was not as wealthy as England, money was essential for constructing the fashionable male identity, as a certain George Boswell of Balmuto acknowledged in August 1614. Boswell sought to redeem some gold buttons and other items that he had pledged to Sir Duncan Campbell of Glenorchy for £100 because he wished to visit the king having been 'advertisit that I wilbe wecome', adding that 'the laik of money stayes me'.[14] For men like

0.4 Bible and Book of Common Prayer, printed by Robert Barker, London, 1607, cover c.1607, British. Satin worked with silk and metal thread, spangles, 34.3 × 23.5 cm. Metropolitan Museum of Art, New York. This richly embroidered cover, depicting Adam and Eve, epitomises what objects meant to Anglicans and Episcopalians.

Boswell, when cash was not readily available, credit was often an option, thereby allowing them to buy new clothes and accessories to engage in a range of social and political activities. While Linda Colley has well observed that 'identities are not like hats' because an individual only wears one hat at a time, a man of substance could and did own many hats during the course of his lifetime.[15] Indeed, an extensive wardrobe allowed a man to change his clothes and headwear to suit the place, the occasion and the activity in which he was engaged.

Stuart fashion did not develop in isolation, and from 1603 there were the English men, alongside the Scots, at or around the court.[16] They jostled with their Scottish counterparts, helping to shape and disseminate royal style. For men like the royal favourite George Villiers, 1st duke of Buckingham (1592–1628) and upwardly mobile men about town who keenly observed and emulated the fashionable habits of the elite, such as the diarist, Samuel Pepys (1633–1703), clothes played a central role in self-presentation.[17] In contrast, Thomas Howard, 21st earl of Arundel (1586–1646) 'wore and affected a Habit very different from that of the time'.[18] These three men typified the style leader, the dedicated follower of fashion, and the fashionless, with the last seeking to distance himself from such frivolous concerns. Arundel was, however, unusual, and most men across the three kingdoms bought into aspects of the Stuarts' style by wearing the same core group of garments and accessories. However, this was not a style that created a corporate elite look, as the patrician toga or the robes *a ducal* of the Venetian Republic did.[19] Rather, there was ample scope for individuality, demonstrating a degree of independence and agency within the fashionable Stuart framework.

Defining the Stuarts' Style

According to James VI, king of Scots, a monarch should 'keep a proportion as well with the seasons of the year as of your age, in the fashions of them being careless, using them according to the common form of the time, sometimes richer, sometimes meanlier clothed, as the occasion serveth'.[20] The subtle nuances of time, place and fashion were to be carefully, and effortlessly, addressed, thereby ensuring that the king was appropriately dressed at all times. Self-awareness and self-expression were also central features of elite male identity in the Stuart kingdoms. In early July 1636 Sir Alexander Gordon of Navidale wrote to his brother, Sir Robert Gordon of Gordonstown, about what he planned to wear at his nephew's wedding. He urged Robert:

> to caus ask for one Johne Turnour, tealzeour in Edinburgh … with whom I left ane suit of black figuirit silk and ane taffatie cloik … And faill not send me ather as mutch skarlet or fyin gray Lundon cloith with beas to lyin it, and sillwer leas and buttons to serw it, conform to the best and newest fasion.[21]

The Stuarts' style is hard to define, so it is easier to start with a brief statement of what it was not. It was not uniformly sombre or plain, it did not involve large quantities of tartan or specifically Scottish items of dress, it was not modestly priced and it was not inferior to, or a natural progression from, Tudor dress. So, what was it? The motivations behind Stuart style were shared with other monarchies, as well as republics and commonwealths: a desire to be seen, a need to be dignified and a belief that the Stuart kings would ensure the stability and wealth of the state. These concepts underpinned a growing uniformity in dress and jewellery styles in seventeenth-century Europe that was linked to the role of print in disseminating fashionable ideas quickly. Stuart style can therefore be presented as a set of possibilities and preferences linked to a degree of openness to external, European, influences.

One way to tease out what Stuart clothing was like is to consider the wool suit that James, duke of York wore for his marriage to Mary of Modena (1658–1718) in 1673 (fig. 0.5).[22] The coat and breeches provide a sense of the duke's height and size in a way that a portrait cannot. The quality of the materials indicates that the ensemble was expensive, as appropriate for clothes ordered for a special occasion in royal circles. However, this wedding was modest because of its political and religious ramifications, arising from James's recent conversion to Catholicism and Mary being recommended as a suitable bride by Louis XIV of France. The combination of probably home-produced cloth for the outer fabric, an imported silk lining and silver and silver gilt embroidery were the height of fashion. The floral and foliate design ensured that this suit was tasteful and elegant, while examination of the construction reveals that it was well made. It was the product of a skilled tailor, working with an embroiderer, who drew on a range of suppliers for the various materials and accessories required to complete the outfit. However, the suit is incomplete, and while the coat and breeches remain, the vest is missing, either reused or discarded. Even so, it may well have been made either from the red/orange ribbed silk used for the coat's lining, or from brocade in similar shades. Elegant and expensive, James's suit compares well with many of the suits listed in Charles II's account for the same year, including 'a stone colour cloth coat and cullet breeches embroidered with gold and silver the coat lined with scarlet padusoy [*sic*] and trimmed with scarlet gold and silver'.[23]

James's suit offers one instance of royal style. As so few garments survive, a broader, more representative view of Stuart fashion can be obtained by looking at a long sequence of portraits. Such a grouping incorporates works by Marcus Gheeraerts the younger

0.5 The wedding suit of James, duke of York, 1673. Wool, embroidered with silver and silver gilt thread and lined with red silk. Victoria and Albert Museum, London.

(*c*.1561–1636) and Paul van Somer (*c*.1577–1621), via Anthony van Dyck (1599–1641) to Sir Peter Lely (1618–80) and Sir Godfrey Kneller (1646–1723), who worked predominantly in London for English and Scottish clients. Equally valuable is the work of John Baptiste de Medina (1659–1710) and David Scougall (1645–1730), artists who were painting in Scotland. These portraits served a range of functions beyond just capturing the monarch's dress, as can be seen in the following three examples. Katherine Gibson has demonstrated just how effectively Charles II managed his image, reinventing the monarch after the Restoration.[24] In contrast, Richard Ollard compared the royal image of Charles I and Charles II, concluding that 'both kings created images of themselves which had a power and a durability that outrange all competition'.[25] Catriona Murray takes a very different approach to Stuart portraiture by highlighting how images of their many children were used to present the family to a wide and sometimes critical audience.[26] The Stuarts' use of clothing functioned in the same way – it was a visual means of promoting the royal family.

The Stuarts' style evolved considerably over the 135 years covered by this book, as the following descriptions of garments sourced from official records of the time make clear: 'a French joup and hose with bands' made for James VI from fine green velvet in July 1591; 'a suit of grass green silk camlet cut upon the same camlet laced with gold and silver lace and garnished with many long buttons and loops of gold and silver' selected for Charles I in autumn 1630; and 'A blake wrought silk French stuffe suite and Cloak lined with the same and richly laced with black Flanders lace' ordered for Charles II in May 1660 (see The Evolution of Stuart Male Dress).[27] Changes in Stuart fashion over time can be summed up in four main ways. First, in terms of the garments worn, it shifted from the doublet, hose and cloak chosen by James VI and I to the coat, waistcoat and breeches favoured by his grandsons.[28] Second, in terms of construction it evolved from the tight-fitting, padded and stiffened doublet of the 1560s, to the looser, softer doublet of the 1630s and the waistcoat or vest of the 1660s.[29] Third, in terms of colour it moved from pale to bright colours in James VI's Scottish reign, and from the pastel shades favoured by Charles I during the 1620s and 1630s to the sombre and muted shades of the 1660s under Charles II and his brother James. And fourth, favouring silk with some wool until *c*.1600, then silk until the 1650s and finally a shift to wool and mixed fibre cloths. These four points stress that Stuart dress, like other fashionable styles, was not static. Rather, it was constantly, if subtly, evolving. In addition, there was a growing sense of the seasonality of fashion that placed an increased emphasis on small, changing details of garment cut, trimmings, accessories and jewellery.

James VI and I clearly felt it was his right to determine what was *à la mode*, as was shown in December 1607 by his response when he was informed that it was traditional to have a masque at Christmas. James exclaimed, '[W]hat do you tell me of the fashion? I will make it a fashion'.[30] In 1628 the Welsh epigrammatist John Owen continued the theme:

All subjects in their manners follow kings
What they do, bids; forbearing forbids things
A king's behaviour sways his subjects lives
As the first mover all the fixt stars drives.[31]

Despite this, while they might have lead fashion, the Stuart kings rarely innovated. Rather, they adopted aspects of an existing style and made it popular, thereby avoiding the danger of fashionable extremes.

The later Stuarts monarchs, from Mary, Queen of Scots (1542–87) onwards, had a charismatic, even romantic, quality for many of their subjects, an idea that Murray Pittock has explored in *The Invention of Scotland*.[32] This could be true *in extremis* as with Mary, Charles I and his exiled sons, but it was also present in good times, such as at the Restoration of the Stuarts in 1660. Loyal supporters preserved pieces of the monarch's clothing and jewellery and these items served a variety of functions ranging from that of memento to relic, while commemorative objects produced on a large scale fostered feelings of identity and loyalty. Jewellery was especially important in this context, serving as it did to commemorate royal acquaintances, lost individuals and seemingly lost causes. As Pittock and Neil Guthrie have demonstrated, the Stuarts and their supporters were particularly adept at exploiting material goods as a means of rewarding loyalty and rallying support to the cause, culminating in the Jacobites' use of clothing, jewellery and a range of other items as a means of promoting sedition against the Hanoverians and memorialising the Stuarts.[33]

Critics of the Stuart monarchy alleged that the kings were variously effeminate, hen-pecked or excessively addicted to the pursuit of women, all claims that appeared at times to be supported by the monarch's clothing choices. Effeminate style, expressed through a fondness for pale colours, tight clothing, perfume and a lack of beards, was linked, of course, to unmanly behaviour.[34] However, as Curtis Perry has stressed, when we consider the influence on fashion of men such as Robert Kerr (or the anglicised Carr), earl of Somerset (*c.*1587–1645), we need to focus on him as a historical figure rather than on the 'emergent cultural stereotype' found in libels and drama.[35] While Charles I was condemned for being dominated by his wife, he was not criticised for his clothes (even though during the Wars of the Three Kingdoms the archetypal cavalier would be). In contrast, Charles II and James VII and II epitomised the overt male sexuality that was exemplified in John Michael Wright's portrait of the merry monarch (fig. 0.6). Wright carefully enhanced Charles II's luxuriant curls, while his long shapely legs were accentuated by white silk stockings and high-heeled shoes.

Was Stuart style Scottish style? Arguably yes, for James VI and for Prince Henry. The answer is more complex for Charles I, who left his homeland aged three. Yet in spite of this, Edward Hyde, 1st earl of Clarendon (1609–74) described Charles I as 'an immoderate lover of the Scottish nation'.[36] James VI and I's grandsons were born in England, which raises the question of how strong their bond was to the Scottish kingdom and its people. Both spent some time as adults in Scotland and they divided opinion there, rather as their great-grandmother, Mary, Queen of Scots, had done. Their appeal to the Scottish elite was founded in the belief that the Stuarts were specifically Scottish kings in an age when loyalty was given to the monarch and dynasty rather than, or as well as, the nation.

The royal body was linked to ideas of nation, meaning that the clothes worn by the monarch could be expressive of nationality and unity. This was an important consideration in light of the challenges the Stuarts faced ruling multiple kingdoms. James VI and I wanted to bind his subjects to him, and in 1607 he referred to the 'Irish, Scottish, Welsh and English, divers in Nation, yet all walking as subjects and servants within my Court'.[37] A shared clothing style, led by the monarch and the court, had the potential to unite the male elite of the Stuarts' three kingdoms. However, while these men might, and indeed often did, dress in a similar way, the sense of unity that this created was often illusory. Considering the clothing of the male elite is another way of contemplating the question posed by Jenny Wormald when she asked whether James and his successors ruled over three kingdoms or a 'core and colonies'.[38] Scotland was never a colony, but all the Stuarts sought to assert their authority by regulating civic dress there, in particular the robes of key royal officials and judges. For example, on 22 November 1619

> the provest, the foure baillies, the deane of gild, and the treasurer, were commandit, by a charge from the king, to prepare everie one of them a reid robe of scarlot lined with furring, and the provest to have a chaine of gold beside, against Christmas nixt, and to weare the same upon Sondays and holie days, as the major and aldermen of London doe.[39]

When James VI and I left Scotland in 1603, he brought Scottish court style with him and found a receptive environment for it. With no king to outshine, the male courtiers of Elizabeth I (1533–1603) had used their opulent wardrobes to compete with each other to gain the Virgin Queen's favour.[40] The length of Elizabeth I's reign, her skilled use of clothing to assert her authority as queen, and the lack of an official male consort between 1558 and 1603 ensured that a high level of interest was placed on female dress throughout that period.[41] Yet men played an essential role at court as a foil to the queen, with Robert Dudley, 1st earl of Leicester (1532–88), Sir Christopher Hatton (1540–91), Robert Devereux, 2nd earl of Essex (1565–1601), and Henry Wriothesley, 3rd earl of Southampton (1573–1624) all acting as fashion leaders.[42] Francis Bacon (1561–1626) alluded to the subtle nuances of their role when he urged Elizabeth to reinstate Devereux 'for society to yourself and for an honour and ornament to your attendance and Court, in the eyes of your people, and in the eyes of foreign ambassadors'.[43] However, the execution of Essex in 1601 meant that there was no leading male courtier in place at

0.6 John Michael Wright, *Charles II*, c.1661. Oil on canvas, 281.9 × 239.2 cm. Royal Collection. Charles II's royal authority is emphasised by his cloth of silver suit, formal robes and the new regalia made for his coronation.

the accession of James VI to challenge the new king's fashion.[44] Instead, there was a competitive, assertive and ambitious set of English male courtiers who were keen to find a place under the new regime.

Sources and Approaches

Stuart Style is all about stuff, specifically all the things used to cover, clothe and adorn the body. These garments, accessories and jewels, whether or not they still survive, are depicted in portraits or described in words, and are highly revealing of the culture that produced them. When Stephen Greenblatt wrote about the self-fashioning of early modern male identities he saw them as being created by, and expressed in, words rather than images or objects. Far more importantly in this context, he argued that the concept did not apply to the elite.[45] Yet royal and elite self-fashioning was achieved as much by the display of the clothed body and its visual image as it was by writing, and, as Catherine Richardson has shown, while most of this clothing is long lost, the documents of the time record vital information about dress and attitudes towards fashion.[46] The technical vocabulary of craftsmen and merchants recorded by royal clerks of the Great Wardrobe and the Wardrobe of the Robes, or the gossipy words of Samuel Pepys, are vital when forming an impression of how the men at court dressed and why they might have chosen to do so. Royal clothes are frequently evidenced by the observations of a third party. Thus James VI and I's fashion choices are revealed in the scathing words of Sir Anthony Weldon (1583–1648) or in the court news passed on by keen letter writer John Chamberlain to the collector and diplomat Dudley Carleton.[47] The Stuarts are also, on occasion, revealed in their own words, such as when Charles II sought the advice of his Paris-based younger sister Henrietta ('Minette') (1644–70), in a bid to ensure that his clothes were *à la mode*.[48]

The importance of male appearance in the seventeenth century – of looking good and being appropriately attired, accessorised and armed – cannot be overstated.[49] While Baldassare Castiglione recommended that the courtier should 'say and do everything with grace', grace required a degree of panache.[50] This was the age of the so-called 'swagger' portrait that reflected the self-confident male, like that of James Hamilton, 3rd marquis and 1st duke of Hamilton (1606–49), a young man who was dressed to impress and who knew it (fig. 0.7).[51] As Andrew Wilton asserts, for early modern male sitters, it was essential that their portraits should express their dignity and worth, the skill of the painter and, in most cases, their Protestantism.[52] Yet the Catholic Anthony van Dyck imparted an irresistible sense of glamour to his sitters.[53] The swagger portrait posed a challenge to the viewer that was often combined with an element of theatre.[54] This links well with Amanda Bailey's concept of flaunting, a style of behaviour and dress that was a young man's game in the late sixteenth and early seventeenth centuries.[55] Arguably, this confident flamboyance applied to Scottish men of all ages throughout the century, as is indicated by the observation of Thomas Kirke, a Yorkshireman, who travelled to Inverness in 1677. He described the Highland men 'strutting' like peacocks in their short doublets 'slashed in the sleeves, and open on the back', a plaid and 'a sort of breeches, not unlike a petticoat that reaches not so low by far as the knees'.[56] While Kirke was something of a Scotophobe, his words unwittingly capture the undeniable flair with which Scottish men wore their clothes.[57] And as the English naturalist John Ray observed in *c.*1662, this was true of men at all levels of Scottish society and 'a fellow that hath scarce ten groats … you shall see … clad like a gentleman'.[58]

0.7 Daniel Mytens the elder, *James Hamilton, 3rd Marquis and 1st Duke of Hamilton*, 1623. Oil on canvas, 200.7 × 125.1 cm. Tate Britain, London. Aged 17, Hamilton shows off his Spanish-style black doublet and breeches, a style he adopted after his visit to Madrid with Prince Charles in 1623.

So *Stuart Style* draws heavily on the evidence of the written word, whether it is Middle Scots, English, Gaelic or Latin.[59] Scots words such as *breiks* ('breeches'), *jupe* ('jerkin'), *sark* ('shirt'), *shanks* ('stockings') and *trews* (close-fitting hose, often of tartan) serve as a reminder of the cultural differences between the two countries. These words are illuminated and expanded upon by reference to portraiture produced in Edinburgh, London and elsewhere, along with surviving examples of clothing, accessories and jewellery.[60] While there are only a handful of garments, jewels and accessories that can be linked with a degree of certainty to the Stuart royalty, there is a larger pool of seventeenth-century artefacts that can augment evidence found in contemporary writings, and the book draws on all of this evidence.[61]

Structure

Stuart Style is divided into three parts. The first presents five clothing case studies running from James VI and I to James VII and II. As fathers, sons or grandsons, these Stuart men spanned three generations of what Pittock has well described as 'a Catholic or Catholic leaning Scottish dynasty'.[62] The garments placed on these royal bodies ranged from robes of state, via shirts, drawers, stockings and, on occasion, socks, to the 'suit' – a subtly evolving combination of garments, variants of which were worn for every occasion from meeting ambassadors, hearing sermons and attending Parliament to dining, hunting and playing tennis (fig. 0.8). In addition, royal clothing choices were linked to specific 'stages' rather than 'ages', a point David Cressy explored in his analysis of the early modern male life cycle.[63] These included youth, marriage and fatherhood – all key points in shaping their relationship with their clothes. These 'clothing biographies' establish each man's contribution to royal or Stuart style while also exploring whether Stuart style was still Scottish style after 1603, and if so, for how long. In addition, this section assesses how far, if at all, these Stuart kings used clothing to create a group identity at court, and whether the success of this varied over time according to who was king and the prevailing political circumstances. In other words, did the Stuarts use dress to create a sense of British and/or Scottish and English identity, and, if so, who bought into this, when, where and why?

Two other men made a bid for inclusion as full case studies but were rejected. William III (1650–1702) was excluded because his accession represented a break in the direct male Stuart line in 1689/90. After this point James VII and II, James VIII and III (1688–1766) and then Charles Edward Stuart (1720–88) sought to regain their throne from William, Anne and then after 1714 with the accession of George I (1660–1727), from the Hanoverians.[64] The subversive potential of clothing was stressed in 1702 when Jacobites drank to 'the little gentleman in black velvet'.[65] This was a nod to William III's horse tripping over a molehill in that year and throwing its rider with fatal consequences. However, evidence from William's reign

0.8 Unknown artist, *Charles II and James Duke of York*, 17th century. Oil on canvas, 238 × 174 cm. Government Art Collection. The royal brothers look very alike in their silk velvet robes, a style of dress that they shared with the male elite in Scotland and England.

is essential when exploring continuities with, and developments from, his Stuart predecessors and contemporaries. It is also vital in providing the context for the rise of Jacobitism – the response by James VII and II and his supporters to the loss of his thrones – a significant example of a style that affected both Scots and English.[66]

Oliver Cromwell (1599–1658) has likewise been excluded because he was not a Stuart and never king, in spite of many his supporters believing that he should be treated as a monarch, in death if not in life. When the royalist collector John Bargrave (1610–80) visited Florence in 1679 he noted unhappily in his memoirs that 'In the Greate Dukes most Famous Gallery, I found Crumwells Picture hanged in amongst the Heros (which vexed me)'. When asked his opinion of the collection, Bargrave stated that Cromwell's portrait 'spoyled all the rest'.[67] In spite of Bargrave's disapproval, Oliver Cromwell and William III undeniably shaped the political landscape in which the later Stuarts operated. Both men had a confrontational relationship with Scotland. They also contributed to, and engaged in, the Stuarts' sartorial story, with neither man being as dowdy as is often suggested.[68] Indeed, using a combination of adoption and adaptation both drew successfully on different aspects of the Stuarts' style to legitimise their position in the Three Kingdoms.

The scope of *Stuart Style* broadens in Part II, and changes to a thematic approach as it explores the production and ongoing care of high-end male clothes. Both the Scottish and English elite clothing trades depended heavily on three things. First, the government's wish to promote domestic textile production, combined with an ever-expanding rhetoric in support of home-produced cloth, shaped clothing choices in both countries. Second, imported materials from Europe and beyond, such as silks, were as significant as new ways of cutting and shaping. Third, the Stuart court cities of Edinburgh and London drew leading Scottish craftsmen and craftswomen, in search of the opportunities on offer to succeed and prosper. The rapid growth of London during the seventeenth century provided many possibilities for Scots to live and work there, making and selling Stuart fashion to willing customers. While Scots did not have a monopoly on royal clothing care and production, relative to their numbers, Scottish royal tailors played a significant role in creating and managing royal style. Equally, Scots shopping in London opted to patronise fellow Scots who had moved south when they could.

Part III concentrates on the spaces, places, times and occasions when these clothes were worn north and south of the border, and the consequences of this for how they were received. It begins with an exploration of the textiles, such as the embroidered nightcap in fig. 0.9 that would have been worn within the bedchamber, and the processes of dressing, undressing in the morning and evening and changing clothes throughout the day. The view opens out in Chapter 10 to consider the king and the elite out and about, engaged in a range of daytime activities including the ceremonial opening of Parliament, in their official robes, as well as informal activities such as riding and hunting. The chapter that follows addresses the contentious topic of liturgical textiles, religion and religious spaces. Chapter 12 considers the clothing and textiles associated with mourning and funerals, with the latter increasingly taking place at night. This last chapter also serves as an epilogue to the book. Focusing on royal deaths, it contextualises them within a wider discussion of elite funerals and surveys the use of dress and display at the final send-offs of all the Stuart monarchs discussed here, from the magnificent funeral cortège of James VI and I to the death of the exiled James VII and II in Paris, one of a number of turning points in the development of the Jacobite cause that would culminate in the defeat of Bonnie Prince Charlie at Culloden in 1746.

0.9 Nightcap, 1600–20, British. Linen worked with silk and metal threads (chain, stem, darning, detached buttonhole and plaited braid stitches), spangles, 20.3 × 19.7 cm. Metropolitan Museum of Art, New York. The thistle and rose reflect an interest in the natural world while also nodding towards the union of the crowns under James VI and I.

PART I

THE EVOLUTION AND SIGNIFICANCE OF STUART STYLE

THE STUART MONARCHS FROM JAMES VI and I to James VII and II are at the heart of *Stuart Style*. Their shared belief in their right to rule Scotland, England and Ireland meant that among the elite, court style became the national style in all three kingdoms. This was not to say that their style was not challenged on occasion; rather, that the Stuarts set a benchmark against which others aligned themselves or not, as it suited them. In practical terms, in spite of periods of civil war, exile and the relocation of the Stuart court, the clothing of these five men is surprisingly well documented in words and images, if not in surviving garments.[1] So, this opening section sets the groundwork by evaluating the evolution of men's clothes from 1566 to 1701 through the wardrobes of three generations of Stuarts. There is inevitably some overlap in terms of chronology when writing each man's clothing biography, but this offers the reader scope for comparison and analysis. For instance, the chapters demonstrate that while the types of clothing worn by infants and young boys remained quite stable, once breeched, sons experienced the adult fashions favoured by their fathers with varying degrees of enthusiasm.

(page 24) See figure I.3.

Another emerging theme is the Stuarts' declining level of Scottishness from James VI and I onwards in terms of their blood, their time spent on Scottish soil and their wider engagement with the Scots male elite, with the exception of James VII and II. However, while the Stuarts became more 'British' or more Anglicised, their courts still provided a draw for Scottish courtiers and craftsmen alike, who helped shape the styles synonymous with the Stuart name. The fashionable Scottish elite consistently presented themselves as the equals of their English, Irish or French counterparts, serving as representatives of the absentee Stuart monarchs on home soil. However, before embarking on the clothing biographies, it is important to set the scene by asking which clothes were considered fashionable in early modern Scottish and English contexts, how clothes and fabrics were linked to national identity and, consequently, how clothes were used, and abused, to promote national stereotypes.

Fashionable Dress, Clothing Regulations and the Lowland Scottish Male

In 1558 George Seton, 7th lord Seton (1531–86), attended the marriage of Mary, Queen of Scots to the dauphin of France as the master of her household. 12 years later he was painted in a sumptuous suit of crimson silk, and the presence of embroidered gold thistles on this set of garments suggests that these were the clothes he had worn for Mary's wedding (fig. I.1).[2] Seton's crimson doublet, hose and cloak are an excellent example of the mid-sixteenth-century suit, the evolution of which was central to the male wardrobe during the long seventeenth century. In its final form of coat, vest and breeches, the suit symbolised modest masculinity among the social elite for contemporaries such as the diarist John Evelyn (1620–1706). Running in tandem with the evolution of the suit was the use of new and traditional accessories, which served as markers of male status and fashionability.[3]

An early modern Scotsman's clothing choices were influenced as much by his status as they were by where he was born. As Thomas Kirke observed in 1677, 'The Lowland gentry go well enough habited', by which he meant that the gentlemen of Lowland Scotland wore fashionable dress of the type to be found throughout northern Europe.[4] An English clergyman, Thomas Morer, expanded on this in 1689, commenting that in the Lowlands 'Their habit is mostly English, saving the meaner sort of men wear bonnets instead of hats and pladds, instead of cloaks'.[5] Indeed, all through Scotland 'the Scots generally (that is, the poorer sort), [wore] … blue bonnets on their heads, and some russet'.[6] The popularity of these bonnets is borne out by examples recovered from archaeological sites including Dava Moor near Cromdale, Tarvie in Ross-shire and Quintfall Hill, Caithness (fig. I.2).[7] While Morer was unenthused, others saw bonnets as desirable, and in 1617 the tailor William Orme stood trial for receiving stolen goods from Margaret Grey, who took oats, meal and 'ane

I.1 Unknown artist, French school, *George Seton, 7th Lord Seton*, 1570. Oil on panel, 120 × 105.7 cm. National Galleries of Scotland. Clad all in scarlet, Seton is dressed in the height of French fashion.

new blew bonnett' from her employer.[8] As a tailor, Orme would have been well placed to sell on this bonnet to a willing buyer.

The value that was placed on propriety in clothing styles in the British Isles was evident from the repeated attempts made by the government to regulate what men wore. While James VI and I repealed English laws regulating clothing in 1604, by 1610 he accepted that it was still necessary to take 'some politic order gainst excess of apparel'.[9] He and his successors did so with varying degrees of success through a series of proclamations. In contrast, James left sumptuary law in place in Scotland, and so it remained until 1701.[10] Why he followed different strategies in the two kingdoms is harder to explain. One possibility lies with how James viewed both nations. He certainly believed that 'Saint george surelie rydes upon a touardlie rydding horse, quhaire I ame daylie burstin in daunting a wylde unreulie coalte'.[11] His decision also reflects that Scottish men had always spent heavily on their clothes, in spite of Scotland's relative poverty compared to larger European countries. When Don Pedro de Ayala (d. 1513) visited Scotland in 1496–7 he noted that 'They spend all they have to keep up appearances. They are as well dressed as it is possible to be in such a country.'[12] Attempts to regulate this wish to be well dressed occurred in

I.2 Not all bonnets were blue, as in the case of this dark green example with a narrow headband decorated with red spots, which was recovered from a bog on Arnish Moor, Lewis. Early 18th century. National Museum of Scotland, Edinburgh.

1581 with the 'Act Aganis the Excesse of Coistlie Cleithing' – a statute that was renewed in 1595 and again in 1612. All three excluded the elite and the officers of the king's household from any sartorial restrictions.[13]

The doublets and hose, and later coats and breeches, described in and regulated by the Scottish sumptuary laws were in keeping with fashionable male dress across Europe.[14] However, there were other styles of clothing open to Scottish men, as is clear from the regulations for merchants trading at Veere, the staple port for Scotland in the Netherlands between 1541 and 1799, that stipulated that 'none seil in merchandise except he be honestly abuillzied like an honest merchant'.[15] 'Honest' business attire was clearly a doublet and hose, as was made evident in a negative comment about merchants from Aberdeen travelling to Edinburgh and Dundee in 1611. It was sniffily observed that these individuals were dressed in 'plaidis and blew bonnatis ... as giff they were landwart men ... and not merchantis'.[16] In contrast, Alexander Barclay, merchant, burgess of Edinburgh and indweller in Mayboill, dressed in the approved style, as revealed in the testimony he made in 1617. Barclay claimed that he was attacked by John Ferguson of Kilcarran and David Ferguson, otherwise known as Davie the Devil, who 'cutit his cloik throw the double neck thairof and doublet and ther claithes into the skyne'.[17] Whether his doublet made Barclay more of a target for the likes of Davie is harder to say.

In spite of the fashionable style of men like Barclay, in *c.*1620 Sir Robert Gordon (1580–1656) wrote a letter of advice to his nephew, John Gordon, 14th earl of Sutherland (1609–79), urging him to 'Purge your countrey piece by piece from the vnciwill kind of cloithes, such as plaids, mantels, truses and blew bonnets ... Cause the inhabitants of the countrey to cloith them selfs as the ciwill prowinces of the kingdome do, with doublet, hoise, cloiks and hats'.[18] In Sir Robert's view, lowland clothing was preferred to highland dress and, as Stana Nenadic has observed, this style of 'civil' – and fashionable – appearance was still viewed 'as a mark of status' by many Scots at the end of the seventeenth century.[19]

The Distinctive Appearance of Highland Dress and its Significance in Stuart Society

Early modern concepts of identity and civility were closely linked to language, dress and the types of textiles used to make clothing. James VI revealed some of the underlying tensions within sixteenth-century Scottish society, and the Highland–Lowland divide, in his *Basilikon Doron* (1599) when he commented:

> As for the highlands, I shortly comprehend them all in two sorts of people: the one that dwelleth in our mainland, that are barbarous for the most part, and yet mixed with some show of civility: the other, that dwelleth in the isles, and are utterly barbarians, without any sort or show of civility.[20]

When Sir William Brereton travelled to the Highlands in 1635 he described the local men's distinctive clothing as 'a kind of loose flap garment hanging loose about their breech, their knees bare'. However, unlike James, Brereton considered that the Highlanders were 'proper, personable, well-complexioned men, and able men, the very gentlemen in their blue caps and plaids'.[21]

Seventeen years earlier, former London boatman John Taylor, the water poet, had recorded Highland dress more fully, noting unfamiliar garments made from distinctive textiles.[22] He described men wearing

> stockings (which they call short hose) made of a warm stuffe of divers colours which they call Tartane; as for breeches, many of them, nor their forefathers, never wore any, but a jerkin of the same stuffe that their hose is of … [with] a plead about their shoulders, which is a mantle of divers colours, much finer and lighter stuffe than their hose, with blue flat caps on their heads.[23]

Aspects of this style were shared between the Highlands, islands and Ireland. Thus Randal MacDonnell, 1st marquis of Antrim (1609–83), wore 'neither hat, cap nor shoe, nor stocking' until he was 7 or 8 (arguably the time when he might have been breeched) because he was 'bred the highland way' and wore their distinctive style of dress.[24]

By the 1670s the plaid was worn, belted to form a cloak and kilt, with a short waisted doublet of a style that had dropped out of fashion in the 1660s. John Michael Wright (1617–94) captured this short doublet in his portrait of Lord Mungo Murray (1668–1700), which he painted while he was in Ireland (fig. I.3).[25] Thomas Kirke saw this style of dress when he travelled to Inverness in 1677. He wrote that the men's doublets were

I.3 John Michael Wright, *Lord Mungo Murray (Am Morair Mungo Moireach)*, 1683. Oil on canvas, 154.3 × 24.8 cm. National Galleries of Scotland. In addition to his bonnet, belted plaid and tartan hose, Lord Mungo also has an impressive set of Highland weapons including a dirk, basket-hilted sword, two pistols and a flintlock sporting gun.

> slashed in the sleeves, and open at the back … [worn with] a sort of breeches, not unlike a petticoat that reaches not so low by far as the knees, and their stockings are rolled about the calves of their legs, and tied with a garter, their knee and thigh being naked … with a plaid over the left shoulder and under the right arm, and a cap a-cock.[26]

As the seventeenth century progressed it became common for some Scottish gentlemen to own a distinct set of 'Highland clothes', as opposed to clothes for elsewhere. One very interesting example from 1682 is that of Charles Home, of Ayton in the Border region, who asked his nephew George for a suit of Highland clothes and laces.[27] More details of Highland clothing appear in the inventory of Colin Campbell of Glenure of 1740, including a kilt and a short kilt jacket.[28] Of all the elements of Highland dress, the plaid was most distinctive. Many men, including John Campbell, 1st earl of Breadalbane and Holland (1635–1716), wore their plaids regularly. In 1690 he bought a waistcoat to wear under his coat 'as his plaid has grown threadbare'.[29] By the 1720s the significance of the plaid as the key part of a man's Highland identity was such that when one man abandoned his plaid, to the fury of his neighbours, he observed that 'his greatcoat was the cause of their wrath; and that their reproach was, that he could not be contented with the garb of his ancestors, but was degenerated into a Lowlander, and condescended to their unmanly fashions'.[30] Here the role of Scottish geography and Highland dress are very clearly linked in creating a sense of identity.

The weapons a Scotsman carried were an essential marker of social standing that the crown, again, tried to regulate. On 22 March 1617 James VI and I renewed the ban on a certain Lauchlan MacLean, stating 'that he nor his sone sall not beare nor weare hacquebutis or pistolettis bot in the Kingis service', although they were permitted a sword as a reminder of their place in society.[31] Over half a century later attempts at control were still in place. For instance, in February 1656 Sir David Ogilvy, laird of Inverquharity, was permitted to 'passe with his sworde in the shire of Angus & to keepe a fowling peece for his Game'.[32] Even so, by the 1670s most Highland men carried 'a durk or skean, of about a foot and a half a yard long, very sharp … nor is this honour sufficient, if they can purchase more, they must have a long swinging sword'.[33] Scottish weapons were distinctive in style in terms of type of blade and style of hilt.[34] Many also had characteristic decoration, as is indicated by an inventory taken at Gordon Castle in 1699 that recorded six old guns 'with highland works' – a distinctive feature worthy of note.[35]

While weapons were significant, plaid and tartan were two of the most distinctive yet elusive features of early modern Scottish dress. Regulations controlled the quality, colour and lengths of plaids in use, as is evident from a ruling made by the town council of Stirling on 18 August 1661 that stated that 'plaids are to be of good yarn, that the red, blue and yellow colours thereof are to be dyed by litsters [dyers] of the burgh, at a cost not exceeding 5s Scots per pound, that each pair of plaids is to be 12 ells long and ¾ ell broad and that the weavers are to give ready service to the plaid-makers in the burgh'.[36]

Plaids were often worn draped around the body, but they could also be cut and made into garments. While seventeenth-century household accounts distinguished between purchases of plaid and tartan, indicating that they were different products, the exact nature of the tartan was less certain.[37] It was a checked, wool cloth that was produced in a variety of weights, ranging from fine to coarse. Worn throughout the seventeenth century, it was the fabric used in hunting dress for the Highland elite and in everyday clothing for much of the rest of the population. By the 1690s the elite were accustomed to giving lengths of tartan to members of their household. For instance, in 1697 the earl of Breadalbane bought 10 ells of tartan for his footmen and scholars, while in April 1698 he charged Colin Campbell to buy 3 ells of plaid to make a waistcoat for John McComie, the butler's man.[38] The earl also clad his pipers in tartan. Thus, Little Johnny McIntyre, piper, received a plaid, while tartan was sent with Johnny McIntyre, piper, to be given to McCrooman, piper in the Isles, for his breeches and hose.[39] Here, at

I.4 John Michael Wright, *John Lacy*, c.1668–70. Oil on canvas, 233.4 × 173.4 cm. Royal Collection. Lacy's choice of trews for the part of Sauny the Scot reveals a lot about the character's status and wealth.

the end of the seventeenth century, we see the first tentative steps towards what Michael Lynch identified as 'the cult of tartanry'.[40]

By the mid seventeenth century, Scottish dress and tartan were present in London too. In January 1659, for example, John Duncan Campbell of Glenorchy, 1st earl of Breadalbane and Holland (1635–1717) paid James Campbell, merchant in Edinburgh, for carriage of his cloak and waistcoat to London by land, along with a fine plaid.[41] Fifteen years later a Highland plaid was bought for Dougal Campbell in London at a cost of £12 Scots. He also received a short coat of blue cloth, 9 ells of ribbon to trim the plaid and coat, trews and hose of fine tartan, a dirk with a sheath, a powder horn and belt, a targe and a broadsword. A bonnet, two pairs of Lorn brogues, a belt and a purse completed the outfit.[42] The acceptability of this stylish dress is evident in John Michael Wright's triple portrait of the actor John Lacy (*c.*1615–81) in the clothes associated with his most famous roles: the lead from *Sauny the Scot* (an adaptation of *The Taming of the Shrew*), Monsieur Device from *The Country Chaplain* and Scruple from *The Cheats* (fig. I.4). Like Campbell,

Lacy wore a pair of trews, a very distinctive element of Highland dress and one that was typically considered an elite garment because of its tailoring. Commissioned by Charles II, it is most unlikely that this painting – or the actor it depicts – were mocking the Scottish nation. Rather, Lacy was surely shown here clad in the way that Scots could, and often did, dress. Indeed, copies of this painting, depicting as it did Scottish, French and very subdued English clothing, were popular in Edinburgh in 1697 when two examples were for sale.[43] In short, Wright's painting summed up three significant and contrasting strands of the Stuarts' style, of which Highland dress was a distinctive and increasingly acceptable option.

Dressing the Part? A Multitude of Stuart Types

If clothes reflected a man's place of birth, social position and good character, then mocking distinctive aspects of a person's dress was associated with national stereotypes in early modern literature, drama and libels.[44] English poems and songs commenting on Scottish men of the middling sort emphasised their provincial, functional and inexpensive accessories. This suggests that there was less to ridicule in terms of their clothing, while acknowledging that the correct accessories were essential in making a man fashionable. Bonnets, shoes and swords all came under close scrutiny, indicating that they were distinctively different and that aspirational Scottish men discarded them when presented with an alternative. Consequently, the blue bonnet was replaced by the socially aspirant Scot with 'a hat and feather', rough footwear was exchanged for shoes of Spanish leather 'decked with roses', and a sword with 'a great basket hilt of iron' was swapped for a rapier. Sartorial adjustments like these prompted some Englishmen to make the provocative claim:

> Bonny Scot, we all witness can,
> That England hath made thee a gentleman.[45]

The importance of these accessories meant that the stock figure of the middling sort of Scot on the English stage was distinguished by his blue bonnet and whinyard (a hanger or short sword), his accent and dialect.[46] In contrast, high-ranking Scots were presented as 'gentlemen in their own countries' with no reference to specific clothing, mannerisms or speech indicating that they exemplified the fashionable Stuart look.[47]

The change in accessories described above was linked to a shift in social status to a gentleman, a recurrent theme that indicated that many of the Scots who had come to London had done well for themselves. In the anonymously penned verse below, it was the transition from a naturally coloured or 'pied motley' jerkin to one made of scarlet that affected the transformation and made it apparent to all:

His pied motley jerkin all threadbare and old
Is now turned to scarlet and o'er-laced with gold
His straw hat to beaver, his hat band to pearl
And Jockey can caper as high as an Earl.[48]

Scotland and England were both wool-producing countries, with raw wool, yarn and woven cloth making up a significant part of their exports. There was also a close link between home-produced cloth, patriotism and dress. In death, the wool trade was promoted by the English government's insistence on the use of woollen burial shrouds.[49] In life, Englishmen were encouraged to wear broadcloth, as is made clear in the subtitle of Robert Greene's *A Quip for an Upstart Courtier. A Quaint Dispute between Velvet Breeches and Cloth Breeches* (1592). Here, the character of Cloth Breeches, a stalwart and Protestant Englishman, is stoutly opposed to the silk fabrics imported from Catholic countries represented by his rival, Velvet Breeches.[50] In a similar vein, Scottish wools and linen were staples in many Scots' wardrobes. However, the elite shopped more widely as was indicated in 1640 when Sir Colin Campbell, 8th laird of Glenorchy, 2nd baronet (*c.*1577–1640) settled his account with James Rae, merchant and burgess of Edinburgh. The laird's purchases included the finest black satin, silver-plate breast buttons, purple ribbons, Holland cloth, purple Spanish taffeta and a fine, black English hat.[51] Fashioned from a range of European goods, the laird positioned himself among the well-dressed Scottish elite.

Unlike the Scots, the English did not have a distinctive national style of dress. However, English men (and women) did have a clothing weakness that could be exploited in turn – their susceptibility to fashionable novelty and innovation. European visitors mocked this trait, while a group of English commentators who felt they were above such things wrote scathingly about this national failing. In 1562 Welsh physician Andrew Boorde mockingly observed:

I am an English man, and naked I stand here,
Musyng in my mynd what rayment I shal were;
For now I wyll were this, and now I wyl were that;
Now I wyl were I cannot tel what.[52]

Accompanying Boorde's text was a woodcut of a scantily clad Englishman brandishing a pair of scissors. Driven by a desire for the novel, the result was inelegant confusion. Matters had not improved by the time Daniel Defoe wrote *The True-born Englishman* (1701), in which he declared:

A true-born Englishman's a Contradiction
In Speech an Irony, in Fact a Fiction.[53]

Another very important pair of figures, from 1642 onwards, was that of the cavalier and roundhead.[54] These political terms could sum up a distinctive look created by a man's choice of clothes and hairstyle, both north and south of the border. The name 'cavalier' was derived from the Spanish word *caballero*, meaning 'a swaggering soldier'; at times this could be seen as a good thing.[55] For instance, Scottish general Robert Monro addressed a summary of his life written in the 1630s 'to the use of all worthie Cavaliers favouring the laudable profession of Arms'.[56] However, during the Wars of the Three Kingdoms the term 'cavalier' was used to describe and denigrate the followers of Charles I, many of whom wore sumptuous clothes and had long hair. In contrast, the soubriquet 'roundhead' was used to disparage the shorter-haired, simply dressed followers of Parliament. Tamsyn Williams and Christopher Breward have successfully challenged the stock images that these terms conjured up by demonstrating that the terms and the types, or stereotypes, were not as cut and dried as they might appear to be.[57] Even so, they had ongoing use, for example, with the Cavalier Parliament that was in session from 1661 to 1679, and was so-called because of the number of royalist MPs.

The plainly dressed roundhead has often been associated with a third distinctive group, the Puritan or, in Scotland, Presbyterian. Both Puritans and Presbyterians were opposed to luxurious clothing and personal adornment for the laity and liturgical textiles for the church or kirk. The cover of Samuel Ward's 1622 sermon, *Woe to Drunkards*, appears to gesture towards this Puritan view by making a direct link between changes in men's fashion and a decline in moral standards. The high-heeled shoes, shoe roses, garters, lace cuffs and satin doublets of the 1620s were equated by some moralist commentators with smoking, dice and drink.[58] However, Francis Bremer has challenged this view by citing the work of Puritan clergyman William Perkins.[59] Perkins stressed the value of clothing 'in respect of place, calling and condition, for the upholding and maintenance thereof'.[60] So, for the elite there was a permissible level of luxury that was required to maintain one's position in society.

This was equally true for Puritans and Presbyterians. When Suffolk gentleman Edward Lewkenor died, in 1634, he was described as not only 'honest, devout, holy and [of] christian life' but also as being 'somewhat above the ordinary garbe and fashion of gentlemen of his age and quality'.[61] His everyday clothing was 'far from baseness' but it was 'normally much lower than the height of his meanes'.[62] While these words from Lewkenor's funeral sermon were likely to play down worldly concerns such as clothing, his portrait records him posed nonchalantly in an elegant doublet, breeches and short cloak.[63] In a similar, if more exalted manner, William, 3rd duke of Hamilton, a committed Presbyterian, dressed the part of Scotland's leading peer. An inventory of his clothes, dating from 1693, included 'a fine scarlet embroidered coat with gold, with a gold stuff waistcoat fringed with gold [and] a fine scarlet cloak embroidered with gold and lin'd with blue velvet'.[64] This shared attitude to clothing meant that, while there were clear doctrinal differences between Puritanism and Presbyterianism, one might be confused for the other by non-Protestants.

Many Puritans and Presbyterians adopted black, but it is important to note that they did so for a range of reasons. While donning black could represent a rejection of colour, black clothing had significant social and financial value.[65] When Archibald Campbell, 8th earl of Argyll (1598–1661) was painted in the 1650s (fig. I.5), his fine quality linen was accentuated by an understated yet expensive black doublet and gown that commanded the respect due to his place in society. Dyed black textiles were costly and elegant, and they gained in desirability when embellished with embroidery, lace and passementerie, either black, coloured or of metal thread. In 1601 the tensions between a certain John Weillands and the Reverend John Gibson at Haddington were expressed by their clothes. A witness reported that Gibson 'said errant knave ar ye cummit heir to schaik yowr breiches with … satein doublet, and the said Jhone Weillandis ansuerit quhay maij I not weir this … dowblet, as weill as ye weir blak klaithis'.[66] Both men felt equally justified in their choice.

I.5 David Scougall, *Archibald Campbell, 8th Earl of Argyll*, 1650s. Oil on canvas, 73.7 × 67.3 cm. National Galleries of Scotland. Sombre yet elegant, Archibald Campbell's fashionable black doublet, nightcap and gown are paired with a very fine linen collar and tassels.

The perceived opulence, colourfulness and fashionability of Catholic dress were compared by contemporaries with the plainness of Anglican and Puritan style. George Savile, 1st marquis of Halifax (1633–95) summed up the danger faced by Charles II during his European exile when, he claimed, 'the outward appearance of such unfashionable [Anglican] men was made an argument against their religion; and a young prince more susceptible to raillery, was the more susceptible of contempt for it'.[67] As this discussion reveals, nationality, political views and religion divided and drew together Stuart society. Your dress could indicate what sort of man you were, thereby inviting criticism and compliment alike.

Scottish Military Men

The Scottish soldier was a well-known, if not an especially well-liked, figure in England, chiefly because Scottish armies crossed the border on four separate occasions between 1639 and 1651.[68] Some of the rank and file were well equipped, as is indicated by the comments of John Spalding on troops who mustered in Aberdeen on 16 February (*c.*1640) when 'Ilk soldiour wes furneshit with tua sarkis, cot, breikis, hoiss and bonet, bandis, and schone'.[69] An image of a Scottish soldier in 1651 that features in a print of the Covenanters holding Charles II's nose to the grindstone, is in a similar vein. 'Jockie', as he was styled, wears a short coat with a centre back seam and buttoned back vent, sleeves with a turned-back cuff, simple loose-fitting knee-length breeches and a bonnet (fig. I.6). Overall, the English view of Scottish soldiers was not positive, and vice versa.

Scottish troops also played a significant role in European armies, where, again, some of the rank and file were distinctive because of their dress. This was the case of the professional soldiers fighting for Gustavus Adolphus, king of Sweden (1594–1632) during the Thirty Years War (fig. I.7).[70] In addition, many Scots held high rank, including Patrick

Ruthven, 1st earl of Forth (*c.*1573–1651), Alexander Leslie, 1st earl of Leven (1580–1661), David Drummond (1593–1638) and Sir John Hepburn (*c.*1598–1636). Ruthven and Leslie returned to Scotland dressed in the height of European fashion. Scots also held commands in the French and English armies.[71] In the case of the latter, Scots led five of Sir William Waller's 11 regiments, so making them very visible in society south of the border.[72] They also held commands in the Royalist army, but as Newman has observed, they were less prominent.[73]

From the mid seventeenth century onwards, the development of military uniforms associated with the king's Scottish and English standing regiments exerted a growing influence on fashionable male clothing. In 1699 Archibald Campbell, 10th earl of Argyll (1658–1703), arranged a contract to clothe his Horse Guards with the Edinburgh merchants Hugh Blair and Samuel McLellan. The uniforms were stylish, with each gentleman receiving 'ane fashonable coat of fine scarlet cloth … mounted with fashonable double guilded princes mettle buttons'.[74] Everything about the cut and decoration of this coat was influenced by fashionable male dress.

Running in parallel to this development was the option for elite men to be portrayed in armour, as William Dobson (1611–46) and Sir Peter Lely frequently painted them. Armour asserted a man's knightly status, alluded to his military skill and emphasised his honour. Therefore, it did not matter if it was one's own, or was outdated. The value placed on such a portrait is evident from the group of three-quarter-length pictures of men in armour

1.6 Unknown artist, 'The Scots holding their young king's nose to the grindstone', 1651, broadside. The clothes of the three protagonists – the simply dressed soldier, the Covenanting minister in black gown and cap, and their young, cavalier king, dressed fancy breeches, long boots and spurs – correspond to contemporary stereotypes.

1.7 Unknown artist, *Scottish soldiers in the service of Gustavus Adolphus*, 1631. Woodcut. New York Public Library. Prized for their ferocity, Scottish troops were heavily armed with bows, halberds or lochaber axes and muskets, and distinctively dressed in bonnets and belted plaids.

painted by John Michael Wright in the 1660s.[75] This includes his portrait of Robert Bruce, 2nd earl of Elgin and 1st earl of Ailesbury (*c*.1623/7–85). Sir John Baptiste de Medina produced similar work, including a portrait of his leading Scottish patron, David Leslie, 3rd earl of Leven (1660–1728), painted in 1691. Leven persuaded Medina to come to Edinburgh, pleading with him 'only to stay so long as to doe all the faces of his pictures … If you can condescend upon the persons to be drawn, the size and the garb, a good many be so blocked as that he'll finish them before he goes'.[76]

Medina painted a number of his male sitters in very similar armour, with their collar or cravat, sash and sword belt offering an impression of individuality, as in the 1694 portraits of Thomas Hamilton, 6th earl of Haddington (1680–1735) and Charles Hope, 1st earl of Hopetoun (1681–1742).[77] While this generic style might speak to ideas of chivalry and elite masculinity, their behaviour and reputation determined how others viewed the man in question. David Paton's portrait of the professional soldier, John Graham of Claverhouse, viscount Dundee (*c*.1649–89) presents a good-looking man with his long, dark hair falling onto his armoured shoulders. However, his reputation divided opinion. To the Covenanters, whom Graham defeated at Bothwell Bridge or Brig on 22 June 1679, he was 'Bloody Clavers', while his supporters called him 'Bonnie Dundee'.[78]

Clothes as Disguise

'I thought myself to be like a crow in the middes of a great many golden feathered dove'.[79] These words summed up how one Wiltshire MP felt when he attended the ceremonies marking Henry's creation as prince of Wales in 1610. At an event such as this, clothes served as a display of magnificence and loyalty to the crown. On other occasions the Stuarts used clothing as a disguise to allow them to step outside their usual place in society, to take part in court entertainments and even to escape capture *in extremis*. They also used clothes and jewellery as a means of asserting their cause during the Wars of the Three Kingdoms, the Commonwealth, and after 1688 when James VII and II became 'the king across the water'.

Prior to 1603 the Stuart kings occasionally used clothes as a disguise, to give them freedom to act outside the usual constraints that were placed upon them. Consequently when Elizabeth I said that she would like to meet Mary, Queen of Scots, the Scottish ambassador Sir James Melville offered 'to convey her secretly to Scotland by Post, clothed like a Page, that under this disguise she might see the Queen as James the Fifth had gone in disguise to France with his own Ambassador, to see the Duke of Vendom's sister, who should have been his Wife'.[80] However, disguise outside the royal family was generally associated with subversive behaviour. On 22 March 1606 false rumours of James VI and I's death circulated and it is interesting to note that 'Some said the treason was performed by English Jesuits, some by Scots in women's attire, others by Spaniards and French'.[81] Coming only a few months after the Gunpowder Plot, such rumours easily gained credence among the public.

The masque flourished at the Jacobean and Caroline courts. As an art form, it was used to explore ideas of nationality both in terms of the subject matter and the participants. In 1613 the diarist John Chamberlain described Ben Jonson's *The Irish Masque at Court* to Alice Carleton, informing her that 'yesternight there was a motley maske of five English and five Scotts (which are called the high dancers) amongst whom Sergeant Boide, one Abraham crummie and Ackmoutie (that was at Padoua and Venice) are esteemed the most principall and loftie'.[82] William Davenant's *Salmacida Spolia* (1639) included 'an ancient Scotishman, presented by Mr Atkins', while Inigo Jones drew costume designs for an Englishman, an Irishman and a Scot.[83] While quite sketchy, the contemporary design for the Scot suggests that the masquer was dressed in a belted plaid over trews in order to evoke the sense of the Stuarts' homeland.

The masque also allowed the royal family to take centre stage. Masked and in costume, everyone knew who they were because of the quality of their clothes, as is evident from Inigo Jones's extant design for Charles I's costume for the Shrovetide masque.[84] At this time the king was described as having 'his hair all gauffred and frizzled, which he never used before'.[85] Four years later, when the queen and her ladies performed Aurelian Townshend's *Tempe Restored* on 14 February 1632, observers reported that 'The king himselfe by gaily taking part in the dancing, proved the pleasure which he took in it'.[86] George Kirke, yeoman of the robes, similarly provided masquing apparel 'for his Majesty's oune Royall person and others' for *Coelum Britannicum*, performed on 18 February 1634.[87] Not everyone approved of these entertainments and the use of costumes to play a part. Indeed, some saw the court as 'a nursery of lust and intemperance' where courtiers 'were entertained with masks, stage playes and sorts of ruder sports' and 'wantonnesse in things belonging to the bodie is shewed in costly apparell ... in no estate or degree may one be so excessive as to forget holinesse and Christian sobrietie'.[88] From a Puritan perspective, these costumes embodied everything that was wrong with the Stuart court.

The Stuarts also resorted to disguise when they were in great danger or difficulty, the most celebrated occasion being when Charles II masqueraded as a countryman during his escape after the battle of Worcester in 1651. It was acceptable for prisoners to dress as women when attempting to escape, as was the case of James, duke of York in 1648.[89] And it was not just the monarchs who sometimes had to resort to such tactics. In 1690, Mary Carew's son Alexander joined his brother George at Spithead in the Solent after escaping from Spain by cutting his hair and dressing as a friar.[90]

While costumes and disguises were often problematic, adopting Scottish dress in London could serve as 'a compliment' to the Stuart kings.[91] The dramatist Thomas Dekker (*c.*1572–1632) suggested this in *The Gull's Hornbook* performed in 1609, when he described a 'true humorous gallant' wearing trews because he 'desires to pour himself into all fashions' and consequently was 'ingenious in the trussing of a new Scotch hose'.[92] In a similar vein, John Taylor revealed that elite figures from across Scotland 'doe conforme themselves to the habite of the High-land-men' when they went hunting because it was expected.[93]

The monarchy also adopted this style when it suited them. Before our period, James V and his daughter Mary, Queen of Scots chose to wear a form of Highland dress on occasion. In August 1538, for example, 'The expensis on ye kingis personne deliuerit to Thomas Authnore' includes reference to the purchase of Highland tartan for the king.[94] No evidence has so far been found to indicate that the later Stuart kings wore this style of dress when hunting in Scotland, but they did want to see it being worn. On 29 June 1633, the Scottish privy council wrote to the 8th laird of Glenorchy to inform him of Charles I's request that he wished to see 'a show and muster made of hieland men' when he was at Perth. They were to be 'men personable for stature and in thair best array and equippage with trews, bows darlochs [quivers] and other thair ordinarie weapons and furniture'.[95] Even an Englishman such as Taylor could dress the part successfully with a little help. He noted that 'My good Lord of Marr ... put me into that shape [i.e. Highland dress]'.[96] Dressing the part, whether it was to fit in with a hunting party, take part in a masque or evade capture, played a significant role in Stuart society.

Each of the Stuarts shaped fashionable dress during their lifetime, and it was their style that much of the elite followed. It was a style that reflected the tensions between the three kingdoms and national stereotypes that were often associated with specific types of clothing. However, in the Scottish context elite men, especially those from the Highlands, had an alternative to the fashionable 'Stuart' style suit in Highland dress, which they could wear as an expression of distinctly Scottish culture or as a lack of engagement with or rejection of Stuart (or later, Hanoverian) authority.

CHAPTER ONE

James VI and I (1566–1625)

JAMES VI AND I IS OFTEN PRESENTED as less significant than Charles I and Charles II in dress histories that focus on either the seventeenth century or the Stuarts. This is largely because by taking an Anglo- or London-centric view, these studies start with his arrival in England, thus missing 37 years of James's clothing history, and then analyse a king who was middle-aged at his accession. As a result, James is frequently regarded as passively following his more glamorous, clothes-conscious cousin, Elizabeth I, and studies tend not to look at how he added to and drew upon the clothing traditions established by his recent Scottish, Francophile predecessors – in particular James V and Mary, Queen of Scots.[1] When Jenny Wormald considered whether James VI's style of kingship was radically different before and after 1603, she actively compared his Scottish and English reigns.[2] However, when thinking about his clothing it is more helpful to divide his life into three: from birth to the point when he gained control of his own wardrobe in 1584; from then until 1603, thereby encompassing his life as a married man and a father in Scotland, presiding over a court with a particular style; and after 1603 when he was a mature figure living at Whitehall, dealing with the challenges of ageing and competition from younger men (fig. 1.1). This chapter argues that rather than embracing London fashions in 1603, James brought the distinct style of the Scottish court to the English capital, and imposed this look on his new court, thereby shaping what we think of as early Stuart fashion. This is very much in keeping with Linda Levy Peck's argument that in that year James created a new court, a new elite and a new culture.[3] Far from being the scruffy king that Sir Anthony Weldon mocked, James was clothes conscious and elegant, and his court, whether in Edinburgh or London, was his showcase.

1.1 Adam de Colone, *James VI and I*, after 1622. Oil on canvas, 109.3 × 83.5 cm. National Galleries of Scotland. James's doublet has a peasecod belly and small shoulder wings, typical of the 1620s.

James VI's and I's Clothing

'Remember, that as I am your kinsman, so am I a true prince.'[4] These words, addressed to Elizabeth I in December 1591, demonstrate James VI's absolute belief in his royal dignity and the honour of Scotland. As a true prince of the Scottish people, James had his own fashionable style, which he brought south with him in 1603. If his new subjects chose to adopt this sartorial look, it had the potential to visually bind his three kingdoms together. James, who described himself as the father of his people, certainly thought they should follow his example. So it is no surprise that he wrote a good deal about the importance of clothing in the *Basilikon Doron*, or kingly gift, a work which, while ostensibly for the benefit of his son, provides a clear record of his beliefs on all things pertaining to the exercise of royal authority.[5] James urged his reader to 'return to the purpose of garments' because 'they ought to be used according to their first institution by God, which was for three causes: first, to hide our nakedness and shame; next and consequently, to make us more comely; and thirdly to preserve us from the injuries of heat and cold'.[6] In addition to their practical virtues, James acknowledged the ability of clothes 'to make us more comely', thereby stressing their visual appeal for the wearer and their audience. James's tailor created the king's elegant appearance, so making him the focal point of his court, while the king took time to admire well-dressed men around him. The defining characteristics of James's clothing style were eye-catching colour, enhanced by the generous application of trimmings, and jewellery.

The *Basilikon Doron* was written for a very specific Scottish audience, so James's views on clothing did not always tally with how the English thought their sovereign should look or how the Tudors had used dress to project a sense of magnificence.[7] Even so, the ideas underpinning Scottish royal male dress, including the need for opulence and swagger, would have been familiar to James's London courtiers, and James acknowledged the source of these ideas when he stated, 'we imitate the French fashion, in fashion of clothes'.[8] The 'auld alliance' ensured strong links between Scotland and France, a place where many young Scottish men travelled and in the process acquired an appreciation of French style. Take the son of Lady Faudonside, Jon Ker, who was 'pransing in his French garb, with his short scarlet cloake and his long caudie rapier'.[9] This French influence would remain a constant feature of Stuart fashion throughout the seventeenth century.

The 'Cradle King': From Birth to the Start of James's Majority, 1566–1584

Parents usually shape their child's views on clothing, but this is unlikely to have been true in the case of James VI. While both his parents took a keen interest in clothes, their direct influence on their son was short-lived. His father, Henry Stuart, lord Darnley (1545–67), was murdered on 10 February 1567 when James was less than eight months old. Darnley's strangled body, dressed in his nightshirt, was found outside his lodgings at Kirk o' Field, along with the body of his page, William Taylor. Prior to his marriage, Darnley had lived in France, and his double portrait with Mary, *c.*1565, presents a young man who carefully managed his appearance (fig. 1.2). Small hints remain of Darnley's clothing, including an order in January 1567 for linings for two gowns of satin and velvet, and cambric for his shirt ruffs.[10] His elegance and good looks caused Mary to describe Darnley, shortly after she first met him, as the 'lustiest and best proportioned long man that she had seen'.[11] Sir James Melville of Halhill (1535–1617) was less easily impressed by Darnley's boyish looks, observing laconically that 'na woman of sprit wald mak choice of sic a man, that was lyker a woman than a man; for he was very lusty, berdles and lady facit'.[12] Melville's words rang true, and Mary soon came to regret her marriage.

Mary's direct maternal influence ended when she abdicated on 24 July 1567, making James a 'cradle king', but prior to this she lavished clothing and furnishings on her young son. In September 1566 she ordered a bed and bedding for James.[13] Six months later a 'Memorandum for my lord Prince' recorded the delivery of 60 ells of Holland, 10 ells of white Spanish taffeta and 80 ells of white Florence ribbon.[14] The items

1.2 Unknown artist, *Henry Stuart, Lord Darnley and Mary Queen of Scots*, c.1565. Oil on panel, 110.5 × 150.5 cm. Hardwick Hall, Derbyshire. Darnley's tight-fitting pink doublet, decorated with slashing and pinking, and very full hose contrast with the black gown of his wife.

made from these materials were probably similar to those described as 'my Lord Prince geir' in an inventory dating from 1542. Possibly made for James, duke of Rothesay (1540–41), Mary's short-lived, older brother, the inventory includes 'ane wylicoit of scarlet', 'ane bonat of blak velvot' and 'twa litill bonattis of quhyte satyne'.[15] While sumptuous, they were not personal, unlike a set of embroidered child's reins often said to have been made by Mary for James. These are embroidered with a crowned harp, sceptre, roses, carnations, pomegranates and thistles and the text 'Angelis Svis Devs Mandavit De Te Vt Cvstodiant Te In Omnibvs Viss Tvis' ('God hath given his angels charge over thee: to keep thee in all thy ways'). However, Margaret Swain has convincingly argued that while Mary may have made these reins, she probably did so for one of Anne Dacre's children, rather than for her own son.[16]

More influential were the four regents who oversaw the young king's clothing orders from 1567 to 1578: James Stuart, 1st earl of Moray (*c.* 1531–70); Matthew Stuart, 4th earl of Lennox; John Erskine, 17th earl of Mar (1558–1634) and James Douglas, 4th earl of Morton (1525–81) (fig. 1.3). Three of the four were the king's relatives, and familial bonds explain the amount of time they spent in Stirling with young James.[17] Payments for some of their clothes appeared in the royal accounts and relate to garments worn to promote their roles as regents. For instance, on 14 April 1568, 12 ells of black figured velvet were bought for Moray 'to be my lord regent ane goun'.[18] On 13 September 1569, 2 ells, 2 quarters of violet in grain were supplied, 'to be his grace ane cloke', and 12 double hanks of silver for decoration.[19] Both garments are more opulent than those Moray was painted in by Hans Eworth eight years earlier, in 1561. The earl of Mar favoured a similar dignified appearance. In 1571 John Murdo, tailor, was paid for 8 ells of fine black velvet 'to be his grace breikis and bordering the breikis'.[20] The sombre clothes of the regents served as a foil for the brightly dressed boy-king.

1.3 Attributed to Arnold Bronckorst, *James Douglas, 4th Earl of Morton*, 1580. Oil on canvas, 106.3 × 82.1 cm. National Galleries of Scotland. Douglas's close-fitting, high-necked black doublet and full hose are accessorised with a tall crowned hat and gloves.

The regency began when James acceded to the throne on 24 July 1567. Two days later James Inglis, 'master tailliour to the prince', received material for the cradle king's coronation, including 'Fyve elnis of fine cramosie veluet, five elnis of blew fyn veluet, off red armosie taffeta thre elnis two quarters, of blew armosie taffeta thre elnis thre quarter, off plen pietticks' for the 'abilliaments to the prince'.[21] For his first appearance in the Scottish parliament in August 1571 James had miniature robes.[22] The order included

1.4 Livinus de Vogelaare, *The Memorial of Lord Darnley*, 1567. Oil on canvas, 142.3 × 224 cm. Royal Collection, Palace of Holyroodhouse. Dressed in full mourning attire, the earl and countess of Lennox, along with their son Charles Stuart, kneel behind James.

'fine purpour crammosie velvot to be his grace ane side coit' and 'foure elnis of purpour Armosie taffatie to lyne the same coit' for £56 Scots.[23] He was depicted in pale blue robes kneeling before his father's tomb with his grandfather (fig. 1.4). Having royal robes such as these was essential for such a young king to stress his right to the throne, but his everyday clothes acknowledged his youth. In October 1567 he received gowns, including one made from 4 ells of 'grosgrane taffeteis', embellished with gold and silver 'practikis' and gold buttons.[24] By March 1568 James was receiving coats including 'blak welvote to be ane cote', an incarnate coat decorated with 8 oz of silver 'cordonis', and a red satin coat lined with 'reid Armosing' taffeta and trimmed with 4½ oz of gold passements. He also received six leather belts and six pairs of small cut gloves. Over the next couple of years his clothes became more sophisticated, and in January 1572 he received a doublet of slashed black satin laid over black corded taffeta, while in July 1573 he received a cloak.[25]

The breeching of the young king took place by, or in, May 1574, when the accounts record the first order for adult clothing, consisting of 3½ ells of red figurate taffeta for a pair of breiks and an ell of red Spanish taffeta for a doublet.[26] Aged 8, James was painted in clothes of this type in *c*.1574 (fig. 1.5). He was dressed in a simple yet elegant white satin doublet, or a doublet and jerkin, and green velvet breeches.[27] These breeches compare well with an order placed in November 1574 for a pair of breiks of grey figured velvet and in November 1575 for a pair of provincials of grey figured velvet.[28] They continued to be popular over

1.5 Unknown artist, *James VI*, late 16th century, after an original of c.1574. Oil on canvas, 118.1 × 73 cm. National Portrait Gallery, London. From his jaunty black bonnet to the dark green velvet Venetians and sparrowhawk on his left fist, a young James's love of hunting is already clear.

the coming years, with a preference for satin doublets worn with provincials made of patterned, fancy fabrics, such as a pair of provincials made from black figured velvet on crimson satin in November 1576 paired with a red cramosie satin doublet.[29]

James officially came of age on his twelfth birthday in March 1578, when Morton lost the regency. The following month his clothing orders, reflecting his increased influence, included a Spanish cloak of black grosgrain taffeta, an Almain cloak with sleeves of the same black taffeta, along with orange velvet provincials and three orange satin doublets.[30] His coming of age saw Lady Annabel, countess of Mar, deliver the clothes still in her care to James Murray, master of the wardrobe, at Stirling Castle in September 1579.[31] While his minority did not end until 1584, James was increasingly involved in court life, including the Maundy celebrations, revels, progresses and hunting, and this was reflected in his clothing.

It was at this time that Mary sent her son *Tetrasticha, ou Quatrains à sons fils*. According to the bishop of Winchester, 'The Quene his Majesties Mother wrote a book of verses in French of the Institution of a Prince, all with her own hand, wrought a cover of it with a needle, and is now of his Majestie esteemed as a precious jewel'.[32] While his mother might offer advice on French style from a distance, Esmé Stuart, 1st duke of Lennox (1542–83), was much closer at hand. James was 13 when he met his second cousin, who quickly became a royal favourite, along with Captain James Stuart, the second son of Lord Ochiltree, who was made captain of the guard in 1580. The young king's clothes became increasingly sophisticated, and in December 1579 he ordered a black velvet Almain cloak, a gown of black figured velvet upon grey satin, and a pair of black velvet provincials.[33] November 1583 saw a change in style and terminology. Lennox may have returned to France, but the king wore a doublet and breeches of white velvet upon white satin and a cloak, jupe and breeches of Paris scarlet.[34] James's clothes during this phase of his life reflected his physical progression through infancy and childhood, while asserting his royal status. His style was influenced by the men around him, with the regents and Esmé Stuart shaping the young king's views.

Adult King of Scots, 1584–1603

James settled into his role as king, a position that was consolidated by becoming a husband and father of sons. In many ways his wardrobe continued as it had been, with an emphasis on expensive, high-quality, fashionable materials. His cloaks, for instance, were made of velvet or very good quality wool, with the latter often lined with velvet. Velvet was used for the 'neck' or collar, as well as forming decorative bands placed down each front and around the hem. While the styles of the doublet and hose remained fairly stable in the 1580s, during the 1590s they started to be cut from layers of fabric, with the top fabric slashed or pinked to reveal the layer below.

It was unusual for the clerk to record why clothes were ordered. However, hunting was always a priority, with green suits, boots and boot hose. A royal appearance at Parliament called for new clothes, such as the columbine satin doublet and hose ordered on 16 May 1592 for 'his majesty for the time of the parliament'.[35] Travel was important, as in August 1596 when the king received two pairs of silk hose to wear 'in the time of his progress'.[36] Church attendance and a celebration of spring were marked by a green grosgrain taffeta cloak, doublet and breeches supplied against the first Sunday in May 1597.[37] Summer and winter riding clothes also featured regularly in orders, indicating the amount of time the king spent in the saddle, and in May 1597 the king received a riding garment of tawny velvet and a riding cloak of sad violet French cloth 'at his majesty riding to Dundee'.[38] James needed these clothes because he had called the General Assembly of the Scottish Kirk, and Dundee was a strategic choice because its distance from St Andrews and Edinburgh reduced the number of ministers attending from either place.[39]

In August 1584 Mary's envoy Monsieur de Fontenay informed her that her son disliked 'dancing and music … or curiosities of dress'; he attributed this sad state of affairs to 'a lack of proper instruction'.[40] While this might have been a jibe at James's tutor George Buchanan, Fontenay believed that James lacked the polish and skills essential for the ideal, preferably French, courtier. However, his comments do not tally with the king's wardrobe or portraiture. It was true that royal style needed to be managed, and that expensive clothes were not enough in themselves. They had to be worn with regal elegance, which required good deportment and a fine physique, and James projected all these qualities in a half-length portrait from *c.*1586. Painted when he was a young man of 20, possibly as part of the early negotiations for his marriage to Anna of Denmark, James was dressed in a tawny-coloured doublet. However, true magnificence was to be found in the jewelled band which features on his black velvet bonnet and appears to disprove Fontenay's view that James did not appreciate the 'curiosities of dress' (fig. 1.6).

When James went to Denmark in 1589 to collect his bride, he was able to show off his courtly skills. He made a good impression, being described as 'a tall, slim gentleman' who dressed stylishly in 'a red velvet coat appliquéd with pieces of gold so that there was a row of golden stars and another row

1.6 *(above, left)* Unknown artist, attributed to Adrian Vanson, *James VI*, c.1586. Oil on panel, 35 × 25.5 cm. National Trust for Scotland, Falkland Palace, Falkland, Fife. James's ruff is an exemplar of the starcher's craft, while the tawny satin is decorated with short slashes and silk-thread-wrapped buttons.

1.7 *(above, right)* Unknown artist, *James VI and I*, c.1595. Oil on panel, 72.9 × 62.3 cm. National Galleries of Scotland. Over his doublet James wore a short cloak with wide fur guards.

where the velvet could be seen. He also wore a black velvet cloak lined with sable'.[41] On his wedding day, James dressed with a sense of poise and he 'walked first on the red carpet where he stood with his hands on his hips'.[42] A half-length image presents him in a doublet of pale, patterned silk embellished with applied bands of narrow gold lace and slashing, suggesting this style continued after his marriage. This was topped off with a tall-crowned felt or beaver hat with a jewelled hatband at the centre of which was an A made of diamonds, for his wife Anna (fig. 1.7). The accounts reveal that James's style as a married man was influenced by Anna on many levels, not least of which was her appreciation of fine clothes. James also used clothes to mark becoming a father, selecting four sets of sumptuous clothes in 1596 to celebrate the birth of his daughter. These included a cloak of 'rose peach' colour velvet and a suit of purple velvet.[43]

While James was aware of European fashions, he also looked across the border towards England. In 1597 a group of items were made for him in London, including a cloak of black velvet lined with black pan velvet and another in grey. Both were decorated with embroidered guards costing '£10 sterling made in Scots money – £100'. Other purchases included olive, grey and sand colour velvet costing £1,104.[44] Shopping in London was expensive but offered insights into what men of taste were wearing there, and added a further nuance to James's style.

Courtiers and Favourites in Jacobean Scotland

During this period the king's own views were clearly established but the influence of certain male courtiers on court style was still important. Most significant were the royal favourites, perhaps most notably George Gordon, 1st marquis and later earl of Huntly (1562–1636). Educated in France, Gordon was a Catholic, and while he signed the Scottish Presbyterian Confession of Faith (1560) in 1588, he supported a Spanish invasion of Scotland. Even so, James paid for Huntly's marriage to Henriette Stuart the same year, which cost 5 per cent of the royal annual household's expenditure.[45] Talented and handsome, Gordon was described by James as his 'good sonne', one of the early instances of the king using his role as father figure to frame personal and political relationships, even when the individual in question was older than him.[46] The same was true of his friendship with George Home, earl of Dunbar (*c.*1556–1611; also known as George Hume), who James met when he was 16 and the earl was 26. Home travelled with James to Denmark, and his portraits suggest that he was very interested in his appearance (fig. 1.8). Equally important was Ludovic Stuart, 2nd duke of Lennox (1574–1624), who had lived at court since his father's death in 1583. James demonstrated their friendship with small gifts of clothing, including a velvet-lined black castor hat with a hatband and a pair of long Naples silk hose in October 1590 and another pair of these hose on 25 February 1591.[47] Two years later Ludovic and 15 friends swore an oath not to wear gold and silver trimmings for a year, which is suggestive of how highly rich clothing was valued at James's court.[48]

1.8 Unknown artist, *Sir George Hume, Earl of Dunbar*, after 1590. Oil on canvas, 128.3 × 102.2 cm. National Galleries of Scotland. The striped effect on Dunbar's doublet and trunk hose was achieved with applied bands of passementerie.

The clothing choices of royal favourites helped develop and perpetuate court style, a style that was emulated in the purchases of others. For instance, Sir William Douglas, laird of Lochleven, earl of Morton (*c.*1540–1606) half-brother of James Stuart, 1st earl of Moray, ordered his clothes from the Edinburgh merchant, George Wauchope. His account dated 1583 came to £534 18s Scots, and listed the materials and clothes that George had supplied since 1581 for the laird and his sons. From these, their tailor John Douglas had created a number of items, including 'thrie standis' (sets) of clothes for the laird. While these were mostly black, there was also a gown of hunscott, a fabric from the Low Countries, riding clothes trimmed with green Spanish taffeta and 'nycht geir'. Sir William's son Robert received a more chic mandilion cloak with an embroidered lining and garments in green, grey, violet and white.[49] In the same year Douglas, the laird of Lochleven, received a bill for items including 13 ells of incarnate satin to make a doublet, a pair of hose and a cloak lining, 13 ells of black satin for the other stand of clothes, and 4 ells of incarnate passements and buttons for the incarnate doublet.[50] Edinburgh tailors and merchants helped disseminate court style to a receptive Scottish male elite.

King of Scots and King of England (1603–25)

In 1594 the English gentleman Robert Carey described James as a king only to add 'yet he is but a king borne in Scotland and so a Scottes man' and to be treated warily.[51] In turn, the Scots believed that the English did not deserve James because 'this people will spoil a gud king'. The English lawyer Sir Roger Wilbraham feared the same and hoped 'that nether the welth and peace of England make him forgett God, nor the painted flatterie of the Court cause him forgett himself'.[52] Sir Roger's prayers fell on deaf ears: prior to 1603 James was addressed as 'our soverane lord' in Scotland, but after he was 'his sacred majesty', following the English style.[53] Even so, while James embraced certain aspects of English court culture, especially those that suited his idea of kingship, he did not change his style of dress.

James travelled south with three stands of clothes and a cloak made for him by his tailor, Alexander Miller, in Edinburgh in April 1603. These garments reflect how the king viewed this period of transition. First and foremost was his official mourning for Elizabeth made from 21½ ells of purple velvet – his 'dule' coat, cloak and breiks. These items were worn with a riding cloak of fine violet cloth lined with purple velvet and trimmed with fur. The second was 'a stand of ryding claithis' of feuillemort velvet and a 'fine color de roy frenche claith to be a riding cloak, lined with color de roy velvet' for the king's journey. The third was entirely the colour green: 'green satin to be dowblet and breiks lined with green Spanish taffeta with a pair of green silk shanks'.[54] His choices were respectful and fashionable, suitable for travel while also allowing him to take advantage of good hunting as he rode through England.

On his arrival in London, James had a new audience for his style. What his English subjects saw was an individual dressed in an elegant, French style suitable for a mature family man aged 37. James's style was echoed in the clothes of his Scottish favourites, advisors and nobles, who had accompanied him south, and together these men set the visual appearance of the core group at court. Miller travelled with James, and once in London he set to work making 15 doublets and 14 pairs of hose of satin 'of sundry colours', along with a jerkin and a pair of velvet hose and five suits of grosgrain of sundry colours, one suit of silk grosgrain brocaded with gold and silver, one jerkin and breeches of cloth with a doublet of satin. All the suits were decorated with lace, pinked and lined with taffeta.[55] In terms of quantity and materials, this order set the tone for the years between 1603 and 1615, when the evidence relating to the king's clothes is patchy, but after 1616 it is minimal.

The suit, consisting of the doublet and hose, was central to James's wardrobe, and he ordered significant numbers, ranging from 65 in 1603/4 and 51 in 1613/14.[56] While the accounts provide little detail on cut, portraits suggest that his doublets were fairly close fitting with a peasecod belly. They were lined with taffeta and the tailor also supplied stitching and sewing silk, ribbon, baize, fustian, rug, hair stiffenings and Holland cloth.[57] Equally, there are only a few hints about the style of hose being ordered. For example, in 1605/6 James appears to have favoured long hose, including a doublet and pair of long hose of hair satin slashed with taffeta upon cloth of silver.[58] Paned hose of the type depicted by John de Critz appear, along with occasional pairs of bullion hose and canions, and in 1613 there was a single pair of the full breeches known as Venetians (fig. 1.9).[59]

1.9 Attributed to John de Critz the elder, *James VI and I*, c.1606. Oil on canvas, 200.5 × 129.5 cm. Dulwich Picture Gallery, London. James's cream doublet, paned trunk hose and shoes show off the sable-lined cloak very effectively.

Successive orders reveal fancy cloaks, such as a tawny velvet example with three embroidered borders and furred with sable, and opulent suits, including a doublet of pinked carnation silk grosgrain and hose of uncut carnation velvet trimmed with embroidered silk lace.[60] Essentially the same in terms of cut, the all-important differences lie in the details of colour, combinations of fabrics and applied decoration. In part this reflects the way in which the fashionable look changed subtly year in, year out, but it may also suggest that James knew what he liked and wise tailors provided him with that. It may have been a reflection of his age, although in Fontenay's opinion James was always 'an old young man'.[61] However, James was not alone in prizing familiarity and good materials over innovative cut. When Robert, lord Spencer, went to Württemberg in 1603 he ordered 'a white satin doublet of the same fashion that my old one is'.[62] Whether Spencer favoured older styles or was resisting the new court look under James, it is hard to say.

1.10 *(below, left)* Paul van Somer, *James VI and I*, c.1620. Oil on canvas, 226.1 × 149.2 cm. Royal Collection. The king's formal robes contrast with his white suit.

1.11 *(below, right)* Doublet and breeches of satin, slashed and laid over taffeta, of similar style and colour to those favoured by James, c.1618. Victoria and Albert Museum, London.

Equally challenging are the lack of accounts and the small number of portraits between 1615 and 1625, which make it difficult to consider the king's clothing in detail during this period. However, the basic format of his orders probably remained the same, and this is supported by a comment made in 1617 by the Venetian ambassador, Horatio Busino. He described James wearing 'tawny satin, the whole suit being embroidered, while his black velvet cloak was trimmed with lace right up to the shoulders, and lined with sables'.[63]

When Paul van Somer painted the king in *c.*1620, James wore a suit of white satin comprised of a doublet with fitted sleeves, slight peasecod front, small skirts and short points, full, knee-length breeches with slashing and pinking; and fairly flat shoes with a ribbon bow (fig. 1.10). In terms of style and cut this compares very well with a surviving suit from the period (fig. 1.11). Although the king looked much older when painted by Mytens in 1621, he was dressed in a similar white satin suit.[64] This suggests that a pale suit was favoured with state robes, but it also reflected James's fondness for white, a colour often associated with the Stuarts.[65] James also promoted blue as a fashionable colour – especially pale to mid-range bright blues – and he wore it for state occasions. For instance, the king selected a suit of 'watchet satin laid with silver lace' for his meeting on 5 June 1619 with the duke of Lorraine (fig. 1.12).[66] While Sir John Holles complained that the Scots 'filled every corner of the Court with theis beggarly blew caps', he was wise enough not to pass comment on the king's blue satin doublet.[67] More importantly, fashionable younger men such as Nathaniel Bacon embraced Stuart blue, so demonstrating their support for James (fig. 1.13).

1.12 *(above)* Nicholas Hilliard, *James VI and I*, c.1609–15. Watercolour on vellum on card, 4.6 × 3.8 cm. Royal Collection. This blue doublet is decorated with lots of slashing, pinking and jewelled buttons.

1.13 *(below)* Nathaniel Bacon, *Self-portrait*, c.1625. Oil on canvas, 57.5 × 44.5 cm. National Portrait Gallery, London. Bacon's doublet is an excellent example of the style popular in the 1620s.

The Impact of the Stuarts Moving to London

The impact on the king's clothes of his transfer to London was minimal in terms of his personal style, with his wardrobe reflecting the look he had developed in Scotland. However, there were clear differences between James's clothing in Edinburgh and Westminster on a number of practical and administrative levels. Financially, moving to England meant that James had considerably more money to spend on everything, including clothes, although not necessarily as much as he had anticipated. This was reflected in a marked increase in the number of items ordered, and the cost, because the bills were now in pounds sterling rather than the Scottish pound, which was worth a twelfth of sterling. There was also a change in the pattern of when things were ordered, but this was a continuation of changes that had begun in Scotland. From early on, orders were placed when the king required new things, and the frequency of orders increased as his reign progressed, rising from 7 in 1579 to 54 in 1591. Equally, up until 1590 the king's clothes were listed in the Treasurer's accounts. After that, the impact of the king's marriage was felt, and between 1591 and 1600 the materials supplied by Robert Jousie for 'the king's and queen's apparel' were listed in a separate volume of accounts at the instigation of Home, the master of the wardrobe.[68] In England, the king followed the established pattern used by the officers of the Great Wardrobe and the Wardrobe of the Robes since the 1520s, with James placing orders twice a year, in the spring and autumn, as the Tudors had before him.[69]

Miller, James's tailor, travelled with his employer and adopted this new working pattern. In Scotland, the materials required to make the king's clothes were delivered to Miller, so the king acted like other Scottish clients in that he (or a member of his household) supplied the fabrics. On occasions when the royal household had not bought enough, they looked to other suppliers to make up the difference, as on 22 June 1587 when Patrick Nimmo supplied Jousie with fustian, linen, a dozen green silk points and four dozen green silk buttons 'for his majesties grene claithis'.[70] In the Great Wardrobe, the king's tailor supplied all the fabrics and charged their royal client for them, and Miller did likewise.

There was also a change in the range of materials used, especially those used for linings and stiffening. Up until 1603 these had been Scottish fabrics or fabrics that were regular imports into the country. Most notable were plaiding, stenting, caddas and Scottish linen, alongside imports including Naples taffeta, Spanish taffeta and Florence ribbon. After 1603 these changed to fabrics produced in England or those that merchants imported into London. As noted, some English cloth had featured in James's pre-1603 wardrobe, as on 29 September 1591, when Miller received 6 ells of columbine colour (blue) London cloth to be his majesty's winter riding clothes, cloak, coat and breeches at £8 the ell.[71] In tandem with this there was also a change in the measurements used, from the Scottish ell (37 inches or 94 cm) to the English yard (36 inches or 91.5 cm). Finally, the language of the accounts changed from Middle Scots and French to English or Latin. As a result many French terms for colours (such as 'rouge brown', 'fleur de pêche' and 'cramosie') or garments (for instance a 'French joup and hose') found in the Scottish accounts disappear, as do Scots terms such as 'shanks' and 'sarks'. While James and Miller might have influenced the style of the clothes being made, English administrative systems forced changes in the way Miller worked and supplied his king.

The Scottish Male Elite South of the Border

Many of the Scots who travelled with James to his southern kingdom had worked hard to see him succeed Elizabeth.[72] They fell into two groups, with the first consisting of courtiers such as John Erskine, 17th earl of Mar, who was known as Jock o'the Slates, and Thomas Erskine, 1st earl of Kellie (1566–1639), who was captain of the guard and groom of the stool from 1604. The second was made up of civil servants and politicians, including Sir George Home, noted above, and the lawyer

Edward Bruce, 1st lord Kinloss (1548–1611). As Jenny Wormald has observed, James gave most of his Scottish supporters money rather than office, at a time when, in Alexandra Shepard's view, individuals assessed themselves primarily in terms of their wealth and moveable goods.[73] As a result, these Scots had the means and motive to buy clothes in the style favoured by their king at his new court, and in so doing helped promote the Stuart look.

Appointed master of the Great Wardrobe in 1603, Home played an important role in the king's court at Westminster. Dunbar's influence was evident at the wedding of John Ramsey, viscount of Haddington and lord Ramsey of Barns (*c*.1580–1626), to Lady Elizabeth Radclyffe (d. 1618) on 9 February 1608. While the royal children ate with the bride, and the king offered a substantial gift, 'Dunbar's went beyond all, being valued between four and five hundred pounds'.[74] With this present, Dunbar, an established royal favourite, demonstrated his support for another royal favourite and fellow Scot. More importantly, he represented James in Scotland, because the king gave him almost vice-regal powers there.[75] In order to maintain this role, James gave Elizabeth I's 'inestimable Wardrobe' to Dunbar, who, according to Thomas Astle, keeper of records at the Tower, 'wickedlye transporting them to the Low Countrys, sold them for above One Hundred Thousand Pounds'.[76] This was a significant windfall for Home, and added greatly to his standing.

Like Home, the king was well aware of the importance placed on the male body when he observed that should anyone 'set another leg as well made beside mine, I warrant you … [Northampton] will swear the King's sweet leg is the finest'.[77] Sir James Hay, 1st earl of Carlisle (1580–1636), was also blessed with fine legs, and his first patron was Charles Cauchon de Paupas, baron du Tour, a French diplomat sent to Scotland in 1602 (fig. 1.14).[78] Hay's European elegance ensured that James sent him to greet ambassadors in London.[79] He also served as an ambassador and in 1616 was made an extraordinary ambassador to Louis XIII of France. Hay ordered 20 new suits, which needed to be changed to keep in line with French fashion.[80] His wardrobe included a white cloak and hose embroidered with gold and silver thread, a doublet of cloth of gold, also embroidered,

1.14 Unknown artist, *James Hay, Earl of Carlisle*, 1628. Oil on canvas, 194.6 × 120 cm. National Portrait Gallery, London. Hay's love of clothes is evident from his sumptuous doublet and flamboyant collar supported by a pickadil.

1.15 Marcus Gheeraerts the younger, *Alexander Seton, 1st Earl of Dunfermline*, 1610. Oil on canvas, 115.5 × 88.2 cm. National Galleries of Scotland. Seton's expensive accessories include a four-layered ruff, gilt sword hilt, gilt fittings on his girdle and the ring on his right hand.

and a white beaver hat.[81] As one onlooker observed, he 'furnishes himself very sumptuously, and purposes to appear in that court with as muche magnificence, as good clothes, and embroderies can give, being accompanied with Sir Harry Riche, Sir George Gowring, and many others of that humour'.[82] For his 1621 embassy to France, Hay bought his clothes in Paris to ensure that he was stylish.[83]

In 1617 James VI told the Scottish council that his 'salmonlyke instinct' had drawn him back to his homeland.[84] James's approach to the visit is summed up in his request to receive his robes in advance. It was ordered that 'His Majesties robe royall be send up to his Majestie with all convenient [haist] to the effect his Majestie may provyde him self of ane new robe efter the fassioun of the auld'.[85] He intended to wear his Scottish robes, but their condition had to reflect his dignity as king of three kingdoms and of Scotland. His visit was carefully planned but could never truly make up for his prolonged absence.[86] Even so, he used the opportunity to promote the union of the crowns, and while there he noted how many of his fellow Scots 'had learned of the English to drink their healths, to wear coaches and gay clothes, to take tobacco, and to speak neither Scottish nor English'.[87] How much weight to attach to the phrase 'gay clothes' is debatable; the king's attire prior to 1603 was brightly coloured and showy without any English intervention, although the quantity of clothes he owned had increased significantly. While James had always worn a range of colours, bright shades did not suit all tastes, as indicated by the portrait of Alexander Seton, 1st earl of Dunfermline (1555–1622). Seton was lord chancellor of Scotland from 1604 to 1622 and lord high commissioner to the Parliament of Scotland. When he sat for Marcus Gheeraerts, he selected a black, fur-lined gown over a black doublet and hose (fig. 1.15) that added gravitas to his place in Scottish government.[88]

James did not go back to Scotland alone. Sir Robert Gordon (1580–1656), who had been appointed as a gentleman of the privy chamber in 1606, returned to James's northern kingdom with him in 1617, where he won the silver arrow in the archery competition at Holyroodhouse. Archibald Armstrong (d. 1672), who was either from Scotland or Cumberland, was court jester to James VI and I, and he accompanied the king on his visit to Scotland in 1617, where he was a great success. More importantly, the visit was an opportunity for James to meet his subjects and these included James Hamilton, 2nd marquis of Hamilton (1589–1625), who rapidly became James's new favourite, replacing Robert Kerr. James delighted 'at the conquest I have made in drawing in this man to wayte upon me … that I assure myself his service will repaye my liberallitie with a double interest'.[89] As his portrait reveals, Hamilton expressed his loyalty by dressing in Jacobean court fashion (fig. 1.16).

1.16 Workshop of Daniel Mytens, *James Hamilton, 2nd Marquis of Hamilton*, c. 1622. Oil on canvas, 215.9 × 135 cm. Lennoxlove, East Lothian. Hamilton's black suit, striped with silver, demonstrates how fancy black could be.

Englishmen at James's London Court

Not all the men who found favour at James VI's court were Scots. One of James's English favourites was Roger Aston, who was born in Cheshire but had lived in Scotland since he was a boy. He was a trusted servant of James, serving as a private courier to Elizabeth, and he had become the king's master huntsman by 1580. In January 1604, Aston received two suits of clothing as a gentleman of the bedchamber.[90] However, he was in a minority, and most of James's English supporters, such as Robert Cecil, 1st earl of Salisbury (1563–1612), first met him in 1603. While Cecil was vital to James's government, he was not a fashion leader, and his response to Stuart flamboyance is telling. Determined not to be outplayed, in 1603 Cecil bought himself a large diamond ring of 53 carats, so ensuring he looked the part at the new king's court, with further purchases of jewels from Sir John Spilman in 1606 costing £1,257.[91] In contrast, Thomas Howard, 21st earl of Arundel, adopted 'so ordinary a habit', but it was not to his detriment because 'his garb and fashion drawing more observation than did the rich apparel of others, so that it was a common saying of the late Earl of Carlisle, here comes Arundel in his plain stuff and trunk hose … that looks more like a nobleman than any of us'.[92] James's Scottish supporters recognised that Arundel's style provided a distinctive counterpoint to their court dress.

James's court also attracted a competitive group of younger men, such as Richard Sackville, 3rd earl of Dorset (1589–1624), who wore expensive, flamboyant clothes in a bid to stand out.[93] Their ornate attire was, arguably, the product of competitive male dressing at the Stuart court, where there was a need to be noticed by the king. James was certainly appreciative of well-dressed young men, and this resulted in a continuation of the role taken by Robert Devereux, earl of Essex, and the earl of Southampton as taste-makers under Elizabeth, where the need to gain female royal approval had created the same competitive environment. The popularity of tight, white hose can be seen in the Elizabethan Garter portraits of men Castiglione described as wanting to 'cut a figure'.[94] Cutting a figure was the key to male success at James VI and I's court, regardless of whether it was in Scotland or England.

There were ways to resist what was seen as Stuart style, and in the view of Malcolm Smuts, this was to adopt the Spanish fashion. Based on an analysis of courtier portraits of the 1610s, Smuts considers that the increasing quantities of black, in tandem with less brocade, reflected a move towards Spanish style, and gravitas.[95] However, to see Spanish style as the model of understatement needs to be tempered by other viewpoints, such as that of Matthew Bruninge in November 1608. Writing from Madrid, he excused his request for money to buy clothes by explaining that 'here the very shoemakers go in their velvet'.[96] Even so, at times all things Spanish were in vogue, as in early 1617, when Sir John Throckmorton reported that while 'the Spanish treaty is not so forward as reported … the Spanish tongue, dress, &c., are all in fashion'.[97] As Lesley

Miller has shown, Prince Charles briefly promoted Spanish style in 1623 after his return from Madrid. While there were moments such as these, when adopting Spanish dress was a politically and economically prudent move, it could also be a risky option, as a visitor to the capital noted: 'Foreigners are ill regarded, not to say detested, in London, so sensible people dress in the English fashion, or that of France, which is adopted by the whole court'.[98] This fondness for French fashion and French tailoring is reflected in the accounts of Lord Ross, who was supplied with clothes by John Jackson from a tailor in Paris. A bill dating from April 1614 includes details for 'shkerlet clois', 'your lordships tawny satin clocis', and for 'the reid camelet clois'.[99] As noted earlier, France rather than Spain was the significant European influence on James's fashionable look.

Guising: Costumes and Disguises as an Integral Part of Stuart Clothing Culture

Dress played an important part in the Scottish royal guising culture, with the accounts for December 1579 listing an entry for masque clothes requiring 28 ells of red and yellow taffeta, 6 ells 'tock' of silver, and 10 ells of buckram along with six swords and six daggers.[100] While often the primary member of the audience for a masque, James also wrote masques, including those performed at the wedding of the earl of Huntly and the duke of Lennox's sister in 1588 and at the baptism of Prince Henry.[101] Occasionally he participated, as in June 1591 when he dressed in a suit of 'maskerie' clothes of incarnadine Spanish taffeta at a marriage, possibly that of Lilias Murray, daughter of John Murray, the laird of Tullibardine.[102] For participants, the value of attracting the admiring royal gaze was priceless, and tight-fitting clothes on a lithe male body helped to achieve this. Lord Hay recalled how 'the mode was to appeare very small in the wast' and so he was 'drawne up from the ground by both hands whilst the tayler with all his strength buttoned on my doublet'.[103] While James appreciated the merits of the masque, he was not a keen jouster. Even so, as a display of Stuart family pride he did run at the ring on important family occasions such as the visit of Christian IV of Denmark in 1606, and in 1613 to celebrate his daughter's wedding.[104]

Such occasions also saw use of the Stuart livery colours of red and yellow, which were also employed for making clothing for royal household servants. One disadvantage with livery was that anyone wearing it was accepted as being a legitimate member of the royal household, so much so that the conspirators engaged in a foiled plot in November 1603 planned 'after the slaughter of many guards to put on their coats'.[105] However, when Sir Randal MacDonnell issued his troops with crimson and yellow taffeta in 1625 he did so for very different reasons. His stated aim was to ensure that they would not look 'like kernes', the traditional lightly armed Irish foot soldiers, by dressing them in the colours and style of loyal supporters of the Stuart monarchs.[106]

Clothes often served as a cover for something else. According to Sir Anthony Weldon, James was 'more corpulent through his cloathes then in his body' because 'his cloathes [were] ever being made large and easie, the Doublets quilted for stiletto proof, his breeches in great pleats and full stuffed'.[107] While James did have anxieties about his safety, men's suits in the early seventeenth century were padded, so Weldon's comments reflect the fashionable trend as much as a specific royal foible. While it is not easy to assess whether the king's doublets had more padding than usual, he was certainly not out of step with mainstream fashion. For instance, a black and green velvet doublet made for the king in 1604 was lined with taffeta, Holland and bombast, while the hose were lined with Holland, frieze and horsehair.[108] This compares favourably with a doublet of rose-coloured satin ordered for Prince Henry in 1607/8 that was lined and padded with 2¼ ells of Holland, 5 yards of baize, 2 ells of canvas, 2 yards of rug, 1½ lb of bombast, 4 yards of fustian and 2 ells of crine (a type of hair cloth).[109] This is another example of how Weldon's view has coloured James's reputation, and while James may have been keen to prevent more attacks on his safety, his clothes expressed his sense of fashion rather than fear.

Conclusions

James VI and I was certain that, in spite of what Castiglione and others might say, 'if your mind be found occupied upon [clothes], it will be thought idle'.[110] Nevertheless, his mind regularly did dwell upon clothing because it was central to his own self-representation as a Stuart king, and that of his court and countries. James aspired to set the style in Scotland through personal example backed up with the use of sumptuary law; however, he was inconsistent in its application. While present in both countries prior to his accession in 1603, sumptuary legislation ended in England but not in Scotland in 1604. On occasion the king's influence could be negative, as when James expressed his disapproval of women wearing masculine styles.[111] Notable is how James sought to fashion his own image and reputation with words, often expressing his frustration by reference to clothing or nudity. For example, the constant petitioning of suitors caused James to exclaim on one famous occasion: 'God's wounds! I will pull down my breeches and they shall also see my arse.'[112]

In spite of the criticisms made by Weldon, James's clothing accounts reveal a man who was keen to ensure that his clothes upheld his royal authority, whether while young and growing into his role as king of Scots, or as he set about the challenge of ruling three kingdoms. Just as Jenny Wormold has demonstrated that James was a very successful monarch as king of Scotland, the sartorial evidence reveals that he led a fashionable court there too, where male dress was prized and admired.[113] He also succeeded in transferring his style to London, in part because London had elements in common with the Scottish court, but also

because there had been a lack of a strong male fashionable lead with James's level of influence at the court of the Virgin Queen. James's style was shared with most of his older Scottish and English male courtiers, with a few opting out and favouring black over Jacobean opulence. However, as the next chapter reveals, the king's position as leader of court fashion was challenged by his sons as the reign progressed (fig. 1.17). The competition between the young men at court, and in particular Prince Henry and the king's young Scottish favourite, Robert Kerr, soon resulted in the development of a second, rival strand of Stuart style.

1.17 Renold Elstrack (engraver), *James I and Anna of Denmark*, 1651. Engraving, 28.3 × 37.8 cm. Metropolitan Museum of Art, New York. Placed between his fashionable father and mother sits Prince Henry, the hope of Stuart fashion.

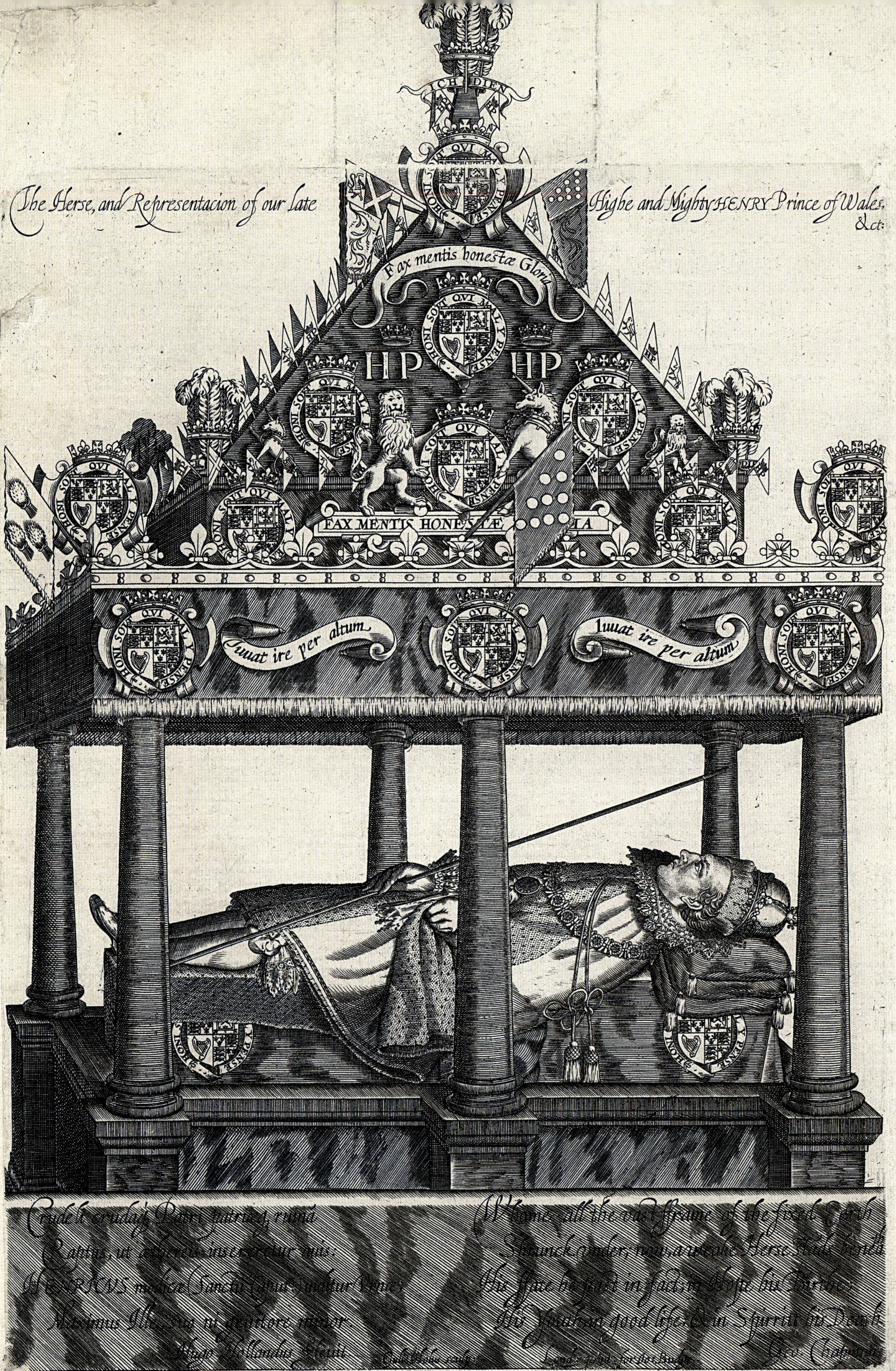

The Herse, and Representacion of our late Highe and Mighty HENRY Prince of Wales. &ct.
ICH DIEN
HONI SOIT QVI MAL Y PENSE
Fax mentis honestæ Gloria
HP HP
FAX MENTIS HONESTÆ GLORIA
Iuuat ire per altum
Iuuat ire per altum
Crudeli crudaq; Patri patriaeq; ruinâ
Whome all the vast Frame of the fixed Earth
His Youth in good life, & in Spirit his Death.

CHAPTER TWO

Prince Henry (1594–1612)

WHEN PRINCE HENRY DIED on 6 November 1612 aged 18, five embroidered suits lay unfinished on his tailor's bench along with '3½ yards of cloth of tissue upon a purple ground for a doublet, the doublet being cut out'.[1] The same account also records the purchase of lengths of carnation, crimson and yellow taffeta to embalm his body, fine scarlet and ribbon to wrap his corpse and more ribbon for tying the effigy to the coffin (fig. 2.1).[2] In life and death, textiles played a central role in presenting this Stuart prince fittingly, although determining what was appropriate was more challenging, then and now, as indicated by the advice James VI gave his eldest son on how he should dress:

> Be also moderate in your raiment, neither over-superfluous, like a deboshed waster, nor yet over-base, like a miserable wretch; not artificially trimmed and decked, like a courtesan, nor yet over-sluggishly clothed, like a country clown; nor over-lightly like a candy soldier or a vain young courtier, nor yet over-gravely, like a minister.[3]

While not the first subject the king offered Prince Henry guidance on, James considered clothing important enough to include reference to it in his *Basilikon Doron*. When James wrote this text he was thinking of courts in general, and of the Scottish court in particular, but his words were equally applicable after the Stuarts moved south.

This chapter explores how far Henry took his father's words to heart, concentrating on the themes of excess or being 'over-superfluous', and the dangers of being like 'a candy soldier or a vain young courtier' who dressed 'over-lightly'.[4] Henry agreed with his father that clothes mattered, but he used them in ways his father had not intended in order to assert his own place at James's court in Westminster, a court where Scots and Englishmen, whether they subscribed to the king's vision of Britain or not, jostled for position and favour. Henry created a parallel strand within Stuart dress, expressive of his youth, thereby posing himself as a rival to his ageing father.

2.1 William Hole, *The Hearse of Prince Henry*, 1612. Print, 32 × 28 cm. British Museum, London. The prince's effigy lays in state dressed in his robes and a coronet.

The Prince and His Clothes

Stirling, 1594–1603

Henry was born at Stirling Castle on 19 February 1594, where, by tradition, the Prince's Tower housed the royal nursery. On the same day a table was established for the mistress of the nursery, the four rockers, Barbara Murray, keeper of the prince's coffer and clothes, and Elspeth Crumney, who made the prince's linens.[5] Shortly after, Henry was placed in the care of John Erskine, earl of Mar, who received £10,000 (Scots) to entertain the prince during 1595.[6] The scale of the prince's household, as appropriate to his role as heir to the throne, is evident from the list of allowances made to Thomas Duddingston, master of the household, and others in 1594,[7] and from the list of the prince's servants to whom Mar had to pay 'feallis' in 1596.[8]

Like most infants, Henry was probably swaddled for the first months of his life, and his first coats were ordered in February 1595. Worn over linen shirts, he also had 'wylicoats' or waistcoats for added warmth. In the period from February 1596 to June 1597 Henry received new coats roughly every five to six months – at a rate of one in February, two in August, two in December 1596 and two in May 1597.[9] The orders included a coat of changeable (shot) Spanish taffeta costing £47 6s 1d to purple Lucchese velvet and 'reid cremosie' velvet costing £186 12s 8d and £175 12s 8d Scots respectively. While they postdate a portrait by an unknown artist painted when Henry was aged 2, they do confirm that he was regularly wearing coats of this type, trimmed with silver, gold or silk passementerie (fig. 2.2). The richness of the metal lace used to trim the coat contrasts with a bunch of cherries in his right hand, symbolising Henry's sweet temperament untainted by his undeniable wealth and privilege.

2.2 Unknown artist, *Prince Henry as an Infant*, c.1596. Oil on canvas, 68.6 × 52.1 cm. Private collection. A fine linen apron heavily trimmed with metal lace covers the young prince's coat.

As Henry got older more fabric was required for the coats that were now worn with accessories selected to stress his increasing maturity and masculinity. Starting with plain velvet bonnets, he progressed to velvet bonnets with gold and silver hatbands and ostrich feathers, and daggers worn from embroidered belts.[10] October 1599 saw the first reference to him having suits, consisting of a cloak, doublet and breeches made from 9 ells of 'weiloreis velvet … of color deory', trimmed with silver passement.[11] Henry also received special suits, including green suits, for hunting in the summer months.[12] Alongside daywear, he received gowns to wear in his bedchamber, a space held to be of great significance by the Stuart royal household (see Chapter 9).

His clothes stress two points. The first is the importance of the bedchamber, even at this young age. A bed of orange velvet and shot or changeable violet taffeta was ordered for Henry in February 1594.[13] In May 1597 he received his first toilet of green velvet, lined with green taffeta and trimmed with a green and silver fringe.[14] The second is the start of his education. James started his son's riding lessons when Henry was aged three and a few months, as is indicated by the provision of a saddle and horse harness covered in velvet in 1597.[15] Three years later he was evidently competent enough to be given boot hose for hunting, like his father.[16] The rest of Henry's physical education started in September 1600 with a delivery of golf clubs and tennis rackets trimmed with velvet and metal passementerie, suggesting that no expense was spared.[17]

Records also reveal when he was breeched, so making the transition from the dress of a child to that of a young man. At this time Henry started to participate in a wider range of social activities. While he spent almost all of his time at Stirling, Henry received a white satin suit to wear to the christening of his brother Robert, one of his first public occasions. Who was behind this? James paid but he appears to have had little personal involvement, and prior to being reunited with her son in 1603, Anna had not seen him 'by the space of five years'.[18] While hard to prove, the timing of the clothing orders and the indication of what was required probably came from the earl of Mar. Mar played an important part in the prince's early life, and when Henry said farewell in 1603 he 'suddenly embraced the said Earl, [and] burst forth into tears, albeit he was known to weep as little as any child whatsoever'.[19] This uncharacteristic display of emotion suggests Mar was much more of a father to Henry than James was.

London, 1603–12

Henry spent half of his short life in Scotland and half in England. This was not what James had intended, but Anna forced the king's hand, with Lennox escorting mother and son to England in 1603. As Pauline Croft noted, 'The queen's forceful maternal action was politically significant, since after May 1603 Henry immediately made the transition to the English court and to an English rather than a Scottish upbringing'.[20] If James had had his way, it is possible that Henry would have remained in Scotland until he became prince of Wales in 1610.[21] As it was, Henry came to London, giving him more independence on the one hand, and more interaction with his parents on the other, something James never had.

Once in the south, Henry had a more public life and this was reflected in his clothing. He received gifts such as a length of satin striped with silver over cloth of tissue of gold and silk. Given to him by his relative Lady Arabella Stuart (1575–1615) some time in 1603–4, the silk was made into a sumptuous doublet, hose and cloak.[22] He also required more specialist items of clothing, such as a black mourning cloak made from very fine

2.3 Marcus Gheeraerts the younger, *Henry, Prince of Wales*, c.1603. Oil on canvas, 161.9 × 116.8 cm. National Portrait Gallery, London. Now breeched, Henry displays fashionable accessories – a tall hat with a jewelled band, gloves and ribbon shoe roses – alongside his robes.

black cloth,[23] or the doublet of white satin cut on black taffeta, trimmed with black embroidered lace and black binding lace that he wore on St George's Day as a Garter knight.[24] His Garter portrait shows him wearing the traditional robes with fashionable white shoes (fig. 2.3). Like all boys of his age, Henry was still growing, as is indicated by the sizeable payment of £34 10s 10d for 'repairs, alterations and mending of divers doublets, jerkins and hose'.[25] By 1611/12 the accounts show that Henry favoured suits consisting of a loose cassock, doublet and hose or doublet, jerkin and hose. The hose were ornate and either paned or bullion with canions. For outdoor wear he selected cloaks and riding coats. For the bedchamber he received his first nightgown in 1605/6, and this garment was then a regular feature of his accounts ending in September 1612 with 'a night gown of crimson velvet all embroidered with gold' and 'a gown of black velvet lined with shag and garnished with silver parchment lace'.[26] These clothes indicate that Henry was at the heart of Stuart social and political life.

Analysis

Colour was a significant part of any suit, and Henry's wardrobe presents a rich range of shades. As a young boy his clothes were made in 18 colours, but half of these only featured once. Of the remainder, red shades (red cramosie, red scarlet and incarnate) predominate, followed by purple and green. Most notable was the colour of his first suit: deroy, a bright tawny otherwise known as *couleur de roi*, a royal colour and one favoured by his father, and, as such, very suitable to mark Henry's transition to adult clothing. Upon his move to England, and when the two partial accounts are taken out of the equation (1603 and 1612), the prince had a colourful wardrobe ranging from between 12 and 22 colours per year. Some colours were seasonal, with green suits mostly ordered in the summer months for hunting. Others had a more symbolic significance, and Aileen Ribeiro has interpreted the colours worn in Robert Peake's portrait of the prince as courtly carnation contrasting with the purity of white (fig. 2.4).[27] The choice also made a nod to his mother's fondness of white and carnation, colours that predominated in her wardrobe, although it took second place to black and green.

While in Scotland his outer clothes, regardless of style, were made from three main silk fabrics: satin, a range of taffetas and velvet. There was only one instance of cloth of silver being used, in the year he was born, and a small amount of wool in the form of serge, frieze and scarlet. The range of top fabrics increased in 1603. A sense of the hierarchy of silks available, rather than their popularity, is evident from an entry in the privy purse accounts for 1608/9. Baptiste Hullip and a Mr Voctrowe, mercers, presented a bill for £821 9s 8d for 'cloth of gold, cloth of silver, silver velvets, all sorts of velvets, satins taffetas and other silks'. Henry's suit orders reveal a lot of silk with satin predominant, along with small amounts of silk camlet, silk grosgrain, velvet and fabrics incorporating metal thread. He favoured a high number of fabric combinations for his suits, especially in 1611/12 when the number of plain satin suits dropped dramatically, as did the quantity of wool. There was a small amount of scented leather, most notably 'One rich suit very richly wrought with gold and silver upon shammy leather', which cost £200.[28] Compared to his father, Henry wore similar amounts of satin but much less velvet and wool (although James did not wear much either). The range of fabrics selected for cloaks was different. Velvet was the most common, with wool including cloth, frisado and scarlet next, followed by grosgrain and satin. This meant that most cloaks were of a complementary, rather than a matching, fabric to the suits they were worn with. In almost all cases these cloaks were a vehicle for display regardless of whether they were made from wool or silk.

The predominant form of decoration while he was in Scotland was applied gold, silver or silk trimmings. These were often very expensive, paid for by the ounce rather than the ell. Slashing and pining were also in regular use. One distinctive change came in September 1600 when there was a payment for goffering 5 ells of purple velvet bought to line a cloak. The descriptions of Henry's clothes become much more detailed than those of his father once he moves to England, a feature also found in his brother's and mother's accounts, suggesting that they shared a greater interest in the little details of their clothes, as well as in the colour and choice of fabric. While passementerie was still important, Henry's suits in 1606/7 also include many references to the slashing of one fabric to reveal one or two other layers of fabric underneath.[29] Stamping was used with increasing frequency, especially for cloak linings.[30] However, the most significant difference was the extensive use of embroidery. For instance, in 1606/7, Edmund Palmer, embroiderer, was paid for embroidering a suit of purple satin with silk

2.4 Robert Peake the elder, *Prince Henry*, c.1610. Oil on canvas, 172.7 × 113.7 cm. National Portrait Gallery, London. Henry wears a matching jerkin and short trunk hose with long carnation stockings along with a fitted doublet, while next to him there is a high-crowned white beaver hat.

and silver and Oes of silver (an O or Oe was a small ring of wire) (fig. 2.5).[31] In 1608/9 Mr Palmer worked on three suits – one crimson satin with silk and silver twist, one green taffeta with red silk, and one white satin with carnation silk and pearl – at a cost of £154 0s 0d.[32] The cost and desirability of embroidering is made evident by a comment made at Henry's creation as prince of Wales, when it was reported that 'embroidered suits were so common, as the richest lace to be gotten seemed but a mean Grace to the wearer'.[33] Henry's clothes, and those of the men around him, were eye-catching, so making the young prince the centre of attention.

2.5 This doublet of c.1600 demonstrates just how striking polychrome embroidery combined with metal lace can be. Eastern European, silk. Metropolitan Museum of Art, New York.

Creating Henry's Style

After the first year of his life Prince Henry had a different tailor to his father, so clearing the way for the gradual creation of his own distinctive style. More importantly, he brought his tailor, Alexander Wilson, with him to England, and later employed another Scot, Patrick Black, as his second tailor. In parallel to other Scots forming a key part of the households of James, Anna and Henry, they also could be found in the groups of royal artificers working for the crown. There was a strong Scottish element in the production of royal wardrobes in London, assisting Henry in his self-fashioning. His arrival in 1603 was particularly significant because there had not been a prince in London for 66 years. He was the same age Edward VI (1537–53) had been when he became king, and so Henry was poised to become the focal point within his own household, and the wider court and political culture.

James wanted to mould his son's development, and in 1607 Sir Thomas Chaloner observed that 'His Highness's household … was intended by the King for a courtly college or a collegiate court'.[34] And it was not just his son that James wished to shape. As the relationship between the king and Kerr deteriorated, James claimed that 'all your being, except your breathing and soul is from me'.[35] However, Henry resisted his father's efforts and as he got older those around him recognised this. In 1606, when the departing Venetian ambassador presented his successor to the king, they also visited the prince.[36] Four years later, in August 1610, aged 16, 'the Prince, who now that he has taken his seat in Council desireth to have to do with some of the more weighty affairs, and he is so strict in his dealings that he pushes aside many difficulties, for all are afraid of falling into his displeasure'.[37] While James was affectionate towards Henry at his creation as prince of Wales, Antonio Correr, the Venetian ambassador, felt their relationship was under

2.6 Attributed to Isaac Oliver, Letters Patent of James VI and I investing his son Henry as prince of Wales and earl of Chester (detail). British Library, Add. MS 36932. While the primary emphasis is on their robes, Henry was depicted in a dark blue velvet doublet, which contrasts with the white suit often worn by his father.

strain (fig. 2.6).[38] He reported, 'It seems that the King has some reasonable jealousy of the rising sun'. And James had reason to be concerned.[39]

If Henry's relationship with his father was difficult, he shared many interests with his mother, Anna of Denmark, including an appreciation of the political and social implications of clothing.[40] Sir Dudley Carleton (1573–1632) informed Sir Thomas Percy (*c.*1562–1605) on 28 June 1603 that Anna gave 'great contentment to the world in her fashion'.[41] Anna drew Henry into her circle, including him in events where the clothing of the chief participants was carefully chosen to assert their importance. On 27 December 1604, Prince Henry and Anna's brother Ulrik, the duke of Holstein (1578–1624), led Susan de Vere (1587–1628/9), daughter of Edward de Vere, 17th earl of Oxford (1550–1604), to her wedding with Philip Herbert, 4th earl of Pembroke (1584–1650). When Anna retired with her ladies to give birth, her sons went with her to Greenwich, so being drawn into part of her displays linked to laying-in and churching.[42] Equally, with his increased independence, Henry, either alone or in tandem with his mother, offered an alternative to those who were concerned about the tone of James's court, the influence exerted by royal favourites and the number of Scots in positions of influence in the

2.7 Unknown artist, *Sir David Murray of Gorthy*, 1603. Oil on canvas, 54.1 × 43.8 cm. National Galleries of Scotland. While Murray's doublet may appear understated at first glance, a closer look reveals a mass of slashing and pinked decoration, making it a very elegant garment.

household. The Scots and English courtiers who clustered around the prince focused more on their shared Protestantism and less on their national differences. Of these, one of the most important was Sir David Murray (1567–1629), keeper of the prince's privy purse, groom of the stool and gentleman of the robes. His own black satin doublet served to accentuate his master's more flamboyant wardrobe (fig. 2.7).

One of the key themes in James's advice was the importance of avoiding excess in dress and, by implication, luxury, because clothes served to display the body. The playwright Ben Jonson (1572–1637) made the point eloquently when he observed, 'It is not powdering and perfuming and everyday smelling of the tailor that converteth [a man] to a beautiful object but a mind, shining through any suit, which needs no false light either of riches or honours to help it'.[43] Yet Jonson, through his collaboration with Inigo Jones (1573–1652), knew that clothes mattered and the clothes of a prince especially so. Getting clothing right was important because, as George Puttenham (1529–90), the author of *The Arte of English Poesie* (1589) observed, 'a king and prince may use rich and gorgeous apparel decently, so cannot a mean person do'.[44] Yet a king or a prince could overstep the bounds, which was why James stressed the importance of 'moderate' dress, a theme echoed by Sir Arthur Gorges when he described prince Henry's clothing as the opposite of 'extreame excess and pride of Apparell'.[45] A contemporary writer signing himself W. H., who may have been William Haydon, groom of the bedchamber, was keen to stress that Henry got the balance right because he loved 'to goe handsome and well cloathed: yet without any manner of superfluity of excesse'.[46] Henry used his clothes to present himself as a model of princely virtue.

The Influence of Chivalric Fantasy on Prince Henry's Image

Henry's heroes were Sir Philip Sidney (1554–86) (fig. 2.8) and Robert Devereux, 2nd earl of Essex, whom Sir Roy Strong described as 'the epitome of militant Protestant chivalry'.[47] The prince may have been familiar with Sidney's poetry before 1603, because it was available in Scotland.[48] More significantly, his household included Sir Thomas Chaloner (1559–1615) as governor and chamberlain, Lionel Sharpe (1559–1631) and John Hayward (*c*.1564–1627), who were drawn from the circles of Sidney and Essex.[49] It was from within this context that Henry stated: 'I know what becomes a Prince. It is not necessary for me to be a professor, but a soldier and a man of the world.'[50] Isaac Oliver captured the prince's military demeanour in *c.*1610 in his half-length miniature of Henry wearing black armour with gilt decoration of the 1570s (fig. 2.9).

With a king on the throne, tournaments changed from the Elizabethan format. Although James did run at the ring, he was not a keen jouster, so providing his sons with an opportunity they exploited.[51] As Malcolm Smuts has argued, it seems likely that Henry favoured outdoor events for self-promotion because they had a larger and more diverse audience than indoor masques.[52] He made his first public appearance in the tiltyard on 5 August 1606 when, aged nine, he ran at the ring before his

2.8 Unknown artist, *Sir Philip Sidney*, c.1576. Oil on panel, 113.9 × 84 cm. National Portrait Gallery, London. The pronounced peasecod belly on the doublet, in tandem with the very full hose with metal thread embroidery on the panes, present Sidney as a man of fashion.

father and his uncle, the king of Denmark, 'gallantly mounted, and [with] a hart as powerfull as any, though that youth denied strength'.[53] Just two years later Sir Henry Lee, former champion to the late Elizabeth I, looked to Henry to revive chivalry at the Jacobean court.[54] He presented the prince with a Greenwich armour of blued steel with fire gilding and a design consisting of bands of strapwork and arabesques in between which were thistles, roses, fleur-de-lys and the prince's monograms, FHP and HP (fig. 2.10).[55]

Henry was described as the 'Prince of th'Isles, the hope and delight / Of all the northern nations' in Jonson's *Tethys' Festival*, which was performed to mark his creation as prince of Wales.[56] Jonson built on this idea in the words he prepared for *The Lady of the Lake* or *The Speeches at Prince Henry's Barriers* (1610). Henry's challenge was issued on 31 December 1609 in the name of Meliadus, lord of the Isles. Meliadus, or Moeliades, was an anagram for *Miles a deo* (soldier of God), stressing Henry's stance as a Protestant prince. The barriers (a foot combat with

2.9 *(above)* Isaac Oliver, *Prince Henry*, c.1610. Watercolour on vellum laid on card, 13.2 × 10 cm. Royal Collection. The exceptionally fine quality ruff and the blue satin ribbon with the lesser George, paired with parade armour, depict Henry as a militant prince.

2.10 *(right)* Jacob Halder, Greenwich workshops, armour garniture for Henry, future prince of Wales, for the field, tourney, tilt and barriers (detail), c.1608. Windsor Castle, Royal Collection. The Tudor roses and Scottish thistles, symbolising the union of the two countries, are equally prominent on Henry's breastplate.

pikes and swords) also demonstrated Henry's support for his father's vision of unity between Scotland and England. Henry and six friends – three Scots and three Englishmen: Sir Robert Gordon; Ludovic Stuart, 2nd duke of Lennox; James Hay, 1st earl of Carlisle; Thomas Howard, 21st earl of Arundel; Henry Wriothesley, 3rd earl of Southampton and Sir Thomas Somerset – took on all comers. It was observed at the time that 'His Highnesse did admirably fight his part, giving and receiving that night 32 pushes of pikes, and about 360 streakes of swords, which is scarce credible in so young yeares, enough to assure the world, that Great Britaine's brave Henry aspired to immortality'.[57] And Henry did so in style. Thomas Bowker received £247 8s for the costumes, with a further £1,986 9s 7d being spent on 'diverse sortes of perles, Silkes and other necessaries' to ensure the success of this event.[58]

The Prince and Disguise

As we have seen, the masquing tradition was rich in both Scotland and England, and Scots took leading roles in James's new court.[59] Shortly after coming to England, Christophe de Harlay (1553–1610), comte de Beaumont and ambassador of Henri IV, reported that on 6 January 1604 there was 'a masquerade of certain Scotchmen'.[60] Masques such as this formed part of a shift from public to private displays of magnificence during James's reign.[61] Participating in them was one way in which Henry could present himself to a select audience of courtiers and ambassadors. However, not everyone saw the masque in such a positive light. In 1593 the Elizabethan pamphleteer Thomas Nashe (1567–1601) summed up the mutability of masque costumes when he used them as a means of criticising what he saw as the Englishman's obsessive following of fashion, which made him 'the ape of all nation's superfluities, the continual masquer of outlandish habilements'.[62] In contrast, Francis Bacon, in his essay *Of Masques and Triumphs* (1625), saw costume in much more practical and also more appreciative terms, advising 'Let the suits of the masquers be graceful, and such as become the person when the vizars are off'.[63] He went on to specify that 'The colours that shew best by candlelight, are white, carnation and a kind of sea-water-greene; and oes, or spangs, as they are of no great cost, so they are of most glory'.[64] Inigo Jones drew on aspects of this advice when he

2.11 Inigo Jones, costume design for prince Henry as Oberon, 1611. Chatsworth, collection of the duke of Devonshire. Henry wore short scarlet hose, white brodequins with silver spangles and white and scarlet feathers on his head, with a scarlet band across his chest.

designed Henry's costume for the leading role in Ben Jonson's *Oberon the Faery Prince* (fig. 2.11), which was performed on 1 January 1611.[65] The sumptuous costumes, which cost £1,412, conjured up a magical world with those styled *à l'antique* like the prince, contrasting with wild, bestial characters.[66]

Just as important as the right costume were well-honed dancing skills. Henry's lessons had progressed well in Stirling, since when he performed in public on 20 June 1603 'the Queen commanded that all of his age who attended him should dance, but no-one taking it on them, Lord Cecil's son stepped forth in a comely and lowly manner, and took the young Princess and danced his galliard'.[67] Six months later Henry took part in *The Vision of the Twelve Goddesses* on 15 January 1604, when Carleton reported that the ladies 'for galliards and corantoes they went by discretion, and the young prince was tossed from hand to hand like a tennis ball'.[68] Henry's prowess was admired at a ball attended by Juan Fernandez de Velasco, constable of Castile and Spanish envoy, on 19 August 1604. Velasco reported: 'The Prince was commanded by his parents to dance a galliard … and this he did with much sprightliness and modesty, cutting several capers in the course of the dance … after this … the Prince stood up to dance a *correnta*, which he did very gracefully'.[69] James and Anna were keen for Henry to participate because dancing in a masque was a well-established way to show off young men of marriageable age.

Clothing as an Expression of Youth Culture at the Jacobean Court

The young or, to be more precise, groups of adolescent, beardless, males – including apprentices, students at the Inns of Court and universities, and younger sons at court – were regarded with caution in early modern society. Their youthful exuberance manifested in a tendency towards drinking, violence and flamboyant clothes that they displayed on the street. They were significant enough, as Amanda Bailey has noted, to have developed as a specific character type in drama, as exemplified by Piers Gaveston, the king's young favourite, 'jetting' in Italian clothing at the heart of 'a corrupt court overrun with young male court hangers-on' in Christopher Marlowe's *Edward II* (1594).[70] Although Prince Henry was not a second son, his father did regard him as his apprentice, and James's court valued male beauty and youth in what Christopher Breward has described as 'a cult of aesthetic masculinity'.[71] Henry epitomised this cult, described as he was by the Doge of Venice as 'an angel in outward form'.[72]

As John Leeds Barroll has noted, James's newly established court in 1603 served 'as a showcase for the younger courtiers whom the king favoured'.[73] These included Ludovic Stuart, duke of Lennox, the king's second cousin, and James Hay, 1st earl of Carlisle. Alongside them was a less acceptable group including Henry Wriothesley, 3rd earl of Southampton, William

Herbert, earl of Pembroke (1580–1630) and Edmund Sheffield, 1st earl of Mulgrave (1564–1646), men Alastair Bellany has described as associating with 'discontented noblemen of the younger sort'.[74] Pembroke and Sheffield may have been the inspiration for the 'fair youth' in Shakespeare's sonnets.[75] What has not really been explored, however, is the presence of boys and adolescents at court, and the ongoing emphasis placed on youth. Starting with the former, a patent issued on 30 January 1604 saw the establishment of a troop of boy actors and choristers. These Children of the Chapel Royal were known as the Children of the Queen's Revels, and Samuel Daniel oversaw their repertoire.[76] Equally, the pages at court were often young, a point alluded to in the text of *Coelum Britannicum* (performed in 1634), which mockingly observed that 'The gods must keep no pages nor grooms of their chamber under the age of 25, and those provided of a competent stock of beards'.[77] More importantly in this context, there was a second wave of young men focused around the prince, his brother, Charles, and their friends, such as the earl of Essex's son, Sir John Harrington, and the new royal favourite, Robert Kerr (*c.*1587–1645).

Characteristics of Youthful Dress at the Jacobean Court

There were several interlinked strands of male fashionable dress at the Jacobean court. They reflected contemporary ideas about the different phases of a man's life and can explain, in part at least, why Henry Howard, earl of Northampton (1540–1614), when writing to Elizabeth and James, referred to himself as an old hermit and wore black.[78] Yet the black he wore was no less elegant than the colours favoured by many of his contemporaries. In contrast, younger men opted 'for good fashion in cloathes … good looks and handsome accoutrements', because the king 'laugheth at the long grown fashion of our young courtiers and wisheth for change every day'.[79] As one observer noted, 'We have lately had many Gallants who failed in their suits for want of due observation of these matters. The King is nicely heedful of such points, and dwelleth on good looks and handsome accoutrements'.[80] James's scrutiny of the young men at his court promoted a competitive environment as each bid to attract his attention.

While Henry's clothes followed his father's style in the period until 1608, he then started to use them to create his own distinctive image. In doing so, he developed a way of expressing his rivalry with young royal favourites, most notably Kerr, and by doing so provided a role model for his younger brother. Between 1610 and 1612 Henry's clothes were characterised as flamboyant, heavily embellished, colourful and elegant. He chose close-fitting doublets with less padding than those favoured by James, and these were worn with short trunk hose. This style of dress was copied by others at court, as is exemplified by the miniature of Richard Sackville, 3rd earl of Dorset, of 1616 by Isaac Oliver (fig. 2.12). Sackville was part of the prince's chivalric circle, he regularly appeared in the tiltyard and his luxurious clothes explain why he was described as 'a licentious spendthrift'.[81] Henry's style was also worn by elegant young Scots at court, including James, 2nd marquis of Hamilton (1589–1625), who was painted in 1610 dressed in a fitted doublet and short padded hose embroidered with a design of flaming hearts and heart's ease (fig. 2.13).[82]

Three specific characteristics were identified by contemporaries as being typical of the styles favoured by young men at court. First, their clothing was 'effeminate'.[83] This word inferred that the individual was

2.12 Isaac Oliver, *Richard Sackville, 3rd Earl of Dorset*, 1616. Watercolour on vellum, 23.5 × 15.3 cm. Victoria and Albert Museum, London. This pale grey-blue doublet and darker blue trunk hose decorated with suns and moons feature in Sackville's inventory, indicating that they were real clothes and not an artistic creation.

beardless and slender, both indicative of a lack of physical maturity. This male body shape was accentuated by close-fitting fine clothes, which according to the pamphlet writer Philip Stubbes 'transnatureth them, makinge them weake, tender and infirme'.[84]

Second, young men were said to favour the distinctive use of colour, in particular pastel colours and white, a view that is backed up by their portraits. Yet this was only a partial view. Dekker and Middleton referred to 'such a kind of light colour summer stuff, mingled with divers colours' in *The Roaring Girl*. This play was performed by Henry's men at the Fortune Theatre in 1611, suggesting the theme was topical but also that these colours were as much seasonal as they were youthful.[85] One of Anna's influences on fashion was the use of ribbon in pale shades by men and women of all ages.[86] Equally, Elizabeth I's favourites Robert Dudley, 1st earl of Leicester and Robert Devereux, 2nd earl of Essex, had used colour to make themselves stand out at court (fig. 2.14). Both Laurence Stone and Malcolm Smuts have linked a perceived shift to black, epitomised by Henry Howard, earl of Northampton, with a

2.13 *(above, left)* After Daniel Mytens, *James Hamilton, 2nd marquis of Hamilton*, 1610. Oil on canvas. Lennoxlove, East Lothian. James's stylish suit is accessorised with a tall-crowned felt hat, gloves, sword, boots and spurs.

2.14 *(above, right)* Nicholas Hilliard, *Youth Thought to be the Earl of Essex*, c. 1588. Watercolour on vellum, 13.5 × 7.3 cm. Victoria and Albert Museum, London. Note the contrast of the black and white, and emphasis on this young courtier's long shapely legs.

rejection of the bright, brash colours worn by younger men.[87] But, not all older men wore black, as is shown by the portrait of George Carew, earl of Totnes, who was painted in 1619–20 in a white satin doublet with a floral pattern and carnation paned hose.[88]

Third, they favoured styles that displayed the full length of their shapely legs, usually short, tight hose worn with fancy silk stockings. The appeal of such a style is revealed by a letter of Sir John Holles to his son Denzel, dated 4 March 1615, which notes that wearing 'a bullion paire of carnation velvet, and satten [hose] all embroderd over with riche embroidery of gould, silver, and silke … and a paire of carnation silk stockins would have done your busines a great deal of honor, and your self grace, for your legg beeing (as it is) the best part of your body'.[89] Youth and clothing were closely linked at the Jacobean court and not always in positive ways, but the competition between Robert Kerr and Henry ensured that it gained even greater significance.

A Favourite's Wardrobe: Robert Kerr

Robert Kerr, or Carr to give the anglicised form of his surname, is usually discussed in relation to his marriage to Frances Howard and the salacious trial that followed shortly afterwards. Yet far too little attention has been paid to his sartorial role at court. Kerr came to England with the king as a page in 1603, and on their arrival James ordered him a doublet and hose of ash colour satin and a cloak of black silk grosgrain lined with taffeta.[90] But Kerr did not remain in the king's service for long because, as one contemporary noted, 'the pages the King brought with him to wait upon his coach in the French manner were discharged and footmen according to the English way supplied in their places'.[91] This comment stressed the importance of French style and Kerr's youth in shaping his outlook. The significance of Kerr's clothing was also central to a poem that mockingly declared:

> When Carr in Court at first a page began,
> He swelled, and swelled into a gentleman.
> And from a gentleman and bravely dight [adorned]
> He swelled, and swelled till he became a Knight.[92]

In addition to elegant attire, Robert Kerr is said to have had a 'fair complexion, equally sharing the beauty of both sexes'.[93] He was also 'straight-limbed, well-favoured, strong-shouldered and smooth-faced'.[94] On the death of Dunbar, the leading Scot at court up until 1611, Correr informed the Doge that 'Robert Carr, also a Scot, a youth of a most modest nature, and always beloved by the king, has made such strides in his favour as it would seem that he alone is to dispose of everything.'[95]

On 20 October 1607 Lord Thomas Howard wrote to Sir John Harington reporting that 'Carr was with him [the king] a boy in Scotland', adding, significantly, that Kerr 'knoweth his taste and what pleaseth'.[96] It was their shared past that gave Kerr influence over the king. By 18 June 1608 one observer was able to state:

> Our English Lords who had hoped for an English favourite (to which end the Countess of Suffolk did look out choice young men whom she daily curled and perfumed their breaths) have now left all hope and turn to adore the rising sun; which is not hard to obtain for Carr is naturally more addicted to the English nation than to the Scottish.[97]

Contemporaries observed that Kerr 'changed his tailors and tiremen many times, and all to please the Prince'.[98] They waxed lyrical on the subject, claiming that 'nothing so costly, no tire so uncouth, but at all costs and charges he obtained it for the increase of favour; new fashions are produced, so that he might show more beautiful and fair; and that his favour and personage might be made more manifest to the world'.[99]

A glimpse of Kerr's elegance can be seen in the slashed, white satin doublet, trimmed with gold lace and jewelled buttons, which he wore for a miniature painted in *c.*1611 (fig. 2.15). Doublets of comparable quality, including a doublet of white cloth of silver laced with silver lace and a doublet of white cloth of tissue with gold flowers, were listed in the inventory taken of his possessions at the time of his arrest on 29 November 1615 for the alleged murder of Thomas Overbury. This included one suit and cloak, 14 doublets with hose, 10 doublets, 7 pairs of hose, 19 cloaks, a jerkin, a riding coat and a nightgown.[100] It was a sizeable wardrobe but it could not compare with Henry's, even if these were only the clothes that Kerr bought in 1615.

A high proportion of Kerr's clothes were made from cloth of gold and silver, including 'a doublet of striped cloth of gold and silver cut with yellow taffeta' and 'a doublet and paned hose of black cloth of gold laced all over with black satin lace'. He also had purple items, including 'a [pair of] bullion hose of purple velvet and cloth of gold embroidered and tissued with gold and silver'.[101] With the abolition of English sumptuary laws in 1604, the colour purple no longer had the exclusive cachet it had enjoyed under the Tudors, but it still possessed royal overtones. Kerr's choice was indicative of his having the king's favour, and there are parallels with the wardrobe of Henry, who could of course wear the colour without challenge. Equally, black was the single most important colour in Kerr's wardrobe, just as it was in Henry's. Kerr owned 19 black garments or sets of garments, while the remaining 33 garments or sets of garments were made from more than

2.15 Nicholas Hilliard, *Robert Carr, 1st Earl of Somerset*, c.1611. Watercolour on vellum, 4.5 × 3.5 cm oval. National Portrait Gallery, London. Carr is the epitome of Stuart elegance, dressed in a magnificent ruff and earring, while his slashed doublet is trimmed with gold passementerie.

11 different colours. So, when John Hoskins painted Kerr at some time between 1625 and 1630 dressed in a very simple black doublet, his clothing reflected a lifelong choice of the colour as much as the change in his circumstances (fig. 2.16).

Not surprisingly, Kerr's robes of state – the scarlet robes for Parliament, the velvet robes of an earl and his St George's robes – were kept 'in the custody of Mr Walter James at [Carr's] lodging in Westminster'.[102] This was where he needed them and where they acted as the most forceful reminder of his social and political success. Kerr's status was compounded by the quality of his furnishings and informal attire, which reflected the importance of his place in the king's bedchamber. These furnishings included a carpet and cupboard cloth of tawny velvet embroidered with cloth of silver and trimmed with silver and silk fringe, and a nightgown of tawny velvet embroidered with gold and lined with unshorn velvet. They were of high quality, co-ordinated, and tawny (*couleur de roi*) was a favourite colour of James V and James VI.[103] Kerr's clothes and furnishings openly proclaimed his influence at court, and he exemplified the youthful version of Stuart style which was so admired by the king.

2.16 After John Hoskins, *Robert Carr, 1st Earl of Somerset*, after 1630, based on a work of 1625–30. Oil on panel, 24.1 × 18.4 cm. National Portrait Gallery, London. Carr's black doublet, close buttoned down the centre front, contrasts with his full, falling ruff.

Prince versus Favourite

Henry's wardrobe accounts for 1611/12 make reference to a black silk grosgrain suit made for Lord Hay, lined with taffeta and with white satin for the collar.[104] This gift for Hay suggests a cordial relationship between the prince and one of the king's well-established Scottish favourites at court, who was 14 years senior to Henry. This partially fits with the observation made by Antoine le Fevre de la Boderie, the French ambassador, in 1606 that 'None of his pleasures savour the least of a child … he despises those of his own age'.[105] However, a letter of 1609 from Henry to Sir John Harrington, who was the same age as him, suggests that this observation was not entirely true, for in it the prince observes, 'When I see you (and let that be shortlie) you will find me your better at tennis and pike'.[106] This friendly competition with Harrington did not apply to Henry's relationship with Kerr, who was seven years older than the prince. On 25 July 1610 it was reported that 'there is little love between the Prince and Kerr, whom once he threatened to have stricken with his racket when they were playing at tennis'.[107]

Henry shared his dislike of Kerr with his mother.[108] On 17 June 1612 Chamberlain stated that 'The Queen and Prince are earnest in Sir Henry Wotton's behalf, and the Lord Rochester is not willing after his late reconciliation to oppose himself, or stand in the breech, against such assailants'.[109] At the same time Rochester could not 'find the right way to please either the Queen or the Prince, but they are both in the conceit of this court not well satisfied with him'.[110] According to the historian

Arthur Wilson, 'Sir James Elphington, who (observing the Prince one day to be discontented with the Viscount) offered to kill him: but the Prince reprieved him with a gallant spirit, saying if there were cause he would do it himself'.[111]

Two years later, in March 1611, Henry actively changed his style of dress to make a specific political point. The Venetian ambassador reported:

> The Prince has abandoned the French dress and has taken to the Italian: in this he has been followed by the Duke of York and by the larger part of their household. He says he will always wear it . . . as he cannot endure the changes in fashion which come every day from France.[112]

The same year the Tuscan agent in London noted that the prince was wearing 'a richly embroidered Italian suit'.[113] The Venetian ambassador's assessment was significant on several levels. First, the repudiation of French fashion was a means of attacking Kerr, who was pro-French in his dress. Second, Henry demonstrated an appreciation of how different national styles of clothing could be used to make a political point – a tactic employed successfully by Elizabeth I and by Anna, who wore Spanish clothing to show her support for a possible Spanish marriage for Henry. Third, the value of this rejection was on a par with that of Charles II when he claimed to reject French fashion in favour of the vest in 1666 – in other words, it allowed Henry to make a point at Kerr's expense, one that when it had served his purpose, he would go back on when it suited him, because French fashion was an underlying feature of the Stuart court. Fourth and last, it may be inferred that the prince's reference to the changing nature of fashion was a sly dig at Kerr's ever-changing style and at his father's encouragement of it.

A Generous Prince: Henry's Gifts for Family and Friends

Henry's accounts indicate that, once he was 16, he started to use clothing and accessories as gifts to manage his relationships with his immediate family. In 1611/12, for example, he bought items for his father and brother and they were carefully selected. He chose a beautiful accessory for his father in the form of 'One verie rich scarff made of green taffeta cutt in little peeces and laid betwixt the peeces with silver broad seaming laces and edgd at the ends with a verie deepe bone lace'.[114] He selected something more practical for his brother: 'One pair [of] wrought hangers and [a] girdle wrought with gold for the duke of York' and a rapier to go with it.[115] Such a gift would have encouraged Charles to develop his military skills and keep his interests in line with Henry's. Most expensive, and so potentially, most significant, was the richly embroidered petticoat Henry procured for his mother in 1610/11.[116] It was lined with carnation shag and trimmed with gold and silver Flanders lace and a deep, gold and silver spangled fringe. Costing £172 18s 7d, it was more expensive than the petticoat given to Anna in 1609 by his father.[117]

Gifts for immediate family were to be expected. However, Henry was also making wider connections through his gift-giving. First, there was 'A rich petticoat wrought with embroidery all over upon white satin ground with gold, silver and silk' costing £116 1s 0d for 'the low countries duke of Brunswick's daughter'.[118] This was probably Henry's cousin, Princess Hedwig (1595–1650), duchess of Brunswick-Wolfenbüttel, and then by marriage, duchess of Pomerania, and daughter of Henry Julius, duke of Brunswick-Wolfenbüttel and his second wife, Elizabeth, daughter of Frederick II of Denmark. This present echoed his mother's pattern of gift-giving. On 10 July 1610 Anna had regifted a petticoat that had been a gift from the earl of Leicester to her sister Elizabeth.[119] Hedwig's gift was paired with another for her father and Henry's uncle: watchet velvet for the armourer to garnish the duke of Brunswick's armour, watchet satin for the same purpose, green cotton for the armour, and watchet baise to cover the armour.[120] This small selection indicates that Henry used gifts of clothing and armour to forge connections with his family, both at home and abroad, with his mother and her relatives playing a prominent part.

Things Left Undone and Unmade

Although Henry died shortly before his sister Elizabeth was to marry Frederick, his presence continued to be felt at several levels. Practically, while his death delayed the wedding, David Lindley has plausibly argued that as Chapman's patron, Henry's anti-Spanish stance was reflected in the content of the masques performed at his sister's marriage (fig. 2.17).[121] Henry had also chosen, but not paid for, his wedding gifts, which consisted of 'a fayre riche chayne all sett with Dyamants … whiche his Hignes did appoynt for his deere and worthy sister' and a chain and tablet of diamonds for the prince Elector.[122]

On the occasion of the wedding itself, the bride and groom 'were both in a sute of cloth of silver richly embroidered with silver'.[123] Anna was dressed 'all in white', while the king had chosen 'a cap and a feather, with a Spanish cape and a longe stocking' (this described only one of the three suits that James wore during the course of proceedings).[124] Male courtiers selected their clothes with a view to catching the royal gaze and that of other interested observers. One of these noted that 'The bravery and richese of that day were incomparable … above all the King's Favourite, Viscount Rochester, and Lord Hay, Lord Dingwell and Lord Dorset dazzled the eyes off [all] who saw the splendour of their Dress'.[125] It is likely that the five unmade suits, mentioned in the introduction to this chapter, were the clothes Henry had ordered for his sister's wedding. Although made of less costly satin than the king's suits (which were cloth of tissue, cloth of gold and cloth of tissue), the heavy embroidery made these suits very expensive. If worn with the hatband of diamonds ordered by the prince with 'a great Jewell toe it in forme of a Rose', which it was later noted were 'not yett payed', Henry would have glittered alongside Kerr and all the rest.[126]

2.17 Robert Peake the elder, *Princess Elizabeth, Later Queen of Bohemia*, 1606. Oil on canvas, 154.3 × 79.4 cm. Metropolitan Museum of Art, New York. Henry's sister Elizabeth dressed as elegantly as her brother, and in this portrait she wears a gown over a drum or French farthingale while her collar is supported with a pickadil.

Conclusions

Henry's clothes were always of the best quality as suited his status as the king's heir – the chief difference between those which were ordered for him in Scotland and those which were made in England at his own direction was the increasing level of control that he had over their style and cost. Always expensive, his wardrobe sat on the boundary of outright luxury, a fact that could be justified by his being the king's first-born son. As we have seen, Henry was starting to fashion his own identity until he reached a point where he was at the forefront of a circle of younger courtiers. His parents and the Scots who served as his tailors, seamstresses, laundress and master of the robes all helped to create his wardrobe. Most significant was James VI and I, whose 'version' of Stuart style offered challenges to Henry, which the prince was happy to embrace. Not wanting to dress like his father, Henry was drawn into the competitive dressing embraced by other young men at court, especially young Scotsmen like Kerr, to attract the attention of the king. The result was that Henry developed a striking, opulent style of his own and used his clothes – in the same way that Elizabeth I had done and which his mother did – to convey a political message. Aspects of his choice looked back to the long legs and close-fitting clothes favoured by Elizabeth's favourites, as they cultivated a chivalric milieu within which they could gain the queen's favour. Henry's style also played upon nostalgic views of Elizabeth promoted by James's critics. However his youthful style was subtly different, being linked to his being a prince and the heir to his father's three kingdoms. He was the most influential supporter of, and rival to, his father at court. And while his early death saw this mantle pass to his brother Charles, it was George Villiers who was to realise the true potential of Henry's tragically short-lived strand of Stuart style. Charles in turn developed his own distinctive Stuart look, which proved far more divisive than that of his older brother.

Gloria
Cœli Specto
Asperam at Levem
Gratia
IN VERBO TUO SPES MEA
Christi Tracto
Splendidam at Gravem
Vanitas
Mundi Calco

CHAPTER THREE

Charles I (1600–1649)

CHARLES I'S EXECUTION on 30 January 1649 ensured that clothing, accessories and jewellery associated with him gained relic status among his supporters.[1] One of the most emotive items is a small, sky blue knitted silk vest or waistcoat, an intimate garment worn for warmth rather than style and hidden from view by outer layers, that Charles is thought to have worn that day (fig. 3.1). Termed 'damask knitting' by Maj Ringgaard, this monochromatic technique was popular in Denmark, a country with close cultural and trading links to Scotland that were embodied in the person of Anna of Denmark, the king's mother.[2] Charles dressed with care for his execution, just as his grandmother, Mary, Queen of Scots had. The manner of Charles's death was reminiscent of Mary's, thereby either legitimising his execution as a traitor or making him a martyr.[3] Charles I divided opinion across his three kingdoms in death, as he did in life. Supporters such as Henry Howard, earl of Northampton, considered him 'a right king' because Charles was 'readie to employ his goods, his bloud and lyfe for his people'.[4] This very quality caused James Hamilton, 3rd marquis and 1st duke of Hamilton (1606–49), to question in 1638 whether Charles could 'clearlie sea hou ye can effeckt your end uithout the haserdding of your 3 crounes'.[5]

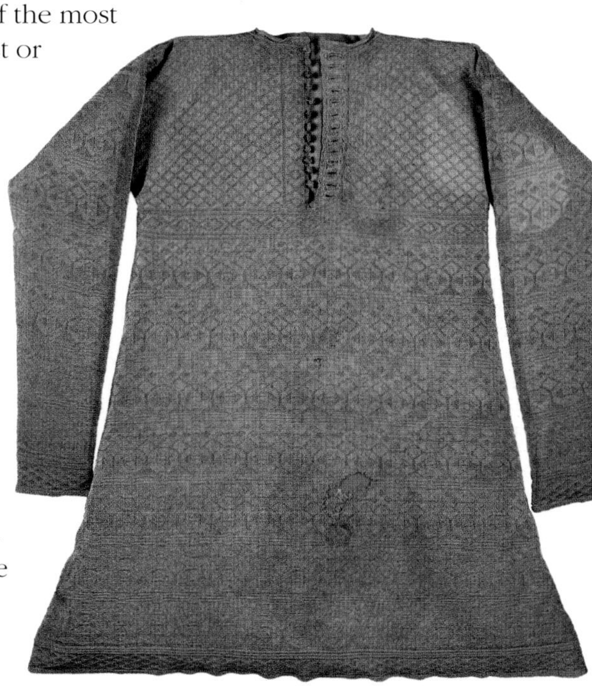

3.1 *(above)* A purl-patterned silk vest associated with Charles I, c. 1630–40. Museum of London.

3.2 *(facing page)* Detail from William Marshall, Charles I in prayer, frontispiece, *Eikon Basilike*, 1649. Engraving. Private collection.

Clothes, ranging from the satin suits recorded by Van Dyck to the robes of state depicted in the frontispiece of the *Eikon Basilike*, were central to Charles I's self-representation (fig. 3.2). In 1980 Sir Roy Strong wrote a very influential article that drew on one of Charles's clothing accounts, paving the way for Kevin Sharpe to observe that 'Charles's dress and behaviour were didactic as well as personal'.[6] Charles used his attire to assert his belief in the divine right of kings, justifying a period of rule without his English parliament and the promotion of the Anglican Church. It was a carefully crafted role, well summed up by Sir Henry Wotton, an English poet and diplomat, who noted that he admired the king for 'your gestures free from affectation; in your whole aspect no swelling, no rigidity, but an alluring and pleasing suavity'.[7] In a different vein, Edward Hyde, earl of Clarendon, described Charles as 'an immoderate lover of the Scottish nation', confident in the belief that Scotland 'could never fail him'.[8] While many of his close Scottish friends such as the duke of Hamilton were loyal to the end, as will be shown in Chapter 11, Charles's insistence on the use of the surplice in Scotland would irreparably divide him from many of his people there.

The king's relationship with clothes was shaped by his ideas about royal authority, and these, in turn, were formed by four significant factors. The first related to his place in the family as the second son. Henry, as the eldest child, had received the privileges accorded to the heir by virtue of his age, a situation that was all the more apparent in a royal family. On his brother's death Charles was then elevated to the position of heir, but Henry's image lived on. Willem de Passe's engraving of James and Henry, prince of Wales, produced in 1625, was a reworking of a 1621 piece depicting the king with Prince Charles.[9] On his accession, Charles's sister Elizabeth was his own heir, and in June 1628 the diarist John Rous noted that there was 'a secret whispering of some looking towards the Lady Elizabeth'.[10] The second key factor in shaping Charles's clothing choices was personal. Charles struggled with a weakness of his legs that he overcame, but not without teasing by Henry, who said he should be archbishop of Canterbury because his legs would be covered by skirts.[11] This stresses how central good legs were to male style. Charles was less successful in addressing his stammer, and he never really overcame his shyness.

The third was how to be a successful king of Scots with only a limited knowledge of the country and its people. While Charles left Scotland aged three, he continued to have Scots in his household for the rest of his life, including the Presbyterian, Thomas Murray (1564–1623), who was the prince's tutor from 1605.[12] This has been linked to his use of Scottish spelling and the suggestion that he had a Scottish accent.[13] Equally, while Gilbert Burnet, bishop of Salisbury, a Scottish historian, considered that Charles did not have James VI and I's 'light and familiar way', he could be informal in more private spaces such as the bedchamber or the tennis court.[14] In Charles I's own view, 'the marks of my favour ... are neither places nor titles, but the little welcome I give to accusers and the willing ear I give to my servants'.[15] Last but not least was his relationship with his mother. As both Leeds Barroll and Steve Murdoch have stressed, Anna took a keen interest in Charles, emphasising to him the importance of his Scottish and Danish heritage.[16]

'Sweet Baby Charles' (1600–12)

Charles was born on 19 November 1600 at Dunfermline Palace in Fife and he received the title of duke of Albany at his christening on 23 December.[17] He grew up in the household of his guardian Alexander Seton, 1st earl of Dunfermline, but his clothes were supplied by the royal household. One order placed in November 1601 consisted of scarlet 'stenning' to make hose, fine white fustian for two-day wylicoats, red French 'stamyng' to be a coat, with white satin sleeves trimmed with silver passement, a pair of 'mariken' sleeves wrought with ribbon, and 'scarlet Inglis staming' to be two pairs of shanks.[18] There is also a selection of white linen items associated with his infancy, including a shirt with a later lace trim, a linen robe, two little shirts and two caps.[19]

Among the first items made for Charles in England were the robes of state 'for his creation' as duke of York that took place shortly after his fifth birthday, on 6 January 1605.[20] Listed on his elder brother's warrant, dated 28 September 1604, he received a crimson velvet robe with a train, furred with 104 timbers of ermines, 13,000 powderings and 12,000 pinks at a cost of £400 6s 8d.[21] However, apart from this occasion, Charles spent much of his time away from court with his guardians Sir Robert and Lady Carey.

In a painting attributed to Robert Peake the elder of *c.*1605, the young prince is shown wearing a coat of flowered silk buttoned down the front (fig. 3.3). Fitted to the chest, with long sleeves and a natural waistline, his coat is accessorised with a sword, while behind him on the table are a gorget, helmet and gauntlets indicative of Charles's future place among the male elite. In this picture Charles is wearing clothes, linen and accessories of the type supplied for him by the Great Wardrobe on two warrants dated 27 September 1606 and 27 September 1607.[22] He was kept well dressed with orders costing £1,437 14s 4½d and £684 14s 2d respectively. On both occasions, Charles received coats – 25 in 1605/6 and 20 in 1606/7 – indicating that he had not been breeched. Even so, these coats could be sumptuous, with the most impressive example being made from cloth of silver branched with silver and gold, with two pairs of sleeves trimmed with gold and silver plate and lined with taffeta. The timing of the order suggests that Charles wore this coat for the visit of his uncle, the king of Denmark, an event upon which his mother placed great importance.[23]

3.3 Robert Peake the elder, *Charles I, when Duke of York*, c.1605. Oil on canvas, 112 × 83 cm. Bristol City Museum and Art Gallery. Although still dressed as a child, Charles also wears a gorget and rests his hand on the hilt of his sword.

3.4 Robert Peake the elder, *Charles I*, c.1610. Oil on canvas, 127 × 85.7 cm. National Galleries of Scotland. The matching red silk cloak and breeches show off the prince's cream silk doublet to good effect.

The two accounts record 19 specified colours, 12 in 1605/6 and 13 in 1606/7. Most colours appeared just once, but carnation, ash, pink and white were popular choices. While impractical for a young child, pale colours were as common in his wardrobe as they were in the orders of his brother and father. In May 1617, Lady Anne Clifford similarly dressed her daughter, known as 'the Child', in 'her white coat'.[24] Possibly because of Charles's youth, there were no black, grey or purple garments, the colours explicitly linked to mourning or royalty, in his wardrobe. Nine different fabrics were used, offering variety, but satin accounted for a third of the coats, making it the most popular, just as in his father's accounts. The chief differences between the accounts are the presence of taffeta, tabby and grosgrain in 1605/6 (all fairly plain silks), and cloth of silver, double the amount of velvet and also velvet with a silver ground in 1606/7. A comment in Lady Anne Clifford's diary suggests that, as the children got older, they were allowed these more sophisticated silks. On 1 January 1619 Clifford noted that 'this day the Child put on her crimson velvet Coat laced with silver Lace, which was the 1st velvet Coat she ever had'.[25]

After 1607 there is a gap in the accounts relating to Charles's clothes, but a portrait of *c.*1610 presents a very elegant prince to the viewer. Dressed in a silver doublet, crimson breeches and cloak, his confident pose emphasises his legs, indicating that Charles had worked very hard, having a regular riding regime, to strengthen his body so that he could emulate his brother's athleticism and equestrianism (fig. 3.4).

Charles as Prince of Wales

The death of his elder brother Henry on 6 November 1612 meant that Charles became heir to the throne and shortly after the funeral he took a prominent role in his sister Elizabeth's betrothal. On 27 December Charles escorted Frederick 'appaireled in a black velvet cloake caped with gold lace. Then followed she in a black velvet gown seeme of crosletts or quatrefoils sylver, and a small white feather on her head'.[26] The following year Peake captured Charles in a swagger pose, dressed once again in crimson, with a cloak on his left shoulder lined with shag or plush, and a fitted doublet worn with very full breeches (fig. 3.5). This portrait offers a glimpse of how Charles fashioned his own image as prince of Wales prior to the block of seven extant clothing accounts that run from 1617 to 1624 with a gap between 1620 and 1622.

After 1612 Charles's clothes were more colourful than before, with 32 different shades plus 13 combinations, where one colour was used for the doublet and another for the hose. Of these, only black was ordered on every account. Black was the most frequently ordered colour, followed by green, rose, tawny, hair and grisdeline. At the other end of the spectrum, 24 colours, including bloom, dove, peach, sage and sky, were only ordered once. Variety was not only present across the time span but also within each account. Suits in 12 to 18 colours were ordered on each account. His use of fabric was also more complex, with 13 types recorded, along with two types of leather. By using them in combination, with one fabric used for the doublet and another for the hose, the range of options increased greatly. The satins in particular were embellished with slashing and pinking in decorative patterns.[27]

3.5 Robert Peake the elder, *Charles, Prince of Wales*, 1613. Oil on canvas, 154.9 × 86.4 cm. The Old Schools, University of Cambridge. Charles is dressed in his late brother's style in this portrait.

Initially, there was marked hostility between George Villiers, 1st duke of Buckingham, and the young Charles.[28] However, later, Buckingham was like an older brother to Charles and this bond was perhaps enhanced by James signing himself 'dad' in his letters to Buckingham. Buckingham also took on Henry's role as a sartorial model for Charles. On 2 September 1614 John Erskine, earl of Mar, noted in passing to Thomas, viscount of Fenton, that 'a youth called Villiers is in favour'.[29] The duke's good looks were the key to his rise, and his modest background is hinted at in a report of 1615 which notes that he was seen 'at a horse race in Cambridgeshire in an old black suit, broken out in divers places'.[30] Buckingham soon learnt, however, how to use clothing to acquire, and then assert, influence;[31] so much so that Francis Bacon advised him to 'Let vanity in apparel, and, which is more vain, that of the fashion, be avoided', while adding that 'if we must be vain and superfluous in laces and embroideries, which are more costly than either warm or comely, let the curiosity be the manufacture of the natives'.[32] The Scots at court were taking notice by June 1616 and the earl of Mar reported that Buckingham was his friend.[33] Bishop Goodman described him as 'the hand-somest-bodied man of England; his limbs so well compacted and his conversation so pleasing and of so sweet a disposition'.[34] By the mid 1620s Buckingham was at the height of his influence with both Charles and James, and his wardrobe reflected his status.[35]

While Buckingham was important, there were still Scots in the prince's household who were promoting Scottish interests.[36] For instance, in July 1613 Sir Robert Kerr, later earl of Ancrum, was appointed to Charles's bedchamber.[37] The earl of Roxburgh wrote to Sir Robert in October 1623 expressing his joy at Charles's safe return from Spain and the hope that 'your Worthe Maester will neuer wrong him self to neglect ane Loyell heart'.[38] Such hopes were not in vain, because, in 1617, Charles had asked James 'to let me see the country where I was born and the customs of it'.[39] While the request was refused, Charles gained a different experience when appointed, along with his mother, to the council that ruled England while James was on his Scottish progress.[40] Charles was also painted a few years later by Hendrik van Steenwijk, *c.*1620, in robes of state (fig. 3.6). When Charles attended debates as a prince 'his affability and courtesy in the Parliament hath won him great reputation and love'.[41] Unfortunately, this happy rapport was not to last.

As a young man, Charles's self-fashioning took a different turn to that of his brother Henry and he developed a distinctive, if short-lived, style on his trip to Spain in 1623 (fig. 3.7).[42] As a choice, it was out

3.6 Hendrik van Steenwijk II, *Charles I as Prince of Wales*, c.1620. Oil on canvas, 219.5 × 174.5 cm. Statens Museum for Kunst, Copenhagen. The prince's scarlet robes are the most important feature of his dress.

of kilter with much of Stuart style because of its overt acceptance and adoption of Spanish fashion. Three suits were sent to Spain marked as 'unmade': a green satin suit, the cassock and cloak embroidered with gold and silver; a tawny satin suit, cassock and cloak embroidered with gold and silver; and a sky colour satin suit cassock and cloak embroidered with gold.[43] Robert Jossey's charges included £9 13s 6d for transporting the prince's trunks from St Andreas to Madrid and back again.[44]

3.7 Daniel Mytens, *Charles I as Prince of Wales*, 1624. Oil on canvas, 70 × 60 cm. Private collection, sold by the Weiss Gallery, London.

However, while Charles was taking centre stage in Spain, he was little more than a name on documents in Scotland in the early 1620s. The documents in question were charters, some of which were issued jointly with his father, as in the case of the letters of gift granted to Elizabeth Macgill, lady Cullane, of single escheat of Alexander Kennedy, brother of James Kennedy of Culzeane, in June 1619 by James VI and Charles, prince and steward of Scotland.[45] Or they could be in his sole name, as in June 1621 with a confirmation of lands in favour of 'James Buchanan, servitor to the king, and Jean Lundie, his spoiuse' by Charles, prince of Scotland and Wales, duke of Rothesay, Albany, Cornwall and York, and lord of the regality of Dunfermline, but accompanied with the signatures of James VI and Charles.[46] Thus, as Charles grew up, his knowledge of Scotland was shaped by his relationships with the Scots in his household and at court, arguably giving him a rather idealised view.

King, Husband and Father

In March 1625, James VI and I died and Charles mourned his father as a dutiful son should. On 5 April Sir William Neve observed that the new king 'kept privately his bed or chamber, at St. James's untill Sunday last, & then dined abroad, in the privy Chamber, being in a plain black cloth Cloke to the ancle'.[47] However, Charles wanted his court and his household to run on very different lines to those of his father, and the change was rapid. On 25 April 1625, Zuane Pesaro, the Venetian ambassador in England, wrote to the Doge and Senate informing them that 'The king observes a rule of great decorum', adding that 'he desires the observance of the rules and maxims of the late Queen Elizabeth, whose rule was so popular and is so vastly famous'.[48]

Plans for his marriage progressed rapidly too. His choice settled on Henrietta Maria (1609–69), the youngest daughter of Henry IV of France, who he had met on his journey to Madrid.[49] For their formal betrothal on 28 April 1625, Henrietta Maria wore a robe of cloth of gold and silver

3.8 *(right)* Sir Anthony van Dyck, *Charles I and Henrietta Maria Holding a Laurel Wreath*, 1632. Oil on canvas, 113.5 × 163 cm. Kroměříž Archdiocesan Museum, Kroměříž, Czech Republic. The king in a 1630s-style salmon-pink doublet with paned sleeves and deep, overlapping skirts.

3.9 *(below)* Paned doublet of the early 1620s. Metropolitan Museum of Art, New York.

with a train, and she wore it again to sign the marriage contract. Three days later Charles and Henrietta Maria were married by proxy at Notre-Dame, the same spot where Mary, Queen of Scots had married the Dauphin.[50] Charles's proxy, Claude de Lorraine, duke de Chevreuse, wore a black striped suit decorated with diamonds, and James Hay was a witness.[51] However, the retinue that received Henrietta Maria on 13 June 1625 included just one Scottish peer, James Hamilton, 3rd marquis of Hamilton, who travelled with 27 English nobles.[52] Endymion Porter was among them and he wrote to his wife on 14 June 1625 noting that he had a souvenir for her: 'I haue sent you two of the kings poyntes one for your selfe and an other for a frend'.[53] These wedding favours were just one of many ways in which the royal marriage was celebrated and promoted at court and more widely (figs. 3.8 and 3.9).

The king's coronation, held on 2 February 1626 at Westminster Abbey, was also distinctive because the king wore a white suit with his formal robes.[54] Indeed, while not that common at the start of the reign, white, and more importantly white combined with a colour, became increasingly popular in the 1630s. Like his father, Charles also owned a few suits in watchet, and more in sky blue. In contrast, black featured every year and was the single most frequently occurring colour in the king's wardrobe. However, when offset against the 80 colours and colour combinations that feature in his accounts for this period, it is always secondary to the very wide range of predominantly pastel shades.

Charles's accounts from 1627 to 1638 reveal that the young man adopted a new look once he became king, with his suits consisting of paned doublet, breeches and a cloak. There is just one named, short-lived fashion in the royal accounts, and that was linked to the ill-fated Île de Ré campaign of 1627, but unfortunately the accounts do not say what was distinctive about this style. Robert Ramsey, Buckingham's tailor, made the king two suits, with cloaks and stockings, in this style, and Charles received two more from his tailor, all in 1627.[55] While Charles and Buckingham used clothes to promote this endeavour, the fashion failed, as did the campaign lead by Buckingham.

The most popular fabrics for the king's suits were satin, then cloth, with satin doublets twinned with cloth hose as third on the list. The satin was usually plain, but satins described as branched, brocaded flowered and wrought were used. The cloth was usually a broadcloth but occasionally he wore mixed or Sergovia cloth. Wool camlets also featured, with a few instances of silk and watered camlets, along with some tabby and taffeta, with watered examples of both (fig. 3.10).

3.10 Daniel Mytens, *Charles I*, 1629. Oil on canvas, 200.3 × 140.7 cm. Metropolitan Museum of Art, New York. Liberal application of metal thread passementerie, to either wool or silk suits, created a sophisticated look.

Charles also occasionally favoured velvet with cut pile, as well as wrought, uncut and figured velvets. There was very little cloth of gold or silver but what there was, was used to good effect, such as the cloth of gold doublet laced with two bone laces and cut in panes worn with a pair of black wrought velvet hose.[56] However, this does not mean that gold and silver were absent from the royal wardrobe; rather, that they just came from different sources including grosgrains. More significantly, gold and silver lace, as well as coloured silk lace, was liberally applied to mark seams and along the edges of panes. Metal thread and silk embroidery was reserved for the most important suits, so there was a peak in the account for the Scottish coronation, demonstrating the significance of this occasion for Charles, both sartorially and politically.

Rivals for the King's Friendship: Competition between the Scottish and English Male Elites

3.11 Michiel Jansz van Miereveld, *George Villiers, Duke of Buckingham*, 1625–6. Oil on wood panel, 69.5 × 57.5 cm. South Australian Government Grant, 1967, Art Gallery of South Australia, Adelaide, 0.2115. Buckingham's dark green satin doublet shows off his love of pearls.

In the early years of the reign Buckingham regularly dressed in a style that was more opulent than the king, as van Mierevelt's portrait suggests (fig. 3.11).[57] Such opulence was in keeping with an entry in his accounts from 1625 paying £20 'to the man that made his lordships network silver suit for altering of it'.[58] The duke was a trendsetter when he went to Paris to collect Henrietta Maria in 1625, making all things English popular, including 'un boukinkan', a hunting cap made fashionable by the duke.[59] Of his 29 suits, one of white satin and velvet was 'set all over both suit and cloak with diamonds, the value whereof thought to be fourscore thousand pearls' while another of purple satin was embroidered with pearls.[60] It comes as no surprise that in 1627 Buckingham spent £3,000 per annum on his clothes.[61] Equally, his preparations for the Île de Ré campaign reveal a close focus on his wardrobe, with him buying new linen, silk and buttons while reusing some of the clothes and the coach made for his trip to Paris in 1625.[62]

However, Buckingham did not have a monopoly on the king's favour. In 1624, on the death of Lennox, James Hamilton, 3rd marquis and 1st duke of Hamilton, replaced him as lord steward.[63] There was little love lost between the two men, and in 1625 George Eglisham (1612–42), a Scottish doctor and poet, who served James, 2nd marquis of Hamilton (1589–1625), accused Buckingham of poisoning his employer.[64] After Buckingham's death, Hamilton was well placed to become master of the horse and the king's new favourite. He

3.12 Daniel Mytens, *James Hamilton, 1st Duke of Hamilton*, 1629. Oil on canvas, 221 × 139.7 cm. National Galleries of Scotland. Elegant in a silver camlet suit, Hamilton shows of his appreciation of Stuart fashion.

was painted by Daniel Mytens in 1629 in a silver suit, paned in the upper body and upper section of the sleeves of the doublet, breeches and knee-length boots (fig. 3.12).[65] In January 1631 his masquing suit cost £6, while his vizard cost £1.[66] His accounts for 1634 included a payment of £40 17s 7d for revamping his clothes for St George's Day.[67] However, alongside his role as a courtier, he had a military career in Sweden. His expenditure included 10s for cleaning two buff coats and 12s for four great gold and silver tags on 29 May 1631, and on 3 July a buff coat and crimson velvet hose laced thick with rich silver lace costing £9 0s 6d.[68] The importance of this was not lost on the English writer and politician Sir Philip Warwick (1609–83), who shrewdly noted that while Hamilton 'carried it very modestly and warily, yet he had a strong influence upon the greatest affairs at Court, especially when they related unto his own country'.[69]

3.13 Unknown artist, after Sir Anthony van Dyck, *George Gordon, 2nd Marquis of Huntly*, after 1640. Oil on canvas, 58.3 × 44.5 cm. National Galleries of Scotland. Huntly proudly wears the red ribbon of a knight of the Bath.

Demonstrative gestures, such as those used by Hamilton, marked him out as a Scot, although according to Sir Edward Stanhope (*c*.1591–1638), even taking another by the hand was 'out of fashion at Court, ever since bleu coats, and swords, and bucklers were laid by'.[70] Patrick Gordon of Ruthven (1606–49) went further, stating that spending time at the English court curbed a Scot's natural exuberance. He believed that George Gordon, 2nd marquis of Huntly (1592–1649) had succumbed to 'that English divell, keeping of state' (fig. 3.13). He added that 'for his excuse, I darre avowe, that his reseruedness, his keeping of distance, and the proud show of affecting steat, was no part of his naturall inclinatione; he was knowen to be both affable, courteous and sociable before he was called to court'.[71]

Charles's third cousin, James Stuart, 1st duke of Richmond, 4th duke of Lennox (1612–55) was a key friend and supporter of the king (fig. 3.14). The portrait of him in a black suit with black cloak with the Garter star marks him out as part of the inner circle around the king, a position reinforced by his marriage to Mary Villiers, daughter of the duke of Buckingham. During the masque *Salmacida Spolia* performed at court in 1640, which stressed the themes of union and obedience, Hamilton danced with the king and queen. In spite of, or perhaps because of this royal favour, Clarendon considered that he laboured 'under the disadvantage of being looked upon as a Scotsman: which he was not in his affections at all, being born in England, of an English mother, and having had his education there, and had indeed the manners and affections of an Englishman'.[72] As the court careers of Hamilton and Lennox demonstrate, Charles had close Scottish friends who shared and promoted his style. However, they were often perceived as being too English for the Scots and too Scottish for the English.

Charles I as King of Scots

In 1628 James Hay urged Charles not to go to Scotland 'in a worsse fashon' than his father. Rather, it was essential that he went 'in grater pompe and stait, being aboute to receave his croune, as also to make his first entrey amongst his native people'.[73] It was sound advice but the resulting delay was frustrating for the king's Scottish subjects. On 15 July 1628 the earl of Mar informed Hamilton that 'the King's majesty is resolved god willing to honour this, his ancient and native country with his royal presence about the hinder end of August next'.[74] Preparations for the royal visit began but by September 1630 progress was slow, with the earl of Mar complaining about Lord Napier's lack of assistance in repairing the royal houses and making preparations for the coronation and parliament.[75] Finally, on 6 October 1632, Lord Drummond assured the earl of Morton that the king was 'fully resolved to see Scotland this next spring and is offended if any seem doubtful of it'.[76]

The trip was planned to run from 11 May to 22 July.[77] The king set out with about 150 Englishmen plus members of the household and the royal guard. From a Scottish perspective the composition of this group reflected

3.14 Sir Anthony van Dyck, *James Stuart, 1st Duke of Richmond, 4th Duke of Lennox*, 1632–40. Oil on canvas, 215.9 × 127.6 cm. Metropolitan Museum of Art, New York. James Stuart displays the embroidered Garter star on the left side of his cloak.

the problems they faced in Westminster. On 20 April 1633 Sir David Cunningham urged Sir David Cunningham of Robertland to settle down with a good wife rather than come to court, because the duke of Lennox would be attended by English people on his visit to Scotland and so 'there is little or no hope for any of our nation'.[78] He was not alone in thinking this, demonstrating that Charles's love of Scotland did extend far enough beyond a small court circle to gain him strong support north of the border.

Even so, the Scots were determined to receive Charles correctly. First, the nobility were summonsed to attend the king by the lords of the privy council. They wrote to Alexander, earl of Eglinton, requesting his presence at the coronation and parliament, and asking that he bring with him 'your Rob of Crymson velvet enamered, and your Croun at the Cownatioun And with your Scarlet Rob at ye Parliament, And neewayes doutting that yow wilbe wanting in anie thing'.[79] The earl of Cassillis dispatched his factor, Fergus Kennedy, to London for his coronation and parliament robes.[80] In addition to robes, new clothes were required for a visit to Edinburgh, and Alexander Campbell of Auchinrire wrote from Dundee to his uncle Sir Colin Campbell of Glenorchy exclaiming his willingness to go to Edinburgh when the king arrives, 'seing I have not spendit my tym in vain sinc I cam to the scooll', adding that he 'will need a pair of boots and a riding coat' to look the part.[81]

Second, an inspection of the royal regalia revealed a number of problems, including the fact that the sword was 'vere faltie both in ye blade and scabbert'.[82] When the 'committee concerning the Wardrobe' met on 23 January 1633 they decided 'to provide sume litill new crymsie velvit and golden walhines for covering of the staves' and 'as for the kingis new rub [robe]' the hope was that 'his maiestie be content that the armine in the king James the fourt rubbis'.[83] Each of the trumpeters needed a cloak of scarlet with gold lace, a satin doublet and cloth hose trimmed with gold lace, stockings, garters, hats and hatbands, points and girdles. They also required new trumpets with silk and gold strings, with trumpet banners 'as we had the last time' to ensure everything was done correctly.[84]

Third, Sir James Balfour, lord Lyon, king of Arms, was keen to stress the importance of the coronation, declaring that it was 'the most glorious and magnificent Coronation that ever was seen in the Kingdom, and the first King of Great Britain that ever was crowned in Scotland, to behold these triumphes and ceremonies, many strangers of great quality resorted hither from diverse countries'.[85] While the coronation was the most significant occasion in the sequence that Balfour co-ordinated, the first key event was the king's entry into Edinburgh on Saturday 15 June. He and his horse were clothed in satin and ermine, while the town's troops were 'all clad in white satin doublets, black velvet breeches, hats, feathers scarves and bands'.[86] For the coronation, on Tuesday 18 June, Charles was the focal point, dressed 'in crimpsone veluett robes, ryding one a riche foote clothe, all embrodred with siluer and pearle'.[87] Then the king was 'disrobed … of his vpper garment, his wunder coate hanging with the loupes opened in the places quher he wes to be anoynted'.[88] Finally, Charles was 'invested with the robes royall of King Ja: 4'.[89] The reuse of James IV's robe emphasised the continuity of the Stuart line, a point that was stressed on the commemorative medals (see fig. 3.15). He was attended by the Scottish nobility in 'long scarlet Robes trailing upon the ground, trimmed with Ermine and lined with white satin'.[90]

The following day the king took part in the traditional riding to Parliament with Charles mounted 'upon a gallant chestnut horse having at its head a fair bunch of feathers with one foot mantle of velvet'. More significantly, 'His Majesty made choice to ride in the Royal robe of James

IV which was purple velvet richly furred and laced with gold'.[91] John Leslie, 6th earl of Rothes (1600–41) carried the sceptre at the opening of the parliament, while William Cunningham, 9th earl of Glencairn (1610–64), carried it at the sumptuous closing ceremony. However, in political terms what the king wanted was at odds with what the Scots required, and his difficulties were not helped by the fall of William Graham, 7th earl of Menteith (*c.*1591–1661) as lord justice general in 1633: prior to this, Graham had been a key supporter of the king.

Charles's Scottish visit was divisive. He showed favour to his personal friends and those who supported his views on the church, including the 10 earls, 2 viscounts, 8 lords and 57 knights who were created at the coronation, the parliament and during the progress.[92] On 17 June 1633 George Hay, chancellor of Scotland, was made earl of Kinoole in the withdrawing chamber at Holyrood and presented with his coronet, red robe and spurs.[93] Then, on 5 July, Sir Robert Kerr of Ancram, gentleman of the bedchamber and keeper of the privy purse, was made earl of Ancram, lord Kerr of Nisbitt, at Dunfermline, the king's birthplace.[94]

3.15 Nicholas Briot, medal commemorating the Scottish coronation of Charles I, 1633. Silver, 2.83 cm diameter. Royal Collection.

Charles visited Scotland briefly just twice more, but under very different circumstances, because the period 1633–9 saw a souring of the relationship between the king and his Scottish people. Indeed, in 1639 Charles was preparing to fight an invading Scottish army and by April Archibald Campbell informed the 8th laird of Glenorchy that the king had arrived at York. The duke of Lennox and Lord Stirling were the only Scots travelling with him – the other Scots nobles were expected to return, having sworn and signed the National Covenant in support of Presbyterianism.[95] On 5 February 1639 a payment of £600 was authorised for George Kirke for clothes for the king's progress to York, 'to be taken without account'.[96] This was followed by another warrant to pay Alexander Heriott, jeweller, for wares delivered and work done for His Majesty's use from the 12 October 1638 until 14 March following.[97]

Charles's complex relationship with his Scottish lords is exemplified by John Leslie, 6th earl of Rothes, who had opposed Charles's introduction of the Scottish Book of Common Prayer in 1638. On 27 August 1640 Leslie accompanied the army that crossed the Tweed.[98] However, by 1641 the possibility of his marriage to Christina, countess of Devonshire, the daughter of Edward Bruce of Kinloss, dominated court gossip to such an extent that Robert Baillie informed his wife, 'The King and Queen begin much to affect him: and if they goe on, he is lyke to be the greatest courteour either of Scotts or English. Lykelie he will take a place in the Bed-chamber, and be little more a Scottish man'.[99] When Charles went to Scotland in 1641 the marquis of Huntly travelled with him. In July the earl of Traquair told Charles I it was a 'poynt d'honneur' that the king would be served by Scots while he was at Holyrood.[100] Charles arrived in Edinburgh on 14 August and two days later the privy council ordered the constable of Edinburgh Castle to deliver the crown, sceptre and sword to Sir James Carmichael, treasurer depute.[101] In spite of the difficulties, as on his previous visits to Scotland, Charles was still treated with all the dignity due to a Scottish king.

The 1640s: The Impact of War on Stuart Fashion

3.16 Sash associated with Charles I, 1635–42. Silk, embroidered with silk and metal thread, 266.7 × 68.6 cm. Victoria and Albert Museum, London.

Lack of documentation makes it very difficult to piece together the contents and workings of the king's wardrobe in the last decade of his life. It is likely that the staff of the robes took many of the king's clothes and parliament robes to Oxford. However, a few items were left behind at Whitehall and these were recorded in the Commonwealth sale inventories. They included 'the King's Coronation Roabe Kirtle and hood', his Garter robes and a selection of items with fur linings for cloaks and a nightgown.[102] The clothes were possibly made for Charles in the months just before he left London and included 'A Satin Coate of a deere Colour laced with Gold lace & embroidered wth order of the Garter & lined wth rich furre'.[103] Similarly, the duke of Hamilton left his Garter robes in London when he left the city at the outbreak of war. His tailor, James Marshall, promised to keep them 'as safe as my own goods by me'.[104]

Charles I was based in Oxford between 1642 and 1646 and from 1643 his main residence was at Christ Church, while the queen lived at Merton.[105] Fleeting glimpses from the cathedral register indicate that the household functioned along traditional lines for the list of burials, including Steven Scanderett, yeoman of the wardrobe, on 24 August 1643 and Robert Josse, yeoman of the robes, on 29 December 1644.[106]

In spite of the king being resident in Oxford and Parliament holding London, the Great Wardrobe still supplied the royal family with some items. On 22 March 1643, £200 was issued to the master of the Great Wardrobe for the king's Maundy and the Wardrobe of the Robes.[107] Three weeks later Elizabeth Wheeler, laundress for the body to the king, was paid £180 for 'diverse parcels of lace purchased for the king for ruffs, bands, cuffs and handkerchiefs and for making thereof'.[108] In the same year a groom of the robes brought the king '4 yds of taby, 2 ells and ¼ of taffety to be a tennis suit, and 2 pairs of garters and roses with silk buttons and other necessaries for making up the said suit'.[109] By July 1644 the irregularity of the situation was apparent to all in the petition of the wardrobe officers – David Murray, David Cunningham and Hugh Ross – to the House of Commons. They sought permission to leave with 'Cloaths, Linen, and other Necessaries' for the king, Prince Charles and James, duke of York that were 'now provided and made ready' with the items 'being first searched and sealed by such as this House think fit to appoint'.[110] The last recorded allocations of money for clothes, a modest £250 and £100, were made to George Kirke, yeoman of the robes, on 4 April and 22 May 1644.[111] In recognition of his loyalty, Charles gave the bride away when Kirke married Mary Townsend on 26 February 1646. He is also reputed to have given Kirke a white lace-edged collar, a handkerchief and a nightcap as a wedding gift.[112]

Belief in the king had long inspired his most ardent followers to band together, and in 1627–8 Sir John Coke called for a 'Loyal Association' whose members would serve Charles I 'with person, goods, and might'. Members would have the right 'to wear in their hats some riband or

3.17 Unknown artist, *Charles I and Sir Edward Walker*, c.1650. Oil on canvas, 151.8 × 226.1 cm. National Portrait Gallery, London. Wearing buff jerkins over their doublets and breeches, Charles and Walker demonstrate the impact of war on male dress.

badge of the King's colour'.[113] Coming shortly after Buckingham's assassination as it did, this grouping reflected the tense political situation. Sir David Cunningham and others evidently acted upon this idea, and on 22 October 1628 Cunningham reported that 'the noble fraternity' held 'a solemn meetinge in London'. Membership was acknowledged by 'these incolsed badges of the noble brothered' that were 'to be worne by you and the Advocate about your hatband till our next meeting which is to be every sixe monthes'.[114] By the mid 1640s the king and his supporters were finding it harder to dress in their lavish, pre-war style, so aiding a shift to a more military style. Dress also became increasingly important in visually defining where a man stood politically. Once fighting began, sashes rather than badges were generally adopted, but the idea of them being 'of the King's colour' persisted. Royalist sashes were usually crimson, while the king's was purple (fig. 3.16), and those favoured by the English parliament were orange.

The king dressed as the leader of the Royalist armies. For the battle of Edgehill in October 1642 Charles wore a black velvet coat lined with ermine and he had a steel cap lined with black velvet.[115] However, there is a small but very good quality buff coat attributed to him of the type depicted in the double portrait of Charles I and Sir Edward Walker, *c.*1650 (fig. 3.17). It may represent a scene from one of the West Country campaigns and in it the king is dressed in a sleeveless buff coat trimmed with two rows of gold lace over a dark grey or watchet doublet, and breeches and long boots coming to the mid thigh. The fighting was dangerous for individuals and their property. After the battle of Naseby in June 1645 'some of his Majesties servants, all the Ordinance, Amunition, the Kings stuffe, Houshold carriages, and all the Baggage of the Army totally lost'.[116]

The Scots subverted the royal entry to mock Charles I's arrival at Newcastle in 1646 after his surrender when 'his Majestie marched with the Generall, and some other Scottish officers, divers of whom also that were neer the King, rid bare [removed their hats]'. The king was modestly dressed in 'a sad coloured plaine suite' and there was less drumming than 'when one troop of Scottish Horse march into Newcastle'.[117] News of this lack of respect travelled fast, with Jean de Montereul informing Cardinal Mazarin, chief minister to the king of France, that 'the Mayors of Durham and Newcastle were prevented from coming to receive his Majesty officially, as is the custom: so that the Scots not only failed in paying the honours required of them, but they prevent other subjects from rendering those they owed to him'.[118]

3.18 Edward Bower, *Charles I at His Trial*, 1649. Oil on canvas, 131.1 × 99.2 cm. Royal Collection. While Charles I wore black throughout his life, these black clothes were chosen to make a dignified statement in the face of adversity at his trial.

Shortly afterwards, in January 1647 the Scots sold Charles to the English Parliament for £400,000 sterling or £4,800,000 Scots.[119] On 19 June 1647 Charles I wrote from Newcastle to James, marquis of Montrose, thanking him for the sword 'ye sent me'.[120] Charles was also kept well dressed throughout his time as an effective captive of the Scots, as is evident from the bill of John Alexander, his shoemaker, who supplied 57 pairs of shoes, 10 pairs of boots and 2 pairs of slippers in the period up to February 1648.[121]

Edward Bower's painting *Charles I at His Trial* (1649) depicts Charles in a black satin doublet, a black cloak with the Garter star on the left arm, and a beaver hat with a tall crown (fig. 3.18).[122] This understated elegance dominated the final months of Charles's life and reflected a growing sense of the king's vulnerability and melancholy.[123] The latter was a trait linked to elite male creativity, as Patrick Gordon of Ruthven observed when he compared Charles I and George Gordon, 2nd marquis of Huntly: 'Never two lived in an age that went nearer to be one in abilities, both of bodie and mynd; they war both near about one pitch, of one stature, of one strength, of one activities, of one constitution, both melancholians, borne under Saturne.'[124] Richard Cust has also convincingly interpreted this choice of black as a visual acknowledgement of military defeat on Charles I's masculinity.[125] Yet this carefully constructed monochrome image was only one facet of the king's appearance. During his time at Newport in 1648, Charles ordered a velvet suit embroidered with gold thread and the cloak lined with satin.[126] The same year, the London diurnal the *Perfect Weekly Account* reported that the king 'hath three new suits, two of them are cloth with rich gold and silver lace upon them, the other is of black satin, the cloak lined with plush'.[127] In other words, up to the last, Charles deftly managed his clothes and royal image.

On 8 February 1649 the laird of Grant learnt of the 'sad and sorrowful' execution of the king and that his son had been proclaimed king of Great Britain, France and Ireland at Edinburgh's Market Cross.[128] It was not just the king who suffered at the hands of the executioner. George Gordon was captured in December 1648 and on the ruling of the Scottish parliament he was beheaded at the cross of Edinburgh on 22 March 1649. James Hamilton, 3rd marquis and 1st duke of Hamilton was defeated at the battle of Preston, captured on 25 August 1648 and beheaded on 9 March 1649. The following year James Graham, marquis of Montrose (1612–50) was beaten at Philiphaugh and was hanged in the Grassmarket in Edinburgh 'in his red scarlet cassock'.[129] If the scarlet cassock was an act of defiance, then it was offset by his lack of a hat. Montrose was taken to the place of execution 'on a cairte beare headit, the hangman in his liverey, covered'.[130] Preceding all four deaths was that of William Laud, archbishop of Canterbury. Wenceslaus Hollar's engraving of Laud's trial was accompanied with the verse from Proverbs 11:8: 'The Righteous is delivered out of Trouble, and the wicked commeth in his stead'. Laud was impeached by the English parliament and as he laid his head on the block on 10 January 1645 on Tower Hill, he wore a red waistcoat and black breeches.[131] For these men, dressing in Stuart style was as important at the time of their death as it had been during their lives.[132]

Charles Stuart: A Master of Guising and Disguise

Guising played a significant part in Charles I's life and he utilised it in three very different ways. First, he made very careful and strategic use of the masque in which he performed with his mother, siblings and wife. At the age of 9 Charles took part in the third dance of *The Masque of Queens*. The dancers were 'graphically disposed into letters, and honouring the Name of the most sweete, and ingenious Prince, Charles, Duke of Yorke'.[133] A year later, in 1610, he took part in the masque *Tethys' Festivale*, held to celebrate his brother's investiture as prince of Wales. On this occasion Charles wore 'a short robe of green satin embroidered with gold flowers, and a round wing made of lawns on wires, and hung down in labels. Behind his shoulders were two silver wings'.[134] Before the Christmas masques held in 1622 and 1623 Charles practised his part and 'the privie chamber on the Quenes side' was made ready 'twoe severall tymes for the Princes practysinge fower dayes, the hall for the Princes maskes twice ten dayes'.[135] Ever the perfectionist, Charles received a pair of under-hose for his own dress rehearsal.[136]

3.19 Sir Anthony van Dyck, *Charles I, King of England, from Three Angles*, 1635–6. Oil on canvas, 84.4 × 99.4 cm. Royal Collection. From the paned sleeve of the black doublet on the left to the cloak with Garter star on the left shoulder on the right, this portrait emphasises key aspects of 1630s fashion.

The masques were magnificent but exclusive, expensive and indicative of a distance from the realities of everyday life. As early as January 1627, Amerigo Salvetti noted that 'Their majesties being occupied with the festivities of Christmas, business is not spoken of in court or city'.[137] This was summed up by the rich suit 'for his majesty's royal person' made for the masque performed on Shrove Tuesday 1633.[138] The bodies, under-sleeves, and upper bases were made from aurora colour satin, while the upper sleeves and under bases were white and embroidered all over with fine silver wire and spangles. Worn briefly, this suit temporarily transformed the king.

Charles's use of tournaments reflects a continuation of his brother's ideas about chivalry as well as a desire to present his body to best effect. In 1616 at the tilt held to celebrate his creation as prince of Wales, the prince was 'not strong enough to put on an impressive display, so his opponents had to hold back lest they outshone him'.[139] Four years later Charles appeared at the tilts 'mounted on a powerful white horse, decked in splendid plumes, and wearing a suit of the finest armour inlaid with gold and silver'.[140] From this point on, horses were a vital part of Charles's royal image, an idea embodied in Van Dyck's equestrian portraits.[141]

Going incognito was accepted royal behaviour in Scotland, and it was an approach that was also found in Denmark. In 1630 Prince Ulrich, Charles's cousin, visited England incognito, and Crown Prince Christian is said to have done likewise in 1639.[142] With this family heritage, Charles's decision to travel this way to Spain with Buckingham in 1623 to woo the Infanta comes as no surprise. Indeed, by temporarily shedding his royal status, Charles could travel more easily. 'Baby Charles' and 'Steenie', as James referred to his son and his favourite respectively, took on the personas of Jack and Tom Smith.[143] Their false names were supplemented with fake beards. At Paris they bought periwigs.[144] At Bordeaux they purchased riding coats, thereby maintaining their fictive identities.[145] In times of dire need, Charles also disguised his appearance to ensure his safety. One such occasion was when the Royalist capital of Oxford fell to Parliament on 27 April 1646. After cutting his distinctive hair and part of his beard, the king left carrying 'a Cloak-bagge or Portmantle behind him like a serving man'.[146] The poet John Cleveland, among others, felt this was below his royal dignity and he asked in *The Kings Disguise*, 'What an usurper to his Prince is wont/Cloyster and shave him, he himself hath don't'.[147] However, freedom was all-important, and the necessity of discarding his distinctive outer clothing embroidered with the Garter was again vital when Charles escaped from Hampton Court on 11 November 1647. Colonel Edward Whalley found 'his Majesties cloake lying in the midst of the floore, which much amazed me'.[148] The king reserved his best performance until last, when he stepped out onto the scaffold for his execution, quietly certain of his own beliefs and vision of kingship.

Conclusions

While not its original purpose, Van Dyck's triple portrait of Charles I brings the king's three kingdoms to mind (fig. 3.19). The 'careless romance' of Van Dyck's style, and the clothing he depicts, presents the viewer with Charles I's vision of kingship. Charles followed much of the advice laid down by James VI and I but times had changed, and many of his subjects, whether Scottish, English or British, resisted his style of rule, so ensuring that his version of Stuart style was doomed. Unlike his father and brother, Charles favoured a number of different styles ranging from his early choices influenced by Henry, to the Spanish fashion after his return from Madrid, or the melancholic style of his final months, but his signature look, captured by Van Dyck, was synonymous with his personal rule. While far from simple, Charles I's strand of Stuart fashion offered a distinct response to Jacobean ostentation while also reflecting changes in European dress, and it is one that was shared with, and shaped by, Buckingham and Hamilton. To consider Charles as being completely English in outlook, as Jenny Wormald did, is to miss the significance of Sir Robert Kerr and others like him who surrounded the king. Indeed, a small group of Scottish friends helped to shape his outlook and shared his fashionable style. However, while James VI and I did little to help his son learn about Scotland prior to his accession, Charles for his part never successfully translated his love of the idea of Scotland into the reality he engaged with when he visited in the 1630s and 1640s. Although his confidence in some of his Scottish subjects proved distinctly misplaced, as we shall see, the Scots and Scotland would play a very important part in ensuring the restoration of the Stuarts to their three kingdoms, and the development of a new phase of Stuart style.

CHAPTER FOUR

Charles II (1630–1685)

ON 13 MAY 1660 a certain Margaret Nixon of Newcastle exclaimed, 'What! can they finde noe other man to bring in then a Scotsman? What! is there not some Englishman more fit to make a King then a Scott?'[1] Although he was born on English soil, his Stuart name and Scottish heritage were more than enough to make Charles II a true Scotsman in Margaret's eyes. Nixon was not alone in holding anti-Stuart, anti-Scottish views or in her dislike of Charles II. A man in Carlisle, on hearing the news of the king's return, held up his sword and declared, 'This is the sword shall run Charles Stuart through the heart blood'.[2] However, others saw things differently, including Lady Monck, wife of General Monck, who prophesied that 'at last there came a tall blacke man up to the dunghill, took up the Crowne and put it upon his head'.[3] Her vision was significant because Oliver Cromwell considered Monck to be 'a cunning fellow in Scotland ... who lyes in wait there to serve Charles Stewart'.[4] Serve him he did, ensuring that Charles II regained the thrones his father had lost, but the Stuarts' three kingdoms were irrevocably changed by the experience of war and the interregnum, not least in terms of how clothes shaped a man's identity and place in society. A new phase in the evolution of Stuart style was about to begin, one in which the elite Scottish dimension, while modest, was still significant. Most importantly, as Maurice Lee has shown, this group was dominated by the Scottish 'Worcester veterans', Charles II having given them offices and power after the Restoration in recognition of their friendship and loyalty.[5]

At the time of the Restoration, fashionable men wore a short doublet and petticoat breeches trimmed with bunches of ribbon, a distinct change from the styles favoured at the pre-war court (fig. 4.1). While Hieronymus Janssens painted Charles II as the epitome of the stylish gentleman, Diane Purkiss has stressed how new or different models of masculinity were in circulation after the Restoration as 'the Cavalier was transmuted into the libertine'.[6] Then, as now, both terms were redolent with meaning for Charles II personally, while also revealing an increasingly moral tone

See figure 4.2.

4.1 Hieronymus Janssens, *Charles II Dancing at a Ball at Court*, c.1660. Oil on canvas, 139.7 × 213.4 cm. Royal Collection. Dressed in the height of fashion, Charles and his sister Mary, princess of Orange, dominate this image, while other family members look on.

underpinning criticisms of the correct behaviour for king and courtier alike throughout the three kingdoms.[7] Clothes were as important as actions in shaping Scottish and English elite male identity, a point the satirist Samuel Butler made in *A Huffing Courtier* (1667–9). Butler claimed that the courtier's tailor was 'his Creator, and makes him of nothing' while the courtier's 'Occupation is to show his Cloathes, and if they could but walk themselves, they would save him the Labour, and do his work as well as himself'.[8] Like Margaret Nixon before him, Butler also made an unhappy nod towards Charles II's Scottishness with his quip that the courtier's 'Legs are stuck in his great voluminous Britches, like the Whistles in a Bagpipe'.[9] While the number of Scots close to the king was small, London's Scottish community was increasingly making its presence felt, thereby garnering the criticism of some English commentators.

A Happy Childhood

The birth of a royal son and heir was cause for personal and national rejoicing and on 15 June 1630 Charles I issued a proclamation informing his people 'it hath pleased Almighty God of his speciall grace and goodness to vouchsafe unto us a Sonne, borne at our Manor of St James the 29th May last past'.[10] At the end of the year, Archibald Campbell of Glencarradale confided in Sir Duncan Campbell, 7th laird of Glenorchy, 1st baronet (1550–1631) that Lady Roxburghe was a lady of the bedchamber caring for the prince along with Lady Dorset.[11] While this particular appointment fell through because of her Catholicism, in 1631 Jean Ker, countess of Roxburghe (*c.*1588–1643), later became governess to Princess Mary (1631–60) and then to Princess Elizabeth (1635–50) and Prince Henry (1640–60), so keeping a Scottish presence around the royal brood. The significance of these children to their parents can be seen in Van Dyck's group portrait of 1635 and their description as 'Three Royall Blossomes ... Whose lookes and sweetnesse, make eternall spring' in the masque *Corona Minervae* performed on 27 February in the same year.[12] As Catriona Murray has noted, the Stuarts promoted and celebrated their children and the young family of Charles I was no different.[13]

4.2 *(above)* Unknown artist, *Charles II as an Infant*, 1630. Oil on canvas, 120.7 × 93.3 cm. National Portrait Gallery, London. Over his white satin coat Charles wore a fine white linen apron, a close-fitting linen cap on his head, and held a teething coral in his left hand.

4.3 *(below)* Sir Anthony van Dyck, *The Three Eldest Children of Charles I*, c.1636. Oil on canvas, 133.8 × 151.7 cm. Royal Collection. Flanked by his elder brother Charles and his elder sister Mary, James here is youthful, as stressed by his pale coat and apron.

Even so, relatively little is known about what Charles wore in the first few months of his life, apart from a portrait painted in 1630. Attributed to Justus van Egmont, the image presents the young prince in a white silk coat with paned sleeves and deep turned back lace cuffs (fig. 4.2). The colour of the coat is supported by a bill submitted by the mercers, Richard Miller and Richard Williams, to Henrietta Maria's Wardrobe of the Robes for the quarter period ending on 1 January 1631. They supplied 6¾ yards of rich white Florence satin and 3 ells of white rich Florence taffeta that Patrick Black made up into a coat for the prince.[14] A slightly fuller picture of who made the prince's clothes, and the scale of the provision, can be gleaned from his mother's wardrobe accounts from October to December 1630. These included five payments for Henrietta Maria's son. The largest bill at £32 5s 7d was from his tailor, Patrick Black, while the others were from Robert Ramsey, tailor; Humphrey Palmer, embroiderer; Alexander Sowtor, shoemaker and William Ardington, pin maker. Against each name was a note acknowledging that the king would pay.[15]

Charles I also took an interest in how his eldest son was depicted. In 1635 Van Dyck painted Charles, James and Mary twice. On the first occasion Charles wore a rose-coloured coat trimmed with silver lace and Henrietta Maria sent the picture to her sister, Christine, duchess of Savoy as a gift. However, Charles I was unhappy because his sons were depicted 'on accoustume aux petit enfens' (in childish dress).[16] The solution was simple. Van Dyck painted the children again, and this time Charles was dressed as a young man in a tawny satin suit of doublet and breeches (fig. 4.3).[17] This was a precursor to Charles II formally making the transition from wearing the coat to adult dress, which took place on 7 December 1635. Sir John Finett reported that 'the women being discharged ... a settled number

of gentlemen and officers' would now be 'attending dayly on his person'.[18] This coincided with the king paying the expenses of the prince and the royal children to mark the change in status of the prince's household.[19] The earl of Dorset received £2,655 17s 1d to pay several persons for clothes for the prince and duke of York for two years ending at Christmas 1635.[20] Both Charles's parents took a keen interest in his appearance, presenting him in his father's version of Stuart fashion.

Growing Up

When Lord William Hamilton left the French court in 1636 he hoped to become master of the horse to the queen, but he received that office with Prince Charles instead.[21] He joined the household of the confident boy Van Dyck painted in 1637, dressed in crimson satin and surrounded by his brothers and sisters (fig. 4.4). Lord William was kept busy, and the young prince's enthusiasm for horses is evident in his letter to William Cavendish, later the duke of Newcastle (1593–1676), sent in January 1639.

4.4 Sir Anthony van Dyck, *The Five Eldest Children of Charles I*, 1637. Oil on canvas, 163.2 × 198.8 cm. Royal Collection. Charles's more adult-style suit with lace collar contrasts strongly with the coat and apron of James, standing to his right, and the gowns of his sisters.

He assured his mentor that 'I ride everyday, and am ready to follow any other directions from you. Make haste to return to him that loves you'.[22] In the same year Charles I approved regulations for his son's household that were modelled on those drawn up for his brother Henry in 1610. Like his father before him, the importance of riding in the prince's daily routine is evident from the instructions given to 'the Quiryes upon Rideing daies when the Prince drawes on or off his Bootes' and the requirement that 'none presume to come booted except at such times when they are to ride abroade with his Hignes'.[23] Apart from this, there were no direct references to how the prince should be dressed or undressed, just that he should not 'receive clothes or any thing' from anyone in ill health because Charles represented his parents' future hopes for the Stuarts.[24]

Charles was painted in 1639 by Cornelius Johnson dressed in a black satin doublet and breeches that came below the knee, with panes to the sleeves and upper part of the doublet and trimmed with silver lace. This sober, fashionable suit stressed Charles's growing maturity, a factor also reflected in his acquisition of formal robes for the Garter and Parliament. Both institutions left a lasting but very different impression on him. Charles was elected as a knight of the Garter aged 8 in 1638 but the planned procession was cancelled.[25] Even so, Charles valued the collegiate nature of the order, and the material markers of being a knight, for the rest of his life. The following year, in February 1639, he received a fine example of the latter when George Kirke paid £550 17s 6d for pearls and diamonds for the St George's Day robes for the king and his son.[26] Charles's early experience of Parliament was equally formative but far less positive. He attended the trial of Thomas Wentworth, 1st earl of Strafford, in 1641. Robert Baillie reported that 'the Prince in his robes' sat 'on a little chyre at the side of the throne'.[27] In contrast, the earl 'was always in the same sute of black, as in doole [mourning]'.[28] The 'Princes Kirtle and hood lined with furre' and 'The Princes Parliament Roabe Kirtle hood and cap' were left at Whitehall when the royal family moved to Oxford. Outgrown and discarded, these items were still valued at £6 and £100 in the Commonwealth Inventory, by a clerk who probably had a more positive view of this institution than the prince.[29]

From an early age, Charles received armour such as the black armour that Van Dyck painted him wearing in *c.*1637–8.[30] He also had a set of harquebusier's armour that was probably made at Greenwich in *c.*1638–40, as well as a Dutch armour of *c.*1616 that had been made for his father.[31] These different types and sizes of armour reflected different fighting techniques and Charles's changing stature.[32] Just as his household was influenced by that of Prince Henry, so this emphasis on his military training harked back to his late uncle, who had taken a keen interest in military strategy and the political situation in Europe. By wearing armour made for his father and uncle, Charles was very aware of his Stuart heritage.

A few years later Charles made the short but very significant step to real warfare, which William Dobson recorded in his portrait of the prince

4.5 *(above, left)* William Dobson, *Charles II as Prince of Wales, with a Page*, c.1642. Oil on canvas, 153.6 × 129.8 cm. National Galleries of Scotland. The cream satin doublet and scarlet breeches offer a courtly elegance that contrasts with the buff jerkin, military sash and armour.

4.6 *(above, right)* Studio of Sir Anthony van Dyck, *Prince Rupert, Count Palatine*, c.1637. Oil on canvas, 216 × 133.3 cm. National Gallery, London. Without a breastplate, the cut of Rupert's buff jerkin is clear.

painted in *c.*1642. The picture is all the more telling because, in spite of Henry practising pike drill and reading about strategy, Charles was the only early modern or indeed modern prince of Wales to actually set foot on a battlefield (fig. 4.5).[33] The look – doublet and breeches under a buff jerkin – was very similar to that captured by Van Dyck five years earlier in his portrait of Prince Rupert (fig. 4.6). Both paintings stress the part played by the younger Stuart men in shaping the idea of the dashing cavalier.[34] By the time James Graham, marquis of Montrose, sat for Dobson in Oxford between August 1643 and March 1644, the realities of war were clear to all. Montrose gazes at the viewer, dressed in half-length armour, with very little emphasis on fashion or swagger.[35]

For the young prince, this military image was central to his role in the conflict. In 1642 Charles went to Raglan Castle where he spoke to his Welsh supporters stating that 'you shall be sure of … my favour as long as I am prince of Wales'.[36] Their support was vital, as Charles acknowledged after the Restoration when he observed 'that in the late troubles the principality of Wales were true to their duty'.[37] He also rallied Cornish troops during the Royalist muster at Launceston towards the end of the war when he 'went to the head of their maine body and made a speech'.[38] In early January 1646 Charles went to Tavistock and it was reported that the Cornish Royalist troops 'call him not the prince, but altogether the Duke of Cornwall'.[39] In both Wales and Cornwall, Charles succeeded in aligning himself with the specific identity of each region, thereby gaining their support for the royal cause. But it was a cause that would fail.

Exile

After his father's defeat in 1646, Charles spent a long, formative period in exile. He visited a number of European cities and courts and his fortunes fluctuated between periods of relative poverty that limited his wardrobe and other times when he was able to buy fashionable clothes, even if in smaller quantities than he needed (fig. 4.7).[40] Charles stayed in Jersey twice: from April to June 1646 and then from September 1649 to February 1650. His second stay was long enough for him to require more clothes. As early as 4 January 1650 Charles II wrote from Jersey to Edward Progers, one of his servants in Paris, to send him 'a plain riding suit with an innocent coat, the suits I have for horse-back being so spotted and soiled that they are not to be seen out of this island'.[41] Even so, his possessions were still meagre and on his departure Robert Long recalled that 'there was but one cart in all allowed for your majesty's robes and necessaries and particular trunks'.[42]

The situation was rather different in France. Montrose joined Charles in exile in France, where he disapproved of the 'lewdness and worthlessness' of his court.[43] Here Charles's household numbered around 300, including tailors, shoemakers and a laundress.[44] Of these, Stephen Besse provided clothes to Charles and his brother costing 10,000 crowns in 1649.[45] He was not paid until 19 July 1661 when a warrant was issued for £2,333 in full for all the clothes Besse had supplied to the king while on French soil.[46]

The pattern was similar in the Netherlands, as became clear at the point when it was time for Charles to leave. On 6 June 1649, 29,900 gilders was distributed among 48 suppliers, while another 26,738 gilders was shared among 98 individuals on 13 June.[47] These were the lucky ones because Charles owed a further 187,126 gilders.[48] This sum included 10,143 gilders

4.7 A good example of the cut of a mid-1640s doublet. British, leather, silk. Metropolitan Museum of Art, New York.

to 'his Majesties Taylor and seuerall other persons for necessaries brought into the Roabes', as well as 539 guilders to Abraham Walkheart, jeweller, 2,779 gilders to Monsieur Isaac Vanlier, mercer, and 3,030 gilders to the seamstress 'for Linnen and makeinge'.[49] Charles was not alone in exile, and William Hamilton, 2nd duke of Hamilton (1616–51), was one of a group of Scots who spent time at Charles II's court at The Hague. Hamilton was made a knight of the Garter in 1650 and the Garter star is prominent on his black cloak in his portrait by Adriaen Hanneman.[50] His accounts for 1649 include mourning, presumably for his brother, who was executed on 9 March. Returning to Scotland with Charles II in 1650, he died of his wounds after the battle of Worcester, but Charles never forgot his support: the duke's portrait hung in the presence chamber at Windsor throughout the king's reign as a reminder of his loyalty.[51]

To Scotland: A Challenging Homecoming

By 1648 rumours were circulating of Royalist attempts to raise money and of the prince of Wales going to Scotland.[52] Everything changed with the death of Charles I. The Scots were furious that English Parliamentarians had executed their king and Charles was proclaimed as king of Great Britain, France and Ireland on 5 February 1649 by the lord chancellor of Scotland, John Campbell, 1st earl of Loudoun (1598–1662). The Scots offered a crown and a kingdom to Charles but on the condition that he accepted the Covenants of 1638 and 1643 promoting Presbyterianism. Robert Baillie, one of the Presbyterian commissioners sent to meet Charles, was optimistic and described the young king as 'a trim person, and of manly carriage; understands pretty well; speaks not much; he might make, with God's blessing, as good a king as Britain saw these hundred years'.[53]

In 1649 and 1650 repairs were undertaken at Holyroodhouse and Stirling in anticipation of Charles's arrival. In May 1650 the Honours were delivered by the marquis of Argyll on behalf of the Commissioners of the Treasury to the laird of Scotscraig.[54] Charles arrived in Scotland in June 1650.[55] He made his court at Perth but it was not a great success, and on 4 October he set out for Fife 'without any change of clothes or linens more than was on his body, in a thin riding suit of stuff'.[56] Robert Montgomery, earl of Eglinton, found him shortly after dressed in his riding suit on a ship, and Charles had to return to Perth.

Even so, Charles was crowned on New Year's Day 1651 at Scone, while Oliver Cromwell and his English army occupied Edinburgh (fig. 4.8). For the ceremony, the crown was carried by Argyll, the spurs by Eglinton and sword of state by Lord Rothes. [57] The ceremony began with Charles dressed 'in a Princes robe' that he put on in his bedchamber, processing to the presence chamber. He then processed to the Kirk of Scone where he swore that 'I, Charles, King of Great Britain, France and Ireland, do assure and declare, by my solemn Oath … my allowance and approbation of the

Nationall Covenant and the Solemn League and Covenant'.[58] He was next 'disrobed by the Lord Great Chamberlain of the Princely Robe wherewith he entered the kirk' and then invested in 'his Royal Robes'.[59]

These robes acknowledged that Charles II was now an anointed monarch, but they could be read in different ways. The cowed figure of the king features in a pro-Parliamentarian English satirical print captioned 'The Scots holding their young king's nose to ye grindstone'. Here Charles is shown dressed in his coronation robes and fashionable, cavalier dress (see fig. I.6). By association, for the peers who attended the coronation, wearing their robes was a symbol of disloyalty to Cromwell, and Gilbert, earl of Erroll was fined £2,000 sterling for attending 'at ye Coronation at Scone'. In his defence, Erroll stated that his 'simple presence at ye action of Coronation could hardly inferre any guilt' because he 'came there only for obedience of ye commands of ye Authority under whose power he was for ye time, and whose commands he durst not then disobey'.[60] Some did dare, including the creator of a Dutch broadsheet who omitted the robe. Instead, Charles is in armour

4.8 Attributed to Jacob van der Ulft, *The Coronation of Charles II as King of Scotland at Scone, 1 January 1651*, c.1651–7. Brush drawing with watercolour, 10.9 × 13 cm. Royal Collection. While the king's coronation was important, it is here seen in context with the prominent position of the preacher, the courtiers and the royal guard.

4.9 *(right)* The role of Charles II as military leader of his Scottish people, a position validated by his coronation, is stressed in this broadside showing the coronation. Allard the Elder, Amsterdam, 1651. British Museum, London.

4.10 *(below)* David des Granges after Adriaen Hanneman, *Charles II*, based on a work of 1648. Watercolour on vellum, 4.5 × 3.8 cm. National Portrait Gallery, London. Worn over his buff jerkin and breastplate, Charles's plain linen collar and blue garter ribbon stress his right to rule and his commitment to recovering his three thrones.

with Robert Douglas by his side as he is offered a pistol by a man kneeling before him who represents Scotland, while in the background the young king takes part in the riding for the parliament held near Johnstone. The message of legitimacy and defiance was clear (fig. 4.9). In this spirit Charles II sent letters during the first half of 1651 from 'our Court at Stirling'.[61] A glimpse of this young king, also in armour, can be seen in a miniature painted in 1651 in Scotland by David des Granges. Des Granges was not paid and in 1671 he petitioned the king for payment of £76 on account of having 'served your Majesty faithfully & diligently before your restauration as your limner in Scotland' (fig. 4.10).[62] In June Charles left Scotland with an army and marched into his southern kingdom only to be defeated on 3 September during the battle of Worcester. He never returned to Scotland, but his experiences were formative for his kingship and many of the men he met there played significant roles in the rest of his life.

Exile Again

Michiel Morosini, the Venetian ambassador, described Charles's arrival at Paris on 20 October in scathing terms: 'His retinue consisted of one gentleman and one varlet, and his costume was more calculated to induce laughter than respect; his appearance, in short, being so changed, that the outriders who first came up with him, thought he must be one of his own menials'.[63] Charles lacked the funds to live as a king and in June 1652 Edward Hyde, 1st earl of Clarendon complained that 'what the King gets being not enough to provide him with clothes and meat'.[64] So much so that when Charles left Paris two years later he did so on horseback with his coach horses pulling 'a light cart' that held his clothes and furnishings.[65] Even when money was limited, small amounts were allocated to the king's wardrobe officers, such as the allowance of 500 livres a month for Charles's journey to Spa.[66] While at Aachen in September 1654 he 'walked a-foot through the streets from his lodgings to Cæsar's bath, where the princess royal was bathing herself' dressed 'in black with a cloak, with his ribband and garter'.[67] As will be shown in Chapter 8, the Garter was central to how Charles II shaped his royal image while in exile.

During the years 1658 and 1659, a number of Charles's clothes came from Paris and he used a variety of tailors. In April 1658 Monsieur Stairs, the prince of Condé's tailor, received 200 florins for a grey suit and 5 florins for 'fitting those cloaks from Paris'.[68] On this occasion Charles was using family connections, because the prince of Condé was Louis de Bourbon, Henrietta Maria's cousin. People also made occasional purchases for him in Paris, including a certain Mr Roberts who bought him a beaver hat and a silver and gold hatband. Charles also received some clothes and lengths of cloth from home and in November 1658 he paid 130 livres for making 'a suit of the sand colour cloth that his majestie had from England, lining the cloak with plush and furnishing all but the cloth'.[69] In December he bought a garniture of 222 ells of ribbon for 68 livres to decorate a new cloth suit from England.[70] His English tailor, Mr Allen, also provided 'a camlet riding cloak for his majestie' in July 1658.

Most important was the king's business relationship with the Parisian tailor Claude Sourceau. In April 1658 Charles ordered a black suit of wrought stuff, laced and lined with velvet, a grey cloth suit, laced and lined with plush, and a grey riding cloth suit for 226 livres and 10 cents.[71] In December 1659 payment was sent to 'Monsieur Sourceau for his majesties winter clothes that arrived'. In March 1660 Sourceau received 200 livres for a riding suit 'entirely furnished for his majestie October 1659' while Mr Allen supplied a tennis suit, two pairs of Holland drawers, three Holland waistcoats, and two pairs of canvas stockings.[72] This was pleasing to the king, but Pepys was less than impressed when he met Charles at The Hague on 16 May; he thought him in 'a sad, poor condition for clothes and money', adding scornfully that his clothes were not 'worth 40s, the best of them'.[73] By June 1660 Charles was able to pay 2,100 livres to 'maistre Jean a Taylor at the Haage for Cloathes for his majestie' and 235 livres 'To two merchants for stuffe to make Cloathes'.[74] The Restoration gave Charles access to a well-stocked wardrobe once more, and he implemented a key lesson he had learnt in exile – the importance of dressing like a king.

Continuity and Change: Charles II's Clothes as King

Once Charles II had been restored to the throne, men had a wide choice of styles including the short doublet and petticoat breeches that the writer and diarist John Evelyn laughingly referred to as 'the short Wast, and Skirts in Pye-crust'.[75] However, the coat that was an option in 1660 became increasingly significant during the 1670s and 1680s. Charles ordered coats throughout his reign, both singly and in over 30 different combinations with other garments. The most discussed innovation came late in 1666. On 15 October of that year Pepys observed that 'the King begins to put on his vest ... being a long cassocke close to the body, of black cloth and pinked with white silk under it, and a coat over it and the legs ruffled with black riband like a pigeon's leg ... it is a very fine and handsome garment'.[76] Just two days later the court was 'full of vests' in a variety of styles, much to the king's amusement because 'only my Lord St Albans not pinked but plain black; and they say the King says the pinking upon white makes them look like magpies, and therefore hath bespoke one of plain velvet'.[77] Shortly after, at the queen's birthday ball, Lord Herbert saw 'a hundred vests that at the least cost a hundred pounds. Some were adorned with jewels above a thousand. The Lord Chamberlain's was one'.[78] While the coat became a central feature of the male wardrobe, the cloak still had a place and was worn with flair by Charles II and men at court (fig. 4.11).

4.11 Man's suit consisting of coat, breeches and a cloak, made from brown wool, c.1680. Victoria and Albert Museum, London.

Charles II managed his appearance differently to his father. When the occasion called for it, he dressed with full royal magnificence. His coronation was one such event when he wore 'a most rich imbroidered suit and cloak [that] looked most nobly'.[79] Pepys's patron, Lord Sandwich, followed the king's example. His French suit cost £200 and 'very rich it is with imbroidery'.[80] However, on other occasions the king valued a degree of informality that Pepys was not reconciled to, and on 19 August 1661 he saw Charles II 'in a plain common riding-suit and velvet cap, in which he seemed a very ordinary man to one that had not known him'.[81] The king's tailors achieved magnificence and informality by a deft choice of materials, colour and varying levels of decoration.

Fabric

During the 1650s Charles's wardrobe had made the shift from the silk suits of his youth to wool so that by 1660 cloth – whether it was the traditional broadcloth or the softer, lighter, new draperies – dominated his clothing orders. There was a nationalistic element to this change, as the king's government was keen to promote home-produced wool over imported silks, but it was not as simple as this. For instance, drugget, which was often a plain or ribbed light-weight wool cloth, was also available in silk, mixed or mixed silk versions, and alongside Norwich druggets, the king owned French, Sergovian and Spanish examples. There is just one reference to openly Scottish cloth, and this appears in 1673 when the king had two waistcoats made of Harris wool.[82] Rather more exotic were the waistcoats made from China tabby, mentioned in 1670, and a rich sad colour, Indian Atlas, flowered with gold, from 1681/2.[83] As this last item reveals, there was a place for silk in the male wardrobe: it was generally used for waistcoats, vests and coat linings, along with a small amount of velvet for coats and suits.

Colour and Pattern

By the mid seventeenth century, the discerning Parisian could buy silk stockings in up to 50 shades with enticing names such as Amorous desire, Lost time, Mortal sin and Sad friend.[84] Selling goods on the basis of their colour meant that, as the seventeenth century progressed, France became increasingly polychrome while Spain was often associated with black.[85] Britain experienced a similar, colourful trend, with the variety of different shades peaking under Charles I. After the Commonwealth the range of fashionable hues decreased slightly and they changed in tonal range. Gone were the pale yellow, green, pink and orange shades, which were replaced with an increased number of browns, greys and creams. This new colour palate also exploited the contrast between muted, sombre, sad colours of the type seen in the double portrait of Charles II and a gardener (who may be John Rose), with pastels for ribbon trimmings (fig. 4.12). Descriptive names continued but now it was a language of ash, cinnamon, lead, olive, russet and stone. However,

4.12 British School, *Charles II Presented with a Pineapple*, c. 1675–80. Oil on canvas, 96.6 × 114.5 cm. Royal Collection. Coats of a similar style to figure 4.11 can be seen here worn by the king and his gardener.

the move towards more descriptive colour names and the availability of a wider range of shades made proxy shopping and shopping by post more difficult. Henry Harper of Edinburgh faced this difficulty in 1659 when a Mrs Inglis wrote requesting a 'douse color' coat for her child. In the hopes of getting the right colour, he sent one pearl-coloured and one dove-coloured coat for her to choose from.[86]

The more subtle Restoration palate saw white and blue shades, favoured by James VI and I and Charles I, fall out of use for the outer fabric for suits. However, blue made an appearance for waistcoats between 1678 and 1685, with plain blue examples alongside blue silks flowered with silver and striped with gold. White also was used from 1664 and was mostly plain, although 1676 saw a fine white silk flowered and striped with gold. These examples also highlight that some of the silks used for vests, waistcoats and coat linings had floral designs or stripes, as well as a few with spots or checks. The use of colour and eye-catching design was offset by plain fabric for the main fabric, usually plain wool – but not all the time, and some top fabrics were flowered or striped, with others from 1674 described as waved, suggesting that they were watered.[87]

Decoration

The cycle of fashionable and seasonable change was created in a variety of ways in the king's wardrobe. One of the most important was the subtle differences in ribbon trimmings every six months made possible by the wide variety of types, colours and combinations. Ribbon garnitures, placed at the waist or in bunches on the shoulder, were the most important part of the decorative scheme of Charles's coats and suits. Consequently, the king's tailor, Sourceau, imported ribbon and other prohibited goods from France for his royal client, although one shipment was seized at a certain Monsieur Shumatt's house.[88] In addition, pinking was used to decorate linings for coats and waistcoats, and Robert Pritchard, a specialist pinker, was listed in the king's accounts from 1662 until 1681/2, with one exception, the account for 1666/7. All the little details noted here were vital to Charles II's contribution to Stuart dress.

The Scottish Elite after the Restoration

Although Charles II did not visit Scotland after the Restoration, the sense of the royal presence was maintained in several ways. For example, in 1662 John Michael Wright produced an oil sketch of Charles II. The coat of arms behind the king is quartered, with those of Scotland in the place of honour, suggesting that it may have been intended for display at Holyroodhouse.[89] Moreover, pensions were distributed to royal officials, supporters and friends.[90] Some such as John Middleton, 1st earl of Middleton (1608–74), who served as lord high commissioner to

4.13 *(left)* Jacob Huysmans, *John Middleton, 1st Earl of Middleton*, c.1650–73. Oil on canvas, 127 × 101.6 cm. National Trust, Castle Ward, County Down, Northern Ireland. Middleton proudly emphasises his military career in his choice of armour and sash for this portrait.

4.14 *(below)* Samuel Cooper, *Charles Stuart, Third Duke of Richmond and Sixth Duke of Lennox*, between 1661 and 1667. Watercolour and gouache with gold on parchment laid down on card, 7 × 5.7 cm. Yale Center for British Art, Paul Mellon Collection. Thick bands of metal braid decorate Charles Stuart's fashionable doublet.

the Scottish parliament, acted almost as the king's proxy. Gilbert Burnet described how Middleton arrived in 1661 'with great magnificence', adding that 'His way of living was the greatest the nation had ever seen: but it was likewise the most scandalous' (fig. 4.13).[91]

Very few Scottish courtiers lived permanently in Restoration London, opting instead to come to the city as they needed. Some were relatives of the king, such as Charles Stuart, 3rd duke of Richmond and 6th duke of Lennox (1639–72), who was appointed as great chamberlain of Scotland in 1660, and he wore a fashionable suit when he sat for Samuel Cooper (fig. 4.14). In 1671 he was sent as ambassador to Denmark, but he drowned there at Elsinore. His wife was Frances Teresa Stuart (1647–1702), daughter of Walter Stuart, a Scottish Catholic royalist, who served in Henrietta Maria's household as her physician. Rather unusually, she resisted becoming Charles II's mistress in spite of his persistence. While her great beauty is often given as the reason why she was chosen as the model for Britannia in 1667, she also had both Scottish and English blood, making her perfect for the role.

Far more influential was John Maitland, 1st duke of Lauderdale (1616–82), a skilled, ruthless politician and keen follower of Stuart

4.15 Sir Peter Lely, *John Maitland, 1st Duke of Lauderdale and His Wife Elizabeth Murray, Countess of Dysart and Duchess of Lauderdale*, c.1672. Oil on canvas, 138.4 × 165.1 cm. National Trust, Ham House, Richmond, Surrey. Lauderdale is dressed in a wig, a partially buttoned coat, lace cravat and breeches with ribbon at the waist and knee, while Elizabeth wears a nightgown over her smock.

fashion (fig. 4.15). He was very powerful in Scotland, and when there, Sir Robert Murray looked after his interests in London.[92] Early in 1664 Pepys noted that Lauderdale had 'got the whole power of Scotland into his hand'.[93] More significantly, the philosopher and bishop Gilbert Burnet noted that 'The duke Lauderdale had kept the Scotch nation in such a dependence on himself, that he was not pleased with any of them that made an acquaintance in England, and least of all in the court'.[94] Lauderdale assured Charles in 1669 that the Supremacy act made him 'Soveraigne in the Church', adding that 'never was [a] King so absolute as yow are in poor old Scotland'.[95] Lauderdale's association with fashionable court style may explain why Lauder of Fountainhall described Charles II's support for Lauderdale in clothing terms. Fountainhall noted how the king refused 'to hear all his ennemies, cloathing him in purple royall robes, making him a Duke, and partaker of his dominions, and his chief friend'.[96]

For all of his political acumen, Lauderdale's looks were against him because 'he was very big, his hair was red, hanging oddly about him … and his whole manner was rough and boisterous, and very unfit for a court'.[97] However, he knew how to make the king laugh, and he danced dressed in women's petticoats to amuse the king after the Dutch burnt the fleet at Chatham in June 1667. The previous year Pepys had been unimpressed by the Scottish songs playing when he visited Lauderdale, but he was amused by the duke's admission that 'of all the instruments he hates the lute most, and next to that, the Baggpipe'.[98] Music apart, Lauderdale's taste in architecture and furnishings was impressive, as demonstrated by the interior of his London home, Ham House. In 1679 the inventory listed 'Two sleeping chayres carv'd and guilt frames covered with Crimson and gould fringes, Cases of Crimson sarsnet'. According to Geoffrey Beard, these were probably made by Jean Poictevin (fl. 1677), who had made similar examples in 1675 and 1677 for the king, on the basis that 'What the king had, the Duke of Lauderdale presumably wanted too'.[99] Both in England and Scotland, Lauderdale played a key role in promoting and disseminating the Stuart style.

Opposition to Lauderdale was led by William Douglas, 3rd duke of Hamilton, who had married Anne Hamilton, duchess of Hamilton, in 1656. He received the title of duke of Hamilton after the Restoration, making him the leading duke in Scotland.[100] Matters came to a head in 1679 when the royal army marched into Scotland behind the duke of Monmouth to put down the revolt at Bothwell Brig. This unrest was caused by Lauderdale's use of a 'Highland Host' to put down a rebellion in the south west. While Kneller's portrait of 1679 shows the duke in armour (fig. 4.16), he often wore the height of fashion to court.[101] For instance, in October 1678 Charles Carmichael sent silks, velvet caps and muffs to Mr Smith, the duke's secretary.[102] Like the king, Hamilton was tall, dark-haired and charming. Having initially supported Lauderdale, he came to oppose his repressive policies towards his fellow Presbyterians, so much so that in autumn 1678 Lord Cochrane urged the duchess of Hamilton to persuade her husband to spend the winter at court. His reasoning was that, should Charles II look favourably on the duke, 'there is nothing will vex d. L. [the duke of Lauderdale] mor'.[103]

While aristocrats were the most influential Scots in England, they were not the only ones to capture the public imagination. When the poet and politician Andrew Marvell (1621–78), wrote *The Last Instructions to a Painter* in 1667, he celebrated the bravery of Archibald Douglas, who had died when Michael de Ruyter, the Dutch admiral, attacked the fleet in the Medway. Marvell contrasted the valour of Douglas, and his company of Royal Scots, who defended the *Royal Oak*, with the shame of the English sailors who ran away.[104] The previous year Scotland was in the news in London for different reasons. On 30 November Pepys noted that 'people have no mind to observe that Scotch saint's day till they hear better news from Scotland'.[105] He was referring to the Pentland Rising, which took place after Sir James Turner's heavy-handed attempts to enforce the oath of allegiance. However, indirectly Pepys indicates that in other years the St Andrew's Day celebrations did occur. One place where they were observed was in the household of Catherine of Braganza (1638–1705), Charles's official wife.[106] Equally, the Royal Society chose to hold its annual general meeting on St Andrew's Day, while in 1673 Evelyn noted that 'It being St Andrews day I saw first the new Diutchesse of York'.[107] It was a reminder to London society that James was both duke of York and of Albany.

4.16 Sir Godfrey Kneller, *William Douglas, 3rd Duke of Hamilton*, 1679. Oil on canvas, 127 × 102 cm. Hamilton Collection, Lennoxlove, East Lothian. A glimpse of the duke's taste is revealed in his fine lace cravat, Garter ribbon and fancy sash.

Acknowledging Welsh Loyalty to the Stuarts: Celebrating St David's Day and Wearing the Leek

Wearing an embroidered leek on St David's Day was a feature of the royal household under both Charles II and James VII and II. The leek symbolised the principality of Wales, and the habit is referred to in Shakespeare's *Henry V* when the king tells Fluellen that he is wearing a leek, 'for I am Welsh, you know, good countryman'.[108] However, this was a new development under Charles II, and all his clothing accounts include payments for embroidered leeks to wear on St David's Day. In 1668 they are described as being made from pearl, gold wire and green Naples silk.[109] They were given to all members of the wider royal family, including the king and queen, the duke and duchess of York, Prince Rupert, Prince Edward and the duke of Monmouth and in 1662/3 they cost £13 7s 4d.[110] James VII and II continued to mark St David's Day, and the recipients of embroidered leeks reflect the scope of the family group. In 1686/7 William West embroidered leeks for the king and queen, queen dowager, the prince and princess of Denmark, the king's illegitimate sons Mr FitzJames and Mr FitzHenry, the master of the robes and master of the leeks.[111] In terms of the king's clothes, Charles took this opportunity to remember the loyalty of Wales by marking St David's Day and wearing the Welsh national symbol in a way that he did not do with the Scottish thistle.

Following in the Family Tradition: A King in Disguise

Charles II appreciated the anonymity that travelling without pomp brought and he took advantage of this in September 1655 when he wrote,'My sister and I go Monday next to the Fair at Frankfurt incognito'.[112] However, while this type of deception might work for a short time, the king was less certain of success when he was waiting in Saragossa in October 1659. A ship, as he explained to Sir Edward Hyde, would be 'so great a convenience' because of 'the hazard I might run of being known in so long a passage through France'.[113] He had learnt this lesson the hard way in 1651 when he was on the run after the battle of Worcester. Indeed, how he eluded capture became part of the Stuart myth surrounding the king after the Restoration, a story that spread through works such as Thomas Blount's *Boscobel* (1660). The antiquarian, Blount, described how 'His Majesty had been advised to rub His Hands on the Back of the Chimney, and with them his Face, for a Disguise, and some Person had disorderly cut off His Hair'.[114] Charles II later recalled how he threw his clothes 'into a Privy-House, that noe Boddy might see that any boddy had beene Stripping themselves'.[115] He told an attentive Pepys of his travels 'every step up to the knees in dirt with nothing but a green coat and a pair of country breeches on and a pair of country shoes that made

4.17 Isaac Fuller, *King Charles II and Jane Lane Riding to Bristol*, 1660s. Oil on canvas, 212.1 × 237.8 cm. National Portrait Gallery, London. Disguised as Jane Lane's servant, Charles wore the simple clothes of a groom.

him so sore all over his feet that he could scarce stir'.[116] His height was undisguisable, but not his good deportment, and 'They had much ado all that day to teach and fashion his Majesty to their country guise and to order his steps and straight body to a lobbing Jobson's gait' (fig. 4.17).[117]

Dressing incognito was not for everyone. The aristocratic poet, John Wilmot, later earl of Rochester (1647–80), declared that he would not adopt a disguise because 'he should look frightfully in it'.[118] However, others successfully followed in the Stuart tradition, including Archibald Campbell, 9th earl of Argyll (1629–85). He escaped from Edinburgh Castle in 1681 assisted by his stepdaughter Sophia Lindsay, who was given permission to visit him, walking out of the fortress dressed as her page.

Charles was not the only member of his family to be linked with disguise, but in the case of Prince Rupert it had more sinister overtones that were developed and exploited by Parliament's propagandists. The pamphlet *Prince Rupert's Disguises, Or A … True Relation of the Severall Shapes he has taken* (1642) assured readers that the prince dressed as a gentleman, an apple vendor, a cabbage seller and a woman in order to spy on Parliament's troops. However, as Mark Stoyle has observed, the pamphlets went further than this and suggested that Rupert did not need disguises because he was a shape-shifter.[119] The myth developed by early 1643 in the work of T. B., who claimed that the prince's poodle, Boy, could breathe 'a black cloud around Prince Rupert … in which he goes … invisible' so allowing his disguises to work.[120] But T. B. went further, asserting that it was Boy who changed shape, noting that 'one day he is *Philip* the Shoomaker, and another day he is *Tom* the Barber'.[121] With this association with witchcraft and conjuring, the Stuarts' use of disguise took a dangerous turn.

As a Father and an Uncle

Charles II was a father many times over, but none of his offspring were legitimate. Even so, his children played an active role at court and were painted by the leading court artists. Most important in the Scottish context was Charles II's eldest son, James Croft. His marriage to Anne Scott brought him the titles of duke of Buccleuch and Monmouth, and then in 1673 he was appointed as high chamberlain of Scotland on the death of the hereditary holder of the title, the duke of Lennox and Richmond.[122] Charles II's attitude was reminiscent of how James V had promoted James Stuart, 1st earl of Moray (*c*.1531–70), his son with his mistress Lady Margaret Erskine. Moray served as regent for his half-nephew, James VI, from 1567 to 1570, and attended the wedding of his half-sister, Mary, in Paris in 1558. Acknowledging illegitimate children was usual in Scotland, as can be seen when Sir John Seton thanked Alexander, 6th earl of Eglinton, in September 1634 for sending his illegitimate son to a boarding school in Prestonpans, along with the earl's child. Such care was warranted because the boy's mother was from a good family in Germany and Seton intended to make the lad his sole heir.[123]

4.18 John Michael Wright, *James, Duke of Cambridge*, 1666 or 1667. Oil on canvas, 130.3 × 104.7 cm. Royal Collection. James's cloth of silver Garter suit and velvet robes stress his place at the heart of the Stuart family.

While never his father's heir, Charles FitzCharles, 1st earl of Plymouth (1657–80), was Charles II's son with Catherine Pegge, fathered during the king's Spanish exile in 1657–8.[124] FitzCharles, or Don Carlos as he was known, had a short court career. Elevated to the earldom in 1675, he married the earl of Danby's daughter in 1678 and died of dysentery in Tangier in 1680.[125] Even prior to receiving his title, he dressed the part of a courtier as a bill from William Watts, the king's Scottish tailor, dated 6 September 1672 to 8 October 1674, indicates.[126] The bill records details of suits for the earl and his associates costing a princely £1,062 7s 11d.[127] Many were sumptuous, as indicated by the suit listed on 13 July 1673 consisting of a feuillemort, bloom, gold and silver striped and flowered brocade coat and breeches. The coat was lined with black and white checked lutestring, while the breeches were trimmed with sky-shaded ribbon.[128] While Don Carlos dressed the part of a prince, there was no hope of taking on his father's mantle.

More likely to take on this role were his brother James's sons, most notably James, duke of Cambridge and baron of Dauntsey (1663–1667) (fig. 4.18). The boy was brought up as an Anglican, making him a potential heir for Charles II, but any thoughts in this direction were cut short by his early death. His was one of six funerals that Charles paid for between 1660 and 1671 for his nephews and nieces. The sad pattern continued during James's second marriage, including their four daughters – Catherine Laura (1675), Isabel (1676–81), Elizabeth (1678) and Charlotte Maria (1682) – and Charles, duke of Cambridge (7 November – 12 December 1677). The lack of a legitimate male heir saw Charles II's thrones pass to his Catholic younger brother James.

Conclusions

The pink quilted waistcoat said to have been given by Charles II to Colonel Thomas Veel of Alverstone, near Bristol, in 1645, is a remnant of the king's wartime adventures that culminated in his escape after the battle of Worcester and his bid to regain London backed by a Scottish army (fig. 4.19).[129] While the campaign was a failure, Charles II's Scottish 'Worcester veterans' played a significant, if under-sung role in shaping his court, and they did so dressed in the style promoted by their king. During the course of his lifetime, Charles II and his brother experienced a substantial shift in men's clothing from the doublet and breeches to coat and breeches that, in sartorial terms, was on a par with the big political changes of this period. While Charles II is best known for his innovation in terms of the vest and for pushing against French fashion, what is most distinctive about his adult wardrobe is the variety – in terms of combinations of garments ordered, colours and fabrics – and the conflicting wish for formal and informal clothes. All of these points can be attributed to his time in exile and enforced European travel, an experience that he shared with many Scots of the same generation.

While Charles did not return to Scotland after 1651, the significance of his time there is undeniable, both in terms of receiving the crown of his ancient kingdom but also by reforging the bond between the Stuarts and their Scottish people. His new brand of Stuart style, including the advent of the vest, was embraced in Scotland in two key ways. The first was via Lauderdale and Hamilton, who served as a conduit between Charles and Scotland, and the second was the increased appeal, both to Scots and English, of London as a place to shop. While he lacked a son, Charles's decision to send James, his brother and heir, to Edinburgh played a key part in the next stage of the ever-evolving Stuart style.

4.19 Whether it belonged to Charles II or not, this quilted satin waistcoat is a very fine example of a piece of informal male dress, c.1640–80. Burrell Collection, Glasgow.

CHAPTER FIVE

James VII and II (1633–1701)

THERE IS A SIGNIFICANT and a poignant gulf between the rich silver and silver gilt metal thread embroidery that decorates the cuffs, pocket flaps, skirts and centre front of James, duke of York's wedding coat (fig. 5.1) and the scrap of 'the Flannell wastecoate he dyed in'.[1] One represents an understated opulence appropriate for the heir to the Stuart thrones, who was making a politically and religiously charged marriage; the other is the choice of a man forced by exile to reassess his life. Yet both garments were associated with occasions when James's Catholic faith was foremost in his mind, whether it was expressed through the words of the wedding ceremony to Mary of Modena or the last rites. James's conversion to Catholicism in 1668 or 1669 had several long-term consequences for his relationship with the Stuarts' style. Ultimately it split support for the Stuarts, and while William III chose to relaunch the suit as a symbol of Stuart Protestantism, James's exile in France consolidated the influence of French fashion on his Catholic court. However, these events were not a certainty in 1685, and for some James's accession was a blessing, as indicated by this inscription placed inside a mourning ring for his late brother:

> Charles is reviv'd while Royal James does reign;
> And all our loss well paid in such a gain.[2]

Of the five men considered in *Stuart Style*, the written material recording James VII and II's clothing choices is the most fragmentary. In contrast, as Aileen Ribeiro notes, James exploited portraiture in ways that his elder brother did not.[3] Reflecting a combination of personal preference in tandem with the freedom of being a younger brother, the paintings reveal several distinct facets to James's clothing style. His early portraiture stresses his role as the second son in a close group of siblings. Between 1652 and 1659, and then 1660 and 1673, James, like many second sons in Scottish elite and middling families, shaped his image

5.1 Detail from the wedding suit of James, duke of York, 1673. Victoria and Albert Museum, London. The stylised design of flowers and leaves is created with couched silver and silver gilt threads and metal strips wrapped over strips of parchment, so making the embroidery three-dimensional.

with the uniform, insignia and armour associated with his military and naval careers. Emulating his own father, he also presented himself as a fashionable husband with his wife and children, a comfortable image that was complicated by there being two wives and two sets of children, who would split the Stuart family. James may be the last Stuart considered here, but his contribution to Stuart fashion both in his own lifetime and in the long term was not insignificant, and it had implications for the development of Jacobitism.

Following in his Brother's Footsteps: Childhood and First Period of Exile

If Charles I's outlook was influenced by being a second son who idolised his elder brother, James was a younger brother who got on well with his siblings. Born on 14 October 1633, James was three years younger than Charles II and almost seven years older than Henry, duke of Gloucester, whose birthday fell on 8 July 1640. James received titles and offices suited to his status: he was made the lord high admiral in 1636, elected as a knight of the Garter in 1642 and created duke of York on 22 January 1644. However, he was not given the title of duke of Albany until December 1660.

The earliest image of James is with his elder siblings, Charles and Mary, in Van Dyck's painting of the king's three eldest children from 1635 (fig. 5.2). James is dressed in a blue satin coat with a square neckline and

5.2 Sir Anthony van Dyck, detail from *Three Eldest Children of Charles I*, 1635. Oil on canvas, 151 × 154 cm. Galleria Sabauda, Turin. James is also dressed in a coat, and the simpler neckline, lack of lace collar and hanging sleeves that could be used as leading strings all stress that he is the younger son.

hanging sleeves, marking him as the younger brother who was learning to walk. This picture must have been significant to James because the inventory of his goods taken in 1701 included 'A picture of king Charles the Second when prince of Wales with the duke of York and princess Royal afterwards Princess of Orange, by Vandike'.[4] James was still wearing coats in Van Dyck's *The Five Eldest Children of Charles I*, dated 1637, this time of dark orange satin, and they serve to stress his youth compared to Charles (see fig. 4.4). However, by the time Cornelius Johnson painted his full-length portrait in 1639, James had been breeched (fig. 5.3). He is dressed in a blue satin suit, and just as he serves as a foil to his elder siblings in Van Dyck's group portraits, so here his portrait is paired to that of Charles, who Johnson paints dressed in more adult black.[5]

5.3 Cornelius Johnson, *King James II*, 1639. Oil on panel, 28.9 × 20 cm. National Portrait Gallery, London. James dressed all in blue, from his doublet to his shoe roses, his suit embellished with silver embroidery and silver lace.

A suit like this blue example would have been expensive, but it is uncertain whether the £2,000 issued to William Feilding, the 1st earl of Denbigh (*c*.1587–1643) on 14 March 1639 for 'the speedy providing of divers necessaries for the queen and children' from the Great Wardrobe included items for James. Even so, it gives an indication of the scale of expenditure on clothing for the royal offspring.[6] The belief that they should be suitably dressed remained firmly entrenched even when the royal family faced serious financial difficulty, and on 18 January 1645 John, lord Byron, gentleman of the robes to the duke of York, received £50 in part payment of £5,000 for the robes and privy purse. He received a further £200 on 28 February and a final £100 on 28 March 1645.[7]

After the fall of Oxford in June 1646, Parliamentary forces captured James and he was placed in the care of Algernon Percy, 10th earl of Northumberland (1602–68). Percy only agreed to look after the king's children on the proviso that he could do so in a manner 'in all respects as was agreeable to their quality and his duty', and so he was granted £7,500 a year.[8] Captivity brought a return to the style of life James had known before the outbreak of war, and the earl 'presented His Highness with a very rich French embroidered coach and six excellent coach horses, wherewith His Highness and the rest of the King's children here have appeared *en princes* like themselves in Hyde Park'.[9] Lely captured hints of this pre-war style when he painted James with his father in 1647 while they were prisoners at Hampton Court.[10]

Dressed as a woman, James escaped, and by September 1648 he was in The Hague with his elder brother. When Charles left in June 1649, he was presented with debts of 20,902 gilders 4 stivers 'Oweing to seuerall persons by his highness the Duke of Yorke as wille appeare by the particular Bills'.[11] Of these Charles agreed to pay 855 gilders to settle three tailor's bills, 135 gilders to an armourer for 'a suit of arms', 312 gilders 'to Mr Armourer', 299 gilders to the shoemaker and 2,655 gilders to the sempstress.[12] The brothers were still in mourning for their father when they were in Jersey in September 1649. The 15-year-old duke was described as being 'attired in an entire suit of black, without any other ornament or decoration than the silver star displayed upon his mantle. He also wore a purple scarf across his shoulders'.[13] The brothers were unified in their loss.

During the next decade James moved round Europe and his fortunes and funds fluctuated, meaning that he often had to manage on considerably less than he was used to as a boy. He went to Brussels in 1650, where the poet Abraham Cowley (1618–67) reported that the duke was 'in all extremities of want' and that it would be better if he went 'into Germany, or indeed Japan, or the West Indies' rather than return to Henrietta Maria in Paris.[14] While in Brussels he attended Catholic services sitting in 'a private place, where he might neither give nor receive offence', and he chose to dress incognito.[15] In 1652 James joined the French army after receiving a loan of 300 pistoles.[16] With this he purchased 'a camp bed and his small baggage', which were carried by two mules.[17] In April 1654 he left Paris to fight for the French and went 'with bag and baggage' requiring four mules.[18] He also spent some time in Breda where his household was 'in all the confusion imaginable, in present want of everything'.[19]

Despite this lack of possessions, during this period James developed his reputation as a soldier. While fighting in the Spanish army at the Battle of the Dunes, he sat for his portrait (fig. 5.4). The military look was adopted at this time by many of the Scottish elite who were earning a living by the sword. At the siege of Étampes in 1652, 'An attack was believed so imminent that the Duke of York who was on an ambling horse did not think he had time to change his mount, although a war horse had been brought for him, or to put armour on. This they put on him while he was still mounted.'[20] In such an environment his possessions were often vulnerable, although, after the Battle of the Dunes, in June 1658 a companion noted ironically, 'as for the baggage and cannon, wee had none to lose … our baggage being left behind at Furnes'.[21]

Religious beliefs apart, his life was similar to that of his younger brother Henry, duke of Gloucester, except that in the months after Charles I's execution, Henry had been suggested as a possible king of Scots.[22] This came to nothing and in 1652 Cromwell allowed Henry to go to France where he lived for a brief time with Henrietta Maria. Henry soon left to fight with Louis de Bourbon, prince of Condé, in support of the Huguenots, and in 1653 Adriaen Hanneman captured his military style (fig. 5.5). In this portrait his princely rank is hinted at by the blue silk ribbon, which identifies him as a Garter knight. Whether Henry would have been a rival to James in later life is unknown, because he

died of smallpox on 18 September 1660: Burnet recalled that 'The duke of Gloucester's death seemed to touch him much'.[23] When Henry's death was followed by that of Mary a few months later, it served to strengthen the relationship between Charles and James, and James was described as 'a young man of good spirit, loving and beloved by the King, his brother'.[24] The strength of the family bond between the Stuart siblings endured in spite of religious differences and shared financial difficulty.

5.4 *(above, left)* Attributed to Charles Wautier, *James, Duke of York*, c.1656–60. Oil on canvas, 124 × 93 cm. Royal Collection. Wearing black armour over a buff jerkin with a falling band trimmed with lace, James points to the commander's baton in his right hand.

5.5 *(above, right)* Adriaen Hanneman, *Henry, Duke of Gloucester*, c.1653. Oil on canvas, 104.8 × 87 cm. National Gallery of Art, Washington, DC. Henry's buff jerkin, worn over a tawny-coloured doublet and grey breeches, trimmed with silver gilt metal thread, braid and buttons, echoes the style of his older brothers.

Loyalty to Caroline Style: James's Clothes after the Restoration

James, his first wife, Anne Hyde, and their two daughters offered an image of Stuart family life as a counterpoint to Charles II and his childless marriage with Catherine of Braganza (fig. 5.6). James and Anne had a reputation for extravagance, and in the years immediately after the Restoration the duke regularly overspent. In 1663 he had to economise and limits were set for key areas of expenditure, with £12,000 allocated for clothes, accessories and linen for his person and for sheets.[25] By 1665 his account books record that £2,000 was allowed for the duke's clothes and linen.[26] In 1667 Pepys estimated the duke's income at approximately £40,000 a year but it was closer to £47,000 and it increased steadily in the period up to 1685.[27] His expenditure can be gauged by looking at the salaries paid to his household. For instance, in July 1664 James Carlisle,

5.6 Peter Lely and Benedetto Gennari II, *James II when Duke of York with Anne Hyde, Princess Mary and Princess Anne*, c. 1668–85. Oil on canvas, 168.6 × 194 cm. Royal Collection. Lely has stressed the full sleeves of James's shirt, visible through the open seam of his doublet sleeves.

the sergeant of the hounds, received £250 a year, while Edward Sanders, a foot huntsman, received £30 per year for attending the foxhounds and £25 for the buckhounds.[28] Equally, not all bills were paid on time, because on 18 December 1682 Anne Hargreaves petitioned for £129 still owing to her for goods listed on three bills from June 1665 to Lady Day 1667 – her case was upheld.[29]

While there are no known clothing accounts from this period, Pepys indicates that James followed important court fashions. On 2 November 1663 he 'heard the duke say that he was going to wear a perriwigg; and they say the king also will' and on 15 February 1664 he wrote 'to White-hall to the Duke; where first he put on a periwigg today but methought his hair cut short in order thereto, did look very prettily of itself before he put on his periwig'.[30] James also adopted the vest and Pepys 'stood and saw him dress himself and try on his vest which is the king's new fashion'.[31] His taste was in line with that of the Right Honourable William Russell, whose clothes were made by James Blacklaw and recorded on three bills dating from 1664 to 1669.[32] James also shared his brother's love of horses and hunting, and used his riding clothes for other leisure activities, as in November 1661, when Pepys reported that he had gone 'this morning to wait upon the duke of York which we did in his chamber as he was dressing himself in his riding suit to go this day by sea to the downs'.[33] In the late 1660s James expressed the fashionable opinion that 'there was no hope for a leg unless it was clothed in green'.[34] So, Stuart style was a family style, with James emulating his older brother.

His Brother's Heir: James's Time in Scotland

On 12 March 1679 Elizabeth Maitland, duchess of Lauderdale, told the earl of Caithness that Charles II had sent the duke of York to Brussels, a state of affairs that pleased neither the Catholics nor other 'malcontents'.[35] The king did so in response to the Exclusion Act that sought to remove James, as Charles's heir presumptive, from the succession. As the crisis continued, James and his family moved to Scotland where they lived from November 1679 to February 1680 and then from October 1680 to March 1682.[36] While this was not the original intention, these two lengthy stays in Scotland fulfilled one of the points listed in the Engagement Treaty of December 1647, namely that the king or prince would spend time on Scottish soil.[37] The Scots prepared for James's arrival and on 16 October 1679 the privy council sent out letters stating 'yt his Royall highness ye Duke of York is expected to be verie shortlie in this Kingdom And conceaving it fitt yt his entries and reception be with ye respect and honor due to his dignitie they have resolved to met him at ye Border of England'.[38] More significantly, the Scots nobility showed their loyalty by returning to Edinburgh so much so that one of their number noted, 'I do not hear of one who stays [in London]'.[39]

While James was effective as his brother's representative in Scotland's government, his religion was divisive, and on Christmas Day 1680 the Reverend Robert Law described how 'the youths of the Colledge of Edinburgh havin caused make the pope's effigies of timber, with a painted face, lyke a man, the head covered with a lyert pirewig, on his head a triple crown of timber ... This the Duke of York took ill, as a reflection on him.'[40] James provoked a mixed response in Scotland, with one underwhelmed individual describing him as 'dismal Jimmy'.[41] However, others supported James and his family, and when in 1680 John Elphinstone, 8th lord Elphinstone, had a daughter, she was christened Mary Beatrice Anna Margaret Frances Isabella after the duchess of Albany.[42]

The impact of James's presence in Scotland was felt in several other ways. Most significantly, Charles II appointed him to the Scottish privy council and made him high commissioner of Scotland, a position previously held by the duke of Lauderdale. Shortly after his arrival the earl of Rothes advised the earl of Caithness that James was actively engaging in Scottish politics, confiding that 'the duik intends to hear all persons himself that are Concerned in the Heighlands, a great many whairof are in toun already and uthers will be advertised to come, among which number your lordship and your Antagonist will certainly be'.[43] James presided at the parliament held in summer 1681 that passed 'An Act acknowledging and asserting the right of succession to the imperial crown of Scotland', which stated that 'the kings of this realm deriving their royal power from God Almighty alone, do succeed lineally thereto, according to the known degrees of proximity in blood, which cannot be interrupted, suspended or diverted by any act of statute whatsoever'.[44] This was a clear statement of support for Stuart rule.

5.7 Pair of leather gloves embroidered with metal wire said to have belonged to John Graham of Claverhouse, Viscount Dundee, 17th century. 27 × 32 cm. National Museum of Scotland.

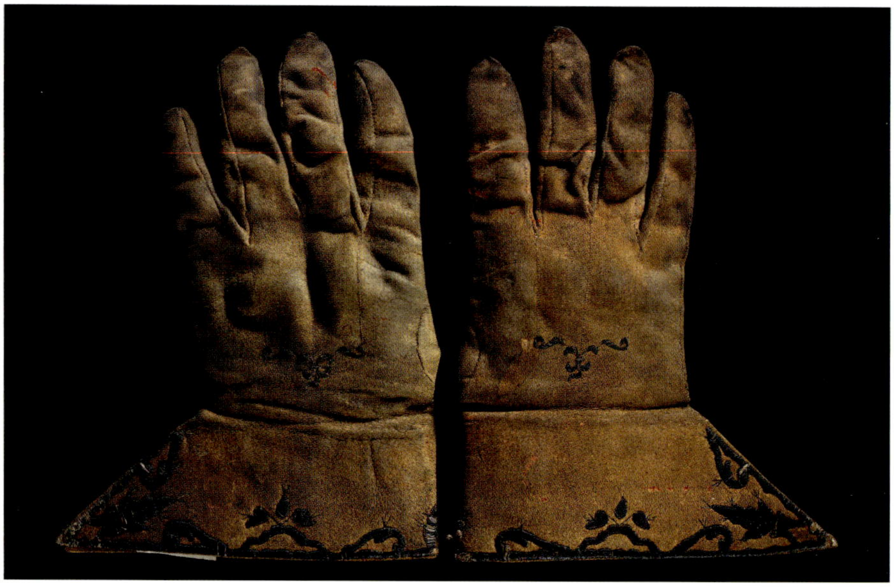

James also held court in Edinburgh and during this time, in keeping with the Stuart masque tradition, his younger daughter Anne (1662–1714) performed Nathaniel Lee's *Mithridates: King of Pontus*. During this interlude James brought Stuart style directly to Edinburgh, and the impact of his court on Edinburgh society may well explain attempts to regulate textile imports into Scotland planned for September 1681. Edinburgh's merchants petitioned James in April, complaining about the impact this would have on their businesses.[45]

On James's return to Whitehall, members of the Scots elite still looked to the duke to promote their particular concerns. John Graham of Claverhouse, for example, spent the spring of 1683 at London, Newmarket and Windsor with James and his brother.[46] Graham embraced Stuart style, as was demonstrated by the expensive clothing and accessories he wore, such as a pair of high-quality gloves that are associated with him (fig. 5.7). James acted as a patronage broker for many Scots, including the 3rd duke of Hamilton, who wrote to his wife Anne describing how the duke of York has prevailed upon the king to see him and three others.[47]

A Style of His Own? James VII and II's Royal Wardrobe

Charles II died on 6 February 1685, and the same day James wrote to his nephew William informing him that 'it has pleased God Almighty, to take out of this world, the King my Brother'.[48] At the same time, the royalist politician Sir Justinian Isham observed that 'Never king was proclaimed with more applause … He has made a speech to the Councell that did charm everybody concerning his intentions of maintaining the Government as it was established in Church and State'.[49] James ordered four suits for his coronation, the most splendid of which consisted of a gold and silver rich brocade coat and breeches lined with taffeta and decorated with rich gold brocade lace.[50] However, his young queen outshone him. Mary recorded that her 'dress and royal mantle were covered with precious stones, and it took all the jewels all the goldsmiths of London could procure to decorate my crown'.[51] Hopes of using the Scottish regalia were mooted but dashed as Lauder of Fountainhall reported that 'Our Commons took up a jealousie that the Scots croun was to be sent up to Windsor, that he might also be crouned with it'. As a result a new 'massie croun of gold is making for hir'.[52]

Differences in style between the brothers were noticeable from the outset of James's reign, including James's greater formality as expressed in his use of hat etiquette. Francesco Terriesi, the envoy from Tuscany, reported that James VII and II 'receives all foreign representatives who come to compliment him on his accession, seated, with his hat on, and in a special room; not like the late king, standing in his own bedchamber and with his hat in his hand'.[53]

His clothes, however, followed the pattern of the last decade of Charles II's reign with the suit, consisting of coat, waistcoat and breeches, dominating the royal wardrobe (fig. 5.8). The king's coats and breeches were usually wool and listed as cloth, serge or drugget, a choice in keeping with promoting the domestic wool trade. Cloth alone accounted for 61 per cent of the orders. Some included their place of origin in their name, such as Farnham drugget and Taunton serge. However, the names can be misleading – not all 'Spanish' cloth, for instance, was made in Spain; some was made in England using Spanish or merino wool.[54] Camlet, which could be either wool or silk, was the second most frequently ordered fabric and was used for 22 suits, or a quarter of James's orders. Only three suits were definitely made of silk, with one example each of brocade, tissue and velvet, and it was a coat of this type that he wore when he sat for a painting by Anne Killigrew (fig. 5.9). His colour choices reveal a different trend to that of his predecessors in that black was not predominant – indeed, suits of sad colour were by far the most common.

While wool might have been the most popular choice for the outer fabric of the king's suits, it concealed linings and waistcoats that were frequently made from French and Italian silks. 16 different fabrics, or variants, were used as coat linings. The most popular were rateen, a thick woollen cloth, crêpe, taffeta and lutestring. Where the design is mentioned, it reveals a preference for stripes in 1686/7 and 1687/8, along with spots and floral patterns. Variety and change were evidently important, with most colours or patterns only featuring once. The two colours that stand out because of the frequency with which they were ordered are black and purple.

Not surprisingly the most expensive materials, including those with complex patterns and metal thread, were used for waistcoats, which were ordered as an integral part of James's suits. The fabrics selected for waistcoats were more highly patterned than those for linings, and it was quite common for the waistcoat not to match the coat lining. As with the coat linings, there was a preference for stripes, often combining colour with metallic threads. While the popularity of purple remained constant, the use of black was noticeably less.

James's accounts also include separate orders for waistcoats, which were ordered in considerable numbers. While some were quite plain, others were fancy; similarly, some were made with sleeves and others without. When a waistcoat had sleeves, these were often longer than the coat sleeves.[55] An example of a sleeved waistcoat made of the type of fabrics favoured by James VII and II and William III can be found in the collection of the Museum of London.[56] This item was made from a flowered silk in shades of brown with flowers in metal thread. A slightly different fabric was used at the end of the sleeves, and the sleeves themselves were cut in two pieces and had no cuffs. The waistcoat was lined with a striped silk, and an interlining of dark brown linen. A strip of blue linen was placed behind the 36 buttonholes on the proper left front.

5.8 The cut of James's coats was similar to this brown wool coat dating from 1680 to 1690, with pocket flaps and cuffs of the same wool and a brown/blue shot silk lining. Platt Hall, Manchester.

James's suits were at times quite plain, but with fancy buttons and ribbon as the main types of decoration. For special occasions, such as Catherine of Braganza's birthday in 1688, he ordered 'rich broad French gold purl point lace' for his coat costing £30 2s 6d.[57] Some suits had specific accessories, such as a pair of purple shammy gloves trimmed with purple ingrain taffeta ribbon that were worn with 'a sad colour camlet coat lined with black rateen, breeches and waistcoat of rateen'.[58]

James did not relinquish his military career once he was king. Indeed, he used it to shape his royal image. His purchases after his accession included a harquebusier armour made by Richard Holden of London in 1686 and the buff coat associated with it.[59] A year later his accounts for 1687/8 include altering a buff coat and making new sleeves of shammy, and a burlet 'to bear armour on the shoulders'.[60] James also ordered a large scarlet camlet coat lined with fine shalloon and a crimson camlet surtout lined with the same shalloon, both of which are described as being designed 'to wear with armour'. This is very much of the type of military coat with gold embroidery that James chose for his portrait by Gennari, and would have been suitable for the annual review of the army (fig. 5.10).[61] He also had two surtouts (an outdoor coat popular after *c.*1680), which were probably worn for the same purpose.[62] The surtout was thigh length and loose in cut with a downturn collar and wide sleeves.[63] It had two side seams and a slit at the centre back to allow for extra ease when riding a horse.[64] James's taste was in keeping with that of many of his contemporaries who had fought abroad. For example, George, earl of Winton, ordered a campaign coat for Robert Duncan in 1678–9 from George Grey of Edinburgh,[65] while in 1680 John, earl of Caithness, ordered a campaign coat from Mr Munro, in London.[66]

Throughout his life James was an enthusiastic huntsman. In May 1686 it was reported by one who had observed his activities in the

field that 'His Majesty kept pretty near the dogs, though the ditches were broad and deep, the hedges high, and the way and fields dirty and deep; but most of the lords were cast out again and amongst them the Duke of Albemarle'.[67] In 1687/8, James's accounts included 'a light colour camlet coat, breeches of French rateen, and a tabby waistcoat for hunting'.[68] The time spent in the saddle took its toll on the king's clothes and in 1685/6 Mr Chavois, brusher to the robes, was paid extra for 'cleaning and liquoring boots and shoes, cleaning hunting clothes, mending cloaks and silk and thread'.[69] In addition, Mr Rogee, the king's tailor, repaired three hunting suits.[70] James's clothes reveal his Stuart pedigree, as he followed his brother's love of sport and informality, and his grandfather's obsession with the hunt.

5.9 *(above, left)* Anne Killigrew, *James II*, 1685. Oil on canvas, 104.8 × 86.4 cm. Royal Collection. The straight lines of the coat, cut without a waist seam, show off the patterned fabric well.

5.10 *(above, right)* Attributed to Benedetto Gennari II, *James VII and II*, c.1685. Oil on canvas, 241.5 × 149 cm. National Army Museum, London. James's scarlet coat with metal thread embroidery and blue turned-back cuffs demonstrates how military uniforms were developing and starting to influence male fashion.

Support for James VII and II in Scotland

While there was not much support for Catholicism in Scotland in 1685, there was also a lack of enthusiasm for Archibald Campbell, 9th earl of Argyll, who landed on Scottish soil in May in an attempt to depose James. His invasion coincided with the unsuccessful rebellion led by the king's nephew, James Scott, duke of Monmouth and Buccleuch (1649–85). When Monmouth was captured after his defeat at the battle of Sedgemoor he was much changed from the dashing young courtier of the early 1660s, with 'his beard being grown so long, and so grey as hardly to be known, had not his George discovered him'.[71]

James looked to a small group of men in Scotland for support, many of whom were converts, such as John and James Drummond. John Drummond, 1st earl of Melfort (1649–1714), had a career of royal service starting as a captain in the Scottish Foot Guards in 1673, moving to become deputy governor of Edinburgh Castle in 1679 and master of ordnance in 1680. John was secretary for Scotland in 1684–8 and one of the founder knights of the Order of the Thistle in 1687. He later went into exile with James and was his ambassador in Rome. His brother James, 4th earl of Perth (1648–1716), was lord chancellor of Scotland until James VII's abdication and prior to this he had been a member of the Scottish privy council. However, the brothers posed a problem for

5.11 Henri Gascar, *George Douglas, 1st Earl of Dumbarton*, c.1676. Oil on canvas, 127 × 102 cm. Lennoxlove, East Lothian. Dumbarton's buff jerkin and long leather gauntlets contrast with the opulence of his sleeves and sash.

James because in 1686 they had provoked anti-Catholic riots, having failed to persuade the Scottish parliament to agree to toleration of Catholics. Another important supporter was George Douglas, 1st earl of Dumbarton (1635–92) (fig. 5.11). He had shared experiences and interests with the king, having spent much of the 1670s fighting in Europe or hunting with his pack of terriers, and like James, he chose the military option for his portrait. He was appointed as a gentleman of the bedchamber to James in July 1687.[72] James's Scottish supporters shared his religion, his military interests and his love of riding, all of which were reflected in their use of Stuart fashion.

Emulation and Appropriation: William III, the Williamites and Stuart Style

James had a rival in the person of his nephew and son-in-law, Prince William III of Orange-Nassau. William was younger, a Protestant, and he was familiar with the Stuart court at Whitehall, having visited his uncles twice. His trip in 1670 provoked comment because he wore plain suits and his own hair, rather than the fashionable wig favoured by his uncles. However, his clothes had been made in Paris, indicating that French style did not have to be flamboyant. Two years later William made his mark on French fashion when, in 1672, Louis XIV banned anything orange after problems with his campaign in the Netherlands.[73] When he married James's daughter Mary (1662–94) in 1677, William was described as 'the plainest man ever seen and of no fashion at all'.[74] Fashionable or not, he, along with his wife, were regarded as the Protestant alternative to James and his version of Stuart style, and on 5 November 1688 he landed at Brixham to claim his father-in-law's throne.

William III's image makers promoted his preference for plain cloth suits and for the reading of the Declaration of Right, which outlined the wrongs committed by James. On 13 February 1689 William 'probably wore a simple cinnamon-coloured suit'.[75] A week later rumours about a coronation were circulating, and on 21 February Walter Scott, earl of Tarras (1644–93) learnt that 'Its supposed the K. and Q. of Ingland (now soe called) will be crouned speedilie if not on Mvnday last. Its thought the robes being gone was the reason it was not on Saturday'.[76] Instead, they took their time to prepare appropriately, thereby ensuring that William and Mary's joint coronation, which took place on 11 April, compared favourably with that of James and Mary, which had taken place only four years earlier.

Once crowned, William used his clothing as one way of stressing the legitimacy of his claim to the Stuart thrones. He reverted to Robert Graham, the Scottish tailor who had served Charles II from 1677 to 1685 and for the early months of James VII and II's reign.[77] However, this did not represent a complete rejection of French tailoring, because he employed a French tailor occasionally.[78] William emulated Charles

II's court in other ways. He restored the household to how it had been under Charles II, so making a break with the reforms made by James. William was aware that his court needed to create a positive, legitimate image to counter charges of his being a usurper. In spite of fighting against Louis XIV, William looked to Versailles as a model for court entertainments and on 7 January 1692, James Fraser told Henry Hyde, 2nd earl of Clarendon (1638–1709) that 'There were great doings last night at Kinnington [Kensington] in Imitation of the apartments of Versailles'. However, William, like James before him, did not opt for formal court style as Louis did on such occasions, and so 'all the rooms were full of Ladies & men ... The Ladies were the more numerous, in regard they had the liberty to come in Manto's [mantuas]'.[79]

David Kuchta argues that James VII and II's clothes were symbolic of his reign and so different to the 'oppositional' style adopted after the Glorious Revolution, which became 'the dominant culture'.[80] William is credited with bringing back the vest, thereby emulating Charles II by turning away from French fashion. However, like his uncle, it was more complicated than a simple rejection once William was king. This is because James's personal dress was more restrained than Kuchta suggests, while his son-in-law's was more flamboyant, as the patterned silk suit captured in Jacob de Later's mezzotint of William III indicates (fig. 5.12).

In 1689 John Blanch praised William and Mary for coming 'to rescue the glory of the English nation from that stupidity, that luxury, that effeminacy of the late reigns'.[81] This comment reflects Blanch's Whig politics and the association of Catholicism and luxury, rather than an actual assessment of what James spent on clothes. His clothing accounts record an upward trend from £1,909 12s 7d in 1685/6 to £3,692 10s 4d in 1687/8.[82] In contrast, William III's costs for a comparable time span were £4,483 4s 4d in 1688/9 and £4,196 3s 9d in 1689/90.[83] Equally, the costs the Wardrobe of the Robes incurred for their coronations reveal a similar pattern, with James's bill coming to £1,695 2s 8d and that of William £2,627 19s 1d.[84]

During the course of 1689 the choice between James VII and II and William split families. William, 3rd duke of Hamilton, supported Mary II and William III and the duke demonstrated his loyalty to the new regime when he wore 'a new sute with gold buttons and brocade wastcoat to complement his majestie with' when he attended the king's birthday ball.[85] In contrast, the duke's eldest son followed James and on 8 January 1689 the earl of Arran addressed the Scots nobility and gentry in the council chamber at Whitehall speaking against the overtures being made to the Prince of Orange to govern Scotland.[86]

The accounts of Scottish men shopping in Scotland reveal a preference for French clothing terms, especially the 'justaucorps', a knee-length coat. In 1682 John Clarke made 'a fine flowered justicoat' for the laird of Dean.[87] By the early 1690s Dougal Campbell's tailor supplied a coat and justaucorps for his coachman, as well as a

flowered example for his lordship.[88] Another European fashion, the Brandenburg (a loose overcoat) also featured. In October 1690 the countess of Caithness paid James Marshall for a Brandenburg coat for Mr Colin made from Irish frieze, and also for enlarging a coat and vest for him.[89] Three months later Marshall made a Brandenburg for Mr Gregory.[90] While the terms might be French, this did not mean that the resultant look was always in line with Paris fashion, as suggested by James, 1st earl of Seafield's choice of a tight-fitting coat worn with a simple cravat (fig. 5.13).[91]

Challenges to William's rule came from several directions including the ongoing presence of James in exile, periodic assassination attempts, and rival claimants to the throne. In December 1691, the captain of the Edinburgh town guard learnt that 'ther is one Maitland, who keepes choopp at the Head of Blackfriers wynd, whom to his Cabball yeasterneight declaired his having intelligence from the E. of Lauderdall that King James wold be hear shortlie and that he hade prepaired some stands of armes for his use'.[92] Potentially of greater concern was the proclamation of James Scott, earl of Dalkeith (1674–1705) in 1692 by 'thirty of forty wild people' at Sanquhar Cross, Dumfriesshire.[93] Dalkeith was the second son of the duke of Monmouth, and more importantly, Charles II's grandson. Little came of it, but when Anne revived the Order of the Thistle in December 1703, young James was made a knight the following year. As such, Anne was following William's use of pre-existing Stuart dress and ceremony to bind the Scottish and English elites to her cause.

5.12 *(above, left)* Jacob de Later, *William III*, c.1690. Mezzotint, 33.8 × 26 cm. Private Collection. William's embroidered coat, fringed gauntlets, fine shirt, lace cravat and big beaver hat all proclaim him as very elegant.

5.13 *(above, right)* Sir John Baptiste de Medina, *James Ogilvy, 1st Earl of Seafield*, 1695. Oil on canvas, 125.7 × 103.1 cm. National Galleries of Scotland. A plain dress, with an understated shirt and cravat, suit Seafield's self-presentation.

Embracing French Fashion: Life and Death in Exile

When Mary arrived in France she was dressed in a black silk gown. Louis XIV sent her a French court dress so she could be received at Versailles suitably attired.[94] Having failed to leave England on 11 December 1688, James succeeded on 23 December, so beginning his exile. He wrote to Lord Dartmouth on 19 January 1689 asking if William III would send him his coach and horses, and these were sent, along with plate and hunting things.[95] Other items were retained including 'a Cabinet of silver Fillgrene' that John Evelyn saw in July 1693 in Mary of Orange's library, 'which I think was our Queen Marys, & in my opinion with other Things, Cabinet pieces, should have ben generously sent her Majestie'.[96] Some of the perks taken by Charles Sackville, 6th earl of Dorset, as lord chamberlain included two beds that had been used by James.[97] Others to profit included Simon de Brienne, housekeeper of Kensington Palace, who claimed an ebony table, stands and a looking glass garnished with silver and marked with James's cipher as duke of York.[98]

At Louis XIV's prompting, James subsequently landed in Ireland in 1689 in a bid to recover his three kingdoms. When he entered Dublin on 24 March James wore a cinnamon suit trimmed with silver lace, the Order of the Garter and a black hat.[99] At the time of his death, six years later, he still owned 'A case of travelling plate' that was 'marked with the king of France his arms and was given to the late king when he went into Ireland'.[100] After his defeat at the Battle of the Boyne on 1 July 1690, James returned to France for a second and final period of exile.

Louis gave James the château of Saint-Germain-en-Laye, which had been the French king's chief palace from 1666 until Louis relocated the court to Versailles in 1682. As Edward Corp has revealed, James used the antechamber for the levée, the formal dressing ceremony, suggesting that he had a suitable wardrobe to maintain this level of display.[101] The ground floor plan of the Château-Vieux de Saint-Germain records that three rooms served as his wardrobe.[102] By necessity, James now adopted his cousin's style, including big wigs, knee-length coats, sleeves with big cuffs and large beaver hats (fig. 5.14).[103] The opulence of French court dress was clear on state occasions such as the marriage of Monsieur de Chartres and Mademoiselle de Blois in 1692. The groom 'was in black velvet embroidered all over in gold and trimmed with rubies' while Louis XIV wore 'a coat of gold brocade embroidered with silver, and a strap of very large diamonds as a shoulder knot, instead of the ribbon loops usually worn there'.[104] On this occasion James and Mary were the highest-ranking royalty present and so they handed the couple their chemises as they prepared for their wedding night.[105] This careful attention to precedent extended to Louis, permitting James and his son to wear purple for mourning (the colour worn by English kings) rather than black (the colour worn by French kings).[106]

James received a pension of 600,000 livres a year from Louis XIV, and the French king also maintained and furnished the chateau. James also received money from Italy, France and England.[107] Louis XIV accorded

James the place at court reserved for a ruling monarch. Mary was popular at court and had a role because of the lack of a queen or a dauphine between 1690 and 1711. In contrast, James was regarded as boring and one Frenchman unkindly commented that 'when one talks to him, one understands why he is here'.[108] There was a need for a level of formality in James's dress in order to maintain his position, for when he was received at the French court by Louis XIV.

The Scots who accompanied James into exile, such as Sir David Nairne, clerk of the foreign office at Saint-Germain (1655–1740), also dressed in the French style. On 6 November 1699 Nairne bought himself a black coat and breeches, he spent £58 14s on a new sword and a new suit in October 1702, and on 25 January 1697 and 6 January 1700 he bought new wigs

5.14 Nicolas Langlois, *La Reception faite au Roy d'Angleterre par le Roy à St Germain en Laye le VIIe janvier 1689*, 1690. Engraving, 32 × 49 cm. Bibliothèque Nationale de France, Paris. As James (on the left) and Louis greet each other, the similarities in their dress are evident, while Louis's added opulence makes him stand out.

costing 39 livres and 52 livres respectively.[109] However, the king could only support a small group of attendants, and James was forced to give up his Scottish guard consisting of 150 men who would be victorious at Killiecrankie, a key victory in the first Jacobite rising of 1689. In May 1691, Francis Scott sent lists of the Scots officers who had 'gone in' to the French army to his brother Tarras.[110] There was an ongoing interest in the exiled court among the Scottish elite, and in March 1696 Dougal Campbell bought 'A view of the Court of St Germans' – whether a book or a print, this item demonstrates that there was a market for Jacobite material in Scotland.[111]

However, in 1699 Louis XIV made peace with England, and the new ambassador, Lord Halifax, reported he had 'faced old James the other day at St. Cloud', adding contemptuously that 'You never saw such a strange figure … lean, worn and ravelled … their equipages are all very ragged and contemptible'.[112] James II died aged 67 on 16 September 1701, and his probate inventory reveals both his relative poverty and the importance to him of his faith.[113] In addition to owning religious paintings and texts, as George Scott has revealed, James chose to wear a metal cilice on certain days as part of his devotional life. Concealed from the casual gaze, this garment placed James on the first stage of the spiritual life, known as 'praxis'.[114] James's second period of exile combined French court style in public with private expressions of piety.

James and the Ups and Downs of Fatherhood

Unlike his older brother, James had legitimate as well as illegitimate children, and it was the former who caused him the most difficulties. Maureen Waller has, with some justification, described his Anglican daughters, Mary and Anne, as 'ungrateful'.[115] However, it was the birth of a son in 1688 that proved the catalyst for their behaviour. Rumours at court whispered that the child was 'a prince of Wales' because during her pregnancy Mary of Modena 'longs for tosted chees'.[116] The predictions were correct and when James Francis Edward Stuart (1688–1766) was born at St James's Palace, he received the traditional titles of duke of Rothesay, earl of Carrick, lord of the Isles and great steward of Scotland. James acquired his own household in 1696 under the control of James Drummond, 4th earl of Perth. Alongside his father, young James represented the Stuarts' future hopes, and in 1695 Nicolas de Largillière captured this potential when he painted the prince, breeched and formally dressed in a red suit with his Garter ribbon (fig. 5.15). The presence of a new Stuart family was reinforced by the birth of a daughter and Andrew Hay related to his nephew Sir Patrick Aikenhead, the commissary clerk of Edinburgh, how on 5 September 1692 there was 'a great solemnitie at St. Germans' for Louisa Maria's christening. Louis XIV was her godfather, the duchesse of Orleans was godmother and 'the wholle court of France was present'.[117]

James had simpler, loving relationships with his illegitimate children, as his letters from Edinburgh to Charlotte Lee, countess of Lichfield

5.15 Nicolas de Largillière, *Prince James Francis Edward Stuart and His Sister Princess Louisa Maria Theresa Stuart*, 1695. Oil on canvas, 192.8 × 145.7 cm. National Portrait Gallery, London. James Francis Edward wears his own hair, rather than a wig, but his lace and ribbon cravat, elegant suit, tricorne hat and sword are in the French style.

indicate.[118] His sons included James FitzJames, 1st duke of Berwick (1670–1734), his son with Arabella Churchill, who was brought up in France. Lord Perth relayed a rumour circulating in Scotland in September 1687 that there were plans to 'have His Grace the Duke of Berwick Considder'd As other than his majestys naturall son'. However, Perth believed that 'The King is too just to have such a thought & that sueet young man too good ever to have such a vanity'.[119] James's trust in his son was evident as he sought to recover his throne, and in November 1689 the king assured General Cannon that 'Wee have resolved to send our Right Trusty & intirely beloved Natural son the Duke of Berwyck to your ayde'.[120] James's sons, legitimate and illegitimate, proved loyal to their father and helped sustain Stuart style as it developed into Jacobite style.

Playing Multiple Parts: James's Relationship with Disguise

Disguise played a very significant role in James's life in moments of need. Like Charles, he too had his great escape from Cromwell when he slipped the leash in 1648 dressed as a girl. Anne, lady Halkett, recounted in her memoirs how she received 'the bigness of the duke's waist and his length to have clothes made fit for him', adding:

> when I gave the measure to my tailor to enquire how much mohair would serve to make a petticoat and waistcoat to a young gentlewoman of that bigness and stature, he considered it a long time and said he had made many gowns and suits, but he had never made any to such a person in his life ... his meaning was, he had never seen any woman of so low a stature have so big a waist.[121]

In spite of his doubts, the tailor made the scarlet petticoat that the prince wore with a waistcoat of black- and hair-colour mohair. His uncommon clothing nearly gave him away when the owner of the barge taking him to France saw him 'laying his leg upon the table, and plucking up his stocking in so unwomanish a manner'.[122] Gossip reported in Scotland asserted that 'the Duke of York is gone from St. James betwine eight and nyne of the clocke and it is constantlie reported that he is eithere gone for holland or for Wales'.[123] James's need for disguise continued during this first period of time he spent in exile. For instance, when he arrived in Brussels in 1659 he 'enter'd privately into the Town' and on receiving news that he was to go to Calais to meet Charles 'he made no longer stay than just to put on his disguise, in which he was resolved to go to England'.[124] On reaching Calais, a rumour circulated that he was 'there in disguise'.[125] Henri, viscount de Turenne, lent him 300 pistoles and encouraged him to return to Brussels.[126]

James went into exile for a second time in March 1679 as a consequence of the Popish Plot, hoping that 'God would give me his grace to suffer death for the true Catholic religion as well as banishment'.[127] When Charles II was taken ill unexpectedly in late August, James 'left Brussels in a disguise of a black perruque only and a plain stuff suit without his Star and Garter'.[128] It is telling that the removal of the Garter was considered sufficient of a change to his appearance to make James blend in. He also demonstrated a wish for anonymity as an expression of his humility when he visited the English Benedictine priory in Paris. It was raining and he wore a cloak so that the porter 'taking him only for a Gentleman [and] not aware of his Star ... trudged to acquaint [the] worthy superior ... The King followed him into the Cloister ... where H.M.'s great Piety took great delight in the pleasantness of the mistake'.[129] This wish to worship freely, and being prepared to take risks in order to do so, means that James would have understood the motivation that drove the Covenanter preacher, Alexander Peden (1626–86), who wore a wig and a mask with a false moustache and beard to protect his identity.[130] Both men demonstrate the significance of guising in Scotland and the world of the Stuart kings.

Conclusions

Although James VII and II had the shortest reign of the later Stuart kings, his time as king and the years preceding it were very significant. For James personally, the high point of his political career was his time in Scotland. While there he made a surprisingly positive impact, and afterwards he played an important part in promoting Scottish interests at Westminster. However, James's kingship also demonstrates the significant challenges that he and all of the Stuarts faced as a consequence of ruling multiple kingdoms. For James, this was exacerbated, as it had been for his great-grandmother Mary, by his Catholicism, which alienated him from many of his subjects. In addition, as Alasdair Raffe has argued, after 1688 the people of the three Stuart kingdoms had a choice between James, their *de jure* sovereign, and William and Mary, the *de facto* monarchs, and many chose William.[131]

James was much more ambitious in his use of portraiture than his brother, demonstrating a personal interest in his image and the freedom available to the heir to the throne. Henri Gascar portrayed James as a Roman emperor or general, giving lustre to his post as admiral (fig. 5.16). This style resonated with his Scottish subjects, including John, 1st marquis of Atholl, in 1680, and Archibald, 1st duke of Argyll with his sons John and Archibald in 1689, who were painted in the same way.[132] However, in terms of his contribution to Stuart style, prior to his accession James echoed his brother in favouring French taste and fashion. His own clothes between 1685 and 1689 were more conservative than his brothers' and cheaper than William's, and set the style that William followed. James's most important contributions were made after 1688. On a personal level he made use of disguise to change or conceal his appearance, which he took one step further as part of his image as a penitent. In the context of his three kingdoms, his last period of exile divided opinion and resulted in two stands of Stuart style – his own and the counter-style of William III and the Williamites. The circumstances in which James lost his thrones ensured that a new strand of Stuart style developed in the eighteenth century, one that would visually define the Jacobite cause in Scotland and in which jewellery played a central role.[133] The part played by jewellery in Stuart fashion and the Jacobite legacy is central to Scottish demonstrations of male agency, which is a key theme in Part II.

5.16 Henri Gascar, *James Duke of York*, 1672–3. Oil on canvas, 229 × 173 cm. National Maritime Museum, Greenwich, London. Combining classical imagery with the Stuart's love of guising, James set a short-lived portraiture style when he was painted in Roman-style dress.

PART II

CREATING THE STUART LOOK

STUART STYLE OFFERS THE READER a story of Scottish cultural influence and agency, and in Part II, the narrative moves beyond the Stuart kings.[1] While the royal body was perfect for displaying fashionable clothes, a large group of craftsmen, -women and merchants was essential for the creation and maintenance of the king's wardrobe. The tricky question of what to wear, and when, was not restricted to royal palaces, as is clear from the advice Sir Robert Gordon gave to his nephew, John, earl of Sutherland in *c.*1620. The ideas Robert put forward, along with the words he used, were reminiscent of those found in James VI's *Basilikon Doron* on the one hand, and the work of the English poet and writer Henry Peacham (1578–*c.*1644) on the other. He urged John to be 'not superfluous in your rayment lyk a deboshed waster', adding that his clothes should be 'rather meane, to change often, then costlie to keip them long and out of fashion; keeping the seasons of the yeir and of your age'.[2] Most interesting was the need to be well dressed at 'hie tymes' and when the Scottish parliament met, offset with the caveat that John should 'repair to parliaments als rarlie as yow can'. The following three chapters demonstrate the role of Scots within the Great Wardrobe, Wardrobe of the Robes and in the Office of the King's Tailor in shaping Stuart style, regardless of which side of the border the court was located. The Stuarts used Scottish, English and European materials for their clothes and accessories, the most significant of which was jewellery.

(page 150) See figure 7.5.

A Tale of Two Stuart Cities: Edinburgh and London

The location of the Stuart court, which had a direct bearing on how accessible it was, changed dramatically with the move to London in 1603, so much so that David Stevenson has claimed that Scotland was a country without a court after this time.[3] By implication, the ramifications of such a change were profound for the elite, as well as for the merchants and craftsmen who supplied them with fashionable clothing, and on the sartorial reputation of Edinburgh. However, Julian Goodare's view that, in both the short and long terms the absence of the court and monarch had a much less drastic impact on Edinburgh, and Scotland as a whole, is compelling, and one that is borne out in the following chapters.[4] Indeed, as Goodare has argued, the absentee Stuart monarchy offered the Scottish elite greater latitude than their English counterparts, and it was a freedom that they exploited sartorially as well as politically.[5]

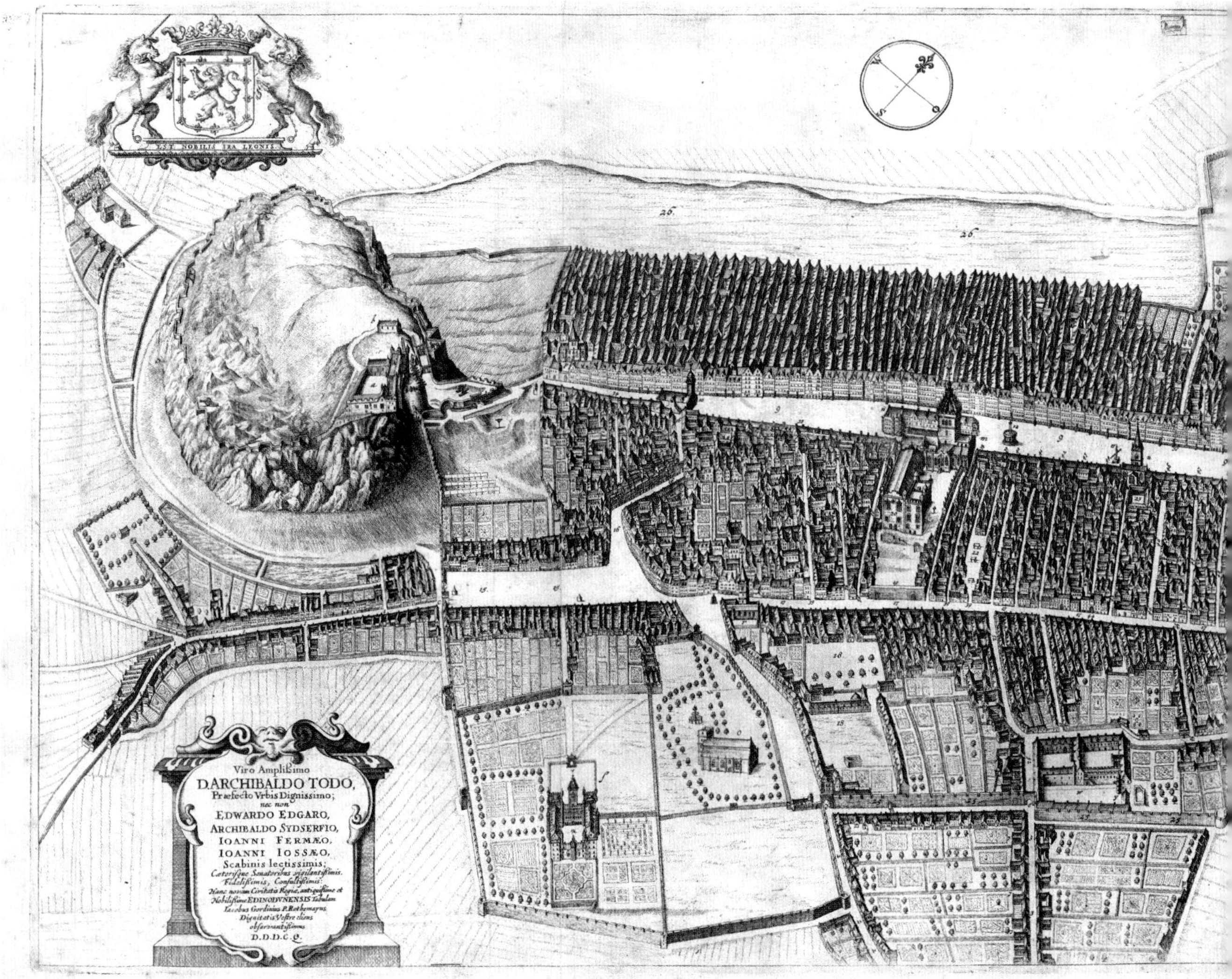

Edinburgh and London were capitals and court cities and these qualities dictated how people decided to dress when they were there. The distinctive shape and topography of Edinburgh is clear in the bird's-eye view produced in 1647 by James Gordon of Rothiemay, as is the size and sense of a bustling place of business (fig. II.1). Such a city always provoked a range of opinions about the merits of urban living, and in January 1634 Archibald Campbell of Glencarradale hoped that the 8th laird of Glenorchy could 'remain out of Edinburgh, where there is nothing but vanity and vexation of spirit'.[6] In contrast, half a century later, David Erskine, 4th lord Cardross, wrote from Edinburgh in December 1695 berating Sir Alexander Jardine, saying, 'I think it very strange that you keep the Country so close & so long at a season when every body almost is in toun & the country has nothing that is agreeable or pleasant'.[7] Cardross was not alone in promoting the virtues of city life.

II.1 James Gordon of Rothiemay, *Bird's Eye View of Edinburgh*, 1647, printed by W. and A. K. Johnston, c. 1870. 35 × 72 cm. National Library of Scotland. Gordon's view of Edinburgh is dominated by the castle on the left, Holyroodhouse on the right and the main processional route between the two.

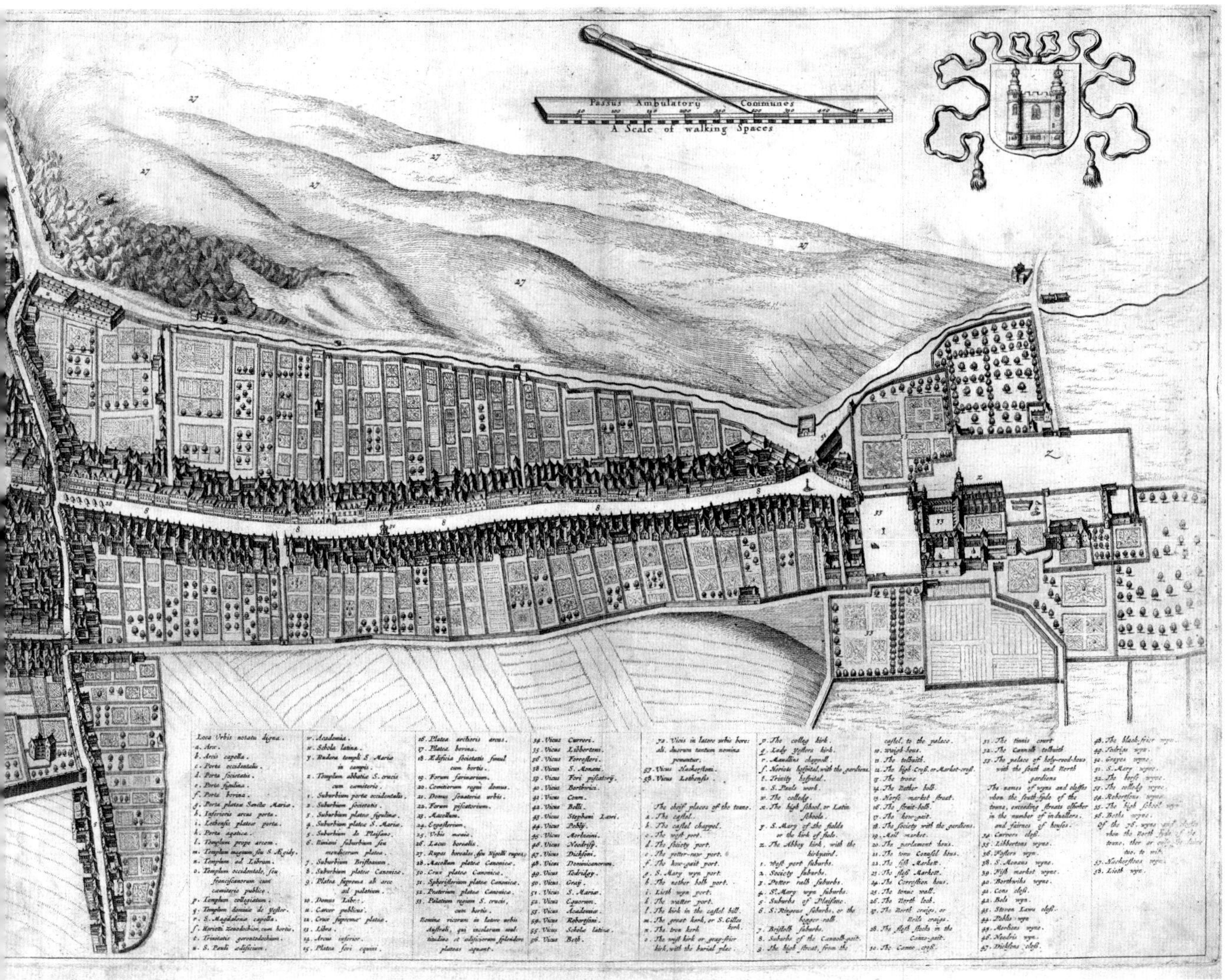

II.2 Wenceslaus Hollar, *London from Arundel House*, 1643. Etching, 7.8 × 13.3 cm. Metropolitan Museum of Art, New York. From their broad-brimmed hats to their boots, the men here are displaying their engagement with Stuart fashion.

In parallel to the development of Edinburgh, London grew in importance during the reign of James VI and I as the setting for court culture in the three kingdoms.[8] Hollar's London panorama gives a sense of the city's size by 1647, while his more intimate view, illustrated here, drawn from the perspective of Arundel House, shows well-dressed men enjoying a stroll by the river (fig. II.2).[9] The city of London and the suburb of Westminster played a significant role in the formation of the Stuarts' fashion narratives, providing, as they did, an ever-expanding pool of suppliers of clothing and textiles and customers keen to purchase their goods. During the course of the seventeenth century London developed as the arbiter of fashionable ideas, and this was reflected in the shopping patterns of Scots and English alike, including the high-born 3rd duke and duchess of Hamilton, and Samuel and Elizabeth Jeake of Rye, who came from the middling sort.[10]

Seventeenth-Century Ideas about Stuart Fashion

As noted above, Sir Robert Gordon evidently felt knowledgeable enough about fashion to give guidance on the topic, so raising the question of where an interested, well-informed Scottish gentleman acquired such opinions. One option was fashion dolls, but dolls dressed in the most recent styles were mostly aimed at women.[11] Certainly almost all surviving examples are female with the exception of 'Lord Clapham', and there is some debate over whether 'he' was a fashion doll (fig. II.3).[12] Fashion plates were also a possibility. Samuel Pepys started buying French prints in 1670, and these included the 'Habits de France d'environ l'année 1670 d'entre les Années 1693 & 1696, l'une et l'autre incluse'.[13] While Louis XIV used fashion plates as a means of self-promotion, many of the early examples are of women, suggesting a primarily female audience here too (fig. II.4).[14]

A third potential source of information were the newsletters and newspapers that were sold by subscription. The latter included *Mercurius Caledonius* produced in 1661 by the stylish Thomas Sydserff, the *London Gazette* from 1665 and the *Edinburgh Gazette* that flourished briefly in the spring and summer of 1699.[15] While their fashion content was limited, they demonstrate the thirst for news in Scotland, as is evident from John Kirkwood's promise to send a *Gazette* from London to Sir John Campbell, 10th laird and 4th baronet of Glenorchy (1606/7–1686) in February 1672.[16] By the 1690s copies of the *Gazette* dated at Whitehall were being reprinted in Edinburgh.[17] Information travelled in both directions, with Scots in London consulting the publication for news of home, and on 15 September 1691 Sir John Campbell of Glenorchy reported from London to Barcaldine, his chamberlain, that 'I find it in the Gazet that non of the Highlanders hav taken the Indemnitie wherat many rejoyse'.[18]

Best placed to give their male customers advice on what to wear were tailors, mercers, drapers and haberdashers, and discerning individuals like Pepys exploited their services to the full. On 23 April 1669 the diarist went 'to the Exchange and [he] helped me to chose a summer-suit of coloured Camelott, coat and breeches, and a flowered tabby vest, very rich'.[19] Men higher up the social hierarchy asked friends to consult the tailors of the men above them. On 6 December 1679, for example, Francis Gwyn informed Edward Conway, 1st earl of Conway (1623–83) that he had visited 'Lord Ranelagh's tailor to-day and have bespoke two suits for you', one for riding and the other of black cloth, 'with the waistcoat, sleeves and breeches to be laced with a new fashion black and white bone lace'.[20] Not surprisingly, the role of tailors in spreading new ideas was not always seen in a positive light. In 1620 the author of *Hic Mulier* blamed tailors for the recent trend of women adopting male fashions, such as the doublet, which he termed a

II.3 Doll known as 'Lord Clapham', 1690–1700. Turned, carved, gessoed and painted wood, wool, linen, silk, and human hair. Victoria and Albert Museum, London. Fashion doll or not, Lord Clapham is dressed as the quintessential fashionable gentleman.

II.4 Wenceslaus Hollar, *Muffs and Articles of Clothing on a Table*, 1647. Etching, 10.8 × 20.3 cm. Metropolitan Museum of Art, New York. Hollar presents the viewer with a range of fashionable accessories worn by men and women, including fur muffs, gloves and lace collars.

'new disguise'. The tailor's craft metamorphosed acceptable male garments into unacceptable female fashions.[21]

Passing on fashionable clothes to others played an important role in spreading ideas about clothing styles. Anthony Wood recorded how 'Endymion Porter, Esq., ... a servant of the King, a person also of most generous spirit' gave Robert Dover 'some of the King's old clothes, with a hat and feather and ruff purposely to grace him and consequently his solemnity'.[22] In this instance, clothes passed from James VI and I to Porter and then to Dover, and from the court to the Cotswold Olympic Games held at Whitsun 1610, where Dover played a key role. While these luxurious hand-me-downs helped spread knowledge of court fashions, ultimately, word of mouth, whether in person or contained in letters, was vital for the circulation of male knowledge of Stuart fashions.

Being Fashionable

The Stuarts were keen to set the fashion and their Scottish subjects, in turn, discussed what was in vogue. Accessories formed a key part of any male outfit and their changing style was carefully noted. In 1642 Sir Robert Campbell, 9th laird, 3rd baronet of Glenorchy (*c.*1575–1657) bought a range of items from Andrew Reid, a merchant trading in Perth, including two dozen new fashioned points (fig. II.5).[23] When James Campbell sent a group of items from Edinburgh to Henry Cheristy of Cragtoune in 1659, they were all 'of the best and newest fashion', unlike fringed belts, which were dismissed as old news.[24] This interest in the fashionable was also evident in the 1701 accounts of the barony of Lude, which included payment for a pair of buckles 'fashionable' for shoes.[25]

New trimmings were also essential, as Michael Young's letter of October 1654 to the countess of Lothian reveals. Having explained that her sons 'will be as frugal as honesty will permit', he adds that 'their suits, though plain, must be in the fashion with ribbons and other things'.[26] Subtle seasonal changes in trimmings were carefully observed, so in January 1665 the laird of Glenorchy paid for 12 dozen 'fine new fashioned mandell buttons' purchased from Alexander Ranken, a merchant in Perth.[27]

How did individuals get fashionable items? One option was to employ people who knew what was in favour, as in 1676 when the 10th laird of Glenorchy asked a cousin to send Mr Patrick Campbell's widow to James Row's shop 'wher shee is to get camrick to maik cravatts of the newest fashion of plain ons which ar not to imitat laiced ons and send 3 yards of camrick for handkurchifs to me'.[28] Another was to receive regular updates from someone who had impeccable judgement. In May 1671 Mr Campbell assured the 10th laird of Glenorchy at Balloch that 'light hair stuff quhairof the coat very short & the breeches narow the justicoat plaine without lace of flour'd silk stuff unstript & the hatts very

II.5 George Jamesone, *Sir Robert Campbell of Glenorchy with Sir Robert Campbell*, after 1640. Oil on canvas, 107 × 128.6 cm. National Galleries of Scotland. The elegant dress of Sir Robert and his son, which Jamesone captures, was the product of the knowledgeable shopping recorded in the family's letters.

brod' was the height of fashion in Edinburgh.[29]

Benchmarks of fashionability were set by the court and reflected by individuals who chose to follow royal style. Alice Smith sent Lady Jane Digby Gerard 'a suite of flourished gauze as fashionable as any lady in London does wear' in August 1689, along with pictures of William and Mary for her son.[30] However, not everyone felt that the newest look was desirable, preferring to stick with what they knew and liked. The earl of Breadalbane was one such man who prized the familiar over the fashionable. In December 1690 he was quite certain about how he wanted his new coat to look, stating firmly that 'I will hav no buttons abov the arms in the sleevs but under in the old fashion'.[31] Then again, some were aware of the sartorial failings of their wardrobe, as was the case with William Littill who sent a hat to his brother Edward, a merchant in Paris, in 1613. He noted that 'my caster quhlk beand out of faschion I thocht not meit to keip it and I culd not get it sauld have and reformit it. I wald ye suld put it away the best ye may' and asked for a replacement of Spanish wool.[32]

Even so, being male and fashionable was not always a good thing because being well dressed could conceal a lack of useful masculine skills such as military ability. Lord Archibald Hamilton certainly thought this was the case in July 1695 when he wrote to the earl of Arran. Two days earlier Hamilton had captured a French privateer with ten guns that belonged to the 'Postilion' of Saint-Malo. The reasons for his success, Hamilton declared, were twofold. First, the vessel was only carrying a little powder and shot, and second, the captain was 'a very prittey fellow' and his crew 'so many men of fashion' who did not put up much of a fight.[33] John Evelyn described one such 'man of fashion' in *Tyrannus* in 1661 as 'a fine silken thing' that he saw 'walking th'other day through Westminster Hall that had as much ribbon about him as would have plundered six shops and set up twenty country pedlars' (fig. II.6).[34] Being a fashion victim could damage your reputation as well as your pocket.

Creating a Seasonal, Fashionable Stuart Wardrobe

II.6 This suit, consisting of a doublet and petticoat breeches of cream figured silk and associated with Edmund or Mun Verney, epitomises the style that Evelyn is mocking. c.1660–62. Verney Collection, Claydon House, Buckinghamshire.

Getting fashionable clothing right, however, usually enhanced a man's social position, and à la mode dress meant engaging with the idea of a seasonal wardrobe. Clothes needed to reflect the changes in temperature that the seasons brought in the Scottish and English climate. Hints of this can be seen in Thomas Dekker and Thomas Middleton's *The Roaring Girl* (1601), which mentions clothes made of 'a kind of light-colour summer stuff', while Hollar's fashionable women in winter clothes wore furs to keep them warm (fig. II.7).[35] In keeping with this pattern, Pepys tended to wear silk in the summer and wool in the winter and on 29 September 1667 he specifically linked this to the seasons when he wrote 'up and put off first my summer's silk suit and put on a cloth one' to mark the start of autumn.[36]

Scottish men followed a similar pattern, as is evident from the letters sent by Alexander Campbell of Auchinrire to his uncle Sir Colin Campbell of Glenorchy while Campbell was at school in Dundee. Alexander had a clear sense of ordering clothes according to the needs of the seasons. This was very much linked to the change in temperature rather than reflecting changes in fashion, although this may also have been a consideration. In September 1633 he asked for winter clothes.[37] As none were forthcoming he wrote again adding that he needed them because 'the weather is cold in that country'.[38] At the start of April 1634 he announced that he would require his summer clothes at Easter.[39] A month later they had arrived, and were made of 'thik cloth becaus that thine stuffe wold be very unlestie & slycht' in the bracing Dundee summer.[40] The need for warm winter clothes was an important feature of a letter sent nearly 20 years later by the earl of Kinghorne. He and his servant kept warm in St Andrews with a delivery of clothing in November.[41]

Clothes also followed a pattern of change every season, each of which brought the consumer a new range of colours and patterns for fabrics and trimmings. When John Clarke advised the laird of Dean in 1682 about his 'fine flowered justicoat', this may have included a careful discussion of the most recent floral designs.[42] Such decisions reveal that the consumer had a choice, and there are hints of how this worked in the royal wardrobe. On the one hand, choice was given to the consumer (in this case the king), usually in the form of samples of trimmings or embroidery patterns. For instance, in September 1606 John Parr and William Broderick provided two sets of embroidery samples on velvet costing 44s to James VI and I.[43] Then in 1662–3 Francis Manby received 40s 'for divers patterns of gold and silver lace' and 30s for 'Patterns of black Flanders bone lace'.[44] This was also the case with large, expensive furnishings such as the new bed made for the king's bedchamber at Whitehall in May 1678. The bed, with its matching wall hangings, chairs, stools, and door curtains, was to be made of crimson damask fringed with silk fringe 'as his Majesty shall like'.[45] The following year the king's closet at Windsor was decorated with flowered silk 'as his Majestie shall make choice of'.[46] This level of royal involvement could extend to diplomatic gifts for favoured individuals, and in 1672 the mercer Richard Alchorn received £150 in 'ready money' for a quantity of scarlet Morella mohair that his majesty 'made choice of and gave unto Monsieur Colbert'.[47] On the other hand, there was an element of flexibility given to royal suppliers, especially after the Restoration. Orders for clothes often used vague wording, in relation to colour in particular, such as stating that a particular suit would be in 'a sad colour'. As this term encompassed any muted shade, this gave them the option to supply a 'sad' colour that they had in stock or one that was in fashion.

II.7 Wenceslaus Hollar, *The Winter Habit of ane English Gentlewoman*, 1644. Etching, 20.4 × 9.8 cm. Metropolitan Museum of Art, New York. With her stylish hood, vizard, tippet, lace collar and large fur muff, this elegant woman is very eye-catching. Two decades later Pepys was not above borrowing his wife's fur muff when he wanted to be seen with the latest accessory.

The use of samples to allow customers to exercise choice when purchasing material is also evident among Scottish consumers. Margaret Bissit wrote on behalf of her husband, Andrew Reid, to the 8th laird of Glenorchy in 1638, sending him samples as desired of various materials with prices. She offered any sort of silk stuffs, either black or coloured, adding 'praissed be god we neid not go to no neighbour to seik it'.[48] Furnishings were bought in the same way. Thus, Anthony Crackerode, a draper of St Paul's, Covent Garden, arranged to deliver 150 yards crimson broadcloth 'agreeable to [the] Patterne already delivered to his lordship', at a price of £169 5s to James, marquis of Montrose.[49] The alternative was to use existing garments as a template, and in 1689 Henry Balfour advised David, earl of Leven, to 'send up the stokings you desyr with your own seall on them' for the knitters in Aberdeen to work from.[50] The next chapter explores how Stuart men, both Scottish and English, selected their clothes and dressed in the royal style.

CHAPTER SIX

Choice and the Stuart Male Consumer

A SET OF LATE SEVENTEENTH-CENTURY men's cloths recovered from a bog on the Barrock Estate, near Keiss, Caithness, provides a rare opportunity to study an ensemble as worn from head to toe.[1] Wool predominates from the bonnet to the coat, jacket, breiks, plaid and stockings, and most or all is likely to have been Scottish. The same is true of a similar set of finds made at Gunnister in Shetland (fig. 6.1).[2] Both sets of garments contrast with the clothes chosen in Edinburgh in 1606 by Colin Campbell, fiar of Glenorchy. Campbell's new wardrobe combined imported silks with home-produced cloth and linen in items for everyday wear and more formal occasions. A doublet and breiks of 'cannie' fustian, with the collar and pickadil (a separate support for the ruff or band) made from Spanish taffeta and lined with 'tueill', represents the former. The breiks were lined with plaiding and reinforced at the knee with 'bukasie'. The latter consisted of a black satin doublet and breiks and a velvet cloak.[3] All of these garments represent a sequence of choices made by their respective owner about what type of suit they wanted or needed. Considerations such as cost, availability, fashionability and the type of garment required influenced a person's decisions. And the decisions did not end there, because the suits were incomplete without a range of accessories, whether they were bespoke items or off the peg. Once the items were purchased they could be worn in a variety of combinations, so creating multiple outfits that were subtly different.

The king was the most important Stuart consumer, although the clothing he purchased had much in common with that purchased

6.1 *(above)* Brown wool jacket found at Gunnister, Shetland, late 17th century. National Museum of Scotland.

(facing page) See figure 6.9.

by the wider male elite. He had access to a group of suppliers and craftsmen and -women who aimed to provide the best of what was available at the time. So, satin dominated James VI and I's London suit orders. Most used satin for the doublet and breeches but on occasion it was combined with cloth, cloth of gold and velvet. If not satin, velvet and grosgrain were also in vogue. However, by the reign of James VII and II cloth reigned supreme, followed by camlet, with other fabrics used very rarely. The most popular linings were rateen, crêpe and taffeta. In other words, this 90-year period witnessed a shift from silk to wool for the outer fabric, while retaining silk for fancy linings for coats to add colour and glamour.

Although the king and his court set the fashionable male standard, this became couched in a discourse relating cloth and national identity, on the one hand, and to anxieties about the cost and luxurious nature of silk, on the other.

John Evelyn encouraged Charles II to set the tone by wearing home-produced goods and avoiding European imports. The king obliged in 1673, stating that 'by his own example' he would 'encourage the constant wearing of the manufacturers of His own kingdom … excepting all foreign points in bands and sweet gloves or fans which cannot be found in this kingdom'.[4] Charles ultimately failed as a role model, but James Butler, 1st duke of Ormonde (1610–88), was more successful. As viceroy of Ireland, Butler encouraged the purchase and wearing of local fabrics, in particular Irish frieze, poplin and linen.[5] Lauderdale did not attempt the same in Scotland, and Sir George Mackenzie in *Aretina* (1660) condemned the court as a source of luxury so that 'the mony which the poor country men buy with their sweat, must be sold for silk and spices' (fig. 6.2).[6] 30 years later he went further, complaining in 'A discourse concerning the Three Unions 'twist Scotland and England' that his fellow Scots 'carry our Money to England' to buy 'spices, silks and other commodities' that 'we may not only want, but likewise we are the worse for having'.[7] While revealing concerns about consumerism, the views of Evelyn and Mackenzie also stress the importance of men as consumers of fashion who went shopping for themselves, their families and their homes, all of which were decked out in variants of Stuart style, the key theme explored in this chapter.

6.2 After Sir Godfrey Kneller, *Sir George Mackenzie*. Oil on canvas, 73.2 × 61.8 cm. National Library of Scotland. While Mackenzie complained about luxury, he was not above wearing fashionable dress.

Textiles and the Royal Consumer: The Role of the Stuart Wardrobes

Throughout the seventeenth century there were two royal wardrobes or textile stores, one in Edinburgh and the other in London. They had many qualities in common, but as the Edinburgh wardrobe declined in importance after James's departure in 1603, so Scots started to run the London site. However, prior to 1603 the Scottish royal wardrobe was an important part of the household, supplying clothes and furnishings for the monarch, and it came under the financial control of the Treasurer. The officers of the wardrobe cared for the fabrics stored there, as in 1566 when Balthazar Hullin, valet of the queen's chamber, received materials for packaging and looking after the wardrobe.[8] On occasion things went missing, as during the early years of James's minority, when James, lord of Torphichen, acquired bed hangings, tapestries and books from the royal wardrobe that had to be recovered in the summer of 1573.[9] Six years later James sent James Murray, master of the wardrobe, to Elizabeth I and his journey cost £766 13s 4d.[10] He was dispatched again the following year, when his expenses came to £266 13s 4d.[11] Murray also paid £321 for three garments of cloth of gold silk and silver damask bought from the merchant James Dalziell.[12] As Murray's keepership demonstrates, the wardrobe dealt with large sums of money, and this continued under his successor Sir William Keith, who was in post by 1587.[13] In 1590 Sir William made a part-payment of 10,000 merks to Robert Jousie, merchant burgess of Edinburgh, for silks 'to the apperrelying of our awin bedye'.[14] Jousie continued to be the key royal supplier as revealed by the accounts of Sir George Home from 1590/2, 1594/6 and 1596/1600.[15]

After 1603 the wardrobe stopped making the king's clothes but the keeper continued to oversee the furnishings in the palace of Holyroodhouse and other royal properties. It was next called upon seriously for James's visit in 1617, when its holdings included 20 sets of hangings, 80 small carpets, 3 furnish bedsteads, 120 pairs of Holland 'Scheittes', 60 pairs of 'Wollen blankettes', 40 pairs of 'fustian blankettes', 6 'Clothes of Stait' and 10 'beir hydes and taut canveses for carriages'.[16] Another list from *c.*1617 included 'damask of xx shilling the yard for the kingis table'.[17] The wardrobe offered secure storage and in 1622 John, earl of Mar, was authorised by the privy council to deliver the king's silver plate to John Auchmuty of Scoughall, master of the wardrobe.[18] In April 1624 the king wrote to the earl of Mar, treasurer, and Sir Archibald Napier, treasurer depute, about the fees of keepers of tapestry and moveable goods in the king's wardrobe in Scotland.[19] The year after his Scottish coronation, Charles I issued instructions for the disposal of the king's wardrobe, but this did not mark the end.[20]

In 1685 Patrick Murray, 3rd lord Elibank, drew up his will and appointed John Auchmuty, master of the wardrobe, and Peter Murray, a merchant in Edinburgh, as tutors to his son.[21] The same year the inventory of His Majesty's goods in the wardrobe, council chamber and session house in the custody of John Auchmuty, master of the wardrobe, included a crimson velvet cloth of state and another of blue flowered.[22] The wardrobe continued after the accession of William III and Mary II with Samuel McAdam appointed as clerk of the wardrobe in June 1691, and Walter Stirling was in post in the early 1700s.[23]

In a similar way, the Great Wardrobe had played an important part in making clothes for the English monarch and his family, livery for the king's household and furnishings for the royal palaces since 1359. The keeper had a substantial budget and oversaw large-scale purchases of wool, silk and linen. The choices the keeper made helped to shape the fashionable world of the king and his court, and the post was held by a number of Scots after James's accession – men who helped to develop and perpetuate Stuart style. Elizabeth's last keeper, Sir John Fortescue, served up to 1603.[24] He was replaced by Sir George Home, later earl of Dunbar, who had been master of the king's wardrobe in Scotland from 1601 (fig. 6.3).[25] Two years later, the justices of the peace of London were asked to assist him in taking up workmen and provisions for the Great Wardrobe at reasonable prices.[26] By the time of the 1606/7 account Dunbar had been succeeded by Sir Roger Aston. English by birth, Aston had been brought up in Scotland and he was a close confidant of James VI.[27] On his death, the wardrobe owed Aston nearly £12,000.[28]

6.3 Unknown artist, *George Hume, 1st Earl of Dunbar*, 1610. Oil on canvas, 124.5 × 100 cm. Paxton House, Berwick-upon-Tweed. Elegant in a white suit of the style favoured by the king.

In April 1607 James Hay received a reversion in the office, and the position became vacant in March 1613.[29] The wardrobe was the ideal location for him to operate from. On 16 February 1617 Chamberlain informed Dudley Carleton that the previous night the duke of Lennox feasted the French ambassador in the king's presence 'and this night he is solemnly invited by the Lord Hay to the Wardrobe to a supper and a Masque'.[30] Hay was the last of the Scottish keepers and his successor, Sir Lionel Cranfield, was a very successful English silk merchant who brought his knowledge of textiles to the office in 1618.[31] When Cranfield was accused of fraud in 1624 he declared that he had bought 'cloth of gold, silver and tissues, my velvets, satins, damasks, and taffetas, and my hangings, carpets and all other things of value of the merchants at the first and best hand with ready money and charged His Majesty with no other prices than I paid them'.[32]

He was followed by William Feilding, 1st earl of Denbigh and brother-in-law of the duke of Buckingham. He was appointed as master of the Great Wardrobe in January 1622, made a gentleman of the bedchamber, and his daughter Mary married James Hamilton, marquis of Arran, so linking him to one of the leading Scottish families at court.[33] Even so, Feilding was frequently absent from the wardrobe, travelling to Spain in 1623 with Charles and Buckingham and then undertaking a series of naval postings from 1625. From January 1631 to August 1633 he journeyed to India and Persia, and the influence of the former was evident in the distinctive style he wore for his portrait by Van Dyck painted in *c.*1633–4 (fig. 6.4).[34]

From Feilding's tenure onwards, the office was held by Englishmen and one example serves to demonstrate how they fared. Sir Edward Montagu, later 1st earl of Sandwich (1625–1671/2), was appointed at the Restoration. Montagu had supported Cromwell but prospered under Charles II.[35] On 27 November 1660 Pepys went 'to Whitehall where I find my lord gone abroad to the wardrobe whither he doth now go every other morning and doth seem to resolve to understand and look after that business himself'.[36] However, Montagu ran into difficulties with the wardrobe's finances and on 15 July 1664 Pepys noted that 'he hath been at great charges in getting things to this pass in his estate … he says he hath now evened his reckonings at the wardrobe till Michelmas last and hopes to finish it to lady day before he goes'.[37] Whether in Scottish or English hands, the Great Wardrobe played an important role in reinforcing trends in which fabrics were fashionable.

6.4 Sir Anthony van Dyck, *William Feilding, 1st Earl of Denbigh*, c.1633–4. Oil on canvas, 247.5 × 148.5 cm. National Gallery, London. Feilding is dressed in an Indian-style jacket that also incorporates elements of the fashionable doublet, and loose 'trousers' of the pyjamas type.

Stuart Royal Suppliers

Linked to the royal wardrobes were the clusters of craftsmen and -women and suppliers working for the monarch, their spouse, siblings and children. The seventeenth century saw the rise of the king's woollen draper, linen draper, mercer, haberdasher and laceman, among others. Such people were the supplier of choice for their particular products, thereby giving them a small 'monopoly'. By the 1670s some received a salary in addition to the profit on their sales, making these very desirable positions to hold.[38] So much so, that in December 1682 Joseph

Hindermarsh, stationer, and Edward Hayes, skinner, applied for 'the honour to be called his Royal Majesty's tradesmen'.[39]

Part of the appeal of the Stuarts, from the point of view of the hopeful artificer, was that there were several royal households, resulting in parallel sets of craftspeople, including Edmund Harrison, embroiderer to Charles I, and John Shepley, embroiderer to Charles II as prince of Wales.[40] These groups of makers and suppliers did not have to be mutually exclusive, and individuals could move from one master to another, as the cutler Robert South did. When Prince Henry died, South became cutler to James I. Similarly, leading figures like George Villiers shared suppliers with the king.[41]

Many of the royal suppliers and craftsmen and -women were English, such as the goldsmith and banker, Sir Robert Vyner (fig. 6.5).[42] His family portrait captures a sense of his undeniable wealth but nevertheless his clothes are a step away from those worn by the court elite. He worked alongside men and women of many other nationalities. The accession of James VI and I, and the Restoration of his grandson prompted the migration of Scottish craftsmen and -women and merchants to London. While only a small number entered royal service, most made a good living with the Scottish courtiers as their key clients. A number of French artisans and merchants worked for Charles I and Charles II prompting

6.5 John Michael Wright, *The Family of Sir Robert Vyner*, 1673. Oil on canvas, 144.8 × 195.6 cm. National Portrait Gallery, London. Sir Robert Vyner is dressed in a loose robe or nightgown tied with a sash, while his son wears a vest with elbow-length sleeves and breeches.

the Puritan William Prynne to link Henrietta Maria's reluctance to give up French style after her marriage to the increase in popularity of foreign styles in England.[43] Lucy Hutchinson went further, observing that 'a French queen never brought any happiness to England'.[44] However, not everyone agreed with her and in 1642 'many thousands of courtiers, citizens, gentlemens and trades-mens wives inhabiting within the cities of London and Westminster' drew up a petition 'concerning the staying of the Queenes intended voyage into Holland' and the negative impact this would have on their businesses.[45]

A third wave of foreign suppliers tied to tastes of the royal family appeared after the accession of William and Mary, who were followed from The Hague by an influx of Dutch craftsmen and -women.[46] However, their presence was evident earlier and in 1672 Charles II appealed to 'subjects of the United Provinces of the Netherlands' to move to England 'paying only native customs' on the goods they brought with them. In return they would receive 'all privileges and freedoms of a natural born subject'.[47]

The fashionable and the upwardly mobile looked to royal suppliers to give them an edge in the sartorial world. Samuel Pepys bought fabric from the draper, Sir William Turner, who was also a royal supplier and a relative by marriage to the diary writer. However, there were dangers attached to serving the crown and their supporters, as Thomas Morton, laceman, discovered. He sold gold and silver lace to James VII and II and members of the elite including John Drummond, earl of Melfort, who followed James into exile in December 1688. In 1691 Morton petitioned that 'some of the goods belonging to the Earl of Melfort, lately seized for their Majesties' use, may be disposed of amongst the said Earl's creditors'.[48]

One area where the Scots maintained an interest after 1603 was jewellery, a luxury commodity that was made and sold by goldsmiths and jewellers. In particular, the Edinburgh goldsmith, George Heriot, whose work was favoured by James VI and I and Anna of Denmark, excelled at styles which placed big stones in small mounts. Heriot brought this Jacobean fashion to London when he moved with the king, and it was embraced warmly by a new circle of clients (fig. 6.6). This did not mean that there was not a market for high-quality jewellery in Edinburgh, and by the 1680s and 1690s there was a cluster of jewellers based in the Canongate including William Grant, Walter Scott and Walter Graham.[49]

6.6 John Scougall, after Paul van Somer, *George Heriot*, late 1690s. Oil on canvas, 127 × 95.2 cm. George Heriot's Trust, Edinburgh. Heriot displays examples of his work, the key to his wealth and success.

London-based Scottish goldsmiths included John Campbell, whose business was at the Three Crowns, on the Strand.[50] Like many other goldsmiths, Campbell also acted as a banker, and he provided loans secured on jewels to Breadalbane in 1698.[51] However, jewellery sales were still an important part of his business, as indicated by the bills he sent to Lord Glenorchy between 1695 and 1699 for a wedding ring, a cornelian ring, a ring set round with diamonds and a hair ring.[52] During the same period Campbell sold two diamonds to set in an emerald ring, a wedding ring that later needed adjusting, and a locket set round with turquoises set in gold to the laird of Grant.[53] As these examples indicate, the choice offered by London-based goldsmiths meant that the Scottish elite often bought wedding jewels there.

The belief that James's accession in 1603 saw a legion of 'hungry Scots' descend upon London and Westminster fails to appreciate that Scots were there already, although in fairly modest numbers. The Return of Aliens lay subsidy rolls of 1568 had listed 47 Scots including John Tronyon, hat maker, and James Clarke, skinner, in the ward of Farringdon Without, and James Wylson, tailor, Garret Skotts, button maker, and George Lynse, hat maker, in Lord Montague's Liberty.[54] Indeed, by 1584 Scots had migrated in large enough numbers for there to be a vibrant Scottish community in the city, and after James's arrival another developed in Westminster.[55] So much so that by 1617, interpreters translating between Scots and English were no longer required at the port of London, because they were now 'not so far different but ane understandeth ane uther'.[56] This Scottish presence continued, ranging from a Scottish feather supplier working in 1647[57] to James Kynneir, a master weaver, probably from Edinburgh, who was named in the records of the Weavers Company in London taking an apprentice between 1665 and 1670. In 1684 his bequests included 12s for meat and drink on St Andrew's Day for poor members of the company.[58] There were also families who had been trading successfully for several generations, including James Fowles and James Heriot, Scottish goldsmiths, who were listed in the 1677 London trade directory.[59] James Fowles had links to William Paterson, who was a 'pedlar or incipient merchant', and to John Paterson. James Heriot was related to the previously mentioned George Heriot, banker, goldsmith and jeweller to James VI and I. Over the course of the seventeenth century Scots like Heriot and his family established themselves and thrived in the Stuart's new capital.

Selecting Textiles: Domestic Production and National Identity

Early in 1601 James urged the earl of Mar and Edward Bruce, 1st earl of Kinloss, to 'use all means to get me a party there [in London] and assure them that I can neither with honour nor surety disguise myself any longer'.[60] James's ambassadors and emissaries dressed with care, promoting themselves and their king as fashionable men. Bruce, for example, was a lawyer and very much looked the part in his portrait of *c.*1604, while his tomb effigy stressed his post as master of the Rolls. Mar and Bruce were successful and by 1601 there was a pro-Scottish group in London consisting of Lord Henry Howard and Lord Cecil, among others. Irish chieftain Shane O'Neill had adopted a very different strategy when he visited Elizabeth I in 1562. While he was in fashionable dress, O'Neill was accompanied by 'a troupe of Galloglassorum, who had their heads naked, and curled haire hanging on their shoulders, yellow shirts, as if they had beene died with Saffron … wide sleeues, short Cassockes, and rough hairy Clokes'.[61] As he demonstrated, choices of colour, fabric and garment type reveal a lot about a man. In this case O'Neill used characteristic Irish clothing to make his retinue stand out at the English court and in order to challenge Elizabeth's authority in Ireland.[62] Under James VI and I a similar clash of clothing styles was evident in the distinction between Scots wearing Lowland fashionable dress or Highland, national, clothing. However, perceptions change. By the death of James VII and II the plaid and tartan were becoming more fashionable and both were worn to show allegiance both to Scotland and to the king over the water.

Wool, linen and mixed fibre textiles were very important in the early modern economy of the Stuarts' three kingdoms, and loyal subjects were encouraged to wear home-produced fabrics. Each country had its own distinctive textiles ranging from English broadcloth to Scottish wadmol, a coarse woollen with a napped surface. A speciality of the Shetlands in the sixteenth and seventeenth centuries, most wadmol was exported and in 1629 the crown official sold 209 packs of 60 ells each within the Scottish islands and further afield, including Norway, for just over £1,622 Scots.[63] However, the quality was variable and when Andro Smyth sent 64 packs to Bergen in 1642 the agent reported that the locals 'complaineth much of the unsufficiency thereof'.[64] Other Scottish woollens included kelt, a coarse black or grey cloth of frieze, tuidling or tweedline, a twill weave, and plaiding, the cloth that plaids were made from.

Of these, plaiding was the most significant, especially in Glasgow and Galloway. The plaid, a length of fabric worn by men and women, was a key element of Highland dress that Sir William Brereton dismissed in 1636 as 'a garment of the same woollen stuff whereof saddle cloths in England are made'.[65] Its importance as part of the Scottish economy was confirmed in the 1641 Act of Parliament standardising the width or 'breadth of plaiden to be three quarters of an ell'.[66] From the mid seventeenth century the male elite were purchasing plaids regularly. In January 1662 Archibald Campbell wrote from London to the 10th laird of Glenorchy informing him that certain plaids had not yet come.[67] By the end of the century selecting a specific plaid was possible, and in 1693 John Hamilton promised David Crawford that he would bring with him 'a pattern of the plaids his grace commanded me to tray [try] for him'.[68] Two years later Crawford was busy explaining to the earl of Arran why there was a delay in sending certain plaids that his lordship wanted.[69] By July 1709 the *Female Tatler* proudly informed readers that 'night-gowns ready-made' and 'right Scotch plaids' were for sale to gentlemen in London.[70]

Knitted stockings formed another important part of Scotland's textile production. From the 1580s Shetland regularly sold stockings to Dutch fishing ships in Bressay Sound and by the seventeenth century the Netherlands was the major purchaser.[71] However, Aberdeen was an important centre of production of quality stockings. Other Scottish products were more specialised and distinctive, such as the black sealskin cloak pledged to Robert Kers in Borroustonnes by Alexander Abercrombie, eldest son of deceased James Abercrombie, fiar of Kerssie, in 1612.[72]

Scotland also produced a range of linens including harn, a coarse fabric made from the flax and better-quality 'linin' or 'lining'. David Forrest sold Duddingstone harn along with fancier fabrics such as fine stamped yellow crêpe, crimson and blue crêpe, and fine blue stamped stuff.[73] Linen production was seasonal, as is revealed by the purchases of Marie Hume in 1661. She spent £40 Scots of the 10th laird of Glenorchy's money on 36 ells of ticking, explaining that she 'had much ado to get anie att thes time the market being past befor the lad came ... If my lady desire anie more ye may let us know befor the first of march or anie dornick brod or nerow'.[74] A similar pattern is evident in the purchases made for the laird of Glenorchy. His account from 1668/70 included kelt bought at Fillan's market.[75] The countess of Caithness followed a similar pattern. She commissioned dornix from John Taylor, a weaver at Alichroy, Perthshire, in February 1690, and four years later she ordered dornix from Inverkeithing fair.[76] The elite also took an interest in promoting home-produced linen on a larger scale and in July 1694 George Livingstone, 4th earl of Linlithgow authorised the viscount of Tarbat to act as his proxy at the next meeting of the Scots Linen Manufactory in Edinburgh.[77] The following year the Scottish parliament passed an act in favour of the Scots Linen Company in a bid to meet local demand.[78]

The potential for Scottish textiles to evoke a bond between the wearer and their sense of nationhood is evident among those Scots who moved to England but wanted Scottish goods to remind them of home. Thus, Jane, countess of Sutherland, assured her son Sir Robert Gordon that on

> the xv of this instant November I result ane lettir of youris daitit at Salisberie the xvij of June, quhairin ye desyir mair of the small lining cleith. Trevlie gif I had gottin aduerteisment in tyme I vald not haue slipit sic ane turne, bot this tyme of yeir it is not in my power to get it.[79]

In a similar vein, in 1690 Mary, countess of Caithness, hoped to persuade her husband that they could live more quietly and cheaply in London than in Scotland, if they took lodgings of their own. These they could furnish with items from home, including tapestries, blankets and Scots linen.[80] Scottish textiles furnishing a London home offered the best of both worlds.

Stuart Imports and the Wish for Silk

The Stuarts were keen to promote Scottish textile production as an important part of national trade. Consequently, wearing and using Scottish cloth was linked to national identity in the sumptuary legislation.[81] However, mid sixteenth-century Scotland did not produce high-quality patterned silks, the fabric of choice across Europe. This explains James VI and I's endeavours to promote sericulture by paying £100 for silkworms in 1608/9 and encouraging the planting of mulberry trees.[82] Others looked further afield for a solution and in June 1640 Edward Bernard, who was based in Aleppo, described his investments in the 'Plantations in the Islands' to Archibald Hay. In his view 'Rice is much better in Italy than here ... but it may prosper there, and so mullberrys for silkworms'.[83] By 1668 Charles II received a gift of 'four hundred weight of silk' grown in Barbados.[84] Home-based silk weaving also developed and in 1633–4 George Melville of Garvock, a royal patent holder, was producing silks in Scotland 'to good perfection' but his business was struggling.[85] This was just the first of a number of ventures. For instance, in 1681 Hugh Jackson, an Englishman who had gone to Scotland to weave gold and silver leaves in a bid to develop Scottish manufacturing, requested a licence to continue his business.[86]

In spite of these attempts, the lack of a flourishing silk weaving industry producing high-end silks in Scotland or England resulted in large-scale imports. In 1661 Samuel Howard and partners sold velvet, 'bunbazen' and striped silk.[87] 15 years later Sir John Campbell bought Genoa velvet, rich gold brocade and morella tabby from Nicholas Fownes.[88] The sumptuary law of 1673 confirms the view that a wide range of luxury silks was available in Edinburgh, including flowered and striped fabrics as well as brocade, silk lace and embroidery. Not surprisingly, some individuals, including Sir John Colquhoun of Luss, fell foul of the law, which was enforced with unusual vigour. In July 1673 Sir John was brought before the privy council for wearing 'a blak justicat whereupon there was black silk or gimp lace' and fined 500 merks.[89] In contrast, Alexander Heriot was more savvy and paid 'for a horse to myself to go to Edinburgh to get some new furnishing' for the clothes of Alexander Gilmour of Craigmillar, which were altered in order to comply with the act.[90]

While there was a wide range of silks on offer, large quantities were not always available. In June 1597 Patrick Nimmo, an Edinburgh tailor, supplied a number of items to Robert Jousie, a merchant and a leading royal supplier, including 'delyvert to Thomas Scot messenger iij elles and ane half of grey fustiane at xlvjs viijd ye ell' and 'vij quarters of lynning deluverit to [James seyvne] at vjs viijd' and most interestingly, 'ane dossane of grene silk poyntes to his maiesties grene claith' and 'to James Seyane iiij dossane of grene silk buttons to his maiesties clayth'.[91] Periodic shortages remained common throughout the century, as Katharine Kerr's apologetic letter to the countess of Lothian in 1693 reveals. She had searched high and low in Edinburgh but there was 'no more off the plush left but 5 ells and we cannot get it matche in the town and Mrs Trotter has no other at all'.[92]

For those not tempted by silk there was a range of other desirable goods on offer throughout the seventeenth century, including cotton. In 1640 James Rae sent red calico from Edinburgh to the 8th laird of Glenorchy.[93] Over 40 years later Lady Glenorchy bought stamped calico from John Bouie.[94] At the start of the eighteenth century the Cupar merchant James Robertson sold 3 ells of broad calico with stamped flowers at Kendrochit, to make frocks for the children of the barony of Lude.[95] While Edinburgh might have been the first port of call for fashionable textiles, by the end of the seventeenth century they were readily available across Scotland.

Shopping and the Scottish Male Consumer

The presence of a shopping list jotted on the back of a letter sent in 1669 to Sir John Sinclair of Hermiston by John Stevenson is telling.[96] It highlights the importance of the seventeenth-century retail experience, an activity that was increasingly significant in men's lives and where the Stuarts led by example. When James V went shopping in Paris in 1537, he thought he did so incognito, but 'any carter pointed with their finger saying, "Younder goes le Roi d'Ecosse"'.[97] Shopping was a family affair under James VI and I and in 1609 he was accompanied by both his sons as well as his wife and daughter when he attended the opening of the New Exchange, or Britain's Burse (fig. 6.7). James and his family hoped for a degree of anonymity but with little success, and in 1618 Chamberlain reported how 'The Queen was yesterday at the Exchange; and though she meant to go privately, yet being discovered, she was no sooner in the Pawn above, than the press grew so great, that they were fain to shut the doors.'[98] However, there was a downside to this association of royalty with retail therapy, and in July 1628 Alexander Gill, the high master at St Paul's School, claimed at his trial that the king 'has enough wit to be a shop-keeper and ask "what do you lack" and that is all'.[99] Undeterred, Charles I's sons liked to shop, and their time in exile ensured that James, duke of York was well acquainted with the Parisian boutiques. In 1655, when Charles II directed Henry Bennet to buy him a sword from a particular shop, it is no surprise that he noted: 'My brother can tell you where it is'.[100]

While Alexander Gill regarded shopping as frivolous, Pepys viewed the activity very differently. His shopping forays combined the pleasures of window shopping, making canny purchases and flirting with female shopkeepers. On 4 April 1664, for example, Pepys went 'to the Change to buy a pair of cotton stockings, which I did at the husband's shop of the most pretty woman there … and I was glad of the occasion and bespoke some bands of her entending to make her my seamstress'.[101] While Pepys may have hoped to make her more than his seamstress,

6.7 Wencelaus Hollar, *The Royal Exchange*, 1647. Etching, 14.8 × 25.6 cm. Metropolitan Museum of Art, New York. Like the New Exchange, the Royal Exchange was another fashionable place in London to go shopping and be seen out and about.

he actively enjoyed the mechanics of shopping and he was not alone in spending many a happy hour looking at, selecting and purchasing fabrics, trimmings, ready-made items and accessories.

The best way to benefit from the purchasing power of men like Pepys was to own a shop, and in 1629 Archibald Hay of Strowie applied for 60-year leases on the houses and shops on 'a common street or ditch' between Aldgate and Tower Hill – and in 1632 he was successful.[102] In March 1642 shopping for fashionable clothes was still possible in London and William Rollo sent his elder brother James some bracelets and earrings.[103] However, by August the following year John Tolly was calling in the accounts of his Scottish clients, because he had been forced to shut his shop and he needed money.[104] Even so, in 1652 Sir James Murray still kept a house 'in the Strand by the New Exchange in Londoun'.[105] The Restoration gave the market a boost, and on 10 December 1660 the Londoner Andrew Cole asked the earl of Selkirk where he should send his furred mantle to.[106] While the New Exchange was a popular place to shop, it was equally important as a venue for meeting people, as in 1666 when Frances, lady Paget, informed her brother-in-law, the 10th laird of Glenorchy, that she had met one of his cousins there.[107]

After the Restoration, many wealthy Scots came to London during the winter months. After attending to business, politics and social obligations, shopping was high on their list of things to do. For example, the 3rd duke of Hamilton bought shoes from Louis Leclerc, hats from Monsieur Chaigneau, jewellery from Richard Beauvoir, who traded at the Silver Ball in Pall Mall, and wigs from Monsieur Laborde.[108] While French sellers offered him particular goods, the duke also frequented the premises of fellow Scots trading in London, including the goldsmith James Heriot, and he bought muffs from James Donaldson and clothes from a tailor called Munro.[109] The appeal of goods from London, in terms of both desirability and choice, is evident from the number of people that the duke of Hamilton went shopping for when he was there.[110]

Edinburgh offered a similar experience, both for shopping in person and by letter, as in the case of John Andrew, tailor, writing to Macintosh of Dunachton in the Highlands about clothing and some gold bracelets.[111] More illuminating is the account book of the Edinburgh-based tailor Patrick Nimmo who, in 1601, made items from 'Scots claith' for the laird of Stanehouse and a grey satin doublet for Sir James Hamilton of Letterick, the style and quality of which was very much on a par with those being made for James VI.[112] At the end of the seventeenth century the countess of Caithness bought a range of goods from Mary Campbell in the New Exchange, Edinburgh, including striped muslin, quilted tape, 'tiffiny' pins, scarlet ribbon, black silk and stockings.[113] Some of the stock was imported directly into Edinburgh while other items came from London. William Whiting at the Griffin in the Royal Exchange sold a range of goods to Alexander Campbell in Edinburgh, including a dozen velvet masks for 15s 6d and eight pairs of spectacles in shagreen cases costing 18s.[114] Whiting supplied everything Campbell wanted 'excepting the whyt crape which I could not meet with it Being scarse till some come over which is dayly expected'.[115] Clearly, then, even London did not have an infinite supply of fashionable goods.

At the other end of the shopping experience, chapmen or peddlers offered a range of small yet desirable goods for sale in towns and villages throughout the three kingdoms. They travelled widely, as the writer Martin Martin recounted in his *Description of the Western Islands of Scotland* (*c.*1695). He asserted that 'there are some peddlers from the shire of Moray, and other parts, who of late have fixed their residence in the isle of Skye, and travel through the remotest isles without any molestation; though some of these peddlers speak no Irish [Gaelic]'.[116] The wish to buy their goods helped overcome any differences in language.

Links between Scotland, England and Beyond

Just as the Stuarts spanned their kingdoms, so their subjects crossed national boundaries looking for trading opportunities to produce and sell textiles. Yet trade between the two countries was not as straightforward as it should have been after 1603 because of the imposition of trade tariffs. In September 1663, for instance, James Padie and John Corse felt the impact of a new duty of nine pence an ell on Scots cloth at the customs house at Bo'ness, where they could neither unload nor sell their packs.[117] However, entrepreneurial Scots were undeterred, and many either had relatives in Scotland and England working for the family business or formed partnerships with merchants south of the border. For example, in 1644

Sir Adam Hepburne of Humbie and James Riddell of Edinburgh joined with William Sykes, an English clothier, who oversaw their cloth works at New Mills beside the burgh of Haddington.[118] Towards the end of the century, the range of Robert Blackwood's business connections is evident from his letter-books. Blackwood, an Edinburgh silk and cloth merchant, was an original member of the Darien Company (an overseas trading company), and in 1711–13 he served as lord provost. In the mid to late 1690s he had a number of significant clients, including the laird of Kilbirnie,[119] the laird of Wemyss[120] and Lord Bargainy.[121] In 1699–1700 the laird of Dean bought a range of exotic goods from him, including a fan with ivory spokes, 5 ells of 'snuffish' cloth, stamped plush, a Carolina hat and some buff-coloured Persian.[122] He also traded further afield for other clients, as in the case of the viscount of Tarbat, whose man of business, Charles Hay, settled a bill with Blackwood for goods bought in London costing £8 11s 8d.[123]

6.8 Abraham Lambertsz van den Tempel, *Sir William Davidson of Curriehill with His Son Charles*, c. 1664. Oil on canvas, 140 × 108 cm. National Galleries of Scotland. William's son Charles wears a stylish coat trimmed with ribbon.

Scottish merchants traded in Europe and their well-established links to the Netherlands played an important part in this. In 1615 James VI and I ratified that Scots ships would use Veere, making it the staple port for Scottish goods in the Netherlands, and so wool, woollen cloth, wool and linen yarn, as well as plaids and stockings, went by this route. Trading in Amsterdam, Sir William Davidson of Curriehill was rewarded with the post of conservator of Veere by a grateful Charles II in 1661, and he dressed the part of a successful Dutch merchant (fig. 6.8). By the 1680s Andrew Russell was the Scottish factor in Rotterdam and his correspondence with Hugh Blair reveals the various facets of his business. In 1682 Blair was in London assessing what was in fashion, then buying it in the Netherlands and shipping it to Leith for sale in Edinburgh. Blair demonstrates a very detailed knowledge of both fashion, taste, and the law. He had clear views on what would sell and of his profit margin, and both considerations explain comments such as, 'I would neither have it a fiery redis collour not a blueish pale ash colour but a lyvely mixture of near to the sattine pattern as can be'.[124] In turn, Russell had many contacts, including Balthazar, Daniel and Matheus de Neufville, who were based in Amsterdam, so allowing him to fulfil this type of order.[125]

The Scots had many other European connections, as two brief examples demonstrate. The first looked to the 'Auld alliance' with France, which meant that during times of war Scottish merchants were often welcomed in French ports when their English counterparts were not.

Clothing and accessories were among the goods they looked to buy, as in 1610 when James Broun wrote from Edinburgh to Archibald Cokky asking him to buy a range of goods in Rouen for him. He had a good knowledge of the market, asking for two dozen hats lined with velvet at £42 per dozen and a dozen hats of 'conninghair' (probably felted rabbit hair) at £3 10s each.[126] New markets further afield were also attractive, and one of the younger brothers of John Campbell of Glenorchy, 1st earl of Breadalbane, was apprenticed to a London merchant who traded with the Levant.[127] Scottish elite families, like their English counterparts, not only bought luxury goods during the seventeenth century, but also started to trade in them, so making them an integral part of the Stuarts' fashionable style.

Stuart Men and the World of Accessories

6.9 Sir Anthony van Dyck, *Lord John Stuart and His Brother Lord Bernard Stuart, Later Earl of Lichfield*, c.1638. Oil on canvas, 238 × 146 cm. National Gallery, London. Lord Bernard's short cloak is draped over his doublet with panache, while his older brother John wears the fashionable doublet of the 1630s.

A full-length portrait of Lord John Stuart (1621–44) and his brother Lord Bernard (1622–45) offers a clear sense of how clothes, boots, gloves, swords and fine linens combined to create the well-dressed man (fig. 6.9). Both men are clothed in royal Stuart style, and both lived and died supporting the king. In contrast, Robert Rich, 2nd earl of Warwick (1587–1658), was a Puritan and openly critical of Charles I in 1628 over the Petition of Right. Yet when he posed for Van Dyck in *c.*1632–5 his clothes, with co-ordinating garters and shoe roses, were the epitome of court fashion (fig. 6.10).[128] Rich wore Stuart style because it denoted his place in society, even though it was a society he increasingly wished to change.

Accessories were essential in completing all three outfits discussed above, but they were also singled out for criticism by some contemporary writers, such as the playwright Ben Jonson, as unnecessary and frivolous. When, in *c.*1620, Jonson penned 'An Epistle to a Friend to Perswade Him to the Warres', he urged his friend to renounce 'his Combes, his Curling-irons, his Glasse, Sweet bags [and] sweet Powders'.[129] As this list suggests, a man's hair was indicative of his temperament and nationality, and according to the well-travelled Fynes Morison, while Italians 'weare very short haire, as all nations doe that live in hot climes, the contrary vice of wearing long haire [is] proper to the French, English, and the Scots, but especially to the Irish'.[130] From the mid seventeenth century the wig was the fashion item of choice, an item that required regular maintenance. Dougal Campbell paid for dressing Breadalbane's periwig in 1691 and three years later Robert Moray asked his mother to send him 3 ounces of hair and 10 shillings to complete and pay for a wig.[131]

Headwear was equally important because it was central to male displays of courtesy and honour.[132] When James went to collect Anna of Denmark he attended a number of church services and his polite behaviour prompted favourable comments, as on 19 November 1589 when 'His majesty took off his hat, immediately put it on again and paid close attention to what the bishop was saying; and when the oration was finished, his majesty once again took off his hat, gave his hand to the bishop and thanked him respectfully'.[133] However, on New Year's Day 1590 things were slightly different; on this occasion 'he did not take his own hat off or replace it, since one of his attendants did it for him'.[134] Royal taste could also serve to regulate excessive expenditure, as on 5 July 1620 when it was reported from court that 'The king … will take order by proclamation that no beavers shall be worn but by men of certain quality and that himself, the prince and my Lord of Buckingham will give the first example of wearing felts'.[135] Here the shift was from expensive, imported hats made from felted beaver fur to those made at home from rabbit.

A range of accessories was essential for male hands, of which gloves were the most important. Worn to protect and accentuate the hands, gloves were popular gifts (fig. 6.11). At New Year 1627 Charles I received 70 pairs of gloves including pairs from Thomas Caldwell, his barber, Robert Hutchinson and William Huggins, perfumers, and James Heriot and Philip Jacobson, jewellers.[136] They were also exchanged or rejected by lovers or prospective love interests. Prince Henry snubbed Frances Howard at a ball in April 1612 where she dropped a glove. It was offered to Henry 'by one

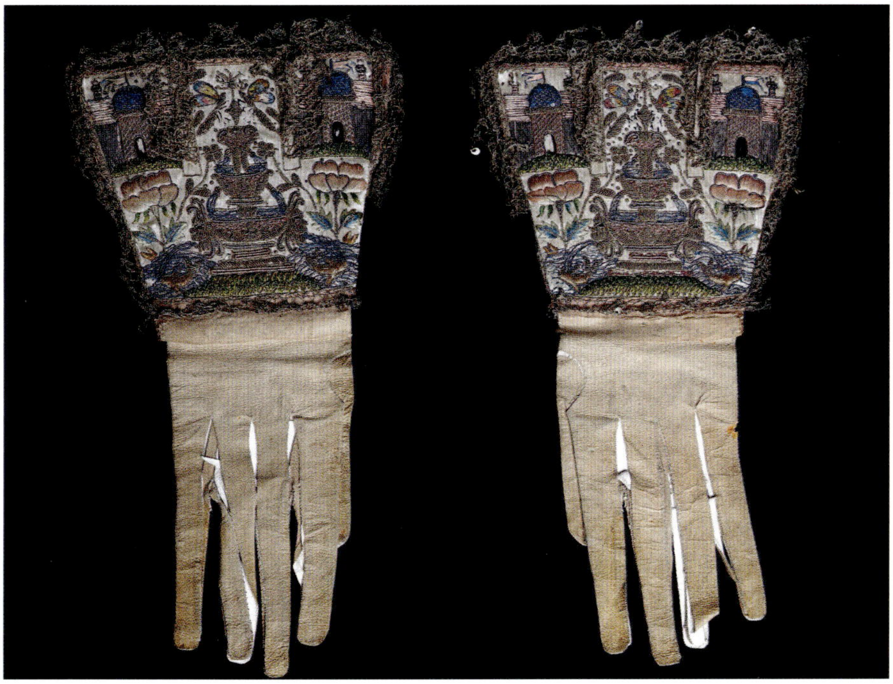

6.10 *(above)* Sir Anthony van Dyck, *Robert Rich, 2nd Earl of Warwick*, c.1632–5. Oil on canvas, 208 × 128 cm. Metropolitan Museum of Art, New York. Rich's cloth of silver doublet, scarlet breeches and scarlet mantle demonstrate his adoption of Stuart style even though he did not support the king's political views.

6.11 *(left)* Embroidered gauntlet gloves presented to Sir Henry Wardlaw by Charles I, c.1600–30. University of St Andrews.

that thought he did him an acceptable service; but the Prince refused it, saying publickly, He would not have it, it is stretcht by another'.[137] Equally popular were fine linen handkerchiefs that had a range of uses apart from the obvious: Sir William Douglas kept his money tied in his.[138] By the 1660s muffs joined the ranks of male accessories and they remained popular for some time. In 1697 Dougal Campbell reminded his cousin Alexander, an Edinburgh merchant, that he had 'promised me a muff when I was at Edinburgh', adding 'pray send me on now aither in a gift or for money for the weather is very cold, and yow use to have on to spair'.[139]

No man was well dressed unless his legs and feet were displayed appropriately. Good-quality stockings were essential and the quality on offer is evident from a green silk pair linked to William III: here the personalised clocks consist of a floral design and a crowned W (fig. 6.12).[140] Linen boot hose were worn over fine stockings like these to protect them from rubbing when worn with boots, and of the many ordered for Charles I a single surviving example may be attributable to him dating from *c*.1630–40.[141] All the Stuarts had their own shoemakers making them bespoke footwear, but for Charles I and II there were times when the shoes on their feet painfully reminded them of the vulnerability of their royal position. When as a young boy Charles I had problems with his feet and legs and was late learning to walk, he wore specially made boots.[142] In contrast, the memory of the ill-fitting, borrowed shoes that Charles II wore during his escape after the battle of Worcester stayed with him for the rest of his life.[143]

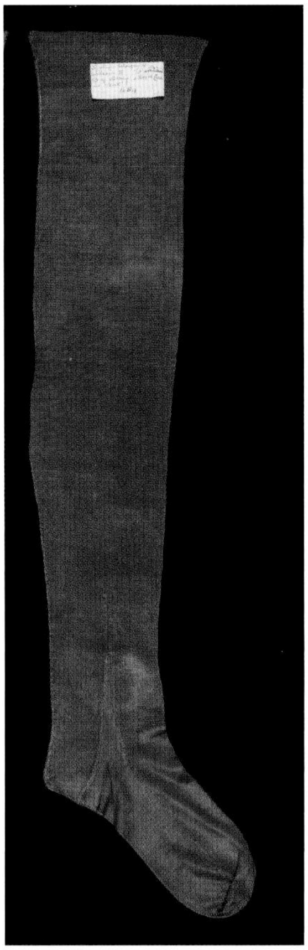

6.12 Green silk stockings associated with William III, c.1690. Royal Ceremonial Dress Collection, London.

James I's portraits suggest that he favoured pale-coloured leather shoes with a low heel and latchet fastenings tied with white ribbon. These were in marked contrast to the wonderful shoe roses and tightly gathered bunches of ribbon and lace favoured by his sons and the younger courtiers. Not surprisingly, large shoe roses were the subject of ridicule and one of the characters in John Webster's *The Devil's Law Case* (1623) mocked men who wore 'overblown roses' to hide their 'gouty ankles'.[144] Even so, for men like Richard Rich, with shapely ankles, roses served to accentuate them, making a pair the final flourish to his ensemble that he wore with flare.

Conclusions

After the death of Elizabeth I, the Stuart kings placed the focus firmly back on men as the primary consumers of fashionable goods, either for themselves or, bought by them, for others, and Scottish men were no exception. This close relationship between male consumers and their suppliers is summed up deftly in *The Funeral Obsequies of Sir-All-In New-Fashions* where a lengthy procession of tailors, shopkeepers, mercers and drapers follows respectfully behind the deceased (fig. 6.13). In contrast, when Lord Neill Campbell died in 1696, John Tyller, a merchant in Dumbarton, submitted his accounts from the time when Campbell was governor of Dumbarton Castle, revealing that he catered

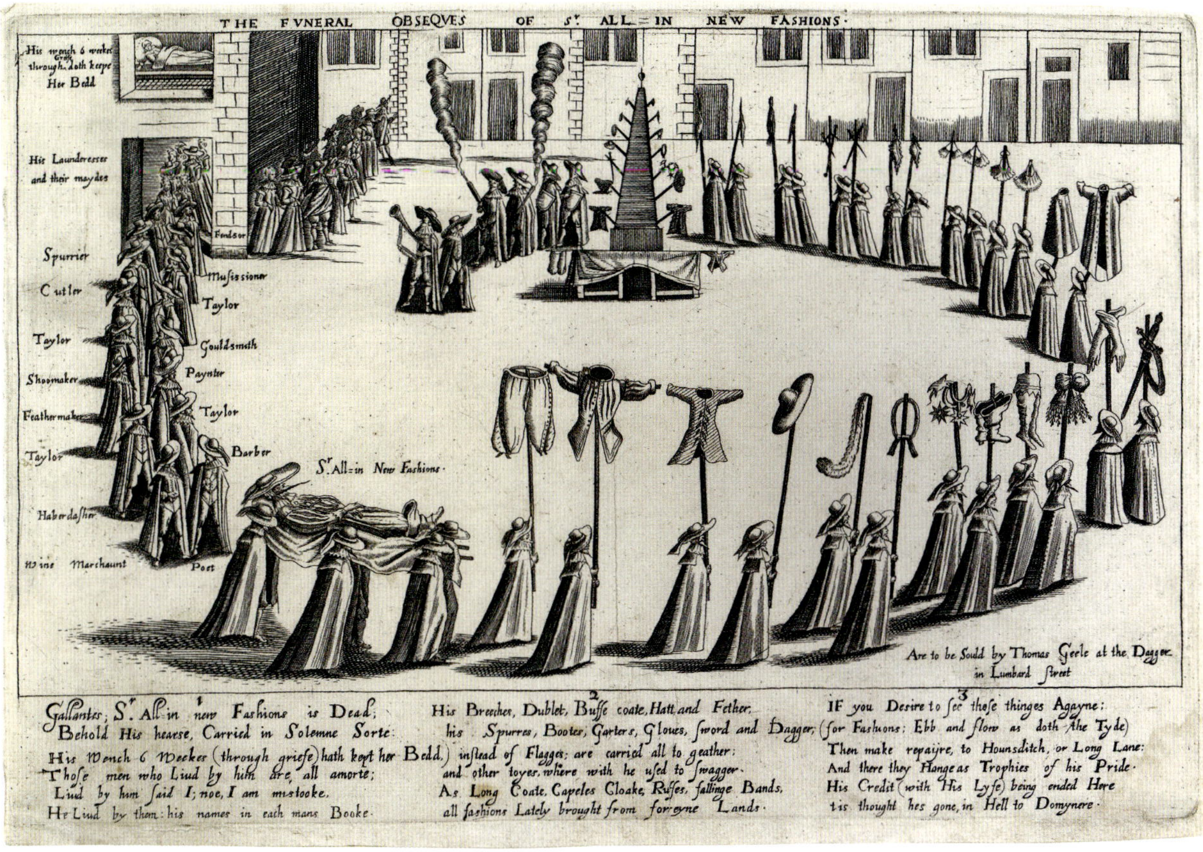

6.13 Unknown artist, *The Funeral Obsequies of Sir-All-In New-Fashions*, 1620s. Engraving, 20.9 × 30.3 cm. Ashmolean Museum, Oxford.

to all his needs ranging from soap, thread, linen and pins, to tartan plaids and shirt making.[145] The presence of tartan plaids among his purchases demonstrates the importance of home-produced Scottish cloth alongside other fabrics that would have made up Lord Neill's wardrobe.

It also contrasts well with the order placed in London by Mr Campbell for a rich brocade waistcoat.[146] David Carnegie's account notes that it was made with 'large gold buttonholes', making it very specific to his Scottish client's requirements and revealing how the Stuarts' court cities of London and Edinburgh offered customers choice. This meant that they could buy into the strands of Stuart style that appealed to them and their pocket. Under the Stuarts the concept of the court supplier developed and, in tandem with the masters of the Great Wardrobe (many of whom were Scots until the 1620s), helped shape the sense of what was fashionable. Many of the Scottish shoppers coming to London looked out their fellow countrymen to do business with, thereby helping to secure and enrich the Scottish community there. Stuart fashion reflected the taste of this cosmopolitan royal family and it was received enthusiastically by buyers, sellers and tailors alike, as the next chapter shows.

CHAPTER SEVEN

Making and Maintaining Stuart Style

BUNCHES OF PRIMROSE YELLOW RIBBONS decorate the waist of Charles I's brown wool jerkin and the knees of the matching breeches and compliment his doublet in Daniel Mytens's full-length portrait of 1628 (fig. 7.1). The stylish cut of the doublet and elegant lines of the jerkin are in keeping with the garments made for Charles by Patrick Black, his Scottish tailor, at the time this portrait was painted. Charles I's personal taste, in tandem with the advice and skill of his tailor, created a specific phase of Stuart style that has come to be regarded as synonymous with the image of the cavalier and the paintings of Mytens and Van Dyck. Together, king, tailor and artist set and promoted the fashion that others followed, modified or rejected as political, religious and national allegiance dictated. Evidence that men did look and take note can be found in their bills, accounts and, most tellingly, in surviving pieces of clothing such as a cream silk doublet dating from around 1620, with links to the Stuarts of Urrard. This garment has the same distinctive pointed waistline, deep skirts and high collar as Charles's jerkin (fig. 7.2).[1] It is a fashionable, well-made doublet that formed part of the wardrobe of a Scotsman who was aware of current clothing trends at court and who included them as part of his regular clothing choices.

This chapter considers the role of the tailor and in particular the relationship between the Stuarts and their tailors, most of whom were Scots, in creating a fashionable look that spread throughout the three kingdoms. The office of gentleman of the robes, which was also held by Scots, also aided the development of royal style and its dissemination. Having achieved the Stuart look, men then had to keep garments like the cream silk doublet, in tandem with the white linens it was worn with, clean and presentable. The second half of this chapter demonstrates how sumptuous royal and elite wardrobes were maintained, thereby rejecting Sir Anthony Weldon's negative view of Scotland as inelegant and unhygienic.

7.1 *(above)* Daniel Mytens, *Charles I*, 1628. Oil on canvas, 219.4 × 139.1 cm. Royal Collection. Charles I's appearance is testament to the skilled work of his staff, who kept his clothes in pristine condition.

7.2 *(facing page)* This cream satin doublet would have been the height of fashion at James VI and I's court, c.1620. Perth Museum.

Selling Royal Style to the Scottish and English Elites

While Charles I planned his Scottish coronation carefully, there are surprisingly few specific references to his visit to Edinburgh in his clothing account for 1632/3. The most obvious is a payment of £50 to Patrick Black as a reward to him and his servants for making up the king's clothes for the Scottish journey, and for his travel and expenses attending Charles 'to see all things fitted to his majesty's royal person'.[2] Robert Jousie, yeoman of the robes, and his servants attended the cart loaded with his majesty's apparel.[3] While there, Black lined a cloak for the king with plush, Edward Ash supplied three feathers, Joseph Atkinson provided embroidered gloves and Thomas Robinson delivered some 'very rich garters with roses and points for the journey to Scotland'.[4]

No clothes in the account are specifically described as being for the coronation. However, as the suits are probably listed in the order that they were made and the most expensive suits in the 1632/3 account come quite late on, they may well be the clothes for this event. The most expensive was certainly a suit of distinction, being embroidered all over with gold and silver and costing £475 6s 5d.[5] Other items ordered at this point include a suit and cloak of watchet satin, laced all over with gold and silver lace and priced at £241 6s 3d, and a scarlet cloak and pair of hose worn with a doublet of gold and silver stuff that was slightly cheaper, at £195 3s 8¾d.[6] Whether Charles chose to emulate his English coronation by dressing in white is harder to tell, but the account does include a suit of white satin, cut and trimmed with silk passementerie, the doublet open on the shoulder seams and centre back and worn with round hose, which would have been appropriate.[7]

The king's choices set the tone for everyone else to follow, and the way in which the Scottish elite emulated royal style is revealed in two letters sent by Sir David Cunningham to his brother. In the first, dated 20 April 1633, he complained that 'yor instrctions are come so late and so generall neither expressing what nor how much that I know not how to behave myself'.[8] Even so, he planned to send 'suits of sattin or silke of severall sorts with cloaks suitable'. However, Sir David was diligent and by 1 May his advice had changed significantly, 'having aswell seene all his majesties apparel newlie made as sundry other noble mens and lykewise haveing taken advice of Patrik Blak his majesties Taillor'. As a consequence, he sent

> a very rich cloth of silver dowblet with black sattin breaches and sattin Cloake much laced as the fashion is this suite is for all great daies and holly dayes and when for varietie you please to make this suite somewhat worse there is a black sattin dublett suitable. Also yow shall have another fair new kinde of wrought sattin suite willow collour with silver lace dublett breaches and cloake to which for change and varietie your silver dublett will suit very well yow shall have stockings & garters, roses, points, girdles, hat bands and some few falling bands to make yow compleate.[9]

It was evidently good advice because John Kennedy, 6th earl of Cassilis, made a similar selection, choosing a cloth of silver doublet, a gold-coloured satin suit and a cloak lined with plush.[10] It also makes the suggestion that the gold-coloured satin suit at Claydon House was worn at the Scottish coronation plausible. Both fronts are cut in panes, while the high waistline curves down at the centre front (figs. 7.3 and 7.4).[11] Like the suits mentioned above, the doublet is trimmed with braid made from silver metal thread and cream silk. While it does not appear on Sir Edmund Verney's bill for clothes ordered in May 1633 that might have been for this occasion, a willow-coloured satin suit and cloak laced all over and double cut in small panes is mentioned, similar to the suit ordered by Sir David.[12] Loyal subjects emulated the king's style for this very important occasion.

7.3 *(above, left)* Front of a gold satin doublet with paned sleeves, 1630s. Verney Collection, Claydon House, Buckinghamshire.

7.4 *(above, right)* Back view of figure 7.3 showing the paning in the upper back.

Making Royal Style: Scots and the Office of the King's Tailor

Sir David Cunningham's letter reveals that the royal tailors were seen as the quickest, most reliable route to learning what was fashionable, so placing them at the forefront of shaping male style. Their role under the Stuarts was twofold. First and foremost, they made the king's clothes and guided his choices on what was stylish and suited to his age and status. Second, they helped disseminate royal style by making clothes for other men. It was a close working relationship, and usually a stable one, with royal tailors staying in post for long periods of time. Under the Stuarts the office was held by a high proportion of Scots, and this had important implications for the development of royal style and its appeal to the Scottish male elite. Monarch and tailor worked together to develop and promote the fashionable male look. For the king, this offered an opportunity to unite the male elite, sartorially if in no other way, while for these tailors, their office provided a priceless opportunity to further their own careers.

Before James VI reached his majority his tailors were based in Edinburgh; his clothes were made in the city and then taken to Stirling by horse by William Murray, valet of the chamber. His tailor Alexander Miller had wide-ranging business connections, and in 1587 he purchased woollen cloth from Hugh Hyndley, citizen and Merchant Adventurer of London, for £124 12s.[13] By 1598 Miller was a burgess of Edinburgh and in 1601 he bought land in Langhirdmanstoun and Currie.[14] Although Miller travelled south with James in 1603, he retained his role as an Edinburgh burgess.[15] In 1604 Robert Erskine received the office of king's tailor 'with survivorship' and began working in tandem with Miller.[16] Keen to cement his place, Erskine gave the king a nightcap of tawny velvet embroidered with Venice gold and silk in 1606 as a New Year's gift – a gift of comparable quality to the pair of pantofles embroidered with Venice gold presented by Alexander Hume.[17] He also settled into London life and by 1608 was described as a merchant tailor of London in an agreement with John, lord Erskine, son and heir of the earl of Mar.[18] As late as January 1639, his widow Agnes received £50, part of £210 owed by the late James VI and I.[19]

Patrick Black is one of the best-documented Stuart tailors. The bond between him and Charles I began with a gift of 25¼ ounces of plate ordered on 31 December 1606 as the prince's christening gift for Patrick's child.[20] In or around 1611, Patrick and Richard Black were appointed as tailors to the duke of York.[21] Two years later, in July 1613, Patrick was granted the office of tailor to Prince Charles.[22] However, not everything was straightforward and in July 1615 Martin Lumley, alderman of London, applied for a licence to arrest him for a debt of £400.[23]

Black maintained his interests in Scotland and in 1618 he petitioned for the conditions in two contracts with Sir William Anstruther to be enforced. These stipulated that Sir William would renounce the lands and barony of Anstruther to Patrick.[24] He did so the following year, when Patrick Black was described as 'now of Largo'.[25] Black made the transition from tailor to Charles as prince to tailor to Charles I. In August 1625 Charles I authorized Conway to pay £1,000 to Black and Richard Seymer, who went to France 'for necessaries requisite for the King's speedy use and service'.[26] He also took on the role of making livery for the household and 'horse clothes'.[27]

Robert Ramsey appeared in George Villier's accounts in 1626 when £5 was given to 'Mr Ramsey's man that brought his lordship's clothes'.[28]

The following year he received £356 towards the duke's preparations for going to the Île de Ré.[29] By 1630 he was making clothing for Prince Charles.[30] He also worked for Henrietta Maria, creating costumes for some of her entertainments, including 'her Maiesties pastorall since the 6th of October 1632'.[31] On Black's death in 1636, Ramsey worked for the king, and towards the end of his career he and David Murray were made tailors to His Majesty, the prince and the duke of York, and the two men made livery for the servants of the king and his children.[32] This kept a Scot in the office of king's tailor (fig. 7.5).

7.5 Anthony van Dyck, *Charles I and Henrietta Maria with Their Two Eldest Children, Prince Charles and Princess Mary*, 1632. Oil on canvas, 303.8 × 256.5 cm. Royal Collection. Charles and his son are dressed in clothes of the type made for them by their Scottish tailors.

By April 1636 David Murray was established as a tailor on the Strand.[33] Four years later, on the death of Ramsey, he received livery worth £4 5s 4d as His Majesty's tailor.[34] He served Charles throughout the civil war period and in February 1648 it was noted 'That the King's escape is designed, the manner thus, by one Napier and a servant of David Murray, whom we take to be the King's tailor'.[35] He also bought goods from the Commonwealth sale including two sets of horse harnesses made by Tennant, the king's saddler.[36] His time as the king's tailor saw the creation of short doublets, such as the example shown in figure 7.6, of an embroidered cream linen, probably made in London in the late 1640s–1650s.[37]

William Watts was the king's tailor from 1671 to 1678, and he was also part of the

7.6 *(above)* The high-standing collar, close-buttoned front and open seam of the sleeves are the distinguishing features of this 1640s–1650s linen doublet. National Museum of Scotland, Edinburgh.

7.7 *(right)* Gilbert Soest, *John Hay, 2nd marquis of Tweedale*, 1670s, oil on canvas, 125.9 × 105.2 cm, Glasgow Museums Resource Centre. While Watts may well not have worked for Hay, the marquis is dressed in the height of fashion, something William was very familiar with.

Scots community in London (fig. 7.7). He helped train his countrymen, including Daniel Sage of Kilmarnock, Ross, who was apprenticed to him in 1670. He had links with Edinburgh including bonds with and from Thomas Fisher, an Edinburgh tailor. In his will he bequeathed 'To the Scots corporation the foundation of Charles II the interest of £100 due unto me on a bond from the corporation for 10 years'.[38] He also left £80 to the minister of Forfar to buy land or houses for '4 poor people from the parish … and if any poor people be of the name of Watts, they should be the persons' to live there, plus £20 for a cross in the parish of Forfar 'after the best manner and form as may be and as the best of the crosses in Scotland' as a memorial to his life, his piety and the family of Watts.[39]

While James, duke of York and Albany was in Scotland, there is a suggestion that he employed a local tailor. The account of the earl of Lowden Caw covering the period from 26 October 1675 to 1682 records what he owed to 'Allexander Hoom his Majesties Tayllor'.[40] In June 1678 Alexander Hoom was appointed as parliamentary commissioner for the royal burgh of Lauder, a position he held until 1681.[41] Equally elusive is Robert Graham, who was appointed as Charles II's tailor on 3 December 1678.[42] He also worked briefly for James II and William III – however, it is likely that he is the Robert Graham who served as master of the Royal Scottish Corporation in 1694.[43] So, while not a complete monopoly, the office of king's tailor under these Stuart kings was firmly in Scottish hands, thereby ensuring a Scottish component in the development of royal style.

Scottish Tailors in London and Edinburgh

The influence of Scottish tailors at Whitehall and in the city of London was so well known that Monsieur Device, a character in William Cavendish's play *The Country Captain,* described himself as 'an English Monsier, made vp by a Scotch taylor that was Prentice in France'.[44] This sentiment rang true for London audiences not only when the play was first performed in *c.*1639–40, but also when it was published in 1649 and when it was revived after the Restoration. The significance attached to Scottish tailors also explains a mock epitaph penned several years earlier for James Hay, earl of Carlisle, and his tailor, Patrick Black, the same Black who had served Charles I. Tailor and client died within an hour of each other in 1637, and the epitaph's author claimed that even though 'in the wither world they were no clothes' Black still chose to 'hunt' Hay there in the hope he would finally 'pay his bill'.[45] This close link between Scottish elite client and Scottish craftsman was not unique; rather, it was central to Stuart self-fashioning.

Black and the other royal tailors were not the only Scottish tailors living and working in seventeenth-century London. Drawn there by the presence of the Stuart court and by the sheer scale of the city, many Scots settled in and around the church of St Martin-in-the-Fields. London was a place in which to do business and succeed, with the added benefit that one could serve fellow Scots coming to court, which meant bonds of kinship could be maintained. The evidence indicates that the tailors prospered and that they offered their customers more than just tailoring skills. In some cases they served as bankers. For instance, in 1633 George Balfour, 'tailor in Blackefreres', was described as 'sometime resident at the Blak Freiris in London'.[46] He signed bonds with Robert, lord Dalkeith, for £137 14s sterling in 1633 and three with William, earl of Morton, and Robert, lord of Dalkeith, with the consent of Sir William Scott of Clerkingtoun, in 1633, 1637 and 1639.[47]

The career of John Hay, tailor of St Martin-in-the-Fields, indicates that this pattern continued after the Restoration. Hay was tailor of the robes for Charles II and James VII and II with a specialism in making liveries for the royal household. According to a bill from July 1673, he also provided liveries for the duke of Lauderdale.[48] He had a number of other Scottish clients, such as James Graham, 3rd marquis of Montrose.[49] From 1689 Hay's customers included John Campbell, 1st earl of Breadalbane and Holland, and his son Colin Campbell. He also made liveries for their footman, groom of the chamber, coachman and porter.[50] Hay also made loans to Scots including a bond in 1685 for £101 5s sterling that James, earl of Airlie, pledged to pay from his pension.[51] On occasion Hay had to resort to the law to get the debts paid, as was the case in 1697 with the earl of Linlithgow in respect of money owed by the late earl, George.[52]

When John Hay died he remembered Scotland in his will, leaving a bequest of £20 to 'the Scotch hospital or corporation' in London for the poor living there, with another £100 to be distributed among his poor relations 'if any there be'.[53] This reflects a long-standing relationship, because in 1684, as master of the Scots Corporation in London, Hay had acknowledged a gift from George, earl of Panmure.[54]

Hay made fashionable clothes for James Graham, 3rd marquis of Montrose (1657–84). He also made court clothes, specifically two suits Montrose wore while at Windsor with the king and the duke of York. The first was made from silk prunella. The coat was lined with pinked, coloured lutestring and the waistcoat made of gauze. The second had a coat and breeches of rich brocade silk stuff, the coat lined with cherry gold lutestring and the waistcoat and canons laced. Hay's experience in making liveries made him a good choice for uniforms. Montrose commanded the king's troop of guards and he ordered scarlet uniforms for his men in 1680–81.[55] In June 1680 he ordered a scarlet coat laced over with silver lace and lined with blue tabby, blue cloth breeches and a scarlet cloak embroidered with silver and gold from Hay.[56]

Montrose came to London regularly and ordered clothes from Hay in person. However, there were other options for members of the Scottish elite who did not travel down, including proxy shopping. A good example of this took place in March 1641 when William Rollo was shopping in London on behalf of his brother Sir James.[57] William stated confidently that 'your velvet is of the best sort of that kinde which I have boght for all both linen [lining] and outside' rather than a 'thrid plush' lining. In terms of style he opted for 'that new forme of cassike which is called Mantle de gard, it is of the lastest forme for when you ride it will serve for slives if yow button it right'. However, while tailors helped make a man fashionable, they would also 'radiely deceave'. William was wise to this, however, noting how the tailor 'gained ane yeard and half' according to how he cut the garments out. The closeness of their relationship becomes evident in April 1680 when Montrose's servant John Smith attended the christening of Hay's child 'where I stood for my lord'.[58]

7.8 An opulent cloth of silver suit worn for the Order of the Garter consisting of doublet and trunk hose, 1661. National Museum of Scotland, Edinburgh.

Hay stored clothes for Scots as they travelled between England and home. In April 1679 he took delivery of a large number of clothes and accessories belonging to Montrose with instructions that they were 'to be sent to Scotland by the first ship'.[59] The following February, on arrival in London, Montrose left his baggage with Hay until he had secured lodgings.[60] While no garments can be associated with Montrose, the silver Garter suit of Charles Stuart, 6th duke of Lennox and 3rd duke of Richmond (1639–72), a close contemporary, does survive. While it does not offer evidence of his fashionable taste, it does demonstrate how clothes placed men like Lennox and Montrose at the heart of the Restoration court (fig. 7.8).[61]

For Scots preferring a tailor closer to home, the best in Edinburgh had premises on the Canongate, the main shopping thoroughfare. In 1642 General Patrick Ruthven, earl of Forth, ordered clothing from John Steill on the 'Cannogait'.[62] Over 40 years later Robert Polson, tailor burgess in the Canongate, submitted his bill to Hugh Fraser, younger of Belladrum.[63] Other desirable addresses included the abbey of Holyroodhouse, where James Kilpatrick was based; he worked for the earl of Breadalbane.[64] Skilled tailors were based across Scotland, for example Thomas Pollock, a tailor in Glasgow who worked between 1689 and 1691 for the earl of Kilmarnock, the late earl, Captain James Boyd and Captain Robert Boyd.[65] Wherever they were based, skilled and knowledgeable tailors played a vital part in ensuring their clients were dressed in a variant of the Stuarts' style to suit their pocket and their personality.

Politics and the King's Clothes: The Role of the Gentleman of the Robes

Since the Stuarts' style was shaped by predominantly Scottish or French tailors, it is not surprising to find a Scottish presence within the Wardrobe of the Robes, the household department that ordered and cared for the king's clothes. The staff of this wardrobe came into daily contact with the king while he was dressing, a process that is discussed further in Chapter 9, and had close ties to the royal laundress and the other individuals who ensured that the king looked, and smelt, as good as possible.

In 1603 James appointed Sir George Home, 1st earl of Dunbar, master of the Great Wardrobe and gentleman of the robes, following the Scottish pattern.[66] He was followed in this role in 1605 by the clothes-conscious James Hay, later 1st earl of Carlisle.[67] Hay's interest in clothes meant that he was well suited to this role. On 29 April 1616 Sir John Holles grumbled that Hay 'furnishes himself very sumptuously, and purposes to appear in court with as muche magnificence, as good clothes, and embroideries can give'.[68] John Chamberlain provided more details on 6 July when he informed Dudley Carleton that Lord Hay 'had twenty suits of apparel made for so many days, and then heard the French had changed their fashion'.[69] James's brother, Robert, succeeded him in the office in February 1617.[70] At some point between November 1623 and James's death, Robert was succeeded by George Kirke. In April 1625 Kirke petitioned Charles I that he might continue as gentleman of the robes, 'for which last office he had £500 a year'.[71]

The significance of the office of gentleman of the robes, and the access it brought, explains why the Villiers family sought to control it. Sir John Villiers, later viscount Purbeck, the elder brother of George Villiers, was made gentleman of the robes to Prince Charles in 1616. In January 1620 there was a rumour that Christopher Villiers was to succeed Purbeck as master of the robes.[72] However, it was Spencer Compton who succeeded him in 1622. The previous year Compton had married George Villiers's cousin Mary Beaumont, so making him part of the family circle. Consequently, it was Compton who served Charles while he was in Spain seeking the hand of the Infanta. On 19 March 1623, Carey informed him that 'The Marchioness of Buckingham says that her lord's robes and collar are packed up and given in charge to his servant, Mr. Crow'.[73] A few weeks later, in acknowledgement that arriving in Spain incognito was 'unexampled', Compton and others arranged to send jewels, clothes and his Garter robes along with horses, tilting armour and caparisons to Charles in Madrid, so that he could dress the part of a Stuart prince.[74]

Buckingham suggested to Charles that his nephew William, lord Feilding should become the next gentleman of the robes after Compton.[75] But when Compton became the 2nd earl of Northampton on his father's death in June 1630, he was succeeded by George Kirke as gentleman of the robes.[76] In 1628 Kirke was naturalised, which meant he paid less tax as an English citizen,[77] and in September 1648 he was appointed to serve the king in Newport.[78] In 1664 Kirke appealed for payment of a pension of £500 a year, granted by Charles I, that was approved 'in consideration of the low condition and straitness of fortune to which he is reduced by his loyalty'.[79]

There was a shift in the nature of the office after the Restoration, or rather in the prestige of the men who held the office. Charles II's gentlemen of the robes were Henry Cavendish, viscount Mansfield (1660–62), Laurence Hyde, 1st earl of Rochester (1662–78), Sidney Godolphin, 1st earl Godolphin (1678–9), and Henry Sydney, 1st earl of Romney (1679–85). The appointment of these high-ranking Englishmen may reflect the growing importance placed on the levée and couchée. This trend continued during the first phase of his brother's reign. On 10 February 1685 Catherine Radclyffe learnt from a London newsletter that James VII and II had made Arthur Herbert master of the robes.[80] The pattern changed a little once James was in exile, when Richard Hamilton of Ulster (*c.*1655–1717) took on the role.[81] Hamilton had served with the king in Ireland in 1689–90 and he was given responsibilities for the robes in 1696 after the death of William Herbert, 1st duke of Powis.[82]

If Scots had lost their influence within the Wardrobe of the Robes by the end of the seventeenth century, outside the confines of court members of the Scottish elite were engaging with French ideas on dressing. This was reflected in their wish for a trained valet, and in January 1690 the earl of Sunderland hoped to get 'a good valet de chambre over from France'.[83] Two years later the earl of Breadalbane had evidently succeeded because he gave a guinea to 'Mr La Valet' as a Christmas gift in 1692.[84] By 1723 the clothes of Alexander, 2nd duke of Gordon, were in the capable hands of William Dean, his *valet de chambre*.[85] French influence, in terms of fashion if not politics or religion, was still significant in Scottish society.

Cleanliness

One of Sir Anthony Weldon's many slurs on James VI's character was the claim that 'he would never change his cloathes untill worn out to very ragges'.[86] The king's perceived failure to wash or care for his clothes was not unique, as Lady Anne Clifford noted when she went to Theobalds, the home of Robert Cecil, in 1603 to meet James: '[there is] a great change between the fashion of the Court as it is now and that in the Queen's time, for we were all lousy by sitting in the chamber of Sir Thomas Erskine'.[87] However, it is important to set these points in context by considering contemporary views on washing, on the one hand, and allowing for an element of bias on the part of both writers. In the following century Louis XIV bathed very infrequently but he and his brother Philippe changed their shirts three times a day, so conforming to current thinking about cleanliness.[88] In comparison, Charles II's bathing room at Whitehall was newly furnished in May 1663.[89] Five years later 14 yards of gold-coloured serge were supplied for this room and in 1675 the room was painted and gilded, suggesting that it was in regular use and that its decor was important.[90] In a similar vein, the duchess of Lauderdale installed a bathroom at Ham House in the 1670s that was designed for use rather than show.[91] It may have been a sweating bath, because the duchess furnished the room with a 'bathing tubb & little stoole'.[92] Comparable developments were taking place in Scotland. Charles Wilson and Thomas Chirnsyd carried out building work at Newbattle Abbey, Dalkeith, in 1696–7 that included 'upputting the franch painters scaffoll' and 'a Littell Caiss and Caisments in the Clossit of the bathing roumb'.[93]

During the seventeenth century the staff of the bedchamber undertook an important role in managing royal hygiene by caring for the king's linen. The ordinances of James VII and II stipulated that the grooms of the bedchamber were to 'keep Our Lynnen for Our Bedchamber and Our Person in such manner as the same hath been used heretofore'.[94] They also received the royal bed linen and in 1678 their allocation consisted of 30 pairs of fine Holland sheets, 24 pairs of fine Holland pillow beres, 12 pillows, 12 blankets, 7 fustians, 12 sweet bags, 4 trunks, 1 bed case and 2 Spanish leather cases 'for his majesty's service for this present year'.[95] This quantity of linen made regular changes of bedding possible as one of the ways of ensuring cleanliness and by association the king's good health.

The groom of the stool played a key role in supplying the king's linen. In January 1663 it was formally noted that the groom provided linen lace to the king, and was to be reimbursed for it.[96] This was not a modest undertaking. In May 1667 a warrant for £1,000 was authorised for John, earl of Bath, to cover the cost of this lace.[97] As ever, the money was slow to arrive, and in August 1670 John received £385 9s 2d, for point lace and linen purchased between 18 February and 3 December 1667.[98]

Quality was an important consideration with regards to the king's linen. The household ordinances of William III stipulated that the master of the Great Wardrobe was to provide linen and lace 'for Our Person' but if the goods were not up to standard, the groom of the stool was 'to be allowed money out of our Privy Purse, or by the Privy Seal to buy the same'. In addition, no linen draper was to be appointed without the groom of the stool's permission and approval, and he could 'buy of any other Tradesman he shall think fit'. With the authority to 'appoint, remove, place or displace the said Linnen Draper and Lace Draper as well as our Sempstress & Laundress', the groom of the stool played a key role in maintaining the king's health and the appearance of his linens.[99]

7.9 Adam de Colone, *George Seton, 8th Lord Seton, and 3rd Earl of Winton, with His Sons George Lord Seton and Alexander 1st Viscount Kingston*, 1625. Oil on canvas, 113 × 83.8 cm. National Galleries of Scotland. George Seton and his sons wear immaculate, lace-edged falling ruffs.

Laundresses

Shirts, along with separate collars, cuffs, ruffs, ruffles and cravats, to name but a few of the linen items a man of fashion would own, had several functions linked to comfort, hygiene and health (fig. 7.9). In order to serve well in these capacities they needed to be clean, white, smooth and starched, as Samuel Pepys made clear in his diary. The problem with

Ætatis 40
Ætatis 12

7.10 Man's lace collar, linen edged with bobbin lace, with tassels of knotted linen thread, Honiton, Devon, 1630–40. Victoria and Albert Museum, London. This example demonstrates why the laundress's skill in bleaching, smoothing and starching was so important.

pristine white linen was that it was very easily soiled, as was the case on 3 May 1665 when Pepys drank his 'morning draught in good chocolate and slabbered my band'. Finding himself at a sartorial disadvantage, Pepys 'sent home for another'.[100] Fine linens could also suffer at the hands of careless artisans. On 29 October 1663 Pepys was getting dressed 'and wanting a band, I found all my bands that were newly made clean, so ill smoothed that I crumpled them and flung them all on the ground'.[101] It was men like Pepys that John Taylor, the water poet, had in mind when he described how hard laundresses worked to keep their clients looking presentable in spite of the men's best efforts to the contrary (fig. 7.10). In his play *The Praise of Cleane Linnen, With the Commendable Use of the Laundresse* (1630) Taylor berated 'man-monsters' who were 'monstrous Linnen soylers' and 'shirt polluting tyrants' and urged them to 'Remember that your Laundresse paines is great, / Whose labours onely keepe you sweet and neat', adding that 'By her thy Linnen's sweet and cleanely drest, / Else thou wouldst stinke aboue ground like a beast'.[102]

Laundresses have a close relationship with the people whose linen they wash because in the process things may often be revealed about their customers' health and private lives. As such, they are often the guardians of an individual's secrets and have a valid reason for seeing someone regularly. Until recently, Charles I was always considered to have been very loyal to his wife. Yet Sarah Poynting's research suggests that after Henrietta Maria had left the country, and Charles was imprisoned, his relationship with Jane Whorwood, who posed as his laundress, developed into something more.[103] Charles described her as 'Sweete Jane Whorwood', while her husband referred to her as 'whore, bitch, [and] jade'.[104] Some years later, George Monck was rumoured to have met Anne, his future wife, when she was his laundress while he was imprisoned in the Tower.

Sir Anthony Weldon's view of Scotland was unflattering and succinct: 'The air might be wholesome but for the stinking people that inhabit it'.[105] However, this only serves as evidence of Weldon's dislike of the king and his homeland, rather than exposing a lack on the part of the royal laundresses and royal laundry. An early reference to James VI's laundress can be found in May 1577 when Margaret Duchall, the king's 'lavender', received £30 Scots 'to buy her clothing'.[106] His Scottish laundress, just like his tailor and other royal artisans, came to London with him. The household lists for his sons suggest that they also used the services of Scottish laundresses. On 26 March 1608 'Bessie Moncreiff lavindres of the prince maiestie' acknowledged receipt of £116 Scots from Sir Robert Melville of Murdocarny.[107] In 1610 Prince Charles's laundress for the body was named as Agnes Seaton and she received an annual salary of £40, while his seamstress was Julian Elliott, who also received £40.[108] His laundress for the board was Agnes Joffy, with a salary of £10 and board wages of £27 7s 6d.[109] The pattern continued after he became king, because in July 1625 Anne Josey received a grant as the king's laundress for his table linen with a stipend of 3s a day.[110]

Many of the royal laundresses stayed with their masters in spite of the difficulties the Stuarts faced in the 1640s and 1650s. In July 1643 Elizabeth Wheeler, 'laundress for His Majesty's body', was allowed to go with her servants to Oxford.[111] According to Thomas Coke, Wheeler did more than the king's washing; she 'brought letters to him on the Isles of Wights'.[112]

When Dorothy Chiffinch petitioned Charles II for back pay in January 1659, her writ reveals how the king's laundry worked during his exile. Her predecessor, a Mrs Freeman, had received 4 livres a day while in Paris, along with a place to do the washing, while Dorothy received 20 sous a day for mending the queen's laced linen, and a piece rate for making, the rate set by the queen. When she served as a laundress to the king and queen she received 4 livres on the proviso that it was paid constantly, so that she could keep servants to do the work, and that a place would be provided.[113] The amount of work meant that the laundress managed a team of staff, and when Mary Chiffinch was sworn to the queen's household the warrant issued by the lord chamberlain included her right to choose the laundry maids.[114] The number of maids is hinted at in Henrietta Maria's household listing that recorded three laundry maids, who received £10 with £25 for livery, and a starcher who was paid £8 4s.[115]

Laundresses washed the king's new sheets, shirts and other linen items before they were delivered for his use. Dorothy's bill that was paid on 26 October 1668 included £2 10s for the first washing of the linen. She received a further £1 5s for fine thread and silk to make up the linen and embroider it with the king's mark.[116] Being the king's laundress meant that the recipient received livery which, as the grant made to Eleanor Wall in 1680 indicates, was quite stylish. She received 3 yards of picke for a gown at 16s a yard, 7 yards of silk grosgrain at 10s a yard and 7 yards of tawny camlet at 4s a yard that was to be delivered 'at every Feast of St Andrew'.[117] She also received two trunks 'lined with silk and quilted with perfume to keep his linen in'.[118] In April 1681 Eleanor petitioned for payment of £1,000 for building a house for the king's laundry.[119] As with the Wardrobe of the Robes, Scottish influence within the office of the royal laundresses gradually declined, with the Restoration being the key turning point.

Doing the Laundry in Scotland

The large households run by the Scottish elite made provision for the laundering of clothing and household linens such as sheets in the form of a separate laundry or wash house. For instance, in March 1675 the 10th laird of Glenorchy authorised Robert Stirling to give John Williamsone £48 11s Scots, for 'theiking the washing house, runroof of the stable and mending the wester pyramid'.[120] In 1681 Mungo Campbell of Kenloch paid James Deor, mason, for work on the washing house.[121] The various royal officials who had lodgings at Holyroodhouse needed to ensure that they had access to all the necessary facilities to ensure both their own dignity and that of the king whose representatives they were. On 25 October 1692 John Hamilton wrote from the palace to a Mr David Crauford, passing on the chancellor's enquiries about where the earl of Perth had his washing house when he had lived at Holyrood.[122] While Crauford's reply is now lost, the request reveals the importance placed on clean, white linen.

When away from home, whether they were in Edinburgh, London or elsewhere, most men used a local laundress on a more or less ad hoc basis to do their washing. In 1692, when Lord and Lady Breadalbane were in Edinburgh, they employed Margaret Ross.[123] Two years later Margaret worked for Breadalbane and the countess of Caithness, including washing and dressing linens from 12 May to 22 July 1694.[124] A bill for a longer block of washing running from 23 July 1694 to 12 November 1694 revealed that Margaret lived on the Canongate.[125] When Lord Breadalbane and his son, John, were in Westminster in 1685 they employed Jean Dunbar to wash and dress their 'points', including cravats, ruffles, stocks and shirts.[126] A laundress often took on the laundry for a whole family. In 1686 Mrs Douglas was employed by Lord Abbotshall to wash and dress his linen, as well as the linens of Lady Abbotshall and the young ladies.[127] However, not everyone who took in specialist laundry had the requisite skills, as Erementiana Mayne discovered in 1678. She had retrieved Lady Garard's lace headdress from cousin Bedwell because she 'was washing it with more willingness than skill'.[128]

White linen was highly prized, so large households such as that of Alexander Montgomery, 6th earl of Eglinton, employed specialist bleachers to whiten new linen. In 1626 the 'blicher wyffe' bleached 'tua webis of small Linian of sarking clothe' at 16s the ell.[129] However, this was not a straightforward process as Margaret, dowager countess of Winton, revealed. She was reluctant to bleach 35 ells of her daughter-in-law's new linen because 'last yere I had ane great quantite of my cloith rottin and spoilt with Lyme so that it was goode for no service'.[130]

Margaret was not alone in her struggles to get white linen, and in 1633 the Scottish parliament passed an 'act and proclamatioun discharging all bleitching with lyme under the pane of punishing the contraveenners thairof in thair persons and goods'.[131] The lime was too harsh for the linen that 'is so brunt with the lyme that it hes no continuaunce bot is eaten up and spoyled afoir it be halfe worne'.[132]

Using the sun to bleach fabric was safer but required space to lay the cloth out so that it could absorb the light, and in 1677 an ingenious group of linen bleachers decided to make use of the kirkyard in Linlithgow, much to the annoyance of the minister. He complained bitterly about a former bailie, who had pulled down part of the churchyard wall in order to admit 'certain persons' who were 'defiling the church and sepulchres in a most prophane and indecent manner' by 'bleaching cloth upon the graves of the dead'.[133] Most bleaching was more decorous than this, but it does serve to show the high premium placed on white linen in Scotland.

Achieving flat, crease-free white linens required careful ironing with smoothing irons. When James VI returned to Scotland in 1617 James Baillie received £16 Scots for 'four smoothing irones for the kingis landres'.[134] Irons of this type were still in use at the end of the century, as indicated by Mungo Campbell sending two smoothing irons from the house at Balloch to Castle Kelcharn 'for my lord's use' in the summer of 1690.[135] Ironing required skill, and it took its toll on the irons, which periodically needed repairing. In 1677 Donald Tosh, smith, was paid 'for helping' two smoothing irons belonging to Lord Neill Campbell.[136] This was a small price to pay in order to keep Campbell's wardrobe presentable.

Soap and Starch

Soap played an important role in personal hygiene and while doing the laundry. Efforts to promote soap making in Scotland included the grant of a soap-making monopoly in 1634 to Patrick Maule of Panmure.[137] In 1650 General Lambert permitted James Riddell, master of the Leith soap works, to set his servants to work and to transport materials from his warehouses and 'two myllis beyound the Queinsferie'.[138] Soap was still being produced in Leith in 1695 when Robert Douglas, soap boiler, petitioned the king to honour the act of parliament exempting him and his father from all duties on soap for 19 years.[139] Alongside domestic production, soap was also imported, as indicated in a letter sent in April 1623 by Thomas, viscount Fenton, to John, earl of Mar, about 'bringing in soap'.[140] Port books indicate the scope of the Scottish soap trade. For instance, in 1617 soap was brought into the port of Ayr on the west coast, while by the late 1680s a significant percentage of it came from Rotterdam.[141]

Large households bought soap in bulk. In 1675 Anna Mackenzie, countess of Argyll, ordered two firkins of soap from John Campbell at Rosneth.[142] Four years later William Baillie, master of the duke of

7.11 *(right)* Pieter van der Borcht, *Monkeys Starching Ruffs*, c.1600-37. Etching, 9.3 × 12.3 cm. British Museum, London. While van der Borcht satirises ruff preparation, his print very effectively shows the various stages in the process.

7.12 *(below)* Paul van Somer, *Elizabeth, Countess of Kellie*, c.1619. Oil on canvas, 205.7 × 123.2 cm. Yale Center for British Art, Paul Mellon Collection, New Haven, Connecticut. A yellow ruff and matching cuffs put the finishing touches to Elizabeth's fashionable gown, with its fitted and hanging sleeves, while an open-fronted skirt reveals the petticoat.

Hamilton's household, ordered a firkin of soap from Robert Douglas in Leith.[143] On occasion there are hints about the type, such as the black soap that Breadalbane bought in 1686–7 from Robert Broune, a merchant in Inveraray.[144] More specialist washing items, including washballs, were also available. In 1677 the marquis of Atholl bought washballs from John Blair of Wester Gormak, while by 1700 Lord Glenorchy's accounts included a box to keep the washballs in.[145]

Many linens were starched after washing, and from the late sixteenth century pure white starch was usually made from good-quality wheat. It was soluble in hot water and essential for making ruffs, cuffs and cravats stiff and smooth, and to hold a specific shape. As Pieter van der Borcht's etching indicates, the process was complex (fig. 7.11). However, the problem with making starch from wheat was stressed in 1661 when the Corporation of White Starch Makers was re-established. They were only allowed to make starch from bran, pollard, imported or defective grain, and the import of white starch was forbidden.[146] This did not stop Edward Gareth and William Gallway petitioning two years later for permission to import the product.[147] The demand for starch is evident from the scale of purchases, such as the barrel of starch Andrew Russell bought from John Melville in Edinburgh in 1681.[148] Five years later Lady Glenorchy received a pound of starch and a bag to put it in from John Bouie.[149] Starch was one of a range of luxury dried goods, and during 1697–8 Mungo Campbell of Kenloch bought spices, sugar, dried fruit and starch from Charles Stuart in Perth.[150]

By adding indigo or saffron the starch became pale blue or yellow. The result was subtle, attractive and frequently denounced as the 'devil's fashion' in the 1610s and 1620s.[151] George Villiers wore a yellow-tinged ruff for his portrait of 1616, and critics associated the popularity of yellow starch at court with Scotland, Ireland and Catholicism.[152] More spectacular was Elizabeth Pierrepont, countess of Kellie's use of yellow starch. Here, van Somer captures the popularity of this fashion with women as well as men (fig. 7.12).

Royal Perfume Use

Casting bottles for sprinkling rose water were very popular from the sixteenth to the mid seventeenth centuries, when they dropped out of use.[153] This reflected a change in both how perfumes and cosmetics were used and how they were displayed in fancy bottles on dressing tables from the early seventeenth century onwards (fig. 7.13). These changes were in turn linked to developments in distilling that resulted in stronger, longer-lasting perfumed waters in tandem with an increasing use of musk.[154] The scale of perfume use after 1660 is evident from the accounts of John Jones, apothecary to the king's household, who supplied perfume and rose water for his majesty's barge on 303 occasions from Midsummer 1677 to Christmas 1679.[155]

The rise of the professional perfumer reflected the increased importance placed on scent and the fact that specific perfumes could be made to suit individual tastes. Under the Stuarts this process started at quite a low level that followed on from Tudor patterns in London, with Robert Hutchinson receiving £15 6s 8d in 1623/4 for perfuming the king's parliament robes.[156] While his post might have been modest, the scale of his business was not. In 1639 the earl of Denbigh paid Hutchinson £100, part of £635 owing to him.[157] After the Restoration the situation had changed, and in June 1673 Abraham Dehyninge was appointed groom of the robes in ordinary and perfumer in ordinary in place of Paul Ferrine.[158]

Working alongside the perfumer was the king's apothecary, and in 1607 John Wolfgang Rumler received the money owed him 'for physical things, perfumes, &c' since the death of John Clavee, the late apothecary.[159] After the Restoration John Chase, the king's apothecary, rented 'a small parcel of land next the tennis court in St James's Fields' previously granted by Charles I to John Parkinson, his botanist, as a garden for plants.[160] Charles II also had a French apothecary by the name of Monsieur Le Febvre who imported 36 bales of goods, drugs and 'chemical materials' from France in 1661.[161]

7.13 The cost of the perfume was enhanced by expensive containers such as this gold and enamel early 17th-century perfume bottle from the Cheapside hoard. Enamelled gold, opals, opaline chalcedony, diamonds, rubies, pink sapphires and spinels. Museum of London.

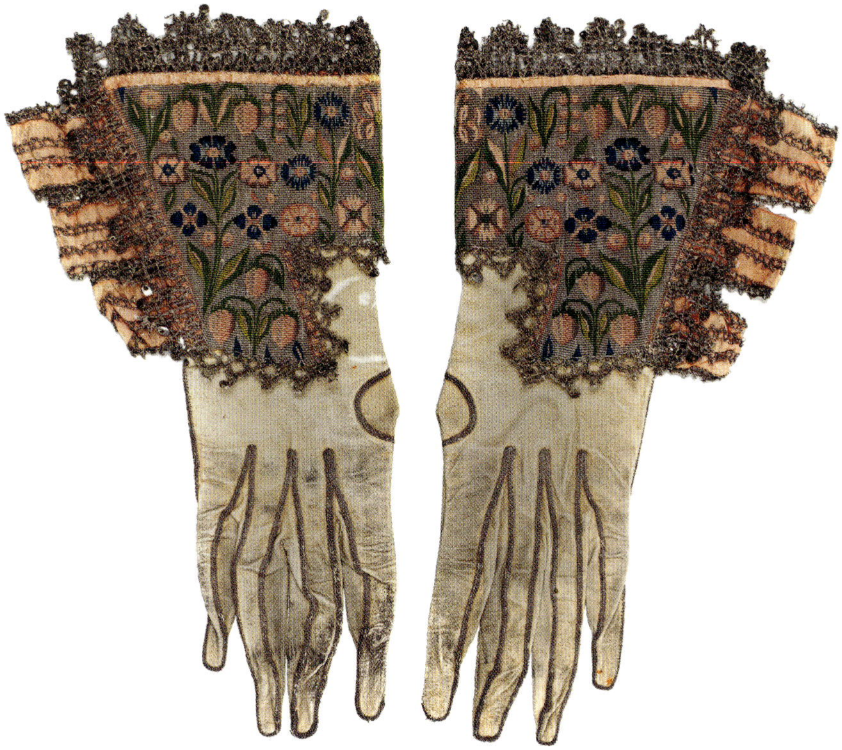

7.14 Pair of gloves, leather, silk and metal thread, early 17th century. Metropolitan Museum of Art, New York. Leather gloves like this pair were often perfumed as well as being decorated.

Perfuming in Scotland

There is fairly limited evidence of perfume use in Scotland before the mid seventeenth century, with the exception of the court. However, from then on it is possible to get a sense of how such scents were used. Scented waters were one option, with Queen of Hungary water, an alcohol-based perfume, predominantly perfumed with rosemary, being popular. Scottish customers included the earl of Breadalbane, who purchased a bottle in 1691.[162] In 1701–3 the laird of Grant's younger brother, Ludovick, bought rose water and Queen of Hungary water from James Gordon the elder in Elgin.[163] In the same period a certain John Gordon, who described himself as a 'chirurgeon apothecary', sold medicines and a glass of Queen of Hungary water.[164] Perfumed oils were also available, with the earl and countess of Lothian purchasing sweet oil from William Dunbar in 1688.[165] Scented products, especially perfumed leather goods, were also in demand. For instance, Sir Robert Campbell of Glenorchy bought two pairs of sweet gloves from Andrew Reid in Perth in 1642.[166] The choice had increased by 1669–71, when John Graham of Edinburgh sold George, earl of Caithness, oiled French gloves, jessamy gloves, double chamois gloves, muffs and sweet kid gloves (fig. 7.14).[167]

Many fresh and dried flowers are heavily scented, as were the 'sweet flowers' sent in May 1642 from Chelsea by Sir John Danvers to the marquis of Hamilton.[168] A growing appreciation of private and royal gardens explains the creation of the royal botanic or physic garden in Holyrood park in 1670. Early in 1704 the botanist James Sutherland received an annual pension of £50 for tending the gardens at Holyroodhouse, establishing a physic garden in Edinburgh and teaching others about plants.[169] Perfumed products were also sold as a vital part of the embalming process and for bodies while they lay in state prior to burial. In 1677 John Foulis, an apothecary in Edinburgh, supplied 'Imbalming pouders Balsame and oyles', as well as 'Sweet gumes for perfuming the Roomes' at Seton, the home of George, earl of Winton, an order costing over £145.[170] An interest in perfumed plants and products, to cheer the living and mask the scent of the dead, played an important role in Stuart society.

Conclusions

When John Goddard drew the Seven Deadly Sins, he chose a well-dressed man accompanied by a peacock to personify Pride, who tells the viewer, 'The Taylors Sheers I should have held in hand' (fig. 7.15). While he did not approve, Goddard acknowledged the central role of the tailor in male self-fashioning, and the most influential tailors were those working for the king. Samuel Butler went further, asserting that 'Sin and he [the tailor] are Partners; for as Sin first brought him into employment, so he by cheating and contributing to Pride and Vanity works to Sin, and the old Trade is still kept up between both'.[171] As this chapter has demonstrated, the style promoted by the Stuart kings was created by a group of predominantly Scottish tailors, so ensuring a pro-French approach. London was growing in importance as a centre of fashionable Stuart tailoring, and Scottish tailors were a part of the developing Scottish community in this city. While happy to work for Englishmen, many had significant numbers of Scottish clients, and they worked together to provide work and support to their fellow countrymen. While not dominating the Wardrobe of the Robes to the same extent, Scots were nonetheless significant here, and through their networks helped spread ideas on court style and the growing sophistication of laundering and starching. Jewellery, often made by Scottish goldsmiths, also played a key role in shaping and perpetuating the Stuart image, as the next chapter reveals.

7.15 John Goddard, 'Pride' from *The Seven Deadly Sins*, c.1629. Engraving, 14.9 × 9.1 cm. British Museum, London. A walking advert for Stuart fashion, this fashionable gentleman personifies pride in Goddard's view of society.

SAL·OBTEIN·VICTORIE·IN·YAIR·PRETENCE·QVHA·HOPIS·STIL·CONSTANLY·WITH

CHAPTER EIGHT

Jewellery and the Romance of the Stuarts

THE LENNOX OR DARNLEY JEWEL is a remarkable piece of sixteenth-century Scottish goldsmith's work. Whether George Heriot, Michael Gilbert II or James Gray made it, the jewel serves as a testament to the talents of Edinburgh craftsmen in the 1570s (fig. 8.1). This small, colourful and visually complex piece was expensive, bespoke and resonant with meaning for the Lennox family and for aspirational Stuarts in the late sixteenth century. The family's wishes are expressed succinctly in the inscription, which reads QVHA. HOPIS. STI. CONSTANLY. VITH PATIENCE SAL. OBTEAIN. VICTORIE. IN YAIR. PRETENCE (Who hopes still constantly with patience shall obtain victory in their claim). In 1603, the Lennox plans were realised when their grandson became king of Great Britain and embarked on what Murray Pittock has styled 'the Stuart myth'.[1]

Stuart male jewellery, consisting of rings, slides, earrings and jewelled buttons, formed an essential part of male adornment. Its appeal was linked to the quality of the workmanship and materials, a reflection both of the ability of Stuart monarchs to attract leading craftsmen to their courts, and of the vibrancy of the gemstone trade and jewellery market. It was an eye-catching style, as John Michael Wright noted when he accompanied Lord Castlemaine, James VII and II's ambassador to Rome, in 1686. For the Easter celebrations the earl 'had great store of Excellent Diamonds in his Hat, Wrists, Sword, Shoes &c. and where ever else they could well appear'.[2] With rock crystal and paste versions readily available, jewellery was accessible to most men in Stuart society. More importantly, jewellery could express loyalty to members of the royal family, past and present. Some pieces incorporated a miniature, initials or symbols, such as the oak tree or butterfly representing Charles II's escape after the battle of Worcester and hopes of his restoration. Royal portraits were produced in a variety of media, and while valuable in their own right, because of the significance of the sitter these portraits

8.1 The Lennox or Darnley jewel, Scottish, c. 1571–8. Gold, enamel, Burmese rubies, Indian emerald and cobalt blue glass, 6.6 × 5.2 cm. Royal Collection.

8.2 Jacobite pincushion and ribbon, c.1745–50, silk, British, probably Manchester. Cushion 10.2 × 5.1 cm; ribbon 24.8 × 1.3 cm. Metropolitan Museum of Art, New York. Embroidered with the words 'God bless PC', a reference to Bonnie Prince Charlie, the sentiments of this pincushion's owner are clear.

were made more precious when combined with a sumptuous, often diamond-rich, setting.[3] Many were openly given and worn with pride. Others were private gifts or commissions, concealed under clothing or inside another piece of jewellery, and contemplated in secret. The latter became increasingly important in the context of the Wars of the Three Kingdoms and periods of Stuart exile culminating with the development of the Jacobite cause. As Pittock has shown, jewellery and other small, personal items such as the pincushion shown in fig. 8.2, were regarded as 'treacherous' by the Williamites and Hanoverians, but both Guthrie and Pittock are in agreement that Stuart jewellery was inspirational for the Jacobites.[4]

The Stuarts had a long-standing appreciation of jewellery, with James V's personal collection from the mid sixteenth century demonstrating the value and appeal of well-set gems.[5] He shared his love of jewellery with his daughter, his grandson and his cousin, Elizabeth I.[6] The result was competitive collecting, and when Mary, Queen of Scots was forced to sell the pearls given to her by Catherine de' Medici as a wedding present in 1568, Elizabeth I was keen to purchase the necklace. In 1603 all of Elizabeth's jewels passed to James VI and I. Whether he looked for his mother's pearls or not, James did not waste much time before going through the late queen's collection. He entered London on 7 May 1603 and on 19 May 'a jewel of gold like a Crossbow garnished with diamonds' was 'Taken by the Kings Majestie'. Van Somer depicted Anna with a similar crossbow jewel in her hair when he painted the queen in *c.*1617.[7]

According to Scaramelli, the Venetian ambassador, James VI prized jewellery over clothes so much so that 'from his dress he would have been taken for the meanest among his courtiers, a modesty he affects, had it not been for a chain of diamonds round his neck and a great diamond in his hair'.[8] As Chapter 1 demonstrated, James VI and I's clothes were not as modest as Scaramelli suggests, but his love of diamonds was undeniable. During the course of the seventeenth century, the Stuarts' relationship with jewellery changed from serving as an expression of power and magnificence to something much more significant. Jewellery, in its many forms, became one of the most potent ways of celebrating and commemorating individual monarchs, and the house of Stuart in good times and bad. This chapter explores how and why jewellery became such a potent expression of Stuart style.

Royal Jewels: The Honours of Scotland

Regalia played a central role in the Scottish coronation, the monarch being crowned king or queen of the people, rather than the land, with the Honours of Scotland. The Honours consisted of 'The sceptar contening thrie pecis with ane stane of cristell', 'The swerd of estait' and 'The croun compleit and furnist with stanis and perle'.[9] These richly jewelled objects were symbolic of the Stuarts' long Scottish lineage and, thereby, their right to rule the three kingdoms. By selecting Scottish gold from Crawford Muir in South Lanarkshire for the changes made to the Honours, John Mosman and James V stressed the bond between the regalia and their country. This was reinforced by the use of seven Scottish or Tay pearls, so called because they came from the River Tay in Perthshire, alongside 13 oriental pearls on the fillet and two rock crystals with green foil to suggest emeralds.[10]

The Honours were present at the coronations of James VI, Charles I and Charles II, and they had a significant history. When the crown was refashioned for James V, the arches of the older crown were added to a new fillet with fleur-de-lys and crosses fleury (fig. 8.3).[11] The sceptre was a partially reworked gift from Pope Alexander VI, while Julius II had sent the sword.[12] Keeping the Honours secure was central to the dignity of the Scottish monarchy, and in March 1646 the governor of Stirling Castle was ordered to deliver them to the earl of Callender, who was to 'appoint his troop to escort them' en route to Edinburgh Castle.[13]

During the ride to and opening of the Scottish parliament, the Honours represented royal authority in the absence of the monarch and asserted the importance of the Scottish elite. For instance, on 2 September 1639 Robert Campbell of Glenfalloch described how Argyll carried the crown, Crawford the sceptre and Sutherland the sword in the opening ceremony.[14] The process was exactly the same in 1641 when Charles I was present, except on this occasion Hamilton carried the crown, Argyll the sceptre and Sutherland the sword.[15] Once in exile Charles II wrote to the keeper of Dunnottar Castle, asking him to give the 'Crowne Scepter, and other the Honors of that our ancient Kingdom' to the captain of a ship that he was sending specially from Paris.[16] His request fell on deaf ears, as had that of Mary, Queen of Scots when she asked for the Honours to be sent to France to crown the Dauphin in 1559.[17]

8.3 The Scottish crown, 1503 with alterations and additions 1532 and 1540. Gold, pearls, gemstones; part of the Honours of Scotland, Edinburgh Castle.

James VI and I and Charles I both wore the regalia of St Edward the Confessor, housed at Westminster Abbey, and the Tudors' personal regalia, kept in the Jewel House at the Tower of London.[18] The latter was listed in the 1547 inventory of Henry VIII and depicted in

8.4 Daniel Mytens, *Charles I*, 1631. Oil on canvas, 215.9 × 134.6 cm. National Portrait Gallery, London. The Tudors' personal crown, orb and sceptre are displayed on a table to Charles's right.

Mytens's portrait of Charles I (fig. 8.4).[19] The Stuarts made this regalia their own by commissioning new pieces, including 'A Crowne sett with Dyamants, Saphirs and Emerandes' made for Prince Henry at his creation as prince of Wales.[20] Charles I made his mark, adding three swords to the St Edward's regalia: Curtana and the Swords of Temporal and Spiritual Justice.[21] New regalia was made at the Restoration and in 1671 it was in the news again. Colonel Thomas Blood's daring raid on the Tower was foiled, but word travelled fast and on 17 May the 10th laird of Glenorchy received 'news from London of an attempt to steal the crown'.[22]

The Stuarts' relationship with the English regalia was complex. On the one hand, it symbolised their success in unifying the three kingdoms, something the Tudors had never achieved. The Stuarts were regularly depicted either wearing or standing next to the regalia, and it was James VI and I who established the concept of the 'crown jewels' being inalienable.[23] Even so, the history of the ruby coronation ring associated with James VII and II, that may also have been worn by Charles I and Charles II, demonstrates that the Stuarts did remove items of great significance to them (fig. 8.5).[24] On the other hand, Stuart rule resulted in the destruction of the English regalia, and its recreation, while the Scottish Honours survived, serving as a permanent reminder of which country was the Stuarts' 'ancient kingdom'.

8.5 The Stuarts' coronation ring, c. 1660 or earlier with later additions. Gold, silver, a ruby and diamonds, 2.3 × 2.2 cm. Royal Collection.

A Surrogate for the Regalia: Stuart Uses of the Order of the Garter

The English and Scottish chivalric orders had immense social and political significance because their membership included royal friends and favourites drawn from the male elite. By 1603 the Order of the Garter had a long pedigree associated with ideas of Englishness, chivalry and elite masculinity. Its membership included James VI, who was made a Garter knight in 1590 by Elizabeth I, just as James V had been in 1535 by Henry VIII. Yet on his accession, James was elevated from knight to head of an order that he then used to bind the English and Scottish elites together, in a bid to promote the idea of Great Britain. He began by putting Lennox and Southampton forward in 1603, and the earls of Dunbar and Montgomery in 1608. According to the Venetian ambassador, James believed 'that nothing can more contribute to the Union than the idea and demonstration of an equality of rank between the two nations'.[25] This pattern continued in 1611 with the appointment of Thomas Howard, 21st earl of Arundel, and Robert Kerr, 1st viscount Rochester, and in 1615 with the election of William Knollys and Thomas Erskine, 1st viscount of Fentoun.[26]

James VI and I commissioned Garters and Georges for the six new Garter knights created at his accession. The details of this commission reveal how James viewed his heir and Stuart blood over that of other royal houses. Henry's Garter was 'to be garnished and sett w[i]th pretious stones and Jewells fittinge the dignity of his p[er]son', while that for the Danish king was 'to be garnished w[i]th other Matter of meaner value'.[27] After a time James was happy to introduce innovations into the order, reflecting his absolute authority combined with a wish for less formality. In 1622 he stipulated that because 'the blue or sky-colour had been used for some years past, the ribband shall in future always be of a blue colour'.[28] While blue bonnets might be criticised, blue ribbons were now associated with the highest chivalric honour. However, not all change came from the king. Henry Howard, earl of Northampton, for instance, had a watch placed inside his George, thereby combining tradition with technical innovation.[29]

8.6 Great George made by Robert Vyner for Charles II, c.1661. Gold, enamel and diamonds, 7.2 × 6.4 cm. Royal Collection.

James shared his interest in the Garter with his sons. Prince Henry's enthusiasm for the order was reflected in the quality of his regalia, including 'A Chayne of Spanish work sett with Dyamants with a great George hanging thereat' and 'One Garter of gold letters with Dyamants thynne sett'.[30] In 1626 Charles I ordered the placement of the order's badge on the left shoulder of his coats and cloaks and Buckingham followed the king's lead, paying John Crane £26 'for embroidering the new order on divers of his lordship's clothes'.[31] After the outbreak of fighting in 1642, Charles I came to appreciate how the jewelled Garter and lesser George could substitute for the royal regalia. Its significance to the king and those supporting his cause explains the actions of John Maitland, earl of Lauderdale, after the surrender of Oxford. Maitland received £500 sterling from Crawford, the lord high treasurer, that he paid to Lieutenant Colonel Robert Hammond 'for releiff of his Majesty's George, his collar of S.S. and garter pawned to him by those Lords who treated for the giving up of Oxford'. He then sent them to the king at Newcastle.[32] Some years later the king went to his death wearing the lesser George.[33]

Almost a year after Charles I's execution, Charles II wrote from Jersey on 12 January 1650 'To our right truly and entirely beloved cosen, James Marquis of Montrose'. He authorised Montrose to use and wear the Garter on his left leg, place the embroidered star within a Garter on his cloak and upper garments, and to place the Garter about his arms, 'in as ample a manner as if he had been installed in the Castle of Windsor'.[34] Two months later Charles II created eight new Garter knights including the earls of Derby, Newcastle and the duke of Hamilton, 'at which prodigall imparting of that Honour, 'tis thought the Scottish Nation will not be well pleased, and in particular that it is not also sent to the Marquesse of Huntley, who perhaps may be thereby much alienated from the Royall Interest'.[35] To make matters worse, the duke of Hamilton 'received this Honour as Earle of Cambridge, and not as a Scotch Duke'.[36] When Charles II hoped to gain the support of the elector of Brandenburg in 1652 he sent him a gift of the George and Garter. It failed because, as Hyde noted, 'it is a thousand pities that the King should send such a George, which cost but six pistols', so undermining the prestige of the order.[37]

In addition to their symbolic worth, royal Garter jewels had significant financial value and in the summer of 1658 Charles II and James, duke of York and Albany, pawned their Georges.[38] In December the following year, 125 florins were due in interest on a loan of 2,000 florins secured 'on his majesties George' at a rate of 6¼ per cent.[39] At the Restoration Charles II commissioned new Garter regalia including a diamond-studded greater George made by Robert Vyner (fig. 8.6). Yet in spite of this financial value, their sentimental worth was often far greater. James VII and II took his father's Garter insignia with him into exile.[40] He continued to create knights of the Garter at Saint-Germain, including John Drummond, 1st earl of Melfort, in 1691, and left his best Garter to his son James VIII and III, thereby demonstrating the significance of the Garter to the Stuart story.[41]

The Stuarts, St Andrew and the Order of the Thistle

St Andrew, with St Ninian, was the patron saint of the Scots in the later Middle Ages.[42] As a result his saint's day was an auspicious choice for events such as the creation of Charles as duke of York in 1605, and it served to promote James's wish for stronger ties between Scotland and England.[43] However, the day itself was not celebrated in a specific way each year, as John Nicoll's comments in 1662 indicate:

> The threttie day of November this yeir fallin upone ane Saboth day, and being a day callit Sant Androis day, many of our nobles, barones, gentrie, and utheris of this kingdome, pat on that day ane liveray or favour for that day, and for reverence thairof. This being a novaltie, I thought guid to record, because it wes nevir in use heirtofoir since the Reformatioun.[44]

It was not until 1687 that the Order of the Thistle, established by James IV but lapsing under James V, was re-established by James VII and II in a bid to strengthen his links with the Scottish aristocracy.[45] Knights received a robe of 'green velvet … pasemée or powdered over the thistles of gold embroidered', a surcoat of purple velvet and doublet and trunk hose

8.7 Sir Godfrey Kneller, *John Drummond, 1st Earl of Melfort*, 1688. Oil on canvas, 243.7 × 147.2 cm. Duff House, Banff, Aberdeenshire. Drummond wears the Thistle robes over a cloth of silver suit, similar to that worn for the Garter.

of cloth of silver trimmed with loops of blue and silver ribbon.[46] James VII and II's accounts for 1687 included a payment for 'embroidering thistles all of gold and silver wire for the St Andrew which is on the breast of the robe'.[47] The earliest surviving set of robes is associated with James Drummond, 4th earl of Perth, and may well be those worn by his brother John, 1st earl of Melfort (fig. 8.7). Made of green velvet, the mantle has the figure of St Andrew on the shoulder surrounded by the words *Nemo me impune lacessit* (No one attacks me with impunity), the Scottish royal motto. The king's jeweller, Christopher Rose, supplied gold for the Thistle regalia.[48]

St Andrew's significance was made clear in the statutes. The knights were 'in honour to the Holy Apostle St Andrew' and 'his Maiestie shall wear the Collar of that Order on the day of the Feast of St Andrew being the 30th November yearly'.[49] The knights swore to 'fortify & defend the Christian Religion & Christs most holy Evangelist'.[50] The king's titles were given as 'James the Seventh by the grace of God king of Scotland, England, France and Ireland, defender of the Faith & Soveraigne of the most ancient & Noble Order of the Thistle'.[51] Members of the order were 'to carry & wear the Rebben, Medalls, Badge, Habit, Collar and all other Ornaments whatsoever now belonging, or that hereafter shall happen to pertain to the said Noble Order' (fig. 8.8).[52] Men who were members of both orders were to 'wear the said Order on the Ribbon of the Order of the Garter, or otherwayes in any manner that his Maiestie shall think fitt'.[53]

The impact of the order in Scotland was significant on two levels. First, James VII and II used it as a means to promote the Scottish elite and bind them to him by including Catholics and Protestants. The response was positive and in 1687 the earl of Melfort enthused that 'The Order ... has had effects beyond My expectatione so that I wold not Giv a farthing betwixt the Garter An it if both wer in My Choise'.[54] However, by October the duke of Hamilton reported to his wife that his brother George, earl of Dumbarton and Melfort, was extremely ill-pleased at the direction to resume wearing the Order of St Andrew about the neck.[55] Second, the order became associated with the Jacobites because Dumbarton, Melfort and Perth went into exile with James. While William and Mary made no new knights, Anne did, and in 1704 Charles II's grandson, James Scott, earl of Dalkeith, paid the goldsmith John Campbell for 'changing and new making the St Andrew the queen gave' and for making 'a gold' St Andrew.[56] Other new appointments included John Murray, 1st duke of Atholl (1659–1724) and George Douglas-Hamilton, 1st earl of Orkney (1666–1737), both of whom fought for the Williamite cause in 1689, thereby demonstrating Anne's wish to counter the Jacobite connections with the order.

Male Jewellery as an Integral Part of Stuart Fashion

Jewellery types and styles changed significantly from the mid sixteenth century to 1700, partly in response to changes in hairstyles and fashionable clothing. Wealthy men went from wearing a lot of jewellery to much less, and from favouring formal ceremonial pieces to less ornate items.[57] They may have been simpler in design but they needed to be big and significant. Enamel, such as *champlevé* and *email en résille sure verre*, gave way to faceted gemstones.[58] Rings, consisting of a single large stone or a cluster, were designed to be seen at a distance, while miniature cases and watches expressed what Joan Evans termed the 'majestic dignity of the Baroque'.[59]

Men displayed jewellery worn on the body or placed on clothing and accessories. Both methods were expressive of an individual's taste, especially when these were bespoke pieces made by the best craftsmen. Earrings were fashionable from the 1580s, yet the pamphleteer Philip Stubbes dismissed the men who wore them as 'another sort of dissolute minions and wanton sempronians, for I can term them no better', adding that they were 'so faire bewitched as they are not ashamed to make holes in their ears whereat they hang rings and other jewels of gold and precious stones'.[60] James VI and I shared Stubbes's view, which may explain why both Henry Frederick and Charles I wore a single earring.[61] They were possibly encouraged in this by their mother, who on 20 June 1603 'took Lord Cecil's little son in her arms, and kissed him twice, and bestowed a jewel on him, tying it herself in his ear'.[62] As an adult, Charles I favoured a single drop pearl topped with a gold imperial crown enamelled blue that he was painted wearing by Van Dyck in several portraits, including his three views of the king (fig. 8.9, see fig. 3.19).[63] Some years later Mary II gave this earring to Hans-Willem Bentinck, 1st earl of Portland, with a note recording that 'This pearle was taken out of ye King my grandfathers ear after he was beheaded & given ye Princess Royall'.[64] This gift demonstrated how both strands of the Stuart family valued their ties to Charles I.

James VI and I, Prince Henry and the young Charles I all favoured hat jewels. When John de Critz painted James in *c.*1605–10 he depicted the king wearing the Mirror of Great Britain in one version and with the Feather 'one fayre jewell, like a feather of gould, contayning a fayre table diamond in the middest and five and twentie diamonds of divers forms made of sondrous other jewells' in another.[65] Gradually hat jewels were replaced by jewelled hatbands such as Prince Henry's example with 'a great Jewell toe it in forme of a Rose'.[66] They were still in favour in 1657 when the 9th laird of Glenorchy bought a counterfeit hatband from Mr Brand.[67]

Jewellery fashions saw the chains, carcanets and collars, often with pendant jewels, favoured in the sixteenth-century fall out of use by the early 1600s, although they were retained for ceremonial use, such as the gold chain bought in 1664 for Lord Lyon, the leading Scottish herald.[68] However, men continued to wear jewels pinned to the doublet or coat.

8.8 An oval jewel or badge of gilt brass with the figure of St Andrew, associated with the Order of the Thistle, late 17th century/early 18th century, 5.2 × 3.7 cm. National Museum of Scotland, Edinburgh.

8.9 Pearl drop earring worn by Charles I at his execution in 1649. The Portland Collection, Harley Gallery, Welbeck, Nottinghamshire.

8.10 Set with 25 diamonds, the Lyte jewel is a pendant piece containing a miniature of the king by Nicholas Hilliard. *James VI and I*, 1610–11. Watercolour on vellum, 10.5 × 4.8 cm. British Museum, London.

8.11 Diamond signet ring made by Francis Walwyn for Henrietta Maria, c.1628. Gold, diamond and enamel. Royal Collection.

In 1611, Thomas Lyte (1568–1638) was painted wearing the jewel that James VI and I had given him in 1610 for tracing James's descent from Brute, the 'most noble founder of the Britons' (fig. 8.10).[69] While the Lyte jewel was unique, James planned to distribute gold badges to the members of his newly formed Order of Baronets. Members received a title and badge in return for 2,000 merks as part of the colonisation of Nova Scotia.[70] In 1685 John, earl of Breadalbane, pawned 'a medal of gold or a baronet's badge'.[71] James VI also wanted to make his knights of the Bath more distinctive, and he did so by giving them an insignia worn on a red silk ribbon.[72] An example of such a ribbon can be seen in Van Dyck's portrait of George Gordon, 2nd marquis of Huntly, who was made a knight of the Bath at Charles I's English coronation (see fig. 3.13).

Rings served as symbols of power and authority, as in the case of coronation rings, but they could also be very personal. While often highly decorative, they also had many practical functions. Signet rings were often set with engraved gemstones – diamonds for James VI and I, Charles I as prince of Wales and Henrietta Maria (fig. 8.11); topaz for James VII and II; and a sapphire for Mary II.[73] The signet Paul van Vianen made for Charles II was rather different, with the royal arms on a steel bezel set in gold, and the lion and unicorn on the shoulders in steel. However, these rings served the same purpose in authenticating letters and official documents.[74] Royal wedding rings were fashionable as well as functional, and Mary, Queen of Scots left her ring of diamonds set in red enamel to Darnley when she made her will before the birth of James.[75] This combination was still popular in 1608, when Christian Bruce married and she received a diamond wedding ring with black enamel.[76] When James married Mary of Modena he gave her a ring made of gold interlinked chains and a similar wedding ring was listed in the inventory of Margaret Scott of Rossie.[77]

Gem-set buttons, another item regularly recorded in Scottish inventories, do not seem at first glance to be the most expensive form of ornamentation, but closer inspection reveals that the materials and the quantity they were used in made them a very significant form of embellishment. In 1579 James VI received 'Threscoir and aucht buttonis of gold sett with a perll in every ane of thame emailed with quheit and blak' and 'Fourscoir and threttene buttonis of gold sum triangle and sum round everie ane divisit for thre perll and want and of the haill threttie five perllis'.[78] 30 years later, Henry's jewel list included 'Twelf great Buttons all sett with Dyamants' and 'Fyfteen dissone of gold buttons with a Dyamant in top of everie one of them for his highnes owne wearing'.[79] The appeal of such buttons is evident in Henrietta Maria's comment to Charles I in 1642 when she told him: 'You cannot imagine how handsome the buttons were, when they were removed out of the gold and strung into a chain'.[80]

Precious metal buttons continued to be a staple of the male wardrobe. In 1653 Hew Craig, merchant burgess of Edinburgh, received the final £3 owing for three dozen great and two dozen small gold buttons.[81] John Strachan paid 37s for four pairs of gold buttons set with stones for the use of Lord Breadalbane's son in March 1685.[82] Towards the end of the seventeenth century, male fashions demanded large quantities of buttons, causing the laird of Grant to purchase 12 dozen silver buttons in November 1686 from the Edinburgh goldsmith Alexander Reid.[83] Leading by example, the Stuart kings ensured that fashionable men used jewellery as an expression of wealth, status and loyalty to the crown.

Novelty Supplied by Stuart Goldsmiths and Jewellers

Jewelled brooches, rings and buttons were traditional forms of male jewellery that remained in fashion by changes in design and materials that reflected current taste. They were joined by new items that became popular under the Stuarts. By the mid seventeenth century, most men of means had small gold or silver pocket watches that often had decorative, jewelled cases. Some were bought new, as in the case of the two clocks and gold and silver watches that the laird of Grant owed £59 to Henry Massy for in 1699.[84] Others were passed down, and in March 1692 Alexander Bruce, son of the laird of Blairhall, received a gold watch from his late sister Dame Catherine Bruce, countess of Menteith.[85]

Shoe buckles became desirable in the early 1660s. Charles II's shoe buckles were usually made from polished or cut steel and they were supplied by his spurrier. However, occasionally they were more sumptuous and were made to match other accessories, as in 1671 when John Hengood supplied the king with a sword and a set of shoe buckles, both inlaid with gold.[86] Buckles continued to be a staple of the male wardrobe until the end of the century. In July 1690 John, lord Bargany, settled a bill for £8 12s Scots that he owed to the late William Law of Lauriestoune, goldsmith and burgess of Edinburgh, for two pairs of silver shoe buckles.[87] Sword hilts also came within the goldsmith's remit, as indicated by the laird of Grant owing money to Alexander Reid for two sword hilts in December 1686.[88] In 1705 Colin Mackenzie, a goldsmith in Edinburgh, repaired the young laird of Grant's whinger (a short stabbing sword), knife handle, cane and sword, and received the hilt and backguard of another sword in partial payment.[89] Canes of the type bought by the laird of Grant feature in full-length portraits of Charles I such as Van Dyck's *Le Roi à la chasse* (*c.* 1636). A hint of their appearance can be gleaned from the cane head associated with Charles I now housed at Carisbrooke Castle (fig. 8.12).[90] Or they could have gold fittings, as in the case of a cane belonging to the duke of Gordon, who paid George Main, an Edinburgh jeweller, £13 10s for a gold 'verrill [ferrule] to a kain' in 1694.[91] While Charles I's cane served primarily to accentuate his elegant posture, it had other uses and while 'at St Mary's in Oxford, he did hit [Prince Charles] on the head with his staff when he did observe him to laugh (at sermon time) upon the ladies that sat against him'.[92] As these examples reveal, the Stuarts readily embraced new jewellery styles and the Scottish elite followed their lead with enthusiasm.

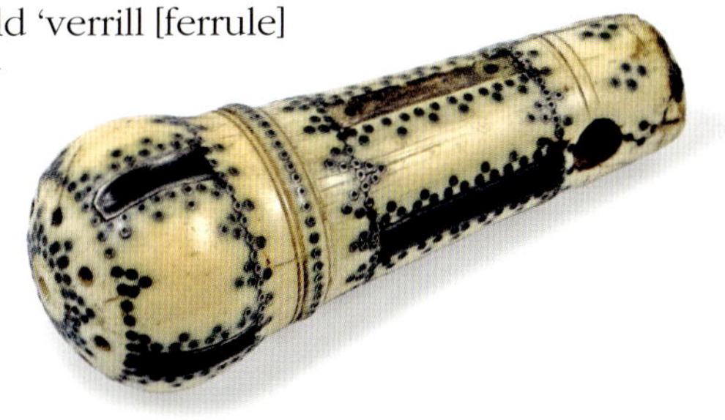

8.12 Bone cane top associated with Charles I, 1640s. Carisbrooke Castle Museum.

Scottish Jewellery as Part of the Stuarts' Style

The jewellery depicted in Scottish portraits and listed in inventories suggests that elite taste closely followed European trends. However, there were very occasional references to brooches, which may have been indicative of a distinctly Scottish strand of jewellery also owned by the male elite. Unfortunately, it is not possible to tell whether they were ring brooches used to hold a draped plaid in place. Even so, in 1649 Sir Robert Campbell of Glenorchy left 'a silver brooch set with precious stones and pearls',[93] while on 1 December 1661 Robert Campbell of Glen Lyon asked Mr Curtis to send his clothes and to borrow a little gold brooch with the promise of a better one.[94] The latter is suggestive of the small brooch pinned to Lord Mungo Murray's shirt in his portrait by John Michael Wright (see fig. I.3).

As Julian Goodare has noted, there have been few studies of the beliefs of the Scottish elite in relation to witchcraft, and jewellery believed to have protective or healing qualities does not feature often in elite records, with one famous exception.[95] This is the 'stone of the quantity of half a hen's egg set in silver, being flat at one end and round at the other end like a hen, which Sir Colin Campbell first laird of Glenurquhay, won when he fought in battle at the Rhodes against the turks'.[96] Another look at the material shows that there are a few items set with semi-precious stones that were believed to have healing properties. For instance, the 1680 inventory of John, earl of Caithness, listed two heliotropes or bloodstones set in gold and valued at £2.[97] There are a few other examples, but these were in the possession of women, including the pair of bloodstone bracelets owned by Dame Anna Stuart, lady Lawers, *c.*1691, and the cornelian ring repaired by George Main, jeweller, Edinburgh, for the countess of Aboyne.[98] Talismanic jewellery played a small but significant role in the lives of the male and female Scottish elite.

Stuart Uses of Jewellery

Stuart jewellery use drew, intentionally or otherwise, on several factors present in seventeenth-century society. First, an interest in the meanings attached to particular stones could influence a buyer's choices, as indicated by the popularity of lapidaries such as Thomas Nicols's *A Lapidary* or *The History of Pretious Stones* (1652) and Robert Boyle's *An Essay on the Origins and Virtues of Gems* (1672). Works like these combined classical ideas with Christian interpretations, so rubies were symbols of beauty, love and passion, diamonds of constancy and virtue, and pearls of purity and innocence. Consequently, combinations of rubies and pearls, or rubies, diamonds and pearls were popular symbols of marriage and married love.[99] Pearls, in particular, offered a variety of interpretations ranging from a symbol of Christ or Venus, of fertility and the tears of the gods, or of death.[100]

Second, jewellery often incorporated devices, initials and heraldic badges. James VI and I, his wife and sons were all very fond of symbolic jewels displaying initials, which they wore pinned to clothing, hats or ruffs, including Prince Henry's 'ballat Rubie in forme of an H with perles upon everie syde with a great perle hanging theretoe'.[101] Some pieces expressed their links to Scotland, including several diamond rings with St Andrew's crosses belonging to Anna of Denmark.[102] Prince Henry had a jewel shaped like 'A Thistle with Dyamants and Rubies', while Henrietta Maria's diamond signet ring was decorated on the shoulders with a rose and a thistle.[103] In a similar vein, the griffin jewel of rubies and sapphires owned by Alexander Seton, Charles I's guardian, was a reference to his family's badge and served as a reminder of his family background.[104]

Third, Stuart jewellery was associated with sentiment.[105] Jewels gained significance from where they were worn, whether it was close to the heart, the head or the wrist. Mary, Queen of Scots exchanged rings with Elizabeth I in 1564 and she wore Elizabeth's ring 'hanging at her breast with a lace of white and black about her neck'.[106] James VI and I demonstrated the importance of Buckingham to him by wearing the duke's miniature 'in a blue ribbon under my waistcoat next my heart'.[107] A similar proximity between monarch and wearer was achieved when wearing a slide, which was essentially a small locket. The example shown in figure 8.13 contains a double portrait of Charles I and Charles II and was threaded on a ribbon and then tied around the neck or the wrist.[108]

8.13 Slide pendant of Charles I and Charles II, c.1650–60. Gold and enamel, 2.9 × 3.1 cm. Victoria and Albert Museum, London.

Linked to this was the increasing value attached to locks of hair as an expression of love for the living and the dead. A strand of hair served as a relic or token and could be made into rings or bracelets, placed inside lockets or be used as a background for motifs.[109] The intimate nature of hair jewellery ensured there were conventions about giving and receiving it.[110] Such a gift among close family was to be expected. Indeed, Mary Verney asked her husband Ralph to send some of their dead daughter's hair 'to make bracelets' because 'I know you could not send a more acceptable thing than every one of your sisters a bracelet'.[111] This was a belief shared among the Stuart elite.

Celebration of the Living

Jewellery stressed family ties, and in September 1578 Mary requested a jewel of gold and enamel to be made in France and sent to her son.[112] In 1616 Charles ordered a piece 'in fashione of a crowned hert set with 200 diamonds of dyvers sorts and conteyning the king, queene, prince and ladye Elizabeth's pictures'.[113] Prince Henry's early death made his relatives prize each other more, and in December 1623 Elizabeth of Bohemia placed a lock of Prince Charles's hair 'in a rich jewel and wore it as an earring'.[114]

The Stuarts believed that royal generosity was a virtue and they used gifts of jewellery to broker friendships and maintain networks of acquaintances. Mary, Queen of Scots had this in mind when she wrote to James Beaton, archbishop of Glasgow (1517–1603) in 1575 telling him that 'There are some of my friends in this country who ask for my portrait. I pray you have four of these made which must be set in gold and sent to me secretly'.[115] While Mary's use of jewellery after her imprisonment in England was covert, her son and his family openly used jewels in this way, and the items they gave were kept and prized by recipients. In February 1651 the goods of the late Robert Kerr, earl of Roxburgh, included a chain of 120 diamonds and rubies; a 'picture case set full of Diamonds the midle stone like a heart bigger then [*sic*] the rest, in it Q: Anns picture', and 'a valentine sett with diamonds in a croune with the Duke of Yorks name in it'.[116]

Gift-giving at New Year grew in importance as James VI got older. In January 1578, 12 gold rings were provided for the king costing £17 Scots.[117] The number doubled the following year: in December 1578 William Murray supplied 24 rings of gold to be distributed on 1 January for £41 14s.[118] The following year Mungo Brady charged £58 14s 8d for 25 rings, which was a notable increase.[119] However, this was minimal in comparison with the princely bill of £763 15s submitted by Thomas Fowles for tablets and rings set with diamonds and rubies and other precious stones and bracelets and other goldsmiths work to be given in New Year's gifts in December 1582.[120]

Jewellery was often given to reward exceptional acts of loyalty. It could be a specially commissioned piece such as the ring given by James VII and II to John Graham in acknowledgement of his support. Inscribed GREAT DUNDEE FOR GOD AND ME J. REX on the hoop, and with a coronet on the bezel, the ring held a lock of the king's hair.[121] Sir Peter Halkett of Pitfirrane, who helped James VII and II to escape from William on 10 December 1688, received a ring with the king's monogram in gratitude.[122] James also rewarded his chaplain with a rectangular emerald ring with his cipher surrounded by table cut diamonds, a style favoured by Louis XIV.[123]

There was an expansion in the use of the royal miniature that was usually painted but could also be in cameo, as on a ring of Charles I worked in black jasper and a pendant of Charles II with his cameo on onyx.[124] Examples were also made in intaglio, as with portraits of James VII and II on emerald and topaz.[125] The value of the miniature was emphasised and enhanced by placing it in a jewelled setting. In 1680 the inventory of John, earl of Caithness included 'a picture case set with rubies and diamonds consisting of 4 rubies and 28 diamonds, great and small, valued at £30'.[126] During James VI and I's reign departing ambassadors regularly received gifts in the form of portrait miniatures in jewelled settings.[127] The duke of Lennox observed that James VI had been prevented from sending portraits to fellow monarchs prior to his accession to the English throne because of the lack of artists in Scotland.[128] Groups of miniatures could be used to form a group identity, thereby perpetuating the Stuart cause,[129] and this usage continued during the Commonwealth and during James VII and II's second extensive period of European exile. The Stuarts and their supporters converted the traditional pattern of miniature gift exchange into a very specific method of asserting legitimacy.

Whether these miniatures were worn openly or concealed under clothing, their small size helped associate them with secrecy and intimacy. In turn, the emotions or sentiments they evoked were more significant than the cost, although this could be considerable. Such an association of ideas made the royal portrait the perfect royal gift and indication of favour. On 27 April 1622 Carleton was informed that 'The Marchioness of Buckingham was churched, and dined in the bedchamber of the King, who has given a diamond chain, with his picture, worth £3,500, to the duchess of Lenox, for making broths and caudles for her in her sickness'.[130]

Many of the pieces discussed so far were bespoke, but the Stuarts also appreciated how to exploit mass-produced pieces that more of their people could own. These included commemorative medals, which were distributed to celebrate royal occasions such as Charles I's Scottish coronation in 1633. Made in silver and British gold by Nicholas Briot, these medals stressed the role of the coronation in uniting Scotland and England.[131] More important to the Stuart cause were the pieces designed to keep Royalist hopes alive during the Commonwealth, such as a copper gilt locket of *c.*1660 showing Charles II and Major Williams Carlos hiding in the oak at Boscobel House.[132] By the 1660s Scots were collecting medals, as the will of Joseph Herriott, dated at Robertland on 2 February 1660, reveals.[133] In 1684 Colin Campbell deposited 115 silver medals with Albert Gladstaines, an Edinburgh merchant, 11 of which were 'large and curious', and the rest small in a silver box of raised work and valued at £144 Scots.[134] The collection included two with Lauderdale's head that might have been examples of the medal made of the duke in 1672 by John Roettier. The duke combines classical dress with a long, curly wig in a style reminiscent of Charles II (fig. 8.14).

8.14 John Roettier, silver medal depicting John Maitland, 1st duke of Lauderdale, 1672. 3.7 cm diameter. National Galleries of Scotland.

However, the Stuarts did not have a monopoly on using jewellery as gifts, and Parliamentarian leaders proved adept at following their example. In February 1646 Francis Allen made the jewel that the English Parliament presented to Alexander Leslie, the 1st earl of Leven: 'On the backside … is drawn the general on horseback and the Army upon their marche with this inscription Donum Domus Co. Parl. Angliae An. Dom. 1646. On the other side of the cover is an emblem of the present union of the kingdoms of England and Scotland'.[135] In a similar vein, life in London under Cromwell was not always dull and subdued. In 1653 Christian, countess of Devonshire, assured her brother Edward Bruce, 2nd baron Bruce of Kinloss, that 'the garb in town is Ladies all in scarlet, shining and glittering as bright as at "anty maske". You would wonder to see such stars in these our cloudy days'.[136] Christian's belief that these were dark times demonstrates that her Royalist sympathies remained strong under the Commonwealth.

Commemoration of the Stuart Dead

The darkest point in these 'cloudy days' was 30 January 1649, marking, as it did, the execution of Charles I. The *Eikon Basilike* asserted the king's status as a martyr at this point, and the book was still selling a hundred years later when William Lorimer, tutor to Master James Grant, bought a copy of it for Lady Margaret.[137] However, commemorative jewellery was equally important in the *memento mori* tradition that developed around Charles I. Some pieces, such as a spray of enamelled flowers with a miniature of Charles I in the central striped pink rose *c.*1650, subtly demonstrate loyalty to the Stuarts (fig. 8.15).[138] Others were more overt, such as a heart-shaped silver locket, *c.*1650, with a heart pierced with arrows and the inscription *I live and dy in loyalty* on the reverse and an image of the king inside.[139] Simpler, but no less direct, were rings with cameo portraits of Charles I and the date of the king's death carved into the mount.[140]

8.15 Gold and enamel flower spray, mid 17th century. National Museum of Scotland, Edinburgh.

The nature of Charles I's death ensured the rich variety of commemorative jewellery. In contrast, Charles II died in his bed, but nonetheless this did not prevent popular expressions of grief and loss. Mourning jewellery, both bespoke and mass-produced, was purchased on a large scale. Slides, a type of pendant popular from *c.*1660 to 1714, were worn on a ribbon tied around the wrist or the neck, and were ideal for displaying portraits with funerary imagery.[141] This is evident on a slide of Charles II that combines an image of the king with a skull on a table to his left on one side and a skull placed on a coffin, along with the initials *CR*, on the other.[142] Charles's widow, Catherine of Braganza, owned two slides of this type when she died in 1705.[143] Slides were popular across society and often combined standard imagery with personal elements. One such item commemorates Margaret Keith, the wife of George Graeme of Inchbrakie. Decorated with her initials, it depicts a skeleton climbing out of a tomb, flanked by angels and the phrase *Come ye blessed.*[144] Mourning rings were personalised with the inclusion of dates, initials or coats of arms of the person being remembered.[145]

Most highly prized were items that had a proven royal provenance, and where possible they were kept within the Stuart family. The mathematician Richard Delamaine made a ring consisting of concentric bands that could answer 'many questions in arithmetick'.[146] Charles bequeathed it to his second son just before his execution. If given away, items with royal provenance were presented to family. Charles II favoured the 1st duke of Grafton, his son with the duchess of Castlemaine, with a ring that had belonged to Mary, Queen of Scots.[147] He also bought several pieces of jewellery from the executors of his sister Mary, including a pair of great diamond pendants and a pair of pearl pendants costing £9,750 and £1,200 respectively.[148]

Stuart gifts of jewellery were often prized enough by the recipient to be kept for long periods of time and then passed on to a friend or relative in their will. The inventory of Sir Colin Campbell of Glenorchy, for example, included a target of gold set with 3 diamonds, 4 topazes, a ruby and a sapphire, given by James VI and I to one of the laird's ancestors. He also had a round jewel of gold set with precious stones containing 29 diamonds, 4 great rubies and a gold ring set with a great diamond shaped like a heart, and 4 small diamonds given by Anna to Sir Duncan Campbell of Glenorchy.[149] These jewels were the proof of long-standing ties between the Campbells and the Stuarts that Sir Colin was proud of. He was not alone. When Lady Jean Wemyss drew up her will in 1655 her bequests included 'The king's picture which is set with 80 small diamonds' that could have been a portrait of either Charles I or Charles II.[150]

This bond was one that resonated across the Stuart kingdoms. When Henry, earl of Northampton, died in 1614 he left his 'best George' to Prince Charles and a 'Jewel of three stones, one of them being that Ruby which his excellent Majestie sent me out of Scotland as his first token' to his nephew.[151] Sir Thomas Sackville's will from 1608 records the gold ring set with 20 diamonds sent by James, delivered by Lord Hay and 'this Royall message vnto me namelie that his highnes wished a speedie and a perfect recouerye of my healthe'.[152] Remembering the dead played an important role in Stuart society, and jewellery had a key part in this process.

Conclusions

After the execution of Charles I, his hair was cut from the back of his head and was possibly taken for use in souvenirs such as the heart-shaped pendant with hair, blood-stained linen and a miniature of Charles I shown in figure 8.16. This example emphasises how jewellery could be very personal and emotive in times of crisis for the Stuarts and their supporters throughout the three kingdoms. More generally, it was an essential accessory for the Stuart kings that they used on both a personal and a popular level to stress ideas about royal authority and to create a bond between themselves and their people. For many Scots, this bond was the product of what Murray Pittock termed 'the Stuart myth'. Whether these pieces of jewellery were bespoke or mass-produced, expensive or cheap, many were designed to engage with the wearer's emotions and thereby foster feelings of loyalty and acts of remembrance. In addition, men used jewellery to assert their place in society and their ties to the Stuart monarchy – in good times and bad, in life and death – so creating memories that would last over the generations. In a Scottish context, the ways in which James VI and I and his successors used jewellery would take on a new, more poignant significance for the Stuarts once they became 'the kings over the water' to their Jacobite supporters.

8.16 Heart-shaped pendant depicting Charles I, c. 1650. Gold, pearl, enamel, porcelain, linen, hair. National Museum of Scotland, Edinburgh.

PART III

CLOTHES ON SHOW: THE SPACES AND PLACES OF STUART MASCULINE DISPLAY

BY COMPARING LONDON with the 'kinges chamber' the historian John Stow (*c*.1524–1605) like the poet John Lydgate before him, was stressing the city's importance to the Stuart monarchs. London was central to the king's relationship with Great Britain, or it was from the perspective of an Englishman like Stow, while the bedchamber was at the core of the royal household.[1] For the Scots, as Julian Goodare has shown, Edinburgh was equally significant, just as Dublin was for the monarch's Irish subjects.[2] In this final section, Edinburgh and London form the main backdrop for the clothes of the Stuart kings and the men who comprised the Scottish elite. Stuart, or royal, style did not exist in isolation and it was not restricted to the royal body. Rather, for it to work, it had to be shared, as was the case with Robert, lord Bruce, who was painted in 1633 aged seven and dressed in the height of fashion (fig. III.1). In other words, the Stuarts' style had to be seen and emulated, modified or rejected by men at court and all the other places that elite men were to be found, whether that was at home, in the street or while they worshipped. The remaining chapters explore the social, political and sartorial value of clothes in four different contexts, which focus on particular times of day and specific activities that men engaged in.

Place

III.1 *(page 220)* Cornelius Johnson, *Robert Lord Bruce, Later 2nd Earl Elgin*, 1633. Oil on canvas, 73.5 × 62 cm. National Galleries of Scotland. The silver lace and points contrast with the pink satin to make a subtly striking combination.

III.2 *(below)* John Michael Wright, *John Maitland, Duke of Lauderdale*, c.1670. Oil on canvas, 127 × 102 cm. Private collection, sold by Christopher Foley, Lane Fine Art, London. Maitland's clothes are far more flamboyant here than they are in figure 4.15, giving a fuller sense of the scope of his wardrobe.

There were a variety of places in which to observe seventeenth-century royalty, the elite and the aspirational, with palaces being of particular importance as the location of the court and the home of the courtier. Some, like Whitehall and Holyroodhouse, were situated close to capital cities, others in key towns or burghs, such as Windsor and Stirling castles, while Hampton Court and Falkland Palace were in the countryside.[3] Fynes Moryson described the latter as 'the Kings House for hunting', adding that he 'did gladly see James the sixth King of the Scots, at that time lying there to follow the pastimes of hunting and hawking'.[4] As these examples demonstrate, the form and function of royal palaces was very similar either side of the border.

The most important Scottish palace, both before and after 1603, was Holyroodhouse. Damaged during the Commonwealth, the palace was revamped by Sir William Bruce (*c*.1630–1710), who was appointed in 1671 as Surveyor of the King's Works in Scotland. Bruce converted the existing building into a baroque palace by working with leading European craftsmen including the painter Jacob de Wet and the sculptor Jan van Santvoort.[5] As Steve Bruce and Steve Yearley have shown, the value placed on Scotland's long royal history was evident in the 1683 commission to de Wet to paint the Scottish kings.[6] The result was impressive and contemporaries observed how 'In our gallery of the Abbey there is set up the pictures of our hundred and eleven Kings since Fergus I'.[7] This display of Scottish royal lineage was very traditional, and a permanent reminder of the portraits displayed in 1633 at Charles I's Scottish coronation.

Charles II did not visit Holyrood after the Restoration, although his brother did, and the leading Scottish royal officials had apartments there as a symbol of their delegated authority. The research of Iain MacIvor and Bent Peterson demonstrates how Lauderdale used Holyrood to assert his position in Edinburgh over the other Scottish officers of state in 1669–70, and he did so dressed in the latest court fashion (fig. III.2).[8] Relations were not always cordial among the king's officers, as in May 1687, for example, when the duke of

Hamilton occupied the rooms that the earl of Perth wanted.[9] Even from a distance, James VII and II made his mark on Holyrood by designating the royal chapel as 'the Chappell of that most Noble Order' of the Thistle when he revived the Scottish order of chivalry.[10]

After 1603 Whitehall, Hampton Court and Windsor became central to the Stuart world. Although these palaces ringed the English capital, the Stuarts' relationship with the city was not always comfortable, and by the early 1640s the king's court had, perforce, relocated to Oxford in the first phase of the civil war.[11] The court's changed location was implicit in the safe conduct granted by Charles I to Patrick Maule for a journey to London and Scotland and 'to returne bake againe to our Court where it shall happen to be for the tyme'.[12] By July 1646 the letter Alexander Hay sent from Charing Cross to Archibald Hay revealed that the king and 'His Court [was] at Newcastle'.[13] After the Restoration, London's place still was not secure and Charles II considered plans for a new court city and a new palace in Winchester that only ended with his death in 1685.[14]

Out of necessity rather than choice, James VII and II held court at Dublin and then at Saint-Germain-en-Laye. While he would have preferred to remain within the Stuarts' three kingdoms, James was familiar with French royal palaces and Saint-Germain had a history of Stuart residents. Mary, Queen of Scots had apartments there during her marriage to the dauphin, Charles II spent time there while in exile, and Louis XIV gave the palace to James VII and II for his residence in exile.[15] It remained the home of James VIII and III, the Old Pretender, until after the Jacobite rising of 1715, when he moved first to Avignon, then to Pesaro and Urbino, finally settling at Rome.

Scots in London

London was the largest city in the Stuarts' three kingdoms and many Scots settled there. After James VI and I's arrival in 1603 the Anglo-Welsh writer James Howell described how the Scots were 'multiplying here mightily' in Charing Cross and Aldwych, and that they had 'nested themselves about the Court'.[16] As Claire Jackson has argued, the Restoration saw another wave of Scottish migration to London and the expansion of their community there. The Royal Scottish Commission received its charter in 1665, a Scottish hospital was established near Blackfriars in 1672 and the first Scottish coffee house opened in Newgate in the 1670s.[17] London was also home to the Royal Society, whose first president was the Scotsman Sir Robert Moray (1608/9–73) – a soldier, a natural philosopher and a supporter of Charles II; other founder members included Alexander Bruce, the brother of William Bruce. Less famous Scots also made their mark, as in the summer of 1665 when plague was rife in the city. Sir John Reresby recalled the fate of a piper who 'being dead drunke, fell on sleep, wher betimes in the morning he was taken up and thrown into the cart amongst the bodys founde dead of the sicknesse'. When he woke, the piper 'takes out his pipes, raiseth himselfe, and begins to play', much to the consternation of those around him.[18]

Other Scots caused less of a stir on their trips to London. Some journeys were for pleasure, such as the visit of the royalist Sir John Gilmour of Craigmillar (1605–71) in 1660 that included an outing to the Queen's House at Greenwich where he listened to the organ.[19] Two years later Gilmour made the journey again, this time summonsed by Charles II and Lauderdale, to give advice on Scottish affairs.[20] Large numbers of Scots attended the English parliament of 1675, although their actions were not always seen favourably by fellow countrymen, one of whom described them waiting at 'the Commons doores' like 'as many porters, ambitious to be slaves to them, to betray their own cuntrey and cuntryemen'.[21] This comment hints at tensions over the influence of the Westminster parliament.

Attendance at court brought a number of advantages for the Scottish elite, whether it was in Edinburgh or London. Proximity to the king and those in favour around him gave a man a chance to bid for patronage that might result in offices, marriages and gifts. However, there were undeniable disadvantages. Being at court was expensive, especially once the Stuarts moved to Westminster, and it took men away from home and their interests. Sir David Cunningham spent most of his time in London, but in June 1628 he complained that he was 'very much wearied of a vaine court life and gladlie would retire before it be too late'.[22] However, having a son at court or in London brought enhanced cultural possibilities for siblings back at home in Scotland, either through visits to their brother or by using him to shop for clothes in London on their behalf.

Being successful at court required having the correct clothes, the right social graces and the benefits of an appropriate education, and this was nothing new for the Scottish elite. Most would have agreed with the poet and cleric John Donne (1572–1631) when he commented in *The Courtier's Library* (*c*.1603/4) that 'the natural occupations of court, in which you spend your time, do not allow you the leisure for literature, because, after sleep, which by custom must not be shaken off until after ten in the morning' you would have to be 'dressed in the clothes appropriate to the day, place, and passions'.[23]

After the Restoration, the clan elite made annual visits to Edinburgh.[24] Lord Lyon, king of arms, managed their attendance, which was marked by an annual procession.[25] They spent the month of August hunting.[26] Some, such as the earl of Leven, also went to London in the winter months, returning home in March. He was not alone in feeling the need to come to London for the 'season', a concept that developed in the early seventeenth century and was linked to the sessions of the law courts.[27] Others, like the royalist Angus MacDonald of Glengarry, who lived near Inverness, received a pension of £3,600 Scots and went to court.[28] While there he adopted court fashions and was criticised accordingly by associates who would have preferred him 'in a coat and plaid than in a cloak which fastens, and that you should walk in a sprightly manner in trews made of tartan cloth'.[29] The link between trews, as more elite wear, and a confident walk is reminiscent of Thomas Kirke's reference to the peacock-like strut of Highland men dressed in their finery (see Introduction).

A writer from Peebles, on the Borders, commented in January 1685 that he 'newer was ane grat nor good courtier but my affection and deutie to his Maiestie and Haynes and ther interest taucht me to be zealus and faethful in my station to ther service'.[30] Men with court connections felt it was their duty to promote friends and relatives. In November 1695 William Kerr, 2nd marquis of Lothian (1661–1722) wrote to his wife about the young men he planned to present at court. He had already taken Mark and Robert but not John. However, he believed that they would all succeed because they were 'all pretty laddes' and that male good looks were an asset at court.[31]

III.3 L. Schuneman, *Sir Thomas Dalyell, of Binns*, 1670. Oil on canvas, 124.4 × 101.6 cm. National Galleries of Scotland. A clean-shaven Dalyell here very much has his own, unfashionably grey hair.

The accession of a new monarch brought fresh opportunities. In mid May 1660 the earl of Airlie was encouraged to secure court positions for his sons Lord Ogilvie and Sir David Ogilvie because 'Ther ar many goeing vp to meitt with the Kings Majestie at his arryvall in England … for seiking of offices and place'.[32] When the monarch, or his heir, was in Scotland, access was cheaper and easier. So, in October 1679 Sir James Graham informed his nephew, William, 8th earl of Menteith, 'that His Royal Highness intended to leave for Scotland soon' and urged him 'to pay court to him'.[33] Equally, for those not at court, royal gossip was always of interest, as when the earl of Middleton assured the earl of Perth in December 1685 that the duke of Monmouth was in disgrace and had been forbidden from appearing at court.[34]

A key benefit of court attendance was the opportunity for personal contact with the monarch. Conversation was good but the opportunity for a public display of royal favour was better. In October 1693 the duke of Hamilton told his wife that after he had kissed the queen's hand, 'all the great men about the toun and Court has made me vissits'. In addition the archbishop of Canterbury had invited him to dinner and he had had another long audience with the queen.[35] Keeping away from court often attracted royal disapproval. In September 1647 Charles I rebuked the earl of Lanark for not coming to London.[36] Absence also provided a man's enemies with opportunities to make negative comments, as the marquis of Hamilton was all too aware of in October 1641. He apologised for his delayed return from Edinburgh and hoped that his 'enemies may be deterred from longer snarling at mee'.[37]

Snarling and snipping could take many forms and it was not always deserved. After Charles I's execution, Sir Thomas Dalyell of Binns (1615–85) swore that he would never trim his beard again as proof of his loyalty to the Stuarts (fig. III.3). In addition, even though he was balding, Sir Thomas did not wear a wig, favouring instead a beaver hat and a short coat rather than the fashionable new style of suit. His devoted, yet idiosyncratic, dress sense meant that he stood out at court, prompting Charles II to enquire why he could not look 'like other Christians' who dressed in the king's brand of Stuart style.[38]

Time and the Public Scene

Time, both in terms of the time taken to undertake an activity and the daily cycle of night and day, became increasingly influential in how people engaged with society. On the one hand, the male elite spent a lot of time travelling, whether it was from house to house, going to Edinburgh or to England, Europe and beyond. Their mode of travel related to how much time they had, the seasons and the weather. Patrick Maule of Panmure's expenditure on travel both in England and between England and Scotland in 1620–5 and 1625–38 consisted of short local coach trips costing 2s or 4s, saddle horses for mid-range journeys, and sea voyages when going to Scotland that cost around £1 12s.[39] In contrast, John Leslie, 7th earl of Rothes, went on a progress in 1665 in his capacity as lord high chancellor (fig. III.4). He travelled for 18 days accompanied by men from the Life Guard and a large retinue to display his authority in this role.[40]

On the other hand, the seventeenth century saw the growing popularity of social events taking place in the evening and at night, in response to what Craig Koslofsky terms the 'nocturnalisation' of life.[41] This partly reflected changing attitudes to night time and darkness that were accompanied by new, more effective methods of lighting and telling the time. This linked to ideas about burgh curfews, as is evident from a petition by John Jackson, town piper of Perth, for restoration of his weekly pension, which had ended in March 1690 when the garrison had stopped him 'doing his dewtie in goeing about the towne evening and morning with the pype'.[42] Jackson's petition was reminiscent of similar trouble in Haddington earlier in the century.[43] The added appeal of night-time activities meant that a firework display in St James's Square was chosen to celebrate the capture of Namur in 1695.[44] Equally, masque costumes were designed to sparkle in the candlelight, such as the 'pairlit' (pearled) mask bought by Shairp of Houston in 1635.[45]

Morning and evening were equally important in different ways. In clothing terms, these were the times for dressing and undressing, activities that young Lord David Hay evidently spent serious time on (fig. III.5). For those travelling, the idea of morning and evening

helped specify departure times, as in April 1650 when General Major Sir John Hurry and his men were ordered to board a ship and set sail with the evening tide for the coast of Caithness.[46] Daily worship also took place at the start and end of the day. In 1637 Archibald Campbell of Glencarradale noted the arrival of the bishop of St Andrews in Edinburgh. He had authorised the reading of prayers at morning and evening in the accustomed form, 'whiche praysit be god is ane gud begineinge' because the previous Sunday the bishop of Brechin had used the new service books.[47]

This growing emphasis on the passage of time and specific times for specific activities made demands on a man's clothing, and affected style by determining different clothes for different occasions. As a result, men needed to know the time. Taking note of the chimes of public clocks or the pealing of church bells was one way to monitor the hours, but wealthy men also had pocket watches. These might be royal gifts, as in the case of a silver watch James VI and I had given to a member of the Hay family, or a purchase such as the silver watch the earl of Winton bought from Paul Roumieu for £6 in 1679.[48] Either way, these small, fashionable accessories ensured that the male courtier was in the right place at the right time, in the right clothes. As this final section of *Stuart Style* demonstrates, Scots played a central role in the development and reception of the Stuarts' style through the growth and sustenance of a cross-border courtly group. This group had a distinct cultural identity that had to be displayed to be effective, and clothes were vital to this.

III.4 *(above, left)* L. Schuneman, *John Leslie, 7th Earl and 1st Duke of Rothes*, 1667. Oil on canvas, 126 × 102 cm. National Galleries of Scotland. Two years after his progress, Rothes was still making a mark with his opulent wardrobe.

III.5 *(above, right)* David Scougall, *Lord David Hay*, c.1665–70. Oil on canvas, 91.5 × 76.1 cm. Private collection, sold by Sotheby's. Hay shows that Stuart fashions appealed to men of all ages (see also figure III.1).

CHAPTER NINE

Dressing, Undressing and the Significance of the Stuart Bedchamber

THE COMBINATION OF CRIMSON GENOA velvet, ivory Chinese silk damask and silk trimmings on the state bed at Melville House, Fife, is a testament to how opulent seventeenth-century Scottish bedchambers could be (fig. 9.1).[1] Made in 1700 for George Melville, 1st earl Melville (1636–1707), the bed reflects the newly created earl's wealth and political standing under William III. The men had first met when Melville went into exile after being implicated in the Rye House plot of 1683, which aimed to replace Charles II and his brother with the duke of Monmouth. Medina's portrait of the earl presents him proudly wearing the crimson sash of a royalist over black armour (fig. 9.2). However, as his story reveals, Melville was a royalist whose idea of monarchy was defined by his Presbyterian beliefs and his Whig politics. He was at the forefront of William's supporters in Scotland and he may have commissioned the bed in the hope of a royal visit in 1700. While the visit did not take place, the bed remained as the focal point of the main bedchamber and serves as a reminder of Melville's taste and ambition.

Dressing and undressing marked the start and finish of Melville's day just as it did for Scotsmen across the social order. Putting on and taking off clothes usually took place in the bedchamber or dressing chamber, and men received frequent advice on how to undertake these simple but significant acts. Richard Day stressed the moral and religious value of clothing in his *Booke of Christian Prayers* (1578), writing: 'Clothe me with thy self O my redeemer and sanctifier … Be thou our clothing and apparel, to keep us warme from the cold of this world'.[2] Meanwhile Philip Stubbes exhorted his readers that once undressed they should 'thinke, that as thou puttest off, and laiest aside thy material garments … put off, and lay away the earthlie mansion of thy bodie'.[3] In contrast,

9.1 Daniel Marot, state bed from Melville House, Fife, 1700. Victoria and Albert Museum, London. The height of French style, this bed asserts Melville's support of William over James.

James VI and I was more pragmatic, commenting in the *Basilikon Doron* that 'Next followeth to speak of raiment, the on-putting whereof is the ordinary action that followeth next to sleep'.[4] By the end of the seventeenth century, however, the guidance focused on how to manage clothing in social situations. For instance, the French diplomat Antoine de Courtin maintained that when in company it was inappropriate to 'pull off your Cloak, to pull off your Periwig, or doublet, to pair your nails … to mend your Garter or Shoo-string, or to call for your Gown or your Slippers to put yourself at ease'.[5]

As de Courtin reveals, a man's gown and slippers were comfortable, so allowing him to relax in the relative privacy of his home. This chapter focuses on activities that were centred on domestic spaces within the elite home or palace. While the early modern home is often regarded as a female space, this chapter will show how the male Scottish elite, like Melville, used their homes to assert their status and taste, either in support of or in challenge to the power of the Stuarts. Linked to this, while Susan Vincent has noted that clothing marks the key transitions in a person's life, it was equally relevant in denoting the shift between being dressed and undressed, formality and informality, and moving from one activity to another.[6] This chapter considers how and why, when dressing and undressing was common to all, the Stuarts elevated these daily processes to a different, ceremonial level. The answer to the latter is linked in part to the importance of the bedchamber as part of the royal household in Scotland and the impact of Scottish bedchamber politics, and the Scots who served there, after 1603, south of the border. The social and political significance of the bedchamber led to the development of a range of special garments and textiles that any wealthy and fashionable man, whether Scottish or English, had to have and be seen to have, thereby promoting a very significant strand of the Stuarts' style.

Defining the Stuart Bedchamber

The bedchamber, whether as a physical space or a department of the royal household, was very important under the Stuarts. With James VI's arrival in 1603, it replaced the privy chamber as the room where the most important decisions were made.[7] As such, the officers of the bedchamber were very influential because they controlled access to the king, they oversaw the activities that took place within the bedchamber, and they managed the objects associated with this space. However, the ways in which the bedchamber was used continually evolved, reflecting the personality of the monarch. After the Restoration, Charles II's bedchamber developed a more public, ceremonial role. As Anna Keay states, this was very different to its role under James VI and I and Charles I, 'who would never have countenanced receiving a civic deputation in their bedchambers'.[8] What did stay constant was the fact that the king's bedchamber remained an almost exclusively male space in terms of

9.2 John Baptiste de Medina, *George Melville, 1st Earl Melville*, 1691. Oil on canvas, 127 × 101.8 cm. National Galleries of Scotland. Melville's very fine lace cravat hints at the quality of his everyday wardrobe.

its staff and those who attended the ceremonial activities held there. It was complemented by the separate bedchamber of the queen, and the apartments of the royal mistresses of Charles II, as centres of more informal politics.

Official business took place in the king's bedchamber. For instance, on 19 September 1579 Robert, commendator of Dunfermline, Robert Erskine and John Drummond witnessed an Instrument of Resignation of Sasine 'in the King's bedchamber'.[9] The same was true of the bedchamber in elite Scottish society. On 20 July 1571 Alexander, earl of Glencairn, and 'Jayne Cwnygham his honorable spous' signed a letter of reversion in the earl's bedchamber in Kilmarnock Castle, for 800 merks in favour of David Cunningham of Robertland.[10] The royal bedchamber was also where James VI received family news that was both personal and highly political. On hearing of his mother's execution, 'he went to bed that night without supper; and on the morrow by seven o'clock went to Dalkeith, there to remain solitary'.[11] When Sir Robert Carey arrived with tidings of Elizabeth I's death he recalled that 'The King was newly gone to bed … I was quickly let in and carried up to the King's chamber. I kneeled by him, and saluted him by the title of England, Scotland, France and Ireland'.[12]

Once James VI moved to Westminster, the king's bedchamber became one of the most contested spaces in the royal palace. Arguments raged over access to the king and the control his Scottish entourage appeared to have. In 1604 the earl of Southampton was arrested because he had 'been rumoured by his enemies to be plotting to slay several Scots much about the person of the king'.[13] In the months after the Gunpowder Plot, James lived 'in the innermost rooms with only Scots about him'.[14] Five years later, in February 1610, Sir John Holles requested that the 'Bedchamber may be shared as well to those of our nation as to them … and that the same chamber may have, the same brotherly partition which all the other inferior forms of the court, the Presence and Privy Chamber have'.[15] Family members such as Ludovick Stuart had access, and he demonstrated his confidence with the bedchamber system by wearing a nightgown over fashionable clothes for his portrait of 1623–5 (fig. 9.3).

9.3 Studio of Daniel Mytens, *Ludovick Stuart, 2nd Duke of Lennox and Duke of Richmond*, 1623–5. Oil on canvas, 218.8 × 137.9 cm. Royal Collection. In addition to his nightgown, Ludovick also wears a fancy nightcap, an essential item when relaxing.

Scots with positions in the bedchamber promoted themselves, their family and the interests of fellow Scots. Marriage often furthered family ambitions, as was the case in 1605 when George Prestoun, James Hay of Kyngask and his son, Sir James Hay, gentleman of the bedchamber, agreed that George would marry Agnes Hay in August of that year.[16] Business was also an important consideration, as is clear from an indenture drawn up on 9 June 1614 between Sir John Bruce of Airth and Henry Gibb, groom of the bedchamber, to export coal from Scotland to London.[17] Bedchamber men also served as a conduit for news to and from Scotland. In June 1639 the earl of Airth asked James Livingston of Biel, of the bedchamber, to expedite a dispatch that he was waiting for.[18] Finally, preferment to an office in the royal household was desirable, as was indicated in September 1641 when Count Leslie from Regensburg, Germany, thanked the marquis of Hamilton for helping his brother to become a gentleman of the bedchamber.[19]

A position in the bedchamber brought a man undeniable influence and opportunities to broker patronage, and this process could be initiated from the outside, as in June 1626 when John Douglas thanked Sir James Fullartoun, gentleman of the bedchamber, for using his influence with Morton on Douglas's behalf,[20] or it could also originate from within, as when Sir David Cunningham wrote to Alexander, 6th earl of Eglinton in December 1635 offering to help the earl's second son, Henry, get a position in the prince's bedchamber.[21]

When the Scottish deputation met Charles II in Breda in May 1650, they were met at the outer door of the king's residence by Lord Wentworth and then taken to the king's bedchamber.[22] The commissioners understood how the Stuart bedchamber worked and tried to control its membership to make it more biddable to their point of view. For example, on 18 May the Scottish parliament asked their commissioners to inform Charles that a number of his Scottish supporters would not be welcomed on his return. They insisted that the following 'remain abroad' because they were the 'instruments of the former or late defection and divisorn in this kingdom', namely 'the duke of Hamilton, the earls of Seaforth, Forth, Callendar, Traquaire, Lauderdale, [Drumfreis] the lords Carnegie, Naper, Ithan, Sinclar, Gevi, Monro, Henryfield, Cononall, Cuchvier, St James, Lockhart, and Cononell Dalzell of Bruds, [and] Bryme'.[23] This was followed in short order by a demand in August that Charles appoint men who were God-fearing, had signed the Solemn League and Covenant, and who could not claim that they had been appointed by Charles I or fought against the Covenant. Furthermore, the grooms of the bedchamber were to consist of two Englishmen and two Scotsmen.[24] There was a clear wish that when the king was in Scotland, he would be served by Scots. The offer of such a position often acknowledged loyal service, as was the case with the promise made by Charles II on 24 September the same year to make the marquis of Argyll a duke, a knight of the Garter and a gentleman of the bedchamber in addition to repaying £40,000 sterling.[25] However, some men were only prepared to accept a post on their own terms. On 22 November Colonel Gilbert Ker thanked William, 3rd earl of Lothian, secretary to Charles II, for recommending him for a place as a groom of the bedchamber that would bring him 'near the King whom he desires to serve faithfully so long as he is a servant to the King of Kings'.[26] Indeed, royal service was not for all, as in December when Sir Archibald Campbell explained that 'owing to the infirmities of old age' he could not act as a groom of the bedchamber.[27]

During these months in 1650 Charles II learnt how the bedchamber worked in Scotland. It served to create friendships and to form memories. On 17 February 1652 John, earl of Lauderdale, wrote from the Tower to Anne, duchess of Hamilton, describing when her uncle, the late 2nd duke of Hamilton, had made a resignation into the king's hands in the bedchamber at Dundee.[28] Occasionally royal service was used as an excuse not to return to Scotland, as in the case of the earl of Arran, who persuaded Charles II to make him a gentleman of the bedchamber in January 1679.[29] While his parents did not approve, Arran's younger brother viewed things differently. Lord William saw it as one of a number of opportunities open to Arran and in August 1681 urged Arran to accept the offer of a regiment in Holland as long as he could continue as a gentleman of the bedchamber.[30]

Charles II's reign saw a decrease in access to the king's bedchamber in the 1670s. Even so, when Sir Charles Lyttleton briefed Lord Hatton in 1683 about who had free access to it, Scottish interests were still represented: 'No body except ye Duke, Ld Ormond, and I think Halifax, the 2 Secretaryes of England, and ye Secretaries of Scotland are to come into ye bedchamber without leave first asked'.[31] If the bedchamber was less open, the withdrawing room was more so: 'Wee are pleased that soe many persons more then formerly are admitted to waite in Our Withdrawing Roome'.[32] However, in 1690 after the establishment of James VII and II's court at Saint-Germain-en-Laye, the royal household underwent more significant changes. The king and queen still had a formal bedchamber and a common bedchamber, but the bedchamber ceased to exist as a separate household department.[33] In contrast, William III used Charles II's household as a model for his own, thereby stressing that his rule represented continuity with the main Stuart line.

Dressing and Undressing, Rising and Retiring

Getting up and going to bed are essential parts of a day's activities, and during the period the form of both events developed in response to the personality of the king and how household ordinances and court ceremony were used to aid or hinder access to the monarch. Periods of informality were followed by periods of formality. For instance, James VI and I complained about how accessible his bedchamber was, and his choice of a metaphor linked to undressing was fitting: 'I would you had first my doublet and then my hose and maybe when I was naked you would leave me alone'.[34] This changed, according to the Venetian ambassador, under Charles I. Etiquette in the royal household as a whole, and in the bedchamber in particular, was enforced: 'The King observes a rule of great decorum … the nobles do not enter his apartments in confusion, as heretofore, but each rank has its appointed place … the king has also drawn up rules for himself, dividing the day from his very early rising, for prayers, exercises, business, eating and sleeping'.[35] When advising the young Charles II, the duke of Newcastle acknowledged that there had been a shift back towards informality, adding: 'he is a fool that is too bold with your Majesty even in your bedchamber, and those that are so, I know your Majesty's wisdom will give them a check for it, and if they do not mend, put them out'.[36] The household regulations issued nine days after Charles's Scottish coronation stipulated 'That none presume to goe unto the withdrawing rooms but Gentlemen of the Bedchamber and Groomes therof, and there pages and Noblemen'.[37] However, by 1661 the pattern was much less regulated, as the Spanish ambassador noted. People 'came to the king at all hours, and spake to him when and as long as he would, without any ceremony … but came into the bedchamber whilst the king was dressing himself'.[38] Evelyn enjoyed this freedom in 1665 when he was called to Charles II's bedchamber to tell the king about the fleet 'as he was dressing'.[39] Five years later Evelyn still had easy access, noting on 14 September 1670 that 'the King arriving from New Market, we both went up into his Majesties Bed-Chamber, it being now almost night'.[40]

The duke of York and Albany followed his brother's relaxed approach. Samuel Pepys was in regular attendance on James and his diary makes regular references to his being present at his master's dressing and undressing. On 20 April 1661 Pepys noted that 'we went up and saw the duke dress himself and in his night habit he is a very plain man'.[41] Pepys's comment confirms that James favoured the simpler style of dress that his elder brother used, as noted in Chapter 5.

As Anna Keay has shown, by the mid 1670s Charles II had adopted French royal dressing ceremonies in the form of the levée and the couchée.[42] While ostensibly to dress and undress, the levée and couchée also provided the king with an opportunity to receive a range of individuals in his bedchamber. Charles II woke early, at or around 6.00 am, and the levée beginning shortly thereafter; couchée usually started at 11.00 pm.[43] A key difference with France was that Charles and his successors were dressed by the members of the household, not the princes of the blood. Charles II's ordinances were reissued by William III and stated that the groom of the stool was 'to put on the Shirt we wear next our Body, Evening & Morning or as often as we shall change Our Body Linnen'.[44] The gentleman of the robes should come every morning into the bedchamber and then 'put on Our Doublet & to stay in our Bed Chamber until we shall be apparelled & dressed', while 'the yeoman of the robes is to wait in the withdrawing room every morning and bring the apparel into the bedchamber'.[45] The reference to a doublet reveals that the regulations did not keep up with fashionable changes in the king's wardrobe, failing as they did to mention the shift to the coat, vest and breeches.

James VII and II's household ordinances offer additional information, stipulating that 'during the time of Our dressing and undressing none of the Groomes of Our Bedchamber do presume to come into Our Bedchamber with their Cloakes, Hatts or Swords'.[46] This ensured that those in attendance on the king were in the same state of 'undress' as he was. On 7 February 1685 when Evelyn visited the king 'he had ben on the bed, but was now risen & in his Undresse'.[47] Evelyn did not describe this undress, but it is likely to have consisted of a nightgown and slippers. In his first account as king, James VII and II ordered two rather sumptuous examples: one of 'rich gimp Brocade' lined with green morella tabby and the other of rich purple Mantua.[48] By his third and last account, James's choices were cheaper: two purple nightgowns, one of cloth and one of silk, one of black cloth and a blue striped nightgown of unspecified fabric.[49]

The value of attending the levée and the couchée for courtiers, and politicians, is made clear in the diary of Yorkshireman Sir John Reresby.[50] He often noted who else was present, what he discussed or hoped to achieve, and which of the ceremonies he went to. Reresby chose Charles II's couchée for preference, recording just one attendance at the levée.

He also went to the couchée of James VII and II, and aspired to go to those of William III. In a similar vein, the diary of Thomas Cartwright, bishop of Chester, that ran from 1 August 1686 to 31 October 1687, records his attendance at James VII and II's levée on 47 occasions in this 15-month period.[51]

However, the most telling episode associated with the Stuart bedchamber relates not to a man but to a woman. When Mary of Modena gave birth to a healthy son in 1688 the child's legitimacy was challenged, causing James to declare 'That very many do not think this Son with which God hath blessed Me, to be mine, but a Supposed Child'.[52] The king held a tribunal to refute the claims that his son had been smuggled into the bedchamber in a warming pan. Many of the witnesses cited their attendance at the queen's levée and couchée as having allowed them to observe Mary's pregnant body. Penelope, countess of Peterborough, swore that she had seen 'the Milk often upon Her Majesty's Smock, when she, the Deponent, took it off from the Queen, and often saw Her Majesty's Belly, so as it could not be otherwise, but that she was with Child'.[53] Others testified that they had witnessed the birth and seen the child at all times, thereby asserting that the infant was the queen's child. Later, Jacobites referred to 10 June 1688, young James's birthday, as White Rose Day, demonstrating their loyalty to the 'Old Pretender' and affirming the legitimacy of his birth.

So far, the focus has been on formal dressing in the morning and undressing in the evening, but the king also changed his clothes during the course of the day, depending on what he was doing. For instance, riding and hunting were daily activities requiring specific clothes and footwear. James VI and I's ordinances stipulated that unless their name was on the roll no one could enter the privy chamber or 'presume to come in booted excepte It be at suche tymes when they are to Ride with us'.[54] It added that

> at any time we shall please to come into our privy chamber to pull one our bootes then it shalbe lawfull for the Querrie of out stable to come in And yf it shall please vs to pull one our botts in the privie lodgings to thendes to be more private, then the Querry to forbare to come in to the privie lodgings.[55]

Ever impulsive, James was quite prepared to break his own rules. At his first meeting with Anna of Denmark in 1589 he 'immediately at his coming passed quickly with boots and all to her highness'.[56] Charles I sought to prevent this type of behaviour in 1631 when new regulations stated that 'none wait upon the King to Chapel in boots and spurs, or enter booted into the presence or privy chamber'.[57] The need to change out of riding boots created delays, as on 10 February 1669 when Pepys recorded that he went 'to Whitehall, where I stayed till the duke of York came from hunting, which he did by and by; and when dressed did come out to dinner'.[58] By 1720 the niceties of when and where boots should be worn were carefully defined, as Adam Petrie's *Rules of Good Deportment, or of Good Breeding for the Use of Youth* reveals: 'It is rude and impudent to enter the house or chamber of a great person wrap'd up in a cloak or big coat, or with boots or whip, or with dirty feet, or without your gloves on your hand'.[59] Dressing and undressing were very social processes for the Stuart kings. These daily events offered a select group of men the chance to see the king's clothes and accessories in close detail. It is not surprising, then, that a doll such as Lord Clapham had a nightgown as part of his wardrobe, ensuring he promoted the idea of being suitably dressed at all times (fig. 9.4).

Dressing the Part: The Royal Nightgown

Of the clothes seen almost exclusively in the bedchamber, the nightgown or chamber gown was the most important.[60] Worn by men and women alike, the nightgown has been described as 'home wear' in acknowledgement of its role in the domestic sphere, but it was a much more significant garment than this designation implies.[61] Although not a Stuart innovation, the social and political significance given to the king's bedchamber under the Stuarts gave this gown added importance within royal palaces and in the lives of the elite and the middling sort. The nightgown, often made en suite with a nightcap and slippers, was an informal garment with a public role that was seen in the intimate setting of the bedchamber. Here royal opulence was displayed through the use of expensive, often highly patterned silks in tandem with fur linings to combine warmth with luxury in winter. In contrast, in May 1597 James VI ordered a sumptuous summer nightgown made from 16 ells of blue satin wrought with damask gold and silver. Lined with double Jean argentine taffeta, this sumptuous gown was decorated with gold and silver passementerie, seven dozen buttons and gold and silver loop.[62]

9.4 Doll known as Lord Clapham dressed in a nightgown, 1690–1700. Turned, carved, gessoed and painted wood, linen, human hair, wool and silk. Victoria and Albert Museum, London.

This luxuriousness continued after James's accession to Elizabeth's throne. Between 1603 and 1613 James ordered 18 nightgowns. Most were made from velvet or wrought velvet with a few of cloth of gold, cloth of silver and wrought satin. They were often fur-lined, such as 'One night gown of very rich rose colour wrought velvet wrought with gold lace with fur paid for in the Great Wardrobe and long buttons of gold on the sleeves'.[63] This example, excluding the fur, cost £148 2s 3d and offers a hint of the king's appearance when, in 1605, he visited the bedchamber of Sir Philip Herbert and Lady Susan the morning after their wedding night 'in his shirt and night-gown'.[64] The link between the nightgown and the sensuous side of the bedchamber may explain Mary, Queen of Scots' gift of 'ung manteaux de nuyct' on 15 May 1567 to James Hepburn, 4th earl of Bothwell (*c.*1534–78), to mark their wedding.[65]

Nightgowns were the most consistently expensive items in James VI and I's English wardrobe, ranging in price from £65 16s 8d to £143 6s 3d. In 1606–7 he acquired two gowns of rich velvet wrought with silver and gold lace about the skirts and with long buttons on the sleeves costing £114 19s 2d and £118 17s.[66] This was a relatively private magnificence because the rules governing access to the bedchamber stipulated that 'no person of what condition soever do at any time presume or be admitted to come to us into Our Bed-chamber, but such as … are … sworn of it, without our special licence, except the Princes of Our Blood'.[67] However, James clearly felt it was money well spent and he was consistently richly dressed while in his bedchamber. In contrast, by the reigns of his grandsons, the royal nightgown had a larger, if still select, audience.

Nightgowns were also worn during periods of illness, when visits to the royal bedchamber continued. In October 1605 Prince Henry was to be found 'in his bedchamber in his nightgown, out of temper, and with much hoarseness in his throat, so as the Doctor stands in doubt that it may turn to the smallpox'.[68] When the chapter of the Order of the Garter met on St Thomas's Day 1612 and elected Frederick of the Palatinate 'they accompanied him into the Bed-chamber, where the King sitting up in his bedd, after a few wordes putt the George about his neck'.[69] Some years later, when Charles I was convalescing after a bout of smallpox in 1632, he received visitors 'in a warme roome with a furr'd gowne on his back'.[70] The cost of this gown would have ensured that Charles had the upper hand in these meetings, even though he was only informally dressed.

The Fashionable Nightgown in Stuart Society

While notably less opulent than the royal examples, two surviving nightgowns offer a glimpse of this Stuart glamour. The first, at Claydon House, Buckinghamshire, dates from *c.*1605–15 and may have belonged to Sir Ralph Verney (d. 1615).[71] This nightgown is made from purple silk damask with a dark grey shag lining and has matching slippers and nightcap. The fabric is pleated and stitched into the shoulder seam to create fullness at the back, while the hanging sleeves are open from the armhole to the cuff. In comparison, the loose gown at Hardwick Hall, Derbyshire, *c.*1600–1610, is made from pink/red satin and lined with velvet of the same colour, with guards of velvet edged with satin placed down the centre front and around the hem.[72]

By the second half of the seventeenth century the desirable nightgown of choice was an Indian gown modelled on the Japanese kimono. Often knee length, these gowns overlapped at the front, and could be left to hang open or secured with a belt.[73] On 1 July 1661 the ever-fashionable Pepys confided to his diary, 'this morning I went up and down into the city to buy several things' including 'an indian gown for myself' costing 34s.[74] This was not the only example Pepys owned and in November 1663 he 'put on my new shagg purple gown with gold

buttons and loop lace'.[75] He also admired his associates dressed in similar attire. On 21 November 1666, for example, he 'went to wait on Sir Philip Howard whom I find dressing himself in his night-gown and Turban like a Turke; but one of the finest persons that ever I saw in my life'.[76] The nightgown's social cachet ensured that when Pepys was painted by John Hayls on 30 March 1666 he sported a golden-brown silk example 'which I hired to be drawn in', adding that it was 'an Indian gowne and I do see all the reason to expect a more excellent picture of it' (fig. 9.5).[77]

Nightgowns were equally popular among the Scots, as is revealed by a bill dated 13 May 1583. William Douglas, the laird of Lochleven, bought 4 ells of 'red cramosie' satin costing £26, and paid a further £3 'for making the night gown'.[78] Their choices followed the fashionable trends, with this example in keeping with those at Claydon and Hardwick. 80 years later, John Michael Wright painted Sir William Bruce in a nightgown of striped silk reflecting the taste of the 1660s (fig. 9.6). However, by the end of the century some Scots favoured tartan nightgowns. For example, purchases for William Campbell's voyage to Darien aboard the *Caledonia* in 1698 included two razors and 11 ells of tartan for a nightgown.[79] By the early eighteenth century, cotton made an appearance and by December 1723 Alexander, 2nd duke of Gordon, owned a calico nightgown.[80]

The demand for nightgowns resulted in the development of specialist shops offering a range of ready-made plain and patterned garments for men and women, such as that of Edward Gunn, 'Indian gown maker', of London.[81] The author of an undated letter from about 1670 reveals some very specific nightgown requirements. This knowledgeable Scottish

9.5 *(above, left)* John Hayls, *Samuel Pepys*, 1666. Oil on canvas, 75.6 × 62.9 cm. National Portrait Gallery, London. The three-quarters pose shows off the sleeve of Pepys's nightgown very well.

9.6 *(above, right)* John Michael Wright, *Sir William Bruce*, c. 1664. Oil on canvas, 72.4 × 61 cm. National Galleries of Scotland.

shopper wanted '2 tuilted nightgowns on for myself and another for my wyfe both Long and Large. They ar to be of stuff'. He added:

> The Register, Advocat and Sir Robert Sinclair bocht thaim at 20s peice; they wer had at the Exchange which is keiped at Gressum Colledge. If they be not already maid large anough yow may caus make thaim large expresslie as they did. I desyre thaim of this sort because we have bettir already.[82]

In 1685 the earl of Breadalbane also looked to a London maker, one John Singleton, for his nightgown needs, indicating how a London-made nightgown was a desirable item in the wealthy Scotsman's wardrobe.[83]

Nightgowns were usually worn with slippers or high-heeled mules, and both terms appear in Scottish accounts. In August 1631 Mungo Lockhart sent his master, the 8th laird of Glenorchy, two pairs of mules from Edinburgh.[84] A salmon-pink satin pair associated with Charles II gives a good indication of what mid-century mules were like (fig. 9.7).[85] John Paterson, a cordwainer in the Canongate, presented the laird of Dean with a bill for shoes bought in 1688–9 that included a sumptuous pair of purple 'turkey' slippers.[86] Equally fine is the pair of square-toed blue satin mules with silver gilt lace owned by the 1st duke of Perth, indicating how important and expensive items worn in the bedchamber were.[87]

Textiles and Accessories Associated with Dressing

The increased interest in, and time taken over, dressing and undressing saw a rise in the number of specialist items associated with the dressing room and a person's toilette, either at home or while travelling. In November 1577, the royal wardrobe supplied 1½ ells of 'red cramosie velvet' to make 'a polk [bag] to his majesty's night gear'.[88] Royal cloak bags, night bags and toilets formed part of the page of honour's remit. Giving the care of these textile items to high-profile household servants stressed their mutual importance. By the same token, these items made excellent gifts and in 1626/7 Charles I received 'a white Satten night bag richlie embroidered with gold siluer and coulered silke and lined with carnation Taffety' from Lady Connisby.[89]

While a night bag might sound like quite a modest item, it was not, as revealed in an exchange in November or December 1660 between Charles II and Edward Hyde, 1st earl of Clarendon. The king planned to visit his sister Minette at Tunbridge, announcing that he intended 'to take nothing but my night bag'. Hyde replied, 'you will not go without forty or fifty horse' to which the king acknowledged 'I count that [as] part of my night bag'.[90] Night bags were often sumptuous affairs, as in the case of the 'crimson velvett nighte bagge' and the 'orenge tawney nighte bagge imbrodered with silver piramides and flowers both sides alike' listed in Henry Howard's inventory.[91] More practical was the 'road' night bag ordered on 5 June 1649 for the 2nd duke of Hamilton. During his time in exile in the Netherlands, he acquired this fully lined night bag made from six pounds of Russia leather and fastened with ties.[92]

9.7 Salmon-pink satin mules, c.1640–60. Burrell Collection, Glasgow.

Cloak bags were not restricted to royalty. In 1633 the household books of Lord William Howard of Naworth Castle included a payment of 2s 'For makeinge 2 clock bagges and harden for lyninge them'.[93] In January 1644 Thomas Halyburton informed Lothian that he had sent a cloak bag for the deputy governor to Bristol, along with some open letters that contained 'nothing prejudicial'.[94] In August 1644 Sir John Maitland and the other Scots commissioners in London signed a pass for John Wood to return to Scotland with two servants, three horses and a cloak bag.[95]

The king's clothes were taken from the wardrobe to the bedchamber wrapped in a special cloth. For instance, in 1609 changeable taffeta sarsenet was supplied 'for a cloth to carry his majesty's clothes in', along with fustian to line it.[96] This may have served the same purpose as the bearing cloth made of 'grideline figured satin' in the 1635/6 accounts.[97] Toilets, in contrast, had several uses. Fancy examples such as 'a great toilet of cherry colour satin with a great double sweet bag and a little one all richly embroidered with gold and silver and garnished with lace' covered the dressing table, but others, such as 'two more purple taffeta toilets to carry his majesty's clothes in', were more like bearing clothes.[98] Whatever their form, their opulence reinforced the importance of the dressing process.

Sleeping and Relaxing in Style: Stuart Beds and Bedchambers

Men's bedchambers were places in which to sleep, dress and undress while also serving as a space to display and store important items reflecting a person's interests. In 1690 Breadalbane's bedchamber at Kilchurn Castle, at the north-eastern end of Loch Awe, housed a selection of guns, including a long gun called 'Dundie', and a brass blunderbuss was propped in a corner.[99] Looking up, the male gaze often fell on a painted ceiling of a type that had a long history in Scotland and which James VI brought to England.[100] Floral, heraldic or allegorical painted ceilings were designed to make the individual contemplate what was depicted and appreciate its significance. Most royal bedchamber ceilings presented messages about love, kingship and God. On 3 October 1662 John Evelyn saw John Michael Wright's allegory *Astraea Returns to Earth*

9.8 John Michael Wright, *Astraea Returns to Earth (The apotheosis of Charles II)*, c.1660. Oil on canvas, 228.6 × 142.2 cm. Nottingham Castle Museum and Art Galleries. This allegory of the Restoration, including an oak tree and the portrait of the king being taken up to heaven, was a very suitable subject for the king's bedchamber.

on the ceiling of the king's bedchamber at Whitehall (fig. 9.8), a story that was carefully chosen to celebrate the Stuart Restoration.[101] In 1673 the ceilings at Holyroodhouse were painted by the Dutch artist Jacob de Wet, with *The Apotheosis of Hercules* placed in the king's bedchamber.[102]

Having contemplated the ceiling, the viewer's gaze would be drawn to the bed, a very important status symbol because of its size and the expenditure that it represented, most notably in terms of the quantity and quality of the fabric and trimmings involved.[103] Beds were the focal point for specific aspects of court ceremonial, resulting in the concept of the bed of state or state bed in royal palaces and the homes of the elite, a development that in turn saw private apartments focusing on the bedchamber in the seventeenth century. The state or formal bed consisted of a joined wooden bed frame that was dressed with a complex assemblage of mattresses, sheets, pillows, bed hangings, valances and plumes of feathers. Sumptuous royal beds were central to how Mary, Queen of Scots presented herself as a legitimate monarch while imprisoned in England. Her goods at Chartley Manor, when she was imprisoned there, included 'furniture for a bed wrought with needlework of silk, silver and gold, with divers devices and arms, not thoroughly finished' that was 'to be delivered to the King of Scottes' on her death.[104]

James VI slept in equally sumptuous beds as an example from May 1580 reveals. This required 23 ells of green figured velvet upon satin, green Spanish taffeta for curtains, 3¾ lbs of green silk for the fringe and black velvet for the coverlet.[105] Some beds had family significance, such as the Hercules bed which James took to England in 1603, where it gained curtains of gold and crimson silk: it was still at Hampton Court in 1659, when it was described as 'a bed all moade of broderie work of gold of the history of the works of Hercules furnished with six pands, roof, headpiece and three underpands which is neither stuffed not garnished'.[106] When James returned to Scotland in 1617 he needed suitable beds to sleep in. Consequently a payment of £66 13s 4d was made to 'Johne Sawers for furnessing all maner of colloures for painting of his Majesties bed that wes sent up from Londoun'.[107] In 1619 William Drummond of Hawthornden related to Ben Jonson that Mary's bed had been sent to London along with three other beds 'to be mendit and providit with furnitour answerable and sutable to the beddis' so that it could be used for the king's visit.[108]

After Henrietta Maria's death 1669, Ralph Montagu, ambassador to

Louis XIV, acted swiftly to secure the best of her furnishings for Charles II. He informed Lord Arlington about 'some pieces of crimson and gold brocard, a very fine stuff, and will make his Majesty a very fine bed', adding that 'If the king pleases I will have it made up for him here much handsomer and cheaper than it can be in England'.[109] Montagu moved fast, soon reporting that 'The stuff that the King would have a bed made of is in my hands. I believe I shall make up the bed with a rich gold campane which is in the nature of a fringe … and have enough to hang the King's new little Bedchamber, where he dresseth himself.'[110]

This was just one of Charles II's beds, and in October 1677 a new bed was ordered for Whitehall of figured velvet, the ground blue and the flowers black and gold, lined with cherry-coloured satin and finished with a deep-twisted fringe. The bedchamber was hung with the same velvet that was used for a sleeping chair.[111] In addition to sleeping chairs, Charles II also had a field bed that was sent to Portsmouth for his use in June 1675.[112] A few years later 'his majesty's travelling bed' was left with Colonel George Legg, governor of Portsmouth.[113] There was also the king's 'progress bed', which was revamped with a new tick in July 1678.[114] More poignantly, and practically, during James VII and II's illness Mary of Modena told her mother in 1700, 'I spend my nights on a little bed in His Majesty's bedchamber'.[115] The Stuarts had beds for all occasions.

A small group of Stuart beds survive and Knole, in Kent, is home to two, including the gold and silver bed associated with James, duke of York and the figured green and gold velvet bed made for James in 1688.[116] Very similar in date is the red damask bed that was listed as part of the furnishings of the duke of Hamilton's apartments at Holyroodhouse in 1684, and is now displayed in the king's bedchamber in the State apartments designed by Sir William Bruce (fig. 9.9) as a reminder of Stuart bedchamber style.[117]

9.9 The king's bedchamber, Holyroodhouse, Edinburgh. Crimson was very popular for royal beds, and consequently for elite bedchambers.

9.10 *(above)* George Jamesone, *Lady Anne Erskine, Countess of Rothes with Her Daughters Lady Mary and Lady Margaret Leslie*, 1626. Oil on canvas, 219.4 × 135.3 cm. National Galleries of Scotland. Red furnishings add to the opulence of Lady Anne's room.

9.11 *(facing page)* Wall hanging of red wool with black silk velvet appliqué and silk embroidery, associated with Mary, Queen of Scots' bed at Lochleven Castle, early 17th century. National Museum of Scotland, Edinburgh.

Scottish Beds and Bedchambers

George Jamesone's painting of Lady Anne Erskine, countess of Rothes (*c.*1595–1640) with her daughters offers a hint of the richness of Scottish homes in the 1620s (fig. 9.10). While it is hard to tell which room Lady Anne stands in, the paintings, jewel box and rich textiles would not have been out of place in a bedchamber.[118] As in the royal household, the main bedchamber was an important room in the homes of the Scottish elite, with the bed taking centre stage.[119] As with the Stuarts, beds were about more than status because they stressed family bonds. A very good example of this is provided by the black velvet bed with black damask curtains that Gilbert, earl of Cassillis, granted to his mother in August 1559 'for the love and favor he bears to her'.[120] Love of a wife for her husband probably explains three surviving embroidered foot valances from a bed belonging to Sir Colin Campbell and Katherine Ruthven. With depictions of scenes from the story of Adam and Eve placed on either side of their initials and coats of arms, the valances probably celebrated the couple's wedding, which took place in 1550.[121]

While best known for his scandalous marriage to Frances Howard, Robert Kerr's pavilion bed in his lodgings at Whitehall makes no references to love or devotion. Rather, it was covered with white silver velvet and carnation silver velvet laced with open gold lace, while his nightgown (of tawny velvet embroidered with gold and lined with unshorn velvet) and waistcoat (of tawny satin embroidered with gold) were made to match the carpet and cupboard cloth, also of tawny velvet and embroidered with cloth of silver. As a final flourish there were six hangings of green velvet embroidered with China gold and silk 'after the manner of China work'.[122] This bed and nightgown demonstrates how profitable Kerr's service in the royal bedchamber had been while also showing off his excellent taste and a passion for the exotic. It comes as no surprise that Kerr was one of the important Scottish collectors at the Jacobean court.

Kerr was not the only one with fashionable taste. A mid seventeenth-century inventory of the house of Strathbogie, Aberdeenshire, lists a 'chapel bed' with an embroidered roof and pand (valance), a headpiece of yellow flowered velvet embroidered with gold and five pieces of damask red and yellow curtains, with a fringe of silk and gold and

laid with gold lace.[123] Further changes could be seen by the end of the century, when John Kello, embroiderer, burgess of Edinburgh, was paid for embroidering 12 slips for bed hangings in 1695.[124] By 1709 mohair was in favour and the duke of Gordon's room was furnished with 'Ane Bed hung with yellow Moyhair'.[125]

Good-quality materials and trimmings of the type described above were available in Scotland at reasonable prices. In 1632 Nicolas Herman sent 34 ells of red and yellow passementerie and 34 ells of black and yellow passementerie from Perth to Duncan Campbell. The remainder would follow in ten days' time, along with the assurance that he 'sall not paye no more nor all the gentillfolks in Scotland hes payet afoir'.[126] The necessary craftsmen and -women were also available, as indicated by the Lochleven hangings that date from the late sixteenth/early seventeenth century. These hangings combine red wool with silk embroidery and black velvet appliqué to very striking effect (fig. 9.11).[127] A hint of the cost of these hangings can be gleaned from the bill for £18 4s Scots submitted by Janet Morison, indweller in Edinburgh, to Robert Stirling, chamberlain to the 10th laird of Glenorchy, for embroidering 12 pieces of 'stript' on a suit of curtains.[128]

Some, including the laird of Pitfodels in Aberdeen, looked further afield for a new bed. In 1664 Mr Mitchell shopped in France for rich scarlet Avignon taffeta to line a bed and make a quilted 'courtpoint' and rich gold and silver 'dentel of the newest fashon' to trim it.[129] London also provided opportunities to buy items made by French craftsmen and items in the French style. In August 1694 Thomas Crosse and Stephen Langley wrote to the earl of Breadalbane about shipping two beds costing £173 12s 1d. The headboards and cornices could travel by land if the curtains and valances were removed and packed in suitable boxes. The bedsteads, chairs and other things would go by sea.[130] However, wherever the bed was made, the taste and opinion of the customer was all-important and as these examples indicate, discerning Scottish customers were keen to be fashionable.

Closets, Dressing Rooms and Garde-robes

From the 1660s a cluster of small rooms, including the closet, dressing room and *garde-robe*, developed in the space beyond the royal bedchamber.[131] This arrangement can be seen in the private apartments at Ham House furnished in the 1670s for the earl of Lauderdale.[132] They were also to be found in Scotland. For instance, in 1682 Lady Katherine Hamilton lost the key to her father's clothes closet at Hamilton Palace.[133] The dressing room could be used for the toilet, as in 1683 when John Evelyn saw the duchess of Portsmouth 'in her dressing-roome within her bedchamber, when she was in her morning loose garments, her maids combing her, newly out of bed, his Majesty and the gallants about her'.[134] On occasion Charles II put dressing rooms to other uses, as Pepys reported on 8 February 1662: 'the good Queen will of herself stop before she goes sometimes into her dressing-room till she know whether the king be there, for fear he should be, as she hath sometimes taken him, with Mrs Stuart.'[135]

The set of apartments prepared for James, duke of Albany and York, at Lyme Park, Cheshire, included a dressing room that was furnished with a Japanned cabinet, a pair of stands, a large black mirror, table and pair of stands, three caned chairs, a portrait of Richard Legh and eight little pictures.[136] Once king, James enjoyed the same arrangement at Hampton Court, with his dressing room next to the 'paradice' chamber and pictures hanging up the staircase to it.[137] Similar opulence featured in the 1681 inventory of Hamilton Palace, where the listing for 'My Lord's dressing room' included damask hangings, a bed and an iron grate.[138] Also recorded were two warming pans and a little skillet to offer added warmth and comfort while dressing.[139]

Conclusions

9.12 Satin nightcap with metal thread embroidery, 1640–45. Burrell Collection, Glasgow.

A nightcap associated with Charles II offers a glimpse of the cost and quality of items made specifically for use in the Stuart bedchamber, and of the social significance of dressing, undressing and being in 'undress' (fig. 9.12).[140] Both as a space and as a group of individuals who occupied that space, the royal bedchamber was very important politically and culturally to the later Stuart monarchs. Here, in an unparalleled way, the Stuarts' Scottish heritage comes to the forefront. When James VI and I moved to England, his use of the bedchamber ensured that this room bypassed the privy chamber that had been at the heart of Tudor politics. By introducing this Scottish dynamic to the English royal household and promoting Scots within it, James brought about significant changes that were visibly expressed through the textiles associated with the bedchamber. And while the number of Scots in the household declined during the course of the seventeenth century, this did not mean that they lacked influence or access to the Stuart bedchamber.

For king and courtier alike, the bedchamber was the place to see and be seen. As the seventeenth century progressed, royal dressing and undressing were elevated from practical necessities to political theatre. The same performance was played out in the bedchambers of the Scottish elite, surrounded as they were by the full range of textiles and furnishings associated with the Stuart bedchamber. Hints of this opulence remain, including a fragment of a plasterwork frieze in the great bedchamber at Elcho Castle, on the south bank of the River Tay. Thistles, roses and fleurs-de-lys combine, symbolising the Wemyss family's loyalty to the monarchy and their engagement with Stuart bedchamber style.

CHAPTER TEN

Clothes and the Social and Political Life of the King and the Male Elite

ONCE DRESSED, THE SEVENTEENTH-CENTURY Stuart elite lived much of their lives in the public gaze. Whether at court or in the open spaces of Edinburgh or London, public and semi-public places were ideal for men to see, and be seen in, fashionable clothing. In turn, these clothes were often viewed in the context of a man's horse, his horse furniture and the liveries of his servants.[1] Many everyday royal activities were the subject of intense scrutiny by individuals like Frances, lady Paget, who informed her brother-in-law, Mr Campbell, 10th laird of Glenorchy, that the king and queen ate in state publicly three times a week, following the dining habits of Charles I and Henrietta Maria (fig. 10.1).[2] As a result, scandal could make or break an individual's reputation, as Margaret Leslie, countess of Wemyss, feared when she told Sir John Gilmour about the marriage of her daughter. Mary had wed Walter Scott, later earl of Tarras, on 9 February 1659 but, aged just 11, she was very young and her mother feared 'the indignity of having the marriage publicly questioned'.[3] By the same token, public displays could make something legal such as the letters of inhibition against the heritors and tenants of Lindeiff that were read 'publicly' at the door of Cleish kirk in 1622.[4] In a similar vein, James Douglas, 1st lord Mordington, was summonsed to appear before the Estates of Parliament on 4 June 1644 to answer for not 'swearing and subscribing' the Solemn League and Covenant. To make amends, he was ordered do so in the 'open face of Parliament'.[5]

Public demonstrations of status were central to the Scottish elite's place in society, and the clothes that were worn on these occasions, whether they were new wedding clothes, formal robes or fashionable sporting attire, played a key part in this. It was a successful strategy, with Keith Brown showing how aristocratic power increased during this

See figure 10.12.

10.1 *(right)* Gerrit Houckgeest, *Charles I, Queen Henrietta Maria and Charles II when Prince of Wales Dining in Public*, 1635. Oil on panel, 63.2 × 92.4 cm. Royal Collection. Attending the monarch at dinner was an excellent opportunity to observe royal fashion and show off your own clothes, as the men in the foreground are doing.

10.2 *(below)* Statue of James VI, National Museum of Scotland, Edinburgh. Crowned, and with the collar of the order of the Garter over his formal robes, James is displaying his authority as king in a very traditional way.

time.[6] From the perspective of the Stuart monarchs, it was the scarlet parliament robes and the black gowns of the judiciary and government officials that served as a demonstration not only of elite power but also of royal authority. As Julian Goodare has argued, the Stuart monarchs made increasing use of their royal prerogative during the seventeenth century in a concerted bid to make their government more effective.[7] While Charles I's use of this tool was successfully challenged in both Scotland and England, the robes survived and continued to demonstrate royal and elite authority after the Restoration.

Present Yet Not Present: How the Stuarts Made Their Presence Felt

Displaying statues of the monarch in public spaces made the royal body, and the clothes placed upon it, a permanent part of daily life. Different styles of sculpture, in tandem with particular clothes, conveyed different messages. Seated figures, such as that of James VI in his red robes of state (fig. 10.2), served as a reminder of traditional Stuart authority in Scotland. Classical forms, as in the case of the equestrian statue of James VI and I erected outside London's Royal Exchange in 1625, conjured up Roman ideas of imperial authority.[8] Similarly, the crowned figure of James VI and I by John Clark placed in 1620 on the Tower of the Five Orders at the Bodleian Library kept the royal intellect in the minds of students and academics. Multiple figures conveyed a sense of the Stuart family, for example the brass statues of Charles I and his father in fashionable dress placed on a portico erected by St Paul's Cathedral or Hubert le Sueur's statues for Winchester Cathedral.[9] Whether it was in Edinburgh, London or Oxford, the Stuarts made very effective use of statues to assert their authority and remind their people that while they might be physically absent, their authority was undeniable.

Grinling Gibbons's equestrian statue of Charles II dressed as a Roman emperor at Windsor received a mixed response in 1685 if the pithy comments of Sir John Lauder of Fountainhall are anything to go by.[10] Yet this did not stop a lead version of this very statue being commissioned for Edinburgh, where it still stands in Parliament Square, bringing garden-style sculpture to important civic spaces (fig. 10.3). The elite also placed royal statues in their gardens as a token of their loyal support for the crown, and in 1686 Arnold Quellin made a statue of Charles I for the earl of Strathmore.[11] While the monarch was not present in Scotland, their statues, dressed in various versions of Stuart style, were to be found across the country as a reminder to the Scottish people of who their sovereign was.

Royal celebrations were equally significant in promoting the Stuart 'brand' to the populace regardless of national boundaries. There were clear precedents: for example, Elizabeth I and her courtiers had made effective use of Accession Day from the 1570s. However, as Ronald Hutton has observed, James had a choice of anniversaries, including his accession to Elizabeth's throne and the anniversary of his coronation on 25 July, the 'king's nights' that marked his escape from the Gowrie conspiracy on 5 August 1600, and Guy Fawkes on 5 November 1605.[12] James brought Gowrie Night to London and the Venetian ambassador noted that he attended chapel every Tuesday 'in memory of his escape' from the Gowrie plot.[13] Celebrations continued in Scotland as the records from Haddington reveal, though it seems that observation of Gowrie Night had to be enforced in areas where affinity with the family endured or where Presbyterian ministers (who doubted the king's account of the supposed assassination attempt) held sway.[14] James's fortuitous escape from Guy Fawkes captured the public imagination and was depicted, alongside the Armada, on a diptych in St Faith's Church, Gaywood, on the outskirts of King's Lynn.[15] It was also the subject of a print published in Amsterdam in 1621 by the

10.3 Grinling Gibbons, lead monument of Charles II on horseback in Parliament Square, Edinburgh, 1685. By depicting Charles as a Roman general or emperor, Gibbons is linking Charles II's kingship with the authority of imperial Rome.

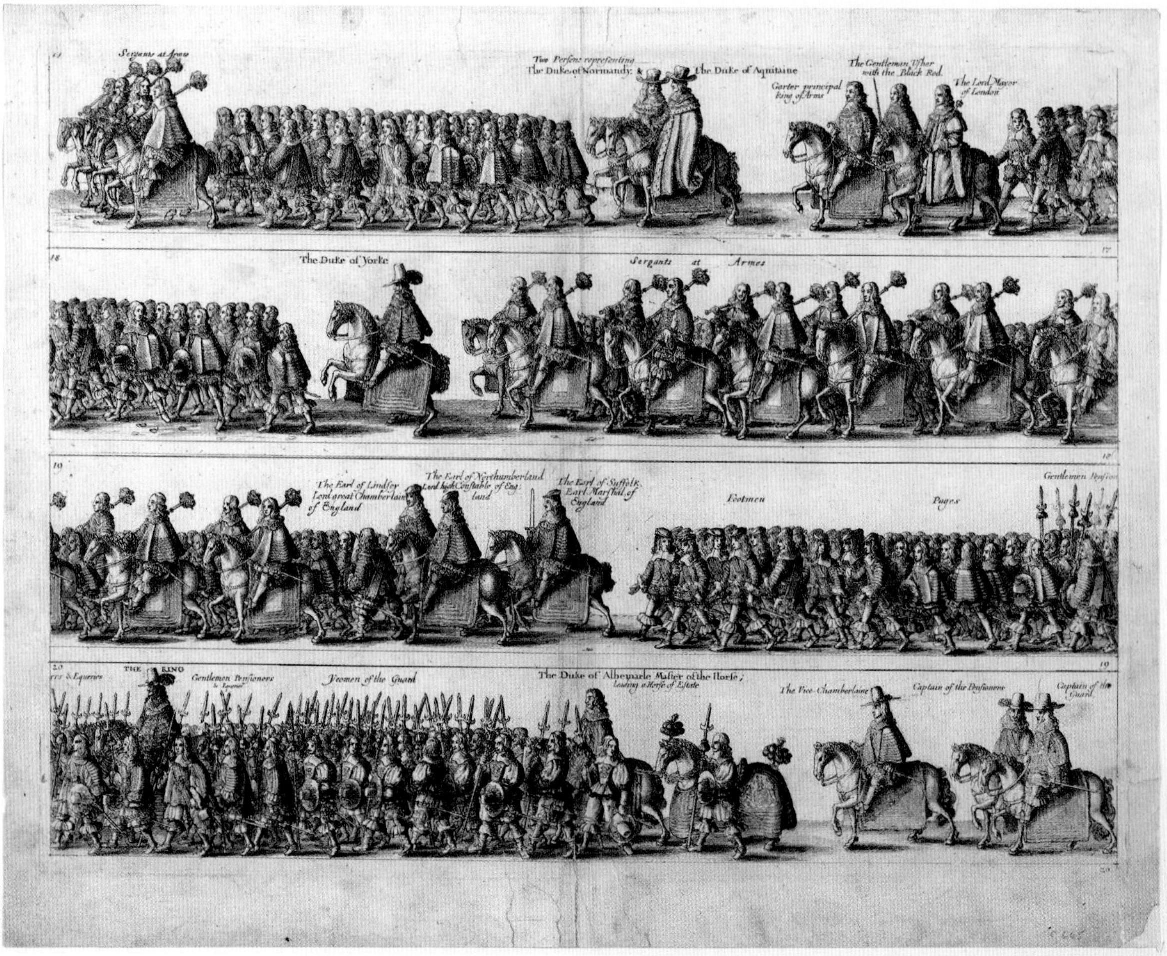

10.4 Wenceslaus Hollar, *Coronation Procession of Charles II through London*, 1662. Etching, 44 × 53.7 cm. Metropolitan Museum of Art, New York. Preceded by his brother, Charles, along with his household and General Monk, display Stuart fashion to the London crowd.

Puritan Samuel West called *The Double Deliverance* that inspired an embroidered picture on very similar lines.[16] Two more royal red-letter days were added to almanacs after the Restoration: 30 January, marking Charles I's execution in 1649; 29 May, Charles II's birthday; Royal Oak Day and the anniversary of his English coronation.[17]

Charles II's decision to enter London on 29 May 1660, his 30th birthday, is in keeping with the Stuart's use of the calendar and was an event that was celebrated with traditional pageantry and reinforced with a flurry of souvenirs. Hollar's etchings of the coronation procession two years later record in minute detail who was present and what they wore (fig. 10.4). Cheap, ephemeral dress accessories, such as fans, also proclaimed national joy. One such example has a leaf decorated with oak leaves, acorns, crowns, orbs, sceptres and the phrase *The Hapy Restoration* on a streamer running through the design (fig. 10.5). Public devotion was also encouraged with the issue of 'a prayer for the king's majesty, proper for the birthday, January 30th, May 29th etc., public days'.[18] All looked equally promising in the months after James VII and II's accession, and when Sir William Scott read his copies of the London newsletters he learnt that 'This being the 5 of November it was kept and observed very stricktly by all people in this citty, no shops being open and sermonds preached in every church, the flagg being outt on the Tower and the gunns all discharged'.[19]

In sartorial terms, the Stuarts made royal birthdays important social occasions. This may have been helped by Charles I's birthday falling on 19 November, with Henrietta Maria's just three days earlier, so making a double celebration the obvious choice. The queen often marked these days with a masque with opulent costumes, such as Walter Montagu's *The Shepherd's Paradise* held in January 1633 and Ben Jonson's *Florimine* in December 1635.[20] However, in 1627 the Suffolk clergyman John Rous noted that the city of London celebrated the anniversary of Elizabeth I's accession to the throne with bonfires and bells on 17 November while failing to observe the king's birthday just two days later.[21] After the Restoration royal birthdays were celebrated more regularly and lavishly with varying degrees of success. In 1680 there were fewer celebrations than usual in London, with some shops remaining open, which, as Ronald Hutton notes, was 'a blatant insult to the king'.[22] For other members of the royal family, especially the queen and the king's brother, birthday balls were an opportunity for a show of fine clothes and jewels. On 14 October 1669 Pepys commented that 'the court [was] mighty full, it being the duke of York's birthday and he mighty fine'.[23]

10.5 This Restoration fan uses the oak tree as a symbol of Charles's escape after the battle of Worcester, c.1660. Bone and paper. Fan Museum, London.

Once king, James continued to celebrate his birthday and in 1685 Evelyn recorded that 'Being the Kings birth-day, [there] was a solemn Ball at Court'.[24] However, the following year he noticed that 'there was a Ball that night but small appearance of qualitie'.[25] Perhaps knowing that James's unpopularity had been revealed by this noticeable indifference to his celebrations, William used the notion of royal birthday celebrations to establish himself. In 1692 a firework display in Edinburgh overseen by Captain John Slezer marked the happy day.[26] Even so, courtiers could opt out for personal or political reasons, as Lord Lothian did the following year. While he noted that there was 'great bravery at Court', Lothian 'did neither make Cloathes nor goe there' because his wife was unwell and he was not in a party mood.[27]

In Scotland, official birthday celebrations focused upon Holyroodhouse and they were managed by the palace underkeeper, Robert Kennedy, who spent £10 sterling on bonfires at Abbey Close and Arthur's Seat on 29 May 1680. A further £44 Scots was spent on 'wine drunk and glasses broken' at the bonfire by the nobility, provost and aldermen, officers and soldiers.[28] Other towns held celebrations, including Linlithgow in 1662 and Inverness in 1663.[29] These public events continued throughout the reign, with the earl of Aberdeen taking part in festivities on 29 May 1682.[30] As in England, not everyone was enthused and in 1681 David Spence, the town clerk of Rutherglen, refused to mark Charles II's birthday saying he did not give 'a fart' for these days.[31]

The Political Life of the Stuarts and the Male Elite

Serving in Parliament was the most important civic responsibility of the elite, and in 1455 an Act of Parliament laid down what the robes for the Scottish parliament should be. The carefully graded use of fur and fabric reinforced the social and political hierarchy. Earls were permitted 'mantles of "grained" brown, open at the front, furred with white', the other lords of parliament were to have 'a mantle likewise of red, open at the front, lined with silk or furred with grey "gris" fur or "pured" fur' and the burgh commissioners were allowed 'a pair of cloaks of blue furred to the foot side, open on the right shoulder'.[32] In 1587 James VI reviewed the parliament robes.[33] He did so again in June 1605 and now dukes, marquises and earls were to wear 'reid cramsie velvit robs lyned with quhyte armings and taffety', while lords were to appear in 'reid scalet robs lynit after the same fashion'.[34] The consequence of this change is evident from the fact that the 1606 parliament held at Perth was known as the 'red parliament'.[35] David Calderwood, the minister of Crailing, feared that the Catholics believed that this red parliament 'sould mend all again'.[36] His concerns were not helped by the attendance of Bishop Graeme of Dunblane and Bishop Lindsay of Dunkeld, dressed in silk, and with velvet 'foote mentles'.[37] The visual impact of these robes is clear from the full-length portrait of Charles Seton, 2nd earl of Dunfermline, *c.*1640 (fig. 10.6).

10.6 Sir Anthony van Dyck, *Charles Seton, 2nd Earl of Dunfermline*, c.1640. Oil on canvas, 220.7 × 134 cm. National Galleries of Scotland. To Seton's right Van Dyck has included his coronet, in further recognition of his rank as earl.

The Scottish parliament remained important after 1603 and in March 1604 David Williamson, burgess of Edinburgh, was confident that while all the nobles were in England they would return for the assembly.[38] Attendance was required but it was also expensive. The accounts of the Maitland earls of Lauderdale record the following statement:

> I Adame Rea merchand burges of Edinburgh grantis me to haif Ressauit … The somme of tuelff hundredth pundis guid & vsuall money of scotland and that as for ye pryce of ane parliament Rob of skarlot lynit with quhyt Satene With ane fitmantle of blak velwot pasmentit & frenyeit with gold & silk & harnessing conforme yairto.[39]

The social value associated with a set of parliament robes saw them passed from father to son, as in the case of James Drummond, 1st lord Madertie (*c.*1540–1623), whose estate

10.7 The 'riding of parliament' from c.1680–85, from Nicholas de Gueudeville, *Atlas historique, ou Nouvelle introduction à l'Histoire à la chronologie & à la Géographie ancienne & moderne* (Amsterdam, 1720). National Library of Scotland. This procession emphasises the importance of the parliament robes, with the train being held up, as the member of parliament walks into the parliament building.

included his parliament robes, a doublet and breiks of black satin and a two-handled sword.[40] Lord Lyon, the leading Scottish herald, also played a central role and in 1661 Sir Robert Murray provided him with a new coat of arms, robe and footmantle so that he looked the part as he fulfilled his ceremonial duties.[41]

It was particularly important that James and his parliament acquitted themselves well when the assembly met in 1617 after an absence of 14 years. The privy council was anxious that all the members looked the part and issued instructions to 'the Commissionaris for the Small Baronis and Burrowis' requiring then to 'attend his Majestie thairfra to the Parliament House upoun horseback and with footemantillis'. If they failed to do so 'thay salbe noted as absentis and accordinglie salbe unlawit, and thay sall haif no place nor voit in this present Parliament'.[42] The king also needed to impress and he 'rode thither in great state on the first day … in as honourable fashion, as I have seen him in England'. However, James had made changes because 'All the Lords rode in English robes' and while Buckingham was in attendance on the king he did not wear his robes.[43] This is another example of James seeking to bring the Scottish and English elites closer together.

The most distinctive feature of the Scottish parliament was the riding of parliament that went from Holyrood, along the Royal Mile, to the parliament house built in the 1630s. The chancellor was in the lead, with the honours in the middle and the high commissioner, the king's representative, at the rear. The procession was intended to impress, and Sir John Clerk of Penicuik thought the riding had 'a very grand appearance … such as I never saw the like in any foreign place' (fig. 10.7).[44] Precedent was hugely important in determining who rode where, as is made clear in the 1681 orders for the riding of parliament.[45] By the turn of the century it was such a spectacle that in March 1703 the Master of Banff was encouraged to 'bring the young ladies to see the parliament ridden' because it was a sight not to be missed.[46]

The relationship between monarch and parliament was built on precedent and right, as is evident from Calderwood's regular statements recording who carried the various appurtenances of kingship. This was very apparent when Charles I was present at the 1641 parliament, at which questions arose over the royal prerogative and whether 'the putting of the Scepter to Acts is but a Ceremony signifying the Royal Assent'. More importantly, if the king put the sceptre to acts past since his last visit it would 'make them acts of his present session of parliament and as much as if they had not been Laws of sufficient force to bind the subjects from the time wherein they were made'.[47]

James, duke of York believed that Scotland and her parliament had an important role to play in making 'men of estates consider well before they engage against the King'.[48] The riding of the 1681 parliament was spectacular, attended as it was by Scots and by a 'great many gentlemen ... from the north of England'.[49] However, the problem with parliament robes was that they were left in storage for long periods of time, thereby attracting moths. The earl of Lothian paid £4 for work 'mending your lordships parlliment Robs and skarllet cloth to fill up the hools'.[50] William, 8th earl of Menteith found he did not have any robes and asked James, 3rd marquis of Montrose to borrow 'sume Earles robes onley for a day to ryde in the parlyment and they shall be cearfulie keipt be me that none of them be spoylt'.[51] Attendance dressed in the correct robes was important.

Public Life: Officers of State and Royal Officials

The Stuarts were keen to regulate the dress of all royal officials and in 1610 James VI and I wrote to Alexander, earl of Dunfermline, the lord chancellor of Scotland, and also to the president and lords of the College of Justice on the subject. Some lawyers and writers to the signet wore cloaks rather than the 'decent habits' promoted by the king. His ordinance was to be obeyed and the extraordinary lords and lords of parliament would wear 'black gowns of velvet, satin or other rich stuff appropriate to their office'.[52] Charles I also took an interest in official dress and in November 1629 he ordered his lord treasurer, John, earl of Mar, to give £500 to the earl of Menteith for the robes provided for the judges of the circuit courts.[53]

When William Cunningham, 9th earl of Glencairn posed for his portrait in 1661, he did so in the black robes of lord high chancellor of Scotland (fig. 10.8). Next to him on the table was the embroidered seal bag, the most important symbol of his office. The appearance of royal officials continued to be important and in 1668 new guidelines appeared governing the robes of the justice general. He should have a long gown of red velvet with two inches of white ermine down the breast. The gown of the justice clerk was of red cloth 'of the same fashion and trimmed with white ermine', while the three justice deputies had unlined red cloth gowns trimmed with white ermine.[54] Shortly after John Graham, 2nd marquis of Montrose was appointed as an extraordinary lord of session in June 1668, James Cuming ordered the necessary robes for him: a black velvet gown laced with gold lace, trimmed with gold embroidered buttons and loops.[55] By 1680 the cost of gowns for the Lords Justiciary and mace bearers had increased to £678 8s Scots.[56] These sartorial markers of office extended further down the hierarchy with the sheriff clerk of Fyfe receiving £20 from Robert Broun and Thomas Thomeson, bailies of Inverkeithing, 'in respect of sheriff gloves' for 1656.[57] Gowns were often passed on, as in 1699 when Margaret, countess of Rothes and Haddington, signed a discharge to Alexander Home of the session gown belonging to her family, lent to the chancellors, Lord Aberdeen and Lord Marchmont.[58]

10.8 John Michael Wright, *William Cunningham, 9th Earl of Glencairn*, 1661. Oil on canvas, 127 × 102.2 cm. National Galleries of Scotland. Fashionable accessories such as the cravat, gloves and his sword complete Cunningham's outfit.

Like members of parliament, some royal officials also had foot mantles, so including their horse within their official dress. In September 1670 George Drummond sent the 10th laird of Glenorchy a bill for £320 15s for a foot mantle: it was made from 'fine blak 3 pyll welvet', lined with broad black buckram and trimmed with black silk and fringe. In addition, 'the horse furnitor' required one ounce of gold thread.[59] The sumptuous materials explain Calderwood's scorn over Bishop Gladstains, who never went to preach without a foot mantle.[60]

The spaces associated with royal government also had to be suitably 'dressed', and after the Restoration Sir Robert Murray took charge of furnishing the rooms at Holyroodhouse with a cloth of state, cushion and footstools for use by the king's commissioner.[61] In 1668 Lauderdale and William Bellenden, 1st lord Bellenden, the treasurer depute, were in London purchasing hangings, carpets, chairs and a 'Crimson-velvet Chair of State', as well as sconces, candlesticks and a clock for 'the Councill and Session house'. Particular care was taken to ensure that 'the Masse [mace] shall be provided of the bignes they use them here [i.e. London] with the Armes right quartered'. Lely was working on the king's portrait at the time, and Lauderdale hoped that its progress would 'be quickened'.[62] While the furnishings asserted the significance of these rooms, royal officials displayed their standing by processing before the people. The importance of doing so is evident in the comment of Patrick, 1st earl of Marchmont, on 1 December 1702: 'The patents to the earl of Seafield for Lord Chancelour, [and] the viscount of Tarbat for secretary

… came here upon Sunday which hapened to be the last day that I appeared in publict as Chancelour in the Church and on the streets.'[63]

The Stuarts' interest in royal officials can also be seen in the work of John Michael Wright. He was commissioned to paint 22 full-length portraits of judges by the aldermen of the City of London.[64] They were noteworthy enough for Evelyn to pay a visit 'to see the Pictures of all the Judges and Eminent men of the Long robe newly painted by Mr Write'.[65] Evelyn was impressed, as he was meant to be, by this project that demonstrated the place of the elite in Stuart government, an elite that could be made to look more uniform than it was by the use of similar robes in Scotland and England.

Sounding Allegiance: The Role of the King's Trumpeters in Scotland

Trumpeters were essential for formal Stuart events, dressed as they were in royal livery and with heraldic banners hanging from their trumpets. In April 1598 new banners were made for the king's four trumpeters from red and yellow damask, painted with gold, silver and oil paints at a cost of £200 Scots.[66] A later embroidered example with the Scottish royal coat of arms and the initials *CR* for Charles II, and another associated with the Council Chamber in Edinburgh, demonstrate that this tradition continued after 1603 (fig. 10.9).[67] Indeed the role that trumpeters played in civic ceremonial is borne out by George Drummond charging £1,580 6s 6d Scots in 1679/80 for liveries for His Majesty's trumpeters.[68] Royal trumpeters gave added formality to the reading of royal proclamations as indicated by payments made by His Majesty's solicitor in November 1677.[69] Trumpeters, along with kettle drummers, who were associated with the Horse Guards, were also given livery asserting their position as members of the king's armed forces.[70]

The Stuarts distributed titles and knighthoods in Scotland to reward supporters, and the ceremonies served to reinforce royal authority. Thus John Andrews, John Fox and Henry Whyte, pages of the presence to Charles II, received £18 Scots from Sir James Drummond as the fee for his knighthood in June 1651.[71] Nine years later the price had more than doubled when Sir John Urquhart of Cromartie paid £40 Scots to Robert Cunningham, gentleman usher, for his knighthood.[72] The trumpeters' role in validating these ceremonies was equally important in times of war and peace. On 28 May 1648 Alexander Ferguson received £50 Scots on behalf of himself and the king's trumpeters from Patrick Maule, earl of Panmure, when he was made 1st earl of Panmure and lord of Brechin and Navar in 1646.[73] Equally important was the provision of drink money worth £19 12s Scots to the men who brought the sword of honour from Edinburgh Castle to dub Sir John Lauder of Woodhead on 10 March 1680.[74] Just as they ushered a man into his new rank, so trumpeters could mark the passing of his relatives, as on 8 June 1700 when Andrew Lamb was paid along with his fellow trumpeters for playing at the funeral of the countess of Lothian.[75]

The heads of the clans also kept trumpeters to assert their position. In May 1639 Archibald Campbell of Glencarradale, Edinburgh, told the 8th laird of Glenorchy about the arrival of a trumpeter from the earl of Holland, with four of the earl of Lothian's gentlemen delivering a letter to the earl of Argyll.[76] These trumpeters were given eye-catching livery, as in the case of the earl of Breadalbane, who bought yellow and black ribbons for his trumpeter in January 1665.[77] However, trumpeters looking for work could outstay their welcome. Patrick Scott of Tanlawhill, who looked after the finances of Francis, 2nd earl of Buccleuch, had to pay 'two or three trumpeters at night, who my lord could not be rid of'.[78]

10.9 *(above)* This silk trumpet banner with the arms of Charles II proudly displays the Scottish arms supported by a unicorn and lion, c.1660. National Museum of Scotland, Edinburgh.

While trumpeters often had ribbon on their livery, men across the social spectrum expressed their political allegiance by wearing coloured ribbons, sashes or cockades with increasing frequency during the seventeenth century. This habit was apparent during the Wars of the Three Kingdoms, and in a group portrait Colonel William Murray dips his grey, black and pink cockade in a glass of wine in a pledge to Prince Rupert and Colonel John Russell (fig. 10.10). During the subsequent fighting the followers of George Gordon, 2nd marquis of Huntly, 'weir ane blak teffetie about thair crag, quhilk we sane signe to fight to the death, bot it provit utherwayes'.[79] On 8 January 1644 Sir Thomas Hope issued 'the soiours of craighall, quho goes under Captain Moffat, ilk of them thair collers of blew and zellow

10.10 *(below, left)* William Dobson, *Prince Rupert, Colonel William Murray and Colonel the Honourable John Russell*, c.1640. Oil on canvas, 151.8 × 208.3 cm. National Trust, Ashdown House, Berkshire. Russell, seated on the right, has the same cockade on his hat as William Murray, while Prince Rupert's scarlet cloak is visible on the left.

silk ribbons, quhilk cost 4 merks'.[80] According to John Spalding, 'the Lord Gordon, and sum utheris … [had a ribbon] of ane red flesche cullor, which thay weir in thair hatis, and all it the royall ribbin, as a signe of thair love and loyaltie to the King'.[81] In contrast, the Covenanters under Montrose wore blue ribbons so that 'few or none of this haill army wantit ane blew ribbin hung about his crag doun under his lefte arme, quhilk thay callit the covenanteris ribbin'. Some in Aberdeen went as far as to tie blue ribbons round dogs' necks in mockery.[82] This is reminiscent of Protestant children tying red ribbons to a dog's tail on St Patrick's Day 1628, thereby provoking the Irish troops stationed at Witham, Essex.[83]

This politicised use of ribbon continued after the Restoration when it started to denote political allegiance. During the Exclusion Crisis the supporters of James, duke of York, who were predominantly Tories, wore red ribbons, while the Whig followers of James Scott, duke of Monmouth, wore blue.[84] Unrest in Edinburgh in 1682 was linked to the Popish Plot and Lauder of Fountainhall recalled how the students wore blue ribbons in their hats and members of 'the Episcopall and Court party have in opposition got rid ribbans'. A verse in the book of Numbers, where the Israelites wore a blue fringe, influenced the zealous Protestants' choice. This idea spread and the Scots reported that 'the watermen and apprentices of London, in this far have imitate us' by wearing blue ribbons to show support for excluding James.[85] Other colours featured too; green ribbons were first used by the Levellers in the late 1640s and were subsequently adopted by members of the Green Ribbon club, a group of radical Whigs, who met in the King's Head Tavern on Chancery Lane from 1675.[86] Not surprisingly, William's supporters including James's daughter Anne, and her ladies chose orange ribbon in 1689 as a challenge to her father.[87]

Exercise as a Means of Displaying the Well-dressed Male Body

When Nell Gwyn took the role of Almahide in *The Conquest of Granada*, one of the speeches that John Dryden wrote for her summed up Charles II's wish for informality:

> Yet princes may retire, whene'er they please,
> And breathe free air from out their palaces:
> They go sometimes unknown, to shun their state.[88]

Once outdoors, the king and men of leisure regularly engaged in a range of sports that provided them with opportunities to show off their skill, physique and clothes to a discerning audience. Walking was increasingly popular, offering as it did a means of gaining healthy exercise and of being seen. James VI and I liked to pace up and down and in 1604 he wrote that the long-suffering Cecil 'hath best cause to complain of my being a peripatetic, for I oft times walk so fast roundabout and about with him that he will be like to fall down dead upon the floor'.[89] Charles II inherited his grandfather's restless disposition, a fact acknowledged in 1651 when his household regulations stipulated that 'the Kyng have constantly a proportion of his gardes to waitt upon him to and garde att the church, as also when he goeth to the fields to walke or [play] goff'.[90] His fondness for a brisk walk influenced the design of royal parks, and in August 1670, while at Windsor, he 'passed most of his time in hunting the Stag & walking in the Parke which was now also planting with walks of Trees'.[91] Charles II resented his constitutional being interrupted by too much business, and so 'he walked by his watch, and when he pulled it out to look upon it skilful men would make haste with what they had to say to him'.[92] Equally unwelcome was rain, and a downpour on 6 April 1668 saw Pepys lending his cloak to James as they made their way through St James's Park.[93] Walking, as Pepys observed, was a great leveller, and rain no respecter of royalty.

When Pepys travelled with Charles II and his brother by barge in July 1665 he noticed that there was no 'difference between them and other men'.[94] And like many other men of the period, they loved horses. The Stuarts' passion for all things equestrian ensured that racing was the sport of kings. James VI and I took the opportunity to attend various races during his progress to Scotland in 1617. At Lincoln, for example, he stood on a specially erected stand while the public was held back behind a rope, so ensuring that 'the horses that ronned were seen faire'.[95] Races, like those held at Lincoln, usually took place on the edge of market towns and contributed to the social and economic life of such places.[96] Newmarket was the most important racing town in England, developing from modest origins in the sixteenth century, slumping during the civil war and rising again from 1680 onwards.[97] Spring and autumn meetings were common from the 1620s, and they benefited from royal support.[98] James Hamilton, 1st duke of Hamilton, on his return from Sweden, was reunited with Charles I on 18 October 1632 at the Newmarket races.[99] The races offered opportunities for more informality, and Sir John Reresby observed that when at Newmarket, Charles II 'mixed himself amongst the crowd, allowed everyman to speak to him that pleased, went hawking in the mornings, to cock matches in the afternoons (if there were no horse races), and to plays in the evenings, acted in a barn'.[100] Windsor, or Datchet Ferry, was another popular venue for racing, as shown by a print of Charles II watching the horses from his box in 1684, dressed on this occasion in a more formal court style (fig. 10.11).

Racing was equally popular in Scotland, and here it was Leith that was the most important venue.[101] In the early 1670s Alexander Gilmour of Craigmillar went to the races at Leith.[102] Later in the decade James, duke of York and Albany attended these races, and in 1680 a set of rules was drawn up for the Leith horse race.[103] Other towns wanted to hold races, and in May 1673 the earls of Mar and Glencairn and 13 others signed a subscription bond to secure the prize money for an annual race at the Brighaugh of Stirling.[104] Increased opportunities encouraged

10.11 Francis Barlow, *The Last Horse Race Run before Charles II*, 1687. Etching, 36.9 × 51.5 cm. Royal Collection. The more informal style that the king often favoured is being worn by the men in the foreground.

men like George Gordon, 1st earl of Aberdeen (1637–1720) to keep racehorses.[105] His horses ran at Leith from 1684 and sack was served after a race in February 1686, suggesting a victory.[106] The opposition included the laird of Powrie's 'running horse'.[107] Specific textiles also came to be associated with these events, and in 1704 the young laird of Makerston paid £1 to Thomas Morton for 'making a jockie coat'.[108]

When not at the races, the Stuarts enjoyed playing golf, and in 1618 James VI and I confirmed the right of people to play on Sunday. In the same year he granted the privilege of making and selling golf balls in Scotland to James Melville and William Berwick.[109] It was a passion they shared with members of the clergy, including William Couper, bishop of Galloway, who was often to be found on Leith Links. Charles I learned to play as a boy and in 1641 he was playing golf at Leith when he received the news of the Irish rebellion. Five years later, while he was held captive in Newcastle, a woman 'seeing the King at Goffe … said that it was better for the King to be with his Parliament than to be there'. After this rebuke, it was reported that 'The King seldome goes out to goffe'.[110] Even so, around this time the earl of Dalhousie bought a pell-mell set for the king.[111] James, duke of York shared the passion, playing pell-mell (a forerunner of croquet) at St James's and golf at Leith.[112]

As noted in Chapter 2, while at Stirling Prince Henry played golf and tennis, the latter on a court his father had also played on. Several other Scottish royal palaces had courts, including Dunfermline, Holyrood, Linlithgow and Falkland. The latter, which is still standing, was built for James V between 1539 and 1541 and was used by Mary, Queen of Scots and her successors.[113] While golf did not require specific clothing, Charles I and his eldest son were such keen tennis players that they regularly ordered special tennis suits. Charles I favoured suits made of silk or silk mixes, such as three of wrought satin flowered with coloured silk and two of tawny grosgrain flowered with silver that he purchased in 1628–9 and another of carnation damask in 1630.[114] In contrast, Charles

II's tennis clothes were mostly made from Holland or barmillion and trimmed with bobbin lace.[115] The tennis suit, consisting of a doublet and breeches, was quite stable in form until 1671, at which point there is a small gap when none are ordered, and when the item reappears, in 1674, it reflects the changes in the fashionable suit, with a tennis waistcoat and breeches being ordered in the accounts.[116]

Tennis was significant in other ways. Edward Sydenham believed that Charles I was unlikely to have 'anie favorite but the queene' because 'they are seldum a sunder, for when he goes to tennis she is ever with him'.[117] This made the demolition of the tennis court at Denmark House in 1629 in order to make a chapel and lodgings for the queen's priests all the more newsworthy.[118] However, it did not stop the king playing or making a wager with Marie de Rohan, duchess of Chevreuse, on a tennis game. Charles lost and Sir Robert Kerr of Ancram paid her £80.[119]

The sport formed an important part of a young gentleman's education, and in May 1676 James Forbes informed the duke of Hamilton that he had found suitable mathematics, language and tennis masters for the earl of Arran at Blois.[120] Not all fathers approved, though, and in 1654 Michael Young assured Lord Lothian that his sons walked in the fields 'being forbidden tennis'.[121] Tennis was considered an elegant sport. Football, on the other hand, was not, although this did not mean wealthy men refrained from playing it. In 1568 the earl of Cassillis reported that when Mary, Queen of Scots arrived at Carlisle, she saw the lord there playing 'at the fuit ball and othir games, bayth without the toun and within'.[122] However, playing football was not without risk, and when Sir David Cunningham took part in June 1629 he injured his left side, subsequently suffering 'much paine and trouble'.[123]

Hunting was a year-round activity. In 1621 Sir Robert Kerr of Ancram, gentleman of the bedchamber to Charles I, received a horse

10.12 Robert Peake the elder, *Henry Frederick Prince of Wales with Sir John Harington*, 1603. Oil on canvas, 201.9 × 147.3 cm. Metropolitan Museum of Art, New York. Henry and his companion are both dressed in fashionable suits of green wool.

10.13 Daniel Mytens, *Charles I and Henrietta Maria Departing for the Chase*, c.1630–32. Oil on canvas, 282 × 408.3 cm. Royal Collection. Stylish but in muted shades suited to the hunt, Henrietta Maria's gown compliments her husband's choice of doublet.

10.14 The very high-quality goldsmith's work on this hunting pouch of James VI and I could have been by George Heriot (see fig. 6.6), c.1600–19. Leather, silk, silver, silver gilt, glass, gold, wood; 37 × 45 cm. Burrell Collection, Glasgow.

for 'summer hunting', while in November 1631 John, earl of Mar, asked his cousin the 8th laird of Glenorchy for 'a cuppill of good earth doggs' because he planned to spend much of the winter in Stirling hunting foxes.[124] The Stuarts were all keen hunters and they set the style for hunting dress. James VI and I, Prince Henry and Anna of Denmark all favoured green for hunting (fig. 10.12), but Mytens's painting of Charles and Henrietta Maria dressed for hunting presents them not in this colour but in muted shades, and this was a trend that continued under Charles II and James VII and II (fig. 10.13). Charles II ordered black velvet caps 'to ride in' but supplied a beaver hat to the master of the harriers and a half-beaver for the sergeant of the buckhounds.[125] In contrast, the 1st earl of Perth owned a dashing red satin riding cap decorated with silver gilt lace.[126]

Hunting accessories were often of very high quality, as with the hawk hood, lures and hunting bag associated with James VI (fig. 10.14).[127] This bag is embroidered with brambles and mistletoe, while the gold mount is enamelled in black, green, white and yellow.[128] Not everyone bought new, as was the case with Anne, countess of Errol, who thanked the earl of Airlie for 'those gloves your Lordship is pleased to give our children the lend of' and promised that 'they shall be as litle the worss as is possible and cairfuly return'd uhen they have learn'd uhat is necessair from them'.[129] As this overview shows, the Stuarts' sporting activities had a direct influence on fashion in terms of developing special clothes for riding and tennis, while also being flexible enough to allow for personal preference.

Dressing the Part: Stuart Men and the Social World

During the seventeenth century, a combination of several lengthy European wars and the domestic Wars of the Three Kingdoms promoted a military career as a way for some men to make a living. The Restoration saw the beginnings of a Stuart standing army, with troop displays serving to display uniforms and military bearing. When Charles II 'saw the Scots Regiment exercise in the French Way, and it pleases so well that the King says he likes it far better than ours, which the Prince, Col. Russell, and all the English officers almost do not'.[130] The royal guards were highly visible when they escorted the king to Newmarket for the races or to the opening of the English parliament in 1669.[131] Military men were on view during musters and army parades such as those held on Hounslow Heath in May and June 1678 and on Blackheath in 1684. The appeal of such events is evident from Alexander Gilmour of Craigmillar's hiring of a horse in 1673 to go to the mustering of the militia at Musselburgh.[132] It also explains why the Edinburgh town guard gradually gained a more formal look. In 1694 James Reede supplied Captain Bayly with 40 hats, hatbands and red coats, two of which were too small and were returned to be made larger.[133]

Dressed in scarlet, James, duke of Monmouth led a brigade of Scottish and English troops in 1672 during the third Anglo-Dutch War (fig. 10.15). The 1670s and 1680s also saw the establishment of a number of Scottish regiments, each with their own distinctive uniform. In May 1683 the privy council agreed to send '150 ells of red cloth, 40 ells of white cloth and 550 dozen of buttons' for Dundee's troops.[134] In contrast, General Dalyell's dragoons were kitted out with 2,536 ells of grey cloth from the New Mills factory near Haddington.[135] The value of these uniforms ensured that they were passed on, and in 1688 David Gourlay received on behalf of Sir William Paterson the scarlet cloak and other clothing owned by the late Kenneth McKenzie of Suddie.[136] When John Graham, 1st viscount Dundee, married Jean Cochrane, daughter of William, lord Cochrane, on 10 June 1684 at Paisley, he was accompanied by his troopers, who were dressed in new red tunics, while the kettle drummers and trumpeters wore grey.[137] While a military career and uniform might attract the female gaze, they could also get in the way of a man's marriage plans, as Sir James Turner informed the duke of Hamilton in 1682. George Macwharne had 'come to Straven to buy shews and other things for his wedding' but his name was on the list of men to be called for military service prepared by the duke and so his marriage plans were spoiled.[138]

10.15 Jan Wyck, *James Scott, Duke of Monmouth and Buccleuch*, c.1675. Oil on canvas, 79 × 103.8 cm. National Portrait Gallery, London. In addition to his scarlet coat, Monmouth also sports a tricorne hat and mid-thigh-length boots.

10.16 Sir Anthony van Dyck, *John Hamilton, 1st Baron Belhaven and His Wife Margaret*, c.1640. Oil on canvas, 124.5 × 146.7 cm. Duff House, Banff, Aberdeenshire. Hamilton's black satin suit is the perfect contrast to his wife's red satin gown.

Van Dyck's double portrait of John Hamilton, 1st lord Belhaven, and his wife Margaret presents the viewer with a fashionably dressed couple (fig. 10.16). It is likely that their wedding clothes had been in keeping with John Gauden's advice in *Christ at the Wedding* (1654) where he stipulated that the happy couple should wear their most 'comely adornings' because 'it would be very grievous to bridegrooms and brides, to be denied the use of their best clothes, their richest adornments and jewels, which God permits and scripture alludes to'.[139] The quality of the groom's clothes stressed that he could afford to marry and support a family. References to Scottish men's wedding clothes are quite rare, but those there are indicate that considerable care was taken over them. In 1582 Jean Forbes, lady Ogilvy, paid £40 Scots to William Betoun, the king's embroiderer, for 'ane hat string … at the mariage of hir sone'.[140] In the mid 1670s John Dalme had a new wedding suit trimmed with 4¼ ells of pink ribbon.[141] In a similar vein, the Englishman Sir Thomas Isham also ordered a new white silk coat and breeches brocaded with silver gilt thread for his wedding, but he died on 8 August 1681, the day before his nuptials (fig. 10.17).[142]

10.17 This detail of a narrow, horizontal pocket flap, 1681, shows how decorative the use of silver gilt buttons could be, and how they enhanced the silver gilt brocading on Thomas Isham's wedding coat. Victoria and Albert Museum, London.

While God might approve of rich wedding clothes, James, duke of York, like many before him, announced his concern in May 1681 at the 'great extravagancy and expenses used and bestowed upon burials, mareages and christnings' in Scotland that was 'to the great impoverishment of the nobility, gentry and burrows'.[143] On 12 January 1688 the duke of Hamilton described the wedding two days before of his son the earl of Arran to Lady Ann Spencer, eldest daughter of the earl of Sutherland, noting how uneven the expenses for bride and groom were: 'The bride was very fine & they say they have bestowed 1000 li on her for clothes, Tweelet & points … our son had but to find a Tollet & night gown'.[144]

Ribbon also played a part in people's romantic lives, and ribbons were popular as wedding favours. On the occasion of Arran's marriage 'any body that came gote a faver of the bride & bridegrooms Ribons that wer on their clothes that day they wer married & there wer many aane given of the same kinde more then they had on their clothes'.[145] These ribbons were distributed widely, with John Evelyn commenting happily that he had received the 'most glorious favours' and that the wedding was celebrated 'with extraordinary splendour'.[146]

By the end of the seventeenth century Henri Misson de Valbourg observed that 'Persons of quality, and many others who imitate them, have lately taken up the custom of being marry'd very late at night in their chamber'.[147] This was certainly true of the marriage of Margaret Hamilton to the earl of Panmure that took place 'this night' on 5 February 1687. Her father recorded that it was 'absolutely privat', adding, 'for we have no body at it but Cassillis and [Donald] Donald and his wife and those within our owen family and he has with him only E. Mar & his own brother Hary'.[148] In a similar manner Lord Yester married 'on Satterday night in ye viscount of Panmuirs lodgings & went to the Canagat Church on Sunday' in 1697 and then dined in her father's lodgings. Patrick Aikenhead added that 'the weding was very privat which hes saved a vast charge'.[149] While these weddings were described as being modest, many in fact were not. Indeed, Scots were often at the forefront of Stuart society weddings on both sides of the border. When Anna, countess of Buccleuch, married the duke of Monmouth in 1663, for example, her purchases included 'high lace to my holland waistcoat on the wedding night', 'broidering my wedding petticoat', rich wedding garters and shoestrings and silver garters.[150]

Most couples hoped for a family in the months and years after marriage. As the seventeenth century progressed there was a growing sense of the social significance of christenings, an idea fostered by the royal court, where Charles I oversaw the christenings of his friends' children. In March 1632, for example, the king arranged the christening of James Hamilton's daughter.[151] When James, duke of York's son, the earl of Cambridge, was christened on 1 January 1661, Charles II and the duke of Albemarle were his godfathers.[152] In Scotland the importance of christenings was reflected in the significance placed on the textiles required for the infant. In 1679 Alexander Gartshore charged £30 Scots for a 'fyne least [laced] chyldbed sewit'. His receipt was more precise, describing the items as a 'chrisning suit'.[153] In the same month Mungo Campbell paid William Menzies of Edinburgh £42 Scots for '1 fyne laced Cristening suit'.[154] In 1693 Katharine Kerr informed the countess of Lothian of her purchases including a christening suit.[155] As with weddings, fathers took pleasure in inviting friends and family to these events: for example, Alexander Falconer asked his father-in-law, the earl of Airlie, to attend the christening of his son.[156]

While Scottish men played a key role in family affairs, they also took a leading role in public social spaces such as those at Bath and Tunbridge Wells. The fame of the latter as a spa town is evident in a letter sent by

Glenorchy when he was in Brussels to his cousin Carwhin. He described the spa at Aix-la-Chapelle (Aachen) as 'the Tunbridge of these countries where all doe meet in spring and summer, to drink the waters there'.[157] The 3rd duke of Hamilton went to both.[158] During his visit to Bath in 1678 he bought a 'bathing suit' costing £1 6s.[159] While John Campbell, 1st earl of Breadalbane was at Bath in 1693, the local tailor was paid for making bathing linen including '2 bath shouls' (10s) and 'a flaning stoumadger' (1s).[160] In addition to health benefits, the spas at Bath and Tunbridge offered other attractions including the opportunity for gossip. On 13 August 1693 Lord Lothian discussed the other Scots in Bath, including Breadalbane and his son, Lord Glenorchy, whom he described as 'a sparke'.[161] Three days later he added, 'The Jacobites have great expectations, but they may be disappointed'.[162] The holiday atmosphere led to rejoicing in May 1684, when Robert Chapman described the celebrations in Bath to Sir Edward Hungerford when people heard of Sir William Bassett's victory over a certain Mr Noseworthy, 'upon which all the bells of this cittie was sett on ringinge and now all our streets are in flames with bonfiers … all persons burninge theyer hatts and periwiggs'.[163] Enterprising artists took advantage of the popularity of Bath, and in the winter of 1687/8 John Graham sat there for his portrait by Sir Godfrey Kneller. Evidently pleased with the resulting picture, Graham's wife Jean described Kneller as 'the best that was in England'.[164]

While most male relationships were cordial, when things went wrong a duel was regularly turned to as the way to resolve a slight to a man's honour. Violence could occur on national lines, as in 1612 when the tensions at court caused by Kerr resulted in duels at Croydon races fought between the Scots and the English.[165] However, duels were usually more personal, as with the quarrel in 1620 between Sir Robert Kerr, later 1st earl of Ancram, and Charles Maxwell at Newmarket.[166] Combatants often fought in a shirt and breeches that allowed freedom of movement but little protection. Consequently, Donald Mackay, 1st Lord Reay's decision to fight in a corselet 'reflecteth on him much shame and derision' and was seen as evidence of his 'base guilt and fear'. In response his opponent David Ramsay chose to 'fight in his shirt'.[167] The symbolic significance of the clothes men wore was still important in 1712 when the 4th duke of Hamilton prepared for his duel against Charles Mohun, 4th baron Mohun: 'his whole dress changed from a long wig and velvet clothes to a riding wig and stuff coat, without either star or ribbon, only a St Andrew's cross on a long white cloak'. What Hamilton described would prove to be his last sartorial choice, making him '*en cavalier*'.[168]

Conclusions

A portrait of John Hay, 1st marquis of Tweeddale, with his wife and children epitomises a family life built up through a pattern of weddings and christenings (fig. 10.18). Hay first joined Charles I at Nottingham

in 1642, fought for Parliament at Marston Moor but survived to take a full part in the Scottish parliament, the privy council and the treasury after the Restoration, as well as being a member of the Royal Society. His life encompassed all the activities that seventeenth-century elite men were expected to engage in, and he undertook them dressed in the official and fashionable elements of Stuart style. This combination of robes of office and stylish suits was not new in the seventeenth century, but the Stuarts still made their mark in both sartorial areas. Most significantly, they were keen to unify the robes worn by government officials in Scotland and England, thereby giving Stuart style a ministerial and legal component while also seeking to draw the two countries closer together. The impact of the Wars of the Three Kingdoms saw the development of military uniforms, especially that of the New Model Army, and the growing influence of military dress on civilian style. There was increased emphasis on the development of specific clothes for sport, an idea that would develop further in the eighteenth century. These were three key ways in which male clothing developed under the Stuarts and these fashionable trends were embraced by men on both sides of the border, with leading Scots at court helping to develop and disseminate the styles.

10.18 Attributed to John Baptiste de Medina, *John Hay, 1st Marquis of Tweeddale and His Family*, c.1695. Oil on canvas, 114 × 184 cm. National Gallery of Scotland, Edinburgh. Faces dominate this picture, stressing the importance of family to John Hay, while the inclusion of the seal bag reminds the viewer of his role as lord high chancellor of Scotland.

CHAPTER ELEVEN

Stuart Religion and Ceremonial: Restructuring or Rejection?

THE TIME FRAME FOR *Stuart Style* sits well with Margo Todd's view of Scotland undergoing a 'long reformation' running from 1560 into the seventeenth century.[1] More importantly, her view of the Scottish Reformation as a 'restructuring' rather than a 'rejection of ceremony and image' is significant for the argument presented here.[2] The ceremony in question, which was heavily underpinned by copes, chasubles and, most importantly, the surplice, was integral to the religious beliefs of the Stuarts. These beliefs brought them into conflict with many of their subjects and this was expressed through the use of textiles during religious worship. Charles I's views were encapsulated in the Bible that he allegedly gave to the family of Sir Henry Wardlaw, 1st baronet of Pitreavie (1565–1637), Fife, for his service to Anna of Denmark (fig. 11.1). Richly embroidered with silver and silver-gilt metal thread, the quality of the crimson velvet slip cover announces that this is a kingly present and the text was chosen with its Scottish recipient in mind, combining as it did *The CL. Psalmes of David in meeter, according as they are sung in the Church of Scotland* produced in Edinburgh, with the Geneva Bible and New Testament printed in Amsterdam in *c*.1640. Treasured by the Wardlaw family, this Bible is resonant of the religious tensions in seventeenth-century Scottish society, at the heart of which were the Stuart kings. Lavish decoration was placed over a simple binding. The Geneva Bible was selected over the contentious Scottish edition of the King James Bible issued in 1633, while the Psalms followed the biblical exhortation to 'sing Psalms unto Him' (1 Chron. 16:9).[3] The timing of the gift suggests a conscious attempt by the king to demonstrate an understanding of his Scottish subjects, coming as it did three years after the highly provocative introduction of the Scottish Book of Common Prayer in 1637, resulting in the First Bishops' War of 1639 and the Second Bishops' War a year later.

11.1 Embroidered front cover of the Wardlaw Bible, a copy of the 1640 Geneva-Tomson Bible presented by Charles I to Sir Henry Wardlaw of Pitreavie for his service to Queen Anne. University of St Andrews.

Religious tensions between a Stuart king and his Scottish people were not new. 20 years earlier, James Cathkin had exasperated his sovereign by not attending church on Christmas Day 1619. On hearing of this, James VI and I exclaimed, 'The devil take you, both soul and body! For you are none of my religion … Ye are worse than Turks and Jews! I can never get an order of this people of Edinburgh'.[4] Christian names apart, the gulf between the religious beliefs of king and subject was deep and wide. Their failure to agree on how and when a man should worship characterised religious tensions throughout the Stuarts' three kingdoms. With the national churches of Scotland, England and Ireland falling under the leadership of one man from 1603, the personal beliefs of the monarch became increasingly divisive. Royal religion, focusing upon the Chapel Royal and the cathedrals associated with coronation and burial, relied heavily on well-established ceremonial and ceremonial textiles, including the vestments worn by the clergy. In contrast, many others felt little or no need for this facet of Stuart style, and therein lay the rub.

Worship was central to daily life, and the spaces where it took place, in chapel, church or kirk, were where the congregation carefully scrutinised their ministers and their neighbours. Some judgements were social and focused on the visual distractions on offer, as in August 1693 when Lord Lothian informed his wife that 'there ar an great show of weomen in the great Church' at Bath. He was swift to add, reassuringly however, that because he was 'playing non [i.e. cards] nor drinking which is not usid hair, I am lonly enough att evenings'.[5] However, more often it was something people heard during a service that caused a stir. On Sunday 23 July 1637, Jenny Geddes allegedly threw her folding stool at James Hannay, dean of Edinburgh, when he read the Collects from the Book of Common Prayer in St Giles' collegiate kirk. Church attendance was usually a less volatile experience, but with Jenny Geddes in mind, this chapter explores the centrality of liturgical textiles and other appurtenances of worship, along with clerical dress, to religious debates in the three kingdoms. The part played by the Scottish people, many of whom clashed with their Stuart kings in this area, as in no other, is clear in the words of Presbyterian pastor Samuel Rutherford, who asked the pointed rhetorical question, 'Christ got a charter of Scotland from his Father, and who will bereave him of His heritage?'[6]

Objects and Faith

When Eamon Duffy considered the impact of the Reformation in England he stressed the significance of liturgical textiles, books and plate in traditional worship and the consequences of their loss.[7] These objects inspired faith by elevating 'the soul towards the Lord' and reflecting the glory of God.[8] This was the purpose of visual expressions of faith such as the scene of the Annunciation from the Beaton panels (fig. 11.2). The same is true of the Fetternear banner, the only known

11.2 Beaton panel of the Annunciation depicting the Angel Gabriel telling the Virgin Mary that she will conceive a child who will be the son of God, 1530s. Carved oak, 145 × 67 cm. National Museum of Scotland, Edinburgh.

surviving church banner from pre-Reformation Scotland. Dating from *c.*1520, it depicts the scourged figure of Christ surrounded by the symbols of the Passion (fig. 11.3).[9] Thought to have belonged to the confraternity of the Holy Blood in St Giles's collegiate kirk, banners like this formed the focal point of parish processions and accompanied civic processional pageants of the saints organised by the guilds. Post-Reformation, textiles, especially vestments, altar cloths and the surplice, continued to occupy a powerful place in the religious debate.[10] For Catholics, Anglicans and episcopalians these textiles were central, while for Presbyterians, Puritans and other nonconformists they were idolatrous and superstitious. However, it was more complex than that, and James VI and I was keen to assert his Protestantism to his people through anti-Catholic legislation. His language of disapproval associated with Catholic religious objects is evident in the powers of search that

11.3 Fetternear banner, c. 1520. Linen embroidered with silk threads, 188 × 96 cm. National Museum of Scotland, Edinburgh. The three borders around the central panel consist of a rosary motif, then knotted corn alternating with hearts and scallop shells, and then scallop shells and columbines.

he granted in 1605–6 to his English justices of the peace. When seeking out Catholics, the king ordered that 'if any Altar Pix Beades Pictures or suche like Popish Religques … shall be thought unmeete for such Recusants as aforesaid to have or use, the same shall be presently defaced'.[11] At the same time, James's bishops were using (or in the case of Scotland, introducing) regalia that more radical Protestants regarded as 'Romish rags'. To more strict Presbyterians like David Calderwood, such anti-Catholic injunctions were mere attempts to distract Protestant attention from the king's episcopalian ceremonies, which were worrying steps along the road to full Catholicism.

James's ban on Catholic objects encompassed small crosses similar to the sixteenth-century silver crucifix decorated with niello that was found at Craigmillar Castle, 3 miles south-west of Edinburgh, that has tentative links to Mary, Queen of Scots (fig. 11.4). Whoever it belonged to, this cross serves as a very good example of a small devotional object that was of great significance to its owner. By the 1670s fear of such items resulted in their often wilful misidentification, as the Royalist pamphleteer, Sir Roger L'Estrange noted during the hysteria associated with the Popish Plot in London. At this time, L'Estrange testified that 'Guinneys pass'd for Popish medalls, crucifixes for the reliques of superstition; … ordinary drinking-plate pass'd for chalices; and men were rifled and robb'd and undone, by the basest of felons under the masque of zeal and conscience'.[12] While Puritans and Presbyterians did not favour liturgical textiles, they did appreciate how talking about textiles conveyed ideas of purity and simplicity and how textiles could be used as metaphors for spiritual exercise. This approach was used by Herefordshire gentlewoman Lady Brilliana Harley when she gave her son Edward advice on clothing in 1638, urging him that God 'is the best master, and will give the best wages, and they wear the best livery, the garment of holiness, a clothing which never shall wear out, but is renewed everyday'. Shifting to fashionable dress, she added: 'it is very well done that you submit to your father's desire in your clothes' because it is good 'to be contented with plain clothes and, in the wearing of better clothes not to think oneself better for them'.[13]

11.4 Silver crucifix decorated with niello and mounted on an ebony cross found at Craigmillar Castle, 16th century. National Museum of Scotland, Edinburgh.

The same tactic is evident in the letters of Samuel Rutherford, who counselled Lady Kenmure, his patron's wife, to 'be content … every day to be adding and sewing a passment to your wedding garment'.[14] He took a more brusque and polemical tone, appropriate to male conversation, with the earl of Carlisle, assuring him that 'One of our tribes, Levi's sons, have sold their mother and their father also, and the Lord's truth, for their new velvet-world and their satin-church'.[15] Rutherford was not alone in using this ploy. The Quaker William Penn expressed similar views in simpler terms. When Charles II asked Penn how their religious beliefs differed he was told: 'The difference is between thy hat and mine; mine has no ornament'.[16] In 1693 Penn continued the theme in *Some Fruits of Solitude*, stating 'Chuse thy cloathes by thine own eye, not anothers.

The more simple and plain they are the better'.[17] Anglican royalists such as Humphrey, 'Silver Tongue' Sydenham, the rector of Puckington in Somerset, also used this style of language. In *The Christian Duell* (1635), Sydenham declared 'that it is a time of Sackcloth and Ashes and casting earth upon the Head, for the humbling and macerating of the Sinner; not of putting on the glorious apparell, your vaine shinings in silks and tissues, for the ruffling of the Gallant'.[18]

In short, clothes and textiles, liturgical and secular were contested ground under the Stuarts, and where you drew the line depended on your religious and political outlook. In a liturgical context, textiles were closely associated with ceremony, an equally problematic subject. In 1636 Sydenham referred to 'Ceremonies, harmlesse Ceremonies' in *The Foolish Prophet* as having 'gotten their former lustre and state againe', while the 'Surplesse, so long in exile and disgrace amongst us, is visible here in our Congregations'.[19] The earl of Clarendon took a different approach when he advised the young Charles II that 'Ceremony, though it is nothing in itself, yet it doth everything. For what is a king more than a subject but for ceremony and order? When it fails him, he's ruined'.[20] As Anna Keay has demonstrated, Charles II successfully negotiated this path, unlike his father, younger brother and later generations of Jacobite exiles.[21] Their respective adherence to Laudianism and Catholicism provided them with lasting spiritual comfort, but the price was their political downfall.

The Stuarts and Religion

James VI and I appreciated the value of textiles to stress both his personal piety and his absolute belief in the divine right of kings, and used a clothing metaphor, an approach culturally embedded in the period, to convey the constancy of his religious views when he asserted: 'I am not a Monsieur who can shift his religion as easily as he can shift his shirt when he comes in from tennis'.[22] The Flemish artist Peter Paul Rubens (1577–1640) captured the essence of James's view of his religious authority in his design for the painting on the ceiling of the banqueting house at Whitehall. In the final scheme, James was 'sett out in Royall robes' in panel two, depicting *The Wise Rule of James I* and the central panel of *The Apotheosis of James I*.[23] In his own lifetime, the miniaturist Nicholas Hilliard (1547–1619) presented James as the guardian of the Elizabethan Church by juxtaposing a portrait of the monarch with an image of the ark, a motif used by the Virgin Queen to promote a similar idea (fig. 11.5).[24] Items produced outside of royal control conveyed the same message by less sophisticated but equally effective means. For example, the piety of the royal family was stressed in an independently produced diptych showing James, Anna of Denmark and Prince Charles listening to a sermon at Old St Pauls.[25]

11.5 Enamelled gold locket with miniatures on vellum of James VI and I and the ark by Nicholas Hilliard, c.1610. Victoria and Albert Museum, London.

James appreciated a beautiful church that included the appurtenances and material objects associated with ceremony, and this caused problems when a group of Scottish ministers visited the royal chapel in August 1607. It was noted at this time that 'The next day, which was the feast of St Michael, the ministers were brought again to the Chapel and there saw on the altar two books, two basins, and two candlesticks, which moved M. Melville to make certain satirical verses'.[26] Undeterred by Andrew Melville's disapproval, James VI intended to redecorate Holyrood to reflect his taste prior to returning in 1617.[27] A contemporary declared that the king intended to include 'all manner of furniture for a Chapel, which Inigo Jones tells me he hath charge of, with pictures of the apostles, Faith, Hope and Charity, and other such religious representations', adding 'how welcome they will be thither God knows'.[28] Sir Anthony Weldon highlighted with glee the tension such changes caused, reporting that 'for the graven images in his new beautified Chappell, they threaten to pull them downe soone after his departure … to appease the indignacion they imagine is conceived against them in the breast of the Almighty for suffering such idolatry to enter their Kingdom.'[29] James was unimpressed, deploring how many of his Scottish subjects could 'endure lions, dragons and devils to be figured in your churches, but will not allow the like place to the patriarchs and apostles'.[30]

James shared his religious beliefs with his sons. When Henry was confirmed on 3 April 1607 at the Chapel Royal in Whitehall, the service was led by the archbishop of Canterbury, and he, the dean of the Chapel Royal and the other clergy at the service processed dressed in 'rich copes', the traditional vestment for such occasions.[31] Two days later the prince received Holy Communion kneeling on a cushion 'at the left hand of the King and somewhat lower'.[32] Prince Henry was a staunch Protestant as his household ordinances of 1610 make clear. These state that 'His gentlemen shall attend him and be present at times of prayers when he goes to his private chapel' and no exceptions were made.[33] Henry's own chapel was run on similar lines to his father's, with purchases including two 'fair church Bibles bound with silk strings', a large service book with psalms and four gilded books with 'singing psalms'.[34] Other acquisitions consisted of 22 ells of Holland for surplices along with diaper, and diaper towelling, for the vestry.[35] At Henry's funeral the gentlemen of the chapel walked in the procession 'in rich copes' to mark the solemnity of the occasion.[36] The memory of Henry's fervour was invoked by his chaplain Daniel Price when he preached on the first anniversary of the prince's death. Price claimed that Henry's 'Magnetique virtue drewe all the eies, and the hearts, of the Protestant world'.[37] However, Henry's Protestant virtue was expressed through visible signs of some richness rather than the plainness of the Scottish kirk.

A hint of the difficulties that Charles I would encounter with the Scots over religion became apparent at his coronation in Edinburgh in 1633. John Spottiswoode, archbishop of St Andrews, along with the bishops of Brechin, Ross and Dunkeld, received a cool reception from the assembled audience when they appeared in their 'white rotchetis and white sleives, and koopis of gold, having blew silk to thair foot'.[38]

11.6 Gold ampulla used at Charles I's Scottish coronation in 1633, possibly made by James Denneistoun, an Edinburgh goldsmith, 12.5 cm. National Museum of Scotland, Edinburgh.

Potentially still more problematic was the tapestry placed behind the altar 'wherein the crucifix was curiously wrought'.[39] All that remains of this finery is the gold ampulla used to anoint the king in 1633 (fig. 11.6).[40] In the years immediately after the coronation, William Laud tried to implement the king's religious policy in Scotland, and on 19 May 1635 he informed Adam Bellenden, bishop of Aberdeen, that 'The King hath been acquainted with your care of the Chapel Royal, and is very well pleased with the conformity that hath been there at the late reception of the blessed Sacrament'.[41] Four months later, in September, Laud noted curtly to Bishop Maxwell of Ross that if he did 'not see the Chapel well furnished, the blame for ever be yours'.[42]

However, many felt the blame for the ceremonial changes lay with Laud and everything changed after the Second Bishops' War, when Charles perforce became a Covenanting king. In September 1640 prayers were offered seeking to bring the royal family into the fold: 'Good Lord bless our King and open his eyes, that he may see the truth of our Covenant. Good Lord bless the Queen, open her eyes that she may fly her idolatory. Good Lord bless the King's bairns'.[43] The following year, on 10 June the Scottish parliament authorised the Presbytery of Edinburgh to dispose of 'all the monumentis and badges of idolatrie' in the Chapel Royal.[44] This removal of liturgical objects was personally very significant for the king. When Charles I was in Edinburgh a few months later, Alexander Henderson, one of the authors of the National Covenant, served as the king's personal chaplain, and it was observed with approval that he 'does daylie say prayer, read a chapter, sing a psalm, and say prayer againe. The King hears all duellie, and we hear none of his complaints for want of a Liturgie, or any Ceremonies'.[45]

After England collapsed into civil war in 1642, the Scottish Presbyterian minister and theological scholar Robert Baillie (1602–62) reported that 'Paul's and Westminster are purged of their images and organs, and all which have offence. My Lord Manchester made two fair bonfires of such trinkets at Cambridge.'[46] The Parliamentary writer T. B. took things further when he claimed that Prince Rupert's white poodle, Boy, 'carries himselfe most Popishly and Cathedrally … he is much taken with their Copes, & Surplices, and singing books, & (since some of the Gentlemen of the Chapel are come down) with the singing men too'.[47] While the lines of battle were drawn up about more than church textiles, these examples demonstrate how passionately people felt about the visible signs of religious nuance. They also provide the context to the observations made by Gilbert Burnet while Charles II was in Scotland bargaining for a crown: 'The king was not allowed so much as to walk abroad on Sundays: and if at any time there has been any gaiety at court, such as dancing or playing at cards, he was severely reproved for it'.[48]

In England, the Restoration saw a return of the Anglican Church, bishops and liturgical textiles.[49] However, Charles II's religious beliefs were the subject of debate at court. George Saville, 1st marquis of Halifax, was of the opinion that the king 'was as certainly a Roman

Catholick, as that he was a Man of Pleasure'.[50] A commonly held view was that 'He seemed to have no sense of religion'.[51] As Alasdair Raffe has noted, irreligion posed a challenge to contemporary religious attitudes, which in a post-Restoration Scottish context added to a 'culture of controversy' between Presbyterians and episcopalians.[52] Equally problematic was the fact that Charles II had sworn the Solemn League and Covenant that was first drawn up in 1643. This was a religious and political settlement that offered Scottish military support to Parliament in return for support for the kirk and Presbyterianism. While many thought the king ungodly, which undid the Covenant to which he had sworn, the fact that he had done so made him equally disliked by others, as the minister Robert Douglas learnt in June 1660. James Sharp, who would soon be made archbishop of St Andrews, informed Douglas that 'Dr Crofts preaching before the King, said that for the guilt he had contracted in Scotland, and the injuries he was brought to doe against ye Church of England, God had defeated him at Worcester, and punished his controversy upon that account aginst him to a Nyne years exile.'[53]

As early as February 1661 Pepys considered the duke of York to be 'a professed friend to the Catholiques', although James did not convert until 1669.[54] Widespread anxieties about Catholicism within the king's family and the court circle resulted in the Test Act of 1673, which stipulated Catholics could not hold office and resulted in calls for James to be excluded from the succession. These attempts failed, and once James was king he re-equipped the royal chapels. The altar plate made for his chapel at Holyroodhouse embodies all the visual, audible and olfactory aspects of the Catholic Mass in the form of a silver-gilt monstrance set with semi-precious stones, a ciborium, an incense burner, a boat and spoon, a chalice and paten and a sanctus bell (fig. 11.7).[55] The arrival of William of Orange on English soil triggered a purge of these chapel goods as a symbolic rejection of James and his religion, and 'the rabble got together there, as they had done in London. They broke into all popish chapels, and into the church of Holy Rood House, which had been adorned at a great charge to be a royal chapel' and purged them.[56]

William assured the duke of Hamilton that 'he had no friends in Scotland but

11.7 Holyrood plate of silver for James VII and II's chapel royal, made in London and Edinburgh c. 1686–7. Lent by the Scottish Roman Catholic Hierarchy, National Museum of Scotland, Edinburgh.

the Presbyterians'.[57] It was a view that the magistrates, town council and inhabitants of Ayr shared. On New Year's Eve 1688 they addressed Sir James Montgomery of Skelmorlie earnestly, declaring that they were 'deeply sensible of the great pious and generous undertakeings of His Hynes the prince of Orange for releiving of these kingdomes from poperie and slaverie'.[58]

The King's Seat and Family Pews

When Fynes Moryson visited St Giles's in Edinburgh in 1598 he described 'the Kings seate [which] is built some few staires high of wood, and leaning vpon the pillar next to the Pulpit'.[59] Prior to the king's visit in 1617, 'certane crammassie velvit Spanies teffitie and clinking pasmentis' was purchased 'to be ane cloth to hing befoir his Majestie in the kirk'.[60] However, the execution of Charles I in 1649 and the abolition of the monarchy brought about a radical shift in attitudes, and on 7 February 1652 John Nicoll noted that 'maissones, carpentaris, and hammermen' were sent 'to the kirk of Edinburgh quhair the Kinges sait was erectit, and to the mercat croce of Edinburgh quhair his airmes and unicorne with the croun on his heid wes set; and thair pulled doun the Kinges airmes'.[61] With the Restoration, the king's seat was reinstated and the town council of Edinburgh presented Charles's representative, the earl of Lauderdale, with a desk seat and pew in St Giles's 'for his good offices'.[62] When Charles II died in February 1685, this seat was covered in black at a cost of £4 16s, with a further £5 12s for covering the pulpit, the Baillies' seat and the Elders' table in solemn recognition of the king's passing.[63]

While the royal presence denoted by the monarch's seat was challenged during the course of the century, the elite and middling sort increasingly wished to have their own seat or pew. This ranged from a folding stool of the type associated with Jenny Geddes in 1637 to the 'great cramoisie velvott cuschiounes for the kirk, ij with thair great silk knops at the nooks and silk fosses about them, with thair reid callico coverings' belonging to the Campbells of Glenorchy in 1640.[64] More wealthy citizens also aspired to having their own pews and in August 1673 the town council of Linlithgow sold a pew in the parish church to Thomas Eduard of Longcraft.[65] In seventeenth-century Scotland, where a man sat and what he sat on said more about his social standing and less about which side of the religious debate he stood on.

Baptisms and Christenings

Christenings symbolised the continuity of the royal line. The most flamboyant later Stuart christenings were those of James VI and his son Henry, and both these events took place in Scotland. Those held in England were less magnificent. In part this reflected a change in fashion and in part the lack of legitimate male (or female) heirs born after the 1630s. The significance of James VI's birth is evident in the amount of money required to fund the celebrations.[66] In October 1566 Henry and Mary, king and queen of Scots, sent out letters to raise £12,000 by taxation for christening 'of oure darrest sone the native prince of our realme'.[67] Purchases included 'fourty elnes of taffetas off the cord' and fireworks costing £190 17s 5½d provided by John Chisholme, controller of artillery.[68]

In his turn, James VI proudly described Henry's birth as 'the blessing of God shawne to his Hienes, this haill realme and natioun in graunting unto him successioun of his body, to posses his crowne'.[69] James's sons, along with his Protestant faith and his bloodline, made him the strongest contender for Elizabeth's throne. All these considerations explain the letters from James VI summoning the Master of Grey, and others, to the baptism of Prince Henry at Stirling on 27 July 1594 in which he tellingly observed, 'Scns it standis we in soe point of honor as we wenst ye will not refuse nor dissapoynt we'.[70] In contrast, the evening christening of Charles I on 23 December 1600 was much more modest. The guests included Alexander Seton, who paid £4 'for twelf torches to convoy the Provest the nicht of the baptisme'.[71] In the years after James's move to Whitehall, the abbey church at Holyroodhouse continued to be used for christenings by the nobility. In March 1612 a payment of 4s Scots covered the cost of 'foure lossones [lozenge shaped panes] in the gret hall at the baptisme of the Earle of Glencarnes barne'.[72]

The birth of Charles II saw plans for the first christening of a prince in England since that of Edward VI in 1537. Orders for the christening were issued on 15 June 1630, requiring that the chapel and all the rooms along the processional route were to be hung with tapestry; an organ and a stage were to be set up in the chapel, along with a font. After the christening the prince was carried to his parents and received their blessing, with Laud and the other clergy in their copes, the mayor in velvet and the aldermen in their scarlet gowns. Artillery at the Tower was fired, as it was by ships on the Thames immediately after the christening, the *feu de joie* being a basic form of celebration common in western Europe, and bonfires were lit at night.[73] James Hamilton attended in the place of the king of Bohemia.[74] Even so, Henry Rich, earl of Holland, was underwhelmed and on 3 July he informed Robert Devereux, earl of Essex, that 'the Cristening of the Prince was no great seremonie'.[75] Rich's comments hint at his growing unease with the importance that the Stuarts attached to ceremony.

Three years later the future James VII and II was christened by William Laud on 24 November 1633 in the chapel at St James's Palace. The remaining official Stuart christenings were of James's children, and in 1688 a prayer of thanksgiving was issued for the safe delivery of the queen and the happy birth of a young prince.[76] A combination of lack of legitimate heirs, the Catholicism of James and a sense that christenings were more private ceremonies all contributed to a further reduction in the significance of christenings under Charles II and his brother. However, this contrasts significantly with the carefully orchestrated images of Elizabeth of Bohemia's children, who Catriona Murray has styled as 'the Palatinate brood'.[77] James VI and I's daughter maintained the older extravagances (perhaps for political reasons, to bolster her family's image in the context of their disastrous continental fortunes) whereas his son, as monarch, could afford to prefer private celebration allied to standard public expressions, such as the firing of cannon.

The Stuarts and Liturgical Ceremonies

Stuart monarchs did not make use of the royal touch prior to 1603, but then they quickly came to appreciate its value as a means of asserting their royal authority.[78] Significantly, William Shakespeare alluded to touch and healing in *Macbeth*, which was first performed in 1606.[79] James VI and I also realised the virtues of dressing the part and when he touched for scrofula (a tuberculosis infection of the lymph nodes in the neck) at Theobalds in 1613 he wore 'a satin robe of an ash colour, thickly covered with gold lace chevronwise, and a rather long cloak of black cloth lined with velvet'.[80] Charles I continued the practice and importantly chose to touch for the king's evil 'in state' on 24 June (St John the Baptist's Day) 1633 as part of the celebrations for his Scottish coronation, so presenting his healing powers to an Edinburgh audience.[81] Charles II touched regularly for the king's evil (fig. 11.8) and the importance contemporaries attached to these ceremonies is evident from the gift of 10s given in 1663 by Anna, duchess of Buccleuch, 'To ye blind maid that receaued sight by ye kings touche'.[82] Other recipients of the royal touch included the son of Henry Alexander, 3rd earl of Stirling.[83] However, there were critics, as is evident from Madam Fanshaw's 'wonderful account of the cureing the kings-evil' offered as a rebuttal of 'a scoffing and lying lybell' published in 1681.[84] James VII and II made very significant use of these ceremonies.[85] Evelyn noted his concerns about the ceremony becoming more Catholic when he 'saw his Majestie touch for the Evil' on 8 November 1688 accompanied by Edward Petre and John Warner, who were both English Jesuits.[86]

The high point of the Lent cycle was Maundy Thursday, or Skerthursday as it was known in Scotland. Traditionally this was a day when the monarch demonstrated their humility, as in 1567 when Mary, Queen of Scots' household purchased the linen required by the queen, her household and 25 poor women, for the Mass of the Last Supper.[87] The first reference to James VI marking Maundy Thursday dates from 1579 when he was 13. Peter Young, the king's almoner, received blue cloth to make 13 gowns 'to be distributit vponn certane aigit and decayit parsons'.[88] This continued after James moved to England. For instance, on 11 July 1611 Lord Hay received 'stuff' for the Maundy.[89] Lent was formally marked at Charles II's court. For instance, the Great Wardrobe account for 1661/2 received 60 yards of black velvet for four cushions, two altar cloths, a pulpit cloth, a desk cloth and for covering a canopy

11.8 Robert White, *Charles II Touching a Patient for the King's Evil Surrounded by Courtiers, Clergy and General Public*, 1684. Engraving. Wellcome Collection, London. Dressed in a fashionable suit, and with clergy in surplices to his right, Charles heals his people.

and litany desk in the chapel royal 'to bee used in tyme of Lent and daies of Humiliation', cost £105.[90] In 1662/3 a further 108½ yards of black cloth was received to hang the chapel royal against Lent, costing £72 16s 2d.[91] In the same year Anna, duchess of Buccleuch, paid £15 19s 6d 'For a rich bewgell gown of fferander for lent'.[92] Charles revived the practice in Scotland after the Restoration by proxy. For example, Robert Gilmour and Patrick Barnes, tailors, received £896 5s for blue cloth for gowns to His Majesty's poor men or 'bedesmen' and for making them against 29 May.[93] Finally, Lauder of Fountainhall witnessed James VII and II display his piety on 18 April, 'being the vigil before Easter', by washing '52 poor men's feet, according to the number of the years of his oune age'.[94]

Vestments in Scotland

As the portrait of William Elphinstone, bishop of Aberdeen (1431–1514) (fig. 11.9) demonstrates, prior to 1560 the Scottish clergy dressed in the same way as their European counterparts. Consequently, when George Thomson was appointed as the chaplain of St Nicholas's altar, in Ayr, in the early sixteenth century, he was given 'possessioun of … the vestmentis bukis and challeis'.[95] A few decades later James Strachauchin, parson of Fethercarne, owned a black gown, vestments and silver chalice.[96] These items marked out a man of the church but they also had financial value and in September 1544 Thomas Charteris of Kinfawnis and John Charteris of Cuthilgurdy were accused of stealing two stands of vestments, worth £10 each, from John Moncur of Ballumy, at Knokhill.[97] The monetary value lay in the high-quality silks often used to make vestments, a fact which in turn led, on occasion, to their being made from recycled clothing. At her mother's urging, Mary, Queen of Scots sent some of her old gowns for making into vestments to the abbess of Saint-Pierre, in Reims, and to Antoinette, the abbess of the Benedictine house at Faremoutiers. Both women were the sisters of Mary of Guise, so Mary's largesse helped maintain spiritual and familial networks.[98]

11.9 Flemish School, *William Elphinstone, Bishop of Aberdeen*, 1480–1505. Oil on panel, 69.5 × 41 cm. University of Aberdeen. Dressed in cope and mitre, Elphinstone wears all the textile trappings of a pre-Reformation bishop.

After 1560 most kirks disposed of their vestments. The items associated with the Skinners' altar in St Giles's, Edinburgh, were sold in August 1560 for £65 to John Loch, who was deacon of the guild. Five years later, Loch was discovered celebrating mass with them in his home.[99] He was not alone in keeping faith with the old ways. Indeed, much of the turmoil in the latter years of James VI's reign in Scotland centred on his reluctance to take decisive action against the Catholic nobility, most notably the earl of Huntly. In 1562 the earl of Mar's chapel contained 'ij Mess buikis, an image of the babe Jesus, an image of our Lady, and a great image with an image of St Anne, a little image of "ewir bane" (ivory), that stood upon a "chandlar"'.[100] Abbot Gilbert Brown, the last abbot of Sweetheart Abbey, near Dumfries, remained in situ with the support of the Maxwell family. When his chamber was searched in 1609, 'a great number of Popish books, copes, chalices, pictures, images and such other Popish trash' was recovered.[101] On this occasion the vestments were burnt, but Scottish Catholics, especially those living in Europe, continued to buy and commission vestments abroad. As Peter Davidson and Prue King argue, a sense of the opulence of these vestments is clear from the late seventeenth-century chasuble and dalmatic owned by count James Leslie (*c.*1621–94).[102]

Both sides of the religious divide were engaged in public dispute over their rights and preferences. A vehement dislike of 'Popish trash' caused John Elphinstone, 2nd lord Balmerino (d. 1649), to protest against the possible reintroduction of vestments in Scotland during Charles I's reign. In 1634 he was imprisoned while waiting for John Maxwell, bishop of Ross to preside over his case.[103] The same year, Robert Maxwell, 1st earl of Nithsdale (1586–1646), made a visual protest about not being able to practise his faith on the walls of Caerlaverock Castle, Dumfries. The facade of the east range of his Nithsdale lodging includes caved pediments depicting Prometheus in chains and the corpse of Patroclus pecked by vultures, and John Hunwicke has plausibly suggested that both items refer to James VI's attack on the family's Catholicism, the earl's father having been left unburied for five years while Maxwell himself was incarcerated.[104] As these two men make clear, whatever side you were on, your beliefs had to be expressed in relation to visible signs, since they were what their Scottish audience would see.

While vestments provoked fierce debate, other church textiles were acceptable to some, although hardliners like Calderwood were unlikely to approve. Regular tailors' bills record the making and repair of a range of items for the Canongate kirk in Edinburgh. These included a green pulpit cloth, a green cover for the magistrate's seat, linen to place over the communion table and black mort cloths to drape the dead during their funeral service.[105] Simple in style and materials, these textiles served to honour the community, the church, civic leaders and the preaching role of the minister.

Problems with Bishops

When Celia Fiennes visited Canterbury in 1693 she admired the textiles given to the cathedral by 'our good Queen Mary'. The gift consisted of 'a Cloth and Coushons of purple figured velvet, the books the same, there is a broad tissue border of orrace work gold and purple, and the edge is fine knotted fringe of purple silk and gold, the Bishops seate and Cushon the same'.[106] While there were some items in common with those in the Canongate kirk, the richness of the velvet and the emphasis placed on the bishop's seat put this gift in a very different category. Bishops symbolised royal authority over the church and their dress became shorthand for their many perceived failings. As Sally Tuckett has shown, Scottish bishops were unpopular between 1625 and 1638 because they were royal counsellors and supporters of royal absolutism.[107] In part, it was the surplice and vestments that the Presbyterians disliked. In 1633 Robert Campbell of Glenfalloch informed his brother of 'sum act made conserning sum seremonies quhairto the Bischoppis is thocht till have takin on sik as weering of quhyt showis in tyme of sermon quhilk most be done by the ministeris with sum uther seremonies according to the ffascion off England'.[108]

Six years later he reported the passing of an act annulling the service book along with common prayers and books of canons and consecration, and which discharged the episcopacy and bishops, while he continued to pray for the king and his succession.[109] As the Anglo-Welsh historian James Howell (*c.*1594–1666) observed, 'The bishops are all gone to wreck, and they have had but a sorry funeral: the very name is grown so contemptible that a black dog if he hath any white marks about him, is called Bishop'.[110] In a similar vein, Robert Baillie dismissed the bishop of Ross as 'a bower at the altar, a wearer of the cope and rochett, a deposer of godly ministers, ane admitter of fornicators, [and] a companier with papists'.[111]

Sir Thomas Lake, secretary of state to James VI and I, informed the diplomat Sir Ralph Winwood while he was visiting Scotland with the king in 1617, that the bishops were 'much misliked, but more for their person than their calling'.[112] Was this a reference to their personality or

11.10 *(below, left)* After Sir Anthony van Dyck, *William Laud*, after an original of 1636. Oil on canvas, 123.2 × 94 cm. National Portrait Gallery, London. Laud's white linen surplice would have required a huge amount of care to keep it pristine.

11.11 *(below, right)* Sir Anthony van Dyck, *Alexander Henderson*, c.1641. Oil on canvas, 127 × 105.4 cm. National Galleries of Scotland. Henderson's multi-layered ruff contrasts with his simple cuffs and the simpler collar selected by Laud.

their clothing? If it was to their clothing, then it was not the black clothes that were the problem but the surplice that they wore over them. During this visit James was also accompanied by William Laud and 'exception was taken to Dr Laud's putting on a surplice'.[113] When Laud was painted in 1636, the artist captured the trademark white linen surplice under a black gown (fig. 11.10). Some years later, Sergeant Henry Foster, who belonged to the Parliamentary-trained bands, recalled how his men often attacked local churches and on one occasion returned wearing the surplice, hood and cap as a jibe at Laud.[114] In contrast to Laud, Patrick Forbes, bishop of Aberdeen, dressed in black.[115] So too did Alexander Henderson, who sat for Van Dyck while he was in London negotiating with Charles I in 1641 (fig. 11.11). His portrait demonstrates Van Dyck's skill in capturing the essence of his clients. Finally, Samuel Rutherford's black was alleviated by just a simple linen falling band (fig. 11.12).

11.12 Robert Walker, *Samuel Rutherford*, mid-17th century. Oil on canvas, 52 × 50 cm. University of St Andrews. Rutherford's falling band is simple neckwear when compared with Laud's or Henderson's.

While James VI and I wanted to promote the surplice as appropriate clerical dress, he also wanted the clergy to stop wearing 'licht and undecent apparrell'. Instead, he insisted in 1609 they were to select 'blak grave and semelie apparel besemyng men of their estait and Conditioun'. It was also important that when attending Parliament bishops should wear 'grave & decent apparrell aggreable to their functioun and as appertenis men of thair rank dignitie and place'.[116]

The Surplice: The Sticking Points

The white linen surplice is one of the simplest liturgical garments, but over the course of 50 years it slowly became the most contentious element of clerical dress north and south of the border (fig. 11.13). When William Horman published the *Vulgaria* in 1519 he described how a priest should dress for Holy Communion: 'Fyrst do on the amys, than the albe, than the gyrdell, than the maniple, than the stoole, than the chesybyll'.[117] This was simplified slightly in the English prayer book of 1549 where the priest was required to 'put vpon hym the vesture appoincted for that ministracion, that is to saye: a white Albe plain, with a vestement or Cope'.[118] Three years later the second prayer book stipulated that the minister 'shall use neither albe, vestment, nor cope; but being archbishop, or bishop, he shall have and wear a rochet: and being a priest or deacon, he shall have and wear a surplice onely'.[119]

From the 1560s onwards there was much discussion about clerical dress even within the Church of England. When Robert Horn, bishop of Winchester, sent the Swiss reformer Heinrich Bullinger the order of administration of the Church of England, Bullinger replied, 'I do not approve of the linen surplice, as they call it, in the ministry of the Gospel, inasmuch as those robes copied from Judaism, savour of popery, and are introduced and established with injury to Christian liberty.'[120] By 1606 the situation was polarised between those who considered the surplice crucial and those who hated it like the devil. Thus, the godly Andrew Melville remonstrated with Archbishop Bancroft by 'taking him by the quhyt sleives of his rocket, and schaiking them, in his manner, frielie and roundlie, callit them "Romishe ragis, and a pairt of the Beastes mark"'.[121]

11.13 The white alb, similar in some ways to the surplice, symbolises purity. The linen could be decorated with pleating and lace, as is the case with this Italian example from the late 17th century. Metropolitan Museum of Art, New York.

With or without lace, it was the colour of the alb, surplice and rochet that was distinctive, resulting in them being referred to as 'the whytts' in the 1633 Scottish parliament. Bishops were to dress in the rochet and chimere (a sleeveless gown), while ministers were to wear surplices for communion, divine service and burials.[122] Such rulings fell on deaf ears, with Thomas Kirke summing up the predominant view in Scotland when he observed: 'They use no service-book, no whore of Babylon's smock (as they term a surplice), nor decency, nor order in their divine or rather contumelious service'.[123] It is telling that Kirke's disapproval of the downplaying of the surplice was accompanied by an anti-Scottish jibe at the blue bonnet. Equally, it is not surprising that Humphrey Sydenham came to the defence of the surplice in a volume of sermons published in 1637 and dedicated to Laud where he posed the question: 'If Schismaticall hands be catching at the Mytre and the Rotchet, how will they rend the comtemptible Hood and Surplesse?'[124]

Serious discussions on episcopal dress took place during conferences at Hampton Court in 1604 and the Savoy Palace in 1661, and on both occasions the surplice was one of the 'storm centres'.[125] The garment returned to everyday use in England after the Restoration, by which time some, including Pepys, found it comical. On 26 October 1662 he felt 'it seemed absurd for him [the minister] to pull [his surplice] over his eares in the reading-pew, after he had done, before all the church, to go up to the pulpit to preach without it'.[126] However, the surplice was not widely reintroduced in post-Restoration Scotland and in 1691 Sir George Mackenzie of Rosehaugh complained that he and like-minded countrymen had 'no Ceremonies, Surplices,

Altars, Cross in Baptisms, nor the meanest of those things [that were] allowed in England by the Dissenters, in way of Accommodation'.[127]

In contrast, a communion cup and basin were central to the celebration of the sacraments of communion and baptism in Scotland, as was made clear by an act passed by the Scottish parliament in 1617 requiring that 'all the paroche kirkis within this Kingdome be prowyditt off Basines and Lavoiris for the ministration of the Sacrament of Baptism, and of couppes, tables and table clothes, for the ministration of the holie Communion'.[128] As a consequence, many of the surviving seventeenth-century Scottish communion cups were bought and hallmarked in 1617–19. On 22 March 1618, William Balfour, who later fought in the Scots Brigade, paid 4 guineas, the sum levied upon the lands of Wormiston, for the purchase of baptism basins and communion cups for the local kirk,[129] while the process of making these items is evident in a letter from James Mowat to Sir John Campbell dated 18 March 1619, which notes that 'becaus the communion approches I have maid you tua cupis' costing £86 6s 8d.[130] Over the decades cups were given as bequests, as in August 1640 when Elizabeth Purdie presented a silver communion cup left by her husband Ninian McMurran to the Cramond kirk.[131] On occasion promised gifts were not forthcoming, and in 1694 Sir Charles Erskine of Alva owed money for a new pulpit and a silver communion basin in the kirk of Alloa.[132]

Religious books also flourished. John Knox, who led the move towards the Reformation in Scotland in 1560, was strongly influenced by John Calvin and Heinrich Bullinger, and all three men valued reading and were determined to focus religious practice on religious texts. Demand grew, and in May 1678 John M'cure wrote from Glasgow to Andrew Russell, a merchant based in Rotterdam, because 'the bookbinders of our towne came to me and intreats me to sie to gett them fyre hounder bibls with three hounder scots psalms and two hounder Inglish psalms'.[133] Many religious books had opulent bindings, such as the psalm book with a tortoiseshell cover owned by the laird of Lundy in 1652.[134] The importance of the volumes determined where they were kept, as is demonstrated by the Dons of Neton keeping their 'great house bible' and a psalm book visible and accessible, in the 'laich [low]' hall of their home in 1680.[135]

Expressions of Penance by Kings and Communities

Acts of penance, for individuals, communities and countries played an important part in the religious life of everyone from the king downwards, and had the potential to offer a significant challenge to royal authority.[136] For instance, in September 1650 Robert Douglas informed Charles II that 'As soon as God shall give a breathing time' the general assembly of the Church of Scotland would 'appoint a humiliation to be kept in reference to the guiltiness of the King and royal family'.[137] This was duly set for 26 December, with a solemn fast and humiliation 'to be kept by king and whole congregation of this kirk'.[138] As a prerequisite of his coronation,

Charles II had no option but to attend a ceremony designed to challenge many aspects of Stuart ceremonial. Attendance at days of fasting was carefully monitored, so much so that in September 1638 the marquis of Hamilton chose to remain in Dalkeith during the solemn fast because if he had been in Edinburgh and stayed away 'it would have infuriated the covenanters, but to have gone would not have been consonant with loyalty to the king'.[139]

Individuals did penance for their sins in acts which were expressed visually through their clothing, such as when James IV did penance for the guilt he felt at the death of his father dressed in James III's shirt. The more extreme wearing of sackcloth instead of, or over, everyday clothing demonstrated guilt and the public performance of penance, and sackcloth was one form of 'religious textile' that reformers appropriated from Catholicism and made their own. For instance, in December 1638 the bishop of Moray was compelled to sit in sackcloth for wearing a surplice.[140] Eight years later in December 1646 James, lord Ogilvy 'sat in sackcloth' for his sins.[141] Alexander Sinclair suffered the same fate in February 1669 when he was ordered to appear dressed in sackcloth, and barefooted, before the congregation in the kirk of Kinloss. Once there, he had to admit to telling lies and pay a fine of £100 Scots.[142] The appearance of these gowns is evident from the loose, brown, sackcloth garment Jonet Gothskirk allegedly wore for her public repentance for adultery in 1677 (fig. 11.14).[143] While the Stuart kings never wore sackcloth, the language of royal repentance was central to the letter sent from 'Jocke a Bread Scotland' to Charles II in May 1674. Here, the character described simply as 'Jocke' assured the king that 'Your Majestie will be brought to the stool of repentance not only for your predecessors sins but your own breach of Covenant, Coronation oath etc.'[144] Times had changed, and while James IV's displays of piety served to strengthen his position as king, no amount of public penitence would have resolved the complex religious position that Charles II found himself in.

11.14 Gown of repentance, 18th century. National Museum of Scotland, Edinburgh. Loose fitting and plain, this sackcloth marked out the sinful from the rest of the congregation.

Conclusions

In 1637 Edmund Harrison, the king's embroiderer, made a set of *or nué* embroideries celebrating the life of the Virgin. Associated with Lady Alethea Talbot, these pictures are an exceptional example of Catholic devotional objects (fig. 11.15).[145] Charles I's Laudianism meant that he appreciated objects like this, for both their religious significance and their aesthetic appeal, but it was an approach that brought him into conflict with many of his subjects, especially his Scottish people. As a result, religion,

11.15 'The Annunciation', from Edmund Harrison's series *The Life of the Virgin*, 1637. Linen, silk, gold and silver thread. National Museum of Scotland, Edinburgh.

whether it was the king's personal beliefs or the patterns of worship that the Stuart kings sought to impose on their people, was the most controversial aspect of their fashionable and cultural style.

The Stuarts' religious style was loved and loathed in equal measure throughout the period from James VI's birth to the death of his last grandson in 1701, and beyond to the kings over the water. It was expressed through a range of ceremonies, public and private observances, significant objects and signs visible in clothing, and it constituted the arena in which the religious, social and national distinctions of the time were played out. Its historical significance is proved by the very fact that there was extensive contemporary discussion of it, so much so that clerical dress became a sticking point, or rather a splitting point, in the Three Kingdoms. Many Scots opted for a religious world with minimal liturgical textiles, a world of simplicity and purity, while their Stuart kings favoured a church with vestments and surplices and valued adornment as an integral part of their faith. However, it was not a complete rejection of liturgical goods. Rather, it was a shift from a rich array of textiles to a much simpler set, used alongside plates and books including the Book of Common Order, psalm books and the Bible. The gulf between these perspectives was often hard to reconcile and played a significant role both in James VII and II losing his thrones and the ongoing attempts of the Old and Young Pretenders to recover them.

CHAPTER TWELVE

Mourning and Funerals for the Stuart Dead

WHEN JAMES STUART, 2nd earl of Moray, was killed on 7 February 1592 at the culmination of a feud with George Gordon, earl of Huntly, his mother commissioned a painting of her son's corpse and left his body unburied as she sought justice (fig. 12.1). His almost naked body served to highlight his wounds and his family's desire for revenge. In contrast, having recovered John Graham of Claverhouse's body after the battle of Killiecrankie in 1689, 'white and shameless and all unclothed', his supporters wrapped him in a plaid.[1] He was then laid to rest in St Bride's Kirk near Blair Castle. These examples demonstrate two ways in which the living could mark the passing of a friend or relative but in most cases, the funerals of the Scottish elite, like those of their Stuart kings, played a significant part in seventeenth-century spectacle. So, just as a funeral marks the end of a life, so this present chapter draws *Stuart Style* to a close by exploring how the Stuarts and the Scottish elite engaged with the textiles and ceremonies associated with death, and how this engagement impacted on wider Stuart society.

Mourning Clothes

Royal Stuart funerals, like other similar ceremonies, focused upon the body – or rather the effigy – of the monarch, dressed in their robes of state, a point of colour surrounded by black, the colour associated with death and mourning. Consequently, the term 'blacks' was synonymous with the paraphernalia required to clothe mourners' bodies, furnish the state apartments and line the route along which the cortège passed. While royal funerals signify an end, they also mark change and transition: from the living to the dead; from being the heir to being the monarch; from the old household to the new. While much of their value came from

See figure 12.2.

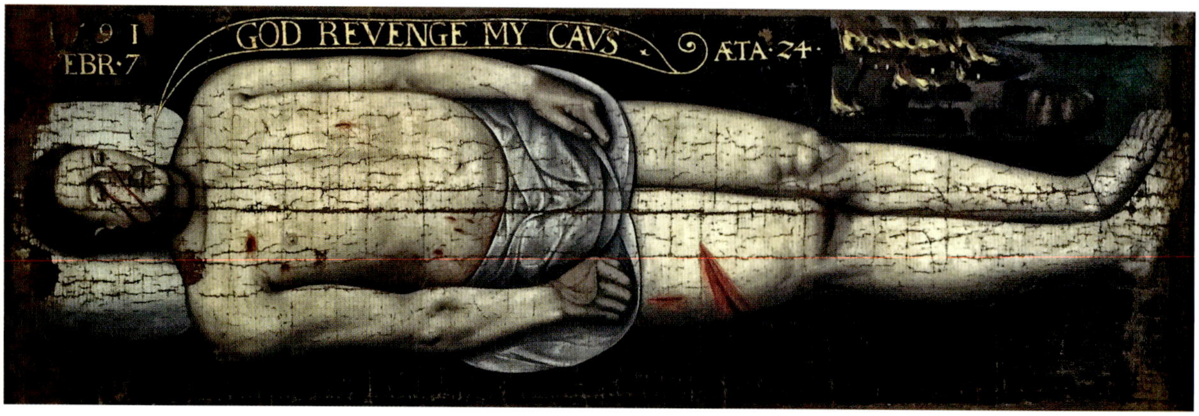

12.1 Unknown artist, *The Bonny Earl of Moray*, 1592. Oil on canvas. Private collection.

tradition, the funerals of Stuart kings in England and those of the Stuart elite were also defined by innovation and change, much of which can be linked to their Scottish heritage.[2]

The quantity of black material given as mourning at a royal funeral was the best indicator of the status of the deceased. Stuart funerals up to 1685 reveal two main trends in terms of the 'mourning' that was distributed. The first relates to how many people were given mourning, with the funeral of James VI and I seeing the largest number of individuals receiving black in the households of the late and the new king, as well as the aristocracy, the clerical elite, ambassadors, city officials and poor mourners. Everyone was grieving for the loss of the sovereign. This followed the model adopted for Elizabeth I and it was echoed for Mary II's funeral on 5 March 1695, but it was not used for Charles I, Charles II or James VII and II. So the Stuart funeral changed from large, impressive daytime occasions dominated by the clothes of mourners to much smaller, evening or night-time events where black-clad mourners blended into darkness unless illuminated by the torchlight.

The second indicator of status relates to the style and quantity of mourning issued at royal funerals. Traditionally, rank determined how much black fabric an individual was given, whether it was silk or wool, and whether they had an allowance for their servants. The size of the Stuart family meant that precedence played a part at all times, so that at Henry's funeral his servants received less cloth than the members of his mother's household who were in attendance. Each of her pages of the backstairs received a piece of rash, 4 yards of cloth, a pair of stockings and a beaver hat, while her musicians were given 8 yards of serge, 4 yards of cloth, a pair of stockings and a beaver hat.[3] There were also two types of mourning: the black mourning gown and hood or cloak worn during the funeral procession and service and the clothing, closely modelled on fashionable dress, worn during the period of mourning after the funeral.

There were two other ways in which the Stuarts made their mark on the format of royal funerals, especially in the first half of the seventeenth century. The first was that while the king did not usually attend funerals, with the office of chief mourner being taken by a leading member of the aristocracy, Charles I broke with tradition and took this role three times, twice as prince and once as monarch.[4] The first occasion was at his elder brother's funeral, an honour he shared with the Prince Palatine, when both mourners were issued with 18 yards of black cloth.[5] The second was at his mother's funeral and the third was at his father's.[6] Secondly, while it was the funerals of royal men, namely kings, that were the most important, royal Stuart women played a very important role in mourning for their menfolk. William Larkin painted Anna of Denmark in 1612 dressed in black as she mourned for her father Henry IV of Denmark (fig. 12.2). Her daughter, Elizabeth of Bohemia, was painted in a black gown and wearing the pearl earrings given to her by her late husband ten years after his death.[7]

12.2 Unknown artist, *Anna of Denmark*, c.1628–44. Oil on panel, 57.2 × 43.8 cm. National Portrait Gallery, London. Anna wears a small black cap along with a gown, cloak with a high collar, earrings and a broach.

Royal Mourning

Mourning was worn more frequently and became more codified as the seventeenth century progressed.[8] There are several overlapping reasons for this, including the growing fashion for mourning, Charles II's close ties to European royalty either by blood or through his prolonged period of exile, and the high mortality rate among his relatives. One of the most visible changes, after Elizabeth's use of black, was the use of purple to mourn immediate family and fellow monarchs. When Henry IV of France was assassinated in Paris on 14 May 1610, James VI and I went into mourning and he received two suits with cloaks, one of black silk grosgrain, the other of purple, costing £45 4s 10d and £47 4s 10d respectively.[9] In contrast, Charles I ordered suits described as being specifically for mourning on three occasions and in each case they were black.[10] Two of his mourning suits were made of satin but examples were also made in black silk grosgrain and black cloth. Appropriate black accessories were also supplied including a pair of mourning gloves with black tops, two pairs of black hangers and black girdles.[11] However, not all black suits were for mourning, as indicated by a purchase of five pairs of black satin and taffeta garters with great roses and points in 1632–3 'for mourning and other black suits'.[12]

The circumstances of Charles I's death meant that it was vital for Charles II to have appropriate mourning, and in May 1649 Thomas Needham sent the young king two pieces of purple cloth to wear.[13] Mourning was not cheap, as a payment of 15,624 gilders 'for the Mourning with other necessary bills' indicates.[14] According to Jean Chevalier, Charles II was still in the first stage of mourning in September and 'his habiliments were all purple with no embroidery, either of gold or silver, but on the left side of his cloak a silver star was attached'.[15] A prolonged period in black followed, allowing Charles to make a point of marking his father's death while at the same time conveniently avoiding the need to maintain a fashionably coloured wardrobe. In 1654 John Thurloe's spies described Charles II, who was then in Aachen, as 'clad in sobre black with white silk stockings, but adorned with the blue ribbon and garter'.[16] While in exile Charles also mourned fellow monarchs, thereby demonstrating his place as a legitimate ruler. Shortly after the death of the emperor Ferdinand III in April 1657, Sir Edward Hyde reported that 'The King has got himself into mourning, how he will pay for it, God knows'.[17] While vital socially and politically, mourning was a major expense.

By the Restoration, royal mourning had developed significantly and was a much more complex affair. In part this was because Charles II, unlike his father, had far more occasion to wear it. As a consequence he ordered mourning on every clothing account apart from one between 1660 and 1672. After this no suits were specifically described as mourning, although purple suits were made in 1674 and 1676. On 30 November 1682 a newsletter was dispatched to John Squier in Newcastle informing him that 'Last Friday Prince Rupert was at a play, sickened on Saturday and died yesterday morning between 5 and 6 ... On Sunday the Court go into mourning for him. His Majesty will be three weeks in purple and plain linen and three weeks in black cloth'.[18] However, the accounts indicate that this prediction was incorrect. There were no purple suits in the 1682/3 account, although there were several black suits that might have been part of the king's mourning. If the king did wear purple, they were suits he had already. This fits with earlier references in his accounts for repairs and alterations to mourning, as was the case in 1670 when Claude Sourceau and John Allen lined a purple coat with purple rateen, made a pair of sleeves for a crêpe vest and put black buttons on the coat, vest and a plain taffeta waistcoat.[19]

While suits were identified in the accounts as being for mourning, they were not categorised as being for specific phases. Even so, it is evident that Charles II wore purple for full mourning for key family members and black for second mourning and for individuals of lower rank. Significant quantities of grey featured in his accounts. While not described as being for half-mourning, it is likely that they were used for this purpose. The same colour scheme was mirrored in the rooms inhabited by the king, with his bedchamber and other important rooms being hung with purple and the remainder in black and grey.

The Impact of Periods of Royal Mourning

James VI and I did not favour wearing mourning for long periods and he did not appreciate others doing so. In May 1603 he informed Anna of Denmark: 'As for your doole weede [for Elizabeth I], wearing it is utterly impertinent at this time for sic reasons as the bearer will show unto you'.[20] After Henry's death, Archibald Primrose reported that 'the prince salbe buried this nixt oulk and all duell and duel weidis sall ceas at court and heir'.[21] A combination of the king's personal preference and a slower fashion cycle meant that mourning was less disruptive in the early seventeenth century.

However, by mid century, longer periods of mourning and a faster pattern of fashionable change had a marked impact on fashion at court and further afield. Pepys made this clear on 11 May 1662 when he noted that he had met the king, who was just out of mourning for his aunt Elizabeth of Bohemia, who had died on 13 February, observing: 'I saw the king now out of mourning in a suit laced with gold and silver which it was said was out of fashion'.[22] Ever anxious to appear at his sartorial best, Pepys sought to avoid finding himself in a similar situation on 22 October 1663 when he commented, 'this morning, hearing that the queen grows worse again, I sent to stop the making of my velvet cloak, till I see whether she lives or dies'.[23] Trying to predict new styles involved watching the court closely, and the 1st earl of Conway relied on people resident in the city to keep him informed. On 6 May 1671 Edward Wayte sent him 'patterns of all the newest stuffs in the box with Lady Conway's things'. Wayte apologised for the delay, stating that 'the Court being in mourning, no one knew what would be worn that summer'.[24] The same was true in late April 1673 when Patrick Gilmour informed Conway that 'The Court is still in mourning, and no fashions known. Some say they will continue in mourning till 29 May. Mr. Wayte says he will know on May Day what fashions will be, [or] at least give a guess.'[25] Royal mourning also had a marked impact on court ceremonials, as was the case with the reception of Claude Lamoral, prince de Ligne, who arrived in London late in 1660 when Charles II and his court were all in black (fig. 12.3). Unaware, the prince arrived for his audience with his brightly dressed retinue.

Careful choices of clothes could limit the impact of mourning and ensure that mourning clothes could become part of one's everyday wardrobe once the mourning period was over. On 6 December 1679 Francis Gwyn ordered a suit for Conway 'of black cloth lined with black ... which is both mourning enough and fine enough for this expedition'.[26] A week later C. Magenis informed the earl that 'Mr. Seymour does not go out of town till the middle of next week and would have a handsome cloak made for you lined with velvet, which may be of use when you are out of mourning'.[27]

Scots and Mourning Clothes

Mourning required specific colours, matt fabrics and sombre trimmings. Suitable woollens included cloth, serge and baize, while velvet, taffeta and crêpe were appropriate silks.[28] A range of these feature in the account listing the clothes bought for the funeral of the 7th laird of Glenorchy in 1631.[29] Orders for mourning were a regular part of life, and in 1672 the 10th laird of Glenorchy ordered a range of clothes including 'blacks' from James Row.[30] Mourning required a full set of accessories, as the 1677/8 account of George, earl of Winton, reveals. William Ferrie, belt maker, supplied the earl with mourning belts, buckles, garters and

second mourning garters.[31] It also extended to a man's weapons, as in the case of Patrick Birnie, who asked Alexander Campbell of Barcaldine in January 1692 for a mourning sword, a pair of holster tops and a house of sealskin with a black mohair fringe upon both tops and housing.[32]

Wearing mourning demonstrated a sense of family and shared loss, so when Archibald, 8th earl of Argyll, lost his father in November 1638 he asked the 8th laird of Glenorchy if he would 'suffer his foster to wear mourning' for his grandfather.[33] It could also express bonds of friendship, as when Robert Campbell of Glenfalloch assured his brother the 8th laird of Glenorchy that the earl of Argyll's body was being sent to Kilmoun by sea and 'his friends are to wear mourning'.[34]

The deceased, or their families, often supplied mourning for a range of individuals in their circle or who attended their funeral. For instance, in June 1631 David Primrose asked Sir Colin Campbell, 8th laird of Glenorchy when the funeral of Sir Duncan Campbell would take place so 'that at that tyme I may mourne in my mourning weid whiche ye have bestowed upon me'.[35] The poor were desirable as mourners and Sir Hugh Kennedy of Girvanmains (d. 1578) asked for six poor boys 'to convey me to the sepulchre' dressed in gowns of black 'dule claith'.[36] Getting the scale right was important, as indicated by the request of Lord Boyd (d.1590), who wanted to be buried in the parish kirk of Kilmarnock 'in the sepulchre of my forebears … to be careit hidder bot [without] onie order, bot onlie betwixt twa hors and ane black claith abone ane kist, bot [without] onie farder ceremonie'.[37]

Wealthy Scots also went into mourning for the monarch and members of the royal family. When Mary II died on 28 December 1694, the

12.3 Attributed to François du Chastel, *Charles II Receiving the Spanish Ambassador*, 1660. Oil on canvas. Collections des Princes de Ligne, Château de Beloeil. Charles II and his court are all in black while the ambassador and his retinue are in colourful attire.

following month Thomas Kilgoure, tailor to the earl of Breadalbane, made 'his lordship's mourning suit'.[38] If they were at court, they also adopted mourning when the king did. In December 1686 Charles Kerr informed his mother that he had gone into 'court mourning' for the prince of Condé.[39] The cost and inconvenience of mourning was not always welcome, however, and in July 1691 John Campbell, 12th laird of Glenorchy and 2nd earl Breadalbane and Holland (1662–1752) noted unhappily that the death of Henry Cavendish, 2nd duke of Newcastle, put him 'to the charge of mourning'.[40]

Funerals

Funerals and funeral processions were carefully scrutinised, with the scale of the event being very important. The interment of Robert Cecil, the late lord treasurer, at Hatfield in June 1612 was a 'Small funeral, and no great stir', while six years later there was the 'Splendid' and much larger funeral of Sir William Craven (1548–1618), a former lord mayor of London.[41] In contrast, Sir John Graemes, a Scottish courtier who died in 1616, 'was solemnly buried in the night at Westminster with better than 200 torches, the Duke of Lennox, the Lord Fenton, the Lord of Roxburgh, and all the grand Scottish Men accompanying him'.[42] It was a funeral that received both positive and negative responses. The butchers of King Street chose to burn 'a dog in Tothill Fields, in ridicule of the ceremony, saying, the soul of a dog was as good as that of a Scot'.[43] However, another source observed that 'the matter proved not so much in denigration of the Scots, seeing some of them were found to be ringleaders in that foolery'.[44] The clothing worn by the celebrants and the language they used could also provoke a strong response. In 1617 the Scots objected to William Laud wearing a surplice at the funeral of an Englishman in Edinburgh, while they criticised Valentine Carey, the dean of St Paul's, for 'commending the soul of the deceased to God', a phrase too Catholic in tone.[45]

The funeral of Elizabeth I in 1603 was the last Tudor funeral but also the first paid for by the Stuarts in England and the first to be recorded visually.[46] There was a competitive element, with Charles I wanting his father's funeral to be 'the greatest indeed that ever was knowne in England' and, as such, a demonstration of the Stuart's right to rule all three kingdoms.[47] He got his way and James VI and I's funeral was so expensive that it cost almost as much as those of Elizabeth I, Prince Henry and Anna of Denmark combined. David Calderwood's contempt for this political and religious employment of ceremony is shown by his remark, that while magnificent in content, the funeral was 'without forme and order'.[48] Early Stuart royal funerals were far larger and consequently more expensive than those in the period immediately after the Restoration, which were much smaller, reflecting changes in taste, but were no less influential. Indeed, by placing a greater emphasis on mourning after the funeral, deaths had a more significant impact on the living.

Later Stuart Funerals in Scotland

When James V died on 19 December 1542, Lord Lisle cautioned Henry VIII that it would be dishonourable to make war upon a dead body, or a widow, or on a young suckling, his daughter, especially at the time of his funeral.[49] A solemn procession accompanied the king's body from Fife to Holyrood where the Dolorous Chapel had been painted black, his coffin was draped with a black cloth with a white cross and the earl of Arran was the chief mourner.[50] The funeral was impressive in scale and the influence of the French court was evident with the use of a full-sized effigy. However, when Mary of Guise died on 11 June 1560, the religious situation in Scotland had changed. While a pall with a white cross was placed over her coffin as it rested in the chapel of St Margaret, her Catholicism ensured that she would not be buried in Holyrood Abbey with her husband and sons.[51] Instead, her coffin was taken on 16 March 1561 from Edinburgh Castle to Leith, and from there to Fécamp, to Rheims and finally to the abbey of Saint-Pierre-les-Dames, while the preacher at her memorial service in Paris took as his verse 'Dead is Judith, light of all the world'.[52]

When Mary, Queen of Scots' second husband, Henry Stuart, lord Darnley, died in suspicious circumstances on 10 February 1567, she used the funeral and her mourning to suggest an official sense of decorum. Huntly authorised a payment of £40 for items required by the 'pottingar

12.4 Matthew Goodrick's frieze of 1617, and the black fictive hanging and yellow margin of 1625, the Queen's Audience chamber, Holyroodhouse, Edinburgh.

and schirurgens to caus perfume the Kings body'.[53] Darnley's funeral took place four days after his death and he was buried in Holyrood Abbey, and on 25 March John Balfour supplied 'blak dumasi taffeta' to line two gowns, cambric for ruffs, Florence ribbons and black silk for 'the Quuen's gowns'.[54] Other items for 'the quenis grace to be ane duille' included serge of Florence to be 'ane goune and ane cloik mulis and schinine'. Mourning extended beyond the queen's body to her apartments, and the royal upholsterer received black material for mourning drapes for her bed and for covering chairs and stools.[55]

In spite of her requests to be buried in France, Mary's mortal remains were interred in July 1587 at Peterborough Cathedral, six months after her execution at Fotheringhay. In England, concerns over the impact of Mary's execution may partly explain the scale of the funeral held for Sir Philip Sidney, who died fighting for the Protestant cause at the battle of Zutphen. Held on 16 February, and paid for by his father-in-law Sir Francis Walsingham, it overshadowed Mary's death and funeral,[56] and John Buxton asserts that the aim was to emphasise in English minds the difference between the lost Protestant hero and the Catholic, Scottish queen.[57] In contrast, when James VI and I's funeral took place in Westminster, the king's apartments at Holyrood were hung with black velvet and taffeta to mark his death.[58] The textile hangings were supplemented by wall paintings, so ensuring a quick but very effective acknowledgement of the king's passing in his native land (fig. 12.4).[59] However, the mourning was also somewhat curtailed there, reflecting the rather mixed reputation James now had.

Stuart Funerals in England

Very shortly after his accession to Elizabeth's throne, James VI and I gave careful thought to his mother's resting place. On 14 August 1603, a velvet pall embroidered with her arms was 'solemnly carried and laid upon and over the corpse of the said late Queene' at Peterborough Cathedral.[60]

12.5 *(above)* Cornelius and William Cure, marble effigy of Mary, Queen of Scots, 1612. Westminster Abbey, London. Mary wears a ruff and robes over her gown, and has a small fitted coif covering her hair.

This textile demonstrated the reverence that was due to Mary's mortal remains as a queen regnant of Scotland and the current king's mother. However, this was only a prelude to her reburial at Westminster Abbey in 1612 (fig. 12.5). Edward IV had used the reburial of his father in 1476 as a means of asserting the Yorkist claim to the throne, and James did the same to stress Stuart legitimacy.[61] Mary's second funeral procession took place at night, as had her first in 1587.[62] There was no effigy on the coffin; instead, a crown was carried on a cushion. This format was also used for the funeral of Charles II, although he had a standing funeral effigy (fig. 12.6).[63] Another funeral, that of Anna of Denmark, saw further breaks with tradition. Most significantly, her son Charles walked behind the coffin while the chief mourner, the countess of Arundel, was accompanied by the duke of Lennox and the marquis of Hamilton. Between them, they signalled family kinship, Catholic associations, French affinity and Scots status.

More importantly, this was a period of marked change when the traditional form of the English heraldic funeral was challenged on several levels. To begin with, James VI and I brought Scottish ideas with him; more importantly still, his Scottish followers were not bound by the rules imposed by the English heralds.[64] The result was a shift to less formal funerals indicated in part by a move to evening and night-time ceremonies – although this was all relative, and the funerals were still impressive.[65] 40 years later the Wars of the Three Kingdoms had a massive impact on society at every level, breaking some of the older traditional bonds and resulting in simpler funerals with less ceremony and less religious content. There was also a transition from supine to standing effigies that were not used during the funeral but that served as an alternative to a tomb or a marker, until a tomb was erected.[66] Arguably, the innovative elements in Charles II's funeral meant that it was not simply small, as Evelyn believed; rather, it was both suitable and highly fashionable, as suggested by the use of a purple velvet cope that still resides at the abbey (fig. 12.7). In contrast, Mary II's funeral was old-fashioned, being so large. For William III, this intentional harking back to the past was designed to evoke parallels with the funerals of Elizabeth I and James VI and I, and to legitimise his sole rule after the death of his Stuart wife.

The part played by heraldry and heralds changed in subtle ways over time and little innovations, such as the horse trappers at James VI and I's funeral, were described by the clerk as being 'in a new style'.[67] While the organisational role of the heralds declined, they were still in attendance and heraldic banners were important throughout because they stressed the lineage and status of the deceased. Indeed, it could be argued that the level of importance attached to heraldry by the crown actually increased over the course of the seventeenth century. On 6 December 1682 a warrant issued to the earl of Ailesbury, deputy to the duke of Norfolk, earl marshal, required him to ensure that the correct form of coronet was used at Prince Rupert's funeral 'for the greater dignity of the royal family' and 'to distinguish them from others of equal title'.[68]

The Stuarts and the State Funeral

Tudor monarchs had paid for the funerals of members of the elite and for faithful servants, and this practice continued under the Stuarts. From a letter dated 27 March 1611, Sir Dudley Carleton learnt that 'Several Lords of Scotland, spiritual and temporal, are at Court, to arrange the affairs of that kingdom, which were wholly managed by the late earl of Dunbar, for whom, though he is buried in Scotland, the King has appointed a funeral at Westminster'.[69] Further examples followed during the reign of Charles I, and in general the outlay on the funerals of these trusted servants was fairly modest and provoked little comment. For example in 1628/9, John Dixon, surgeon, was paid £98 3s 0d by the king for embalming the body of Sir John Borough.[70] In 1633, Charles I's agent Philip Burlamachi received £1,700 for paying the debts of the late diplomat, Sir Isaac Wake (*c.*1580–1632), and for transportation of his body and family from Paris to Dover.[71]

The trend was revived at the Restoration with the caveat that payments towards funeral costs were usually made as a way of refunding salary arrears. So on 17 May 1667 a warrant was issued to pay £270, arrears of wages and expenses, due to Thomas, late earl of Cleveland for three-quarters of a year, ended March 1667, as captain of the gentleman pensioners, towards the expenses of his funeral.[72] Cleveland may have been favoured in this way because his bravery at the battle of Worcester had allowed Charles himself to escape. Similarly, on 4 July 1684 the king ordered a payment of £125 to a Mrs Margaret Napier, towards her mother's funeral expenses. This sum was the equivalent of the late Lady Elizabeth Erskine's pension for half a year.[73] The king also paid for the funeral of Sir Robert Moray, who died in penury. On 10 July 1673 John Robertson wrote to Lothian with details of Sir Robert's sudden death at 6 o'clock on the evening of 4 July and his subsequent burial in Westminster Abbey.[74]

Not all of the funerals paid for by the crown were attended by suitable displays of public grief. This was especially true of the funeral of George Villiers, duke of Buckingham, in 1628. His executors wisely encouraged the king to spend less on the funeral and use the money to settle Buckingham's debts.[75] The Venetian ambassador noted, with evident satisfaction, that while there was 'some little noise' during the funeral procession, it was 'more like joy than commiseration'.[76] Buckingham was highly unpopular with the Scots at court, as is evident from a letter sent by

12.6 *(facing page, below)* Standing funeral effigy of Charles II dressed in Garter robes, cloth of silver Garter suit and a linen shirt, which may have belonged to the king, 1685. Westminster Abbey, London.

12.7 *(below)* A purple velvet cope used at the funeral of Charles II, c.1685. Westminster Abbey, London.

Sir David Cunningham, who frankly confessed that he had never 'seen such signs of joy at a burial'. Sir David told his brother, 'All the kinges servants were commanded to weare black for fowrteene daies', which he dutifully did, but his 'sorrow exceeded not after the expiration of the said fowrteene days I returned to London from court in a greene Sattin Suite where I was made the more welcome of the Citizens … some have beene beaten latlie by Prentises only for haveing on mourning clothes'.[77]

The state funeral continued to develop during the Interregnum, with the Admiralty Commissioners approving the interment of General Blake in Westminster Abbey on 15 August 1657. They cited the funeral of General Deane as a precedent, and Greenwich House was prepared to receive his body.[78] It cost £550.[79] In contrast, the funeral of Henry Ireton (1611–51), Oliver Cromwell's son-in-law, in Westminster Abbey in June 1653 proved unpopular. John Poortmans complained that the 'vain pomp at the funeral of Lord Ireton was very offensive to many. It will be disowned in the burial of Gen. Deane'.[80]

Two particular funerals of the post-Reformation period stand out: those of George Monck, duke of Albemarle, in 1670,[81] and Edward Montagu, earl of Sandwich, two years later. They were different because these two subjects, even though of high rank, were given a state funeral paid for by the king and organised by the lord chamberlain. They were, thus, early examples of what would become a sequence of funerals for national heroes.[82] With the first, Charles II acknowledged his debt to Monck, who had helped to bring about the Restoration by bringing the army south from Scotland. As befitted a man with a military pedigree, Monck's funeral had a pronounced martial element that was not evident in royal funerals. His effigy wore armour, a buff coat and ducal robes.[83] Soldiers were present, with 401½ yards of black crêpe being distributed to make scarves for 107 officers from the two regiments of foot guard and three troops of horse. Black crêpe was also supplied to cover 26 foot colours and 3 horse colours.[84] Monck's importance to Charles was further recognised by the payment of £120 to Mr Sanford 'for brasse Cutts to represent the Funerall', so facilitating the sale of officially sanctioned images of the cortège.[85] Interest in the funeral meant that, by 19 March 1674 'The solemnities of Generall Monks interrment in cuts' was listed in 'A catalogue of books belonging to me' found among the papers of the Hay family.[86]

Charles II's debt to Monck was evident in the cost of the general's funeral. Sir Ralph Verney informed his son Mun that 'The King sent a Garter to the young Duke as soone as his Father was dead, and will bury him at his owne charge, hee is appointed to lie in State at Somerset House'.[87] On 14 February 1670 a warrant was issued to pay to the earl of Sandwich £5,528 15s 8d for the funeral.[88] On 16 April 1670 a newsletter reported: 'It is not determined whether the General's funeral solemnity shall be performed on St. George's Day or not, but the solemnity of the Garter at Windsor is put off till 3, 4 and 5 May'.[89] On 23 April 1670 another source reported: 'The king and duke of York are still at

Newmarket and return to town for the funeral of the duke of Albemarle, who is at present lying in state at Somerset House'.[90] Adverts placed in the *Gazette* two days later issued guidancc on etiquette to 'the nobility and others … invited to attend' the funeral on 30 April.[91]

Equally important in helping set the Restoration in train was Edward Montagu, earl of Sandwich, who was killed on 27 May 1672 during the battle of Solebay when the Dutch attacked his flagship the *Royal James* with fire ships. He was buried on 3 July 1672 at Westminster Abbey after a procession along the Thames consisting of five barges sailing from Deptford to Westminster and arriving at 5pm.[92] Mourners included Samuel Pepys who received 8 yards of black cloth for mourning to show his respects.

Official Funerals in Scotland

The importance the Stuarts attached to royal office holders was also reflected in these men's funerals. These events were prestigious for Scotland as well as for the officials' families. George Hay, 1st earl of Kinoole (1570–1634) and lord chancellor of Scotland, died in London but was buried at Kinoole, Perth. In order to ensure the funeral cortège was suitably magnificent, Archibald, lord Lorne, made it clear that he expected his relatives to attend. He informed his cousin the 8th laird of Glenorchy on 6 August 1635 that he expected 'his company to the burial' if he was well enough to travel in a week's time.[93]

Charles II was alert to the value of state funerals held in Scotland, and he set the tone by ordering the reburial of James Graham, marquis of Montrose, the Royalist hero who had been executed by the Scottish Covenanters on 21 May 1650 (fig. 12.8). On 4 January 1661 the parliamentary register in Edinburgh recorded that the king had ordered that 'the bodies, bones and head of the late marquis of Montrose and Sir William Hay of Delgatie should be gathered and honourably buried at his majesty's expense'.[94] Three days later, on 7 January, a guard of honour went 'to the Burrow mure quhair [Montrose's] corps wer bureyit' and 'his body and bones taken out and wrappit up … and put in a coffin, quhilk, under a canopy of rich velwet, wer careyit from the Burrow-mure to the

12.8 Studio of Sir Anthony van Dyck, *James Graham, 1st Marquis of Montrose*, c.1636. Oil on canvas, 75.6 × 58.4 cm. National Galleries of Scotland. James Graham does not allow fashionable accessories to detract from the chivalric image.

Toun of Edinburgh'.[95] Montrose's limbs were brought from Aberdeen, Glasgow, Perth and Sterling and his remains lay in state at Holyrood until his burial on 11 May 1661. Charles II's treatment of Cromwell stood in marked, and intentional, contrast. The protector's body was exhumed on 30 January 1661, the anniversary of Charles I's execution.

John Leslie, 7th earl and 1st duke of Rothes, lord high chancellor of Scotland, died on 27 July 1681 at Holyrood, and the following month his state funeral began with a procession on 23 August taking his body back to Leslie, Fifeshire (fig. 12.9).[96] The textiles that represented the high points of his political career took centre stage in this procession, including the embroidered footcloth of the horse he used for attending parliament and his lord chancellor's purse. His coffin, draped with a mort cloth, was placed under a canopy decorated with coats of arms, as was the pall. The estimated cost was £30,000 and the procession was five miles long.[97]

Not all state figures were as well regarded as Leslie. James Sharp, archbishop of St Andrews, was considered a turncoat by many Covenanters and on 3 May 1679, a group of nine men attacked and killed

12.9 Unknown artist, *Funeral Procession of John Leslie, 7th Earl and 1st Duke of Rothes*, 1681. Line engraving on paper, 39.37 × 48.9 cm. National Galleries of Scotland. Heralds, trumpeters, banner bearers and a man carrying Rothes's lord chancellor's gown make up the funeral procession.

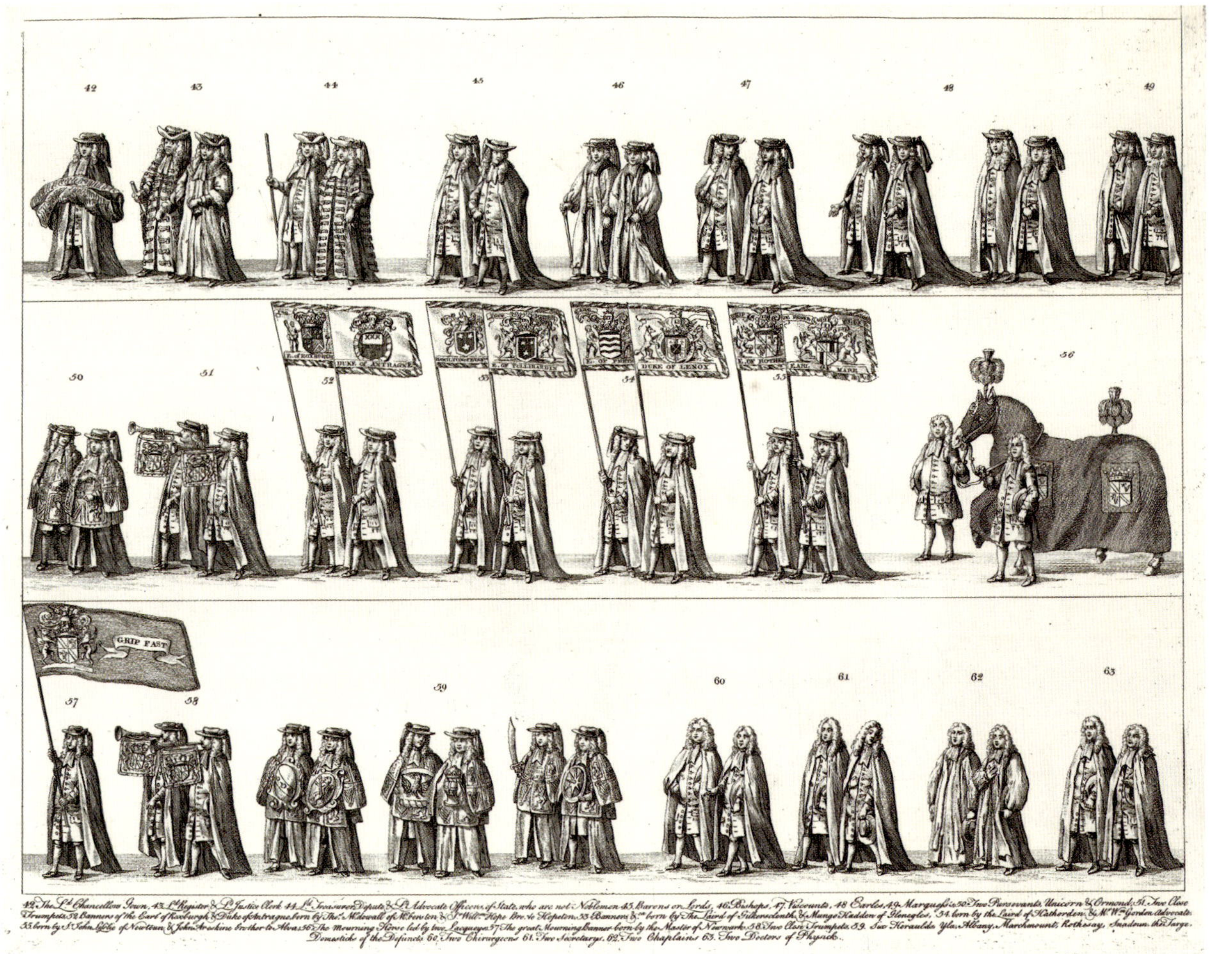

him. His funeral, held two weeks later, was carefully regulated by the town's authorities to prevent any disruptions. It was recommended that the 'tounes men of St. Androwes be drawen upe betuixt the abay and the place of buriall for keiping of the crude [crowd] so that the procession may be made in a lane betuixt the filles without disorder'.[98] The contemporary memorial on Sharp's tomb in Holy Trinity Church contrasts the archbishop's murder, shown in relief, with his serene kneeling figure, asserting his place within the episcopalian church.[99]

Other Scottish Funerals

The importance the Scots attached to funerals is evident from the care James VI took not to disrupt the procession of Robert Seton, 1st earl of Winton, on 5 April 1603. When Seton was buried, 'His Majesty graciously pleased to rest himself att the southwest round of the orch-yard of Seton, in the highway, till the funeral was over, that he might not withdraw the noble company.'[100] After 1603 some of James's Scottish supporters spent much of their lives in England and were buried there, including John Ramsey, 1st earl of Holderness. Ramsey died in January 1626 and was interred on 28 February in St Paul's Cathedral. However, many Scots wished to be buried in their native soil regardless of where they died. For instance, George Home, earl of Dunbar, died at Whitehall in 1611. His funeral service was held in Westminster Abbey in April but afterwards his body was taken north and he was buried in the parish church of Dunbar. This inevitably meant that the whole process was quite drawn out, but it did ensure that leading figures like Dunbar were mourned in both countries.

The funerals of wealthy Scotsmen also demonstrated new fashions, as in the case of James Hamilton, 2nd marquis of Hamilton, who passed away at Whitehall on 2 March 1625. His cortège left London by torchlight and he was buried at Hamilton on 2 September.[101] While there was a very important, public element to these funeral processions, the scale of the event was considered carefully. For instance, in January 1624 Sir Duncan Campbell of Glenorchy declared that he wished to be buried in the chapel of Finlarg and for his corpse to be accompanied to the grave by his 'honest neighbours', such as the lairds of Grantullie, Weyme, Lawers, Glenlyoun and Ballaquhen and others thereabouts, but without any more ceremony.[102] Even if funerals were understated, they needed to befit the status of the deceased. In June 1618 the 7th laird of Glenorchy wrote to a friend about the death of Francis, the son of Argyll. In Glenorchy's absence, the boy had been buried at Clachandysert, alongside some of the children of the lairds of Glenorchy and some of his brothers. The grave was outside the kirk, thereby conforming with the ban on burials inside issued by the General Assembly of the Church in 1576 and 1588, so his son, Robert, was having a chapel built about it.[103] Glenorchy was most anxious that the boy's mother did not think that her son had been neglected by Glenorchy's daughter-in-law and her husband.[104]

Textiles for Burial

On 10 April 1700 Anne, duchess of Hamilton, rebuked her husband for putting up black hangings in his lodgings in Holyrood in mourning for his mother-in-law.[105] Mourning and funerals were expensive and even elite families sought to defray part of the cost by borrowing the necessary textiles and other items from relatives. When Sir Robert Moray of Abercairny arranged a funeral in April 1679 he asked Lilias Drummond, countess of Perth, for help, and she sent him everything he asked for apart from a litter.[106] 12 years later Breadalbane described the preparations he made after the death of Frances, lady Glenorchy, his daughter-in-law, on 4 February 1691. On 11 February he still needed 'mournings' and mourning paper.[107] Several days later he had received his black clothes and had sent for grey clothes because 'death coms in at on dore & hearshipe at the other'. However, while the hearse was not dear, other things were bought in Aberdeen 'at great cost'.[108]

The most important item at a Scottish funeral was the mort cloth, a large rectangular textile that was draped over the hearse at the funeral. These cloths were often made new for a funeral and were expensive because they contained many ells of black silk velvet. On 30 September 1676 Edward Story wrote to Lady Jane Digby Gerard, reminding her that she had not yet paid the bill for Lord Gerard's funeral cloth and noting that he had been instructed to sue her to recover the sum of £151 9s.[109] Some families had their own mort cloth, which they reused for the funerals of family members. When Lady Glenorchy died in childbirth in 1691, for example, her husband asked for the family mort cloth to be sent to Coupar for her and the child 'being a boy'.[110] More often these cloths were hired. In 1686 John Flett, merchant, burgess of Kirkwall and the treasurer of St Magnus kirk there, brought a claim for £12 Scots against Christian Skeine, widow of James Sinclair of Saba, and David Traill, her new spouse, for the hire of the best mort cloth, which was used at James VII and II's funeral.[111]

From 1688 onwards Scots law required the dead to be buried in home-produced linen.[112] On occasion this was described as 'dead linen', as was the case for the funerals of John Kerr, brother of the earl of Lothian, in 1695, and Lady Banff in February 1702.[113] This linen was usually in the form of a winding sheet such as the example made from 7 ells of linen in Caithness in 1685–6 for Mr William Campbell.[114] Several years later purchases in 1691–2 made for James Campbell in Caithness included a coffin and winding sheet.[115] The distinctive appearance of the winding sheet is evident from the cover illustration for the pamphlet *A Messenger from the Dead* depicting Henry VIII and Charles I in their shrouds (fig. 12.10). Cerecloths also served to cover the dead, and in July 1648 Patrick Scott of Langshaw received a bill for a cerecloth to wrap his brother's body in.[116] A cerecloth worth 100 merks Scots was 'made use of' by the late Sir John Campbell of Glenorchy, who died in June 1686.[117] The purpose of the cerecloth is evident from a request of Alexander and John Campbell to David Murray, an apothecary in Perth. After their father's

A
MESSENGER
From the DEAD,
OR,
CONFERENCE
Full of ſtupendious horrour, heard diſtinctly, and by alternate voyces, by many at that time preſent.
BETWEEN THE
Ghoſts of Henry *the* 8. *and* Charls the *Firſt* of ENGLAND, in *Windſore-Chappel*, where they were both Buried.
In which the whole *Series* of the Divine Judgments, in thoſe infortunate Ilands, is as it were by a Pencill from Heaven, moſt lively ſet forth from the firſt unto the laſt.

London, Printed for *Tho. Vere*, and *W. Gilbertſon*, and are to be ſold at their Shops, at the Signe of the Angel, and the Signe of the Bible without *Newgate*, 1658.

12.10 Frontispiece depicting Henry VIII and Charles I in their shrouds, from Richard Perrinchief's *A Messenger from the Dead*, 1659. British Library, London.

death in 1657 they ordered 'ane scheircloth and so much holland as his body may be wraptit in together with so much pulders [powders] as will preserve his corps from putrifaction for ten days space'.[118] However, the linen used could be so much more personal and poignant, as the will of Ludovic Stuart's widow reveals. Frances asked to be dressed in her 'death smock' after her own demise and then wrapped 'vpp againe in those sheets … wherein my Lord and I first slepte that night when wee were married'.[119]

George Porteous had a long career as a heraldic painter in Scotland. He supplied a range of items for the funeral of George Sinclair, 6th earl of Caithness (*c*.1636–76), his order including two great lozenge-shaped coats of arms at £15 each; 54 small arms for the coffin, pall, hearse and horse; gilding and painting two crowns, one for the coffin and the other for the pall; and a large pinsell 2½ yards long with a morthead on both sides.[120] The order was slightly more modest for the funeral of Sir Alexander Done, who died in spring 1687, when Porteous was paid for painting two lozenges with his arms, mortheads and tears.[121] In 1696 Sir William Wallace commissioned Porteous to paint the funeral portrait of Jean Menzies.[122] While these examples all focused on the heraldry of the deceased, it was also possible to display the royal arms as a sign of the king's regard. This happened in March 1669 when Albany Herald was paid for displaying Charles II's coat of arms at the funeral of the earl of Eglinton.[123] The emphasis placed on heraldry led to concerns about individuals seeking to bypass the rights of the heralds. In 1668 William Dugdale described the legal proceedings against Parker, a painter, who had arranged the banners and funeral procession of Lord Gerard, 'thereby usurping the authority of Garter King of Arms'.[124] Surviving examples of these painted funerary textiles are very rare, so making the majesty escutcheon associated with Oliver Cromwell's funeral all the more significant (fig. 12.11).

12.11 A majesty escutcheon from the funeral of Oliver Cromwell, 1658. Westminster School, London.

Funeral Processions

Funeral processions were expected to be dignified and of a scale suitable to the rank of the deceased and their family. The narrative painting of the life of Sir Henry Unton (d. 1596), which shows the black-clad procession that brought his body back to England for burial in his parish church, gives a good impression of how these ceremonies would have looked (fig. 12.12).[125] When Walter Scott, 1st earl of Buccleuch (*c.*1606–33) died in London, bad weather delayed the arrival of the ship taking his body back to Scotland. But once in Leith, he too 'wes carried … to his kirk of Hawick all on fut under a fair velvit pale and the ceremonie with the armes wes set doun by some of his freinds thaimeselffes with advyse of ane painter'.[126] This example stresses the need both for specific textiles and a display of his arms.[127]

There was also a general understanding that it was the men of the family who would accompany the body. John, earl of Mar informed his

12.12 Sir Henry Unton's funeral procession and tomb. Unknown artist, *Sir Henry Unton*, c.1596. Oil on panel, 74 × 163.2 cm. National Portrait Gallery, London. Sir Henry Unton's funeral procession and tomb dominate this painted record of his life.

cousin the 8th laird of Glenorchy of his father's funeral on 2 April 1635. After being collected from Stirling at 10 o'clock, his body would be taken to the burial place at Alloa. Mar asked his cousin to come to Stirling the previous night or by 8 o'clock on the day, to accompany the corpse 'In regayrd Sir thatt yow to repere[sen]t one of my awght Branches I will entreatt yow to provyd some speciall man of yowr name in murning to caryen honores the day of the buriell or els lett me know some dayes befoyr thatt I may employe another'.[128] This letter gives a hint of the planning required for an elaborate funeral procession like that of the earl, which included chief mourners, pall-bearers and gentlemen carrying arms, standards and the earl's collar and robe of the Order of the Garter.[129]

Processions were often long. Seventy soldiers from Edinburgh Castle, under the guidance of their sergeant, lit the route taken by the funeral procession of Duncan Campbell, brother of the earl of Caithness, in 1678 to Greyfriars kirkyard.[130] This was quite modest in comparison with

Highland funerals, when clan chiefs were escorted to the grave along the coffin route by large retinues.[131] The body of Simon, 6th lord Lovat and head of the Fraser clan, was accompanied by over 5,000 cavalry and foot soldiers in 1633, while in 1672 more than 2,700 men formed the cortège for Hugh, 8th lord Lovat.[132] At the other end of the spectrum, in February 1700 Lord Glenorchy paid 5 dollars for a hearse and four horses and a mourning coach for the funeral of an unnamed servant.[133] The valued service of this individual was acknowledged with a fitting burial.

Conclusions

The primary aim of *Stuart Style* has been to reinsert the Scottish element into the traditional fashion narrative that runs through the reigns of James VI and I to James VII and II, and it has done so in two main ways. First, the book is underpinned by an exploration of how significant the Stuarts' Scottish blood, heritage and culture was in giving them an outlook on everything, including clothes, that was different to that of their Tudor predecessors. Second, it considers the role of the Scottish male elite and a multitude of craftsmen and -women, merchants and shopkeepers, who helped develop, promote and display Stuart fashion. It was a team effort and one that was also shaped, positively and negatively, by the interaction of the Stuarts with their English subjects. As such, *Stuart Style* does not challenge the traditional fashion narrative; rather, it argues that the story should be less Anglocentric in full acknowledgement of the impact of the Stuarts ruling multiple kingdoms.

The Stuarts' style was undeniably successful on a superficial level because it was adopted by most of the male elite throughout the three kingdoms. However, men could wear Stuart style without necessarily adhering to the ideas that underpinned it. Or they could change both their political views and their clothes during the course of their lifetime, as was said at the time of the Irish peer Randal MacDonnell, 2nd earl of Antrim, whom Jane Ohlmeyer has so memorably termed an early Stuart 'turn-kilt'.[134] More significantly, it was also a fractured, or fragmented, style, because different Stuarts promoted different strands of it, often at the same time. What is crystal clear, however, is that the fertile Stuarts ensured that there were multiple royal households, namely those of the sovereign, their spouse, siblings and children that individuals could look to for inspiration (fig. 12.13). This meant that, sometimes, Stuart fashion could manifest itself as a competition between older and younger Stuarts, as seen between James VI and I and Prince Henry, a situation that did not reoccur under Charles I because of his untimely death. Or when the Stuarts lost their three thrones and went into exile in the 1640s and 1650s, resulting in several satellite Stuart courts that offered an alternative to Cromwell and kept Stuart hopes alive. Stuart style became fragmented again when James VII and II lost his throne and William of Orange presented his own brand of the style as a means of reuniting the three kingdoms behind him (fig. 12.14).

12.13 Willem de Passe, *James I and His Family – with Charles, Prince of Wales, Elizabeth of Bohemia and Families*, 1622. Engraving, 32 × 38.4 cm. Royal Collection. Three generations of the Stuart family show off their variants of Stuart fashion.

Stuart style was very much Scottish style under James VI and I and in the circle of Prince Henry. However, as a consequence of James's wish to push for the idea of a 'Great Britain', and of the influence of Englishmen like Buckingham, it subtly evolved under Charles I, who also incorporated aspects of his mother's Danish outlook and his wife's French taste. The Stuarts were keen to make links between textiles and nationhood and in both countries home-produced woollen cloth was promoted as the fabric of choice. Silk frequently won out with the fabric-buying Scottish male elite, however, ensuring that variants of fashionable Stuart dress were always the most desirable items in their wardrobes regardless of whether they were from the Lowlands or Highlands. Nonetheless, some did on occasion wear the belted plaid and trews. While far from being a 'national' style in the seventeenth century, these distinctive garments resisted James VI and I's attempts to get rid of them, surviving as hunting dress and among fighting men. Stuart style was also divisive, most notably in the ways in which people responded to liturgical textiles and clerical dress.

Stuart style was a Scottish style in other ways too. Scots held key roles in the formation and dissemination of Stuart style, most importantly as royal tailors, staffing the Wardrobe of the Robes, and as keepers of the Great Wardrobe. In doing so, they contributed to the growing importance of the clothing trade in London and to building a Scottish community there, thereby making London as much their capital as Edinburgh. Through their letters and family connections, they also ensured that their fellow Scots were keen consumers of Stuart style, which people could access on either side of the border. As we have seen, the Scottish male elite were enthusiastic shoppers in both kingdoms, buying clothes in Perth, Stirling, Edinburgh or London. They engaged in the increasingly complex processes of dressing and undressing, while also participating in parliamentary and legal ceremonial and having a significant impact on

12.14 *(above)* Pierre Mignard, *James II and His Family*, 1694. Oil on canvas, 46.4 × 59.8 cm. Royal Collection. This family group promotes the claim of young James, who is wearing a breastplate and the sash of the Garter, as prince of Wales.

12.15 *(facing page)* Sir Anthony van Dyck, *Lord George Stuart, 9th Seigneur D'Aubigny*, c.1638–40. Oil on canvas, 218.4 × 133.4 cm. National Portrait Gallery, London. A Scottish royalist, Lord George embraces the guising element of Stuart style in this portrait.

the scale and timing of elite funerals. They, like their English counterparts, knew and exploited their personal appearance as a marker of self-worth, of family standing and national pride.

There was one more key component of Stuart style that reflected the royals' Scottish heritage: the fantasy element derived from a love of guising. Whether they were playing a part in a masque, travelling incognito for privacy or cross-dressing to evade capture, the periodic adoption of disguise played an important role in the lives of the Stuarts and many of their followers. It is an essential element of what Murray Pittock has termed the 'myth' of the Stuarts and a quality that Van Dyck captured in his portrait *Lord George Stuart, 9th Seigneur D'Aubigny* (fig. 12.15). Dressed as a shepherd, and in clothes reminiscent of a masque costume, George stands poised between a rose bush and a thistle, suggestive of his marriage to Katherine Howard, of the union between Scotland and England and the union between the Stuarts and the Howards.[135] While James VI and I had purposely exploited and encouraged elite marriages like this one, as part of his strategy to create 'Great Britain', developing a specific style of dress cannot be said to have been an intentional policy that was designed to bind the elite together. However, although the Stuarts did not set out deliberately to create a 'Stuart style', that is what they succeeded in doing, and in the process they stamped their mark indelibly upon the age in which they lived. They did so to such an extent that, when we attempt to visualise the people of seventeenth-century Scotland and England today, they stand before us decked out in Stuart style.

ME FIRMIOR AMOR

Timeline of the Stuarts and Their People

THE STUARTS	SCOTLAND
	1560 Reformation in Scotland
	1561 Mary, Queen of Scots returns from France
1566 Birth of James VI	
1567 Accession of James VI as king of Scotland	
	1568 Mary, Queen of Scots travels to England after the battle of Langside
1579 End of James VI's minority	
1587 Execution of Mary, Queen of Scots	
1589 Marriage of James VI to Anna of Denmark	
	1592 James VI recognises Presbyterianism with the 'Golden Act'
1594 Birth of Henry Frederick	
1600 Birth of Charles I	
1603 Death of Elizabeth I; accession of James VI to the thrones of England and Ireland as James I	**1603** Union of the crowns of Scotland and England
1605 Gunpowder Plot	
1612 Death of Henry Frederick	
	1617 James VI and I visits Scotland
	1618 James passes the Five Articles of Perth in an attempt to make the Church of Scotland more like the Church of England
1619 Death of Anna of Denmark	
1625 Death of James VI and I; accession of Charles I; marriage of Charles I to Henrietta Maria	
1630 Birth of Charles II	
1633 Birth of James, duke of York and Albany	**1633** Charles I's Scottish coronation
	1638 Covenanters rebel against Charles I
	1639 First Bishops' War
	1640 Second Bishops' War
	1642 Start of the first English civil war
	1643 The Solemn League and Covenant
	1646 Charles I surrenders to the Scots at Newcastle; end of first English civil war
	1648 Start of second English civil war
1649 Trial and execution of Charles I; start of the Interregnum and the First Commonwealth	**1649** End of second English civil war; start of third English civil war; Scots proclaim Charles II as king of Great Britain
1650 Birth of William III	**1650** Southern Scotland occupied by the New Model Army; defeats at the battle of Dunbar and Hamilton
1651 Charles II's Scottish coronation	**1651** Battle of Worcester (3 September); end of third English civil war

THE STUARTS	SCOTLAND
1653 The Protectorate under Oliver Cromwell	
	1654 Oliver Cromwell proclaimed Protector of England, Scotland and Ireland; Act of Pardon and Grace to the People of Scotland; The Tender of Union, ending Scotland's parliament and joining Scotland with the Commonwealth of England
	1655 Rebellion in the Highlands
1658 Death of Oliver Cromwell	
1660 Restoration of the Stuart monarchy	**1660** Monarchy restored in Scotland (14 May)
	1661 Restoration of the Episcopy in Scotland
1662 Marriage of Charles II to Catherine of Braganza; birth of Mary II	**1662** Restoration of the Church of Scotland; office holders required to renounce the Covenant; Act of Indemnity and Oblivion
1665 Birth of Anne	
1666 Great Fire of London	**1666** Pentland Rising ending in defeat at Rullion Green
1669 Death of Henrietta Maria	
1673 Marriage of James, duke of York and Albany to Mary of Modena	
	1679 Covenanters defeated at Bothwell Bridge; James, duke of York and Albany arrives in Scotland
	1682 James leaves Scotland
1685 Death of Charles II; accession of James, duke of York and Albany as James VII and II	
1688 Birth of James Francis Edward Stuart; deposition of James VII and II; accession of William III and Mary II	
	1689 Jacobite rising, success at Killerkrankie, then defeat at Dunkeld; The Claim of Right and the re-establishment of Presbyterianism
	1692 Massacre of Glencoe
1694 Death of Mary II	
	1695 Bank of Scotland founded **Company** of Scotland founded
1701 Death of James VII and II	
1702 Death of William III; accession of Anne	
1705 Death of Catherine of Braganza	
	1707 Union of the parliaments of Scotland and England
1714 Death of Anne; accession of George I	
	1715 Jacobite rising
1718 Death of Mary of Modena	
1720 Birth of Charles Edward Stuart	
	1745 Jacobite rising ending at Culloden in 1746
1788 Death of Charles Edward Stuart	

The Evolution of Stuart Male Dress, 1560s–1690s

Taking linen neckwear as an example, men could select from a number of alternatives depending on their budget, age, taste and the occasion (Ashelford 1983; Cumming 1984).

DECADE	BODY GARMENTS	LEG WEAR	OUTERWEAR/ INFORMAL WEAR
1560–69 	**Doublets**: close fitting, developing the peasecod belly as the decade progresses, close buttoned, with a standing collar, straight sleeves with wings, could be cut in pickadil **Jerkins**: sleeveless, cut in panes down the chest, with standing collar, could be worn with or without the doublet	**Hose**: full, round, paned trunk hose with codpiece **Stockings**: often matching colour of trunk hose	**Gowns**: long with short sleeves **Cloaks**: hip length, sleeved or sleeveless, worn on both shoulders, could have a high collar **Nightgowns**: loose fitting, full length, often lined
1570–79 	**Doublets**: close fitting, with peasecod belly, buttoned down the front, high collar often with pickadil edging, full or straight sleeves with shoulder wings, with very small or non-existent skirts **Jerkins**: sleeveless, with shoulder wings, downward-pointing waistline and short, overlapping tabs	**Hose**: paned and often heavily paned trunk hose with canions, the codpiece barely noticeable **Breeches**: knee length, known as Venetians, in various styles including fitting, pear-shaped and full **Stockings**: plain and secured with tied garters	**Gowns**: short with fur guards, long with short sleeves **Cloaks**: hip length, sleeved or sleeveless, worn on both shoulders, could have a high collar **Nightgowns**: loose fitting, full length, often lined
1580–89 	**Doublets**: close fitting, buttoned down the front, low curved waistline, peasecod belly, almost no skirts	**Hose**: often very short trunk hose with canions, also wide trunk hose **Stockings**: plain and patterned	**Gowns**: long with short sleeves and hanging sleeves **Cloaks**: often worn on both or one shoulder **Mandilions**: a loose, hip-length garment often worn on one shoulder **Nightgowns**: loose fitting, full length, often lined with shag
1590–99 	**Doublets**: close buttoned down the front with a pronounced peasecod belly, trunk sleeves; as decade progresses the cut gets looser **Jerkins**: close buttoned down the front, with peasecod belly, sleeveless but with hanging sleeves	**Hose**: very short, paned trunk hose, sometimes with canions **Breeches**: fitted, pear-shaped and full Venetians **Stockings**: plain and fastened over the knee-band of the Venetians, boot hose worn to protect stockings when wearing boots	**Gowns**: full length with hanging sleeves with wings **Cloaks**: short and worn on both or one shoulder, lined with shag; longer and in the French style **Nightgowns**: loose fitting, full length, often lined

LINENS	ACCESSORIES
Shirts: not much visible under the doublet, some embroidered on the collar **Neckwear**: single, embroidered ruff, sometimes worn with a pickadil, could be left open at the front, with narrow wrist ruffles	**Hair**: short, often with a moustache and full beard or a small pointed beard **Headwear**: bonnets, with small brims, with feathers, crowned hats **Gloves**: plain leather **Belt** and **sword hanger** with **rapier** **Footwear**: flat shoes with rounded toes
Shirts: not much visible under the doublet, some with embroidery **Neckwear**: small, closed ruffs, lace-edged and falling bands, with wrist ruffles	**Hair**: short, often with a moustache and a small square-cut beard or clean-shaven **Headwear**: high-crowned bonnets, with feathers; crowned hats, getting taller, with a wide brim and feathers **Gloves**: gauntlet style **Belt** and **sword hanger** with **rapier** **Footwear**: flat shoes with rounded toes and slashed uppers
Shirts: not much visible under the doublet, some with V-shaped neck opening **Neckwear**: small, closed ruffs, cartwheel ruffs, lace-edged falling bands, embroidered falling bands, falling bands of cutwork, with matching cuffs	**Hair**: getting longer, often wavy, some with a lovelock on the left shoulder, small moustaches, full beards or pointed beards, some men clean-shaven **Headwear**: velvet bonnets with jewels and feathers, tall crowned hats or capotains, with hatbands and feathers **Gloves**: gauntlet style **Belt** and **sword hanger** with **rapier** **Footwear**: flat shoes with rounded or pointed toes, with pinked uppers, pantofles
Shirts: not much visible under the doublet **Neckwear**: large cartwheel ruffs, smaller ruffs worn with a falling band; plain, lace edged and embroidered falling bands with band strings, sometimes worn open	**Hair**: often short but some had a lovelock, or brushed back from the face, often with a moustache, and pointed or square-cut beards but some men clean-shaven **Headwear**: bonnets, tall crowned hats or capotains with fancy hatbands **Gloves**: plain, with fringed cuffs **Belt** and **sword hanger** with **rapier** **Footwear**: flat shoes with pointed and square toes and slashed uppers; close-fitting boots

DECADE	BODY GARMENTS	LEG WEAR	OUTERWEAR/ INFORMAL WEAR
1600–09 	**Doublets**: deep shoulder wings, longer tabs, just a hint of a peasecod belly **Jerkins**: fastened at the waist to reveal the doublet	**Hose**: padded, paned, trunk hose with canions **Breeches**: knee length or below the knee **Stockings**: with ribbon garters	**Gowns**: full length with hanging sleeves and wings **Cloaks**: shoulder cape often worn across one side of the body **Nightgowns**: loose fitting, full length, often lined
1610–19 	**Doublets**: close fitting, stiffened and padded, long waisted but getting shorter waisted **Jerkins**: could have false hanging sleeves	**Hose**: padded, paned, trunk hose, very full **Breeches**: knee length or below the knee, padded **Stockings**: often with decorative cloaks and fancy garters of ribbon and lace	**Gowns**: ankle length, fur-lined, short sleeves and hanging sleeves **Cloaks**: shoulder capes lined with shag or fur, knee or thigh length **Nightgowns**: loose fitting, full length, often lined
1620–29 	**Doublets**: looser fitting, no padding but with belly pieces, pointed waistline but rising, with longer tabs or skirts but less of them, sleeves full or paned, paned upper body of the doublet, decorative ribbon points	**Breeches**: loose, knee-length breeches replace hose **Stockings**: with decorated ribbon garters	**Gowns**: ankle length, fur-lined, short sleeves **Cloaks**: shoulder capes worn over the doublet, some fur-lined **Nightgowns**: loose fitting, full length, often lined
1630–39 	**Doublets**: shorter waisted, no padding but with belly pieces, tabs replaced by a deep basque, no points, sleeves full or paned, left unbuttoned	**Breeches**: moderately full, knee length; then getting wider at the knee and bulkier, later longer and looser; could be tucked into boots **Stockings**: protected by boot hose	**Cloaks**: shoulder capes, often matching the doublet and breeches **Buff jerkins**: sleeveless, partially laced, some edged with metal lace, gradually getting shorter **Nightgowns**: loose fitting, full length, often lined
1640–49 	**Doublets**: short, no padding but with belly pieces, loose fitting, often worn unbuttoned, front of sleeves left open, panes on the upper body of the doublet	**Breeches**: long, quite full, trimmed with ribbon at the waist and decoration on the side seams **Stockings**: boot hose	**Cloaks**: full, knee length, some with full capes by end of decade **Buff jerkins**: worn over the doublet **Nightgowns**: loose fitting, full length, often lined

LINENS	ACCESSORIES
Shirts: not much visible under the doublet **Neckwear**: narrow ruffs, lace-edged falling bands, with matching ruffles or cuffs	**Hair**: longer, a few having a lovelock, some small moustaches and beards **Headwear**: tall crowned hats with round brim, trimmed with feathers **Gloves**: plain, gauntlet, or with embroidered tabs **Belt** and **sword hanger** with **rapier** **Footwear**: flat shoes with shoe roses
Shirts: not much visible under the doublet **Neckwear**: small ruffs, layered ruffs, falling ruffs, large collars, with matching cuffs	**Hair**: short, or shorter hair often brushed away from the face, with a small beard and a moustache **Headwear**: tall crowned hats with round brim, trimmed with feathers **Gloves**: gauntlet style **Footwear**: heeled shoes with shoe roses; heeled boots
Shirts: not much visible under the doublet **Neckwear**: falling ruffs, falling bands, wide collars with rebatos or pickadils, with matching cuffs	**Hair**: longer for younger men, some with small pointed beard and moustache, some with a longer lock on one shoulder **Headwear**: beaver hats with shorter crown, softer wider brim **Gloves**: gauntlet style with applied braid and fringe; plain **Belt** and **sword hanger** with **rapier** **Footwear**: heeled shoes with shoe roses; heeled boots
Shirts: more is visible, especially the full sleeves **Neckwear**: wider lace-edged collars onto the shoulders, plain linen collars with matching cuffs	**Hair**: asymmetrical with a longer lock on the left shoulder, pointed beards; by late 1630s younger men clean-shaven and with long, full curls **Headwear**: beaver hats with a wider brim and feather **Gloves**: plain leather **Sword** suspended from a **shoulder hanger** not a belt; **walking stick** **Sashes**: silk **Footwear**: soft, heeled boots, developing creased tops, often worn with spurs
Shirts: a lot more is visible, especially the very full sleeves, and ruffle of lace on the front **Neckwear**: lace-edged collars, getting smaller; tied with band strings, linen more like a cravat with a plain collar, with plain cuffs	**Hair**: some asymmetrical styles still, shoulder length, clean-shaven or with small beard **Headwear**: high-crowned beaver hats with narrow brims, along with low-crowned, wide-brimmed versions **Gloves**: plain leather **Sashes**: silk **Footwear**: low-heeled shoes with a ribbon tie fastening; wide-topped boots

DECADE	BODY GARMENTS	LEG WEAR	OUTERWEAR/ INFORMAL WEAR
1650–59 	**Doublets**: short, less fitted, no padding but with belly pieces, elbow or full-length sleeves, centre-back and front of sleeves left open	**Breeches**: wide petticoat by mid 1650s, edged with ribbon loops **Stockings**: plain, protected with boot hose when wearing boots	**Cloaks**: deep-collared shoulder cape **Buff jerkins**: natural waistline, front lacing **Nightgowns**: loose fitting, full length, often lined
1660–69 	**Doublets**: short, no padding but with belly pieces, lots of ribbon **Coats**: loose, straight, worn open or buttoned, elbow-length sleeves developing upturned cuffs **Vests**: 1666: 'Persian', often matching the coat, long, straight cut **Waistcoats**: closely fitted	**Breeches**: petticoat above the knee, very full, lots of ribbon at the waist and lower edge; 1666: knee length **Stockings**: plain, ribbon garters	**Cloaks**: long cape worn with short doublet and petticoat breeches **Nightgowns**: or Indian gown, striped, loose fitting with wide sleeves
1670–79 	**Coats**: plain, quite loose, elbow length or slightly longer sleeves with cuffs that could be turned back, knots of ribbon on the shoulder and cuffs, low-buttoned pockets **Waistcoats**: long, sleeveless and long-sleeved versions; sleeved versions worn with cuffs turned back over the coat sleeves, not always worn	**Breeches**: wide petticoat with ribbon at the waist; close-fitted, quite short, getting fuller at the knee towards the end of the decade **Stockings**: plain, protected with boot hose when wearing boots	**Cloaks**: mostly for travel rather than fashionable wear; more fashionable capes had wide collars **Buff jerkins**: worn by some military men, laced at the front **Nightgowns**: loose, wrap front, tied with a sash
1680–89 	**Coats**: loose, wider at the waist, with or without lapels but becoming more structured by mid-decade, longer sleeves, with wide upturned cuffs, vertical or horizontal pocket flaps, ribbon shoulder knot **Waistcoats**: knee length, sleeveless and long-sleeved	**Breeches**: full, gradually replaced by narrower **Stockings**: plain, protected with boot hose when wearing boots	**Cloaks**: mostly for travel rather than fashionable wear **Brandenburgs**: loose-fitting overcoat/greatcoat **Nightgowns**: loose, wrap front, tied with a sash
1690–99 	**Coats**: closer fitting, with the full skirts formed into side and back pleats, longer sleeves with deep cuffs, horizontal pocket flaps, shoulder ribbons, decorated with frogging; looser styles still available **Waistcoats**: sleeveless and long-sleeved; sleeved versions worn with cuffs turned back over the coat sleeves not always worn	**Breeches**: loose fitting, gathered at the knee **Stockings**: rolled over the edge of the breeches at the knee	**Cloaks**: mostly for travel rather than fashionable wear **Brandenburgs**: loose-fitting overcoat/greatcoat **Nightgowns**: silk, wide sleeves, wrap over front, ankle length, worn with mules

LINENS	ACCESSORIES
Shirts: full with full long sleeves with ruffles **Neckwear**: small falling collars with decorative band strings, matching cuffs	**Hair**: shoulder length, some small beards, others clean-shaven **Headwear**: hats with high crowns and narrow brims, decorated with feathers **Gloves**: trimmed with ribbon, braid, bows and fringe **Sashes**: silk **Footwear**: long-fronted, square-toed shoes tied with ribbon; soft boots with heels for riding
Shirts: very full with full sleeves **Neckwear**: falling collars edged with lace, long linen band with lace edges knotted at the neck, with matching, wide cuffs	**Hair**: longer, fuller, more curly with symmetrical locks on the chest and back; use of false hair, curled wigs; thin moustaches **Headwear**: tall crowned hats with wide brims with feathers and ribbon, small hats with low crowns and small brim **Gloves**: usually trimmed with ribbon, braid, bows and fringe **Footwear**: narrow, square-toed shoes, heels and soft ribbon bows; boots for riding, with boot hose
Shirts: lace-edged fronts, full sleeves, small collar **Neckwear**: linen bands, lace bands, linen and lace cravats, tiered cravats of linen and lace	**Hair**: full, long, curled wigs **Headwear**: beaver hats with large brims, with mid-height to shallow crown **Gloves**: fringed **Muffs**: large, made of fur Broad **sash** as **sword hanger** **Footwear**: square-toed shoes with a deep tongue and buckles; boots for riding
Shirts: full and with narrower sleeves, in response to longer coat sleeves; also with very full sleeves, with ruffled cuffs **Neckwear**: loosely gathered cravats, cravats worn with a flat bow, cravats with ribbons	**Hair**: full, long, curled wigs with a middle parting, clean-shaven **Headwear**: beaver hats with large brims, upturned, with mid-height crown; from c. 1680 no longer worn indoors **Gloves**: plain, then fringed Diagonal **sword hanger** and **sash** **Walking stick** or **cane** **Footwear**: more fitted, high-fronted shoes with a buckle and heels, red heels at court
Shirts: sleeves with ruffles that are visible under the longer coat sleeves **Neckwear**: plain linen cravat tied in the Steinkerk style; lace and ribbon cravat for formal wear; fringed linen cravats	**Hair**: long, curled wig with two high points at the front **Headwear**: hats with large brims, upturned, with low- to mid-height crown, no longer visible, the tricorne **Gloves**: fringed with bullion fringe, lace edged **Muffs**: large, made of fur **Sword belt** and **hanger**, under the coat but over the waistcoat, if worn **Walking stick** or **cane** **Footwear**: more fitted shoes with a heel, red heels at court

Glossary

band/falling band – standing neckband with a collar attached, available in a variety of styles including a falling band or turned-down collar, along with wide and deep versions
band strings – linen tasselled ties to fasten a shirt, ruff or falling band
beaver – the fur of the beaver was felted to make hats known as 'beavers'
bobbin lace – also known as pillow and bone lace; the individual threads are pinned to a pillow and attached to a bobbin and by manipulating the bobbins, the lace is formed by crossing and intertwining the threads
bonnet – very popular soft form of men's headwear, with a brim and crown, often knitted and felted
boot hose – linen overstocking often with decorative tops, worn to protect the stockings/hose from rubbing when wearing boots
boots – footwear, usually made of leather, and usually to the knee or just above
Brandenburg – loose overcoat or surtout
breeches/breiks/breikis – short, often close-fitting garment worn on the lower body, coming to just below the knee, front fastening
buckram/buckasie – coarse fabric made of stiffened linen or hemp, used as a stiffening and a lining
caddas/cadis – light-weight wool fabric
calico – printed cotton fabric
cambric – lightweight, fine, plain-weave linen
camlet – mixed fabric often combining goat hair with wool or silk
canions – extensions to the hose that extended down the thighs; could be various lengths
capotain – sugar-loaf-shaped hat with a tall crown, made from blocked felt
clocks – vertical decoration on the ankle of a stocking
cloth – plain-weave woollen fabric
coat/cote/coit – upper body garment, front fastening with long or elbow-length sleeves
codpiece – attached at the front of the hose by points to conceal the front opening
cramosie – crimson
cravat – strip of linen wrapped round the neck and tied with a bow or a know
crêpe/crape – thin silk gauze or silk and worsted mix used for mourning
damask – patterned textile with a warp and a weft, the pattern created by contrasting binding systems; can be reversible
doublet/dowblet – short, fitted upper body garment with long sleeves worn over the shirt
dule – mourning
feuillemort/filemot/philmote – colour like that of a dead or faded leaf
fustian – union cloth with a linen warp and a cotton weft
garters – usually made from ribbon, or a length of fine silk fabric, tied round the knee to hold up stockings
grisdeline – from the French *gris de lin*, 'grey of flax', 'flax grey'; the colour pale purple or grey violet, occasionally a pale red
grosgrain – silk (or silk and wool/silk and hair) fabric with a ribbed effect created by using a thin silk warp and a thick weft of silk or cotton; often used for ribbons
hanger – often highly decorative, a belt or straps from a belt to suspend a sword from
harden – coarse/heavy-weight linen
harn – coarse linen made from refuse hemp or flax
Holland – medium-weight linen cloth
hose/hois – garment that covered the male body from the feet to the waist, or to above the knees; could be knitted or cut from cloth on the bias
jerkin/jupe – sleeved or sleeveless garment, often worn over a doublet
justaucorps – knee-length coat worn over a vest or waistcoat of similar length
kelt – homespun black or grey cloth or frieze
lawn – very fine linen
lovelock – long curl of hair worn over one shoulder
lutestring – lightweight and very shiny plain weave or tabby silk; a silk ribbon
mandilion – short, loose jacket with a collar and hanging sleeves
mantle – (1) when part of a set of ceremonial robes, a long robe, open at the front; (2) length of fabric, worn round the shoulders, such as the Irish mantle
metal thread – made in several ways: (1) beaten foil cut in strips; (2) foil strips twined together; (3) foil strips wrapped round a fibre core; (4) foil stuck to parchment or paper and cut in strips
mohair – made from Angora goat hair
mules – backless, heeled shoe usually for indoor wear
muslin – very fine, semi-transparent cotton
nightcap – linen cap, often embroidered, worn by men indoors

nightgown/loose robe/Indian gown – all terms for a loose gown worn on informal occasions, usually at home but not always
Norwich stuff – woven textiles, usually worsteds associated with Norwich
paduasoy – fine wool or silk with a tabby weave, popular from the late seventeenth century
pand – a valance, often associated with beds or clothes of estate
panes, paned – (1) separate strips of fabric joined at the top and bottom to make hose and sleeves; (2) long vertical cuts on the upper section of sleeves, doublet fronts
pantofles – high-heeled slippers
passements/passementerie – trimmings of gold or silver lace
peasecod – style of doublet with heavily padded lower fronts creating the rounded, 'peasecod' belly
periwig/wig – worn over a shaved head, the wig came to replace most men's natural hair
petticoat breeches – also called Rhinegraves
pickadil – (1) a wired or soft support for a standing band; (2) small tabs used to create a decorative border, e.g. on the knee-band of breeches or wings on doublets and jerkins
pile on pile velvet – velvet with cut or uncut pile in two or more heights to create a pattern
pinking – a technique for decorating the ground of a fabric with a pattern of small holes or decorating the edges
plaid – a length of cloth (*breacan*) and when worn, belted, called a *feilidh*, worn from the late sixteenth century
plaiding – type of woollen cloth plaids were made from
plush – silk fabric with a long cut pile, in the style of velvet
points – ties with metal ends or tags
Provincials – type of breeches
quhyt – white
rapier – light, thin, sharp-pointed sword
ruff – linen neckwear starched into decorative shapes, could be multi-layered
sark – male or female body garment worn next to the skin; a shirt
satin – fabric, often of silk, with a shiny surface created by floating warp threads
serge – light-weight twill cloth of worsted or wool
shag – pile fabric often used for linings
shoe buckles – from the late 1650s, when they were small and oval, very common after the 1680 when they were large and square, used to fasten shoes
shoe roses – a rosette of ribbon, lace or fabric used to conceal the shoe ties
shoes/schone – footwear, not reaching above the ankle, often with a heal, and changing from a rounded to a square toe
short sword – while longer than a dagger, the blade was usually shorter than a metre (3 feet)
slashing – a decorative technique for cutting fabric with a series of slashes or cuts in order to reveal the lining below, which was often of a contrasting colour
stand – a set of garments, such as a doublet, hose and cloak
Steinkirk – loose style of tying a cravat, with both ends pushed through a buttonhole, allegedly related to the battle of Steinkirk in 1692
stenting – stiffening; often poldavie canvas
stockings/shanks – covered the foot and leg, either knee length or full length
stuff – worsted fabric
suit – a set of toning, matching or accompanying garments, such as a doublet and hose
swaddling/swaddling bands – strips of linen to wrap a baby, usually placed over a shirt
tabby – plain tabbies were known as Florentine, mantua, taffeta; from the late seventeenth century, a watered silk
tabs – overlapping panels making up the skirts of a doublet
taffeta – a plain weave silk with a stiff crisp feel and bright lustrous surface
tartan – a type of cloth, sometimes made of more than one colour, a checked or coloured cloth but by *c.*1600 a striped, wool fabric
tissue – lampas, a patterned textile with weft floats bound by the binding warp on the ground formed by the main warp and weft
toilet/tollat claith – a cloth, often very decorative, used to cover a dressing or toilet table, or to wrap clothes in
trews/truis/triubhas – made from tartan, cut on the bias, very distinctive form of tight-fitting legwear
trunk hose – very full round short hose, often paned
velvet – pile weave; could be figured, stamped, and with several heights of pile
Venetians – knee-length breeches that could be close fitting or full
vest – a sleeved or sleeveless garment often worn under a man's coat from the 1660s
waistcoat/wylecote/wylicoit – (1) informal sleeved or sleeveless garment worn under the doublet; (2) sleeved or sleeveless garment often worn under a man's coat from the 1660s
whinger/whinyard – a short sword or hanger

Conversion Details

MEASUREMENTS

Scottish ell	37 inches (93.9 cm)
English ell	45 inches/1¼ yards (114.3 cm)
English yard	36 inches (91.4 cm)

MONEY

£1 was the equivalent of 20 shillings and each shilling was worth 12 pence.

In 1603 a pound Scots was worth one-twelfth of a pound sterling.

A Scottish merk – valued at 13s 4d, was worth two-thirds of a pound Scots. It·was later raised to 14s. It was worth approximately one English shilling.

Abbreviations

APS – Thomson, Thomas and Cosmo Innes (eds), 1814–75, *The Acts of the Parliaments of Scotland*, 12 vols (Edinburgh: Record Commission)
CBP – Bain, Joseph (ed.), 1894–96, *Calendar of Letters and Papers Relating to the Affairs of the Borders of England and Scotland, 1560–1603*, 2 vols (Edinburgh: General Register House)
CSPD – Lemon, Robert et al. (eds), 1856–1939, *Calendar of State Papers, Domestic Series*, 94 vols (London: Longmans, Brown, Green, Longmans Roberts)
CSP Ireland – Mahaffy, Robert Pentland (ed.), 1871, *Calendar of State Papers Relating to Ireland, 1625–32* (London: HMSO)
CSP Venetian – Brown, Rawdon et al., 1864–1940, *Calendar of State Papers and Manuscripts Relating to English Affairs, Existing in the Archives and Collections of Venice*, 38 vols (London: HMSO)
EHR – *English Historical Review*
HJ – *Historical Journal*
HMC – Historical Manuscripts Commission
IR – *Innes Review*
JWCI – *Journal of the Warburg and Courtauld Institutes*
LP – Brewer, John Sherren, James Gairdner and Robert Henry Brodie (eds), 1862–1932, *Letters and Papers, Foreign and Domestic, of the Reign of Henry VIII, 1509–1547*, 21 vols and addenda (London: HMSO)
PSAS – *Proceedings of the Society of Antiquaries of Scotland*
RPC – Burton, John Hill et al. (eds), 1882–1970, *Register of the Privy Council of Scotland*, 38 vols (Edinburgh: H. M. General Register House)
SHR – *Scottish Historical Review*
SR – Alexander Luders et al. (eds), 1810–28, *The Statutes of the Realm*, 11 vols (London: HMSO)
TRHS – *Transactions of the Royal Historical Society*

LIBRARIES/RECORD OFFICES/MUSEUMS & GALLERIES

Bod. Lib. – Bodleian Library, Oxford
BL – British Library, London
Broth. Lib. – Brotherton Library, University of Leeds
CUL – Cambridge University Library
DHC – Dorset History Centre, Dorchester
Folger – Folger Shakespeare Library, Washington, DC
NAL – National Art Library, Victoria and Albert Museum, London
NGS – National Galleries of Scotland, Edinburgh
NLS – National Library of Scotland, Edinburgh
NMS – National Museums Scotland
NPG – National Portrait Gallery, London
NRAS – National Register of Archives for Scotland
NRO – Northamptonshire Record Office, Northampton
NUL – Nottingham University Library
NRS – National Records of Scotland, Edinburgh
PG – Portrait Gallery
RC – Royal Collection
RCIN – Royal Collection Inventory Number
SoA – Society of Antiquaries of London
TNA – The National Archive, Kew
UoG – University of Glasgow, Special Collection
V&A – Victoria and Albert Museum, London

Notes

Introduction

1 Ribeiro 2005 and Reynolds 2013.
2 E.g. Vincent 2003.
3 Adams and Goodare 2014, p. 1.
4 Pitcairn 1817, p. ii.
5 Lowenthal 1999, pp. 46–7.
6 See Elliott 1992.
7 NRS GD406/1/8017.
8 Morrill 1997, p. 11.
9 Murray 1966, pp. 89–104; Wemyss 2014, pp. 39–53.
10 For the Scottish nobility see Brown 2000.
11 Especially in Chapters 1, 11 and 12.
12 Stewart 2013, p. 33.
13 MacDonald 2005.
14 NRS GD112/39/24/3.
15 Colley 1992, p. 6.
16 Cust 2013 and more broadly see Vale 1977 and Bryson 1998.
17 For Pepys, see and Staniland 2003 and 2005.
18 Smuts 1987, p. 104.
19 Pellumbi 2017, p. 32.
20 Fischlin and Fortier 1996, p. 161.
21 Fraser 1892, p. 168.
22 V&A T.711:1, 2–1995.
23 TNA AO3/919 1673, p. 9.
24 Gibson 1997.
25 Ollard 1979, p. 19.
26 Murray 2017.
27 NRS E35/13, May 1590–May 1592 account, f. 17v; TNA AO3/909/5, f. 2r and AO3/910/6, p. 1.
28 See Byrde 1979, Cumming 1984 and Marly 1985.
29 See Tiramani et al. 2016, pp. 14–19; Waugh 1964, pp. 14–33, 52–85.
30 McClure 1939, vol. 1, p. 250.
31 Owen 1628, p. 31.
32 Pittock 1991, pp. 1–6.
33 Pittock 2013; Guthrie 2014.
34 Perry 2006, p. 155.
35 Perry 2006, p. 160.
36 Richardson 1977, p. 35.
37 Cuddy 1989, p. 122.
38 Wormald 1992, p. 193.
39 Thomson 1842–9, vol. 7, p. 396.
40 Doran 2015, p. 2.
41 Arnold 1988, pp. 110–62; Ashelford 1988, pp. 11–42.
42 E.g. see Williams 1997, p. 357.
43 Quoted in Williams 1997, pp. 357–8.
44 Patterson 2009, p. 114.
45 Greenblatt 1981, pp. 1–9.
46 Richardson 2014, p. 43.
47 For the latter, see McClure 1939.
48 Norrington 1996, p. 36.
49 Woodall 1997, p. 12; Marshall 1981.
50 Castiglione 1976, p. 64.
51 Wilton 1992, no. 4, pp. 70–71.
52 Wilton 1992, p. 12.
53 Wilton 1992, p. 15.
54 Wilton 1992, p. 17.
55 Bailey 2007, pp. 10–13.
56 Anon. 1832, p. 435.
57 Cramsie 2015, p. 264.
58 Hume Brown 1973, p. 232.
59 Quotations retain the original spelling and word use.
60 Macmillan 1990, 2nd edn 2000, pp. 37–89.
61 E.g. Tarrant 2001a, pp. 319–26; Robinson 2015, pp. 8–31.
62 Pittock 1998, p. 1.
63 Cressy 1997, p. 6.
64 Wardle 2002.
65 Pittock 1998, p. 29.
66 See Corp 2009 and Corp 2014.
67 Canterbury Cathedral Archives and Library, Lit MS/E/39, p. 51.
68 Lunger Knoppers 1998 and Little 2008.

Part I

1 This is not the case for James Francis Edward Stuart and Charles Edward Stuart, a key reason for not extending the scope of *Stuart Style* to 1788.
2 Swain 1973, p. 29; Carpenter and Runnalls 2000, pp. 145–61.
3 See Finn 2000.
4 Hume Brown 1973, p. 260.
5 Hume Brown 1973, p. 272.
6 Hume Brown 1973, p. 231.
7 Henshall 1954.
8 *RPC, 1616–19*, p. 52.
9 Harte 1976, p. 150.
10 Chisholm 1891, pp. 290–97; Shaw 1979, pp. 81–115; Hayward 2019, 96–120.
11 Bruce 1861, pp. 31–2.
12 Hume Brown 1973, p. 44.
13 For example *APS* III, 220, c.18; 1581/10/37.
14 Grange 1966; Maxwell and Hutchinson 1958.
15 Lythe 1960, p. 124.
16 Maidment 1837, p. 327.
17 *RPC, 1616–19*, p. 235.
18 Fraser 1892, no. 347, p. 359.
19 Nenadic 2007, p. 42.
20 Fischlin and Fortier 1996, p. 119.
21 Hume Brown 1973, p. 142.
22 McClintock 1949 and 1950; Dunbar 1979.
23 Hume Brown 1973, p. 121.
24 Ohlmeyer 1993a, p. 18.
25 In 1697 Lord Mungo Murray went in search of Simon Fraser, Lord Lovat, 'in a belted plad to the admiration which did encourage the men much'; see Stewart-Murray 1908, pp. 441–2.
26 Anon. 1832, p. 435.
27 NRS GD158/2748.
28 NRS GD170/329; Nenadic 2007, p. 42.
29 NRS GD112/39/149/7.
30 Nenadic 2007, p. 152.
31 *RPC, 1616–19*, p. 74. For the sword girdle and hanger, see Tiramani et al. 2016, pp. 80–87.
32 NRS GD45/16/3028.
33 Hume Brown 1973, p. 260.
34 Blair 1981, pp. 153–252; also Caldwell 1981, pp. 253–314.
35 NRS GD44/49/13/1, no. 8.
36 NRS GD124/18/1.
37 Cheape 2006, pp. 16–17; also Cheape and Quye 2005, pp. 202–7.
38 NRS GD112/29/51, no. 14; GD112/15/74, no. 23.
39 NRS GD112/29/51, no. 6.
40 Lynch 1991, p. 299. His reference links to Stevenson 1980, pp. 294–5, but this is talking about Argyll and Lochiel, which is the sentence preceding the reference to tartanry.
41 NRS GD112/35/10, no. 13.
42 NRS GD112/15/39A, no. 1.
43 Holloway 1989, p. 30.
44 See, for example, McDowell 2006.
45 From Joseph Ritson's 'North Country Chorister' cited in Seton 1882, p. 54.
46 Bartley 1954, p. 80; Lublin 2011, p. 113.
47 Bartley 1954, p. 5.
48 Folger MS V.a.345, pp. 287–8.
49 In 1666, 18 & 19 Cha. II c. 4 (*SR*, vol. 5, p. 598), 1678 30 Cha. II c. 3 (*SR*, vol. 5, pp. 885–6), and 1680 32 Cha. II c. 1 (*SR*, vol. 5, p. 940). Cf. Chapter 12, which discusses acts for burial and Scottish linen.
50 Hentschell 2008, pp. 108–19.
51 NRS GD112/29/15, no. 36.
52 Boorde 1562, A3v.
53 Defoe 1701, p. 13.
54 E.g. Hibbert 1993.
55 Stoyle 2005, p. 6.
56 Berg and Lagercrantz 1962, p. 79.
57 See Williams 1990 and Breward 2009, pp. 33–4.
58 Ward 1622.
59 Bremer 2009, pp. 51, 54.
60 Perkins 1608, p. 97; Cressy 2000, pp. 255–6.
61 Hervey 1904, p. 250.

62 Hervey 1904, p. 252.
63 Unknown imitator of Daniel Mytens, *Edward Lewkenor*, *c.*1630, oil on canvas, 164.7 × 99 cm, Norfolk Museums Service (Ancient House Museum, Thetford); see Moore with Crawley, 1992, pp. 87–8, pl. 58.
64 Marshall 1972, p. 33.
65 Harvey 1995, pp. 71–2.
66 McGavin 2007, pp. 18–19.
67 Rudrum, Black and Nelson 2001, p. 617.
68 Stoyle 2005, pp. 73–90, 198–208.
69 Spalding 1830, p. 381.
70 See Murdoch 2001. While the text described the troops as Irish, they were Scots; see Grimble 1961, pp. 23–38.
71 See Glozier 2004.
72 Stoyle 2002, p. 60.
73 Newman 1983, pp. 952–3.
74 NRS RH15/14/197.
75 See also Stevenson 1981, p. 347.
76 Cust and Hind 1933–4, p. 161.
77 *Thomas, 6th earl of Haddington*, 1694, oil on canvas, 123.2 × 96.5 cm, Earl of Haddington; *John, 8th Earl of Rothes*, 1694, oil on canvas, 116.8 × 96.5 cm, private collection; and *Charles, 1st Earl of Hopetoun*, 1694, oil on canvas, 127 × 100 cm, Earl of Haddington.
78 Holloway 1989, p. 23, fig. 13.
79 Strong 1986, p. 154.
80 Scott 1735, p. 51.
81 Harrison 1941, p. 286.
82 Nichols 1828, vol. 2, p. 78.
83 Bartley 1954, p. 80.
84 Orgel and Strong 1973, vol. 1, p. 395, no. 140.
85 Birch 1848, vol. 1, p. 324.
86 *CSP Venetian, 1629–32*, p. 593.
87 TNA E403/2752, AO3/910/2 and AO3/910/4.
88 Cliffe 1984, p. 151.
89 Loftis 1978, pp. 24–5.
90 NRS GD406/1/11718.
91 Bartley 1954, p. 81.
92 Bowers 1968, p. 88.
93 Hume Brown 1973, p. 120.
94 NRS E21/34, f. 63v. See also Marshall 1994, p. 16.
95 NRS GD112/39/49/12.
96 Hume Brown 1973, p. 121.

Chapter 1

1 For James V, see Rush 2006.
2 Wormald 1983, pp. 187–8.
3 Peck 1991, p. 1; Peck 2005, p. 164.
4 Bruce 1849, pp. 68–9.
5 Wormald 1991, p. 49.
6 Fischlin and Fortier 1996, p. 160.
7 Croft 2003, p. 43.
8 McIlwain 1918, p. 343.
9 Quoted in Mathews 1955, p. 52.
10 NRS E23/3, no. 20.
11 Thomson 1827, p. 134.
12 Fyfe 1928, pp. 37–8.
13 NRS E23/3, no. 10.
14 NRS E23/3, no. 32.
15 BL Royal 18 C xiv, ff. 207r–v.
16 Swain 1973, pp. 86, 122, pls 88 and 89.
17 Blakeway 2015, p. 147.
18 NRS E21/58, f. 34r.
19 NRS E21/58, f. 102r.
20 NRS E21/60, f. 61r.
21 NRS E23/3, no. 46. See also E21/57, f. 20r.
22 NRS E21/60, f. 52v.
23 NRS E21/60, f. 52r.
24 NRS E21/60, f. 36v.
25 NRS E21/60, ff. 74r, 139r.
26 NRS E21/60, f. 180v.
27 Ashelford 1988, p. 58 and fig. 35.
28 NRS E21/72, ff. 25v, 78r.
29 NRS E22/2, f. 62v.
30 NRS E22/2, ff. 135r–v.
31 Thomson 1815, pp. 250–52.
32 Swain 1973, p. 86.
33 NRS E22/3, ff. 84v–85r.
34 NRS E22/5, pp. 178, 181.
35 NRS E35/13, unfoliated.
36 NRS E35/13, unfoliated.
37 NRS E35/13, unfoliated.
38 NRS E35/13, ff. 16v–17r.
39 Patterson 2000, pp. 10-11.
40 Houston 1995, p. 116.
41 Stevenson 1997, pp. 91–2.
42 Stevenson 1997, p. 92.
43 NRS E35/13, unfoliated.
44 NRS E35/13, unfoliated.
45 Croft 2003, p. 33.
46 Wormald 1983, p. 197.
47 NRS E35/13, unfoliated.
48 HMC 1874, p. 527.
49 NRS GD150/formerly box 148.
50 NRS GD150/2727, no. 7.
51 *CBP, 1560–94*, p. 531.
52 Quoted Wormald 1983, pp. 190, 204.
53 Wormald 1983, p. 204.
54 NRS E21/76, ff. 259v–261v.
55 Folger MS X.d.75, no. 8.
56 Stone 1965, p. 563, cited in Jones and Stallybrass 2000, p. 21.
57 Folger MS X.d.75, no. 8.
58 TNA LC9/94, f. 34r.
59 Folger MS X.d.75, no. 8.
60 TNA AO1/2048/2, ff. 8v, 9v.
61 Cumming 1984, p. 23.
62 BL Add. MS 75,303, unfoliated.
63 *CSP Venetian, 1617–19*, p. 79.
64 Daniel Mytens, *James VI and I*, 1621, oil on canvas, 148.6 × 100.6 cm, National Portrait Gallery, London, NPG 109.
65 Pittock 2013, pp. 79, 169.
66 Birch 1849, vol. 2, p. 171.
67 Brown 1993, p. 552.
68 NRS E35/13.
69 Hayward 2012a, p. xix.
70 Sanderson 1987, p. 80.
71 NRS E35/13, unfoliated.
72 Schreiber 1984, p. 7.
73 Wormald 1983, p. 207; Shepard 2015, pp. 1–2.
74 Nichols 1828, vol. 2, p. 189.
75 Croft 1999, p. 90.
76 BL Stowe MS 555, f. 2v.
77 Akrigg 1984, p. 288.
78 Schreiber 1984, p. 6.
79 *CSP Venetian, 1607–10*, no. 918, p. 494; *CSP Venetian, 1610–13*, no. 758, p. 489.
80 McClure 1939, vol. 2, pp. 13–14.
81 Nichols 1828, vol. 3, p. 183.
82 Seddon 1975–86, vol. 1, pp. 125–6.
83 *CSP Venetian, 1621–3*, no. 126, p. 105.
84 Nichols 1828, vol. 3, p. 309.
85 *RPC, 1616–19*, p. 66.
86 For the progress see McNeill and McNeill 1996.
87 Nichols 1828, vol. 3, p. 345.
88 Marcus Gheeraerts the younger, *Alexander Seton, 1st Earl of Dunfermline*, 1610, oil on canvas, 115.5 × 88.2 cm, Scottish National Galleries, PG 2176.
89 HMC 1930, p. 84.
90 *CSPD James I, 1603–10*, p. 65.
91 Croft 1999, p. 89.
92 BL Harley MS 6272, f. 170.
93 See Mactaggart and Mactaggart 1980.
94 Castiglione 1976, p. 111.
95 Smuts 1987, pp. 101–4.
96 HMC 1968, p. 273.
97 *CSPD, James I, 1611–18*, p. 421.
98 *CSP Venetian, 1617–19*, pp. 60–61.
99 NRS GD3/13/2/1/2.
100 NRS E22/3, f. 86v.
101 Barroll 1998, p. 122.
102 NRS E35/13, accounts for 1590–92, ff. 19r–v.
103 Schreiber 1984, p. 10.
104 Young 1987, p. 38.
105 Harrison 1941, p. 74.
106 *CSP Ireland, 1625–32*, p. 64.
107 Houston 1995, p. 117.
108 TNA AO3/1115 (1603–4), unfoliated.
109 TNA LC9/95, f. 39v.
110 Fischlin and Fortier 1996, p. 161.
111 Jones and Stallybrass 2000, p. 75.
112 Wilson 1956, p. 165.
113 See Tiramani et al. 2016, pp. 48–79.

Chapter 2

1 TNA AO3/909/2, pp. 73–4.
2 TNA AO3/909/2, pp. 71, 85.
3 BL Royal MS 18.B.IV; Fischlin and Fortier 1996, pp. 159–60.
4 For the meaning of 'candy' soldier, see Fischlin 1995, pp. 357–61.
5 NRS GD124/10/67.
6 NRS GD124/10/69; Seton 1916, pp. 259, 366–79.
7 NRS GD124/10/68.
8 NRS GD124/10/71.
9 NRS E35/13, accounts for 1596/7, ff. 23r–25v.

10 E.g. NRS E21/72, ff. 39r–v.
11 NRS E21/73, f. 63r.
12 NRS E21/76, f. 160v.
13 NRS E35/13, accounts for 1594/5, f. 1r.
14 NRS E35/13, accounts for 1596/7, ff. 24v–25r.
15 NRS E35/13, accounts for 1596/7, f. 25r.
16 NRS E21/73, f. 106r.
17 NRS E21/74, f. 50r.
18 Thomson 1842–9, vol. 6, p. 230.
19 W. H. 1634, sig. A3.
20 Croft 2003, p. 55.
21 Barroll 1991, p. 199.
22 TNA AO3/1115 1603–4, unfoliated.
23 TNA AO3/909/2, p. 33. It cost £11 12s 7d.
24 TNA AO3/909/2, p. 24. It cost £24 6s 8d.
25 TNA AO3/909/2, p. 42.
26 TNA AO3/909/2, p. 70.
27 Ribeiro 2005, pp. 27–9.
28 TNA AO3/909/1, p. 23.
29 See V&A 378-1898; Hart and North 1998, p. 168.
30 For a comparable example, see Hart and North 1998, p. 178.
31 TNA LC9/95, f. 45r.
32 TNA E101/433/8, f. 19r.
33 Sawyer 1725, p. 182.
34 Cited in McCullough 1998, p.191.
35 Bellany 2002, p. 32.
36 Nichols 1828, vol. 2, p. 34.
37 Harrison 1958, p. 216.
38 Strong 1986, p. 154.
39 *CSP Venetian, 1607–10*, p. 516.
40 Cumming 1989a, p. 18. See also Field 2017.
41 Nichols 1828, vol. 1, p. 190.
42 Barroll 2001, pp. 119, 131.
43 Herford and Simpson 1932, p. 33.
44 Puttenham, Willcock and Walker 1589/1936, p. 285.
45 Trinity College, Cambridge, MS R.7.23* (3), f. 6r.
46 W. H. 1634, p. 9.
47 Strong 1986, p. 14.
48 Pittock 2000, p. 21.
49 Salmon 1991, p. 177.
50 *CSP Venetian, 1603–7*, p. 513.
51 Young 1987, pp. 37–8.
52 Smuts 1991, p. 109.
53 Nichols 1828, vol. 2, p. 80.
54 Chambers 1936, p. 212.
55 Royal Collection, RCIN 72831. See also Evans 1998, pp. 37–8.
56 Orgel and Strong 1973, vol. 1, p. 194.
57 Nichols 1828, vol. 2, p. 270, n. 3.
58 TNA E403/2730, ff. 181v–182r, and E403/2729, f. 137; Young 1987, pp. 57–8.
59 Barroll 2001, p. 76.
60 Barroll 2001, p. 80.
61 Smuts 1991, p. 109.
62 McKerrow 1966, p. 142; Ashelford 1988, p. 122.
63 Bacon 1955, essay no. 37, p. 115.
64 Bacon 1955, essay no. 37, p. 115.
65 TNA E403/2730 f. 181v, AO1/2021/2; Wiggins and Richardson 2015, pp. 105–10, esp. p. 107.
66 Ravelhofer 2009, p. 169.
67 Harrison 1941, pp. 39–40.
68 Ravelhofer 2009, p. 116.
69 Rye 1865, p. 123.
70 Bailey 2007, p. 21.
71 Breward 1995, p. 78.
72 *CSP Venetian, 1610–13*, p. 129.
73 Barroll 2001, p. 81.
74 Bellany 2002, p. 43.
75 Duncan-Jones 1997, pp. 52–69.
76 Barroll 2001, p. 68.
77 Orgel and Strong 1973, vol. 1, p. 67.
78 Peck 1991, p. 166.
79 Ashton 1969, pp. 234–5.
80 Nichols 1828, vol. 2, p. 412.
81 Hearn 1995, p. 198.
82 Marshall 1986, p. 13.
83 Young 2000, p. 5.
84 Furnivall 1877–9, p. 54.
85 Bailey 2007, p. 6.
86 Strong 1986, p. 16.
87 Stone 1965, p. 584; Smuts 1991, p. 9.
88 Unknown artist, *George Carew, earl of Totnes*, 1619–20, oil on canvas, 127 × 102.9 cm, National Portrait Gallery, London, NPG 409.
89 Seddon 1975–86, vol. 1, pp. 62–3, no. 153.
90 TNA LC9/93, f. 37v.
91 Harrison 1958, p. 19.
92 Bellany 2002, p. 169.
93 BL Add. MS 25,348, f. 3v.
94 Harrington 1804, p. 392.
95 *CSP Venetian, 1610–13*, p. 135.
96 Harrison 1958, p. 58.
97 Harrison 1958, pp. 92–3.
98 Harrington 1804, p. 392.
99 Bellany 2002, p. 160.
100 Folger, Loseley MS, L.B. 638, ff. 6v–8r; Peck 1991, p. 167.
101 Folger, Loseley MS, L.B. 638, f. 7v.
102 Folger, Loseley MS, L.B. 638, f. 11r.
103 Marshall 1994, p. 14.
104 TNA AO3/909/2, p. 53.
105 Birch 1760, p. 65; Strong 1986, p. 66.
106 Nichols 1828, vol. 2, p. 268.
107 Harrison 1958, p. 216.
108 For example, Barroll 2001, pp. 12, 133–5, 140, 142–8.
109 McClure 1939, vol. 1, pp. 359–60.
110 HMC 1930, pp. 40–41.
111 Strong 1986, p. 56.
112 *CSP Venetian, 1610–13*, pp. 122–3.
113 Strong 1986, p. 13.
114 TNA AO3/909/2, p. 45.
115 TNA AO3/909/2, pp. 44, 50.
116 TNA AO3/909/1, p. 41; CUL MS Dd.1.26, f. 24r.
117 *CSPD, James I, 1603–10*, p. 488.
118 TNA AO3/909/2, p. 58.
119 CUL MS Dd.1.26, f. 21r.
120 TNA AO3/909/2, p. 58.
121 Lindley 2000, p. 50.
122 Bray 1806, pp. 19–20.
123 McClure 1939, vol. 1, p. 423. See also Cumming 1978, pp. 315–28; Madden 1836, pp. 380–94.
124 McClure 1939, vol. 1, p. 423; Ribeiro 2005, p. 31.
125 Jones and Stallybrass 2000, p. 38.
126 Bray 1806, p. 19.

Chapter 3

1 Staniland 1999, pp. 41–3.
2 Ringgaard 2014, pp. 76–7.
3 Purkiss 2005, p. 85.
4 Peck 1991, p. 156.
5 NRS GD406/1/327, no. 1; Scally 1997, pp. 18–19.
6 Strong 1980, p. 73; Sharpe 1996, p. 191.
7 Wotton 1649, p. 111.
8 Clarendon 1839, p. 743.
9 Willem de Passe, *King James I and VI of Scotland, Henry Prince of Wales*, 1625, line engraving, National Portrait Gallery, London, D9484.
10 Everett-Green 1968, pp. 18–19.
11 See Keevil 1954; Purkiss 2005, p. 101.
12 Sharpe 1996, p. 774. See also Barroll 2001, pp. 153–9.
13 Rubinstein 1975, p. 38; Sharpe 1996, p. 774; Murdoch 2000, pp. 5–6.
14 Sharpe 1996, pp. 191, 774.
15 Knowler 1739, p. 32.
16 Murdoch 2000, p. 6; Barroll 2001, p. 153.
17 He also received the titles of marquis of Ormond, earl of Ross and lord Ardmannoch.
18 NRS E21/76, f. 68v.
19 Museum of London 60.49.1 and 48.88.5.
20 CSPD, James I, 1603–10, p. 186.
21 TNA AO3/1115, 1603–4, unfoliated.
22 Royal Collection, Inventory of Charles II's pictures at Whitehall and Hampton Court, f. 9r.
23 TNA LC9/95, f. 33v.
24 Clifford 1990, p. 55.
25 Clifford 1990, p. 66.
26 Nichols 1828, vol. 2, p. 513.
27 See Arnold 1975.
28 Sharpe 1996, pp. 4–5.
29 NRS GD124/15/27/20.
30 Lockyer 1984, p. 17.
31 Miller 1987, p. 65.
32 Bacon 1778, p. 276.
33 NRS GD124/15/27/28.
34 Lockyer 1984, p. 20.
35 Smuts 1987, p. 104.
36 Murdoch 2000, p. 5.
37 Nichols 1828, vol. 3, p. 166.
38 NRS GD40/9/8, no. 1.
39 Carlton 1983, p. 17.
40 Barroll 2001, p. 153.
41 McClure 1939, vol. 2, p. 359.
42 See Miller 2006.

43 TNA E101/436/1, pp. 65–7.
44 TNA E101/436/1, p. 70.
45 NRS GD25/3/89C.
46 NRS GD224/315/3, no. 5.
47 BL Add. MS 4,177, f. 82 v.
48 *CSP Venetian, 1625–6*, p. 21.
49 Marshall 1990b, pp. 1–15. See also Griffey 2016.
50 Marshall 2003, p. 156.
51 Marshall 1990b, p. 22.
52 Brown 1993, p. 545.
53 *CSPD Charles I, 1625–6*, p. 45.
54 Birch 1848, vol. 1, p. 78; de Lisle 2018, pp. 49–50.
55 TNA AO3/909/3, pp. 17–21.
56 TNA AO3/910/5, p. 15.
57 Scarisbrick 1994, p. 156.
58 BL Add. MS 12,528, f. 25v.
59 Lockyer 1984, p. 236.
60 Hibbert 2007, p. 87.
61 Lockyer 1984, p. 413.
62 Lockyer 1984, pp. 236, 373.
63 HMC 1930, p. 193.
64 Fairholt 1850, p. 20.
65 Marshall 1986, p. 15.
66 NRAS 332/F/1/52.
67 NRAS, F/1/20, no. 28.
68 NRAS 332/F/1/52.
69 Warwick 1702, p. 114.
70 Knowler 1739, p. 237. See also Stevenson 1992.
71 Gordon of Ruthven, 1844, pp. 75, 229–31.
72 Clarendon 1827, p. 215.
73 Balfour 1825, vol. 2, p. 168.
74 NRS GD406/1/100; *CSP Venetian, 1628–9*, p. 190.
75 NRS GD124/15/88.
76 NLS MS 83, f. 41.
77 Brydon 1993, unpaginated.
78 NRS GD237/25/2, no. 10.
79 NRS GD3/5/203.
80 NRS GD25/9/13.
81 NRS GD112/39/48/9.
82 NRS E34/52, no. 8.
83 NRS E34/52, no. 6.
84 NRS E34/52, no. 26.
85 Brydon 1993, unpaginated.
86 Brydon 1993, unpaginated.
87 Balfour 1825, vol. 4, p. 388.
88 Balfour 1825, vol. 4, p. 395.
89 Balfour 1825, vol. 4, p. 396.
90 NRS CH12/12/1019.
91 Brydon 1993, unpaginated.
92 Balfour 1825, vol. 4, pp. 364–7, 370–71.
93 Balfour 1825, vol. 4, pp. 368–9.
94 Balfour 1825, vol. 4, p. 369.
95 NRS GD112/39/69/4.
96 *CSPD, Charles I, 1638–9*, p. 426.
97 *CSPD, Charles I, 1639*, p. 439.
98 Mathews 1955, p. 15.
99 Laing 1830, p. 225.
100 Imrie and Dunbar 1982, p. xxviii.
101 NRS RH15/29/167.
102 Cumming 1989b, pp. 342–4.
103 Cumming 1989b, p. 342.
104 Marshall 1973, p. 88.
105 Curthoys 2012, pp. 104–5.
106 Christ Church, Oxford, Cathedral Register, ff. 42r, 43r.
107 TNA E403/2760, f. 5v.
108 TNA E403/2760, f. 9r.
109 MacGregor 1989, p. 409.
110 Anon. 1767–1830, p. 634.
111 *CSPD, Charles I, 1644*, p. 94; TNA E403/2760, f. 10v.
112 Museum of London 35.147/1 (man's collar), 35.147/2 (handkerchief) and 35.147/3 (man's linen nightcap).
113 *CSPD Charles I, 1627–8*, p. 491.
114 NRS GD237/25/1, no. 5.
115 Bowle 1975, p. 233; Huxley 1959, p. 276.
116 Walker 1660, p. 19. See also Stoyle 2008.
117 Anon. 1646b.
118 Fotheringham 1899, p. 195.
119 Macinnes 2000, p. 109.
120 NRS GD220/3/97.
121 NRS E35/17.
122 Roberts 1999, p. 18.
123 Strong 1972, pp. 95–6; Carlton 1983, p. 17.
124 Purkiss 2005, p. 107; Gordon of Ruthven 1844, pp. 75, 229–31.
125 Cust 2005, pp. 418, 446.
126 Bowle 1975, p. 316.
127 Hibbert 1964, p. 67.
128 NRS GD248/182/1, no. 1.
129 Rogers 1983, p. 44.
130 Balfour 1825, vol. 4, p. 12.
131 Carlton 1987, pp. 225–6.
132 For more on this theme see Hayward 2016.
133 Ravelhofer 2006, p. 197.
134 Orgel and Strong 1973, vol. 1, p. 193.
135 Ravelhofer 2009, p. 76.
136 TNA E101/436/2, p. 4.
137 HMC 1887b, p. 102.
138 TNA AO3/910/2, f. 25r.
139 Carlton 1983, p. 17.
140 Carlton 1983, p. 16.
141 Strong 1972, pp. 45–57.
142 Murdoch 2000, p. 6.
143 James's pet name for Buckingham, the Scots for Stephen, in reference to the beauty of St Stephen: Stewart 2003, p. 280.
144 Halliwell 1846, p. 163.
145 Huxley 1959, p. 79.
146 Anon. 1648.
147 Weber 1995, p. 47.
148 Jesse 1841, p. 58.

Chapter 4

1 Raine 1861, pp. 83–4; Harris 2007, p. 35.
2 *CSPD Charles II, 1660–1*, pp. 37, 39.
3 UoG, MS Hunter 58, pp. 38–9.
4 UoG, MS Hunter 58, p. 10.
5 Lee 2014, pp. 135–7.
6 Purkiss 2005, p. 124.
7 See Curtin 1985 and Bryson 1998.
8 Waller 1908, p. 36.
9 Waller 1908, p. 37.
10 Larkin 1983, no. 132. p. 273.
11 NRS GD112/39/40/25.
12 Brown and Vlieghe 1999, p. 295.
13 Murray 2017, pp. 33–4.
14 TNA LR5/64, unnumbered bill.
15 TNA LR5/63, roll for October–December 1630.
16 Ferrero 1881, p. 43.
17 Sir Anthony van Dyck, *The Three Eldest Children of Charles I*, 1635, oil on canvas, 133.8 × 151.7 cm, Royal Collection, RCIN 404403.
18 *CSP Venetian, 1632–6*, p. 483.
19 *CSPD, Charles I, 1635*, p. 604.
20 TNA E405/285, f. 5r.
21 Rubinstein 1975, p. 45.
22 Bryant 1935, p. 3.
23 Steer 1959, p. 7.
24 Steer 1959, p. 7.
25 Sharpe 1996, p. 222.
26 TNA E403/2757, f. 69v.
27 Fyfe 1928, p. 162; Bowle 1975, p. 182.
28 Fyfe 1928, p. 162.
29 Cumming 1989b, p. 344.
30 Studio of Sir Anthony van Dyck, *Charles II when Prince of Wales*, 1637 or 1638, oil on canvas, 154 × 132.1 cm, Royal Collection, RCIN 404400.
31 Royal Armouries, Leeds, II.92 and II.90, VI.59, VI.117, VI.118.
32 Royal Armouries, II.90; Blair 1958, pp. 204, 216.
33 Evans 1998, p. 17.
34 Purkiss 2005, p. 124.
35 Rogers 1983, pp. 42–4, no. 14.
36 Stoyle 2005, p. 26.
37 *CSPD ,Charles II 1682*, p. 356; Stoyle 2005, p. 12.
38 Stoyle 2005, p. 182.
39 Stoyle 2005, p. 188.
40 Hayward 2012b.
41 Bryant 1935, p. 14.
42 Scott 1905, p. 457.
43 Falkus 1972, p. 31.
44 Hutton 1989, p. 18.
45 *CSPD Charles II, 1661–2*, p. 40.
46 *CSPD Charles II, 1661–2*, p. 40.
47 BL Add. MS 37,047, ff. 5–10; Hutton 1989, p. 39.
48 BL Add. MS 38,854, ff. 30r–51r.
49 BL Add. MS 38,854, f. 33r.
50 After Adriaen Hanneman, *William Hamilton, 2nd Duke of Hamilton*, 1625–50, oil on canvas, 127 × 101 cm, National Portrait Gallery, London, NPG 2120.
51 UoG, Hunter MS 238, p. 83; Keay 2008, p. 207.
52 NRS GD406/1/2443.
53 Laing 1842, vol. 2, p. 334.
54 NRS PA7/7, no. 7.
55 Imrie and Dunbar 1982, p. li.
56 Scott 1905, p. 189.
57 Hutton 1989, pp. 59–60.

58 Hyde 1773, appendix, p. lxiv.
59 NRS CH12.12.1019.
60 NRS GD34/811.
61 NRS GD40/2/16/25.
62 Holloway 1989, p. 13
63 Scott 1905, p. 280.
64 Scott 1905, p. 433.
65 Scott 1905, p. 493.
66 DHC, D.FSI. Box 268, Disbursments at Paris, unpaginated.
67 Birch 1742, p. 591.
68 DHC, D.FSI. Box 268, General household accounts, unpaginated.
69 DHC, D.FSI. Box 268, General household accounts, unpaginated.
70 DHC, D.FSI. Box 268, General household accounts, unpaginated.
71 DHC, D.FSI. Box 268, General household accounts, unpaginated.
72 DHC, D.FSI. Box 267, Accounts for household expenses, unpaginated.
73 Latham and Matthews 1970–83, I, p. 143.
74 DHC, D.FSI. Box 267, Accounts for household expenses, unpaginated.
75 Evelyn 1951, p. 2.
76 Latham and Matthews 1970–83, vol. 7, p. 324, Beer 1938–9.
77 Latham and Matthews 1970–83, vol. 7, p. 328.
78 HMC 1891a, p. 55.
79 Latham and Matthews 1970–83, vol. 2, p. 82; Hutton 1985, pp. 153–4.
80 Latham and Matthews 1970–83, vol. 2, p. 83.
81 Latham and Matthews 1970–83, vol. 2, p. 157.
82 TNA AO3/919, 1673, p. 17.
83 TNA AO3/919 1670; p. 16; AO3/929, p. 24.
84 Chapman 1972, p. 9.
85 Harvey 1995, p. 121.
86 NRS GD406/1/10029.
87 TNA AO3/920, p. 45.
88 *CSPD Charles II, 1661–2*, p. 617.
89 John Michael Wright, *Charles II*, *c.*1662, oil on canvas, 63.8 × 79.0 cm, The Right Honourable the Earl of Wemyss and March; Holloway 1989, p. 20, fig. 9.
90 E.g. NRS GD33/65/38.
91 Fyfe 1928, p. 280.
92 Hutton 1989, pp. 267–8.
93 Latham and Matthews 1970–83, vol. 5, p. 57.
94 Fyfe 1928, p. 288
95 Jackson 2003, p. 117.
96 Lauder of Fointainhall 1840, p. 254.
97 Fyfe 1928, p. 277.
98 Latham and Matthews 1970–83, vol. 7, p. 225
99 Beard 1997, p. 84. See also Rowell 2013, pp. 434–501.
100 Marshall 1972, pp. 32–5.
101 See Marshall 2016.
102 NRS GD406/1/11170.
103 NRS GD406/1/2975.
104 Zwicker 2007, pp. 130–31.
105 Latham and Matthews 1970–83, vol. 7, p. 391.
106 LRO I-Worsley/6, unpaginated.
107 Beer 1959, p. 595.
108 Act 4, scene 7.
109 TNA AO3/917, f. 22r.
110 TNA AO3/911, p. 57.
111 TNA AO3/933, f. 18r.
112 Bryant 1935, p. 41.
113 Bryant 1935, p. 76.
114 Blount 1660, p. 26.
115 Matthews 1966, p. 40.
116 Latham and Matthews 1970–83, vol. 1, p. 155.
117 Scott 1905, p. 227.
118 Fraser 1993, p. 115.
119 Stoyle 2011, p. 39.
120 Stoyle 2011, p. 59.
121 Stoyle 2011, p. 173.
122 NRS GD224/889/5. See also Keay 2016.
123 NRS GD3/5/210.
124 Hutton 1989, p. 125.
125 Hutton 1989, pp. 337–8, 416.
126 Folger MS X.d.478.
127 Folger MS X.d.478, f. 6v.
128 Folger MS X.d.478, f. 3v.
129 Quinton 2013, p. 111.

Chapter 5

1 V&A, T.711.1-1995; Hart and North 1998, p. 80; Graffius 2012, pp. 159–60.
2 Dalton 1912, no. 1415; Scarisbrick 1994, p. 190.
3 Ribeiro 2005, p. 221.
4 Broth. Lib. MS dep. 1984/3/5.
5 Cornelius Johnson, *Charles II as a Boy*, c. 1639, oil on panel, 29 × 20 cm, National Portrait Gallery, London, NPG 5103.
6 TNA E403/2757, f. 93r.
7 TNA E403/2760, ff. 36r, 39r, 41r.
8 Cole 1975, p. 6; Ashley 1977, p. 22.
9 Turner 1948, p. 15.
10 Sir Peter Lely, *Charles I and James, Duke of York*, 1647, oil on canvas, 103.5 × 140.3 cm, the collection of His Grace the Duke of Northumberland.
11 BL Add. MS 38,854, f. 31r.
12 BL Add. MS 38,854, f. 36r.
13 Quoted in Turner 1948, p. 28.
14 Scott 1905, p. 314.
15 Scott 1905, p. 314.
16 Hutton 1989, p. 75; Sells 1962, p. 57.
17 Sells 1962, p. 58.
18 Turner 1948, pp. 41–2.
19 Scott 1905, p. 323.
20 Sells 1962, p. 75.
21 Sells 1962, p. 274.
22 Hirst 1994, pp. 457–8, Adams and Goodare 2014, p. 11.
23 Burnet 1818, p. 233.
24 Turner 1948, p. 60.
25 Miller 1978, p. 42.
26 For example, 1665, Morgan Library, New York, Rulers of England Box 10 James II, unfoliated.
27 Turner 1948, p. 69, n. 2.
28 Turner 1948, p. 63.
29 BL Add. MS 24,928, f. 6r.
30 Latham and Matthews 1970–83, vol. 4, p. 360, and vol. 5, p. 49.
31 Latham and Matthews 1970–83, vol. 7, pp. 320–21.
32 NAL MSL/1935/320.
33 Latham and Matthews 1970–83, vol. 2, p. 213.
34 Latham and Matthews 1970–83, vol. 9, p. 449 and n. 1.
35 NRS GD112/39/126/4.
36 Ogg 1934, pp. 631–2; Ouston 2000, 266–79; Ouston 1982, pp. 133, 136.
37 Young 1998, p. 112.
38 NRS GD16/41/594. See also GD112/39/29, no. 5.
39 Quoted by Brown 1994, p. 87.
40 Fyfe 1928, p. 265.
41 Southcombe and Tapsel 2010, p. 102.
42 Marshall 1976, p. 16.
43 NRS GD112/39/29, no. 12.
44 Douglas 1953, p. 631.
45 NRS PC12/7.
46 Linklater and Hesketh 1992, p. 92.
47 NRS GD406/1/8064.
48 TNA SP8/3, f. 119r.
49 NRO, Isham correspondence, 1379.
50 TNA AO3/932, f. 24v.
51 Oman 1962, p. 94.
52 Lauder of Fountainhall 1840, p. 153.
53 Oman 1962, p. 84.
54 Kerridge 1985, p. 34.
55 Waugh 1964, p. 54.
56 Museum of London, 53.101.4.
57 TNA AO3/934, f. 4v.
58 TNA AO3/932, f. 7r.
59 Royal Armouries, Leeds, II.123 and III.1248; Blair 1958, p. 208, fig. 55.
60 TNA AO3/934, f. 7v.
61 Arch 2007, pp. 100–01.
62 TNA AO3/934, f. 7v.
63 Cunnington and Cunnington 1955, p. 142.
64 Waugh 1964, p. 54.
65 NRS E661/103, no. 4.
66 NRS GD112/35/13, no. 3.
67 Turner 1948, p. 63.
68 TNA AO3/934, f. 5v.
69 TNA AO3/932, f. 18v.
70 TNA AO3/932, f. 14v.
71 Beer 1959, p. 813.
72 NRS GD406/1/6186.
73 Marly 1987a, p. 47.
74 Cumming 1989a, p. 35.
75 Quoted in Kuchta 2002, p. 93.
76 NRS GD157/2181.
77 TNA AO3/935.
78 E.g. Wardle 2002, pp. 29, 107.
79 UoG, Hunter MS 73, f. 86r.
80 Kuchta 2002, p. 93.
81 Blanch 1691, pp. 18–19.

82 TNA AO3/932, ff. 21r–v, and AO3/934, f. 13r.
83 TNA AO3/935, unfoliated, and AO3/936, unfoliated.
84 TNA AO3/932, f. 28r, and AO3/935, unfoliated.
85 Marshall 1972, p. 33.
86 Marshall 1972, p. 33; NRS GD3/10/3/11.
87 NRS GD237/1/14.
88 NRS GD112/15/65, no. 13; see also nos. 7 and 36.
89 NRS GD112/35/14, no. 4.
90 NRS GD112/35/14, no. 6.
91 Marshall 1986, p. 21.
92 NRS RH15/49/2.
93 Marshall 1976, p. 45.
94 Oman 1962, p. 139. Valerie Cumming (1989a, p. 208) describes this as 'the triumph of etiquette over adversity'.
95 HMC 1887, p. 252; Ashley 1977, p. 264.
96 Beer 1959, p. 969.
97 Fryman 2014, pp. 122–3, 125–6.
98 TNA LC5/108, f. 254.
99 Oman 1962, p. 156.
100 Broth. Lib. MS dep. 1984/3/5.
101 Corp 2000, p. 243.
102 Corp 2009, p. 85.
103 Corp 2009, p. 77.
104 Quoted in Waugh 1964, p. 100.
105 Fraser 2006, p. 305.
106 BL Add. MS 10,118; Corp 2009, p. 161.
107 Corp 2000, p. 250.
108 Oman 1962, p. 148.
109 Corp 2009, p. 148.
110 NRS GD157/2187.
111 NRS GD112/15/70, no. 22.
112 Oman 1962, p. 187.
113 Broth. Lib. MS dep. 1984/3/5.
114 Scott 2004, p. 254.
115 Waller 2002, pp. 4–6.
116 NRS GD406/1/11129.
117 NRS RH15/30/1.
118 Folger MS X.c.90, nos. 1 and 2.
119 NRS GD27/7/347.
120 NRS GD26/1/1, no. 45.
121 Hudson 2000, p. 185.
122 Turner 1948, p. 18.
123 NRS GD16/50/38.
124 Sells 1962, p. 283.
125 Sells 1962, p. 285.
126 Sells 1962, p. 289.
127 HMC 1887, vol. 1, p. 36.
128 Quoted in Turner 1948, p. 166.
129 Scott 2004, p. 256.
130 NMS H.NT.239; Linklater and Hesketh 1992, p. 117.
131 Raffe in Adams and Goodare 2014, p. 11 and pp. 173–92.
132 See Jacob de Wet the elder, *John 1st Marquis of Atholl*, c.1680, oil on canvas, 240.4 × 167.5 cm, the collection of His Grace the Duke of Atholl, Blair Castle, Perthshire; John Baptiste de Medina, *Archibald, 1st Duke of Argyll with His Sons John and Archibald*, 1689, oil on canvas, 240 × 158 cm, the collection of His Grace the Duke of Argyll.
133 Nicholson 1998.

Part II

1 Bowie 2013, p. 44.
2 Fraser 1892, no. 347, p. 365.
3 Stevenson 1973, p. 324.
4 Goodare 2004, pp. 110, 115, 141, 289.
5 Adams and Goodare 2014, p. 4.
6 NRS GD112/39/51/8.
7 NRS GD472/68, no. 10.
8 See Fisher 1948.
9 Smuts 1987, p. 54.
10 Marshall 2016 and Tankard 2015.
11 Arnold 1988, pp. 157–8.
12 Snodin and Styles 2001, pp. 114–15.
13 Pepys Library, Cambridge, vol. 2295.
14 Marly 1987b, p. 35.
15 See Buckroyd 1975.
16 NRS GD112/39/118/3.
17 NRS RH18/1/14.
18 NRS GD170/629. See also GD112/39/153/18.
19 Latham and Matthews 1970–83, vol. 9, pp. 532–3.
20 TNA SP29/412 f.107r.
21 Anon. 1620, pp. 13–14.
22 Wood 1820, p. 222; Huxley 1959, p. 130.
23 NRS GD112/29/17, no .20.
24 NRS GD112/39/104/9.
25 NRS CH2/694/10.
26 NRS GD40/2/3/40.
27 NRS GD112/35/11, no. 6.
28 NRS GD112/15/22, no. 31.
29 NRS GD112/39/117/10.
30 NRS GD406/1/3412.
31 NRS GD112/39/149/7.
32 NRS GD122/3/17, no. 11.
33 NRS GD406/1/6326.
34 Evelyn 1951, p. 11. See also Edwards 1985.
35 Dekker and Middleton 2017, p. 5.
36 Latham and Matthews 1970–83, vol. 8, p. 455.
37 NRS GD112/39/50/4.
38 NRS GD112/39/50/34.
39 NRS GD112/39/51/24.
40 NRS GD112/39/52/1.
41 NRS GD45/16/2879 and GD45/16/2882.
42 NRS GD237/1/14, no. 8.
43 TNA LC9/94, f. 30r.
44 TNA AO3/911, p. 29.
45 TNA LC5/65, f. 52v, no. 62.
46 TNA LC5/65, f. 104v, no. 37.
47 TNA LC5/140, p. 121.
48 NRS GD112/39/65/21.
49 NRS GD220/6/689, no. 3.
50 NRS GD26/13/388.

Chapter 6

1 Wilcox 2017.
2 Henshall and Maxwell 1954; see also Tarrant 2001b.
3 NRS GD112/23/7, nos. 12 and 13.
4 TNA LC5/141, p. 402.
5 Barnard 2000, p. 261.
6 Mackenzie 1661, p. 223.
7 Balfour 1825, vol. 2, p. 648.
8 NRS E23/3, no. 28.
9 NRS PC15/3; Thomson 1815, pp. 185–92.
10 NRS E22/3, f. 54v.
11 NRS E22/3, f. 95v.
12 NRS E22/4, f. 29v.
13 NRS GD305/1/29/1.
14 NRS GD111/5/3.
15 NRS E35/13.
16 NRS GD124/10/132.
17 NRS GD90/2/50.
18 NRS GD124/10/223; *RPC, 1619–22*, p. 691.
19 NRS GD124/10/272.
20 NRS SP13/154.
21 NRS GD32/2/25.
22 NRS E35/19.
23 NRS E18/40 and GD1/1237/3.
24 TNA LC2/4/4, f. 71r.
25 TNA SP14/60, f. 3r.
26 TNA SP14/2, f. 1r .
27 Thrush and Ferris 2010, vol. 3, pp. 68–9.
28 Thrush and Ferris 2010, vol. 3, p. 71.
29 TNA SP14/60, f. 35r and SP14/141, f. 50r.
30 Nichols 1828, vol. 3, p. 246.
31 Prestwich 1966, pp. 30, 55; TNA SP14/141, f. 112r.
32 Beard 1997, p. 56.
33 *CSPD, James I, 1619–23*, p. 335.
34 Hearn 2009, pp. 98–9.
35 Hutton 1989, pp. 134–5.
36 Latham and Matthews 1970–83, vol. 1, p. 303.
37 Latham and Matthews 1970–83, vol. 5, p. 206.
38 Folger MS X.d.76.
39 BL Add. MS 24,928, f. 10r.
40 Wardle 1994 and Wardle 2001.
41 BL Add. MS 12,528.
42 See Cumming 2004.
43 Ribeiro 2005, pp. 161–2.
44 Hutchinson 1913, p. 71.
45 Folger MS 26,5630.
46 Wardle 2002, pp. 29, 82.
47 Wardle 2002, p. 101.
48 Wardle 2002, p. 103.
49 NRS GD72/233, GD477/358, no. 17 and GD22/1/133.
50 NRS GD112/39/210/9.
51 NRS GD112/39/177/18 and GD112/39/178/2.
52 NRS GD112/23/77, no. 18.
53 NRS GD248/104/5, no. 21.
54 Kirk and Kirk 1907, pp. 367, 370, 428, 431, 436.
55 Cameron 1979, pp. 4–7.
56 Pittock 2000, p. 21.
57 LMA/CLA/024/06/002 – MCD2/30.

58 Taylor 2003, p. 34.
59 Anon. 1863, pp. ix–x.
60 Akrigg 1984, p. 170.
61 Camden 1625, book 1, p. 90.
62 Flavin 2014, pp. 68, 120–21.
63 Laurenson 2013, p. 46.
64 Laurenson 2013, p. 48.
65 Cheape 2006, p. 23.
66 UoG, MS Murray 147, p. 14.
67 NRS GD112/39/108/1.
68 NRS GD406/1/3841.
69 NRS GD406/1/4005.
70 Cited in Ribeiro 2005, p. 314.
71 Laurenson 2013, p. 52.
72 NRS GD45/17/60.
73 NRS GD112/15/62, no. 85.
74 NRS GD112/15/4, no.11.
75 NRS GD112/29/27, no. 2.
76 NRS GD112/35/14, no. 2 and GD112/15/59, no. 13.
77 NRS GD305/1/167/100.
78 NRS PA7/15, no. 30; *APS*, IX, p. 430.
79 Fraser 1892, vol. 2, p. 124.
80 NRS GD112/39/148/1.
81 Hayward 2019.
82 Peck 2005, pp. 1, 91, 99, 107; Folger MS X.d.587.
83 NRS GD504/9/97, no. 4.
84 Peck 2005, p. 107.
85 *RPC, 1633–5*, 2nd series, p. 253.
86 *RPC, 1681–82*, 3rd series, pp. 687–8.
87 NRS GD112/15/12, no. 66.
88 NRS GD112/15/22, no. 11.
89 *RPC, 1673–6*, 3rd series, p. 68.
90 NRS GD122/3/2, no. 56.
91 NRS RH9/1/7, f. 7v.
92 NRS GD40/9/100.
93 NRS GD112/39/80/12.
94 NRS GD112/29/42, no. 7.
95 NRS CH2/694/10.
96 NRS GD164/1617.
97 Marshall 2003, p. 102.
98 Nichols 1828, vol. 3, p. 477.
99 *CSPD Charles I, 1628–9*, p. 76.
100 Bryant 1935, p. 39.
101 Latham and Matthews 1970–83, vol. 6, p. 73.
102 NRS GD34/840 and GD34/893.
103 NRS GD56/141.
104 NRS GD406/1/1902.
105 NRS GD89/1/119.
106 NRS GD406/1/2549.
107 NRS GD112/39/112/23.
108 Marshall 1973, p. 159.
109 Marshall 1973, p. 159.
110 Marshall 1973, pp. 162–3.
111 NRS GD128/31/2.
112 Sanderson 1987, pp. 80, 83.
113 NRS GD112/15/62, no. 75.
114 NRS RH15/14/39.
115 NRS RH15/14/39.
116 Martin 1999, p. 223. See also Leitch 1990.
117 NRS GD406/1/2573.
118 NRS GD1/395/2.
119 NRS GD20/1/484.
120 NRS GD1/449/326.
121 NRS GD109/2863.
122 NRS GD237/1/40, no. 2.
123 NRS GD305/1/152/195.
124 NRS RH15/106/456, no. 11.
125 NRS RH15/106/349, no. 18.
126 NRS RH15/29/67.
127 Macinnes 2000, pp. 147–8.
128 Hearn 2009, p. 94.
129 Hunter 1963, pp. 87–96.
130 Moryson 1617, p. 129.
131 NRS GD112/15/51 and GD24/1/369, no. 8.
132 See Corfield 1989.
133 Stevenson 1997, p. 91.
134 Stevenson 1997, p. 96.
135 Folger MS X.c.49 (4); Peck 2005, p. 40.
136 BL Egerton MS 2816.
137 Quoted in Strong 1986, p. 55.
138 Sanderson 1987, p. 72.
139 NRS RH15/14/61.
140 Royal Ceremonial Dress Collection, Kensington Palace, London, 2003.8/1&2.
141 Bata Shoe Museum, Toronto, Canada, P06.0001.
142 Museum of London, A18293/4.
143 Latham and Matthews 1970–83, vol. 1, p. 155.
144 Dyce 1830, p. 38.
145 NRS GD112/63/7.
146 NRS GD112/35/15, no. 18.

Chapter 7

1 Payne et al. 2011.
2 TNA AO3/910/1, p. 60.
3 TNA AO3/910/1, p. 61.
4 TNA AO3/910/1, pp. 57–8, 61.
5 TNA AO3/910/1, p. 35.
6 TNA AO3/910/1, pp. 33, 39
7 TNA AO3/910/1, p. 43.
8 NRS GD237/25/2, no. 10.
9 NRS GD237/25/2, no. 11.
10 NRS GD25/9/13, unnumbered bundle.
11 CLA/T/7.
12 CLA 4/5/2/18.
13 HMC 1915, p. 330.
14 NRS GD30/951 and GD124/1/1153.
15 E.g. NRS GD26/6/21.
16 *CSPD, James I, 1603–10*, p. 120.
17 BL Add. MS 8126, pp. 597–8.
18 NRS GD124/7/26.
19 TNA E403/2757, f. 65v.
20 Devon 1836, p. 300.
21 TNA SP14/67, f. 229r.
22 *CSPD, James I, 1611–18*, p. 189.
23 TNA SP14/81, f. 25r.
24 NRS GD63/91.
25 NRS GD63/92.
26 TNA SP16/5 f. 183r.
27 *CSPD, Charles I, 1625–6*, p. 568.
28 BL Add. MS, 12,528, f. 26v.
29 BL Add. MS, 12,528, f. 36r.
30 TNA LR5/63, roll for Oct.–Dec. 1630.
31 TNA LR5/65, unnumbered bills.
32 TNA AO3/910/4, f. 18r; *CSPD Charles I, 1638–9*, p. 485.
33 *CSPD Charles I, 1635–6*, p. 379.
34 *CSPD Charles I, 1639–40*, p. 318.
35 *CSPD Charles I, 1648–9*, p. 14.
36 Norman 1989, p. 360.
37 NMS, K.2004.283.
38 TNA PROB11/356.
39 TNA PROB11/356.
40 NRS GD40/8/360, no. 2.
41 NRS PA7/25/79, no. 9.
42 TNA LC5/143, p. 200; Wardle 2002, p. 98.
43 Taylor 2003, p. 249.
44 Act 1, lines 363–4; Cavendish 1999, p. 11.
45 NRS GD1/616/224.
46 NRS GD29/1251 and GD29/1300.
47 NRS GD29/1251 and GD29/1300.
48 Marly 1978, p. 337, n. 18.
49 NRS GD220/6/884, no. 36.
50 NRS GD112/35/14, nos. 13–14.
51 NRS GD16/42/536. See also GD112/27/99.
52 NRS GD124/2/154.
53 TNA PROB11/471.
54 NRS GD45/17/611.
55 NRS GD220/6/884, no. 3.
56 NRS GD220/6/884, no. 36.
57 NRS GD56/141.
58 NRS GD220/6/884, no. 1.
59 NRS GD220/6/501, no. 37.
60 NRS GD220/6/884, no. 1.
61 Wilcox 2014, pp. 30–42.
62 NRS GD246/26/5, no. 10.
63 NRS GD23/10/263.
64 NRS GD112/35/14, no. 26.
65 NRS RH9/1/69.
66 TNA SP14/2, f. 1r; Cuddy 1987, p. 189.
67 *CSPD, James I, 1603–10*, p. 269.
68 Seddon 1975–86, vol. 1, p. 125.
69 TNA SP14/88, f. 7r.
70 Cuddy 1987, p. 189, n. 41.
71 *CSPD, Charles I, 1625–6*, p. 16.
72 *CSPD, James I, 1619–23*, p. 114.
73 *CSPD, James I, 1619–23*, p. 531.
74 *CSPD, James I, 1619–23*, p. 552.
75 Lockyer 1984, p. 414.
76 Aylmer 1961, pp. 142, 317.
77 Rushworth 1721, p. 633.
78 *CSPD, Charles I, 1648–9, p. 278.*
79 *CSPD, Charles II, 1663–4*, p. 530.
80 *CSPD, James II, 1685*, p. 8.
81 Corp 2009, p. 359.
82 Corp 2009, pp. 70, 108, 216.
83 NRS GD406/1/7639.
84 NRS GD112/29/48, no. 10.
85 NRS GD44/49/13/1, no. 12.
86 Coward 1996, p. 120.
87 Clifford 1990, p. 22.
88 Ashenburg 2008, p. 106.
89 TNA LC5/61, p. 38.
90 TNA LC5/63, p. 11; LC5/141, p. 140.
91 Thornton 1978, p. 317; Thornton 1980, p. 91.
92 Thornton 1978, p. 319.
93 NRS GD40/8/477, no. 1.
94 BL Add. MS 75,391, f. 7r.
95 TNA LC5/143, p. 66.

96 TNA SP29/67, f. 315r.
97 *CSPD Charles II, 1667*, p. 89.
98 *CSPD Charles II, 1670*, p. 365.
99 BL Stowe MS 563, ff. 16v–17r.
100 Latham and Matthews 1970–83, vol. 5, p. 139.
101 Latham and Matthews 1970–83, vol. 4, p. 353.
102 Taylor 1868, p. 169.
103 See Poynting 2006.
104 Fox 2010, p. 25.
105 Nichols, 1828, vol. 3, p. 338.
106 NRS E22/2, f. 91v.
107 NRS GD26/6/17.
108 Turnor 1806, p. 8.
109 Turnor 1806, p. 9.
110 *CSPD, Charles I, 1625–6*, p. 55.
111 Fox 2010, p. 79.
112 Fox 2010, p. 80.
113 *CSPD Commonwealth, 1649–60*, vol. 12, p. 269.
114 *CSPD Charles II, 1661–2*, p. 55.
115 DHC, D.FSI. Box 268, Accounts 1660–64 (which includes some earlier material).
116 TNA LC9/271, f. 70r.
117 BL Add. MS 5,750, f. 35r.
118 TNA LC5/65, f. 122v.
119 *CSPD Charles II, 1680–81*, p. 229.
120 NRS GD112/15/20, no. 3.
121 NRS GD112/15/29, no. 12.
122 NRS GD406/1/3789.
123 NRS GD112/35/14, no. 21.
124 NRS GD112/15/59, no. 1.
125 NRS GD112/15/62, nos. 20–12
126 NRS GD112/15/505, no. 22.
127 NRS RH15/57/3.
128 NRS GD406/1/11514.
129 NRS GD3/6/4.
130 NRS GD3/5/152.
131 *RPC, 1633–35*, 2nd series, p. 305.
132 *RPC, 1633–35*, 2nd series, p. 319.
133 NRS GD215/939.
134 Imrie and Dunbar 1982, p. 111.
135 NRS GD112/29/46, no. 36.
136 NRS GD112/35/12, no. 25.
137 NRS GD45/15/10.
138 NRS GD1/395/4.
139 NRS GD220/6/1749, no. 5.
140 NRS GD124/15/27/149.
141 NRS E71/3/7 and GD1/885/17.
142 NRS GD24/5/63.
143 NRS GD406/1/11823.
144 NRS GD112/15/43, no. 14.
145 NRS GD477/424, no. 59; GD112/23/77, no. 18.
146 *CSPD Charles II, 1661–2*, p. 58.
147 *CSPD Charles II, 1663–4*, p. 42.
148 NRS GD1/885/26.
149 NRS GD112/29/42, no. 7.
150 NRS GD112/15/79, no. 37.
151 Jones and Stallybrass 2000, ch. 3.
152 Bellany 2002, pp. 157–9.
153 Glanville 1997, pp. 354–9.
154 Glanville 1997, pp. 354, 359.
155 TNA LC5/143, p. 456.
156 TNA LC9/98, f. 13r.
157 TNA E403/2757, f. 69r.
158 TNA LC5/140, p. 270.
159 *CSPD, James I, 1603–10*, p. 387.
160 TNA SP29/17, f. 26r.
161 *CSPD, Charles II, 1661–2*, p. 115.
162 NRS GD112/15/51, no. 1.
163 NRS GD248/104/2, no. 7.
164 NRS GD237/11/105, no. 34.
165 NRS GD40/8/404.
166 NRS GD112/29/17, no. 20.
167 NRS GD112/58/30, no. 55.
168 NRS GD406/1/1694.
169 NRS GD220/6/1742, no. 3.
170 NRS E661/103.
171 Waller 1908, p. 123.

Chapter 8

1 Marshall and Dalgleish 1991, p. 17; Pittock 1991.
2 Stevenson and Thomson 1982, p. 27.
3 Scarisbrick 1994, p. 188.
4 Pittock 2013; Guthrie 2014.
5 Thomson 1815, p. 47; Marshall 1996, pp. 79–86.
6 E.g. Arnold 1980, pp. 31–40.
7 Somers Cocks 1980, p. 108.
8 *CSP Venetian, 1603–7*, no. 66.
9 Thomson 1815, p. 288.
10 Finlay 1956, pp. 61–2.
11 Finlay 1956, pp. 61–2, pl. 18; Clark 2014, pp. 21–4, 66.
12 Finlay 1956, p. 63, pls 19a, 20.
13 NRS PA7/23/2/43.
14 NRS GD112/39/74/1.
15 NRS RH15/29/167.
16 BL Egerton MS 2,542, f. 90r.
17 Lauder of Fountainhall 1840, p. 153.
18 Lightbown 1989, pp. 257–8.
19 SoA MS 129, ff. 7r–v.
20 Bray 1806, p. 18.
21 Lightbown 1989, pp. 264, 266.
22 NRS GD112/39/117/10.
23 Scarisbrick 1994, p. 70.
24 Bird 2017, p. 102.
25 *CSP Venetian, 1607–10*, p. 137.
26 Cuddy 1989, p. 122, n. 57.
27 BL Add. MS 29,975, f. 11r.
28 Lightbown 1989, p. 271.
29 Peck 1991, p. 165.
30 Bray 1806, pp. 18–19.
31 BL Add. MS 12,528, f. 31v.
32 NRS E29/2, no. 1.
33 Wellington, 1953, pp. 159–68.
34 NRS GD220/3/122.
35 Gardiner 1894, p. 21.
36 Gardiner 1894, p. 41.
37 Scott 1905, p. 484.
38 Hutton 1989, p. 113; Bod Lib. Clarendon MS 60, f. 127.
39 DHC, D.FSI. Box 268, General household accounts, unpaginated.
40 Scarisbrick 1994, p. 183.
41 Scarisbrick 1994, p. 155.
42 Turpie 2015, pp. 140–53.
43 Cassavetti 1977, p. 77.
44 Fyfe 1928, p. 182.
45 Burnett and Bennett 1987, pp. 4–5.
46 Nicolas 1828, unpaginated.
47 TNA AO3/934, f. 4v.
48 Reid 1974, pp. 51, 55; Burnett and Bennett 1987, p. 8; TNA AO3/934, f. 10r.
49 NRS GD160/529/18.
50 NRS GD160/529/20.
51 NRS GD160/529/19.
52 NRS GD160/529/19.
53 NRS GD160/529/18.
54 NRS GD406/1/9135.
55 NRS GD406/1/7652.
56 NRS GD224/307/5, no. 96.
57 Tait 1986, p. 162; Awais-Dean 2017, pp. 3–5.
58 Evans 1953, 1970, p. 129.
59 Evans 1953, 1970, p. 126.
60 Furnivall 1877–9, p. 70.
61 Scarisbrick 1996, p. 75.
62 Harrison 1941, pp. 39–40.
63 Beneden and Poorter 2006, no. 2, p. 114.
64 Chadour-Sampson 2013, p. 76.
65 Somers Cocks 1980, pp. 107–8.
66 Bray 1806, p. 19.
67 NRS GD112/15/2, no .1.
68 NRS E78/30, no. 195.
69 Unknown artist, *Thomas Lyte*, 1611, oil on panel, 60 × 48 cm, Somerset Museum Service, 108/1998.
70 Marshall 1990a, p. 62.
71 NRS GD112/58/60, nos. 4–5.
72 Scarisbrick 1994, p. 187.
73 Scarisbrick 1993, p. 80.
74 Oman 1974, 51B.
75 Scarisbrick 1993, p. 50.
76 Scarisbrick 1993, p. 82.
77 Curle 1906, p. 58.
78 Thomson 1815, p. 294.
79 Bray 1806, pp. 19–20.
80 Scarisbrick 1993, p. 153.
81 NRS GD66/1/222.
82 NRS GD112/15/505, no. 12.
83 NRS GD248/104/6, no. 14.
84 NRS GD248/104/5, no. 23.
85 NRS GD22/3/717.
86 They cost £18 – TNA AO3/919 (1971), p. 32.
87 NRS GD109/2871.
88 NRS GD248/104/6, no. 14.
89 NRS GD248/141/1, no. 8.
90 Carisbrooke Castle Museum, no inventory number.
91 NRS GD44/51/541/11, no. 1.
92 Turner 1948, p. 12.
93 NRS GD112/3/69.
94 NRS GD112/39/107/5.
95 Goodare, Martin and Miller 2007, p. 249; Marshall and Dalgleish 1991, p. 33.
96 NRS GD112/1/527 and GD112/20/5/5.
97 NRS GD112/35/13.
98 NRS GD112/65/9, no. 9; GD181/196, no. 99.
99 Chadour-Sampson 2013, p. 62.
100 Chadour-Sampson 2013, pp. 63, 67, 74, 75.

101 Bray 1806, p. 19.
102 Scarisbrick 1993, p. 76.
103 Bray 1806, p. 19.
104 Scarisbrick 1996, p. 55.
105 Bury 1985, p. 6.
106 Scarisbrick 1993, p. 42.
107 Akrigg 1984, p. 392.
108 V&A M.253-1975.
109 Bury 1985, p. 33.
110 Bury 1985, p. 44.
111 Verney 1892, p. 316.
112 Swain 1973, p. 86.
113 NRS GD421/2/33, no. 5.
114 *CSP Venetian, 1623–5*, p. 163.
115 Scarisbrick 2011, p. 54.
116 NRS GD40/5/25, no. 3.
117 NRS E22/2, f. 122v.
118 NRS E22/2, f. 172r.
119 NRS E22/3, f. 91v.
120 NRS E22/5, p. 210.
121 Scarisbrick 1994, p. 190.
122 Marshall and Dalgleish 1991, p. 50.
123 Scarisbrick 1993, p. 78.
124 Scarisbrick 1993, p. 81.
125 Scarisbrick 1993, p. 81.
126 NRS GD112/35/13.
127 Sowerby 2015, pp. 119–41.
128 *CSP Venetian, 1603–7*, p. 102; Sowerby 2015, p. 128.
129 Scarisbrick 1993, p. 120.
130 *CSPD, James I, 1619–23*, p. 380.
131 Clifford and Pearson 1991, p. 85.
132 V&A 898-1904.
133 NRS GD90/2/85.
134 NRS GD112/58/57, nos. 21–2.
135 TNA LC5/107, f. 54v.
136 HMC 1898, p. 159.
137 NRS GD248/208/10.
138 Marshall and Dalgleish 1991, p. 37.
139 V&A Croft Lyons Bequest M.8110-1926; Bury 1985, p. 47.
140 Scarisbrick 1993, illus. 253 and 254.
141 Marshall and Dalgleish 1991, p. 49.
142 Murdoch 1991, p. 122, no. 269.
143 Murdoch 1991, p. 122, no. 269.
144 Sharp 1923, pp. 236–7.
145 Scarisbrick 1993, pp. 52–3, 84–5.
146 Wedgwood 2011, p. 181.
147 Scarisbrick 1989, p. 42.
148 *CSPD, Charles II, 1663–4*, p. 189.
149 NRS GD112/1/527.
150 Scarisbrick 2011, p. 109.
151 Shirley 1870, p. 375.
152 TNA PROB 11/113/1.

Part III

1 Kingsford 1908, p. 85.
2 Goodare 2004.
3 See Dunbar 1999.
4 Moryson 1617, Part 1, Book 3, ch. 5, p. 274.
5 Holloway 1989, p. 23.
6 See Bruce and Yearley 1989.
7 Lauder of Fountainhall 1840, p. 156.
8 MacIvor and Peterson 1984, pp. 249–68.
9 NRS GD406/1/9136.
10 NRS GD160/529/19.
11 Barratt 2015, pp. 39–57.
12 NRS GD45/15/14.
13 NRS GD34/832.
14 Thurley 2000, pp. 214–39.
15 See Scott 1905, p. 356; Corp 2000.
16 Howell 1657, p. 346.
17 Jackson 2003, p. 32.
18 Browning 1991, pp. 54–5.
19 NRS GD122/3/2, no. 27.
20 NRS GD122/3/11, no. 42.
21 HMC 1891b, p. 33.
22 NRS GD237/25/1, no. 2.
23 Brown 2008, pp. 858–63.
24 Macinnes 2000, p. 127.
25 Glendinning 2004, pp. 85–91.
26 Macinnes 2000, p. 22.
27 Smuts 1987, pp. 56, 190.
28 Macinnes 2000, p. 127.
29 Quoted in Macinnes 2000, p. 128.
30 NRS GD150/3449, no. 18.
31 NRS GD40/2/8/98.
32 NRS GD16/34/39.
33 NRS GD220/4/172.
34 NRS GD160/529/25.
35 NRS GD406/1/7302.
36 NRS GD406/1/2174.
37 NRS GD406/1/1438.
38 Linklater and Hesketh 1992, p. 73.
39 NRS GD45/22/10.
40 Wodrow 1835, p. 420.
41 Koslofsky 2011, pp. 1–5.
42 NRS B59/24/3/9.
43 McGavin 2001, pp. 49–50.
44 NRS GD40/2/8/97.
45 NRS GD30/16/1536.
46 NRS GD220/3/199.
47 NRS GD112/39/64/11.
48 NRS GD34/843/2/15 and E661/103, no. 41.

Chapter 9

1 V&A W.35-1 to 65-1949; Snodin and Styles 2001, pp. 90–91.
2 Day 1578, sigs Biiiv–Biiiiv.
3 Stubbes 1592, no pagination.
4 Fischlin and Fortier 1996, p. 159.
5 De Courtin 1678, p. 45.
6 Vincent 2003, p. 56.
7 Brown 1993, p. 553.
8 Keay 2008, p. 98.
9 NRS RH6/2530.
10 NRS GD148/302. See also GD60/18.
11 Fyfe 1928, p. 74.
12 Nichols 1828, vol. 1, p. 34.
13 *CSP Venetian, 1603–7*, pp. 165, 168.
14 *CSP Venetian, 1603–7*, p. 293.
15 Cuddy 1989, p. 116.
16 NRS GD122/2/390.
17 NRS GD37/313.
18 NRS GD49/513.
19 NRS GD406/1/1433. See also GD406/1/1402.
20 NRS GD150/3437/13.
21 NRS GD3/5/228.
22 Gardiner 1894, p. 144; Keay 2008, p. 53.
23 UoG, MS Gen. 1769.1.40.
24 Laing 1875, p. 283.
25 NRS GD52/123.
26 NRS GD40/2/4/56.
27 NRS GD40/2/4/59.
28 NRS GD1/499/1.
29 NRS GD406/1/8148.
30 NRS GD406/1/8561.
31 Thompson 1878, pp. 21–2.
32 NUL Portland MS Pw V 93, f. 20v.
33 Corp 2000, p. 242.
34 Quoted in Wilson 1956, p. 195; Smuts 1987, p. 198.
35 *CSP Venetian, 1625–6*, p. 21.
36 Anzilotti 1988, p. 143.
37 Laing 1875, pp. 331–2.
38 Clarendon 1827, pp. 503–4.
39 Beer 1959, p. 474.
40 Beer 1959, p. 546.
41 Latham and Matthews 1970–83, vol. 2, p. 79.
42 Keay 2008, p. 172; Potter and Roberts 1988, pp. 323–4.
43 Keay 2008, pp. 194–5.
44 BL Stowe MS 563, f. 5r.
45 BL Stowe MS 563, ff. 15v–16r.
46 BL Add. MS 75,391, f. 7v, point 17.
47 Beer 1959, p. 791.
48 TNA AO3/932, ff. 15v–16r.
49 TNA AO3/934, ff. 10r–v.
50 E.g. Browning 1991, pp. 134, 208, 224, 246.
51 E.g. Hunter 1843, p. 3.
52 Anon. 1688, p. 5.
53 Anon. 1688, p. 7.
54 BL Harley MS 589, f. 197v.
55 BL Harley MS 589, f. 198r.
56 Stevenson 1997, p. 35.
57 Carlton 1983, p. 130; *CSPD, Charles I, 1629–31*, p. 478.
58 Latham and Matthews 1970–83, vol. 9, p. 443.
59 Quoted in Nenadic 2007, p. 187.
60 Swain 1972, pp. 10–21.
61 Johansen 2002, pp. 398–9.
62 NRS E35/13, 1 February 1596–December 1597, f. 17r.
63 TNA AO1/2048/1, f. 6r.
64 Nichols 1828, vol. 1, p. 471.
65 Robertson 1863, p. 176.
66 TNA AO1/2048/1, f. 2v.
67 NUL, PwV92, f. 7v.
68 HMC 1938, p. 474.
69 Nichols 1828, vol. 2, pp. 511–12.
70 Oman 1951, p. 26.
71 Arnold 1985, pp. 98–100.
72 Arnold 1985, pp. 98–9.
73 Johansen 2002, p. 395.
74 Latham and Matthews 1970–83, vol. 2, p. 130.
75 Latham and Matthews 1970–83, vol. 4, p. 380.
76 Latham and Matthews 1970–83, vol. 7, p. 378.

77 Latham and Matthews 1970–83, vol. 7, p. 85.
78 NRS GD150/2727, no. 7.
79 NRS GD112/64/14, nos. 19 and 20.
80 NRS GD44/49/13/1, no. 12.
81 LMA, AM/P1 (1) 1673/33.
82 NRS GD477/326.
83 NRS GD112/29/41, no. 10.
84 NRS GD112/39/43/2.
85 Quinton 2013, p. 114.
86 NRS GD237/1/19, no. 15.
87 Schnitker and Clayes 2007, p. 17.
88 NRS E22/2, f. 116v.
89 BL Egerton MS 2816.
90 Bryant 1935, p. 104.
91 Shirley 1870, p. 363.
92 NRAS F/1/154/3, no. 5.
93 Cunnington and Cunnington 1955, p. 31.
94 NRS GD40/2/2/8.
95 NRS GD224/173/1, f. 7r.
96 TNA AO1/2048/2, f. 8r.
97 TNA AO3/910/4, f. 11v.
98 TNA AO3/918, ff. 16v, 33v; Wardle 2002, pp. 66–71.
99 NRS GD170/203, no. 15.
100 Bath 2003, p. 1.
101 Beer 1959, p. 445; Stevenson and Thomson 1982, pp. 67–9, no. 14.
102 Holloway 1989, pp. 24–5.
103 See Thornton 1977; Chatenet 1999.
104 Swain 1973, p. 90.
105 NRS E22/4, f. 32r.
106 Swain 1973, p. 46.
107 Imrie and Dunbar 1982, p. 96.
108 Swain 1973, p. 90.
109 HMC 1899, p. 448.
110 HMC 1899, p. 457.
111 TNA LC5/65, f. 27r, no. 97.
112 TNA LC5/141, p. 219.
113 TNA LC5/143, p. 28.
114 TNA LC5/65, f. 57v, no. 79.
115 Quoted in Cassavetti 1977, p. 156.
116 Fryman 2014, pp. 122–3, 125–6.
117 Swain 1988, p. 66.
118 Compare with unknown artist, *Elizabeth Vernon, Countess of Southampton*, *c.*1600, oil on panel, 164 × 110.5 cm, the collection of the Duke of Buccleuch and Queensbury: here Elizabeth stands by her dressing table with her bed behind her.
119 Tarrant 1996, pp. 183–5.
120 NRS GD25/1/577.
121 Belsey 1999, pp. 68–70.
122 Folger, Loseley MS, L.B. 638, f. 11r.
123 NRS GD44/49/13/1, no. 1.
124 NRS GD112/15/62, nos. 80–81.
125 NRS GD44/51/541/11.
126 NRS GD112/39/44/14.
127 NMS A.1921.68; Tarrant 2001a, pp. 89–90.
128 NRS GD112/15/21, no. 5.
129 NRS GD237/11/95.
130 NRS GD112/39/168/9.
131 Thornton 1978, p. 60.
132 Thornton 1980, pp. 48–53.
133 NRS GD406/1/3140.
134 Beer 1959, p. 756.
135 Latham and Matthews 1970–83, vol. 5, p. 40.
136 Rothwell and Westman 2011, p. 17.
137 UoG, MS Hunter 238, pp. 19, 22; for the dating, see Barclay 2010, pp. 1–13.
138 Marshall 1973, p. 251.
139 Marshall 1973, p. 253.
140 For an earlier, embroidered linen example see Tiramani et al. 2016, pp. 152–7, and for a linen nightcap liner see Tiramani et al. 2016, pp. 158–61.

Chapter 10

1 See e.g. NRS GD406/1/3278.
2 NRS GD112/39/113/14.
3 NRS GD122/3/11, no. 17.
4 NRS GD254/375.
5 NRS GD220/3/74.
6 Brown 2000, pp. 271–3.
7 Adams and Goodare 2014, p. 4.
8 Woodward 1997, p. 203.
9 Woodward 1997, p. 203.
10 Jackson 2003, p. 21.
11 Clifford and Pearson 1991, pp. 29, 34.
12 Hutton 1994, p. 182; Cressy 2004, pp. 57, 141–55.
13 *CSP Venetian, 1603–7*, p. 513; McCullough 1998, pp. 116–25.
14 McGavin 2001, p. 47; Thomson 1842–9, vol. 6, p. 185.
15 Tudor-Craig 2004, col. pl. 7.
16 Brooke 1992, pp. 18–20, no. LL5292.
17 Cressy 2004, pp. 171–2.
18 NRS CH12/16/209.
19 NRS GD157/2681.
20 Ravelhofer 1999, p. 94.
21 Smuts 1987, pp. 40–41.
22 Hutton 1994, p. 251.
23 Latham and Matthews 1970–83, vol. 9, p. 328.
24 Beer 1959, p. 829.
25 Beer 1959, p. 854.
26 NRS E96/37.
27 NRS GD40/2/8/72.
28 NRS GD90/2/115.
29 NRS GD157/1700 and GD133/283.
30 NRS GD33/65/47.
31 *RPC, 1681–2*, 3rd series, p. 277.
32 *APS* II 43, c.11; 1455/8.12. See also MacDonald 2010, pp. 49–61.
33 *APS*, III, p. 443.
34 *RPC, 1604–7*, p. 219 n.
35 *RPC, 1604–07*, p. 219 n.
36 Thomson 1842–9, vol. 6, p. 493.
37 Graeme 1904, p. 235.
38 NRS GD112/39/19/1.
39 Quoted in McGavin 2007, pp. 111–12.
40 NRS RH15/123/1.
41 NRS E78/4, no. 3.
42 *RPC, 1616–19*, p. 151.
43 Nichols 1828, vol. 3, p. 345.
44 Gray 1892, p. 46.
45 NRS RH14/89 and RH14/90.
46 NRS GD185/19/6, no. 19.
47 UoG, MS Murray 147, p. 2.
48 HMC 1887, p. 34.
49 Browning 1991, p. 228.
50 NRS GD40/8/360, no. 2.
51 NRS GD220/4/183.
52 NRS GD249/2/1, no. 10.
53 NRS GD220/4/28.
54 NRS E19/37.
55 NRS GD220/6/748, no. 16.
56 NRS E26/11/4, p. 307.
57 NRS B34/20/148.
58 NRS GD158/920.
59 NRS GD112/35/12, no. 4.
60 Thomson 1842–9, vol. 7, p. 177.
61 NRS E78/4.
62 NRS GD90/2/93.
63 NRS RH15/15/16
64 Stevenson and Thomson 1982, p. 22.
65 Beer 1959, p. 589.
66 NRS E23/9, no. 3.
67 NMS A.1988-187 and H.RHB6. See also Henshall and Maxwell 1964.
68 NRS E26/11/4, p. 305.
69 NRS GD214/582.
70 NRS E78/30, no. 178.
71 NRS RH15/123/11.
72 NRS GD305/1/151/111 and GD305/1/151/113.
73 NRS GD45/17/199.
74 NRS E26/11/4, p. 306.
75 NRS GD40/8/366, no. 2.
76 NRS GD112/39/70/19.
77 NRS GD112/35/11, no. 6.
78 NRS GD224/940/16.
79 Reid and Turner 1999, p. 43.
80 Reid and Turner 1999, p. 42.
81 Reid and Turner 1999, p. 39.
82 Reid and Turner 1999, p. 39.
83 Aylmer 1973, p. 139.
84 Southcombe and Tapsell 2010, p. 56.
85 Lauder of Fountainhall 1840, p. 19; Jackson 2003, p. 127.
86 Allen 1976, pp. 563, 568–9. See also Pittock 2013, pp. 80–81.
87 Gregg 1980, p. 68.
88 Act 4 scene 1; Dryden 1763, p. 78.
89 Akrigg 1984, p. 221.
90 Laing 1875, p. 332.
91 Beer 1959, p. 545.
92 Southcombe and Tapsell 2010, p. 67.
93 Latham and Matthews 1970–83, vol. 9, p. 155.
94 Latham and Matthews 1970–83, vol. 6, p. 170.
95 Nichols 1828, vol. 3, p. 265.
96 Borsay 1989, p. 194.
97 Borsay 1989, pp. 180–82, 186.
98 Borsay 1989, p. 187.
99 Rubinstein 1975, p. 261.
100 Browning 1991, p. 259.
101 Burnett 1998; Williamson 2002.
102 NRS GD122/3/2, no. 56.
103 NRS GD50/232/1.
104 NRS GD124/18/2.

105 NRS GD33/65/112/2, nos. 59 and 65.
106 NRS GD33/65/112/2, no. 67.
107 NRS GD33/65/112/2, no. 70.
108 NRS GD477/369, no. 6.
109 NRS PS1/87, ff. 169–70.
110 Anon. 1646a; Terry 1899, p. 126.
111 NRS GD45/18/959.
112 Latham and Matthews 1970–83, vol. 2, p. 64, and vol. 9, p. 542; Mann 2014, p. 139; Ouston 2000, pp. 271–3.
113 Dunbar 1999, pp. 91, 206–8.
114 TNA AO3/909/4, p. 14 and AO3/909/5, f. 4r.
115 E.g. TNA AO3/916, p. 37.
116 TNA AO3/920, p. 20.
117 NRS GD406/1/11134.
118 NRS GD237/25/1, no. 13.
119 NRS GD40/2/13/104.
120 NRS GD406/1/5977.
121 NRS GD40/2/3/27.
122 NRS GD3/5/2.
123 NRS GD237/25/1, no. 10.
124 NRS GD40/2/13/22 and GD112/39/43/17.
125 NRS AO3/919, 1670, p. 36; AO3/919, 1671, p. 32.
126 Schnitker and Clayes 2007, p. 17.
127 Quinton 2013, pp. 83–4, 89–90.
128 Quinton 2013, pp. 86–8.
129 NRS GD16/34/283.
130 Childs 1976, p. 64.
131 Childs 1976, p. 68.
132 NRS GD122/3/2, no. 68.
133 NRS RH15/49/2.
134 Linklater and Hesketh 1992, p. 93.
135 Linklater and Hesketh 1992, p. 93.
136 NRS GD30/2079.
137 Linklater and Hesketh 1992, pp. 107, 110.
138 NRS GD406/1/9392.
139 Gauden 1654, p. 27; Cressy 1997, p. 361.
140 NRS GD16/32/1.
141 NRS E661/103, no. 4.
142 V&A 175-1900; Hart and North 1998, p. 96.
143 *RPC, 1681–2*, 3rd series, p. 110.
144 NRS GD406/1/7808.
145 NRS GD406/1/7808.
146 Beer 1959, p. 874.
147 Misson 1719, pp. 349–50.
148 NRS GD406/1/6164.
149 NRS GD73/1/21, no. a.
150 NRS GD224/906/59, no. 16.
151 NRS GD406/1/266.
152 *CSPD, Charles II, 1660–61*, p. 466.
153 NRS GD112/29/35, no. 4.
154 NRS GD112/29/35, no. 6.
155 NRS GD40/9/100.
156 NRS GD16/31/165.
157 NRS GD112/39/163/6.
158 Marshall 1973, p. 161.
159 Marshall 1973, p. 162.
160 NRS GD112/3/78, no. 15.
161 NRS GD40/2/8/52.
162 NRS GD40/2/8/53.
163 NRS GD406/1/11578.
164 Linklater and Hesketh 1992, p. 142.
165 Stone 1965, pp. 247, 249–50.
166 NRS GD40/2/13/17.
167 NRS GD237/25/2, no. 4.
168 Anderson 1825, p. 167.

Chapter 11

1 Todd 2002; Dransart and Bogdan, 2004, pp. 457–70; Bowie 2013, p. 40.
2 Todd 2002, p. 403.
3 Daniell 2003, p. 458.
4 Cited in Todd 2002, p. 407.
5 NRS GD40/2/8/54.
6 Bonnar 1828, p. 89.
7 Duffy 1992, pp. 128–9, 494–5.
8 Pardailhé-Galabrun 1991, p. 209.
9 McRoberts 1956, pp. 69–88; Tarrant 2001a, pp. 76–9.
10 See Doda 2013, pp. 93–110.
11 *SR*, 3 James I, c.5.
12 L'Estrange 1687, pp. 136–7.
13 Hudson 2000, p. 29.
14 Bonnar 1828, p. 109.
15 Bonnar 1828, p. 520.
16 Mayo 1984, p. 111.
17 Mayo 1984, p. 111.
18 UoG, Bf71–g18, p. 107.
19 UoG, Bf71–g18, pp. 269–70.
20 Bod. Lib., Clarendon MS 109, f. 52.
21 Keay 2011, pp. 105–19.
22 Hibbert 2007, p. 57.
23 BL Add. MS 69,883B, f. 79r.
24 Scarisbrick 2011, pp. 48–9, 70.
25 Tudor-Craig 2004, pp. 13, 27, pl. VI B.
26 Harrison 1958, p. 17.
27 Wormald 2008, p. 373.
28 Nichols 1828, vol. 3, p. 230.
29 Nichols 1828, vol. 3, p. 340.
30 Spottiswoode 1847–51, vol. 3, p. 239.
31 Harrison 1958, p. 21.
32 Harrison 1958, p. 21.
33 Harrison 1958, p. 229.
34 TNA AO3/909/2, p. 61.
35 TNA AO3/909/2, p. 61.
36 Nichols 1828, vol. 2, p. 495.
37 Quoted in Strong 1986, p. 54.
38 Spalding 1830, p. 36.
39 Spalding 1830, p. 36.
40 Finlay 1956, pp. 100–01.
41 Scott and Bliss 1847–60, vol. 6.2, p. 419.
42 Scott and Bliss 1847–60, vol. 6.2, pp. 434–6.
43 *CSPD Charles I, 1640–41*, p. 49.
44 NRS GD25/9/2/13.
45 Fyfe 1928, p. 163.
46 Fyfe 1928, p. 166.
47 Stoyle 2011, pp. 174–5.
48 Fyfe 1928, p. 273.
49 Fincham 2003, p. 34.
50 Halifax 1750, p. 7.
51 Fyfe 1928, p. 274.
52 Raffe 2012, pp. 236–7.
53 UoG, MS Gen. 210, p. 145.
54 Latham and Matthews 1970–83, vol. 2, p. 38.
55 See *McRoberts and Oman 1968;* Finlay 1956, p. 119.
56 Fyfe 1928, p. 290.
57 Goldie 2007, p. 181.
58 NRS GD3/5/784.
59 Moryson 1617, Part 1, Book 3, ch. 5, p. 273.
60 NRS E21/84, f. 56.
61 Fyfe 1928, p. 179.
62 NRS GD103/2/1/12.
63 NRS CH2/122/135, unnumbered bill.
64 Innes 1855, p. 349.
65 NRS GD45/16/2520.
66 Lynch 1990, pp. 1–21.
67 NRS GD160/136/13.
68 NRS E23/3, nos. 18 and 45.
69 *RPC*, 5, p. 116.
70 NRS GD1/212/55. See also Bowers 2005, pp. 3-21.
71 Seton 1882, p. 87. He also attended Margaret's christening in 1599 (Seton 1882, p. 84).
72 Paton 1957, p. 340.
73 *CSPD, Charles I, 1629–31*, p. 283.
74 Anderson 1825, p. 136.
75 Folger MS X.c.132, no. 6.
76 NRS CH12/13/5.
77 Murray 2017, p. 155, and in the title of a paper Dr Murray gave at the Society of Renaissance Studies, University of Glasgow, 2016.
78 Brogan 2015, pp. 67–120.
79 Mapstone 1998, p. 180.
80 Rye 1865, p. 150.
81 Brogan 2015, pp. 85–6; Balfour 1825, vol. 4, p. 360.
82 NRS GD224/906/59, no 6.
83 Keay 2008, p. 115.
84 NRS GD157/1636.
85 Pittock 1991, p. 19.
86 Beer 1959, p. 893.
87 NRS E23/3, no. 39.
88 NRS E22/3, f. 47v; E22/4, f. 42r.
89 *CSPD, James I, 1611–18*, p. 58.
90 TNA LC5/39, p. 106.
91 TNA LC5/39, p. 228.
92 NRS GD224/906/59, no. 6.
93 NRS E26/11/4, p. 303.
94 Lauder of Fountainhall 1840, p. 157.
95 Sanderson 1997, p. 15.
96 NRS GD45/14/779.
97 NRS GD112/3/18.
98 Swain 1973, p. 32.
99 Lynch 1981, p. 29.
100 NRS GD220/2/1/168.
101 *RPC, 1607–10*, p. 301.
102 Swain 1973, p. 51; Davidson and King 2016, pp. 259–77.
103 NRS GD112/39/53/1.
104 Hunwicke 1993, pp. 112–13.
105 NRS CH2/122/135, unnumbered.
106 Morris 1947, pp. 125–6.
107 Tuckett 2014, p. 59.
108 NRS GD112/39/49/13.

109 NRS GD112/39/73/7.
110 Hume Brown 1973, pp. 159–60.
111 Fyfe 1928, p. 159.
112 TNA SP14/92/69.
113 Nichols 1828, vol. 3, p. 344; Mayo 1984, p. 74; Harmes 2014.
114 Peachey 1989, p. 11.
115 Wormald 2008, p. 381.
116 *APS*, IV, pp. 435–6.
117 Mayer-Thurman 1975, p. 53.
118 Anon. 1844, f. Cv.
119 Anon. 1890, p. 29.
120 Robertson 1845, p. 357.
121 Pitcairn 1842, p. 679.
122 *APS*, V, pp. 20–21; Mayo 1984, p. 99.
123 Hume Brown 1973, p. 258.
124 UoG, Bf71–g18, ff. A2v–A3.
125 Mayo 1984, p. 70; Johnstone 2002, p. 19.
126 Latham and Matthews 1970–83, vol. 3, p. 235.
127 Mackenzie 1691, p. 9.
128 Finlay 1956, p. 86.
129 NRS GD203/11/9.
130 Finlay 1956, p. 86.
131 NRS GD90/2/71.
132 NRS GD124/17/230.
133 NRS RH15/106/301, no. 25.
134 NRS GD160/286, no. 1.
135 NRS GD237/7/63, nos 11 and 12.
136 See Young 2016, pp. 136–9.
137 NRS GD40/2/16/23.
138 NRS GD157/1347.
139 NRS GD406/1/10500.
140 NRS GD248/345/1, no. 41.
141 NRS RH15/77/7.
142 NRS GD247/65/13.
143 Johnston 1999.
144 NRS GD30/1716.
145 Tarrant 2001a, p. 88.

Chapter 12

1 Quoted in Linklater and Hesketh 1992, pp. 220–21.
2 Brown 2000, pp. 251–70.
3 TNA LC2/4/6, ff. 26r–v.
4 Woodward 1997, p. 183.
5 TNA LC2/4/6, f. 31r.
6 *CSPD, James I, 1619–23*, p. 45.
7 Gerard von Honthorst, *Elizabeth Stuart, Queen of Bohemia*, 1642, oil on canvas, 205.1 × 130.8 cm, National Portrait Gallery, London, NPG 6362.
8 Taylor 1983, pp. 64–76.
9 TNA AO1/2048.2, f. 9v.
10 1632–3 (AO3/910/1), 1633–4 (AO3/910/2) and 1636–8 (AO3/910/5).
11 TNA AO3/910/1, p. 58.
12 TNA AO3/910/1, p. 57.
13 *CSPD, Charles II, 1660–61*, p. 333; he is also referred to as Francis Needham.
14 BL Add. MS 38,854, f. 31r.
15 Hoskins 1854, p. 324.
16 Scott 1905, p. 13.
17 *CSPD, Interregnum, 1656–7*, p. 342.
18 *CSPD, Charles II, 1682*, p. 556.
19 TNA AO3/919, p. 25.
20 Akrigg 1984, p. 215.
21 NRS GD112/39/23/6.
22 Latham and Matthews 1970–83, vol. 3, p. 81.
23 Latham and Matthews 1970–83, vol. 4, p. 344.
24 *CSPD, Charles II, 1671*, p. 220.
25 *CSPD, Charles II, 1673*, p. 193.
26 *CSPD, Charles II, 1679–80*, p. 300.
27 *CSPD, Charles II, 1679–80*, p. 310.
28 Priestley 1993, pp. 47–56.
29 NRS GD112/22/6.
30 NRS GD112/35/12, no. 7.
31 NRS E661/103, no. 25.
32 NRS GD112/39/157/11.
33 NRS GD112/39/67/16.
34 NRS GD112/39/67/18.
35 NRS GD112/39/42/22.
36 Sanderson 1997, p. 139.
37 Sanderson 1997, p. 139.
38 NRS GD112/15/65, no. 13.
39 NRS GD40/2/7/28.
40 NRS GD112/39/255/11.
41 *CSPD, James I, 1611–18*, pp. 134, 565.
42 Nichols 1828, vol. 3, p. 138; McClure 1939, vol. 1, p. 623; Woodward 1997, p. 145.
43 *CSPD, James I, 1611–18*, p. 361.
44 Nichols 1828, vol. 3, p. 138.
45 *CSPD James I, 1611–18*, p. 473.
46 BL Cotton MS Faustina E.1.
47 McClure 1939, vol. 2, p. 616.
48 Thomson 1842–9, vol. 7, p. 634.
49 *LP* XVII, 1221.
50 Marshall 1977, p. 46.
51 Marshall 1977, pp. 97–8.
52 Marshall 1977, p. 99.
53 NRS E23/3, no. 23.
54 NRS E23/3, no. 34.
55 NRS E23/3, no. 25.
56 Llewellyn 1991, pp. 65–7.
57 Buxton 1989, p. 50.
58 NRS E24/41, f. 82.
59 Personal communication with Dr Michael Pearce.
60 BL Harley MS 293, f. 211r.
61 See Sutton and Visser-Fuchs 1996.
62 Woodward 1997, p. 141.
63 Woodward 1997, p. 201.
64 Gittings 1984, pp. 175, 195–7.
65 Woodward 1997, pp. 144–5.
66 Woodward 1997, p. 201.
67 TNA LC2/6, f. 3r.
68 *CSPD, Charles II, 1682*, p. 565.
69 *CSPD, James I, 1611–18*, p. 18.
70 TNA E405/283, p. 29.
71 TNA E405/284, account 10, p. 40.
72 *CSPD, Charles II, 1667*, p. 104.
73 *CSPD, Charles II, 1684–5*, p. 87.
74 NRS GD40/2/18/1/50.
75 Lockyer 1984, pp. 457–8.
76 *CSP Venetian, 1628–9*, p. 337.
77 NRS GD237/25/1, no. 4.
78 *CSPD, Interregnum, 1657–8*, p. 68.
79 *CSPD, Interregnum, 1657–8*, p. 179.
80 *CSPD, Interregnum, 1652–3*, p. 425.
81 TNA LC5/12, p. 331; LC5/63, pp. 323–38.
82 Fritz 1981, p. 62.
83 Harvey and Mortimer 2003, pp. 73–8.
84 TNA LC5/85, unfoliated.
85 TNA LC5/85, unfoliated.
86 NRS GD477/358, no. 15.
87 Verney, 1968, p. 177.
88 *CSPD, Charles II, 1670*, p. 68.
89 *CSPD, Charles II, 1670*, p. 165.
90 NRS GD406/1/11960.
91 *CSPD, Charles II, 1670*, p. 182.
92 TNA LC5/41, f. 32v.
93 NRS GD112/39/56/14.
94 NRS PA2/26, nos. 7–8.
95 Nicoll 1836, p. 316.
96 NRS GD30/2203.
97 Slater 2013, pp. 46–7.
98 NRS GD157/1373; also GD30/2016.
99 Clifford and Pearson 1991, p. 13.
100 Kingston 1829, p. 60.
101 McClure 1939, vol. 2, p. 604.
102 NRS GD112/3/57.
103 See Spicer 2000, pp. 149–50. It would be repeated in 1631 and 1643.
104 NRS GD112/39/28/10.
105 NRS GD406/1/4604.
106 NRS GD24/1/365A, no. 2.
107 NRS GD112/39/151/15.
108 NRS GD112/39/151/17.
109 NRS GD406/1/11249.
110 NRS GD112/39/151/13.
111 NRS GD217/759.
112 NRS RH14/243.
113 NRS GD40/8/365 and GD185/21/7, no. 2.
114 NRS GD112/29/42, no. 10.
115 NRS GD112/35/14, no. 15.
116 NRS GD224/925/39, no. 7.
117 NRS GD112/29/43, no. 10.
118 NRS GD112/29/24, no. 16.
119 Anon. 1877, p. 246.
120 NRS GD112/26/35.
121 NRS GD237/7/68, no. 7.
122 NRS RH15/112/4/37.
123 NRS GD3/6/14, no. 13.
124 NRS GD406/1/10064.
125 See Strong 1965.
126 NRS GD224/935/6.
127 Williamson 2017, pp. 4–7.
128 NRS GD112/39/54/10.
129 NRS GD124/15/117.
130 NRS GD112/26/36.
131 Spicer 2000, p. 151.
132 Macinnes 2000, p. 22.
133 NRS GD112/38/17, no. 8.
134 Ohlmeyer 1993b, pp. 13–14.
135 Hearn 2009, p. 111.

Bibliography

PRIMARY SOURCES

England

Bodleian Library, Oxford
Clarendon MS 60, 109

British Library, London
Add. MS 4,177, 5,750, 8,126, 10,118, 12,528, 24,928, 25,348, 29,975, 37,047, 38,854, 69,883B, 75,303, 75,391
Cotton MS Faustina E.1
Egerton MS 2,542, 2,816
Harley MS 293, 589, 6272
Royal MS 18.B.IV
Stowe MS 555, 563

Brotherton Library, Leeds
MS dep. 1984/3/5

Canterbury Cathedral Archives and Library, Kent
Lit MS/E/39

Christ Church, Oxford
Cathedral Register

Claydon House, Buckinghamshire
CLA 4/5/2/18

Dorset History Centre, Dorchester
D.FSI Box 267: Account for household expenses 1659
D.FSI Box 268: General household accounts 1658–59
D.FSI. Box 268, Accounts 1660–64
D.FSI Box 268: Dispursements made at Paris for his majesty's journey to Spa, 1654 to 1655.

Lincolnshire Record Office, Lincoln
I-Worsley/6

London Metropolitan Archive
AM/P1 (1) 1673/33
CLA/024/06/002 – MCD2/30

Pepys Library, Cambridge
2295

The National Archive, Kew
AO1 Auditors of the Imprest and Commissioners of Audit: Declared accounts
AO3 Auditors of the Imprest and Successors: Various accounts
E101 Exchequer, King's Remembrancer: Accounts Various
E403 Exchequer of Receipt: Issue Rolls and Registers
E405 Exchequer of Receipt: Jornalia Rolls, Tellers' Rolls, Certificate Books, Declaration Books and Accounts of Receipts
LC2 Lord Chamberlain's Department: Records of Special Events
LC5 Lord Chamberlain's Department: Miscellaneous Records
LC9 Lord Chamberlain's Department: Accounts and Miscellanea
LR5 Office of the Auditors of Land Revenue and predecessors and successors: Vouchers and Accounts
PROB11 Prerogative Court of Canterbury and related Probate Jurisdictions: Will Registers
SP8 State Papers Office, King William's Chest
SP14 State Papers Domestic, James I
SP16 State Papers Domestic, Charles I
SP29 State Papers Domestic, Charles II

National Art Library, Victoria and Albert Museum, London
MSL/1935/320

Northamptonshire Record Office, Northampton
Isham correspondence, 1379

Nottingham University Library, Nottingham
MS PwV92
Portland MS Pw V 93

Royal Collection, London
Inventory of Charles II's pictures at Whitehall and Hampton Court

Society of Antiquaries, London
MS 129

Trinity College, Cambridge
MS R.7.23* (3)

University Library, Cambridge
MS Dd.1.26

Scotland

National Library of Scotland, Edinburgh
MS 83

National Records of Scotland, Edinburgh
B34 Records of Inverkeithing Burgh
B59 Records of Perth Burgh
CH2 Records of Church of Scotland synods, presbyteries and kirk sessions
CH12 Records of the Episcopal Church of Scotland

E18 Commissions for the Exchequer and Treasury, for offices concerned with the revenue and for auditing accounts
E19 Exchequer Records: Exchequer and Treasury Papers
E21 Exchequer Records: Accounts of the Treasurer
E22 Exchequer Records: Accounts of the Treasurer (Leven and Melville series)
E23 Exchequer Records: Treasury Precepts and Receipts
E26 Exchequer Records: Accounts of the Comptroller
E34 Exchequer Records: Household Papers and Accounts
E35 Exchequer Records: Wardrobe Inventories, Accounts and Papers
E71 Customs Books (1st series)
E78 Excise Accounts
E96 Artillery and military stores papers
E661 Exchequer Records: Forfeited Estates Papers 1715: Particular Estates: Winton
GD1 Miscellaneous small collections of family, business and other papers
GD3 Papers of the Montgomerie Family, Earls of Eglinton
GD16 Papers of the Earls of Airlie
GD20 Papers of the Earls of Glasgow (Crawford Priory)
GD22 Papers of the Cunninghame Graham Family of Ardoch, Dunbartonshire
GD23 Warrand of Bught
GD24 Papers of the Family of Stirling Home Drummond Moray of Abercairny, Perthshire
GD25 Papers of the Kennedy Family, Earls of Cassillis (Ailsa Muniments)
GD26 Papers of the Leslie Family, Earls of Leven and Melville
GD27 Kennedy of Dalquharran
GD29 Papers of the Bruce Family of Kinross (Kinross House Papers)
GD30 Papers of the Shairp Family of Houston, West Lothian
GD32 Papers of the Viscounts and Barons of Elibank
GD33 Papers of the Marquess of Aberdeen and Temair
GD34 Papers of the Family of Hay of Haystoun, Peeblesshire
GD37 Papers of the Bruce Family of Airth
GD40 Papers of the Kerr Family, Marquises of Lothian (Lothian Muniments)
GD44 Papers of the Gordon Family, Dukes of Gordon (Gordon Castle Muniments)
GD45 Papers of the Maule Family, Earls of Dalhousie
GD49 Papers of the Barclay Allardice Family of Allardice
GD50 The John MacGregor Collection
GD52 Lord Forbes papers
GD56 Papers of the Rollo family of Duncrub, Perthshire
GD66 Boswell of Balmuto
GD72 Papers of the Hay family of Park
GD73 Papers of the Hay Family of Belton near Dunbar, East Lothian
GD89 Papers of the Carmichael Family of Skirling
GD90 Yule Collection
GD103 Papers of Society of Antiquaries of Scotland
GD109 Papers of the family of Dalrymple-Hamilton of Bargany, Ayrshire
GD111 Papers of Messrs A. O. Curle and J. Curle
GD112 Papers of the Campbell Family, Earls of Breadalbane (Breadalbane Muniments)
GD122 Little Gilmour of Craigmiller and Liberton
GD124 Papers of the Erskine Family, Earls of Mar and Kellie
GD128 Fraser-Mackintosh Collection
GD148 Papers of the Cuninghame Family of Craigends, Renfrewshire
GD150 Papers of the Earls of Morton
GD157 Papers of the Scott Family of Harden, Lords Polwarth, Berwickshire
GD158 Papers of the Family of Hume of Polwarth, Berwickshire, Earls of Marchmont
GD160 Papers of the Drummond Family, Earls of Perth (Drummond Castle Papers)
GD164 Papers of the Sinclair Family, Earls of Rosslyn
GD170 Papers of the Campbell Family of Barcaldine
GD181 Aboyne Muniments
GD185 Papers of the Abercromby Family of Forglen and Birkenbog
GD203 Lindsay Papers
GD214 Papers of Professor Robert K. Hannay
GD215 Papers of James Beveridge, M.A., Linlithgow
GD220 Papers of the Graham Family, Dukes of Montrose (Montrose Muniments)
GD224 Papers of the Montague-Douglas-Scott Family, Dukes of Buccleuch
GD237 Records of Messrs Tods Murray and Jamieson WS, lawyers, Edinburgh
GD246 Records of Gillespie, Macandrew and Co., WS (incorporating Hope, Todd and Kirk, WS), lawyers, Edinburgh
GD247 Records of Brodies, WS (incorporating John C. Brodie and Sons, WS)
GD248 Papers of the Ogilvy Family, Earls of Seafield (Seafield Papers)
GD249 Papers of the Earls of Haddington
GD254 Papers of the Lindsay Family of Dowhill
GD305 Papers of the MacKenzie Family, Earls of Cromartie (Cromartie Muniments)
GD406 Papers of the Douglas Hamilton Family, Dukes of Hamilton and Brandon
GD421 Records of George Heriot's Trust, Edinburgh
GD472 Papers of the Jardine Family of Applegirth
GD477 Papers of the Scott Family of Gala, Selkirkshire
GD504 Papers of the Sprot Family of Haystoun, Peeblesshire

PA2 Acts of the Parliaments
PA7 Supplementary Warrants and Parliamentary Papers
PC12 Warrants of the Committee of Estates
PC15 Privy Council: Supplementary Papers
PS1 Latin and English register, old series, 1488–1651
RH6 Register House charters, 1st series
RH9 Miscellaneous Papers
RH14 Warrants, 2nd series, Mack
RH15 Miscellaneous Papers (formerly known as MP Bundles)
—— RH15/7 Andrew Brown, Edinburgh
—— RH15/14 Alexander Campbell, merchant in Edinburgh, and Alexander Campbell, advocate, his son-in-law
—— RH15/15 Papers of Sir Andrew Home, Lord Kimmerghame
—— RH15/29 Adam Hepburne of Bonhard and lands of Craigmackerrane, 1545–1637
—— RH15/30 Andrew Hay
—— RH15/49 James Baillie, Captain of the Town Guard, Edinburgh
—— RH15/57 George Cessford, writer in Edinburgh
—— RH15/106 Papers of Andrew Russell, merchant in Rotterdam
—— RH15/123 Viscount Strathallan
RH18 Miscellaneous Publications
SP13 State Papers Miscellanea

National Register of Archives for Scotland, Edinburgh

332/F/1/52
F/1/20, no. 28
F/1/154/3, no. 5

Special Collections, University of Glasgow

Bf71–g.18
MS Gen. 210, 1769.1.40
MS Hunter 58, 73, 238
MS Murray 147

USA

Folger Shakespeare Library, Washington, DC

MS V.a.345
MS X.c.49 (4), X.c.90, nos. 1 and 2, MS.X.c.132, no. 6
MS X.d.75, X.d.76, X.d.478, X.d.587
MS 26,5630
Loseley Manuscripts, L.B. 638

Morgan Library, New York

Rulers of England Box 10 James II, unfoliated

PRINTED PRIMARY AND SECONDARY SOURCES

Adams, Sharon and Julian Goodare (eds), 2014, *Scotland in the Age of Two Revolutions* (Woodbridge: Boydell Press)

Akrigg, George Philip Vernon (ed.), 1984, *Letters of King James VI and I* (Berkeley, Calif.: University of California Press)

Allen, David, 1976, 'Political Clubs in Restoration London', *HJ*, 19.3, pp. 561–80

Anderson, John, 1825, *Historical and Genealogical Memoirs of the House of Hamilton* (Edinburgh: John Anderson)

Anon., 1620, *Hic mulier: Or, The Man-Woman: Being a Medicine to cure the Coltish Disease of the Staggers in the Masculine-Feminines of Our Times* (London: Eliot's Court Press)

——, 1646a, *A Continuation of Papers from the Scotts Quarters* (London)

——, 1646b, *A Declaration Published in the Scots Army, Proclaimed by Order from General Leven at Durham* (London: Printed for Matthew Walbanck)

——, 1648, *True Information of the Beginning and Cause of all our Troubles* (London)

——, 1688 *Depositions taken the 22 October 1688 before the Privy Council and Peers of England, Relating to the Birth of the Prince of Wales* (London)

——, 1767–1830, *Journal of the House of Lords: Volume 6: 1643* (London: HMSO)

——, 1832, *Letters of Eminent Men Addressed to Ralph Thoresby*, vol. 2 (London: Henry Colburn and Richard Bentley)

——, 1844, *The Book of Common Prayer Printed by Whitchurch March 1549 Commonly Called The First Book of Edward VI* (London: William Pickering)

——, 1863, *The Little London Directory of 1677* (London: John Camden Hotten)

——, 1877, 'Will of Frances Stuart, countess of Richmond and Lennox', *Archaeologia Cantiana*, 11, pp. 232–50

——, 1890, *The Second Prayer Book of King Edward VI, 1552* (London: Griffith, Farran, Browne & Co.)

Anzilotti, Gloria, 1988, *An English Prince: Newcastle's Machiavellian Political Guide to Charles II* (Pisa: Giardini Editori E Stampatori)

Arch, Nigel, 2007, 'The Wearing of the Red: The Redcoat and the British Brand', *Costume*, 41.1, pp. 99–104

Arnold, Janet, 1975, 'Decorative Features: Pinking, Snipping and Slashing', *Costume*, 9.1, pp. 22–6

——, 1980, 'Sweet England's Jewels' in Jill Hollis (ed.), 1980, *Princely Magnificence: Court Jewels of the Renaissance, 1500–1630* (London: V&A Publishing), pp. 31–40

——, 1985, *Patterns of Fashion: The Cut and Construction of Clothes for Men and Women, c. 1560–1620* (Basingstoke: Macmillan)

——, 1988, *Queen Elizabeth's Wardrobe Unlock'd* (Leeds: Maney)

Ashelford, Jane, 1983, *A Visual History of Costume: The Sixteenth Century* (London: Batsford)

——, 1988, *Dress in the Age of Elizabeth I* (London: Batsford)
Ashenburg, Katherine, 2008, *Clean: An Unsanitised History of Washing* (London: Profile Books)
Ashley, Maurice, 1977, *James II* (London: J. M. Dent)
Ashton, Robert, 1969, *James I by his Contemporaries* (London: Hutchinson)
Awais-Dean, Natasha, 2017, *Bejewelled: Men and Jewellery in Tudor and Jacobean England* (London: British Museum Press)
Aylmer, Gerald, 1961, *The King's Servants: The Civil Service of Charles I, 1625–1642* (London: Routledge & Kegan Paul)
——, 1973, 'St Patrick's Day in 1628 in Witham, Essex', *Past & Present*, 61.1, pp. 139–48
Bacon, Francis, 1778, *The Works of Francis Bacon, Baron of Verulam, Viscount St Albans and Lord High Chancellor of England*, vol. 2 (London: J. Rivington & Sons)
——, 1955, *Essays* (London: J. M. Dent)
Bailey, Amanda, 2007, *Flaunting: Style and the Subversive Male Body in Renaissance England* (Toronto: University of Toronto Press)
Balfour, Sir James, 1825, *The Historical Works of Sir James Balfour*, 4 vols (Edinburgh: W. Aitchison)
Barclay, Andrew, 2010, 'The inventories of the English royal collection, temp. James II', *Journal of the History of Collections*, 22.1, pp 1–13
Barnard, Toby, 2000, 'The viceregal court in later seventeenth century Ireland', in Eveline Cruickshanks (ed.), *The Stuart Courts* (Stroud: Alan Sutton), pp. 256–65
Barratt, John, 2015, *Cavalier Capital: Oxford in the English Civil War 1642–1646* (Solihull: Helion)
Bartley, James Orr, 1954, *Teague, Shenkin and Sawney, Being an Historical Study of the Earliest Irish, Welsh and Scottish Characters in English Plays* (Cork: Cork University Press)
Bath, Michael, 2003, *Renaissance Decorative Ceilings in Scotland* (Edinburgh: National Museums of Scotland Publishing, 2003)
Beard, Geoffrey, 1997, *Upholsterers and Interior Furnishings in England, 1530–1840* (New Haven and London: Yale University Press)
Beer, Esmond Samuel de, 1938–9, 'King Charles II's own fashion: An episode in English–French relations, 1666–1670', *JWCI*, 2, pp. 105–15
——, 1959, *The Diary of John Evelyn* (Oxford: Oxford University Press)
Bellany, Alastair, 2002, *The Politics of Court Scandal in Early Modern England: News Culture and the Overbury Affair, 1603–1660* (Cambridge: Cambridge University Press)
Belsey, Catherine, 1999, *Shakespeare and the Loss of Eden: The Construction of Family Values in Early Modern Culture* (Basingstoke: Palgrave Macmillan)
Beneden, B. van and N. de Poorter (eds), 2006, *Royalist Refugees: William and Margaret Cavendish in the Rubens House 1648–1660* (Antwerp: Rubenshuis & Rubenianum)
Berg, Jonas and Bo Lagercrantz, 1962, *Scots in Sweden* (Stockholm: Nordiska Museet)
Birch, Thomas, 1742, *A Collection of the State Papers of John Thurloe*, vol. 2, *1654* (London)
——, 1760, *The Life of Henry, Prince of Wales, Eldest Son of King James I* (Dublin: G. Faulkner)
——, 1848, *The Court and Times of Charles the First*, 2 vols (London: Henry Colburn)
——, 1849, *The Court and Times of James the First*, 2 vols (London: Henry Colburn)
Bird, Rufus (ed.), 2017, *Charles II: Art & Power* (London: Royal Collection Trust)
Blair, Claude, 1958, *European Armour, circa 1066 to circa 1700* (London: Batsford)
——, 1981, 'The early basket-hilt in Britain', in David Caldwell (ed.), *Scottish Weapons and Fortifications, 1100–1800* (Edinburgh: John Donald Publishers), pp. 153–252
Blakeway, Amy, 2015, *Regency in Sixteenth Century Scotland* (Woodbridge: Boydell Press)
Blanch, John, 1691, *The Character of a Bigotted Prince* (London)
Blount, Thomas, 1660, *Boscobel: Or, the Compleat History of the Most Miraculous Preservation of King Charles II* (London)
Bonnar, Andrew (ed.), 1828, *Letters of Samuel Rutherford* (London: Religious Tract Society)
Boorde, Andrew, 1562, *The Fyrst Boke of the Introduction of Knowledge* (London)
Borsay, Peter, 1989, *The English Urban Renaissance: Culture and Society in the Provincial Town, 1660–1770* (Oxford: Oxford University Press)
Bowers, Fredson (ed.), 1968, *The Dramatic Works of Thomas Dekker* (Cambridge: Cambridge University Press)
Bowers, Rick, 2005, 'James VI, Prince Henry and a true reportarie of baptism at Stirling, 1594', *Renaissance and Reformation*, 29, pp. 3–21
Bowie, Karin, 2013, 'Cultural, British and global turns in the history of early modern Scotland', *SHR*, 92 supplement, pp. 38–48
Bowle, John, 1975, *Charles the First* (London: Little, Brown)
Bray, William, 1806, 'An Account of the Revenue, the Expenses, the Jewels etc. of Prince Henry', *Archaeologia*, 15, pp. 13–26
Bremer, Francis, 2009, *Puritanism: A Very Short Introduction* (Oxford: Oxford University Press)
Breward, Christopher, 1995, *The Culture of Fashion: A New History of Fashionable Dress* (Manchester: Manchester University Press)
——, 2009, 'Fashioning the modern self: clothing, cavaliers and identity in van Dyck's London',

in Karen Hearn (ed.), *Van Dyck & Britain* (London: Tate Publishing), pp. 24–35
Brogan, Stephen, 2015, *The Royal Touch in Early Modern England: Politics, Medicine and Sin* (Woodbridge: Boydell & Brewer)
Brooke, Xanthe, 1992, *The Lady Lever Art Gallery: Catalogue of Embroideries* (Stroud: Allan Sutton)
Brown, Christopher and Hans Vlieghe, 1999, *Anthony van Dyck 1599–1641* (London: Royal Academy Publications)
Brown, Keith, 1993, 'The Scottish Aristocracy, Anglicization and the Court, 1603–38', *HJ*, 36.3, pp. 543–76
——, 1994, 'The Vanishing Emperor: British Kingship and its Decline 1603–1707', in Roger Mason (ed.), *Scots and Britons: Scottish Political Thought and the Union of 1603* (Cambridge: Cambridge University Press), pp. 58–88
——, 2000, *Noble Society in Scotland: Wealth, Family and Culture from Reformation to Revolution* (Edinburgh: Edinburgh University Press)
Brown, Piers, 2008, '"Hac ex consilio meo via progredieris": Courtly Reading and Secretarial Mediation in Donne's *The Courtier's Library*', *Renaissance Quarterly*, 61.3, pp. 833–66
Browning, Andrew (ed.), 1991, *Memoirs of Sir John Reresby: The Complete Text and a Selection from his Letters*, 2nd edn (London: Royal Historical Society)
Bruce, John, 1861, *Letters of Queen Elizabeth and James VI* (London: Camden Society)
Bruce, Steve and Steve Yearley, 1989, 'The social construction of tradition: the Restoration portraits and the kings of Scotland', in David McCrone, Stephen Kendrick and Patricia Shaw (eds), *The Making of Scotland: Nation, Culture and Social Change* (Edinburgh: Edinburgh University of Press), pp. 175–87
Bryant, Arthur (ed.), 1935, *The letters, speeches and declarations of King Charles II* (London: Cassell)
Brydon, Robert, 1993, *The Scottish Coronation Journey of Charles I* (Kirkcaldy: Sporting Partnership)
Bryson, Anna, 1998, *From Courtesy to Civility: Changing Codes of Conduct in Early Modern England* (Oxford: Oxford University Press)
Buckroyd, Julia, 1975, 'Mercurius Caledonius and Its Immediate Successors, 1661', *SHR*, 54.1, pp. 11–21
Burnet, Gilbert, 1818, *Bishop Burnet's History of His Own Time*, vol. 2 (London: J. Nunn)
Burnett, Charles and Helen Bennett, 1987, *The Green Mantle: A Celebration of the Revival in 1687 of the Most Ancient and Most Noble Order of the Thistle* (Edinburgh: National Museums of Scotland)
Burnett, John, 1998, 'The Sites and Landscapes of Horse Racing in Scotland before 1860', *Sports Historian*, 18.1, pp. 55–75
Bury, Shirley, 1985, *An Introduction to Sentimental Jewellery* (London: HMSO)
Buxton, John, 1989, 'The mourning for Sidney', *Renaissance Studies*, 3.1, pp. 46–56
Byrde, Penelope, 1979, *Male Image: Men's Fashion in England, 1300–1970* (London: Batsford)
Caldwell, David, 1981, 'Some notes on Scottish axes and long-shafted weapons', in David Caldwell (ed.), *Scottish Weapons and Fortifications, 1100–1800* (Edinburgh: John Donald Publishers), pp. 253–314
Camden, William, 1625, *Annales: The True and Royall History of the Famous Empresse Elizabeth, Queen of England, France and Ireland* (London)
Cameron, George, 1979, *The Scots Kirk in London* (Oxford: Becket Publications)
Carlton, Charles, 1983, *Charles I: The Personal Monarch* (London: Routledge)
——, 1987, *Archbishop William Laud* (London: Routledge)
Carpenter, Sarah and Graham Runnalls, 2000, 'The entertainments at the marriage of Mary, Queen of Scots and the French Dauphin François, 1558: Paris and Edinburgh', *Medieval English Theatre*, 22, pp. 145–61
Cassavetti, Eileen, 1977, *The Lion and the Lilies: The Stuarts and France* (London: Macdonald and Jane's)
Castiglione, Baldassare, 1976, *The Book of the Courtier*, trans. Sir Thomas Hoby (Harmondsworth: Penguin)
Cavendish, William, earl of Newcastle, 1999, *The Country Captain*, Malone Society Reprints 162 (Oxford: Oxford University Press)
Chadour-Sampson, Beatriz with Hubert Bari, 2013, *Pearls* (London: V&A Publishing)
Chambers, Edmund, 1936, *Sir Henry Lee: An Elizabethan Portrait* (Oxford: Clarendon Press)
Chapman, Stanley, 1972, 'The Genesis of the British Hosiery Industry, 1600–1750', *Textile History*, 3.1, pp. 7–50
Chatenet, Monique, 1999, 'Cherchez le lit: the place of the bed in sixteenth-century French residences', *Transactions of the Ancient Monuments Society*, 24, pp. 7–24
Cheape, Hugh, 2006, *Tartan: The Highland Habit*, 3rd edn (Edinburgh: NMS Publishing)
Cheape, Hugh and Anita Quye, 2005, 'Historical and analytical research of dyes in early Scottish tartans', in Robert Janaway and Paul Wyeth (eds), *The Scientific Analysis of Ancient and Historic Textiles*, AHRC Research Centre for Textile Conservation and Textile Studies Annual

Conference, July 2004 (London: Archetype Publications), pp. 202–7
Childs, John, 1976, *The Army of Charles II* (London: Routledge & Kegan Paul)
Chisholm, J., 1891, 'The sumptuary laws of Scotland', *Journal of Jurisprudence*, 35, pp. 290–97
Clarendon, Edward, earl of, 1827, *The Life of Edward, Earl of Clarendon*, vol. 1 (Oxford: Clarendon Press)
——, 1839, *The History of the Rebellion and Civil Wars in England*, vol. 1 (Oxford: The University Press)
Clark, Neil, 2014, *Scottish Gold: Fruit of the Nation* (Glasgow: Neil Wilson Publishing)
Cliffe, J. Trevor, 1984, *The Puritan Gentry: The Great Puritan Families of Early Stuart England* (London: Routledge & Kegan Paul)
Clifford, David (ed.), 1990, *The Diaries of Lady Anne Clifford* (Stroud: Alan Sutton)
Clifford, Timothy and Fiona Pearson, 1991, *Virtue and Vision: Sculpture and Scotland* (Edinburgh: National Galleries of Scotland)
Cole, Susan (ed.), 1975, *A Flower of Purpose: A Memoir of Princess Elizabeth Stuart* (Ilford: Royal Stuart Society)
Colley, Linda, 1992, *Britons: Forging the Nation 1707–1837* (New Haven and London: Yale University Press)
Corfield, Penelope, 1989, 'Dress for deference and dissent: hats and the decline of hat honour', *Costume*, 23.1, pp. 64–79
Corp, Edward, 2000, 'The Jacobite court at Saint-Germain-en-Laye', in Eveline Cruickshanks (ed.), *The Stuart Courts* (Stroud: Alan Sutton), pp. 240–55
——, 2009, *A Court in Exile: The Stuarts in France, 1689–1718* (Cambridge: Cambridge University Press)
——, 2014, *The Stuarts in Italy, 1719–1766: A Royal Court in Permanent Exile* (Cambridge: Cambridge University Press)
Courtin, Antoine de, 1678, *The Rules of Civility* (London)
Coward, Barry, 1996, *The Stuart Age: England 1603–1714*, 2nd edn (London: Longman)
Cramsie, John, 2015, *British Travellers and the Encounter with Britain, 1450–1700* (Woodbridge: Boydell & Brewer)
Cressy, David, 1997, *Birth, Marriage and Death: Ritual, Religion and the Life Cycle in Tudor and Stuart England* (Oxford: Oxford University Press)
——, 2000, *Travesties and Transgressions in Tudor and Stuart England: Tales of Discord and Dissension* (Oxford: Oxford University Press)
——, 2004, *Bonfires and Bell: National Memory and the Protestant Calendar in Elizabethan and Stuart England* (Stroud: Alan Sutton)
Croft, Pauline, 1999, 'Can a bureaucrat be a favourite? Robert Cecil and the strategies of power', in John Elliott and Laurence Brockliss (eds), *The World of the Favourite* (New Haven and London: Yale University of Press, 1999), pp. 81–95
——, 2003, *King James* (Basingstoke: Palgrave Macmillan)
Cuddy, Neil, 1987, 'The revival of the entourage: the bedchamber of James I, 1603–1625', in David Starkey (ed.), *The English Court from the Wars of the Roses to the Civil War* (London: Longman), pp. 173–225
——, 1989, 'Anglo-Scottish Union and the Court of James I, 1603–1625', *TRHS*, 39, pp. 107–24
Cumming, Valerie, 1978, 'The trousseau of Princess Elizabeth Stuart', in *Collectanea Londiniensia*, vol. 2 (London: Museum of London), pp. 315–28
——, 1984, *A Visual History of Costume: The Seventeenth Century* (London: Batsford)
——, 1989a, *Royal Dress: The Image and Reality 1580 to the Present Day* (London: Batsford)
——, 1989b, '"Great vanity and excesse in Apparell": some clothing and furs of Tudor and Stuart royalty', in Arthur MacGregor (ed.), *The Late King's Goods: Collections, Possessions ,and Patronage of Charles I in the Light of the Commonwealth Sale Inventories* (London and Oxford: Oxford University Press), pp. 322–50
——, 2004, 'The fashionable merchant: a case study', in Mireille Galinou (ed.), *City Merchants and the Arts 1670–1720* (London: Oblong Creative), pp. 121–31
Cunnington, Cecil Willett and Phillis Cunnington, 1955, *Handbook of English Costume in the 17th Century* (London: Faber & Faber)
Curle, Alex, 1906, 'Notes on the Inventories of the House of Rossie, near Montrose, dating from the year 1693 to 1740', *PSAS*, 40, pp. 53–9
Curtin, Michael, 1985, 'A Question of Manners: Status and Gender in Etiquette and Courtesy', *Journal of Modern History*, 57.3, pp. 395–423
Curthoys, Judith, 2012, *The Cardinal's College: Christ Church, Chapter and Verse* (London: Profile Books)
Cust, Sir Lionel and Arthur Mayger Hind, 1933–4, 'Vertue – III. Note-books', *Walpole Society*, 22
Cust, Richard, 2005, *Charles I: A Political Life* (Harlow: Pearson Education)
Dalton, Ormonde Maddock, 1912, *Catalogue of Finger Rings in the British Museum* (London: British Museum Press)
——, 2013, *Charles I and the Aristocracy, 1625–1642* (Cambridge: Cambridge University Press)
Daniell, David, 2003, *The Bible in English: Its History and Influence* (New Haven and London: Yale University Press)

Davidson, Peter and Prue King, 2016, 'The Fetternear Vestments at the Blairs Museum', *British Catholic History*, 33.2, pp. 259–77
Day, Richard, 1578, *A Booke of Christian Prayers* (London)
Defoe, Daniel, 1701, *The True-born Englishman: A Satyr* (London)
Dekker, Thomas and Thomas Middleton, 2017, *The Roaring Girl* (Newton Stewart: Anodos Books)
Devon, Frederick (ed.), 1836, *Issues of the Exchequer Being Payments Made out of His Majesty's Revenue During the Reign of King James I* (London: John Rodwell)
Doda, Hilary, 2013, 'Rounde Heades in Square Cappes: The Role of Vestments in the Vestarian Controversy', *Dress*, 39.2, pp. 93–110
Doran, Susan, 2015, *Elizabeth I and Her Circle* (Oxford: Oxford University Press)
Douglas, David C., 1953, *English Historical Documents: 1660–1714* (Oxford: Oxford University Press)
Dransart, Penelope and Nicholas Bogdan, 2004, 'The Material Culture of Recusancy at Fetternear: Kin and Religion in Post-Reformation Scotland', *Proceedings of the Scottish Society of Antiquaries*, 134, pp. 457–70
Dryden, John, 1763, *The Dramatick Works of John Dryden in Six Volumes*, vol. 3 (London: J. & R. Tonson)
Duffy, Eamon, 1992, *The Stripping of the Altars: Traditional Religion in England, 1400–1580* (New Haven and London: Yale University Press)
Dunbar, John, 1999, *Scottish Royal Palaces: The Architecture of Royal Residences during the Late Medieval and Early Renaissance Periods* (East Lothian: Tuckwell Press)
Dunbar, John Telfer, 1979, *The History of Highland Dress: A Definitive Study of Scottish Costume and Tartan, Both Civil and Military, Including Weapons* (London: HarperCollins)
Duncan-Jones, Katherine, 1997, *Shakespeare's Sonnets* (London: Arden Shakespeare)
Dyce, Alexander (ed.), 1830, *The Works of John Webster*, vol. 2 (London: William Pickering)
Edwards, Lesley, 1985, 'Dres't like a May-pole: a study of two suits of c. 1660–62', *Costume*, 19.1, pp. 75–93
Elliott, John, 1992, 'A Europe of composite monarchies', *Past & Present*, 137, pp. 48–71
Evans, Joan, 1953, 1970, A *History of Jewellery, 1100–1870* (London: Faber & Faber)
Evans, Mark, 1998, *Princes as Patrons: The Art Collections of the Princes of Wales from the Renaissance to the Present Day* (London: Merrell Holberton)
Evelyn, John, 1951, *Tyrannus* or *The Mode* (Oxford: Basil Blackwell)
Everett-Green, Mary Anne (ed.), 1968, *Diary of John Rous, Incumbant of Santon Downham, Suffolk, from 1625 to 1642* (New York: AMS Press)
Fairholt, Frederick William (ed.), 1850, *Poems and Songs Relating to George Villiers, Duke of Buckingham* (London: Percy Society)
Falkus, Christopher, 1972, *The Life and Times of Charles II* (London: Weidenfeld & Nicolson)
Ferrero, Hermann (ed.), 1881, *Lettres de Henriette-Marie de France à sa soeur Christina Duchesse de Savoie* (Turin: Bocca Frères)
Field, Jemma, 2017, 'The wardrobe goods of Anna of Denmark, queen consort of Scotland and England', *Costume*, 51.1, pp. 3–27
Fincham, Kenneth, 2003, '"According to ancient custom": the return of altars in the Restoration Church of England', *TRHS*, 6th series, 13, pp. 29–54
Finlay, Ian, 1956, *Scottish Gold and Silver* (London: Chatto & Windus)
Finn, Margot, 2000, 'Men's things: masculine possessions and the consumer revolution', *Social History*, 25.2, pp. 133–55
Fischlin, Daniel, 1995, The "Candie-souldier", Venice, and James VI (I)'s Advice on Monarchic Dress in *Basilicon Doron*', *Notes & Queries*, 42.3, pp. 357–61
Fischlin, Daniel and Mark Fortier (eds), 1996, *The True Law of Free Monarchies and Basilikon Doron* (Toronto: Centre for Reformation and Renaissance Studies)
Fisher, F. J., 1948, 'The development of London as a centre of conspicuous consumption in the sixteenth and seventeenth centuries', *TRHS*, 4th series, 30, pp. 37–50
Flavin, Susan, 2014, *Consumption and Culture in Sixteenth Century Ireland: Saffron, Stockings and Silk* (Woodbridge: Boydell Press)
Fotheringham, John George (ed.), 1899, *The Diplomatic Correspondence of Jean de Montereul and the Brothers Du Bellièvre: French Ambassadors in England and Scotland, 1645–1648*, 1st series, 30 (Edinburgh: Scottish History Society)
Fox, John, 2010, *The King's Smuggler: Jane Whorwood, Secret Agent to Charles I* (Stroud: History Press)
Fraser, Antonia, 1993, *King Charles II: His Life and Times* (London: Weidenfeld and Nicolson)
——, 2006, *Love and Louis XIV: The Women in the Life of the Sun King* (London: Orion)
Fraser, Sir William (ed.), 1892, *The Sutherland Book*, vol. 2, *Correspondence* (Edinburgh)
Fritz, Paul, 1981, 'From "public" to "private": the royal funerals in England, 1500–1830', in Joachim Whaley (ed.), *Mirrors of Mortality: Studies in the Social History of Death* (London: Europa Publications), pp. 61–79

Fryman, Olivia, 2014, 'Rich pickings: the royal bed as perquisite 1660–1760', *Furniture History*, 50, pp. 119–36
Furnivall, Frederick (ed.), 1877–9, *Phillip Stubbes's Anatomy of the Abuses in England in Shakespeare's Youth AD 1583* (London: N. Trüber & Co.)
Fyfe, James Gabriel (ed.), 1928, *Scottish Diaries and Memoirs, 1550–1746* (Stirling: Eneas Mackay)
Gardiner, Samuel Rawson, 1894, *Letters and Papers Illustrating the Relations between Charles II and Scotland in 1650* (Edinburgh: Scottish History Society)
Gauden, John, 1654, *Christ at the Wedding: The Pristine Sanctity and Solemnity of Christian Marriage* (London)
Gibson, Katherine, 1997, 'Best belov'd of kings: the iconography of King Charles II', unpublished PhD thesis, Courtauld Institute of Art, University of London
Gittings, Clare, 1984, *Death, Burial and the Individual in Early Modern England* (London: Routledge)
Glanville, Philippa, 1997, *Silver in Tudor and Early Stuart England* (London: V&A Publishing)
Glendinning, Miles, 2004, *The Architecture of Scottish Government from Kingship to Parliamentary Democracy* (Dundee: Dundee University Press)
Glozier, Matthew, 2004, *Scottish Soldiers in the Reign of the Sun King* (Leiden: Brill)
Goldie, Mark (ed.), 2007, *The Entering Book of Roger Morrice, 1677–1691* (Woodbridge: Boydell Press)
Goodare, Julian, 2004, *The Government of Scotland 1560–1625* (Oxford: Oxford University Press)
Goodare, Julian, Lauren Martin and Joyce Miller (eds), 2007, *Witchcraft and Belief in Early Modern Scotland* (Basingstoke: Palgrave Macmillan)
Gordon of Ruthven, Patrick, 1844, *A Short Abridgement of Britane's Distemper from the yeare of God MDCXXXIX to MDCXLIX* (Aberdeen: Spalding Club)
Graeme, L. G., 1904, 'Some letters and correspondence of George Graeme, bishop of Dunblane and of Orkney', in *Miscellany of the Scottish History Society*, vol. 2 (Edinburgh: Scottish History Society), pp. 231–67
Graffius, Jan, 2012, 'The Stuart relics in the Stonyhurst collections', *Recusant History*, 31.2, pp. 147–69
Grange, Richard, 1966, *A Short History of Scottish Dress* (London: Burke's Peerage)
Gray, John (ed.), 1892, *Memoirs of the Life of Sir John Clerk of Penicuik, Baronet, Baron of the Exchequer, Extracted by Himself from his own Journals 1676–1755* (Edinburgh: The University Press)
Greenblatt, Stephen, 1981, *Renaissance Self-Fashioning: From More to Shakespeare* (Chicago and London: University of Chicago Press)
Greene, Robert, 1592, *A Quip for an Upstart Courtier, or A Quaint Dispute between Velvet Breeches and Cloth Breeches* (London)
Gregg, Edward, 1980, *Queen Anne* (London: Routledge & Kegan Paul)
Griffey, Erin, 2016, *On Display: Henrietta Maria and the Materials of Magnificence at the Stuart Court* (New Haven and London: Yale University Press)
Grimble, Ian, 1961, 'The royal payment of Mackay's regiment', *Scottish Gaelic Studies*, 9.1, pp. 23–38
Guthrie, Neil, 2014, *The Material Culture of the Jacobites* (Cambridge: Cambridge University Press)
Halifax, George Savile, 1750, *A Character of King Charles the Second: and Political, Moral and Miscellaneous Thoughts and Reflections* (London: J. and R. Tonson and S. Draper)
Halliwell, James (ed.), 1846, *Letters of the Kings of England*, vol. 2 (London)
Harmes, Marcus, 2014, 'Caps, Shrouds, Lawn and Tackle: English Bishops and their Dress from the Sixteenth Century to the Restoration', *Costume*, 48.1, pp. 3–20
Harrington, Sir John, 1804, *Nugae Antiquae*, vol. 1 (London: J. Wright)
Harris, Tim, 2007, '"There is none that loves him but drunk whores and whoremongers": Popular criticism of the Restoration Court', in Julia Marciari Alexander and Catharine MacLeod (eds), *Politics, Transgression and Representation at the Court of Charles II* (New Haven and London: Yale University Press), pp. 33–58
Harrison, George Bagshawe (ed.), 1941, *A Jacobean Journal, 1603–1606* (London: George Routledge & Sons)
——, 1958, *A Second Jacobean Journal, 1607–1610* (London: Routledge & Kegan Paul)
Hart, Avril and Susan North, 1998, *Historical Fashion in Detail: The 17th and 18th Centuries* (London: V&A Publications)
Harte, Negley, 1976, 'State Control of Dress and Social Change in Pre-Industrial England', in David Coleman and Arthur John (eds), *Trade, Government and Economy in Pre-Industrial England: Essays Presented to F. J. Fisher* (London: Weidenfeld & Nicholson), pp. 132–65
Harvey, Anthony and Richard Mortimer, 2003, *The Funeral Effigies of Westminster Abbey* (Woodbridge: Boydell Press)
Harvey, John, 1995, *Men in Black* (London: Reaktion Books)
Hayward, Maria (ed.), 2012a, *The Great Wardrobe Accounts of Henry VII and Henry VIII* (Woodbridge: Boydell Press)

——, 2012b, 'Going Dutch? How far did Charles II's exile in the Netherlands shape his wardrobe, 1646–1665?', in Anna Jolly and Johannes Pietsch (eds), *Netherlandish Fashion in the Seventeenth Century* (Riggisberg: Abegg-Stiftung), pp. 119–28

——, 2016, '"We should dress us fairly for our end": The Significance of the Clothing Worn at Elite Executions in England in the Long Sixteenth Century', *History*, 101.345, pp. 222–45

——, 2019, '"Outlandish superfluities": luxury and clothing in Scottish and English sumptuary law, 1337–1701', in Giorgio Riello and Ulinka Rublack (eds), *The Right to Dress* (Cambridge: Cambridge University Press), pp. 96–120

Hearn, Karen, 1995, *Dynasties: Painting in Tudor and Jacobean England, 1530–1630* (London: Tate Publishing)

——, 2009, *Van Dyck & Britain* (London: Tate Publishing)

Henshall, Audrey, 1954, 'Early textiles found in Scotland', *PSAS*, 86, pp. 1–29

Henshall, Audrey and Stuart Maxwell, 1954, 'Clothing and other articles from a late 17th century grave at Gunnister, Shetland', *PSAS*, 86, pp. 30–42

——, 1964, 'Two seventeenth century embroidered royal coats of arms', *PSAS*, 95, pp. 284–90

Hentschell, Roze, 2008, *The Culture of Cloth in Early Modern England: Textual Constructions of a National Identity* (Aldershot: Ashgate)

Herford, Charles Harold and Percy Simpson (eds), 1932, *Ben Johnson: The Man and His Work*, vol. 4 (Oxford: Clarendon Press)

Hervey, Reverend Sydenham H. A. (ed.), 1904, *Denham Parish Registers 1539–1850* (Bury St Edmunds: Paul & Mathew)

Hibbert, Christopher, 1964, *The Court at Windsor: A Domestic History* (London: Longmans)

——, 1993, *Cavaliers and Roundheads: English at War, 1642–49* (London: HarperCollins)

——, 2007, *Charles I: A Life of Religion, War and Treason* (Basingstoke: Palgrave Macmillan)

Hirst, Derek, 1994, 'The English Republic and the Meaning of Britain', *Journal of Modern History*, 66.3, pp. 451–86.

HMC, 1874, *Fourth Report: Appendix, Mrs. Erskine Murray* (London: HMSO)

——, 1887a, *Eleventh Report, Appendix, Part 1, Manuscripts of Henry Duncan Skrine Esq., Salvetti Correspondence* (London: HMSO)

——, 1887b, *Eleventh Report, Appendix, Part V, Manuscripts of the Earl of Dartmouth* (London: HMSO)

——, 1891a, *Twelfth Report, Appendix, Part VIII, The Manuscripts of the Duke of Athole, Kt and the Earl of Home* (London: HMSO)

——, 1891b, *Twelfth Report, Appendix, Part IX, Manuscripts of the Duke of Beaufort* (London: HMSO)

——, 1898, *Fifteenth Report, Appendix VII, Marquis of Ailesbury* (London: HMSO)

——, 1899, *Manuscripts of the Duke of Buccleuch and Queensberry at Montagu House*, vol. 1 (London: HMSO)

——, 1915, *Calendar of the Manuscripts of the Most Hon. Marquis of Salisbury*, vol. 13, Addenda (London: HMSO)

——, 1930, *Supplementary Report on the Manuscripts of the Earl of Mar and Kellie* (London: HMSO)

——, 1938, *Calendar of the Manuscripts of the Most Honourable the Marquis of Salisbury, vol. 17, 1605* (London: HMSO)

——, 1968, *Calendar of the Manuscripts of the Most Hon. the Marquis of Salisbury, volume 20: 1608* (London: HMSO)

Holloway, James, 1989, *Patrons and Painters: Art in Scotland, 1650–1760* (Edinburgh: National Galleries of Scotland)

Hoskins, S. Elliott, 1854, *Charles the Second in the Channel Islands*, vol. 2 (London: Richard Bentley)

Houston, Stan, 1995, *James I*, 2nd edn (London and New York: Longman)

Howell, James, 1657, *Londinopolis: An Historicall Discourse, or Perlustration of the City of London, the Imperial Chamber and chief Emporium of Great Britain* (London: J. Streater)

Hudson, Roger (ed.), 2000, *The Grand Quarrel: Women's Memoirs of the English Civil War* (Stroud: Alan Sutton)

Hume Brown, P. (ed.), 1973, *Early Travellers in Scotland* (Edinburgh: Mercat Press)

Hunter, Reverend Joseph (ed.), 1843, *The Diary of Thomas Cartwright, Bishop of Chester* (London: Camden Society)

Hunter, William (ed.), 1963, *The Complete Poetry of Ben Jonson* (New York: New York University Press)

Hunwicke, John, 1993, 'Robert Maxwell of Caerlaverock and his fashionable windows', *Transactions of the Dumfriesshire & Galloway Natural History and Antiquarian Society*, 68, pp. 107–21

Hutchinson, Lucy (ed.), 1913, *Memoirs of the Life of Colonel Hutchinson, Written by his Widow Lucy* (London: Everyman)

Hutton, Ronald, 1985, *The Restoration: A Political and Religious History of England and Wales, 1658–67* (Oxford: Oxford University Press)

——, 1989, *Charles the Second: King of England, Scotland and Ireland* (Oxford: Clarendon Press)

——, 1994, *The Rise and Fall of Merry England:*

The Ritual Year 1400–1700 (Oxford: Oxford University Press)
Huxley, Gervas, 1959, *Endymion Porter: The Life of a Courtier, 1587–1649* (London: Chatto & Windus)
Hyde, Edward, earl of Clarendon, 1773, *State Papers Collected by Edward, Earl of Clarendon*, vol. 2 (Oxford: Clarendon Press)
Imrie, John and John, Dunbar (eds), 1982, *Accounts of the Masters of Works: For Building and Repairing Royal Palaces and Castles*, vol. 2 (Edinburgh: HMSO)
Innes, Cosmo (ed.), 1855, *The Black Book of Taymouth* (Edinburgh: Bannatyne Club)
Jackson, Clare, 2003, *Restoration Scotland, 1660–1690: Royalist Politics, Religion and Ideas* (Woodbridge: Boydell Press)
Jesse, Edward, 1841, *A Summer's Day at Hampton Court being a Guide to the Palace and Gardens* (London: John Murray)
Johansen, Katia, 2002, 'In the Lion's Den – on Night-Gowns and Dressing Gowns', in Lena Rangström (ed.), *Modelejon Manligt Mode 1500-tal 1600-tal 1700-tal/Lions of Fashion: Male Fashion of the 16th, 17th, 18th Centuries* (Stockholm: Livrustkammaren), pp. 394–9
Johnston, Flora 1999, 'Jonet Gothskirk and the "gown of repentance"', *Costume*, 33.1, pp. 89–94
Johnstone, Pauline, 2002, *High Fashion in the Church: The Place of Vestments in the History of Art from the Ninth to the Nineteenth Century* (Leeds: Maney)
Jones, Anne Rosalind and Peter Stallybrass, 2000, *Renaissance Clothing and the Materials of Memory* (Cambridge: Cambridge University Press)
Keay, Anna, 2008, *The Magnificent Monarch: Charles II and the Ceremonies of Power* (London: Continuum)
——, 2011, 'The shadow of a king? Aspects of the exile of King Charles II', in Philip Mansel and Torsten Riotte (eds.), *Monarchy and Exile: The Politics of Legitimacy from Marie de Medici to Wilhelm II* (Basingstoke: Palgrave Macmillan), pp. 105–19
——, 2016, *The Last Royal Rebel: The Life and Death of James, Duke of Monmouth* (London: Bloomsbury)
Keevil, John Joyce, 1954, 'The Illness of Charles, Duke of Albany (Charles I) from 1600–1612: An Historical Case of Rickets', *Journal of the History of Medicine and Allied Sciences*, 9.4, pp. 407–19
Kerridge, Eric, 1985, *Textile Manufacturers in Early Modern England* (Manchester: Manchester University Press)
Kingsford, Charles (ed.), 1908, *A Survey of London* (Oxford: Clarendon Press)
Kingston, Viscount Alexander, 1829, *Continuation of the History of the House of Seytoun* (Edinburgh: Bannatyne Club)
Kirk, Richard Edward Gent and Ernest Kirk (eds), 1907, *Returns of Aliens Dwelling in the City and Suburbs of London*, vol. 3 (London: Huguenot Society)
Knowler, William (ed.), 1739, *The Earl of Strafford's Letters and Dispatches*, vol. 2 (London)
Koslofsky, Craig, 2011, *Evening's Empire: A History of Night in Early Modern Europe* (Cambridge: Cambridge University Press)
Kuchta, David, 2002, *The Three Piece Suit and Modern Masculinity: England, 1550–1850* (Berkeley, Calif.: University of California Press)
Laing, David (ed.), 1830, *A Relation of the Proceedings Concerning the Kirk of Scotland* (Edinburgh: Bannatyne Club)
——, 1875, *Correspondence of Sir Robert Kerr, first Earl of Ancram and his son William, third Earl of Lothian*, vol. 2 (Edinburgh: R. &. R. Clark)
Laing, Robert (ed.), 1842, *The Letters and Journals of Robert Baillie, 1637–1662*, 3 vols (Edinburgh: Bannatyne Club)
Larkin, Hilary, 2013, *The Making of Englishmen: Debates on National Identity, 1550–1650* (Leiden: Brill)
Larkin, James (ed.), 1983, *Stuart Royal Proclamations: Royal Proclamations of King Charles I, 1625–1646*, vol. 2 (Oxford: Clarendon Press)
Latham, Robert and William Matthews (eds), 1970–83, *The Diary of Samuel Pepys*, 11 vols (London: Bell & Hyman)
Lauder of Fountainhall, 1840, *Historical Observations* (Edinburgh: Bannatyne Club)
Laurenson, Sarah (ed.), 2013, *Shetland Textiles: 800 BC to the Present* (Lerwick: Shetland Heritage Publications)
Lee, Maurice, 2014, 'The Worcester veterans and the Restoration regime in Scotland', in Sharon Adams and Julian Goodare (eds), *Scotland in the Age of Two Revolutions* (Woodbridge: Boydell Press), pp. 135–54
Leeds Barroll, John, 1991, 'The court of the first Stuart queen', in Linda Levy Peck (ed.), *The Mental World of the Jacobean Court* (Cambridge: Cambridge University Press), pp. 191–208
——, 1998, 'Inventing the Stuart masque', in David Bevington and Peter Holbrook (eds), *The Politics of the Stuart Court Masque* (Cambridge: Cambridge University Press), pp. 121–43
——, 2001, *Anna of Denmark, Queen of England: A Cultural Biography* (Philadelphia: University of Philadelphia Press)
Leitch, Roger, 1990, '"Here chapman billies tak their stand": a pilot study of Scottish chapmen, packmen and pedlars', *PSAS*, 120, pp. 173–88
L'Estrange, Roger, 1687, *A Brief History of the Times* (*The Observator*) (London: Charles Brome)

Lightbown, Ronald, 1989, 'The king's regalia, insignia and jewellery', in Arthur MacGregor (ed.), *The Late King's Goods: Collections, Possessions and Patronage of Charles I in Light of the Commonwealth Sale Inventories* (Oxford: Oxford University Press), pp. 257–75

Lindley, David, 2000, 'The politics of Chapman's *The Memorable Masque*', in Eveline Cruickshanks (ed.), *The Stuart Courts* (Stroud: Alan Sutton), pp. 43–58

Linklater, Magnus and Christian Hesketh, 1992, *John Graham of Claverhouse, Bonnie Dundee: For King and Conscience* (Edinburgh: Canongate)

Lisle, Leanda de, 2018, *White King: Charles I, Traitor, Murderer, Martyr* (London: Chatto & Windus)

Little, Patrick, 2008, 'Cromwell the Dandy', *History Today*, 58.9, pp. 45–51

Llewellyn, Nigel, 1991, *The Art of Death: Visual Culture in English Death Ritual, c.1500–c.1800* (London: Reaktion Books)

Lockyer, Roger, 1984, *Buckingham: The Life and Political Career of George Villiers, First Duke of Buckingham, 1592–1628* (London: Routledge)

Loftis, John (ed.), 1978, *The Memoirs of Anne, Lady Hackett, and Ann, Lady Fanshawe* (Oxford: Oxford University Press)

Lowenthal, Cynthia, 1999, 'Performing nations on the Restoration stage: Wycherley's *Gentleman Dancing-Master*', in Jessica Munns and Penny Richards (eds), *The Clothes that Wear Us: Essays on Dress and Transgressing in Eighteenth-Century Culture* (Newark, Del.: University of Delaware Press), pp. 37–55

Lublin, Robert, 2011, *Costuming the Shakespearean Stage: Visual Codes of Representation in Early Modern Theatre and Culture* (Farnham: Ashgate)

Lunger Knoppers, Laura, 1998, 'The politics of portraiture: Oliver Cromwell and the plain style', *Renaissance Quarterly*, 51.4, pp. 1283–319

Lynch, Michael, 1981, *Edinburgh and the Reformation* (Edinburgh: John Donald Publishers)

——, 1990, 'Queen Mary's Triumph: The Baptismal Celebrations at Stirling in December 1566', *SHR*, 69.1, issue 187, pp. 1–21

——, 1991, *Scotland: A New History* (London: Century)

Lythe, S. G. Edgar, 1960, *The Economy of Scotland in its European Setting, 1550–1625* (Edinburgh: Oliver & Boyd)

MacDonald, Alan, 2005, 'James VI and I, the Church of Scotland and British Ecclesiastical Convergence', *HJ*, 48.4, pp. 885–903

——, 2010, 'Chancellors, Presidents and Speakers: Presiding Officers in the Scottish Parliament before the Restoration', *Parliamentary History*, 29.1, pp. 49–61

MacGregor, Arthur, 1989, 'The King's disport: games and pastimes of the early Stuarts', in Arthur MacGregor (ed.), *The Late King's Goods: Collections, Possession and Patronage of Charles I in Light of the Commonwealth Sale Inventories* (Oxford: Oxford University Press), pp. 403–21

Macinnes, Allan, 2000, *Clanship, Commerce and the House of Stuart, 1603–1788* (East Linton: Tuckwell Press)

MacIvor, Iain and Bent Peterson, 1984, 'Lauderdale at Holyroodhouse, 1669–70', in David Breeze (ed.), *Studies in Scottish Antiquity Presented to Stewart Cruden* (Edinburgh: John Donald Publishers), pp. 249–68

Mackenzie, Sir George, 1661, *Aretina, or The Serious Romance* (London: Ralph Smith)

——, 1691, *A Vindication of the Government of Scotland. During the Reign of King Charles II. Against Mis-representations made in several Scandalous Pamphlets* (London: J. Hindmarsh)

Macmillan, Duncan, 1990, *Scottish Art 1460–2000* (Edinburgh: Mainstream Publishing) (2nd edn 2000)

Mactaggart, Peter and Anne Mactaggart, 1980, 'The rich wearing apparel of Richard the third earl of Dorset', *Costume*, 14.1, pp. 44–7

Madden, Frederick, 1836, 'Warrant of King James the First to the Great Wardrobe for apparel etc. for the marriage of Princess Elizabeth', *Archaeologia*, 26, pp. 380–94

Maidment, James, 1837, *Analecta Scotica*, vol. 2 (Edinburgh: G. Stevenson)

Mann, Alastair J., 2014, *James VII: Duke and King of Scots, 1633-1701* (Edinburgh: John Donald)

Mapstone, Sally, 1998, 'Shakespeare and Scottish kingship: a case history', in Sally Mapstone and Juliette Wood (eds), *The Rose and the Thistle: Essays on the Culture of Late Medieval and Renaissance Scotland* (East Linton: Tuckwell Press), pp. 158–93

Marly, Diana de, 1978, 'Fashionable Suppliers 1660–1700: Leading Tailors and Clothing Tradesmen of the Restoration Period', *Antiquaries Journal*, 58.2, pp. 333–51

——, 1985, *Fashion for Men: An Illustrated History* (London: Batsford)

——, 1987a, *Louis XIV and Versailles* (London: Batsford)

——, 1987b, 'Pepys and the fashion for collecting', *Costume*, 21.1, pp. 34–43

Marshall, Rosalind, 1972, 'Conscience and costume in seventeenth-century Scotland', *Costume*, 6.1, pp. 32–5

——, 1973, *The Days of Duchess Anne: Life in the Household of the Duchess of Hamilton, 1656–1716* (London: HarperCollins)

——, 1976, *Childhood in Seventeenth Century Scotland* (Edinburgh: Scottish National Portrait Gallery)
——, 1977, *Mary of Guise* (London: HarperCollins)
——, 1981, 'Scottish Portraits as a Source for the Costume Historian', *Costume*, 15.1, pp. 67–70
——, 1986, *Costume in Scottish Portraits 1560–1830* (Edinburgh: Scottish National Portrait Gallery)
——, 1990a, *Dynasty: The Royal House of Stewart* (Edinburgh: National Galleries of Scotland)
——, 1990b, *Henrietta Maria: The Intrepid Queen* (London: HMSO)
——, 1994, 'To be the king's grace ane dowblett: the costume of James V, king of Scots', *Costume*, 28.1, pp. 14–21
——, 1996, 'The jewellery of James V, king of Scots', *Jewellery Studies*, 7, pp. 79–86
——, 2003, *Scottish Queens, 1034–1714* (East Linton: Tuckwell Press)
——, 2016, 'The wardrobe of William, 3rd duke of Hamilton (1634–94)', *Costume Society of Scotland Bulletin*, 56, pp. 7–12
Marshall, Rosalind and George Dalgleish (eds), 1991, *The Art of Jewellery in Scotland* (Edinburgh: HMSO)
Martin, Martin, 1999, *A Description of the Western Islands of Scotland* (Edinburgh: Birlinn)
Mathews, David, 1955, *Scotland under Charles I* (London: Eyre & Spottiswoode)
Matthews, William (ed.), 1966, *Charles II's Escape from Worcester: A Collection of Narratives Assembled by Samuel Pepys* (Berkeley, Calif.: University of California Press)
Maxwell, Stuart and Robin Hutchinson, 1958, *Scottish Costume 1550–1850* (London: A. & C. Black)
Mayer-Thurman, Christa (ed.), 1975, *Raiment for the Lord's Service: A Thousand Years of Western Vestments* (Chicago: Art Institute of Chicago)
Mayo, Janet, 1984, *A History of Ecclesiastical Dress* (London: Batsford)
McClintock, Henry, 1949, *Old Highland Dress and Tartans*, 2nd edn (Dundalk: Dundalgan Press)
——, 1950, *Old Irish and Highland Dress*, 2nd edn (Dundalk: Dundalgan Press)
McClure, Norman (ed.), 1939, *The Letters of John Chamberlain*, 2 vols (Philadelphia: American Philosophical Society)
McCullough, Peter, 1998, *Sermons at Court: Politics and Religion in Elizabethan and Jacobean Preaching* (Cambridge: Cambridge University Press)
McDowell, Nicholas, 2006, 'Early modern stereotypes and the rise of English: Jonson, Dryden, Arnold, Eliot', *Critical Quarterly*, 48.3, pp. 25–34
McGavin, John, 2001, 'Secular music in the burgh of Haddington, 1530–1640', in Fiona Kisby (ed.), *Music and Musicians in Renaissance Cities and Towns* (Cambridge: Cambridge University Press), pp. 45–56
——, 2007, *Theatricality and Narrative in Medieval and Early Modern Scotland* (Aldershot: Ashgate)
McIlwain, Charles (ed.), 1918, *The Political Works of James I* (Cambridge, Mass.: Harvard University Press)
McKerrow, Ronald Brunlees (ed.), 1966, *The Works of Thomas Nashe*, vol. 2 (Oxford: Blackwell)
McNeill, William and Peter McNeill, 1996, 'The Scottish Progress of James VI, 1617', *SHR*, 75.1, pp. 38–51
McRoberts, David, 1956, 'The Fetternear Banner', *Innes Review*, 7.2, pp. 69–88
McRoberts, David and Charles Oman, 1968, 'Plate made for King James II & VII for the Chapel Royal of Holyroodhouse', *Antiquaries Journal*, 48.2, pp. 285–95
Miller, John, 1978, *James II* (New Haven and London: Yale University Press)
——, 1987, *Bourbon and Stuart: Kings and Kingship in France and England in the Seventeenth Century* (New York: Franklin Watts)
Miller, Lesley Ellis, 2006, 'Dress to Impress: Prince Charles Plays Madrid, March–September 1623', in Alexander Samson (ed.), *The Spanish Match: Prince Charles's Journey to Madrid, 1623* (Aldershot: Ashgate), pp. 27–50
Misson, M., 1719, *Memoirs and Observations in his Travels over England, With some Account of Scotland and Ireland* (London: printed for D. Brown)
Moore, Andrew with Charlotte Crawley, 1992, *Family and Friends: A Regional Survey of British Portraiture* (London: HMSO)
Morrill, John, 1997, 'Historical Introduction and Overview: The Un-English Civil War', in John Young (ed.), *Celtic Dimensions of the British Civil Wars* (Edinburgh: John Donald Publishers), pp. 1–17
Morris, Christopher (ed.), 1947, *The Journeys of Celia Fiennes* (London: Cresset Press)
Moryson, Fynes, 1617, *An Itinerary Containing His Ten Yeeres Travell through the Twelve Dominions of Germany, Bohmerland, Sweitzerland, Netherland, Denmarke, Poland, Turky, France, England, Scotland, and Ireland* (London: John Beale)
Murdoch, Steve, 2000, *Britain, Denmark-Norway and the House of Stuart, 1603–1660: A Diplomatic and Military Analysis* (East Linton: Tuckwell Press)
——, 2001, *Scotland the Thirty Years' War, 1618–1648* (Leiden: Brill)

Murdoch, Tessa (ed.), 1991, *Treasures and Trinkets: Jewellery in London from Pre-Roman Times to the 1930s* (London: Museum of London)
Murray, Athol, 1966, 'The Scottish Treasury, 1667–1708', *SHR*, 45.1, pp. 89–104
Murray, Catriona, 2017, *Imaging Stuart Family Politics: Dynastic Crisis and Continuity* (Abingdon: Routledge)
Nenadic, Stana, 2007, *Lairds and Luxury: The Highland Gentry in Eighteenth-Century Scotland* (Edinburgh: John Donald Publishers)
Newman, Peter, 1983, 'The Royalist Officer corps, 1642–1660: Army Command as a Reflection of the Social Structure', *HJ*, 26.4, pp. 945–58
Nichols, John (ed.), 1828, *The Progresses, Processions and Magnificent Festivities of King James the First*, 4 vols (London: Society of Antiquaries)
Nicholson, Robin, 1998, 'The tartan portraits of Prince Charles Edward Stuart: Identity and Iconography', *British Journal for Eighteenth Century Studies*, 21.2, pp. 145–60
Nicolas, Nicholas, 1828, *The Statutes of the Order of the Thistle* (London: William Pickering)
Nicoll, John, 1836, *A Diary of Public Transactions and Other Occurrences, chiefly in Scotland, from January 1650 to June 1667* (Edinburgh: Bannatyne Club)
Norman, Alexander Vesey Bethune, 1989, 'Arms, armour and militaria', in Arthur MacGregor (ed.), *The Late King's Goods: Collections, Possessions and Patronage of Charles I in the Light of the Commonwealth Sale Inventories* (Oxford: Oxford University Press), pp. 351–66
Norrington, Ruth (ed.), 1996, *My Dearest Minette: The Letters between Charles II and his Sister Henrietta, Duchess d'Orléans* (London: Peter Owen Publishers)
Ogg, David, 1934, *England in the Reign of Charles II* (Oxford: Clarendon Press)
Ohlmeyer, Jane, 1993a, *Civil War and Restoration in the Three Stuart Kingdoms: The Political Career of Randal MacDonnell, Marquis of Antrim* (Cambridge: Cambridge University Press)
——, 1993b, 'The Marquis of Antrim: a Stuart turn-kilt?', *History Today*, 43.3, pp. 13–18
Ollard, Richard, 1979, *The Image of the King: Charles I and Charles II* (London: Hodder & Stoughton)
Oman, Carola, 1951, *Henrietta Maria* (London: Hodder & Stoughton)
——, 1962, *Mary of Modena* (London: Hodder & Stoughton)
Oman, Charles, 1974, *British Rings, 800–1914* (London: HarperCollins)
Orgel, Stephen and Roy Strong (eds), 1973, *Inigo Jones: The Theatre of the Stuart Court*, 2 vols (London and Los Angeles: Sotheby Parke Bernet and University of California Press)
Ouston, Hugh, 1982, 'York in Edinburgh: James VII and the patronage of learning in Scotland, 1679–1688', in John Dwyer, Roger Mason and Alexander Murdoch (eds), *New Perspectives on the Politics and Culture of Early Modern Scotland* (Edinburgh: John Donald Publishers), pp. 133–55
——, 2000, '"From the Thames to Tweed departed": the court of James duke of York in Scotland, 1679–82', in Eveline Cruickshanks (ed.), *The Stuart Courts* (Stroud: Alan Sutton), pp. 266–79
Owen, John, 1628, *Certain Epigrams* (London)
Pardailhé-Galabrun, Annik, 1991, *The Birth of Intimacy: Privacy and Domestic Life in Early Modern Paris* (Cambridge: Polity Press)
Paton, Henry (ed.), 1957, *Accounts of the Masters of Works: For Building and Repairing Royal Palaces and Castles*, vol. 1 (Edinburgh: HMSO)
Patterson, Angus, 2009, *Fashion and Armour in Renaissance Europe: Proud Looks and Brave Attire* (London: V&A Publishing)
Patterson, William Brown, 2000, *King James VI and I and the Reunion of Christendom* (Cambridge: Cambridge University Press)
Payne, Susan, David Wilcox, Tuula Pardoe and Ninya Mikhaila, 2011, 'A Seventeenth-Century Doublet from Scotland', *Costume*, 45.1, pp. 39–62
Peachey, Stuart, 1989, *The Edgehill Campaign and the Letters of Nehemiah Wharton* (Leigh-on-Sea: Partizan Press)
Peck, Linda Levy, 1991, 'An introduction' and 'The mentality of a Jacobean grandee', in Linda Levy Peck (ed.), *The Mental World of the Jacobean Court* (Cambridge: Cambridge University Press), pp. 1–17, 148–68
——, 2005, *Consuming Splendour: Society and Culture in Seventeenth-Century England* (Cambridge: Cambridge University Press)
Pellumbi, Jola, 2017, 'Revealing and concealing: official male dress in early modern Venice, 1520–1610', unpublished PhD thesis (London: King's College)
Perkins, William, 1608, *The Whole Treatise of the Cases of Conscience* (London)
Perry, Curtis, 2006, '1603 and the discourse of favouritism', in G. Burgess, R. Wymer and J. Lawrence (eds), *The Accession of James I: Historical and Cultural Consequences* (Basingstoke: Palgrave Macmillan), pp. 155–76.
Pitcairn, Archibald, 1817, *The Assembly, or Scotch Reformation* (Edinburgh: D. Webster)
Pitcairn, Robert (ed.), 1842, *Autobiography and Diary of Mr James Melville* (Edinburgh: Wodrow Society)

Pittock, Murray, 1991, *The Invention of Scotland: The Stuart Myth and the Scottish Identity, 1638 to the Present* (London: Routledge)
——, 1998, *Jacobitism* (Basingstoke: Macmillan)
——, 2000, 'From Edinburgh to London: Scottish court writing and 1603', in Eveline Cruickshanks (ed.), *The Stuart Courts* (Stroud: Alan Sutton), pp. 13–28
——, 2013, *Material Culture and Sedition, 1688–1760: Treacherous Objects, Secret Places* (Basingstoke: Palgrave Macmillan)
Potter, David and Peter Roberts, 1988, 'An Englishman's view of the court of Henri III, 1584–85: Richard Cook's "Description of the Court of France"', *French History*, 2.3, pp. 312–4
Poynting, Sarah, 2006, 'Deciphering the king: Charles I's letter to Jane Whorwood', *The Seventeenth Century*, 21.1, pp. 128–40
Prestwich, Menna, 1966, *Cranfield: Politics and Profits under the Early Stuarts: The Career of Lionel Cranfield, Earl of Middlesex* (Oxford: Clarendon Press)
Priestley, Ursula, 1993, 'Norwich and the mourning trade', *Costume*, 27.1, pp. 47–56
Purkiss, Diane, 2005, *Literature, Gender and Politics during the English Civil War* (Cambridge: Cambridge University Press)
Puttenham, George, 1589, ed. Willcock, Gladys Doidge and Alice Walker, 1936, *The Arte of English Poesie* (Cambridge: Cambridge University Press)
Quinton, Rebecca, 2013, *Seventeenth-Century Costume* (London: Unicorn Press)
Raffe, Alasdair, 2012, *The Culture of Controversy: Religious Arguments in Scotland, 1660–1714* (Woodbridge: Boydell Press)
Raine, James (ed.), 1861, *Depositions from the Castle of York*, vol. 40 (Durham: Surtees Society)
Ravelhofer, Barbara, 1999, 'Bureaucrats and courtly cross-dressers in the Shrovetide Masque and The Shepherds Paradise', *English Literary Renaissance*, 29.1, pp. 75–96
——, 2009, *The Early Stuart Masque: Dance, Costume and Music*, 2nd edn (Oxford: Oxford University Press)
Reid, Hazel, 1974, 'A collection of thistle robes from Drummond castle', *Costume*, 8.1, pp. 51–5
Reid, Stuart and Graham Turner, 1999, *Scots Armies of the English Civil Wars* (Oxford: Osprey Publishing)
Reynolds, Anna, 2013, *In Fine Style: The Art of Tudor and Stuart Fashion* (London: Royal Collection Trust)
Ribeiro, Aileen, 2005, *Fashion and Fiction: Dress in Art and Literature in Stuart England* (New Haven and London: Yale University Press)
Richardson, Catherine, 2014, 'Written texts and the performance of materiality', in Giorgio Riello and Anne Gerritsen (eds), *Writing Material Culture History* (London: Bloomsbury), pp. 43–58
Richardson, Roger, 1977, *The Debate on the English Revolution* (London: Methuen)
Ringgaard, Maj, 2014, 'Silk knitted waistcoats: a 17th century fashion item', in Tove Engelhardt et al. (eds), *Fashionable Encounters: Perspectives and Trends in Textile and Dress in the Early Modern Nordic World* (Oxford: Oxbow Books), pp. 73–95
Roberts, Jane, 1999, *The King's Head: Charles I King and Martyr* (London: Royal Collection)
Robertson, Hastings (ed.), 1845, *The Zurich Letters, Second Series* (Cambridge: Cambridge University Press)
Robertson, Joseph (ed.), 1863, *Inventaires de la Royne Descosse: Catalogue of the Jewels, Dresses, Furniture, Books and Paintings of Mary Queen of Scots* (Edinburgh: Bannatyne Club)
Robinson, Claire, 2015, 'An old and faithful servand: a pair of early seventeenth-century gauntlet gloves given by King Charles I to Sir Henry Wardlaw', *Costume*, 49.1, pp. 8–31
Rogers, Malcolm, 1983, *William Dobson, 1611–46* (London: National Portrait Gallery)
Rothwell, James and Annabel Westman, 2011, 'The Ghost of a Royal Visit – the Furnishing of the State Apartment at Lyme Park in the mid-1670s', *Furniture History*, 47, pp. 1–17
Rowell, Christopher (ed.), 2013, *Ham House: 400 Years of Collecting and Patronage* (New Haven and London: Yale University Press)
Rubinstein, Hilary, 1975, *Captain Luckless: James First Duke of Hamilton, 1606–1649* (London: Chatto & Windus)
Rudrum, Alan, Joseph Black and Holly Nelson (eds), 2000, *The Broadview Anthology of Seventeenth Century Prose*, vol. 2 (Peterborough: Broadview Press)
Rush, Sally, 2006, 'French fashion in sixteenth century-Scotland: the 1539 inventory of James V's wardrobe', *Furniture History*, 42, pp. 1–25
Rushworth, John (ed.), 1721, *Historical Collections of Private Passages of State*, 8 vols, vol. 1, *1618–29* (London: D. Brown)
Rye, William Brenchley, 1865, *England as Seen by Foreigners in the Days of Elizabeth and James the First* (London: J. R. Smith)
Salmon, John Hearsey McMillan, 1991, 'Seneca and Tacitus in Jacobean England', in Linda Levy Peck (ed.), *The Mental World of the Jacobean Court* (Cambridge: Cambridge University Press), pp. 169–88
Sanderson, Margaret, 1987, *Mary Stewart's People: Life in Mary Stewart's Scotland* (Edinburgh: James Thin)
——, 1997, *Ayrshire and the Reformation: People and Change 1490–1600* (East Linton: Tuckwell Press)

Sawyer, Edmund (ed.), 1725, *Memorials of Affairs of State … from the original papers of … Sir Ralph Winwood*, vol. 3 (London)

Scally, John, 1997, 'Counsel in crisis: James, third Marquis of Hamilton and the Bishops Wars, 1638–40', in John Young (ed.), *Celtic Dimensions of the British Civil Wars* (Edinburgh: John Donald Publishers), pp. 18–34

Scarisbrick, Diana, 1989, *Ancestral Jewels* (London: Andre Deutsch)

——, 1993, *Rings: Jewellery of Power, Love and Loyalty* (London: Thames & Hudson)

——, 1994, *Jewellery in Britain, 1066–1837: A Documentary, Social, Literary and Artistic Survey* (Norwich: Michael Russell Publishing)

——, 1996, *Tudor and Jacobean Jewellery, 1509–1625* (London: Tate Publishing)

——, 2011, *Portrait Jewels: Opulence and Intimacy from the Medici to the Romanovs* (London: Thames & Hudson)

Schnitker, Harry and Stephen Clayes, 2007, *From Persecution to Integration: The Scottish Catholic Experience as Seen from Perth, 1685–2007* (Edinburgh: Aquhorties Press)

Schreiber, Roy, 1984, *The First Carlisle: Sir James Hay, First Earl of Carlisle as Courtier, Diplomat and Entrepreneur, 1580–1636*, Transactions of the American Philosophical Society, 74.7

Scott, Eva, 1905, *The King in Exile: The Wanderings of Charles II from June 1649 to July 1654* (London: E. P. Dutton)

Scott, Geoffrey, 2004, 'The court as a centre of Catholicism', in Edward Corp (ed.), *A Court in Exile: The Stuarts in France, 1689–1718* (Cambridge: Cambridge University Press), pp. 235–56

Scott, George (ed.), 1735, *The Memoirs of Sir James Melvil of Hal-hill* (Edinburgh: T. & W. Ruddimans)

Scott, William and James Bliss (eds), 1847–60, *The Works of the Most Reverend Father in God, William Laud, Sometime Lord Archbishop of Canterbury*, 7 vols (Oxford: John Henry Parker)

Seddon, Peter (ed.), 1975–86, *The Letters of John Holles, 1587–1637*, 3 vols (Nottingham: Thoroton Society)

Sells, A. Lytton (ed.), 1962, *The Memoirs of James II: His Campaigns as Duke of York 1652–1660* (London: Chatto & Windus)

Seton, George (ed.), 1882, *Memoir of Alexander Seton, Earl of Dunfermline* (Edinburgh: William Blackwood & Sons)

Seton, Walter, 1916, 'The Early Years of Henry Frederick, Prince of Wales and Charles, Duke of Albany, 1593–1605', *SHR*, 13.1, pp. 366–79

Sharp, Andrew, 1923, 'Notes on Stuart Jewellery', *PSAS*, 57, pp. 226–41

Sharpe, Kevin, 1996, *The Personal Rule of Charles I* (New Haven and London: Yale University Press)

Shaw, Frances, 1979, 'Sumptuary legislation in Scotland', *Juridical Review*, 24, pp. 81–115

Shepard, Alexandra, 2015, *Accounting for Oneself: Worth, Status and Social Order in Early Modern England* (Oxford: Oxford University Press)

Shirley, Evelyn Philip, 1870, 'An inventory of the Effects of Henry Howard K. G., Earl of Northampton, Taken on his Death in 1614', *Archaeologia*, 42, issue 2, pp. 347–78

Slater, Stephen, 2013, *The Illustrated Book of Heraldry: An International History of Heraldry and its Contemporary Uses* (Wigston: Anness Publishing)

Smuts, R. Malcolm, 1987, *Court Culture and the Origins of a Royalist Tradition in Early Stuart England* (Philadelphia: University of Pennsylvania Press)

——, 1991, 'Cultural Diversity and Cultural Change at the Court of James I', in Linda Levy Peck (ed.), *The Mental World of the Jacobean Court* (Cambridge: Cambridge University Press), pp. 99–112

Snodin, Michael and John Styles (eds), 2001, *Design and the Decorative Arts: Britain 1500–1900* (London: V&A Publishing)

Southcombe, George and Grant Tapsell, 2010, *Restoration Politics, Religion and Culture: Britain and Ireland, 1660–1714* (Basingstoke: Palgrave Macmillan)

Sowerby, Tracey, 2015, 'Negotiating the Royal Image: Portrait Exchanges in Elizabethan and Early Stuart Diplomacy', in Helen Hackett (ed.), *Early Modern Exchanges: Dialogues between Nations and Cultures, 1550–1750* (Farnham: Ashgate), pp. 119–41

Spalding, John (ed.), 1830, *The History of the Troubles and Memorable Transactions in Scotland, From 1624 to 1645* (Aberdeen: John Rettie)

Spottiswoode, John, 1847–51, *The History of the Church of Scotland*, 3 vols (Edinburgh: Bannatyne Club)

Spicer, Andrew, 2000, '"Defyle not Christ's Kirk with your carion": Burial and the Development of Burial Aisles in Post-Reformation Scotland', in Bruce Gordon and Peter Marshall (eds), *The Place of the Dead: Death and Remembrance in Late Medieval and Early Modern Europe* (Cambridge: Cambridge University Press), pp. 149–69

Staniland, Kay, 1999, 'The King on the Scaffold', *History Today*, 49.1, pp. 41–3

——, 2003, 'Samuel Pepys and his wardrobe', *Costume*, 37.1, pp. 41–50

——, 2005, 'Samuel Pepys and his wardrobe', *Costume*, 39.1, pp. 53–63

Steer, Francis (ed.), 1959, *Orders for the Household of Charles, Prince of Wales* (Lichfield: Dean and Chapter of Lichfield Cathedral)
Stevenson, David, 1973, *Scottish Revolution, 1637–44* (Newton Abbot: David & Charles)
——, 1980, *Alasdair MacColla and the Highland Problem in the Seventeenth Century* (Edinburgh: John Donald Publishers)
——, 1992, 'The English devil of keeping state: elite manners and the downfall of Charles I in Scotland', in Roger Mason and Norman Macdougall (eds), *People and Power in Scotland: Essays in Honour of T. C. Smout* (Edinburgh: John Donald), pp. 126–44
——, 1997, *Scotland's Last Royal Wedding: The Marriage of James VI and Anne of Denmark* (Edinburgh: John Donald Publishers)
Stevenson, Sara, 1981, 'Armour in seventeenth century portraits', in David Caldwell (ed.), *Scottish Weapons and Fortifications, 1100–1800* (Edinburgh: John Donald Publishers), pp. 339–77
Stevenson, Sara and Duncan Thomson, 1982, *John Michael Wright: The King's Painter* (Edinburgh: Scottish National Portrait Gallery)
Stewart, Alan, 2003, *The Cradle King: A Life of James VI & I* (London: Chatto & Windus)
Stewart, Laura, 2013, 'Power and faith in early modern Scotland', *SHR*, 92, pp. 25–37
Stewart-Murray, John, 1908, *Chronicles of the Atholl and Tullibardine Families*, vol. 1 (Edinburgh: Ballantyne Press)
Stone, Lawrence, 1965, *The Crisis of the Aristocracy: 1558–1641* (Oxford: Oxford University Press)
Stoyle, Mark, 2002, *West Britons: Cornish Identities and the Early Modern British State* (Exeter: University of Exeter Press)
——, 2005, *Soldiers and Strangers: An Ethnic History of the English Civil War* (New Haven and London: Yale University Press)
——, 2008, 'Road to Fardon Field: Explaining the Massacre of the Royalist Women at Naseby', *EHR*, 123.503, pp. 895–923
——, 2011, *The Black Legend of Prince Rupert's Dog: Witchcraft and Propaganda during the English Civil War* (Liverpool: Liverpool University Press)
Strong, Sir Roy, 1965, 'Sir Henry Unton and his portrait: an Elizabethan memorial picture and its history' *Archaeologia*, 99, pp. 53–76
——, 1972, *Van Dyck's Charles I on Horseback* (London: Allen Lane)
——, 1980, 'Charles I's clothes for the years 1633 to 1635', *Costume*, 14.1, pp. 73–89
——, 1986, *Henry, Prince of Wales and England's Lost Renaissance* (London: Thames & Hudson)
Stubbes, Philip, 1592, *A Perfect Pathway to Felicitie* (London)
Sutton, Anne and Livia Visser-Fuchs with Paul Hammond (eds), 1996, *The Reburial of Richard Duke of York, 21–30 July 1476* (London: Richard III Society)
Swain, Margaret, 1972, 'Nightgown into Dressing Gown: A Study of Men's Nightgowns in the Eighteenth Century', *Costume*, 6.1, pp. 10–21
——, 1973, *The Needlework of Mary Queen of Scots* (London: Van Nostrand Reinhold)
——, 1988, *Tapestries and Textiles at the Palace of Holyroodhouse in the Royal Collection* (Edinburgh: HMSO)
Tait, Hugh (ed.), 1986, *Seven Thousand Years of Jewellery* (London: British Museum)
Tankard, Danae, 2015, '"They tell me they were in fashion last year": Samuel and Elizabeth Jeake and clothing fashions in late seventeenth century London and Rye', *Costume*, 50.1, pp. 20–41
Tarrant, Naomi, 1996, 'The bedroom', in Annette Carruthers (ed.), *The Scottish Home* (Edinburgh: NMS Publishing), pp. 181–202
——, 2001a, *Textile Treasures: An Introduction to European Decorative Textiles for Home and Church in the National Museums of Scotland* (Edinburgh: NMS Publishing)
——, 2001b, 'The 17th century doublet from Keiss, near Wick, Caithness', *PSAS*, 131, pp. 319–26
Taylor, John, 1868, *All the Workes of John Taylor the Water-Poet*, vol. 2 (London: Spenser Society)
Taylor, Justine, 2003, *A Cup of Kindness: The History of the Royal Scottish Corporation, a London Charity, 1603–2003* (East Linton: Tuckwell Press)
Taylor, Lou, 1983, *Mourning Dress: A Costume and Social History* (London and Boston: Allen & Unwin)
Terry, Charles Sanford, 1899, 'The Visits of Charles I to Newcastle in 1633, 1639, 1641, and 1646–7', *Archaeologia Aeliana*, 2nd series, 21, pp. 83–145
Thompson, Edward Maunde (ed.), 1878, *Correspondence of the Family of Hatton*, new series, 24 (London: Camden Society)
Thomson, J. Thomas (ed.), 1815, *A Collection of Inventories and other records of the Royal Wardrobe and Jewelhouse; and of the Artillery and Munitioun in some of the Royal Castles, MCCCCLXXXVIII–MDCVI* (Edinburgh: General Register House)
Thomson, Thomas, 1827, *Memoirs of his Own Life by Sir James Melville of Halhill* (Edinburgh: Bannatyne Club)
——, 1842–9, *The History of the Kirk of Scotland*, 7 vols (Edinburgh: Wodrow Society)
Thornton, Peter, 1977, 'The royal state bed', *The Connoisseur*, 195, pp. 137–47

——, 1978, *Seventeenth Century Interior Decoration in England, France & Holland* (New Haven and London: Yale University Press) (2nd edn 1981)

——, 1980, 'The Furnishing and Decoration of Ham House', *Furniture History*, 16, pp. 1–194

Thrush, Andrew and John Ferris (eds), 2010, *The History of Parliament: The House of Commons, 1604–29*, 6 vols (Cambridge: Cambridge University Press)

Thurley, Simon, 2000, 'A Country Seat Fit for a King: Charles II, Greenwich and Winchester', in Eveline Cruickshanks (ed.), *The Stuart Courts* (Stroud: Alan Sutton), pp. 214–39

Tiramani, Jenny, Richard David, Susan North and Paul Robbins, 2016, *17th Century Men's Dress Patterns, 1600–1630* (London: Thames & Hudson)

Todd, Margo, 2002, *The Culture of Protestantism in Early Modern Scotland* (New Haven and London: Yale University Press)

Tuckett, Sally, 2014, 'The Scottish Bishops in Government 1625–1638', in Sharon Adams and Julian Goodare (eds), *Scotland in the Age of Two Revolutions* (Woodbridge: Boydell Press), pp. 59–78

Tudor-Craig, Pamela, 2004, *Old St Paul's': The Society of Antiquaries' Diptych, 1616* (London: London Topographical Society)

Turner, Francis C., 1948, *James II* (London: Eyre & Spottiswoode)

Turnor, Edmund, 1806, 'A Declaration of the Diet and Particular Fare of King Charles the First, when Duke of York', *Archaeologia*, 15, pp. 1–12

Turpie, Tom, 2015, *Kind Neighbours: Scottish Saints and Society in the Later Middle Ages* (Leiden: Brill)

Vale, Marcia, 1977, *The Gentleman's Recreations: Accomplishments and Pastimes of the English Gentleman, 1580–1630* (Cambridge: D. S. Brewer)

Verney, Frances (ed.), 1892, *Memoirs of the Verney Family*, vol. 2 (London: Longmans, Green)

Verney, Sir Harry, 1968, *The Verneys of Claydon: A Seventeenth-Century English Family* (London: Pergamon Press)

Vincent, Susan, 2003, *Dressing the Elite: Clothes in Early Modern England* (Oxford: Berg)

Walker, Sir Edward, 1660, *Iter Carolinum being a succinct relation of the necessitated marches, retreats and sufferings of his Majesty Charles the I from January 10, 1641 till the time of his Death 1648* (London: W. Godbid)

Waller, Alfred (ed.), 1908, *Characters and Passages from Note-books* (Cambridge: Cambridge University Press)

Waller, Maureen, 2002, *Ungrateful Daughters: The Stuart Princesses Who Stole Their Father's Crown* (London: Hodder & Stoughton)

Ward, Samuel, 1622, *Woe to Drunkards: A Sermon* (London: A. Math)

Wardle, Patricia, 1994, 'The King's Embroiderer: Edmund Harrison (1590–1667): 1: The Man and his Milieu', *Textile History*, 25.1, pp. 29–59

——, 2001, 'John Shepley (1575–1631): Embroiderer to the High and Mighty Prince Charles, Prince of Wales', *Textile History*, 32.2, pp. 133–55

——, 2002, *For Our Royal Person: Master of the Robes Bills of King-Stadholder William III* (Apeldoorn: Palais Het Loo)

Warwick, Philip, 1702, *Memoirs of the Reign of King Charles I* (London)

Waugh, Norah, 1964, *The Cut of Men's Clothes 1600–1900* (London: Faber & Faber)

Weber, Harold, 1995, *Paper Bullets: Print and Kingship under Charles II* (Lexington: University Press of Kentucky)

Wedgwood, Cecily Veronica, 2011, *A King Condemned: The Trial and Execution of Charles I* (London: Tauris Parke Paperbacks)

Wellington, duke of, 1953, 'The Scaffold George of Charles I', *Antiquaries Journal*, 33, pp. 159–68

Wemyss, Charles, 2014, *Noble Houses of Scotland 1660–1800* (Munich: Prestel Verlag)

W. H., 1634, *The True Picture and Relation of Prince Henry* (Leiden: Christian)

Wiggins, Martin and Catherine Richardson (eds), 2015, *British Drama 1533–1642: A Catalogue*, vol. 6, *1609–16* (Oxford: Oxford University Press)

Wilcox, David, 2014, 'A Suit of Silver: The Underdress of a Knight of the Garter in the Late Seventeenth Century', *Costume*, 48.1, pp. 21–45

——, 2017, 'Scottish Late Seventeenth-Century Male Clothing (Part 2): the Barrock Estate Clothing Finds Described', *Costume*, 51.1, pp. 28–53

Williams, Penry, 1997, 'Court and Polity under Elizabeth I', in John Guy (ed.), *The Tudor Monarchy* (London: Edward Arnold), pp. 356–79

Williams, Tamsyn, 1990, '"Magnetic figures": polemical prints of the English revolution', in Lucy Gent and Nigel Llewellyn (eds), *Renaissance Bodies: The Human Figure in English Culture c.1540– 1660* (London: Reaktion Books), pp. 86–110

Williamson, Eila, 2002, 'Horse Racing in Scotland in the Sixteenth and Earlier Seventeenth Centuries: Peebles and Beyond', *Review of Scottish Culture*, 14, pp. 31–42

——, 2017, 'The funeral of Walter Scott, first earl of Buccleuch: a grand occasion', in Sarah Carpenter, Pamela King, Meg Twycross and Greg Walker (eds), *The Best Pair of Our Play: Essays Presented to John J. McGavin* (Cambridge: D. S. Brewer), pp. 3–21

Wilson, David, 1956, *King James VI and I* (London: Jonathan Cape)
Wilton, Andrew, 1992, *Swagger Portrait: Grand Manner Portraiture in Britain from Van Dyck to Augustus John, 1630–1930* (London: Tate Publishing)
Wodrow Robert, 1835, *The History of the Sufferings of the Church of Scotland from the Restoration to the Revolution*, vol. 1 (Glasgow: Blackie & Sons)
Wood, Anthony, 1820, *Athenae Oxonienses* (London: Rivington)
Woodall, Joanna (ed.), 1997, *Portraiture: Facing the Subject* (Manchester: Manchester University Press)
Woodward, Jennifer, 1997, *The Theatre of Death: The Ritual Management of Royal Funerals in Renaissance England, 1570–1625* (Woodbridge: Boydell & Brewer)
Wormald, Jenny, 1983, 'James VI and I: Two Kings or One?', *History*, 68, pp. 187–209
——, 1991, 'James VI and I, *Basilikon Doron* and *The Trew Law of Free Monarchies*: The Scottish Context and the English Translation', in Linda Levy Peck (ed.), *The Mental World of the Jacobean Court* (Cambridge: Cambridge University Press), pp. 36–54
——, 1992, 'The creation of Britain: multiple kingdoms, or core and colonies?', *TRHS*, 6th series, 2, pp. 175–94
——, 2008, 'The Headaches of Monarchy: Kingship and the Kirk in the Early Seventeenth Century', in Julian Goodare and Alasdair A. MacDonald (eds), *Sixteenth-Century Scotland: Essays in Honour of Michael Lynch* (Leiden and Boston: Brill), pp. 365–94
Wotton, Sir Henry (1649), *A Panegyrick of King Charles; Being Observations upon the Inclinations, Life and Government of our Soveraign Lord the King* (London: Richard Marriot)
Young, Alan, 1987, *Tudor and Jacobean Tournaments* (London: George Phillip)
Young, John, 1998, 'The Scottish parliament and national identity from union of the crowns to the union of the parliaments', in Dauvit Broun, Richard Finlay and Michael Lynch (eds), *Image and Identity: The Making and Re-making of Scotland through the Ages* (Edinburgh: John Donaldson Publishers), pp. 105–42
——, 2016, 'The Covenanters and the Scottish parliament, 1639–51: the rule of the godly and "the second Scottish reformation"', in Elizabeth Boran and Crawford Gribben (eds), *Enforcing Reformation in Ireland and Scotland, 1550–1700* (London: Routledge), pp. 131–58
Young, Michael, 2000, *James VI and I and the History of Homosexuality* (Basingstoke: Macmillan)
Zwicker, Steven, 2007, 'Sites of Instruction: Andrew Marvell and the Tropes of Restoration Portraiture', in Julia Marciari Alexander and Catherine MacLeod (eds), *Politics, Transgression and Representation at the Court of Charles II* (New Haven and London: Yale University Press), pp. 123–38

Index

Acknowledgements

Firstly, I must acknowledge the support I have received for this book. A small British Academy award in 2010 for work on Charles II and a short fellowship at the Folger Shakespeare Library, Washington DC, were very valuable. I am also most grateful to Nell Hoare, and the Textile Conservation Centre, for support for this project prior to 2009. Also very helpful were small grants from the Faculty of Arts and Humanities and the History department, University of Southampton, towards the cost of the illustrations. Particular thanks are owed to the owners of illustrations who generously waived fees, notably the University of Aberdeen; the Archbishopric of Olomouc; Dulwich Picture Gallery; Fan Museum; the Galleria Sabauda; the Gallery of Costume/Manchester Art Gallery; George Heriot's Trust; Lane Fine Art; The Metropolitan Museum of Art; National Gallery of Art, Washington; National Portrait Gallery; New York Public Library; The Old Schools, University of Cambridge; Paxton House; the Royal Collection; Sotheby's; the Textile Conservation Foundation; Wellcome Collection; Weiss Gallery; Westminster School and Yale Center for British Art. In terms of time, I wish to thank the University of Southampton for two periods of research leave.

During the course of my research many people have helped in a wide variety of ways, in particular Patricia Allerston, Natasha Awais-Dean, Andrew Barclay, Sue Baxter, Jutta von Bloh, Christopher Breward, Mary Brooks, Helen Minoki Brooks, Denis Bruna, Tobias Capwell, Sarah Carpenter, Edward Corp, Valerie Cumming, Anne Curry, Hilary Davidson, Jane Eagan, Dinah Eastop, David Forsyth, Hazel Forsyth, Olivia Fryman, Philippa Glanville, Pascale Gorguet-Ballestros, Robert Hill, Susan Jenkins, Alexandra Johnson, Kathryn Jones, Frances Lennard, Renée Lewin, Catharine MacLeod, Joanna Marschener, Lynn McLean, Niki Miles, David Mitchell, Susan North, Michael Pearce, Lena Rangstrom, Alison Rosie, Sally Rush, Emily Taylor, Jenny Tiramani, Edward Town, Sally Tuckett, Rosie Waine, Melinda Watt, Tracey Wedge, Annabel Westman, Gwendolen Whitaker, Lady Willoughby de Eresby and Georgianna Ziegler. The staff at the British Library, National Archive, Society of Antiquaries, Royal Archive, National Art Library, Dorset History Centre, Folger Shakespeare Library and, in particular, the National Records of Scotland have been incredibly helpful.

At the outset of this book, when it was very different, Aileen Ribeiro asked what would make it distinctive – it was an invaluable question, and while it took a while to resolve, I am deeply grateful to her. *Stuart Style* has taken several years to evolve and during that time Naomi Tarrant, Lesley Miller, Joan Tumblety, John McGavin and Mark Stoyle have played a key role. Each of them has helped so much with its development, by discussing ideas, offering suggestions and giving clear feedback, and I wish to thank them for their unstinting generosity and encouragement. I am also very grateful to the two anonymous reviewers who helped me revise the text with their clear, insightful and probing comments. Equally important in shaping this book were Gillian Malpass, Mark Eastment and Sophie Neve, and their colleagues at Yale University Press, in particular Julie Hrischeva, Hilary Hammond and Clare Davis. However, *Stuart Style* would not have been finished on time without Lee Clatworthy, Nutmeg and Gypsy, and it would not have been possible without Mike, who has shared our house, our holidays and many conversations with the ever-expanding cast of individuals who make up *Stuart Style*.

Picture Credits

Art Gallery of South Australia, Adelaide: 3.11 [South Australian Government Grant, 1967, 0.2115]
© Ashmolean Museum, University of Oxford: 6.13
Bibliothèque Nationale de France, supplied by Gallica: 5.14
Bristol Museum and Art Gallery, UK, purchased with the assistance of the National Art Collections Fund (now the Art Fund) and the Victoria and Albert Museum, Bridgeman Images: 3.3
British Library, London, UK © British Library Board. All rights reserved/Bridgeman Images: 2.6 [Add. MS 36932], 12.10
By permission of Dulwich Picture Gallery: 1.9
Carisbrooke Castle Museum: 8.12
Christopher Foley, Lane Fine Art, London: III.2
Collection of the Duke of Devonshire, Chatsworth House, UK © Devonshire Collection, Chatsworth/ Reproduction by permission of the Chatsworth Settlement Trust/Bridgeman Images: 2.11
Collections des Princes de Ligne, Château de Beloeil: 12.3
Courtesy of the Council of the National Army Museum, London: 5.10 [NAM 1987-01-1-1]
Courtesy of the Gallery of Costume/Manchester Art Gallery: 5.8
Courtesy of Perth Museum and Art Gallery, Perth and Kinross Council: 7.2 [2004.107]
© Crown Copyright HES: 12.4
© Crown Copyright reproduced courtesy of Historic Scotland: 8.3
© Crown Copyright: UK Government Art Collection: 0.8 [12789]
© CSG CIC Glasgow Museums and Libraries Collections: 4.19 [29.128], 7.7 [acc. no. 3326], 9.7 [29.144-145], 9.12 [29.133], 10.14 [29.151.1]
© Dean and Chapter of Westminster Abbey: 12.5, 12.6, 12.7
© The Fan Museum, Hélène Alexander Collection: 10.5
George Heriot's Trust/By kind permission of the Governors of George Heriot's Trust: 6.6
© Historic Royal Palaces: 6.12 [acc. no. 3503039.a-b.]
Kroměříž Archdiocesan Museum/Archbishop of Olomouc, photo Olomouc Museum of Art, Zdeněk Sodoma: 3.8
© Lennoxlove House Ltd: 1.16, 2.13, 4.16, 5.11
Lent by the Scottish Roman Catholic Hierarchy. Image © National Museums Scotland: 11.7 [IL.2009.16.1-6]
Licensed by the Ministero dei beni e delle attività – Torino, Musei Reali – Galleria Sabauda: 5.2
The Metropolitan Museum of Art, New York: 0.4 [Gift of Irwin Untermyer, 1964, 64.101.1291], 0.9 [Gift of Irwin Untermyer, 1964, 64.101.1241], 1.17 [28.7.13, Harris Brisbane Dick Fund, 1928], 2.5 [Gift of Bashford Dean, 1923, 23.30.3], 2.17 [51.194.1], 3.9 [The Costume Institute Fund, in memory of Polaire Weissman, 1989, 1989.196], 3.10 [Gift of George A. Hearn, 1906, 06.1289], 3.14 [Marquand Collection, Gift of Henry G. Marquand, 1889, 89.15.16], 4.7 [purchase Irene Lewisohn Bequest, 1982, 1982.183.2a–c], II.2 [Rogers Fund, 1920, 20.81.2(1)], II.4 [Gift of Theodore de Witt 1923, 23.65.36], II.7 [Gift of Theodore de Witt, 1923, 23.65.35], 6.7 [Gift of Junius S. Morgan, 1929, 29.102.128,], 6.10 [The Jules Bache Collection, 1949, 49.7.26], 7.14 [Gift of Mrs Edward S. Harkness, 1928, 28.220.1,2], 8.2 [Rogers Fund, by exchange, 1929, 29.23.7], 10.4 [Harris Brisbane Dick Fund, 1923, 23.89.8], 10.12 [44.27, purchase Joseph Pulitzer Bequest, 1944], 11.13 [2009.300.1667]
Mike Halliwell: 0.2, 10.3
© Museum of London: 3.1 [acc. A27050], 7.13
National Galleries of Scotland: I.1 [NG 2274, Bequest of Sir Theophilus Biddolph 1948, received 1965], I.3 [PG 997, purchased 1925], I.5 [PG 1408, Bequest of the Marquis of Lothian], 1.1 [PG 2172, Bequest of Sir Theophilus Biddolph 1948, received 1969], 1.3 [PG 1857, purchased 1959], 1.7 [PG 156, purchased 1886], 1.8 [PG 816, purchased 1913], 1.15 [PG 2176, purchased 1950], 2.7 [PG 3538, David Lang Bequest to the Society of Antiquaries of Scotland, gifted in 2009], 3.4 [PG 2212, bequeathed by the 13th Baron Elibank, 1973], 3.12 [PG 2722, purchased with help from the Art Fund, the National Heritage Memorial Fund and the Pilgrims Trust, 1987], 3.13 [PG 902, purchased 1919], 4.5 [PG 1244, purchased 1935], 5.13 [PG 1064, bequeathed by Lady Dalgleish to the National Gallery of Scotland; transferred], II.5 [PG 2887 and PG 2886, purchased 1948], 6.8 [PG 2462, purchased 1991], 7.9 [PG 3656, accepted by HM Government in lieu of inheritance tax and allocated to the Scottish National Gallery 2010], 8.7 [PG 1083, purchased 1928], 8.14 [PG 734, purchased 1910], III.1 [PG 3724, purchased 2014], III.3 [PG 2129, purchased 1967], III.4 [PG 860, purchased 1916], 9.2 [PG 1532, purchased 1949], 9.6 [PG 894, purchased 1919], 9.10 [PG 2456, purchased 1980], 10.6 [PG 2222, purchased with assistance from the Art Fund, 1973], 10.8 [PG 661, purchased 1907], 10.16 [PG 1054, bequeathed by Mrs Nisbet Hamilton Ogilvy of Biel, 1921], 10.18

[PG 3155, purchased with the aid of the Art Fund and Heritage Lottery Fund, 1999], 11.11 [PG 2227, purchased with assistance from the Art Fund and the Pilgrim Trust 1974], 12.8 [PG 2418, bequeathed by Lady Malise Graham, 1978], 12.9 [SPL 110.3, provenance unknown]
© National Gallery, London: 4.6 [NG 6363, Bequest of Cornelia, Countess of Craven, 1965], 6.4 [NG5633, presented by Count Antoine Seilern1945], 6.9 [NG 6518]
National Gallery of Art, Washington, Andrew W. Mellon Collection: 5.5 [1937.1.51]
National Library of Scotland: II.1 [EMS.s.52A], 6.2 [PCF2], 10.7
© National Maritime Museum, Greenwich, London: 5.16 [BHC2797]
© National Museums Scotland: I.2 [K.1997.115.F], 5.7 [K.2011.64.2], 6.1 [H.NA 1037], 7.6 [K.2004.283], 7.8 [A.1947.257], 8.8 [K.2001.716], 8.15 [H.NH 12], 8.16 [H.NF 20], 9.11 [A.1921.68], 10.2 [H.KL 21], 10.9 [A.1988-187], 11.2 [H.KL 222], 11.3 [H.LF 23], 11.4 [H.KE 16], 11.6 [H.KJ 164], 11.14 [H.MR 11], 11.15 [A.1963.62]
© National Portrait Gallery, London: 0.3 [NPG 3902], 1.5 [NPG 63], 1.13 [NPG 2142], 1.14 [NPG 5210], 2.3 [NPG 2562], 2.4 [NPG 4515], 2.8 [NPG 5732], 2.15 [NPG 4260], 2.16 [NPG 1114], 3.17 [NPG 1961], 4.2 [NPG 6403], 4.10 [NPG 6276], 4.17 [NPG 5251], 5.3 [NPG 5104], 5.15 [NPG 976], 6.5 [NPG 5568], 8.4 [NPG 1246], 9.5 [NPG 211], 10.15 [NPG 5376], 11.10 [NPG, 171], 12.2 [NPG 4656], 12.12 [NPG710], 12.15 [NPG 5964]
© National Trust Images: 1.2 [NT 1129218], 4.13 [NT 836128], 4.15 [NT 1139789], II.6, 7.3, 7.4, 10.10 [NT 493070]
© National Trust for Scotland: 1.6
New York Public Library Digital Collections: I.7 [PC ARMY-(M-Z)]
Nottingham City Museums: 9.8 [NCM 1953-13]
The Old Schools, University of Cambridge: 3.5
The Portland Collection, Harley Gallery, Welbeck Estate, Nottinghamshire/Bridgeman Images: 8.9 [inv. no. 005669]
Private collection: 12.1
Private collection/photo Antonia Reeve Photography: 2.2
Private collection/photo Mike Halliwell: 3.2
Private collection/Bridgeman Images: 5.12
Reproduced courtesy of the University of St Andrews: 6.11, 11.1 [Bib BS170.C40], 11.12 [HC223]
Reproduced with kind permission of the Trustees of Paxton House: 6.3 [PCF10]
Royal Collection Trust/© Her Majesty Queen Elizabeth II 2019: 0.6 [RCIN 404951], I.4 [RCIN 402803], 1.4 [RCIN 401230], 1.10 [RCIN 404446], 1.12 [RCIN 420039], 2.9 [RCIN 420058], 2.10 [RCIN 722831], 3.15 [RCIN 443097], 3.18 [RCIN 405913], 3.19 [RCIN 404420], 4.1 [RCIN 400525], 4.3 [RCIN 404403], 4.4 [RCIN 404405], 4.8 [RCIN 906544], 4.12 [RCIN 406896], 4.18 [RCIN 404330], 5.4 [RCIN 402572], 5.6 [RCIN 405879], 5.9 [RCIN 403427], 7.1 [RCIN 404448], 7.5 [RCIN 405353], 8.1 [RCIN 28181], 8.5 [RCIN 441925], 8.6 [RCIN 441924], 8.11 [RCIN 65409], 9.3 [RCIN 405664], 9.9, 10.1 [RCIN 402966], 10.11 [RCIN 602686], 10.13 [RCIN 404771], 12.13 [RCIN 601472], 12.14 [RCIN 400966]
© Sotheby's 2019: III.5
Statens Museum for Kunst, Copenhagen: 3.6 [KMS sp184. SMK Photo/Jakob Skou/Hansen]
© Tate, London 2019: 0.7 [NO3474, presented by Colin Agnew and Charles Romer Williams, 1919]
© Textile Conservation Foundation and reproduced by kind permission of the Governing Body, Westminster School: 12.11
© The Trustees of the British Museum. All rights reserved: 2.1 [1870,0514.2896], 4.9 [1868,0808,3358], 7.11 [1873,0614.110], 7.15 [1854,0812.53], 8.10 [WB 167]
University of Aberdeen: 11.9 [ABDUA 30005]
© Victoria and Albert Museum, London: 0.1 [P.147-152-1910, bequeathed by George Salting], 0.5 [T.711-1995], 1.11 [T.28&A-1938], 2.12 [721-1882], 2.14 [P.163-1910], 3.16 [1509-1882], 4.11 [191&A-1900], 5.1 [T.711:1, 2-1995], II.3 [T.847-1974], 7.10 [1126-1903], 8.13 [M.253-1975], 9.1 [W.35.1-61.1949], 9.4 [T.846-1974], 10.17 [175-1900], 11.5 [M.92-1975, given by Dame Joan Evans]
© The Weiss Gallery, London: 3.7
Wellcome Collection: 11.8 [CC BY, inv. no. 184691]
World History Archive/Alamy Stock Photo: I.6 [D98ATE]
Yale Center for British Art, Paul Mellon Collection, New Haven: 4.14 [B1974.2.14], 7.12 [B1981.25.598]